ALEXANDER
III

ALEXANDER III

1249–1286

First Among Equals

NORMAN H. REID

First published in Great Britain in 2019 by
John Donald, an imprint of Birlinn Ltd
This paperback edition first published 2023

West Newington House
10 Newington Road
Edinburgh
EH9 1QS

www.birlinn.co.uk

ISBN: 978 1 910900 38 3

The publishers gratefully acknowledge the support of the
Anderson Dunlop Fund of the Society for Scottish Medieval and
Renaissance Studies towards the publication of this book.

British Library Cataloguing-in-Publication Data
A catalogue record for this book is available on request from the British Library

Typeset by Biblichor Ltd, Edinburgh
Printed in Malta by Gutenberg Press

For Elspeth

Contents

List of Plates

List of Maps

Acknowledgements

Although it appears under my name, this book has been a collective effort. Research and publications by many others have informed and shaped it, and I hope that their inclusion in the footnotes and Bibliography will suffice to acknowledge their contribution. In particular, a number of friends and colleagues have generously shared their knowledge and advice, have tholed my ignorance in patiently answering enquiries, and have engaged in stimulating and informative discussion and debate: in alphabetical order, Alan Borthwick, Dauvit Broun, Rory Cox, Barbara Crawford, Althea Davies, Lucy Dean, Mark Elliot, Liz Ewan, Chris Given-Wilson, Daryl Green, Mathew Hammond, Claire Hawes, Bill Hyland, Chris Jones, Cynthia Neville, Richard Oram, Anne Rutten (and other denizens of the Strathmartine Centre, including Muriel Watson and the bottomless coffee-pot), Simon Taylor, and Rob Wilson are all owed my sincere thanks. I am especially indebted to my auld frien Dauvit Broun for his careful reading of drafts of the first two chapters, and for his detailed and insightful comments. For the plates, I offer my thanks to staff of Westminster Abbey Library, Historic Environment Scotland, National Galleries Scotland, National Records of Scotland, the State Archives of Belgium in Namur, the Library of Corpus Christi College, Oxford, and particularly to the Photographic Collections team in the Special Collections Division of the University of St Andrews Library; and for financial support towards the cost of the plates I am grateful for a generous grant from the Anderson Dunlop Fund of the Society for Scottish Medieval and Renaissance Studies. Gilbert Márkus and Thomas Clancy kindly gave permission to quote from (pp. 248–49), and to reproduce in full (Appendix 2), Gilbert's fine translation of Princess Margaret's wedding hymn. To those I have inadvertently missed from the list, I offer my apologies. The remaining mistakes, omissions and infelicities are, of course, my own responsibility alone.

Hugh Andrew, on behalf of the publisher Birlinn, has consistently pressed me for this book over a period of two decades or more, and I have greatly appreciated his tenacity, encouragement and patience (as well as his own welcome contributions to the historical debate); the lunches and drams were good too. Beyond Hugh, the team at Birlinn/John Donald, particularly Mairi Sutherland, have displayed a winning combination of understanding, efficiency and effective communication, and have produced a book of excellent quality.

Elspeth, my wife, has shared, and at times restored, my enthusiasm and belief in this project. More, she has accepted my mental and physical absence from family life to a degree that was probably unreasonable to expect. Her contribution is greater still, since she has read the whole text several times, has used her skilled editorial pen to help mould it into acceptable prose and, with dogged humour, has persistently challenged me to explain myself more effectively. Without her contribution this would have been a much poorer work, and it is therefore to her that it is fondly dedicated.

List of Abbreviations used in the Footnotes

Anderson, *Early Sources*	Alan Orr Anderson, *Early Sources of Scottish History A.D. 500 to 1286* (Edinburgh, 1922, Stamford, 1990)
APS	T. Thomson and C. Innes (eds), *The Acts of the Parliaments of Scotland* (vol. 1, Edinburgh, 1884)
Arbroath Liber	*Liber S. Thome de Aberbrothoc* (Bannatyne Club, 1848, 1856)
Ash, 'The Church in the Reign of Alexander III'	Marinell Ash, 'The Church in the Reign of Alexander III', in Norman H. Reid (ed.), *Scotland in the Reign of Alexander III, 1249–1286* (Edinburgh, 1990), pp. 31–52
Bannerman, *Kinship, Church and Culture*	John W.M. Bannerman, *Kinship, Church and Culture: Collected Essays and Studies* (Edinburgh, 2016)
Bannerman, 'The King's Poet'	John W. M. Bannerman, 'The King's Poet and the Inauguration of Alexander III', in John W.M. Bannerman, *Kinship, Church and Culture*: *Collected Essays and Studies* (Edinburgh, 2016), pp. 252–82
Barrow, *Kingdom of the Scots*	G.W.S. Barrow, *The Kingdom of the Scots: Government, Church and Society from the Eleventh to the Fourteenth Century* (London, 1973)
Barrow, *Kingship and Unity*	G.W.S. Barrow, *Kingship and Unity: Scotland 1000–1306* (London, 1981)
Barrow, *Scotland and its Neighbours*	G.W.S. Barrow, *Scotland and Its Neighbours in the Middle Ages* (London, 1992)

Bateson, 'The Scottish King's Household'	Mary Bateson (ed.) 'The Scottish King's Household and other Fragments from a Fourteenth Century Manuscript in the Library of Corpus Christi College, Cambridge', *SHS Miscellany*, 2 (1904), pp. 3–43
Broun, *Irish Identity*	Dauvit Broun, *The Irish Identity of the Kingdom of the Scots* (Woodbridge, 1999)
Broun, *Scottish Independence*	Dauvit Broun, *Scottish Independence and the Idea of Britain* (Edinburgh, 2007)
Brown and Stevenson, *Medieval St Andrews*	Michael Brown and Katie Stevenson (eds), *Medieval St Andrews: Church, Cult, City* (Woodbridge, 2017)
CDS	Joseph Bain (ed.), Calendar of Documents Relating to Scotland, 4 vols (Edinburgh, 1881–88); vol. 5, ed. Grant G. Simpson and James D. Galbraith (Edinburgh, n.d.)
Chron. Bower	Bower, Walter, *Scotichronicon*, ed. and trans. D.E.R. Watt *et al.*, 9 vols (Aberdeen and Edinburgh, 1987–1998)
Chron. Fordun	Fordun, Joannis de, *Chronica Gentis Scotorum*, ed. W.F. Skene, 2 vols (Edinburgh, 1871–72)
Chron. Guisborough	*The Chronicle of Walter of Guisborough*, ed. Harry Rothwell (London, 1957)
Chron. Lanercost	*Chronicon de Lanercost, MCCI–MCCCXLVI*, ed. Joseph Stevenson (Bannatyne Club, 1839)
Chron. Man	*The Chronicle of Man and the Sudreys*, ed. P.A. Munch (Douglas, 1874)
Chron. Melrose	Dauvit Broun and Julian Harrison, *The Chronicle of Melrose Abbey: A Stratigraphic Edition*, i, *Introduction and Facsimile* (Edinburgh, 2007) (CD ROM Facsimile)
Chron. Wyntoun	*The Original Chronicle of Andrew of Wyntoun*, ed. F. J Amours, 6 vols (Edinburgh, 1903–14)
Cowan, 'Norwegian Sunset – Scottish Dawn'	Edward J. Cowan, 'Norwegian Sunset – Scottish Dawn: Hakon IV and Alexander III', in Norman H. Reid (ed.), *Scotland in the Reign of Alexander III, 1249–1286* (Edinburgh, 1990), pp. 103–31

CPL	*Calendar of Entries in the Papal Registers Relating to Great Britain and Ireland; Papal Letters*, i, *A.D. 1198–1304*, ed. W.H. Bliss (London, 1893)
Dean, 'Crowns, Wedding Rings and Processions'	Lucinda H.S. 'Dean, Crowns, Wedding Rings and Processions: Continuity and Change in the Representations of Scottish Royal Authority in State Ceremony, c. 1214–c.1603' (unpublished PhD thesis, University of Stirling, 2013)
Donnelly, 'Berwick Shipping Trade'	Joe Donnelly, 'An Open Economy: The Berwick Shipping Trade, 1311–1373', *Scottish Historical Review*, 96 (2017), pp. 1–31
Duncan, *Kingship of the Scots*	A.A.M. Duncan, *The Kingship of the Scots, 842–1292: Succession and Independence* (Edinburgh, 2002)
Duncan, *Making of the Kingdom*	A.A.M. Duncan, *Scotland: The Making of the Kingdom* (Edinburgh, 1975)
Dunfermline Reg.	*Registrum de Dunfermelyn* (Bannatyne Club, 1842)
ER, i	*Exchequer Rolls of Scotland 1264–1600*, vol. i (1264–1329), ed. John Stuart and George Burnett (Edinburgh, 1878)
Fawcett, *Royal Dunfermline*	Richard Fawcett (ed.), *Royal Dunfermline* (Edinburgh, 2005)
Fawcett, *Scottish Medieval Church*	Richard Fawcett, *The Architecture of the Scottish Medieval Church, 1100–1560* (New Haven and London, 2011)
Ferguson, *Papal Representatives*	Paul C. Ferguson, *Medieval Papal Representatives in Scotland: Legates, Nuncios, and Judges-Delegate, 1125–1286* (Edinburgh, 1997)
Foedera	*Foedera, Conventiones, Litterae et Cuiuscunque Generis Acta Publica*, ed. T. Rymer, 17 vols (London, 1816–1869)
Glasgow Reg.	*Registrum Episcopatus Glasguensis* (Bannatyne and Maitland Clubs, 1843)
Grant & Stringer, *Medieval Scotland*	Alexander Grant and Keith J. Stringer (eds), *Medieval Scotland: Crown, Lordship and Community* (Edinburgh, 1993)

Hybel, *The Nature of Kingship*	Nils Hybel, *The Nature of Kingship c. 800–1300: The Danish Incident* (Leiden, 2018)
McDonald, *Kingdom of the Isles*	R. Andrew McDonald, *The Kingdom of the Isles: Scotland's Western Seaboard c.1100–c.1336* (East Linton, 1997)
McDonald, *Sea Kings*	R. Andrew McDonald, *The Sea Kings: The Late Norse Kingdoms of Man and the Isles, c.1066–1275* (Edinburgh, 2019)
McNeill and MacQueen, *Atlas*	Peter G. B. McNeill and Hector L. MacQueen (eds), *Atlas of Scottish History to 1707* (Edinburgh, 1996)
Macquarrie, *Crusades*	Alan Macquarrie, *Scotland and the Crusades, 1095–1560* (Edinburgh, 1985)
MacQueen, '*Regiam Majestatem*'	Hector L. MacQueen, '*Regiam Majestatem*, Scots Law, and National Identity', *Scottish Historical Review*, 74 (1995), pp. 1–25
Markús, *Conceiving a Nation*	Gilbert Markús, *Conceiving a Nation: Scotland to AD 900* (Edinburgh, 2017)
Mayhew, 'A Silver Age'	Nicholas Mayhew, 'Alexander III – A Silver Age? An Essay in Scottish Medieval Economic History', in Norman H. Reid (ed.), *Scotland in the Reign of Alexander III, 1249–1286* (Edinburgh, 1990), pp. 53–73
Melrose Liber	*Liber Sancte Marie de Melrose* (Bannatyne Club, 1837)
Neville, *Land, Law and People*	Cynthia J. Neville, *Land, Law and People in Medieval Scotland* (Edinburgh, 2010)
Neville, 'Preparing for Kingship'	Cynthia J. Neville, 'Preparing for Kingship: Prince Alexander of Scotland, 1264–1284', in Janay Nugent and Elizabeth Ewan (eds), *Children and Youth in Premodern Scotland* (Woodbridge, 2015), pp. 155–72
Oram, *Alexander II*	Richard Oram, *Alexander II, King of Scots 1214–1249* (Edinburgh, 2012)
Oram, *Alexander II Essays*	Richard D. Oram (ed.), *The Reign of Alexander II, 1214–49* (Leiden and Boston, 2005)
Oram and Stell, *Lordship and Architecture*	Richard Oram and Geoffrey Stell (eds), *Lordship and Architecture in Medieval and Renaissance Scotland* (Edinburgh, 2005)

Paisley Reg.	*Registrum Monasterii de Passelet* (Maitland Club, 1832)
Penman, 'Royal Piety'	Michael Penman, 'Royal Piety in Thirteenth-Century Scotland: The Religion and Religiosity of Alexander II (1214–49) and Alexander III (1249–86)', in Janet Burton, Phillipp Schofield and Björn Weiler (eds), *Thirteenth Century England, XII: Proceedings of the Gregynog Conference 2007* (Woodbridge, 2009), pp. 13–29
PoMS	*People of Medieval Scotland, 1093–1314.* Online database – www.poms.ac.uk
Powicke, *The Thirteenth Century*	Maurice Powicke, *The Thirteenth Century, 1216–1307* (Oxford, 1962)
Purser, *Scotland's Music*	John Purser, *Scotland's Music: A History of the Traditional and Classical Music of Scotland from Early Times to the Present Day* (Edinburgh, 1992)
Reid, *Alexander III Essays*	Norman H. Reid (ed.), *Scotland in the Reign of Alexander III, 1249–1286* (Edinburgh, 1990)
Reid, 'Historiography'	Norman H. Reid, 'Alexander III: The Historiography of a Myth', in Norman H. Reid (ed.), *Scotland in the Reign of Alexander III, 1249–1286* (Edinburgh, 1990), pp. 181–213
Reid, 'Political Rôle of the Monarchy'	Norman H. Reid, 'The Political Rôle of the Monarchy in Scotland, 1249–1329' (unpublished PhD thesis, University of Edinburgh, 1984)
Reid and Barrow, *Sheriffs*	Norman H. Reid and G.W.S. Barrow (eds), *The Sheriffs of Scotland: An Interim List to c.1306* (St Andrews, 2002)
RMS	*Registrum Magni Sigilli Regum Scotorum,* ed. J.M. Thomson *et al.*, 11 vols (Edinburgh, 1882–1914)
RPS	K.M. Brown *et al., Records of the Parliaments of Scotland to 1707*. Online database – www.rps.ac.uk
RRS	*Regesta Regum Scottorum* (see Bibliography for individual volume details)

Ruiz, 'Unsacred Monarchy'	Teofilo F. Ruiz, 'Unsacred Monarchy: The Kings of Castile in the Late Middle Ages', in Sean Wilentz (ed.), *Rites of Power: Symbolism, Ritual, and Politics Since the Middle Ages* (Philadelphia, 1999), pp. 109–144
SAEC	Alan O. Anderson, *Scottish Annals from English Chroniclers, A.D. 500 to 1286* (London, 1908)
St Andrews Liber	*Liber Cartarum Prioratus Sancti Andree in Scocia* (Bannatyne Club, 1841)
Stevenson, 'Trade'	Alexander W.K. Stevenson, 'Trade Between Scotland and the Low Countries in the Later Middle Ages' (unpublished PhD thesis, University of Aberdeen, 1982)
Stones, *Anglo-Scottish Relations*	E.L.G. Stones (ed. and trans.), *Anglo-Scottish Relations, 1174–1328: Some Selected Documents* (Oxford, 1965)
Taylor, *Shape of the State*	Alice Taylor, *The Shape of the State in Medieval Scotland, 1124–1290* (Oxford, 2016)
Vet. Mon.	*Vetera Monumenta Hibernorum et Scotorum Historiam Illustrantia*, ed. A. Theiner (Rome, 1864)
Watt, *Graduates*	D.E.R. Watt, *A Biographical Dictionary of Scottish Graduates to A.D. 1410* (Oxford, 1977)
Watt, 'Minority'	D.E.R. Watt, 'The Minority of Alexander III of Scotland', *Transactions of the Royal Historical Society*, 5:21 (1971), pp. 1–23
Watt and Murray, *Fasti*	D.E.R. Watt and A.L. Murray (eds), *Fasti Ecclesiae Scoticanae Medii Aevi Ad Annum 1638* (Edinburgh, 2003)
Welander *et al.*, *The Stone of Destiny*	Richard Welander, David J. Breeze and Thomas Owen Clancy (eds), *The Stone of Destiny: Artefact and Icon* (Edinburgh, 2003)
Woolf, *From Pictland to Alba*	Alex Woolf, *From Pictland to Alba: 789–1070* (Edinburgh, 2007)
Young, *Robert the Bruce's Rivals*	Alan Young, *Robert the Bruce's Rivals: The Comyns, 1212–1314* (East Linton, 1997)

Introduction

In January 1986 the annual Conference of Scottish Medieval Historical Research was on the theme of Alexander III, to commemorate the 700th anniversary of his death. Three of the papers from that conference, with the addition of several more commissioned for the purpose, were published in 1990, in a volume entitled *Scotland in the Reign of Alexander III*. The essays served both to illuminate aspects of the history of Scotland in that period and to highlight the fact that the lack of a coherent study of the reign remained a significant *lacuna* in the historiography of medieval Scotland. For long recognised as a reign of major importance, it was remarkable that no serious published treatment of Alexander III had been undertaken. This book aims to fill that glaring omission.

Since 1990, both understanding and interpretation of the period have been immeasurably improved by the labours of a multitude of historians, many of whom appear in the Bibliography and Acknowledgements to this book. As a result, my own ideas about the reign and its significance have changed markedly since I first wrote about it in the 1980s, and this is far from the book I might have written then.

In my original essay on the historiography of the reign I overconfidently stated that 'the primary importance of Alexander's reign lies in its position at a watershed of Scotland's history; a grasp of the true nature of this settled period is of vital importance to our understanding of the full significance of what followed'. In Chapter 10, I now dispute that statement. The view of the kingdom on the brink of calamity is certainly valuable, but the reign has much more to offer. Now, the key point must be that Alexander III lived at the end of a long period in which Scotland's government and society underwent profound change. That process of change has been studied in great depth, but it is perhaps only in the last few years that its true nature has been recognised, as sources which were previously underused, or misunderstood, have been mined to add further understanding to the picture created through the meticulous analysis of documentary record undertaken by such champions of Scottish medieval studies as the late Professors Geoffrey Barrow and Archie Duncan. What Alexander's reign can tell us is therefore fundamental to the nature of Scottish kingship, government and society; certainly, it offers us a useful portrait of the kingdom in a stable and prosperous condition before the decline which followed dynastic crisis at the end of the thirteenth century, but, more importantly, it provides a window on the character of Scottish kingship and society which allows us to reinterpret the events not only of this reign, but also of other periods, both before and after.

This is not, and could not be, a biography. Rather, it is a deliberately monarchocentric study of kingship as revealed by the conduct of one reign. It is not possible to understand the fruits of twelfth- and thirteenth-century development without a grasp of the foundations upon which it was built. Therefore, in the context of an analysis of the young king's inauguration and what it reveals about the kingship to which he was inducted, the book retreats in time, to begin the story of Alexander III before the Romans invaded Britain. Its first chapter is an attempt to understand the societal traditions out of which Scottish kingship grew. This is followed by a brief portrait of the kingdom as it existed in the mid thirteenth century. The narrative of the reign which occupies the central portion of the book diverges in many respects from the hitherto accepted view. It has emerged from the revised understanding of the societal model gained from the analysis provided in Chapter 1. The nature of the Scottish kingship and its interdependence with the aristocratic community is a consistently binding theme. The final two chapters attempt to analyse the extent to which Alexander achieved the ideals of medieval kingship, to discern at least a little about the man himself and his personal environment, and to discuss the historiography of the reign in an effort to understand why it has achieved its long-held reputation and to what extent that reputation is deserved. The historiographical material covers some of the same ground as the essay written for the 1990 volume but is different both in emphasis and in conclusion. The whole work is a blend of synthesis and original research. The Bibliography is selective, and, although the manuscripts of many of the primary sources have been consulted, they are usually cited in both Bibliography and footnotes in the printed or online forms in which they are most readily accessible.

From the survey of the evolution of kingship which opens the present study, a model of authority emerges which retains powerful elements of election and consensuality, with the king as *primus inter pares*. A very considerable weight of evidence is lent to this model by Alice Taylor's seminal work on *The Shape of the State in Medieval Scotland*, published in 2016, and by other recent research (as yet unpublished) on the political culture of governance in the fifteenth century.[1] Both assert that the relationship between crown and aristocracy in government was one of non-oppositional cooperation, and that they acted for the common good, sharing the principles and values which led them to do so. A firm grasp of this fundamentally consensual nature of Scottish government and society is key to understanding the narrative of Scottish history, arguably until the present day.

One of the greatest impacts of this view of Scottish government is in the contrast which it offers with the society of our southern neighbour. Rooted in conquest, the English monarchical system, and the society that developed under it, was different from that in Scotland. For centuries, however, there have been strong historiographical currents leading towards the categorisation of England as 'core' and Scotland as 'periphery', with societal, governmental and cultural development inexorably travelling in a northward direction. It is an issue which has been exacerbated, particularly in the medieval period, by the relative paucity of native Scottish primary sources and a consequent reliance by Scottish historians on English material. In fact, although it cannot reasonably be disputed that there was extensive borrowing of English and Continental ideas and practices, it is not accurate to regard this as a process of anglicisation, since it is clearly demonstrable that the borrowings were assimilated within existing structures to enhance and yet maintain a distinctive governmental discourse. Part of the drive towards clear identification of Scotland as a kingdom distinct from England in the thirteenth century was supported by those very lords who, having interests in both realms, might have been expected to take the opposite standpoint; their stance was adopted because they wished to avoid in Scotland difficulties being experienced in the crown–aristocracy relationship under the English monarchy.[2]

Having identified the distinctive Scottish model through synthesis of the important work of many historians of the past half century and more, a new narrative can be constructed which reveals, for instance, that the long-recognised politico-dynastic factionalism of Alexander III's minority is a fiction, and that

---

1 Taylor, *Shape of the State*; Claire Hawes, 'Community and Public Authority in Later Fifteenth-century Scotland' (unpublished PhD thesis, University of St Andrews, 2015).

2 See Dauvit Broun, 'Britain and the Beginning of Scotland', *Journal of the British Academy*, 3 (2015), pp. 107–37, at pp. 115–16, where he develops the idea raised by David Carpenter, 'Scottish Royal Government in the Thirteenth Century from an English Perspective', in Matthew Hammond (ed.), *New Perspectives on Medieval Scotland, 1093–1286* (Woodbridge, 2013), pp. 117–59: 'we may wonder whether the perception that, when it came to the demands of the crown, it was far better to be Scottish than to be English, was one of the forces driving the development of a separate Scottish identity in the thirteenth century' (p. 117).

far from being destructively self-serving and inherently opposed to royal power, the thirteenth-century aristocracy of Scotland – a multinational coterie, which was nonetheless coherent in its actions – consistently worked with the crown in the interest of good governance. It is a view which transforms aspects of the reign of Alexander III and may yet prove also to alter our view of the difficult years which followed.

The reign of Alexander III followed a long period which effected a transformation of law, government and society, forging a coherent medieval kingdom out of a patchwork of territorial lordships. As the kingdom gradually emerged, so did an idea of what it meant to be Scottish. The governmental structures which evolved and the national identity which they enabled were to be crucial to the survival of Scotland through the wars of the fourteenth century and have remained a vital element in the deep-seated affinities which have maintained a distinctive Scottish society until the present day. My concluding contention is therefore that Alexander III's reign marks a high-point in Scottish medieval kingship.

CHAPTER 1

Roots of a Kingship

On the west coast of Scotland, just off Oban, lies the island of Kerrera, a tranquil seasonal retreat with a small settled community. Flitting back in time to early July 1249, a scene of startling contrast greets us. In the sheltered waters of the Firth of Lorne lies a fleet of low-gunwaled, high-stemmed, square-rigged galleys, descendants of the once-feared Viking longship. A seaborne army of hundreds, perhaps thousands, of men, from lowly peasants to wealthy noblemen, has been mustered from near and far with the intent of enforcing royal authority. At their head is none other than the king of Scotland himself, Alexander II.[1]

The campaign had required careful long-term planning. Despite the uncertain health of the king, who had been given papal dispensation to be less stringent than was normal with his Lenten diet, plans were actioned, doubtless under the assumption that he would be sufficiently recovered.[2] Quite to the contrary, on Kerrera, with his forces poised for action, on Thursday 8 July at the age of only 50 and in the thirty-fifth year of his reign, Alexander succumbed to a fever and died.[3]

> Shield of the church, giver of peace to his people, guide to the wretched,
> a king upright, strict, wise, prudent, honest,
> a pious king, a brave king, a most virtuous king, a wealthy king;
> he was himself the second of this name (that is Alexander).
> He was himself king for three times ten and five years.
> The island called Kerrera has carried this man off.

---

1 For a discussion of Alexander II's 1249 expedition and of the events leading up to it, see Oram, *Alexander II*, pp. 175–91; see also below, pp. 166–69.

2 *Vet. Mon.*, no. 131; *CPL*, i, 243, cited in Anderson, *Early Sources*, ii, p. 558.

3 *Chron. Melrose*, Faustina B. IX, fo. 55v; *Chron. Man*, p. 103, both trans. Anderson, *Early Sources* ii, pp. 557–58.

His spirit seeks the heights as it joins the heavenly bodies,
But Melrose retains his buried bones.[4]

Without delay, a select few of the nobles who had accompanied him on the expedition crossed to the mainland and rode hard with the news to the widowed queen and her household, likely in either Dunfermline or Scone, and to those in the aristocratic community who held governmental responsibility.

Meanwhile on Kerrera, over the ensuing days the fleet was dispersed and the operation abandoned, most ships and men returning homewards. A more measured and sombre progress began, carrying the late king's body towards its final resting place, a burial site which he had previously identified as the great Cistercian abbey of Melrose in the Scottish borders.[5] In the thirteenth century, Kerrera was remote from lowland Scotland. The journey – over 150 miles at walking pace, or a voyage by sea to Ayr or Dumbarton followed by a further 100 miles overland – would certainly have taken more than a week, lengthened by the pauses demanded by vigils to pray for the deceased.[6] The fleet-footed messengers to the royal court carried out their business more expeditiously. In an impressive feat of organisation, suggesting that the earlier illness of the king had been serious enough to prompt forward planning, within only five days of Alexander's death, arrangements had been completed for the inauguration of his successor. On Tuesday 13 July, before his father had been laid to rest, the young Prince Alexander, a boy still shy of his eighth birthday, became king in a ceremony held at the traditional venue of Scone near Perth. The inauguration rituals duly performed, the royal party proceeded to Melrose for the interment of the king's father. Pause may have been arranged en route for a separate heart burial at Dunfermline.[7]

The precise chronology of death, inauguration and funeral is uncertain, since *Gesta Annalia* claims that Alexander II's funeral took place on 8 July.[8] This is undoubtedly an error, since he was alive on Kerrera on that day, although

4 *Chron. Bower*, v, pp. 192–93.

5 *Chron. Melrose*, Faustina B. IX, fo. 55v; '. . . his body was transported (as he had commanded, before he died) to the church of Melrose, and was committed to the bosom of the earth in it, in royal fashion' (translation from Anderson, *Early Sources*, ii, p. 558).

6 See Dean, 'Crowns, Wedding Rings and Processions', pp. 27–28, and the map outlining potential routes on p. 341.

7 The length of the journey would suggest that the body had to be embalmed before leaving Kerrera, and it is therefore quite possible, although there is no direct evidence of it, that there was a separate heart burial, a common custom, perhaps in Dunfermline. See Dean, 'Crowns, Wedding Rings and Processions', pp. 31–33.

8 *Chron. Fordun*, i, p. 292 (trans. ii, p. 288). For the nature of *Gesta Annalia*, see below, pp. 11–12, n. 25.

probably on his deathbed, when he made a grant to the bishopric of Argyll.[9] That Alexander III's regnal year began between 1 and 11 July also supports the probability that the Melrose chronicler was correct in giving the date of death as 8 July.[10] It is inconceivable, given the distances involved, that both the funeral and the inauguration of Alexander III could have taken place by 13 July, and the funeral must therefore have taken place some days later. This accords with usual practice, so far as can be told. William I, for example, died (at Stirling) on 4 December 1214, and was buried in Arbroath abbey on 10 December. Alexander II, William's son and heir, had already been inaugurated, at Scone, on the day following his father's death.[11] Scone is roughly 40 miles from Stirling (by modern roads), a not inconsiderable journey in the thirteenth century, and the successful holding of the inauguration ceremony (at which we are told at least seven earls and a bishop were present) only a day later, even despite the fact that the king's death was not unexpected, signifies both striking communication and organisation, and a very considerable sense of urgency. There was a practical reason for this: even although it had been increasingly customary for at least a century, the system of primogeniture, by which the eldest son of a deceased king would be assumed to succeed his father, may still have had its challengers. The immediate inauguration of the new king (which included elements of at least nominal election and popular acclamation) therefore reduced the opportunity for any rival to stake a claim to the kingship. There is no evidence of any competition for the throne in 1249 – Alexander's dynasty was apparently secure – but as recently as the late 1220s it had been subject to challenge.[12] There was, however, a further reason to hold the inauguration before the funeral of the last king, which had more to do with the theoretical basis of kingly rule. If a king was laid to rest before the inauguration of his successor, then there would be a theoretical lapse in the rule of the kingdom, during which there would be no authority; no one could wield the abstract ruling authority known, apparently synonymously, as the *regia dignitas* (dignity

---

9 James M. Scoular, *Handlist of the Acts of Alexander II, 1214–1249* (Edinburgh 1959), no. 298.

10 *Chron. Melrose*, Faustina B. IX, fo. 55v. The calculation of the dating of the regnal year of Scottish kings has been debated. A.A.M. Duncan (*Making of the Kingdom*, p. 552) asserted that until 1329 it began with the date of inauguration, but there is evidence to the contrary. *RRS*, iv pt. 1, nos. 136 and 137 are two letters to Edward I, justifying the absence of the earl of Buchan and Alexander Balliol of Cavers from attending Edward's military summons; they must both date from the summer of 1282, and yet are dated respectively 1 July a.r. (i.e. regnal year) 33 and 12 July a.r. 34. For a wider discussion of the dating of the regnal year, see Reid, 'Political Rôle of the Monarchy', Appendix 2, pp. 468–73.

11 *Chron. Fordun*, i, p. 280 (trans. ii, pp. 275–76). See also the detailed analysis of William's funeral procession in Dean, 'Crowns, Wedding Rings and Processions', pp. 27–29.

12 See Oram, *Alexander II*, various index entries to 'MacWilliam family, bids for throne by'.

of the realm) or *corona* (the crown).[13] That the king had to be inaugurated even when still a child indicates that, although the community of the nobility could govern on his behalf until he was capable of personal rule, there was as yet no effective sense that the king's person was separate from his office: without an inaugurated ruler, government could not continue.[14]

The funerary processes following a king's death also reveal attitudes to the concept of kingship itself. Unlike the English monarchy (which, between the Norman Conquest and the reign of Henry III had no recognised 'traditional' royal burial place), the Scottish kings generally followed an established custom. Before 1097 many of them seem to have been buried on Iona, although it is not known when that custom was established, or with certainty when it ceased. Thereafter most chose Dunfermline, beginning with Máel Coluim III and his second queen, Margaret (who was canonised in 1250), and continuing with the whole of the succeeding dynasty until 1371, other than William, who chose to be buried at Arbroath abbey (which he himself had founded), Alexander II and John Balliol (who died overseas in 1314, having lost the throne almost 20 years earlier).[15] The succession of kings who used Dunfermline as their

13 These terms were ubiquitous throughout Europe and, predictably, were used frequently in times of crisis. During the Great Cause, Balliol's pleadings included the statement that the case should be heard according to the law and custom of England, as to do otherwise would be 'to the prejudice of the crown' (*en prejudice de la coroune*). It was quite explicitly the *regia dignitas* which was surrendered by King John Balliol to Edward I of England after his abdication from the Scottish throne in 1296. (*Foedera*, i.i, p. 909; E.L.G. Stones and Grant G. Simpson (eds), *Edward I and the Throne of Scotland, 1290–1296: An Edition of the Records Sources for the Great Cause* (Oxford, 1978), ii, pp. 290, 179).

14 A fully developed theory of 'the king's two bodies' was a feature, particularly of English kingship, which came to its maturity in Elizabethan times, although it had its roots in much earlier political and theological theory. See Ernst H. Kantorowicz, *The King's Two Bodies: A Study in Mediaeval Political Theology* (Princeton, 1997), which traces the development of the theory, finally expounded by Edmund Plowden and other sixteenth-century English jurists, from the twelfth century and beyond. The extent, however, to which such theories were fully assimilated by the Scottish monarchy must be doubted.

15 For a discussion of royal burial places and practices, see: G.W.S. Barrow, *Scotland and Its Neighbours*, pp. 37–39; Dean, 'Crowns, Wedding Rings and Processions', pp. 25–33. Barrow (*Scotland and Its Neighbours*, p. 38), states that Máel Coluim III's body was never returned from England after his death near Alnwick; he does seem to have been initially buried at Tynemouth priory. Different versions of the Scottish king-lists, however, state variously that Máel Coluim was buried in Tynemouth, Iona and Dunfermline (M.O. Anderson, *Kings and Kingship in Early Scotland* (Edinburgh, 1974), pp. 276, 284, 289). Iona seems unlikely, given, by that time, the more easterly focus of the kingship; that his body was indeed removed from Tynemouth to Dunfermline, presumably in the reign of his son Alexander I, is made very likely by the later story regarding the translation of the relics of Margaret in 1250 (see below, p. 94). See also, however, *SAEC*, pp. 111–13, which offers several English chronicle accounts of Máel Coluim's death: William of Malmesbury does state that he was re-interred at Dunfermline during the reign of Alexander I; others cast doubt. See also the discussion in Steve Boardman, 'Dunfermline as a Royal Mausoleum', in Fawcett, *Royal Dunfermline*, pp. 139–53.

mausoleum were those who were descended from Máel Coluim III and Margaret; in later times some of them even asserted that the royal couple were the original founders of their dynasty, ignoring earlier generations.[16] The choice of Dunfermline abbey had doubtless to do with the self-identification of these kings with their saintly royal ancestor Margaret, which bolstered both their sense of dynastic right and their pretensions to the increasingly influential European model of Christian kingship.[17] After an initial struggle with the offspring of Máel Coluim and his first wife, Ingibjorg, daughter of Earl Thorfinn of Orkney (a struggle which was to be reprised several times during the reigns of William and Alexander II), the 'Margaretsons' prevailed, and their close association with Dunfermline (whose first Benedictine monks had been brought there by Margaret herself) therefore had obvious politico-dynastic advantages.

So why did Alexander II break with tradition and choose Melrose? It is certain that he did not lack his family's reverence for his great-great grandmother: it was during his reign that the Scots initiated the diplomatic campaign at the papal curia to achieve her canonisation and began the building of a new sanctuary at Dunfermline to house her relics, perhaps in response to Henry III's extensive rebuilding of Westminster abbey to accommodate the remains both of himself and of his own sainted predecessor, Edward the Confessor.[18] That fact makes the choice of anywhere other than Dunfermline for Alexander's own sepulchre all the more surprising. The selection of a king's burial place, however, was not a matter of whimsy; it was a decision of great significance and symbolism. It may not be irrelevant that almost 40 years later Alexander II's queen, Marie de Coucy, would also opt for burial in a Cistercian house (Newbattle, a daughter house of Melrose), possibly indicating a pious preference by the couple for the more austere, penitential character of the Cistercian order.[19]

---

16 Steve Boardman, 'Dunfermline as a Royal Mausoleum', p. 143. See also below, pp. 40–41.

17 Claiming a saint within the lineage was popular in the twelfth and thirteenth centuries; this was one of the ways in which 'the countries in the European periphery were integrated into the common Christian cultural tradition': Gro Steinsland, Jón Viðar Sigurðsson, Jan Erik Rekdal and Ian Beuermann (eds), *Ideology and Power in the Viking and Middle Ages: Scandinavia, Iceland, Ireland, Orkney and the Faeroes* (Leiden, 2011), Introduction (by Gro Steinsland), p. 10. Olaf Haraldsson, king of Norway (1015–1028), was locally canonised in 1030, with papal confirmation following in 1164. The Norwegian monarchy was relatively recently Christianised, and the presence of royal saints helped to embed state Christianity: 'Royal saints were at the very centre of "state-building"' (p. 10). The argument regarding Christianisation can hardly be applied to Scotland in the thirteenth century, but the development of the Christian ideal of kingship is highly relevant.

18 Penman, 'Royal Piety', p. 20.

19 Penman, 'Royal Piety', p. 22. Alexander II's mother, Ermengarde, had also been buried not at Dunfermline, but at another Cistercian house, Balmerino, which she had been instrumental in founding along with Alexander II. Richard Oram explains Alexander's preference for Melrose in terms of faith rather than politics (Oram, *Alexander II*, pp. 221–22). There is some evidence

More lay behind his choice, however. It must be remembered that Scotland in the mid thirteenth century was still a kingdom in the process of formation: it was not the coherent political or national unit which some historians have depicted. Lothian – the area south of the Forth and to the north of the present-day border with England – had for a couple of centuries recognised the authority of the kings of Scots; that is not to say, however, that there were not still significant cultural differences between Lothian and other areas ruled by them. Previously part of the kingdom of Northumbria, Lothian was predominantly English-speaking and reflected English social custom more closely than it did the predominantly Gaelic society of the greater part of Scotland north of the Forth. There is good reason to believe, based on evidence from the great medieval chronicle written in Melrose abbey itself, that people in that area, while acknowledging that they lived within the Scottish kingdom, nonetheless identified themselves as English. Within the reigns of Alexander II and his son, however, changes in attitude can be discerned in the chronicle which point to a closer association with the kingdom of Scotland; it seems too that innovations in legal practice and the increasing definition of law within the area ruled by the king should be taken as suggestive of a trend towards cohesion, leading to a sense of collective identity throughout the kingdom.[20] In the pages of the Melrose chronicle, therefore, 'it is finally possible to see how allegiance to the king of Scots might make Englishmen become Scottish'. It has been suggested that the favour shown to the abbey by Alexander II in both life and death might have encouraged this trend.[21] Alexander had been a visitor to Melrose not infrequently, observing religious feasts there on more than one occasion, which may have been both part of a royal itinerary that was 'perhaps designed to enhance royal authority and sacrality', and 'a potential strategy for managing Anglo-Scottish relations in the face of inherited and recurrent territorial tensions'.[22]

---

that the mid thirteenth-century promotion of Margaret's cult and tomb at Dunfermline was encouraged, if not initiated, by a Dunfermline establishment which was perhaps nervous at the apparent loss of their monopoly of royal burials (Dean, 'Crowns, Wedding Rings and Processions', pp. 30–31).

20 The significance of the increasing definition of law within a territorial kingdom was decisively demonstrated during Alexander III's reign, by the treaty of Perth: see below, pp. 191–97.

21 Dauvit Broun, 'Becoming Scottish in the Thirteenth Century: The Evidence of the Chronicle of Melrose', in Beverley Ballin Smith, Simon Taylor and Gareth Williams (eds), *West Over Sea: Studies in Scandinavian Sea-Borne Expansion and Settlement Before 1300* (Leiden, 2007), pp. 19–32, at p. 29.

22 Penman, 'Royal Piety', pp. 16, 18. Two of Alexander II's extant royal *acta* are place-dated at Melrose, on 19 March 1231 and 24 February 1236 (Scoular, *Handlist of the Acts of Alexander II,* nos. 146, 211), but other place-dated *acta* and sources such as *Chron. Melrose* make it clear that his itinerary took him there more frequently. 19 March 1231 was during Easter week, and given that the next surviving place-dated act (no. 147) is from Kelso on 29 March, it seems likely that Alexander celebrated Easter at Melrose. It may not be irrelevant that the preceding day, 18

In January 1216 Alexander II had received the homage and fealty of the barons of Yorkshire who were then in rebellion against King John, in the chapter-house of Melrose.[23] Alexander II's wish to be buried at Melrose abbey can be seen as making a point that the southern areas of the kingdom were becoming unquestionably an integral part of the kingdom of the Scots. Melrose in this period was 'at the heart of the spiritual, political and economic world of south-eastern Scotland . . . and beyond',[24] a fact which gave his choice an unmistakeably political dimension.

By the time Alexander II had been laid to rest at Melrose, his son had already been made king of this developing kingdom. Alexander III's is the first Scottish royal inauguration of which a near-contemporary description has survived. An account written probably in the 1260s tell us that:

> The earls, namely lord Máel Coluim, earl of Fife, and lord Máel Ísu, earl of Stathearn, and many other nobles, led Alexander, soon to be king, to a cross standing in the cemetery at the east part of the church, whom they placed in the royal seat adorned with silk cloths woven in gold; the bishop of St Andrews and other assistants with him consecrated [Alexander] as king, as was proper. Also, while the king was sitting on the royal seat, earls and other nobles on bended knee spread their garments under his feet. And behold, after they one by one were finished, a certain highland Scot, kneeling suddenly before the throne, greeted the king in the mother tongue, bowing his head, saying *Bennachd Dé, rí Albanach, Alexanndar mac Alexanndair meic Uilleim meic Énri meic David*, and by proclaiming in this way read the genealogy of the kings of Scots to the end.[25]

March, was the feast day of Edward the Confessor, and 20 March was the feast of St Cuthbert, a saint with strong local connections, and one favoured by the royal house because of St Margaret's connections with Durham. 24 February was the feast of St Matthias, and, perhaps more significantly, it was also during Lent (C.R. Cheney (ed.), *Handbook of Dates for Students of English History* (London, 1978), pp. 47, 49, 56, 86, 100).

23 See Oram, *Alexander II*, pp. 36–37.

24 Penman, 'Royal Piety', p. 21.

25 This account is the contemporary text which Dauvit Broun has extracted by forensic examination of later, inflated texts, in the course of his study of *Gesta Annalia*, or notes of 'annual events' which were until recently regarded as part of – or at least closely related to – the late fourteenth-century *Chronica Gentis Scotorum* (Chronicle of the Scottish People) compiled by John of Fordun. The somewhat complex textual genealogy of Fordun's work and other related texts is discussed in Broun's 'A New Look at *Gesta Annalia* Attributed to John of Fordun', in Barbara E. Crawford (ed.), *Church, Chronicle and Learning in Medieval and Early Renaissance Scotland* (Edinburgh, 1999), pp. 9–30; and further developed in Broun, *Scottish Independence*, especially in chs 6, 8 and 9. It seems indisputable that the source text for the inflated version of the inauguration description contained in *Gesta Annalia I* was written within the reign of Alexander III, since *Gesta Annalia I* itself was completed in 1285. Broun's reconstruction of the

To this text can be cautiously added further details provided by other, not quite so contemporary, writers who have used and expanded it. It is likely, for example, that an oath was sworn, in which the king promised to defend the church and the people through just rule, to make good laws and to continue to use the existing ones until his death.[26]

In addition, important visual evidence is found in two seals. Firstly, the seal made in 1249/50 to authenticate the acts of the young king shows him seated, a sceptre in his left hand and with a sword held in his right hand, lying across his knees.[27] (The great seals used by most Scottish kings, including the adult Alexander III, show them with the sword held upright in their right hand.[28]) The medieval seal of Scone abbey, perhaps in use as early as the 1250s, shows the sceptre (which might possibly have been a golden rose gifted to King William by Pope Lucius III in 1182[29]) in the king's right hand, his left hand holding the cord that fastens his royal mantle, which appears to have been placed around him by two prelates, and the sword and shield held by nobles standing to the sides.[30] Both seals show the young king wearing a crown, a striking image, since Scottish kings were not formally crowned and anointed, a rite which was in the gift of the papacy, and was not granted to Scotland until 1329. The imagery, however, may be more than formulaic, and might be regarded as evidence that some sort of encrowning also took place.[31]

The young prince was thus made king in a ceremony which gave him the symbolic trappings of sovereignty: having first been acclaimed as the true heir,

---

original, thus almost contemporary, description of the inauguration ceremony itself (quoted verbatim above, except for the excision of minor interpolations to indicate his manipulation of the texts) is found in *Scottish Independence*, ch. 6, at pp. 177–78. Broun acknowledges significant debt to the important earlier work of A.A.M. Duncan, and the discussion here of the broader evidence for the nature of the inauguration ceremony also relies very heavily on the analysis in Duncan, *Kingship of the Scots*, pp. 131–50.

26 *Chron. Guisborough*, p. 239: *sanctam matrem ecclesiam populumque sibi subiectum iuste regendo defenderet, leges bonas conderet usitatasque et inventas usque ad mortem continuaret.* Written in the first years of the fourteenth century, this – admittedly perhaps fanciful – abbreviated description of the Scottish coronation oath is from Guisborough's account of the inauguration of King John Balliol in 1292. It seems a plausible précis of the oath which must surely have been sworn by other kings before Balliol.

27 See Plates 1 and 2.

28 See, e.g., Walter de Gray Birch, *History of Scottish Seals from the Eleventh to the Seventeenth Century . . .* (Stirling, 1905), i, plates 2, 5, 7, 9. See also Plates 3 and 4.

29 Duncan, *Making of the Kingdom*, p. 557; Duncan, *Kingship of the Scots*, pp. 137–38.

30 See Duncan, *Kingship of the Scots*, plate 3.

31 The imagery on seals was not entirely formulaic, and was altered to reflect changing situations and attitudes: in the 1250s, for example, Henry III of England changed the depiction on his seal to that of a king bearing a dove-topped rod rather than a sword, in order to stress his association with Edward the Confessor, and to play down his own poor record as a sword-bearing king (D.A. Carpenter, *The Reign of Henry III* (London, 1996), pp. 439–42).

he was seated on the 'royal chair', understood to be a throne constructed to hold the ancient, so-called Stone of Destiny; he received the sword to defend the church and people, the sceptre, crown and mantle (perhaps emblazoned with the royal coat of arms) as symbols of royal authority; his genealogy was publicly read (Plate 18) in order to assert his status within the lineage of Scottish kings; and he swore to uphold the duties of his kingship. A mixture of secular and religious, traditional and modern, this was a ceremony which underlined the king's responsibilities to, and authority stemming from, both the secular community and the church.

At face value, it might seem that the rite of seating on the stone and the presentation of a Gaelic genealogy were symbolic of an ancient Celtic heritage, and that the part played by the ecclesiastics, which closely reflected the rôle of the church in the mainstream European ceremonies of royal anointing and coronation, were elements which had been introduced more recently to reflect the current state of the monarchy. Such a simplistic interpretation, however, would obscure the complexity of the medieval monarchy.

Considering firstly the mythological status which has been achieved by the Stone of Destiny: it has been heralded as a relic from the ancient Dál Riatan past, used for the inauguration of the kings there before their fabled takeover of the Pictish kingdom in the ninth century. In fact, it is a sandstone block which was quarried in the Scone area, and so is very unlikely to have been used – for inauguration purposes, at least – anywhere other than at Scone itself.[32] It would seem to be comparable to other stone seats or chairs used for inauguration purposes in what might broadly be termed Germanic kingship rituals elsewhere in Europe. One of these, the duke's throne of Carinthia (Austria) is formed from the base of a Roman column.[33] It has been suggested that the Stone of Destiny might similarly originally have been used in the construction of a Roman fort; perhaps that of Bertha, which lay close by, at the junction of the Tay and the Almond, or that of the more major, but more distant fort of Carpow, which was near to the important Pictish religious site of Abernethy.[34] That it might subsequently also have been used as part of an ecclesiastical building would have given it an aura both of antiquity and of religious veneration when eventually repurposed for its ceremonial rôle.

32 Emrys Philips *et al.*, 'The Geology of the Stone of Destiny', in Welander *et al.*, *The Stone of Destiny*, pp. 33–40, at p. 39.

33 Stuart Airlie, 'Thrones, Dominions, Powers: Some European Points of Comparison for the Stone of Destiny', in Welander *et al.*, *The Stone of Destiny*, pp. 123–36, at pp. 126–27. See also the discussion of Irish and European analogies in Duncan, *Kingship of the Scots*, pp. 127–29.

34 Ewan Campbell, 'Royal Inauguration in Dál Riata and the Stone of Destiny', in Welander *et al.*, *The Stone of Destiny*, pp. 43–59, at pp. 56–57.

Apart from its local origins, there are other reasons why the stone used at Scone is highly unlikely to have been used in Dál Riatan ceremony. Earlier kings in the Gaelic west had their own distinctive inaugural traditions, which did not include a seat of the type used at Scone. One important inaugural site of Dál Riatan kings was probably at Dunadd in Argyll, where there remains a surviving symbol of ritual – a footprint carved into the rock, a well-attested key element of early Celtic kingship ceremonies, perhaps symbolising the connection of the king to the territory itself, and/or the continuity of the royal line. As the new king stood in the rock footprint, he followed in the footsteps of his predecessors.[35] Dunaverty boasts a similar inaugural relic. It has been convincingly demonstrated that the legends surrounding the Dál Riatan origin of the Stone of Scone date from the thirteenth century, part of a conscious effort to create a sense of 'an impressively deep past' for the Scottish kingdom.[36] There is no direct evidence earlier than the thirteenth century for the use of the stone for Scottish royal inaugurations, but that it was by then an object of sufficient reputation to be worthy of the creation of a fictional past must indicate that it had already been in use for some considerable time.

Ceremonial use of the stone may have been an innovation of the ninth or tenth century, when the southern kingdom of the Picts was pre-eminent among the semi-autonomous provinces which were by then beginning collectively to self-identify as 'Alba'.[37] The earliest reference to Scone as a royal site of Alba comes from a late tenth-century source known as the *Chronicle of the Kings of Alba*, which describes a law-giving assembly which took place in 906 'on the Hill of Faith close to the royal *civitas* of Scone'.[38] Scone, close to the centre of

35 Campbell, 'Royal Inauguration in Dál Riata and the Stone of Destiny', pp. 46–47. See also David H. Caldwell's reconstruction of the inauguration ceremony of the Lords of the Isles, 'Finlaggan, Islay – Stones and Inauguration Ceremonies', in Welander *et al.*, *The Stone of Destiny*, pp. 61–75.

36 Dauvit Broun, 'The Origin of the Stone of Scone as a National Icon', in Welander *et al.*, *The Stone of Destiny*, pp. 183–97, especially at pp. 193–94.

37 See below, pp. 25–27, for further discussion of the development of the kingdoms of 'Alba' and 'Scotland'.

38 The text of *Chronicle of the Kings of Alba* is printed and analysed in Benjamin T. Hudson, 'The Scottish Chronicle', *Scottish Historical Review*, 77 (1998), pp. 129–61; the passage quoted is at p. 150 (translated, p. 156). (See also Broun, *Irish Identity*, p. 167.) I have preferred the translation given by Stephen T. Driscoll, 'The Archaeological Context of Assembly in Early Medieval Scotland – Scone and its Comparanda', in Aliki Pantos and Sarah Semple (eds), *Assembly Places and Practices in Medieval Europe* (Dublin, 2004), pp. 73–94. While the term *civitas* can certainly be taken to indicate an ecclesiastical settlement, even the seat of a bishop (see Norman H. Reid, 'The Prehistory of the University of St Andrews', in Brown and Stevenson, *Medieval St Andrews*, pp. 237–67, at pp. 258–59), Hudson's translation of *civitas* as 'monastery' seems a step too far. Driscoll may well be right to assume, however, that the site was chosen because of its religious significance.

the kingdom of Alba (and also close to what may well have been an earlier assembly and inauguration place, at the impressive hill-top fort of Moncrieff Hill to the south-east), was an obvious choice for a site of royal assembly. Its topography also closely reflects that of other inauguration sites. Govan, for example, sits opposite the confluence of the Clyde and the Kelvin, whereas Scone is opposite the confluence of the Tay and the Almond; both assembly mounds (although Govan's is no longer extant) were close to important early church sites (although that is an assumption, rather than proven fact, in the case of Scone), with royal estates on the opposite side of the river. Govan seems to have become the centre of the British kingdom of Strathclyde in the late ninth or early tenth century, when Dumbarton was destroyed by a Viking siege, and it seems logical to suggest that both Govan and Scone 'are products of the Viking Age and were constructed to celebrate the authority of dynasties that remade themselves in the aftermath of disruptive onslaughts'.[39] The landscape of Scone, with a flat-topped hill built atop a natural terrace sitting above the Tay, and at the time offering clear views of much of the surrounding territory, is analogous to Govan, to Dunadd, and to several other Irish and European inauguration sites. Another feature of the landscape which fits a pattern of developing kingship ritual of the period is the concentration of earlier, prehistoric, monuments close to Scone.[40]

The second element of the inauguration ceremony to be considered is the proclamation of the king's genealogy. The near-contemporary description of the inauguration quoted above states that the genealogy was proclaimed in 'the mother tongue' (*materna lingua*) by a 'highland Scot' (*Scotus montanus*).[41] The portrayal of both the man and his language deliberately set him and the rôle he plays apart from the perceived norm of thirteenth-century lowland-based kingship, and from a ceremony conducted primarily, one assumes, in Latin. This setting apart, along with the subject of his oration – the lineage of the king – has led to the long-held historiographical assumption that the recitation of genealogy was merely an ancient custom, a backward-looking element of the ceremony which lingered within a ritual designed more to reflect contemporary ideas of European kingship.[42]

---

39 Stephen T. Driscoll, 'Govan: An Early Medieval Royal Centre on the Clyde', in Welander *et al.*, *The Stone of Destiny*, pp. 77–83, at p. 82. For analogous attacks in the Dunkeld/Perth area, see below, p. 25.

40 The comments above draw heavily on the work of Driscoll in 'The Archaeological Context of Assembly . . .' and 'Govan: An Early Medieval Royal Centre on the Clyde'.

41 Skene's translation of *Gesta Annalia* translates *materna lingua* as 'his mother tongue' – which emphasises the 'otherness' of the individual even more; the lack of the word *sui*, however, makes Skene's translation somewhat free, and the inclusion of 'his' cannot really be justified.

42 For example, *mea culpa*: 'It was a ceremony which stressed the changing nature of the

Like the Stone of Destiny, however, historiographical tradition has woven a shroud of mythology around the 'highland Scot' and his rôle in the ceremony. The 'highland Scot' was in fact the king's *fili*, or official poet, a hereditary official of the king, a position which was alive and well in the mid thirteenth century; further, he had hastened to the ceremony not from a remote highland glen, but from his considerable estates on the border between Fife and Perthshire, in the heartland of the thirteenth-century kingdom. In earlier society, the king's poet was a high-status position: he would be of a high social standing, but also recognised for his knowledge – 'at the apex of the learned orders'.[43] One of the traditional duties of the *fili* was indeed to maintain the king's pedigree, which was, as it had been for centuries, one of the necessary qualifications for the right to the kingship. The description of the poet as *Scotus montanus* was not intended to indicate rusticity, but was merely an indication that he was a Gaelic-speaker: that he read (*legebat*) the pedigree provides certainty about his literacy, and thus status. This was understood in his own time and later: the illustrator who drew him in the fifteenth-century manuscript of Walter Bower's *Scotichronicon* depicted him with a sword, a signal of nobility.[44] Equally, the account of his 'sudden' (*subito*) appearance does not imply that his part was spontaneous or unrehearsed: this was a part which was deeply entrenched within the model of kingship used by the (Irish) kin-based society. It is more likely that *subito* reflects an unsurprising degree of theatricality in the ceremony, and it may not be too fanciful to imagine that the source text quoted above, which provides our earliest version of events, was written by an eyewitness. In Irish tradition, the poet would also have composed and delivered an inaugural ode accompanied by a harpist (who might be an otherwise unidentified figure on the Scone abbey seal). Additionally, the sceptre (which Alexander is shown to be holding in the images on the Scone abbey seal, on all three of his surviving royal seal designs, and in the later Bower illustration) might typically have been presented to him by the *fili*, who thereby had a rôle in the ceremony completely integral to the bestowal of kingship. It was a rôle which was fully in accord with a much older, more traditional kingship ritual, but also with current symbolism. His duty was both to prove the king's right to rule and to represent the gathered community in the process of making good that right. Alexander had been enthroned by the

Scottish kingship: the "stone", the largely fabulous genealogical recitation, and the part played by the ancient grouping of the "Seven Earls", symbolised the Celtic past, while the homage of the magnates, the consecration by the bishop, and above all the age of the king signified the modern "Anglo-Norman" elements of the monarchy.' Reid, 'Political Rôle of the Monarchy', p. 4.

43 J.W.M. Bannerman, 'The King's Poet'; J.W.M. Bannerman, 'The Residence of the King's Poet', in Bannerman, *Kinship, Church and Culture*, pp. 283–94, where he is more than tentatively identified as Donnchad, lord of Fargie.

44 Bannerman, 'The King's Poet', pp. 252–55.

nobles and invested by the ecclesiastics, 'but it was not until the poet presented him with the sceptre of kingship that Alexander actually became king'.[45]

That the inauguration of the king depended so heavily on traditions which may have been several centuries old does not imply, however, that the ceremony was either immutable or entirely ancient. There is sufficient evidence to be persuasive of the fact, for example, that the ceremony did not take place – as is usually assumed, and as was presumably the case in earlier times – on the 'Moot Hill', but rather by a cross which stood in the cemetery outside the east end of the abbey church. If the English chronicler Walter of Guisborough is to be believed, the next inauguration, that of John Balliol in 1292, took place inside the church rather than in the open air.[46] Another element which it has been suggested was an innovation in 1249 was the strewing of the garments (presumably, cloaks) of the nobility at the new king's feet – a further non-traditional practice, with biblical precedent, which stressed Alexander's God-given right to rule. The ceremony was 'too important an opportunity to miss for making a dramatic statement about the kingship'.[47] This may have been particularly true when the king being installed was a minor, whose grip on power may therefore have been insecure.

Some commentators are reluctant to accept that the inauguration ceremony included any formal bestowal of the crown on the new king. As was noted above, the Scottish kings were not yet crowned and anointed according to what were by then the norms of European kingship. To that extent, it is therefore right to rely on terminology which does not carry any such implication – *inauguration*, rather than *coronation*.[48] There is evidence, however, that the Scottish kings from Edgar (1097–1107) onwards did possess crowns; both David I and Máel Coluim

---

45 Bannerman, 'The King's Poet', pp. 265–67. As far back as 1945 the traditional nature of the ceremony had been acknowledged: 'it reads like an account of the old tribal inauguration blessed by the presence of a bishop' (M.D. Legge, 'The Inauguration of Alexander III', *Proceedings of the Society of Antiquaries of Scotland*, 80 (1945–46), pp. 73–82). Legge points out that, by the time of Charles I, the inauguration had become an amalgamation of tribal inauguration with 'Christian and feudalised coronation', but asserts that, by 1249, that process of assimilation 'had hardly begun' (p. 75). Dauvit Broun has suggested to me (in conversation) that the description of Alexander as *rex mox futurus* as he is led to the Stone might indicate that it was the placing on the Stone which made him king, but equally it could apply to the whole of the forthcoming ceremony.

46 A.A.M. Duncan, 'Before Coronation: Making a King at Scone in the Thirteenth Century', in Welander *et al.*, *The Stone of Destiny*, pp. 139–67, at pp. 145–48; Duncan, *Kingship of the* Scots, p. 150; Broun, *Scottish Independence*, p. 181 (and see also n. 74, where Broun disputes Duncan's suggestion that the Moot Hill may never have been used for the inauguration ceremony); *Chron. Guisborough*, p. 239.

47 Broun, *Scottish Independence*, p. 181. The biblical precedent comes from 2 Kings 9: 12–13.

48 Duncan, 'Before Coronation', pp. 140 (where the use of the term 'coronation' is described as an 'ineradicable error'), 151. Broun, *Scottish Independence*, pp. 179–80.

IV are shown wearing them in the remarkable decorated initial from the 1159 charter confirming the possessions of Kelso abbey.[49] It is possible that the initial is artistically formulaic in its portrayal of the two kings,[50] but there are none-theless aspects of it which are strikingly similar to the consistent portrayal of thirteenth-century Scottish kings and the regalia on their seals. (For example, the fact that the younger king holds his sword flat across his knees is reflective of the 'minority seal' of Alexander III, which will be discussed below.) Perhaps most significantly, previous studies of the inauguration have been heavily reliant on the evidential accuracy of the Scone abbey seal: in common with all of the great seals used in the reigns of Alexander II and III, it clearly shows the king wearing a crown. If the Scone abbey seal is to be regarded as a reliable source for some aspects of the ceremony, then it must also be assumed to present firm evidence that by the end of the inauguration ceremony the young king had a crown on his head.[51] How it got there, of course, is open to question. It is possible that he placed it there himself.[52] If he had been crowned by one of the clerics, this would certainly have been noted in the textual description of the ceremony, as it would have given the event a more ecclesiastical bearing than seems to have been intended and would have been at best controversial, since ecclesiastical coronation was closely associated with the as yet unauthorised rite of unction. A formal request for this rite had been made during the reign of Alexander II, however, and the assumption of a crown during the ceremony, whether it was bestowed on the king by his own hand or by one of the nobility, must be seen as a signal of the pretensions of the monarchy. Even if the portrayal of the crowned Alexander III, David, Máel Coluim IV and the other kings was purely formulaic, which must be doubted, it is still indicative that the Scottish kings regarded themselves as kings equal in status to other monarchs. That does not

49 For the text of the Kelso charter, see *RRS*, i, no. 131; it is reproduced in facsimile in *Liber S. Marie de Calchou* (Bannatyne Club, 1846), i, plate 2. For descriptions of royal seals from Edgar to Alexander II, see John Horne Stevenson and Marguerite Wood, *Scottish Heraldic Seals: Royal, Official, Ecclesiastical, Collegiate, Burghal, Personal* (Glasgow, 1940), pp. 2–5. Edgar is definitely depicted wearing a crown; it is less clear for Alexander I, David and Máel Coluim IV. William is described by Stevenson and Wood (p. 3) as wearing a 'thick cap perhaps of fur'; Alexander II's headgear is not described by Stevenson and Wood. Illustrations of impressions of these seals (excluding Máel Coluim IV) are provided by Birch, *History of Scottish Seals*, i, plates 2, 5, 7, 9 (which show both William and Alexander II wearing headgear very similar to that of Alexander I, described by Stevenson and Wood as 'a small crown').

50 Duncan, 'Before Coronation', p. 151.

51 G.W.S. Barrow, however, cast doubt on the notion that the Scone abbey seal was in fact supposed to represent the 1249 ceremony: G.W.S. Barrow, 'Observations on the Coronation Stone of Scotland', *Scottish Historical Review*, 76 (1997), pp. 115–21, at pp. 116–17. Even if he was right, whether the seal is intended to depict this occasion, another, or is a more general representation, it still provides useful evidence for the nature of the ceremony.

52 For self-coronation, see below, p. 34.

imply, however, that all the traditions of their monarchy, and the nature of their relationship to their nobility and the populace in general, was identical to the monarchies of, for instance, England or France. There was more than one monarchical model, and it is important to understand the nature and development of the Scottish monarchy in order accurately to interpret not only the inauguration ritual, but the course of the reign itself. The Scots kings undoubtedly wished to be counted unambiguously as kings, peers with their European counterparts, but the fact that their inauguration ritual remained 'strikingly different compared with what was increasingly the norm in Latin Christendom'[53] must indicate that they had an equal desire to maintain the distinctive nature and traditions of their kingship.

The kingship to which the child Alexander was initiated in 1249 was one which had developed out of a rich blend of traditions. The significance of the symbolism of the inauguration ceremony, and of its impact on the interpretation of the events of the reign, can only be fully understood through examination of the roots of that kingship, and of the forces that had shaped it and the kingdom over which it claimed authority, across many centuries. Much excellent work has been undertaken recently on the early history of the land we now know as Scotland, and what follows is necessarily only a very brief synthesis of the opinions of many experts on the periods in question, which aims to provide a simplified narrative overview of the complex shifts in power-balance, events and movements which led to the formation of the kingdom.[54]

Well before the Roman invasion of southern Britain, in what now tends to be regarded as the periphery of Europe, but which, through seaborne migration, maritime trade and cultural exchange, was not in fact isolated from the rest of the Continent, a common language (with many dialects) developed. 'Where people brought goods to exchange, the necessary spoken exchanges were perhaps conducted in a variety of Indo-European dialects out of which grew the earliest stratum of the Celtic language.'[55] By the time of the Roman invasion, the

53 Broun, *Scottish Independence*, p. 179.

54 The following passage relies very heavily on a few key works: Gilbert Márkus, *Conceiving a Nation*; Alex Woolf, *From Pictland to Alba*; Barbara E. Crawford: *Scandinavian Scotland* (Leicester, 1987); Broun, *Irish Identity*. I am grateful to the authors of these excellent guides to the complexities of early medieval Scotland. Citations to other sources, and references to quotations and specific parts of these works, are provided in the footnotes. The interpretation of Scotland's early history offered in these works is not uncontroversial, and works offering different views will be found in the Bibliography. The formation of the *Regnum Scottorum* has been described as 'an object lesson in the frustrations of life as an early medieval historian' (Patrick Wormald, 'The Emergence of the *Regnum Scottorum*: A Carolingian Hegemony?', in Barbara E. Crawford (ed.), *Scotland in Dark Age Britain* (Aberdeen, 1996), pp. 131–60, at p. 131). It is not appropriate in this short summary to rehearse the complex arguments involved.

55 Márkus, *Conceiving a Nation*, p. 3.

northern mainland of Britain was inhabited by a number of tribal groupings, all speaking variants of the Celtic language, who were later identified by the Roman occupiers (and gradually began to self-identify) in a generic sense as *Picti*, probably a pejorative term indicating all of the barbaric 'others' beyond the rule of the empire. The *Scotti* were another group, probably seafaring tribes from Ireland and the Western Isles, who would have had extensive contact with the western side of the mainland. The sea was no barrier; rather, it was a means of communication and fostered cultural cohesion. These peoples were not necessarily always hostile to the Romans; they would certainly have traded and at times worked with, and for, the Roman military and civilian presence, and undoubtedly assimilated some of the cultural customs of the Romans, such as alphabet and writing. At other times, as is specifically reported by Roman writers, they were hostile and played their part in exerting the general pressure which gradually forced the Roman retreat by the early fifth century AD. In the ensuing sub-Roman period, northern Briton was occupied by peoples with several cultural ethnic (rather than racial) identifications, who ruled the territories under their control through a series of small, even local, lordships which were maintained through warrior force. In the west, the Gaels (as we describe them from their Q-Celtic language, Gaelic, to distinguish them from their Pictish neighbours, who spoke a dialect of P-Celtic British which was perhaps less Latinised than more southerly variants) were similarly organised in small 'kingship' units, controlled by ruling kindreds who, in time, developed 'genealogical fictions' in order to 'give ancestral legitimacy to new political realities'.[56] These genealogies, the production of which became so integral a part of the kin-based ruling society of the west, and which provide much of our extant documentary evidence for the early Middle Ages, have given a perhaps misleading impression of concerted migration and settlement by long-standing ruling families. There is indeed evidence of some early migration from Ireland into the western fringes of the British mainland, but the development, out of a number of loosely related polities, of a political unit in the Scottish islands and western seaboard identifying itself as Dál Riata, is a later development.[57] The genealogies, however, are

56 Márkus, *Conceiving a Nation*, p. 80. On the Pictish language, see Simon Taylor, 'Pictish Place-names Revisited', in Stephen T. Driscoll, Jane Geddes and Mark A. Hall (eds), *Pictish Progress: New Studies on Northern Britain in the Early Middle Ages* (Leiden, 2011), pp. 67–118, at p. 67.

57 See the discussion in James E. Fraser, *From Caledonia to Pictland: Scotland to 795* (Edinburgh, 2009), at pp. 144–49: 'The early medieval notion of a migration from Ireland can be questioned. Archaeologists have fired salvos against this and other 'diffusionist' models for understanding cultural change. There is no clear evidence that the Roman Iron Age saw the dedicated colonisation of Argyll by a single Irish people.' (p. 147). Ewan Campbell, 'Were the Scots Irish?' (*Antiquity*, 75 (2001), pp. 285–92) similarly challenges the notion of wholesale

undoubtedly evidence of the connection through language and interest, if not through actual kinship, of polities in Ireland and western Scotland and the isles. The idea of ancient and unchanging kingdoms which were internally united through ethnicity, language or culture cannot be sustained: political, ethnic and cultural identities fluctuated over time.

Throughout several centuries, however, it is evident that a degree of stability in kingdoms was achieved.[58] There is archaeological evidence of a level of long-distance trading activity in the west which suggests that 'the northern kingdoms were economically more advanced and integrated by 700 than others further south', which may have been 'a contributing factor to the early development of the unified Scottish dynastic state in the ninth century'.[59] In particular, by the beginning of the eighth century AD, the Pictish kingdom of Fortriu, based on the Moray coast, had been able to extend its power, with some degree of consistency, over most of central and eastern Scotland to the north of the Forth (and including the northern isles); this area was sufficiently under the domination of one ruler for the title of Pictland (or Pictavia) to be appropriate. It was divided into provinces 'roughly corresponding in size to medieval earldoms or modern counties',[60] the rulers of which may, in some cases, have been sub-kings who recognised a greater authority wielded by the kings of Fortriu (and whose positions would in time become known as the 'great stewards', or the *mormaír*, of later kings of Pictland and Alba), or may perhaps have been self-promoted warrior chieftains more in the Scandinavian style. A view which sees Pictavia as 'a loose hegemony centred on a northern kingdom' is consistent with the complex place-name evidence.[61] This Pictish hegemony may also have extended over the more northerly parts of the west coast and islands too, although there is little evidence for who lived there before the late eighth century. By the mid eighth century, Pictland also held sway over the Gaelic

---

displacement of native peoples by Irish migrants in the fifth or sixth centuries. Márkus agrees: he sees the archaeological evidence for large-scale migration as insufficient and prefers the likelihood of trading contacts across the Irish Sea, with cultural separation between east and west (Picts and Scots) being created by the mountains of the central highlands (Márkus, *Conceiving a Nation*, pp. 78–79). More recently, McDonald, *Sea Kings*, p. 21, follows a similar line. I am grateful to the publishers, Birlinn, for allowing me sight of a pre-publication text of this work.

58 For a useful description of the political landscape of northern Britain in this period, see Woolf, *From Pictland to Alba*, especially at pp. 4–13; see also Sally M. Foster, *Picts, Gaels and Scots: Early Historic Scotland* (London, 1996): 'in practical terms the Picts (and indeed Dál Riata) only became truly recognizable as archaeological and historical entities from the sixth century' (p. 13).

59 Ewan Campbell, 'Trade in the Dark-Age West: A Peripheral Activity?', in Barbara E. Crawford (ed.), *Scotland in Dark Age Britain* (Aberdeen, 1996), pp. 72–91, at p. 88.

60 Woolf, *From Pictland to Alba*, p. 11.

61 Woolf, *From Pictland to Alba*, pp. 11–12.

kings of Dál Riata, based in Argyll and holding power over parts of the western seaboard and the islands. Far from the Picts having been wiped out by the encroaching Dál Riatan Scots, as used to be believed, it seems instead that the Dál Riatan kings were in fact 'sub-kings in a Pictish dominion which stretched from coast to coast'.[62] Cinaed mac Ailpín, often hailed as the Scottish conqueror of the Picts in the mid ninth century, was described in the notice of his death given in the Annals of Ulster (one of the key contemporary sources for the period) *sub anno* (s.a.) 858 as 'King of the Picts'; it seems likely that, as a sub-king in Dál Riata, and surely related to the Pictish ruling kindred, he had made good a claim to the kingship. His brother Domnall, who succeeded him, was similarly described on his death in 862.[63] Occasional Dál Riatan counter-offensives also took place, as when, in 768, there was a significant attack on Fortriu.[64]

Notwithstanding, there was a marked shift of cultural and linguistic dominance through the eastward movement of Gaelic-speaking people, and particularly through the spread of the Columban church. The influence of a literate Gaelic monastic clergy would have been felt far beyond the cloister, through their pastoral efforts and their usefulness to rulers as a body of educated administrators; and the existing network of Columban monasteries (which had been being established since the seventh century throughout large parts of Pictland) would have provided 'an *in situ* support system for the advancement of Gaelic kingship as well as Gaelic culture'.[65] Lay settlement would also have impacted on social and economic relationships. In addition, to the south there was another large kingdom (primarily Anglian), Bernicia, occupying most of what we would now call Lothian, Northumbria, Galloway and much of Cumberland, and which periodically exercised some degree of hegemony over the British kingdom of Strathclyde. Pictland may therefore have been under similar cultural, religious and political pressure from the south.

---

62 Márkus, *Conceiving a Nation*, p. 104. This is not an undisputed interpretation of the situation revealed by confusing and contradictory evidence: see, for example, Wormald, 'The Emergence of the *Regnum Scottorum*', esp. at pp. 134–37. See also Fraser, *From Caledonia to Pictland*, pp. 287–305, where a more complex picture – but nonetheless one which portrays Pictish dominance in this period – is painted.

63 Anderson, *Early Sources*, i, pp. 287, 290; for details of the difficult identification of the Dál Riatan and Pictish kings' lineages in this period, see Woolf, *From Pictland to Alba*, pp. 59–64, and Dauvit Broun, 'Pictish Kings 761–839: Integration with Dál Riata or Separate Development?', in Sally M. Foster (ed.), *The St Andrews Sarcophagus: A Pictish Masterpiece and its International Connections* (Dublin, 1998), pp. 71–83.

64 See Máire Herbert, '*Rí Éirenn, Rí Alban*: Kingship and Identity in the Ninth and Tenth Centuries', in Simon Taylor (ed.), *Kings, Clerics and Chronicles in Scotland 500–1297* (Dublin, 2000), p. 66.

65 Máire Herbert, '*Rí Éirenn, Rí Alban*', p. 68; on intermarriage between Pictish and Dál Riatan dynasties, see Bannerman, '*Senchus fer nAlban*', in Bannerman, *Kinship, Church and Culture*, pp. 27–156, at p. 106.

Different concepts of kingship and rule developed out of the infusion of Gaelic and sub-Roman Christian culture into Pictish society, reducing the notion of rule through warrior power, and introducing the idea that the primary rôle of the king was to keep peace, using violence only where necessary to preserve justice or to safeguard the church and people. This shift in emphasis within the kingship from the eighth century is strikingly illustrated by two remarkable artistic achievements. The intricate and magnificent imagery of the St Andrews Sarcophagus, made probably in the first half of the ninth century, is replete with kingly and religious symbolism: the killing of the lion by the youthful David (mirrored by other Pictish art depicting Daniel and Jonah, who were also delivered by divine intervention from wild animals), an elaborate hunting scene, a cross and allegorical animals. It is a monument full of kingly and Christian symbolism for its royal patron. This is Christian art, in a Pictish social and artistic milieu. It is clear, too, that the extraordinary art of the Picts places them in a context of mutual cultural exchange: the artistic and other associations with Pictland are spread widely in Britain and Continental Europe. Pictish society was 'aware of, and fired by, all the cultural stimuli that came with their membership of European Christendom'.[66] The image of King David appears again on an elaborately carved cross from Dupplin, only a short distance away from the Pictish royal centre of Forteviot (and now displayed in the church at Dunning). It also depicts a king, probably Constantín son of Wrguist (*c.*789–820), with ranks of foot soldiers. Its imagery, like the St Andrews Sarcophagus in that it similarly lacks the traditional Pictish artistic symbols, emphasises a new model of kingship which is more authoritarian – 'a strengthening and formalization of royal authority' – and certainly a closer relationship between the Christian church and the kingship than was previously identifiable.[67] Even the name Constantín, borne by several kings of this period, carried unmistakeable reference to the wider Christian world.

The introduction of such overtly Christian elements into the rôle of the ruler would have changed the nature of inauguration ceremonies, as the notion that the king ruled through God's will (as opposed to rule primarily through the will, or election, of the people) took root. Ancient traditions do not disappear completely, however: Christianisation was a slow process, and it involved

66 Charles Thomas, 'Form and Function', in Foster, *The St Andrews Sarcophagus*, pp. 84–96, at p. 95; Isobel Henderson, '*Primus inter Pares*: The St Andrews Sarcophagus and Pictish Sculpture', in Foster, *The St Andrews Sarcophagus*, pp. 97–167 (quote from p. 98). For its political significance, see also Stephen T. Driscoll, 'Political Discourse and the Growth of Christian Ceremonialism in Pictland: The Place of the St Andrews Sarcophagus', in Foster, *The St Andrews Sarcophagus*, pp. 168–78.

67 Woolf, *From Pictland to Alba*, p. 65; Foster, *Picts, Gaels and Scots*, pp. 98–99.

exchange and mutual assimilation of beliefs, customs and cultural traditions. Elements of elective kingship, and of right through lineage (and therefore a continuing importance of the proclamation of the royal genealogy) remained, but within a view of kingship in which the justice which the king was bound to pursue was rooted increasingly in theological rather than in either legal or military terms.

There was a further power-shift of tectonic proportions when, beginning at the end of the eighth century, successive waves of devastating attack and invasive settlement were inflicted on the islands and shores of Scotland by the Vikings. Their predations on the west were first noted in a serious attack on the Hebrides and, specifically, Iona in 794–95, and within several decades they had effectively taken hold of the northern and western islands and were in a position to extract tribute from the inhabitants of neighbouring lands. They did not restrict their activities to the western fringe; they also exerted huge pressure on Pictland, from both east and west, and the earliest raids on British soil, in Northumbria in 793 and 794, should probably be seen as an attempt at invasion. The mistaken, or at best partial, Hollywood view of Viking longships appearing suddenly to pillage and plunder, and then disappearing over the horizon as swiftly as they had arrived, obscures the deep and long-lasting cultural and political effects which the Vikings had on the development of Scotland, and indeed the whole of Britain. There is evidence that in parts there was a sustained policy of what would now be termed 'ethnic cleansing'; in Islay, for instance, place-name, linguistic and archaeological evidence suggests that the local population may have been entirely displaced: the island seems to have suffered 'the physical suppression of native culture through the killing, clearance or enslavement of the native population'.[68] It is certain that throughout much of the Hebrides and western seaboard there was large-scale settlement by Norse-speaking communities which seem to have achieved a fair degree of political stability. Uniquely among Scandinavian settlement areas, the Scottish islands came to be controlled by the developing Norwegian monarchy: 'the northern and western coasts of Scotland were a part of the Scandinavian world', effectively colonies from which war was waged against the neighbouring territories, and it is quite conceivable that (as in England) there was an ambition of overall conquest.[69] It is not

68 Alan Macniven, *The Vikings in Islay: The Place of Names in Hebridean Settlement History* (Edinburgh, 2015), p. 116; Woolf, *From Pictland to Alba*, pp. 12–13: the west coast from Ardnamurchan to Orkney became Scandinavianised 'in as clear-cut a case of ethnic cleansing as can be found in the entirety of British history'.

69 Crawford, *Scandinavian Scotland*, pp. 1–2, 51. Clearly there was close contact between the various centres of Norse activity in Dublin and York and with the polities with which they came into contact. They became 'an established part of the political *status quo* in North Britain in the first half of the tenth century' (*Scandinavian Scotland*, p. 60).

impossible, although evidence is scant, that diplomatic deals were struck through which the Pictish kingdom at times achieved protection in return either for tribute or for allowing settlement in some areas. Throughout the early decades of the ninth century the Viking pressure continued, with violent operations increasingly being launched from bases in Ireland and the Western Isles. In 839, the Vikings inflicted a catastrophic defeat on the Picts in which the king of the Picts, Wen, son of Onuist died alongside Áed, king of Dál Riata; that Áed had been present, fighting a Pictish battle, suggests a continuing dominance of Pictland over the western kingdom. This defeat seems to have brought about the fall of the northern Pictish dynasty and a southerly shift in the balance of power in Pictland.[70] Certainly, as king of the Picts, Cinaed mac Ailpín (who died at Forteviot, not far from Perth) seems to have had his territorial base in the southern part of the kingdom. The Norse pressure continued, however: in the late 840s there were further attacks on the Hebrides, which prompted the removal of Columba's relics to Dunkeld for safekeeping; in the same period there were vicious attacks on Cinaed's heartland in the upper reaches of the Tay; the destruction of Dumbarton in 870 has already been noted; and around 875 there was another decisive defeat at the hands of a Viking force at Dollar. To the south, Northumbria became effectively an Anglo-Danish kingdom in the second half of the ninth century.[71] In this period, under intense pressure both from the west and the south, the Pictish kingdom must have been close to total collapse. Dunkeld, due to the southward shift of Pictish power, was already a royal and ecclesiastical centre, but it is surely significant that in 878 the relics of Columba, which had been moved there from Iona barely 30 years earlier, now found refuge in Kells.[72]

By the end of the ninth century, contemporary writers in Latin and English had more or less stopped referring to Pictland; the Annals of Ulster last referred to the people as *Picti* in 875, after which they became the 'men of Alba',[73] all of which gave rise to the old historiographical tradition, which goes back to the twelfth century, that the Scots had overrun Pictland and obliterated it.[74] The

---

70 Woolf, *From Pictland to Alba*, pp. 66–67.

71 Dollar: Anderson, *Early Sources*, i, pp. 350–53; Hebrides and Northumbria: Woolf, *From Pictland to Alba*, pp. 68–86, 99–102.

72 *Annals of Ulster*: see Anderson, *Early Sources*, i, pp. 279 & n., 356; see discussion in Woolf, *From Pictland to Alba*, pp. 98–102, and pp. 123–24.

73 Dauvit Broun, 'Dunkeld and the Origin of Scottish Identity', *Innes Review*, 48 (1997), pp. 112–24, at p. 112.

74 See Woolf, *From Pictland to Alba*, p. 1, referring to the issue of 'Pictish ethnonemesis' and the work of Henry of Huntingdon, *c.*1140; Woolf's extensive discussion of the end of the Pictish kingdom is at pp. 87–121. See also Dauvit Broun, 'Britain and the Beginning of Scotland'. The idea of a Scottish conquest of Pictland, and of a conscious Gaelic assertion of the 'ideals of Carolingian kingship', are not without support, however: see, e.g., Wormald, 'The Emergence

truth, although challenging to unravel due to the paucity of sources, seems to have been both more complicated and more subtle. It is now doubted that there was, in reality, an early takeover of the Pictish kingdom by the Scots, to found a new Scottish kingdom; that is a notion which is generally now ascribed to the thirteenth century as a part of 'the narrative that was being fashioned to reflect the emerging idea of Scotland as a sovereign kingdom'.[75] The Pictish and Scottish kingdoms having been dynastically linked by the ninth century, and the Gaelic language gradually gaining precedence over the Pictish, it is better to think of Pictland as having been 'reimagined' rather than destroyed: its ruling elite 'had created for themselves a new narrative accounting for the origins of their power, portraying the kingdom's identity in a new way, stressing a Gaelic dimension to their identity'.[76] *Alba* and *Pictland* were effectively different ways of expressing the concept of the same kingdom – that part of Britain which lay to the north of the Forth, which was seen as a separate territory, even as an island, separated from the rest of Britain by the penetrating tentacles of the North Sea and the Atlantic at the Forth–Clyde line. The genealogies of the kings of the tenth and eleventh centuries were extended to offer 'the lustre of antiquity which the kingship required as an expression of its legitimacy' – 'a means for expressing the kingship's royal credentials and for establishing its status in relation to other kingships'.[77] The name which was exclusively used to describe the kingdom, *Alba*, represented this fusion of peoples and cultures; *Alba* did not refer to a single people, either Pictish or Gaelic, but to a political unit, a bounded (although admittedly still fluctuating) territorial area in which the ethnic identities of its inhabitants became subsidiary to the polity itself.[78] It is additionally important that Alba was a name which had previously described the whole of the pre-Roman British island; it thus stressed the fundamentally British nature of the kingdom (in a way similar to that in which the self-adoption of the term *Picti* had earlier identified various peoples as British, non-Roman); but *Alba* was a Gaelic word, certainly reflecting the fact that the Pictish language was by then waning, but, more importantly, proclaiming that the face which the kingdom

of the *Regnum Scottorum*', esp. at pp. 143–45.

75 Broun, 'Britain and the Beginning of Scotland', p. 109.

76 Márkus, *Conceiving a Nation*, pp. 264–65; a different interpretation of events, however, is offered in John Bannerman, 'The Scottish Takeover of Pictland and the Relics of Columba', in Bannerman, *Kinship, Church and Culture*, pp. 209–29; see also Broun, 'Dunkeld and the Origin of Scottish Identity', pp. 122–23; Simon Taylor, 'From *Cinrigh Monai* to *Civitas Sancti Andree*: A Star is Born', in Brown and Stevenson, *Medieval St Andrews*, pp. 20–34.

77 Broun, *Irish Identity*, pp. 189, 192.

78 Herbert, '*Rí Éirenn, Rí Alban*', p. 71: 'the establishment of the kingship of Alba answered an evident need to create a unifying structure which harmonized social and cultural differences. The creation of a political identity laid the groundwork for the definition of further communal bonds.'

now presented to the world was a redefined, Gaelicised but nonetheless British identity.[79]

It is well known that external threat can be a catalyst for political and cultural cohesion, and the constant pressure from the Norse on the relatively disparate elements of Dál Riata and Pictland for well over a century, from the 790s until the gradual dissipation of Norse power during the tenth century, was probably one of the factors which encouraged the creation of what might be recognised as a single kingdom out of the various petty kingdoms of earlier times, with a developing system of 'sub-royal regional power' wielded on behalf of the kings by *mormaír*.[80] In 903, the kingdom of Alba was able to inflict defeat on a significant Viking incursion, perhaps an indication of its growing cohesion and power.[81] It could hardly yet claim to be a culturally, linguistically or politically coherent unit, and was riven with dynastic instability throughout the tenth and eleventh centuries; neither was it yet territorially equivalent to Scotland of the thirteenth century: it may have been in the first quarter of the eleventh century that the kings of Alba finally could claim to rule over Lothian, and another 50 years before the same could be said for Strathclyde. Nonetheless, the Alba which emerged from the cauldron of the Viking Age in the tenth century had more in common with the medieval notion of the kingdom of the Scots than it had with the patchwork of warrior-led territories of sub-Roman Britain.

It is clear, then, that the kingdom which would over another two or three centuries develop into the kingdom of the Scots, and its kingship, were the products of long periods of conflict, assimilation and fusion between a range of peoples and cultures. This raises the question of whose tradition is meant when a 'traditional element' of the kingship, or any of its associated rituals, is discussed. It is easy to say that the roots of the medieval Scottish kingship lay in the Gaelic society of Ireland and the west; but that is to swallow unquestioned the propaganda of the kings of Alba and, further, ignores the possibility that the Gaelic tradition itself may be a cultural amalgam, created over centuries. Equally, to ascribe later Scottish tradition to the Picts would be to ignore the major

79 Márkus, *Conceiving a Nation*, p. 269.

80 Broun, 'Dunkeld and the Origin of Scottish Identity', p. 123: 'the immediate context of the coining of Scottish identity is most likely to have been the instability and social dislocation which followed in the wake of the worst phase of Norse devastation inflicted on southern Pictland in 875–6 and 878.' This is not to suggest that the Norse pressure subsided entirely: strife in the islands was still alive and well in the late tenth century, effectively creating a new 'Kingdom of the Isles' by the end of the century (Woolf, *From Pictland to Alba*, pp. 212–18). On the *mormaer*, see Dauvit Broun, 'The Origins of the *Mormaer*', in Huw Docherty and David Crouch (eds), *The Earl in Medieval Britain* (forthcoming). I am grateful to Professor Broun for giving me sight of this essay in advance of publication.

81 Broun, 'Dunkeld and the Origin of Scottish Identity', p. 124.

influence of both Norse and Gaelic societies. Further impact from more southerly Britons and the Angles of Bernicia/Northumbria cannot be ignored either. There is no single ethnic tradition into which the Scottish or any other kingship type can be packaged: it is a continuously evolving entity. However, by looking at other examples of ritual and rulership, it is possible to identify similarities between the Scottish and other monarchies which might offer clues to the primary influences which shaped the Scottish polity.

The impact of Christian notions of rule, and the effect they had on the nature of kingship from the fifth or sixth centuries onwards, a process which went hand in hand with the increasing spread of Gaelic culture into Pictland, has been mentioned above. But, as is made clear by what is known of the inauguration ceremonies, some older customs retained their position, and their meaning, within the kingship rituals. The use of an inauguration mound, for example, has clear parallels with the earlier Irish/Gaelic custom, but is a feature too of Scandinavian kingship. The mound at Scone, in use as a place of law-giving from at least the early tenth century, is strongly reminiscent of the *thing*-sites of the Scandinavian world, at which popular assemblies took place, where kings might be elected and proclaimed, and at which on a regular basis law was made (not, in earlier times, generally a royal function), promulgated and enacted. There is firm evidence of the Hebrides, for instance, sending representatives to the *thing* assemblies on the Isle of Man during the west's Scandinavian era, and place names from Dingwall in the north to Tinwald in the south indicate widespread and pervasive influence of Scandinavian settlers on customs and governing practices. The Council of the Isles which continued to meet at Finlaggan for centuries thereafter is testimony to how thoroughly such customs permeate a society.[82] A dozen potential *thing*-sites have recently been identified in the areas of Scotland under Scandinavian occupation (excluding Orkney and Shetland, which were not yet part of Scotland in the thirteenth century).[83] The existence of Scandinavian custom in those areas is certainly in evidence; however, the sites often reveal the reuse of existing monuments, especially mounds, indicating that similar custom was already prevalent in those areas. If this was the case in Scandinavian areas, it is likely also to have been the case elsewhere in Scotland where clues provided by Scandinavian place names would be lacking. The identification of early inauguration mounds both in western Scotland and in Ireland, and the mounds at Scone (Pictish) and Govan (British), for example, as well as the likelihood that Moncreiff Hill

82 See Crawford, *Scandinavian Scotland*, pp. 205–09.

83 Alexandra Sanmark, *Viking Law and Order: Places and Rituals of Assembly in the Medieval North* (Edinburgh, 2017), ch. 8 (pp. 194–240), and see map on p. 198.

and Rhynie in Aberdeenshire had fulfilled similar assembly functions in the earlier southern and northern Pictish kingdoms, suggests that some at least of the Scandinavian cultural impositions may not have been as foreign as has been imagined. Dingwall is a particularly interesting example: the place name makes it clear that it was a Norse assembly site; the archaeological evidence, however, seems to suggest that the mound itself is a creation of the eleventh or twelfth century, when Scottish control of that area was being affirmed. If Scottish authority chose to assert control over the area by maintaining continuity through the assimilation of the Norse assembly into its own practice,[84] it is reasonable to envisage that a similar consideration might earlier have influenced the Norse invaders' own choice of sites.

The assembly is a feature of societies in which authority was based initially on localised control by chieftains who gained dominance through might, and who maintained that dominance through the agreement of the ruled. Broadly, this is the pattern of Germanic kingship described by Tacitus, writing in the late first or early second century AD, who described a society in which kings were chosen by the people for their inherited characteristics of leadership as well as their warlike prowess, and whose power was circumscribed by the people, who decided on significant issues as a 'nation', through discussion at assemblies at which all, of any status, might be heard.[85] Several families might achieve dominance at various times, and power would shift between them; the gradual concentration of power within one or several families would be consolidated over time, but the principle of common assent remained and became, in at least a formulaic way, a feature of those monarchies. It was certainly from this model that the Scandinavian monarchies eventually emerged. Since they were late to be Christianised (and thus to receive the overlay of Christian rulership ideals) and have left a rich secular literature as evidence, it is easy to recognise the developmental process.[86] The principle of election remained an element of Germanic kingship for many centuries: as late as 924, the Anglo-Saxon Chronicle claimed that Athelstan was elected king of Mercia, and even in the

---

84 Sanmark, *Viking Law and Order*, p. 225. See also her suggestion that Dingwall had served as an assembly site under different regimes, p. 237, and discussion of the likelihood of assembly as a feature of Gaelic as well as Norse society, pp. 237–38.

85 Paraphrased from the discussion in Hybel, *The Nature of Kingship*, p. 37; see also Hybel's discussion of the elective principle in Danish kingship (pp. 49–56).

86 There is copious literature on the development of the Scandinavian monarchies: see, for example, Sverre Bagge, *From Viking Stronghold to Christian Kingdom: State Formation in Norway, c.900–1350* (Copenhagen, 2010); Sverre Bagge, *From Gang Leader to the Lord's Anointed: Kingship in Sverris Saga and Hákonar Saga Hákonarsonar* (Odense, 1996); Hybel, *The Nature of Kingship*; see also Jonathan Adams and Katherine Holman (eds), *Scandinavia and Europe, 800–1350: Contact, Conflict and Coexistence* (Turnhout, 2004).

1130s the canon of the cathedral of Roskilde who write the *Chronicon Roskildense* seems to have accepted that there was a consensual rôle for the political elite in the justification of kingship.[87] If it had ever been real, the influence of the general populace (or of that portion regarded as worthy) declined; even Tacitus acknowledged that power lay in the hands of a small group of powerful men close to the king.[88] Such a model of rule was in some senses akin to an *aristocracy* in the true Aristotelian sense of the word: authority wielded by a group, rather than by an individual, encapsulating an element of consent – a notion deeply embedded in classical tradition.

The idea of elected monarchy is rarely found in Christian writings, since it contradicted the Christian view that secular power was bestowed by God. There is no doubt, however, that it remained, at least in theory, an important element in some kingship traditions, surviving in the acclamations which became an important part of coronation ceremonies in many kingdoms. In Scandinavian tradition there is little emphasis on genealogy or lineage until the later Middle Ages, when Christian ideals (which stressed the importance of genealogy through the descent of all humans from Adam and Eve) infused the kingship, and when political circumstances made it expedient for the kings to use genealogical arguments to prove their independence from German kings and emperors.[89] In Celtic-speaking societies, however, which undoubtedly shared the elective principle, it seems that there was also a long-standing and powerful tradition of genealogy as an 'ideological weapon verifying that the king was gifted to bring luck and victory to his people', a 'certificate of ability to perform good leadership'.[90] As noted above, genealogy became a fundamental part of the identification of the families and individuals who could achieve the status of potential rulership. The genealogical tradition in kingship can certainly be traced to the early days of Christianity and may indeed have been a feature of leadership in pre-Christian times.[91] Rule in these Celtic-speaking societies, therefore, was based on several factors, which included a dynastic qualification,

---

87 The Anglo-Saxon word is *gecoren* – 'chosen'. *The Anglo-Saxon Chronicle, According to Several Original Authorities*, ed. Benjamin Thorpe (London, 1861), vol. 1 (Original Texts), pp. 198–99; Hybel, *The Nature of Kingship*, pp. 47–48.

88 'About minor matters the chiefs deliberate, about the more important the whole tribe. Yet even when the final decision rests with the people, the affair is always thoroughly discussed by the chiefs.' (Tacitus, *Germania*; https://sourcebooks.fordham.edu/source/tacitus1.html)

89 Hybel, *The Nature of Kingship*, pp. 70–71, 93.

90 See Hybel, *The Nature of Kingship*, p. 74. For the idea of the pedigree as legal title to rule, and its formal presentation as an 'ideological statement', see also David N. Dumville, 'Kingship, Genealogies and Regnal Lists', in P.H. Sawyer and I.N. Woods (eds) *Early Medieval Kingship* (Leeds, 1977), pp. 72–104.

91 Hybel, *The Nature of Kingship*, p. 70.

personal ability to lead (both physical and mental) and, of course, the extent to which the individual was able to control the territory of the kingdom. This last was intricately connected with the group of supporters on whom the king depended. In Scandinavian tradition, it was the *hird*, the close companions or retinue of the chieftain or king. The *comitatus* of a king in Britain was an equivalent group: the supporters who remained primarily in the king's company, who fought with him when necessary, and performed services in return for protection and favour, thereby increasing wealth and standing in their own locale and beyond. From this basis grew a social and military aristocracy, and a governing community.[92]

The kingship to which the child Alexander was initiated on 13 July 1249 was thus one which had developed out of a rich blend of traditions. The traditional elements of the ceremony can be seen as deriving from the Gaelic roots of the kingship; but these and other aspects of the kingship might also reflect Scandinavian, Pictish, British or Anglian heritage. The assumption that *tradition* necessarily means Gaelic is no longer sustainable, if the strongly Irish identity of the kings and their descent is recognised as largely an invention of the tenth century, and if the society of medieval Scotland can be shown to have developed through assimilation and confluence of several ethnic, political and cultural streams. Two elements are particularly clear. Firstly, this kingship placed considerable importance on lineage, influenced by either the Gaelic, kin-based society of the west and/or the British-Pictish background. Secondly, the part played by the church was very limited. Although the church clearly had been influential since at least the sixth century, and probably earlier, and although Christian moral concepts had increasingly infused the outlook and principles of the monarchy throughout several centuries, ecclesiastical influence remained of secondary importance, outweighed by an older political structure which had its roots in the pre-Christian war-band model most familiar from Scandinavian practice. That it was the aristocracy (including the *fili*) who undertook the most fundamental elements of the kingmaking ritual, pushing the ecclesiastical components into the background, emphasises the point: this was a ceremony in which the thirteenth-century Scottish equivalent of the *hird* proclaimed and acclaimed their choice of king at an assembly of the people – or at least of those who claimed to represent them.[93]

The secularity of Scottish kingship should not be overstated: it would be

92 See Woolf, *From Pictland to Alba*, p. 32.

93 Ireland, with similar ritual, has been described as 'a show-case of a "non-mainstream European" Christian ideology of rulership'; Steinsland *et al., Ideology and Power in the Viking and Middle Ages,* Introduction, p. 3.

wrong to say that the Christian model of monarchy was irrelevant. The kings of Dál Riata, Pictland, Alba and Scotland, since the days of Columba and perhaps earlier, had been Christian kings in the sense that they recognised their clear duty to protect, uphold and promote the church and the faith, and to uphold justice within a Christian framework. The dynastic legacy of Máel Coluim III and St Margaret was overtly Christian. When asked to give homage to Edward I of England for his kingdom in 1278, Alexander III himself would retort that he held his kingdom of no one but God and owed homage for it to God alone.[94] The general style which the kings adopted in their public instruments was, until the 1170s, simply *rex Scottorum*; from then on, it was more commonly *Dei gratia rex Scottorum*.[95] On their seals, however, from the early twelfth century they used the style *Deo rectore rex Scottorum* – 'King of Scots under God's guidance', rather than 'by God's grace'.[96]

By the thirteenth century, the Scots were one of just a handful of European monarchies which did not anoint and formally crown their kings. Under Alexander II, as noted above, a formal petition for unction and coronation was lodged with the papacy, probably for the first time. This was a tardy request, however: the Norwegian monarchy, for instance, very much more recently Christianised, had successfully petitioned for these rites in the mid twelfth century. Even in Sweden, where the rites seem to have carried less significance, kings were crowned and anointed from 1210.[97] The Scottish approach to the papacy in 1220 may be seen in the context of increasing political pressure on Alexander II from England in relation to the status of his crown, and of long-standing ecclesiastical claims on the part of the English church to control of the *ecclesia Scoticana*.[98] There is little doubt that the Scottish kings would have welcomed the elevation of St Andrews to an archdiocese, with unction and coronation being carried out by a Scottish archbishop, a clear signal of regnal independence and status. The increase in status of the church in relation to the kingship, however, raised different issues. The serious disputes, for example, between the Norwegian church and crown from as early as the mid twelfth century were symptomatic of the church exerting itself in a polity which was relatively recently Christianised,

94 See below, pp. 225–32.

95 *RRS*, ii, pp. 75–76.

96 See Stevenson and Wood, *Scottish Heraldic Seals*, i, pp. 2–5.

97 Sverre Bagge, *Cross & Scepter: The Rise of the Scandinavian Kingdoms from the Vikings to the Reformation* (Oxford, 2014), p. 57.

98 Duncan, *Kingship of the Scots*, p. 119; see also pp. 88–90, where Duncan conjectures (admitting the lack of evidence) that an earlier request may have been made in the reign of Alexander I. I find his argument unconvincing.

and in which the two worldviews of secular and religious kingship clashed.[99] Conflict between secular and ecclesiastical jurisdiction would also be a feature of Scotland in the early years of Alexander III's reign. While the position of the church in relation to the kingship might provide assistance in bolstering the status of the kingdom and its rulers, the fundamental outlook of the monarchy was not one which demanded the overt symbolism of Christian kingship; as in Sweden, it seems that the monarchy remained primarily secular, kings gaining and exerting their authority through the will and support of the people (or at least the elite among them). It may have been the case that even as late as the reign of Alexander III the issue of unction and coronation was not theoretically important to the Scots, but was pursued as a potentially convenient weapon in the kingdom's struggle for status in relation to England. It was politically expedient to pay lip-service to the more commonly held monarchical ideals, but not of crucial importance to the kingship itself. It is not certain, either, that there was a widespread belief elsewhere that the lack of unction and coronation implied inferior status. As will be demonstrated below, there is good reason to believe that Henry III (Plate 11) understood and respected the model of Scottish kingship which his young son-in-law had inherited, and examples such as the kingdom of Castile, which consciously rejected such symbolism, do not add weight to the idea that kings who were not subject to formal ecclesiastical coronation were generally deemed to represent an impoverished regnal tradition.[100] Such notions were wheeled out from time to time in pursuit of political advantage, but there seems to have been a general recognition that this was different, rather than lesser, kingship.

The nature of Scottish monarchy is not without analogue elsewhere Europe. Perhaps the most striking parallel is with Castile where, as in the case of Alexander III in Scotland, there was dubiety about who might knight a prince

99 For discussion of these disputes, see Bagge, *From Viking Stronghold to Christian Kingdom*, pp. 294–316. For the assimilation of older, pagan elements of rule into the Scandinavian Christian model, see Gro Steinsland, 'Origin Myths and Rulership. From the Viking Age Ruler to the Ruler of Medieval Historiography: Continuity, Transformations and Innovations', in Steinsland *et al.*, *Ideology and Power in the Viking and Middle Ages*, pp. 15–68, at p. 18: '. . . when Nordic culture encountered the European, Christian ideology of rulership, it showed a high degree of independence by retaining native pagan traditions on rulership long into the Middle Ages. Mythological and cognitive elements of the pre-Christian ideology of rulership were perpetuated, transformed, and incorporated into new contexts . . .' Steinsland (p. 63) refers also to the discussion between Robert Bartlett and Patrick Geary regarding the spread of religious and cultural impulses from centre to periphery; Steinsland prefers, in relation to the Nordic experience, Geary's contention that the periphery 'brought its own traditions to the meeting'. The same case can, of course, be made for Scotland.

100 See below, p. 218.

about to be enthroned.[101] The problem was solved in Castile by the ingenious solution of having him knighted by the mechanical arm of a statue of St James.[102] (The act of knighting was seen to place the new knight under obligation and service to the one who knighted him, an obvious problem for a king in terms of his status both within and outwith his kingdom.) In 1332, Alfonso XI of Castile placed the crown on his own head, rather than being crowned, as in most European ceremonies, by a senior bishop or archbishop.[103] As in Scotland, the crown existed as a symbol of status. It was worn, and the kings were depicted with it, but it did not carry the religious significance of the crowns of England or France. The Castilian kings 'consciously rejected the traditional emblems of power and authority in use elsewhere in the medieval West', and while they believed that their kingship was God-given, they did not believe it to be sacred.[104] For instance, they are said to have been dismissive of the belief (strongly held in France and England) that kings had the power to heal, another element of kingship which appears to have been absent in the Scottish model.[105]

The Castilian kings came from the tradition of Germanic kingship in which their predecessors, Visigothic kings, had been 'elected and acclaimed by the assembly of all free men'.[106] As early as the late sixth century they adopted the trappings of Christian kingship, but nonetheless, demonstrating their 'ambivalent and, at times, quite practical approach to institutionalized religion',[107] they also retained elements of election and rejected strict dynastic succession, a policy which led to disruptive instability, and a reputation for deposition and regicide. As would be explicitly stated in early fourteenth-century Scotland, there was a clear principle that unjust, tyrannical kings could be removed from office. In essence, any pretensions held by the Castilian rulers towards a more fully fledged concept of dynastic or theocratic kingship were limited by the law and custom of the kingdom, and the elective principle lingered well into the later medieval period in tandem with an inevitable growth in the acceptance of primogenitive succession. The history of this area,

101 See below, pp. 84–88.

102 The following description of the situation in Castile relies heavily on Ruiz, 'Unsacred Monarchy'. I am grateful to Professor Chris Given-Wilson for drawing my attention to this article.

103 In the 1332 ceremony, Alfonso XI was also anointed with holy oil, but in that respect he was unique among Castilian kings after the mid twelfth century.

104 Ruiz, 'Unsacred Monarchy', p. 110.

105 Ruiz, 'Unsacred Monarchy', p. 128; Michael Prestwich, *The Three Edwards: War and State in England, 1272–1377* (London, 1980), p. 82, cites the fact that Edward I is said to have blessed over 1,700 sick men in a single year.

106 Ruiz, 'Unsacred Monarchy', p. 111.

107 Ruiz, 'Unsacred Monarchy', p. 127.

with migration and conquest by Muslim invaders in the early eighth century, long-standing regional conflict and later revival of Visigothic ritual and tradition, has echoes in ninth- to eleventh-century Scotland. In both cases, a fiercely protected national identity was to arise. By the thirteenth century it is possible to see in the Castilian monarchy, as well as a retention of a strongly physical and martial character of leadership, a deliberate abandonment of some of the features of Christian kingship, such as coronation and anointing, and a conscious re-adoption of earlier customs, secular ceremonials and symbols, some of which were rooted in much older Germanic practice. There was thus a strong principle of contractual and consensual rule, which was clearly in evidence in extant medieval law codes, and which was as important as customs of lineage and notions of divine legitimacy. The elective principle was symbolised in the inauguration ceremony by the lifting of the new king on a shield – a ritual presentation of the newly elected monarch to the assembled people. It is not impossible that an analogous ritual had been performed at Scottish inaugurations before the innovation (perhaps for the first time in 1249) of the more biblically precedented cloak-laying. Both, however, are to be seen as forms of public acclamation and acceptance. It may not be irrelevant, either, that in pre-Roman times the area which later became Castile was populated mainly by Q-Celtic-speaking tribes.[108]

The kingdoms of both Scotland and Castile were forged out of conquest, reconquest, territorial extension and cultural assimilation. Both kingships exercised symbolism, ritual and custom which described a model of authority which was a 'response to the dynamics of a frontier society'.[109] Even if there was an element of deliberate archaicism in the Scottish ceremonies (as seems to have been the case with the exaggeration of the longevity of the Stone of Destiny's use in royal inauguration) in order to offer a validating antiquity to the kingship in an era of changing political relationships, it is clear that this was the model which the Scottish kings wished to promote as their own. The conduct and rhetoric of their rule, as is made clear by the reign of Alexander III, affirms the underlying principles of their monarchy.

The contention that Scotland's monarchy developed out of an elective and consensual model is given added force by recent research relating to the character of Scottish government as it had developed by the mid thirteenth century. It has been persuasively argued that the nature of the changes which were wrought in Scottish government and administration during the twelfth and thirteenth

108 See https://web.archive.org/web/20040609143259/http://www.arqueotavira.com:80/Mapas/Iberia/Populi.pdf; see also https://en.wikipedia.org/wiki/List_of_the_Pre-Roman_peoples_of_the_Iberian_Peninsula.

109 Ruiz, 'Unsacred Monarchy', p. 130.

centuries has been misinterpreted.[110] There has been a prevailing view that royal power and aristocratic power are 'structurally opposed' to each other: the monarch could not gain power without curbing noble power, leading to competition and conflict. This model does not describe the Scottish experience. As government and royal control developed, an existing framework of aristocratic authority was used: 'aristocratic power was, in the Scottish case, constitutive of state power, rather than structurally separate from it'.[111] While changes in land tenure made noble power more territorially based, with consequential development of administrative and judicial practice, there was nonetheless a continuity in the nature of the relationship between the monarchy and its lay aristocracy, and the model of rule which developed was one in which 'the heavy presence of non-royal elite power was not inimical to the emergence of relatively intensive public institutions of government'.[112] As well as innovations, there were continuities with previous centuries in the manner of exercising royal authority: specific examples are the importance of assemblies in the legitimisation of royal power, and the use of local aristocratic power to exercise judicial and administrative royal functions. The thirteenth-century Scottish monarchy was thus in some ways limited, both conceptually and institutionally; the authority of the monarch was circumscribed. It is argued that the limitation was consistent with a 'structural inheritance' from the eleventh century.[113]

If the 'structural inheritance' can be identified as an eleventh-century form, it had its roots in much earlier practice, and must emanate, eventually, from the model of early kingship described above. The central rôle of the aristocracy in the model of Scottish government is a retained aspect of the power base of the much earlier warrior-chiefs of the British, Pictish, Gaelic and Scandinavian societies from which the Scottish monarchy developed.[114] It was more than simply consensus, however: aristocratic authority was 'the key basis on which royal institutional government rested'.[115] It follows, therefore, that the part played in government by the Scottish nobles was not imposed on them by the king; neither was it a new ideology of rule introduced during the twelfth and thirteenth centuries. It was a responsibility which was recognised to be a function of aristocratic status, inherited from their predecessors and ancestors.

---

110 The following paragraph is a very brief summary of the conclusions in Taylor, *Shape of the State*.

111 Taylor, *Shape of the State*, p.20.

112 Taylor, *Shape of the State*, p. 2.

113 Taylor, *Shape of the State*, pp. 444–46.

114 Taylor, *Shape of the State*, pp. 450–51, also recognises this, noting the place of large-scale assemblies and consensus-driven law-making in early societies, and the rôle of 'ritual and symbolic consensus' as tools of early medieval kingship.

115 Taylor, *Shape of the State*, p. 455.

Collaborative rule by king and aristocracy was a long-standing and integral element of the culture of Scottish kingship.

The Scottish royal dynasty of the thirteenth century was merely one of a number of families able to trace their roots (fictitiously and/or genuinely) far back into Alba or earlier times. The earls of Fife and Strathearn, key functionaries in the inauguration ceremony, probably represented branches of the same family, and may themselves have had royal ancestors.[116] They are symbolic of the fact that in a very real sense the Scottish kings and aristocracy constituted a centuries-old governing community. The king was not *apart* from the nobility of the kingdom: he was one of them, and when the *fili* read the royal lineage at the inauguration ceremony, it was not in order to proclaim the distinctiveness or separateness of this man from the others; it was not to declare that he was above them, or different from them. Quite the reverse: it was to make the public declaration that, being one of them, and that being acknowledged (in earlier times, chosen) by them, he was fit to be their king. By the inauguration ceremony at Scone, the boy Alexander was made king, truly *primus inter pares*, the first among equals. It is a contention which is supported by a recent study of the nature of Scotland's political community in the reign of Alexander II, based primarily on analysis of the witness lists of royal charters, which demonstrates that the Scottish court society was 'more politically inclusive' than its more elitist English counterpart.[117]

The fundamental nature of the Scottish kingship is key to understanding and interpreting the reign of Alexander III, as is the fact that it represents an essential point of contrast with the English monarchy. Scottish historiography has failed to address this adequately. Much of the seminal work of the last 50 years, examining the development of Scottish government and society throughout the twelfth and thirteenth centuries, depicts the introduction of 'feudal' landholding patterns and the migration of new, Anglo-Norman families into Scotland as part of a process of anglicising modernisation, promoted by the kings themselves (influenced by their southern rôle-models), in order to increase their power at the expense of the native aristocracy.[118] It is important to note,

---

116 See John W.M. Bannerman, 'MacDuff of Fife', in Grant and Stringer, *Medieval Scotland*, pp. 20–38 (reprinted in Bannerman, *Kinship, Church and Culture*, pp. 230–51); Bannerman, 'The King's Poet', p. 258, where these families are described, perhaps controversially, as 'royal segmental discards'.

117 Keith Stringer, 'The Scottish "Political Community" in the Reign of Alexander II (1214–49)', in Hammond, *New Perspectives*, pp. 53–84.

118 Even the title of Geoffrey Barrow's meticulous and penetrating study of the period in his Ford Lectures, full as it is of insight and revelation, suggests this assumption: *The Anglo-Norman Era in Scottish History* (Oxford, 1980). To be fair, Barrow's final chapter, 'The Other Side of the Coin', does attempt to redress the balance, and makes the point that the continuity of Scottish

however, that there was far more social and familial continuity in this period than has sometimes been suggested. There has been a largely unquestioned view that the supposedly core European governmental models of England and France would overwhelm supposedly peripheral states such as Scotland, leading to their adoption of what is assumed to be a more advanced, dominant political culture. It is a central conclusion of Alice Taylor's work discussed above, however, that the territorialisation (rather than feudalisation) of the Scottish aristocracy did not undermine the essential continuity of Scottish governmental tradition. The Scots did borrow and copy English governmental methods, institutions and procedures, but they adapted them to local circumstances, rather than attempting to recreate them on a smaller scale.[119]

The marked contrast between the English and Scottish monarchies in the thirteenth century was rooted in the Norman Conquest, which imposed on England a model of kingship which was a pre-eminent example of the Continental, Christian monarchy, replete with religious symbolism. Since 1066 England had thus been ruled by a dynasty which had gained, and retained, power by force of arms over native elites. To retain its authority the monarchy had to continue to be above and separate from the aristocratic class, in marked contrast to the Scottish tradition. Without the conquest, the Anglo-Saxon traditions of rule in England may have remained stronger, and the contrast with Scotland been less stark. Failure to recognise the deep-rooted consensual nature of Scottish society and government has had profound consequences for the course of history. Examples might be cited of Edward I's abortive attempts to control Scotland in the 1290s, and even of the abysmal failure of the Thatcher government's attempt to introduce the Poll Tax to Scotland in the late 1980s. There is a traditional Scottish saying, 'I kent his faither' ('I knew his father'), often misunderstood, and misused, as a mocking put-down of someone who has achieved some sort of celebrity. Its true nature is as a mirror to that *primus inter pares* concept which is so clearly identifiable in the medieval monarchy; it is not personally demeaning – on the contrary, it means 'he is one of us'. Unlike in England, where the dominance of the incoming dynasty rendered the old idea of election no more than 'a relic of a distant past',[120] the Scottish king was permitted to rule because he was 'one of us'.

The foregoing discussion of the roots of Scottish kingship has shown that to depict the difference between the English and Scottish monarchies as a simple counterpoint of the Christian conquest model versus the secular consensual

---

governmental development over many centuries resulted in a different nature of feudal settlement and government administration north of the border.

119 Taylor, *Shape of the State*, pp. 446–49.

120 Ruiz, 'Unsacred Monarchy', p. 119.

model would be grossly over-simplistic. The English monarchy is of course as complex in its origins and nature as the Scottish, and the long-standing Christian ethos of the Scottish monarchy has already been emphasised. Nonetheless, there was a fundamental difference in attitude and approach of the two monarchies. Understanding that fact is a prerequisite for understanding the course of events in this or any other reign, and for appreciating that the overwhelming influence of the English social and monarchical model in much past historiography has led to misinterpretation of events, relationships and personal motivations in Scottish history, especially in the thirteenth and fourteenth centuries. The Scottish aristocracy have frequently been portrayed as selfishly and without principle jockeying for power, fighting for their own personal seat at the table. If instead the Scottish nobles are seen as motivated by a responsibility to take part and fulfil their duty to govern with, rather than against, the king, then their actions take on a new light, and many aspects of Scotland's history become more comprehensible.

In 1992, G.W.S. Barrow published an essay entitled 'Kingship in Medieval England and Scotland'.[121] Despite his rôle as a champion of Scottish feudalism, and of the significant influence of English government on the Scottish experience, he argued that the Scottish medieval kingship still displayed traces of the 'common [western European] heritage of non-scriptural and non-classical kingship which came down from their barbarian ancestors, whether Celtic, Germanic, Slavonic or Hungarian (Magyar) . . .'.[122] He also discussed the impact on the English monarchy of the Norman Conquest, and contrasted it with the 'kin-based unity, a peculiar characteristic which the Scots monarchy, as long as it endured, was never to lose'.[123] Along the way he did refer to the likelihood that the Scots kings 'often imitated' the ruling practices of the English, but nonetheless his basic thesis, that the Scottish monarchy was, both in its tradition and its practice, different from the English, demonstrates that the basic contention of this chapter, which has been developed out of much more detailed recent work by a new generation of scholars, is not entirely radical. Indeed, Barrow's 1992 essay was a republication of a work which first appeared in a German journal a decade earlier, itself a slightly abbreviated version of a seminar or conference paper he had prepared at least a year or two previously.[124] That a figure of Barrow's eminence raised these ideas almost 40 years ago, and that nonetheless they still seem new,

121 G.W.S. Barrow, 'Kingship in Medieval England and Scotland', in *Scotland and its Neighbours*, pp. 23–44.

122 Barrow, 'Kingship in Medieval England and Scotland', p. 23.

123 Barrow, 'Kingship in Medieval England and Scotland', p. 44.

124 *Historisches Jahrbuch*, 102 (1982), pp. 362–89; annotated (in G.W.S.B.'s hand) typescript, undated, in author's possession.

is testimony to the overwhelming influence and long endurance of an Anglocentric historiography of medieval Scotland. It is a tradition which goes back to the fourteenth century at least. Scotland's relative paucity of native historical writing in this period has created an inevitable reliance on the much more plentiful English sources, especially the splendid narrative histories of the twelfth to the fifteenth centuries. On these firm foundations has been built an historiographical edifice which has proven hard to shake. It is a key objective of this book to reinterpret the events of the reign of Alexander III through an approach which is rooted in a different understanding of the nature of Scottish kingship and government, and in so doing to reveal the true importance of a period which lies at the end of two centuries or more of rapid and fundamental political, social and economic development, and which, conversely, heralds an oncoming period of political, social and economic catastrophe.

Returning to the ceremony at which the young prince became King Alexander III, its significance takes on a new light. Although there is some reasonably detailed information, there is still much that is unknown. Elements of the ceremony are undoubtedly unrecorded, though of importance to those who attended either as participants or as observers. Despite the persuasive case for innovation within the ceremony, it seems nonetheless that the view of a ritual which was fundamentally rooted in the ancient, and secular, traditions of the monarchy is well founded.[125] The assumption that many of those traditions were wholly Irish, and Gaelic, might now be tempered by the newer understanding of the deliberate fostering of the Irish identity by the kings of Alba. Part of the motivation behind that propagandist message was the fact that the kingship traditions of Alba owed as much to its Pictish/British/Scandinavian heritage, making the appeal to Irish ancestry more important in order to create a clear distinction between the Scottish (Alban) kingship and its English (British) counterparts. By the thirteenth century, however, it was the non-Irish, secular elements of the Scottish monarchy which made it more functionally distinctive from the mainstream Christian monarchy of England than did the elements brought to it by the Gaelic model. In that respect, the identification of the reinstatement of Pictish rulers within Scottish king-lists during the thirteenth century is indeed indicative of a developing view of the kingdom as a territory containing inhabitants who accepted subjection to a single royal authority, rather than as a dynastic possession.

The same requirement to differentiate Scotland from England can be seen in the emphasis placed by some sources on Máel Coluim and Margaret as

125 Bannerman, 'The King's Poet', p. 265: 'It seems to owe little or nothing to the introduction of new ideas that flowed from the Norman Conquest of England; not even the participation of the clergy need be seen in that light.'

dynastic founders, which demonstrated not only that the descendants of the sons of Margaret (rather than of Ingibjorg) were the rightful kings, but also that the Scottish kingship represented a clear dynastic succession from the pre-conquest English ruling family. The assemblage of works known as the 'Dunfermline compilation', dating from within the reign of Alexander III, goes to great lengths to portray the Scottish kings as descendants of Margaret and, through her, of King Alfred, and thereby of monarchs who had been anointed and crowned. These works may have been written specifically in the context of Scottish requests for unction and coronation.[126] The same emphasis is found in the 'Scottish poem' of the *Liber Extravagans*, from the early fourteenth century.[127] Together, they further signal the rising notion of Scotland as a national entity which required to assert its antiquity as a kingdom (and thus confer its kings with a status) independent of the post-conquest English regime.

Whatever the significance placed on the use of the Stone of Destiny, on the bestowal of royal insignia, on the religious affirmation of Alexander's kingship by the ecclesiastics or on the strewing of garments at the new king's feet, the evidence available to us suggests that the key symbolic kingmaking element of the inauguration ceremony was indeed the part played by the *fili*; he did not merely proclaim Alexander's dynastic qualification to rule, but in doing so he also affirmed the status of the monarchy itself as inheriting an ancient right and tradition, and, further, he put forward the more modern assertion of territorial kingship. What has sometimes from an Anglocentric viewpoint been seen as an archaic ritual was in fact the climax of a ceremony which presented a powerful public expression of the self-image and identity of a nation-state, full of significance for the present and future of the kingdom. In 1249 Alexander III's genealogy was still portrayed as Irish; but the re-inclusion of Pictish lineage within king-lists of this period also establishes a sense of forward momentum in the concept of the kingdom. As the idea of a territorial political unit emerged, the ethnic or cultural origins of the people who lived and were ruled within it became less significant. The Scots effectively became the people of Scotland, who lived under the authority of a national, multiethnic royal tradition stretching back into a distant past. This was the kingship to which Alexander III was initiated on 13 July 1249.

---

126 These issues are all rehearsed in much greater detail in Broun, *Irish Identity*, chs 8 and 9. See also Alice Taylor, 'Historical Writing in Twelfth- and Thirteenth-Century Scotland: The Dunfermline Compilation', *Historical Research*, 83 (2010), pp. 228–52; see also Broun, *Scottish Independence*, p. 51. The compilation survives in a manuscript in Madrid; I am grateful to Professor Broun for giving me sight of his transcription of that part of it known as the 'Dunfermline chronicle'.

127 *Chron. Bower*, ix, pp. 58 and (text) 72–75.

CHAPTER 2

Bequest of a Kingdom

Alexander II's long reign had profoundly changed the kingdom of the Scots. Following his death there was for the first time apparently no challenge to the succession: previous reigns, including that of Alexander II himself, had suffered from the dying throes of an older succession system, which saw rebellions by representatives of families laterally related to previous kings attempting to assert their position. The gradual acceptance of the system of primogeniture during the course of the previous century or more had led to a strengthened sense of dynasty and of the personal authority and responsibility of the kings, and consequently to a clearer definition of the geographical boundaries of their rule.

Alexander III's inauguration ceremony displayed signs of a sense of identity which had developed over the previous century or so, and perhaps especially under his father. It was the initiation of a king with a firm dynastic heritage and who, despite the lack of formal unction and coronation, was regarded as the leader of a governing community which saw itself as sovereign within an independent kingdom. Only 60 years previously, however, Scotland had emerged from a period in which she was without question a kingdom inferior to her more powerful southern neighbour. Supporting an internal rebellion against Henry II of England, the Scots king, William, had been captured in July 1174, and was forced under the terms of the ensuing treaty of Falaise to accept the subordination of his kingdom to the English crown in return for his freedom. Not until December 1189, after the accession of Richard I to the English throne, would Scotland be released from this position of subjugation by an agreement known as the Quitclaim of Canterbury. However, the relationships between the rulers of the two neighbouring countries were close, and for many years William's predecessors had held a dual rôle as both Scottish king and English baron, holding large tracts of land within England for which they owed feudal service to the English crown. Owing allegiance to the kings of England in one capacity certainly blurred the lines of royal independence: but the notion was yet to appear that unambiguous definition of such issues was required. There is no clear evidence that Scottish kings prior to Alexander II had a firm belief in the complete independence of their kingdom, or, rather, that the concept of such independence was comparable to that of the present day. Particularly in the period prior to the treaty of Falaise in 1174, evolving and developing personal relationships between the rulers of the neighbouring kingdoms mirrored the fluctuating ascendancy of one over the other.[1]

William's sense that he had been unjustly deprived of the rich earldom of Northumberland (which had for long been held by the Scottish royal dynasty) prompted his participation in the rebellion which led to his capture in 1174. However, it is unclear whether the Scottish kings regarded what are now accepted as the English northern counties as part of the English kingdom, rather than as part of their own realm. When Alexander II went to war with England in 1215 in the quest to reassert his own claim to the same lands, it is by no means certain that he did not have his eye on the long-term goal of holding them as part of the Scottish kingdom, rather than as an English fief.[2] He failed in his attempt, and later, by the treaty of York in 1237, he finally abandoned the claims. That the treaty of York was to be a crucially important factor in the definition of the southern boundary of Scotland signifies that the territorial delineation of both kingdoms was still evolving.

Definition of boundary, and therefore also of authority, requires a certain self-identity in both ruler and ruled. Following the end of the 1215–17 war, Scotland and England were to remain largely at peace until near the end of the century, a period which has been described as 'the most sustained Anglo-Scottish "cease-fire" in the entire Middle Ages'.[3] This period of stability allowed considerable consolidation and development of the Scottish state in administrative, economic and political terms.[4] The relationship between the crowns of Scotland and England had been temporarily settled: after 1237 there was no further English attack on the status of the Scottish kings until the 1250s. Alexander II's authority within his kingdom was less certain, however. The ruthless efficiency – even to the point of vindictiveness – with which he went about quelling opposition and securing his own and his dynasty's ongoing dominance over

---

1 See Broun, *Scottish Independence,* chs 4 and 6; Duncan, *Making of the Kingdom*, pp. 236–37; R.R. Davies, *Domination and Conquest: The Experience of Ireland, Scotland and Wales, 1100–1300* (Cambridge, 1990).

2 See K.J. Stringer, 'Kingship, Conflict and State-making in the Reign of Alexander II: The War of 1215–17 and its Context', in Oram, *Alexander II Essays,* pp. 99–156.

3 Stringer, 'Kingship, Conflict and State-making', p. 151.

4 The judicial and administrative changes, in particular, are analysed in great detail in Taylor, *Shape of the State.*

areas of the kingdom which had previously been at best loosely controlled, does not speak of a coherent nation at peace with itself. It is certainly a measure of Alexander II's success in achieving that dominance that his son's succession in 1249 was unchallenged despite his tender age, presenting a more cohesive and self-assured political attitude than had been apparent at the beginning of previous reigns.[5]

The ambiguity of the status of the Scottish kingship, and of the concept of independence, before the mid thirteenth century is paralleled by the situation of the church. The position of the kingdom in national and international terms was intricately tied to that of the church. The key diplomatic rôle of the pope as arbiter between nations throughout Christendom is evident in the continual involvement of the curia in Anglo-Scottish disputes throughout the Middle Ages. In 1192, by the bull *Cum universi*, the Scottish church (with the exception of the diocese of Galloway) had been designated by Pope Celestine III a *filia specialis* (special daughter) of the papacy. It was thus subject, without reporting to any archbishop, directly to the Roman see.[6] The bull was reissued in 1218 by Honorius II, and in 1225, unusually, further local self-governance was granted to the Scottish church with the right to hold provincial councils, the edicts of which were to be effected by the bishops themselves within their own dioceses.[7] These developments might seem to indicate unequivocal support by the papacy in the early decades of the thirteenth century for the independence of the Scottish church from the metropolitan sees of either York or Canterbury. However, subjection to York or Canterbury had been hotly disputed since as early as the mid eleventh century, and remained so. The twelfth century had seen successive attempts on the part of the papacy to make the Scottish church accept obedience to York, attempts which were strongly resisted in Scotland (except in the case of the diocese of Galloway), especially at St Andrews, which by the early twelfth century certainly had its own archiepiscopal pretensions.[8] As regards the kingdom's secular status, in a letter to King William in 1180, Pope Alexander III (not the first to have done so) had

5 Oram, *Alexander II*, pp. 256–59.

6 I have accepted the most often-cited date for this bull, although it is not without dispute. See A.D.M. Barrell, 'The Background to *Cum universi*: Scoto-Papal Relations, 1159–1192', *Innes Review*, 46 (1995), pp. 116–38; Duncan, *Making of the Kingdom*, pp. 264–65, also argues for *Cum universi* as confirming and amplifying earlier papal statutes, rather than itself being a significant departure in papal policy.

7 See Marinell Ash, 'The Church in the Reign of Alexander III', p. 33; for a study of Scottish church councils, see D.E.R. Watt, *Scottish Church Councils in the Middle Ages* (Edinburgh, 2000), of which the provincial councils are discussed in chs 4–6. (See, however, Duncan's contrary view of this provision, in *Kingship of the Scots*, p. 119.)

8 See Broun, *Scottish Independence*, ch. 4; Barrow, *Kingship and Unity*, pp. 68–69.

drawn a clear parallel between the independence of the church and that of the kingdom.[9] The thirteenth-century papacy could thus be seen to be taking the Scottish side in disputes with the English church. Equally, by making Scotland a 'special daughter', the papacy might be regarded as sitting on the fence: it did not accede to English claims of superiority, nor did it entirely support Scottish counter-claims. It did not go as far as offering St Andrews the desired status of an archbishopric, just as it did not accede to the Scottish request in the 1220s for unction and coronation of the king. By resisting both English and Scottish aspirations, the popes thus endorsed uncertainty and ambiguity in the concept of national independence, while maintaining a level of direct influence in national affairs which at times caused tension between the kings and the papacy.

Of course, while hindsight renders it tempting to assume that there was an automatic resistance to subordination of the kingdom or of the church, in fact there were personal, regional and organisational issues which pulled in diverse directions. The requirement for expeditions to be mounted by William, Alexander II and Alexander III to bring areas of the kingdom under Scottish royal control confirms that there was not necessarily a greater enthusiasm for subjection to a single Scottish authority than there was to an English (or Norwegian) one. Individuals, families and institutions could have their own powerful reasons for providing, or refusing, support for one monarchy or another at any given time.[10] In ecclesiastical terms, the bull *Cum universi*, as well as providing freedom from subservience to York or Canterbury, also offered all the other Scottish dioceses freedom from archiepiscopal dominance by St Andrews. The diocese of Glasgow had actually achieved the highly unusual status of being independent of metropolitan control by *any* archdiocese some years previously, and the suspicion that the architect of the bull *Cum universi* was Bishop Jocelin of Glasgow lends weight to the suggestion that there were forces at play within the Scottish church which objected just as much to dominance by St Andrews as by York or Canterbury.[11]

Policy aimed at exerting royal control over the church in Scotland, and especially the nurture of the ecclesiastical dominance of St Andrews, also

9 Broun, *Scottish Independence*, pp. 113–14; Barrow, 'The Idea of Freedom in Late Medieval Scotland', *Innes Review*, 30 (1979), pp. 6–34.

10 Family was a powerful binding – or fragmenting – force. See, for example, the complex analysis of family relationships and their influence on Scottish, English and French politics in M.A. Pollock, *Scotland, England and France after the Loss of Normandy, 1204–1296* (Woodbridge, 2015).

11 Robert Somerville (ed.), *Scotia Pontificia: Papal Letters to Scotland before the Pontificate of Innocent III* (Oxford, 1982), no. 76 (pp. 76–77). For rivalry between the Scottish bishoprics and the rôle of Bishop Jocelin, see Broun, *Scottish Independence*, ch. 5.

impacted in other ways. The continuing encouragement of St Andrews as a centre for pilgrimage, for example, brought with it a steady revenue stream. More importantly, it was also an internationally visible reminder of the politically convenient status of Scotland's patron saint as an apostle of equal seniority to his brother St Peter, to whom the cathedral of York was dedicated.[12] By the mid twelfth century, St Andrews appears to have dominated the education of Scottish clerics who would go on to study at universities on the Continent and should be regarded as a *universitas* out of which the formal *studium generale* – now known as the University of St Andrews – would evolve in the early fifteenth century.[13] Education of clerics was not irrelevant to the running of the state, since it was from the ranks of these educated men that the officers of state were taken. For example, 12 men are known to have held the office of royal chancellor during the period between *c*.1200 and the death of Alexander III in 1286.[14] Four of them were, either at the time of their appointment or later, bishop of St Andrews; one was archdeacon of Lothian, an important officer of the diocese of St Andrews; all but two can be shown to have had, at some point in their previous careers, a connection with the diocese of St Andrews.[15] Seven of them, all with St Andrews connections, were graduates, including five out of the six chancellors appointed by Alexander III. It was mostly from the ranks of the educated upper echelons of the clergy that ambassadors and others entrusted with international diplomacy (and, most importantly, those who negotiated with the papacy) were chosen. The kings therefore needed to maintain influence over the appointment of ecclesiastical magnates, who were so vital to the administration and governance of the kingdom. The promotion of St Andrews, potentially as an archdiocese, may have been one reason for their ambivalence about the provisions of *Cum universi*: a national church under the leadership of a strong, royally sponsored

---

12 For the development of the cult of St Andrew, and the parallel promotion of the diocese as the senior bishopric of Scotland, see Simon Taylor, 'From *Cinrigh Monai* to *Civitas Sancti Andree*: A Star is Born', in Brown and Stevenson, *Medieval St Andrews,* pp. 20–34. The cult of St Andrew in Scotland (and at the place we now call St Andrews) was certainly far from new in the thirteenth century; but the pilgrimage trade was still encouraged, and healthy. See, e.g., *CDS*, ii, no. 8.

13 Norman H. Reid, 'The Prehistory of the University of St Andrews', in Brown and Stevenson, *Medieval St Andrews*, pp. 237–67.

14 See the list provided in E.B. Fryde, D.E. Greenway, S. Porter and I. Roy (eds), *Handbook of British Chronology* (London, 1986), pp. 180–81. For biographical information, see *PoMS*; and Watt, *Graduates*.

15 Dauvit Broun has pointed out to me that there is also a strong connection between the diocese of Glasgow and royal office; but the evidence of St Andrews as a hub of education for the Scottish church is strong – most of the Glasgow-connected individuals also had previous links with St Andrews.

metropolitan at St Andrews might be more controllable than a *filia specialis* of the Roman see.[16]

The importance to the crown of control over episcopal appointments is well exemplified by a long-running conflict over appointment to the bishopric of St Andrews towards the end of the twelfth century.[17] When Bishop Richard died in May 1178, the canons of St Andrews elected as his successor John the Scot, who had for some time been a member of the late bishop's *familia*. No royal approval had been gained for this election, however, and King William overturned the election, instead nominating and ordering the consecration of his personal chaplain, Hugh. The resulting conflict between King William and the papacy (spanning no fewer than three pontificates) witnessed the temporary excommunication of the Scottish king and a papal threat to subject the Scottish church to the archdiocese of York. After several attempts at compromise, and failed attempts by both king and pope to effect their candidate's hold on the see, the dispute eventually came to an end only when Hugh, on a visit to Rome in August 1188 in a perhaps over-optimistic attempt to seek papal confirmation of his appointment, died of plague. King William's next nominee for the bishopric of St Andrews was Roger, royal chancellor and cousin of the king; it was uncontested by John the Scot, any of the other Scottish bishops or indeed the pope. The dispute had raged for over a decade, with complete determination on the part of the king that his right to control such important appointments would not be compromised. What was at stake was the principle of royal control over the church. For the same reason, the papacy – largely supported by the other Scottish prelates – had been equally intransigent. Thus it can be seen how when in 1192 the bull *Cum universi* made the Scottish church a *filia specialis* of the papacy, although the privilege was probably sought in order to prevent moves by the new archbishop of York to extend his authority over the Scottish dioceses, it may equally have been seen by both papacy and the other Scottish bishops (and particularly by Bishop Jocelin of Glasgow) as a means of limiting the overarching power both of the diocese of St Andrews and of its promoter, the king.

It is thus clear that the nature of the kingdom by the mid thirteenth century was not cohesive. Although major strides had been made towards the concept

16 There is a counter-argument, that the more disparate nature of a church lacking the status provided by a metropolitan would be more controllable in the royal interest. A Scottish metropolitan, however, would bring to an end the dangerous ambitions of York.

17 For a more detailed discussion of this episode, see Duncan, *Making of the Kingdom*, pp. 270–75, and the biography of John the Scot in Watt, *Graduates*, pp. 485–88; much primary evidence for the dispute is contained in correspondence with the papacy, provided by many entries in Somerville, *Scotia Pontificia*.

of what we would now term a nation-state, there yet remained uncertainties about its status and about the geographical and conceptual limits of the king and governing community's authority. With these caveats in mind, a brief portrait of aspects of Alexander III's kingdom can be attempted.

As in the rest of Europe, the Scottish church had undergone a revolution during the twelfth and early thirteenth centuries. From a largely eremitic, monastic tradition of Christianity, the emergence of a secular (or non-monastic) church administered by a Roman-style episcopacy, broken down into local parishes had been encouraged by Alexander III's predecessors from David I (1124–53) onwards. Particularly under David I, there was also a promotion of the great Continental monastic orders throughout Scotland. As a result of endowment from kings and from wealthy nobles (with royal encouragement), around 55 monastic houses were founded in Scotland by 1249. Of those, very few were established before the reign of David I, around 20 during his reign, around 10 each in the reigns of his successors Máel Coluim IV (1153–65) and William I (1165–1214), and about a further 15 in the reign of Alexander II. Some of these were re-foundations of earlier monastic communities, but the totality nonetheless represents a very significant change in the ecclesiastical landscape of the kingdom. Most of the major monastic orders were represented, but with a marked predominance of Cistercians and Augustinians. It is noteworthy that the majority of the foundations farthest removed from the lowland economic and political centres of power came later, predominantly in the reigns of William and Alexander II. Pluscarden in Moray (Plate 5), for example, a foundation (1230) of Alexander II, can be seen as part of an attempt to achieve a sympathetic landholding and commercial presence within an area of the kingdom over which the king wished to strengthen his influence. The same might be claimed for the foundations in Iona, Saddell and Glenluce (in the reign of William), and Ardchattan, Beauly, Fearn and Tongland (in the reign of Alexander II) among others.

The most striking physical symbols of the changing character of the thirteenth-century church are the cathedrals. The diocesan structure was largely in place by the mid twelfth century, partly reflecting older ecclesiastical and political entities: the diocese of Glasgow largely echoed the territory of the former kingdom of Strathclyde, and the diocese of St Andrews was based on the sizeable landholding of an earlier Celtic monastic institution, for example. Other dioceses – Moray, Ross, Caithness and Argyll, for instance – were created afresh, mainly by Alexander I and David I, perhaps motivated 'by a desire to give each frontier province a strong secular government and a bishop to match'.[18] St Andrews had a small twelfth-century church for the senior bishopric of the

18 Barrow, *Kingship and Unity*, p. 68.

kingdom, part of which, known as St Rule's tower, still stands.[19] Its replacement with the largest and most splendid of all of Scotland's medieval buildings (Plate 9) began in the early 1160s; competition for status with York may have been an element in the motivation for its grandeur.[20] Glasgow too had twelfth-century cathedral buildings, overlaid during the middle decades of the thirteenth century by the cathedral which still stands on the site. Construction of the present cathedrals at Dunblane and Dornoch (for the diocese of Caithness) as well as the very splendid Elgin cathedral, the seat of the bishop of Moray, all began in the 1220s; the bishop of Ross's cathedral at Fortrose was started in the late 1230s. Impressive cathedrals and abbeys, in addition to the many smaller, more rustic parish churches were now features of the Scottish built environment. The kingdom traversed by the funeral cortege of Alexander II in 1249 was undergoing a major construction boom, infused with unfamiliar architectural ideas from northern England and the Continent. At that moment veritable armies of stonemasons would have been labouring at the cathedrals of Dornoch, Dunblane, Elgin (Plate 10), Fortrose, Glasgow and St Andrews, with work only recently completed at Brechin and halted, if not completed, at Kirkwall. Monastic building campaigns seem likely to have been in progress at Dunfermline, Holyrood, Pluscarden, Paisley, Inchmahome, Beauly, Inchcolm, Ardchattan and Dundrennan, and perhaps only very recently finished at Dryburgh (Plate 8), Jedburgh (Plate 7), Cambuskenneth and Balmerino.[21] The list cannot be comprehensive, and while it seems likely that an earlier surge of smaller-scale parish church-building was by this stage diminishing, both the difficulty of dating this type of building and the poor survival rate make it impossible to estimate how many such projects may have been current in the mid thirteenth century. Concern for the spiritual well-being of the people in a society infused by Christian belief was a major driving force for these developments, but these buildings were also powerful symbols of a concerted attempt to establish a new level of territorial control over the kingdom, and thus over its economic resources. While dateable evidence is less plentiful for secular architecture, in 1249 building in stone was probably in progress at, for example, Dirleton castle in East Lothian and Hermitage in Liddesdale, perhaps also at Dunstaffnage, Mingary and Castle Sween on the west coast, and doubtless at other centres.[22]

---

19 I have accepted the argument for a twelfth-century date for this building advanced in Fawcett, *Scottish Medieval Church*, pp. 13–17.

20 Malcolm Thurlby, 'St Andrews Cathedral-Priory and the Beginnings of Gothic Architecture in Northern Britain', in J. Higgitt (ed.), *Medieval Art and Architecture in the Diocese of St Andrews* (Leeds, 1994), pp. 47–60, at p. 56.

21 For a detailed guide to the ecclesiastical architecture of the period, see Fawcett, *Scottish Medieval Church*, especially, chs 2 and 3.

22 See Richard D Oram, 'Royal and Lordly Residence in Scotland c 1050 to c 1250: An

Alongside spirituality, learning thrived within the new cloisters. *Registrum Anglie*, a list of books by selected authors held in some British religious houses at the end of the thirteenth century, provides details of almost 500 works owned by the seven Scottish houses surveyed (the abbeys of Dunfermline, Holyrood, Jedburgh, Kelso, Melrose and Newbattle, and St Andrews priory).[23] Some of these are very substantial libraries; yet they represent only a selection either of the houses, or of the books within them. Books were mentioned in an earlier St Andrews context in two mid twelfth-century charters. Bishop Robert's foundation charter of St Andrews priory, *c.*1140, included a gift of his entire book collection.[24] Although his books were not listed, the simple fact of the gift indicated an expectation that study would take place within the new priory. The other charter, a gift to St Andrews of the tiny monastery of St Serf in Loch Leven, *c.*1150, named 17 volumes held there.[25] A few of the St Serf's books were liturgical, but most were mainstream works of European theological and philosophical thought, confirming that even in such a small house, intellectual study was the norm. There is evidence in the thirteenth-century register of St Andrews' cathedral priory of a further work belonging to St Serf's, comprising property records, written in Gaelic.[26] St Serf's was a community of *Céli Dé*, a monastic order with its roots in the Columban church, and it is instructive to see that while these records emphasise its essentially Gaelic cultural identity (as was the case in other *Céli Dé* communities, such as at Brechin and Abernethy), nonetheless the members of the community were learned also in Latin. As the new religious houses, obedient to the incoming Continental monastic orders, appeared in Scotland throughout the twelfth and

Historiographical Review and Critical Revision', *Antiquaries Journal*, 88 (2008), pp. 165–89; http://www.historic-scotland.gov.uk/index/places/propertyresults/propertyabout.htm?PropID=PL_149&PropName=Hermitage%20Castle. See also below, pp. 321–23.

23 R.A.B. Mynors, R.H. Rouse and M.A. Rouse (eds), *Registrum Anglie de libris doctorum et auctorum veterum* (Corpus of British Medieval Library Catalogues, 2; London, 1991), pp. 303–08. See also John Higgitt (ed.), *Scottish Libraries*, Corpus of British Medieval Library Catalogues 12 (London, 2006), pp. xxxvi–xxxix and under each of the relevant library's entry, for comments regarding the Scottish element of *Registrum Anglie*.

24 *St Andrews Liber*, pp. 122–23; For the date, see A.A.M. Duncan, 'The Foundation of St Andrews Cathedral Priory, 1140', *Scottish Historical Review*, 84 (2005), pp. 1–37.

25 See the discussion of these books in Higgitt, *Scottish Libraries*, pp. 222–25. There is also an edition of the text and notes regarding the books in A. Lawrie, *Early Scottish Charters Prior to A.D. 1153* (Glasgow, 1905), pp. 210–11 & 445–46. Barrow, *Scotland and its Neighbours*, p. 119 & n. 80, suggested that the books of St Serf's and those of Bishop Robert were one and the same; I agree, however, with Simon Taylor, with Peter McNiven and Eila Williamson, *The Place-Names of Kinross-shire* (Donnington, 2017), p. 590, that Barrow was mistaken and that the two sets of books are distinct.

26 See Higgitt, *Scottish Libraries*, p. 223; *St Andrews Liber*, p. 113–18; see also Taylor *et al.*, *The Place-Names of Kinross-shire*, pp. 566–86 for the thirteenth-century Latin texts of this originally Gaelic material, with English translations and notes.

thirteenth centuries, they effectively planted centres of Latinate learning throughout the kingdom and, as the older forms of monasticism waned, their communities gradually assimilated into the new. The cathedrals with their chapters (mostly) of secular clergy[27] took over the administration of the secular church, and Latin gradually became the *lingua franca* of academic learning, although Gaelic continued to be spoken and written both within and outwith the cloister. One particular literary form of relevance to the current study was the Gaelic king-list.[28]

The compilers of the Melrose chronicle, written in the twelfth and thirteenth centuries,[29] the historical work of the author known as *Veremundus* (identified as Richard Vairement, a member of the *Céli Dé* community of St Andrews), and of earlier St Andrews writers show that Scotland's Latin written culture was of the same tradition as that in England and Continental Europe.[30] Those teaching in the cathedral and monastic schools produced scholars who progressed to careers in the universities of Europe and who made major contributions to the canon of European theological and philosophical thought. Among important thirteenth-century Scottish scholars are Michael Scot, a polyglot known to have worked in Bologna, Palermo, Toledo and at the court of the Emperor Frederick II in the early part of the century, who has left works on astrology, astronomy and psychology; and, later, John Duns *Scotus*, a theologian who taught in Oxford, Cambridge, Paris and Cologne. Over 400 Scots have been identified as having studied at English and Continental universities during the thirteenth century.[31] Their preparation for those advanced studies would have

---

27 The bishops of St Andrews and Whithorn, unlike all other Scottish bishops, had chapters of regular clergy – Augustinian canons in the case of St Andrews, and Premonstratensians in the case of Whithorn (although note that Whithorn owed allegiance to the metropolitan see of York until 1355).

28 For a description of the complex linguistic situation in thirteenth-century Fife, for example, see Simon Taylor, 'Babbet and Bridin Pudding or Polyglot Fife in the Middle Ages', *Nomina*, 17 (1994), pp. 99–118.

29 See A.A.M. Duncan, 'Sources and Uses of the Chronicle of Melrose', in Simon Taylor (ed.), *Kings, Clerics and Chronicles in Scotland 500–1297* (Dublin, 2000), pp. 146–85; W.W. Scott, 'Abbots Adam (1207–1213) and William (1215–1216) of Melrose and the Melrose Chronicle', in Barbara E. Crawford (ed.), *Church, Chronicle and Learning in Medieval and Early Renaissance Scotland* (Edinburgh, 1999), pp. 161–72; and the excellent introduction to *Chron. Melrose*.

30 For an extensive discussion of Veremundus, see Broun, *Scottish Independence*, particularly ch. 9. There is detailed biographical information about Vairement in Watt, *Graduates*, pp. 559–60. Earlier work includes the writing of the St Andrews foundation legends: see Taylor, *Kings, Clerics and Chronicles*, chs 7 and 8. The *Céli Dé* of St Andrews were in a different position from the other surviving *Céli Dé* communities: see 'The Clergy at St Andrews', in Barrow, *Kingdom of the Scots*, pp. 212–32, for a discussion of the status of this community.

31 Watt, *Graduates;* for Scot, p. 490; for Duns, p. 168. See also D.E.R. Watt, 'Scottish University Men of the Thirteenth and Fourteenth Centuries', in T.C. Smout (ed.), *Scotland and*

taken place in monastic and cathedral schools in their homeland. Baldred Bisset, who in 1301 was one of the key figures involved in pleading the Scottish case at the papal curia against the depredations of Edward I, is said by the seventeenth-century writer David Buchanan to have studied philosophy in St Andrews before crossing to the Continent for his university education.[32]

The royal administration, in which the church played such an important rôle, evolved immensely during the course of the twelfth and early thirteenth centuries and, even during the reign of Alexander III, must be seen as a work in progress. Although a tendency to centralise governmental activity in Edinburgh can be detected from the late twelfth century onwards, the king's court, and thus the royal machinery of government, was still itinerant, an inevitable effect of the requirement to fulfil the fundamental personal duty of the king to provide justice to his people. The place-dates of Alexander II's *acta*, for instance, show him active in over 50 Scottish locations, although only six (Edinburgh, 59 *acta*; Stirling, 27; Forfar, 24; Scone, 18; Selkirk, 18; Roxburgh, 12) account for roughly half of all those identified. The locations are overwhelmingly in the eastern lowlands, with only a few examples in the western or northern parts of the kingdom (including one, on the day of his death, in Kerrera), and none at all north of Inverness.[33] This is a pattern which generally repeats that of previous kings, and is repeated again by Alexander III, who issued acts at around 45 identified locations, out of which only five (Scone, 24; Roxburgh, 14; Edinburgh, 13; Traquair, 10; Haddington, 9) account for around half of the total.[34] Itineration, however, was not the only way in which the legal and administrative bureaucracy of government was non-centralised. As royal authority was largely exercised through local aristocratic power, central organs of government, such as financial and legal administration, were much slimmer than in, for example, the much more centralised bureaucratic state of England.

Nonetheless, a royal household did exist in the thirteenth century, with a set of key officials who held specific responsibilities. Their duties were set out in a document, known as 'The Scottish King's Household', written in French

---

Europe 1200–1850 (Edinburgh, 1986), pp. 1–19, which paints a portrait of a vibrant community of scholars, both at home and abroad.

32 See Watt, *Graduates*, pp. 49–51, citing Buchanan, *De Scriptoribus Scotis Libri Duo* (Bannatyne Club, 1837), pp. 27–28.

33 See this data mapped by Keith Stringer, in McNeill and MacQueen, *Atlas*, p. 162.

34 Acts to 1214: see Geoffrey Barrow's maps in McNeill and MacQueen, *Atlas*, pp. 158–61; Alexander III: Norman Reid's map in McNeill and MacQueen, *Atlas*, p. 163 and the map in *RRS*, iv pt.1, p. 275 give marginally different distributions (based on interpretations of the authority supporting some of the place-date attributions); yet the pattern remains the same, and is consistent enough to be generally informative. See below, pp. 214–15, for further comments on place-date evidence of itineration.

probably for King John Balliol, *c.*1292.[35] The first official named in the treatise is the chancellor:

> wise, suitable and of good discretion, impartial to rich and to poor, as head of his [the king's] Council, and who ought to know the Chancery forms and know the laws of the land . . . one of the wisest and most discreet of the realm; for if this office be well governed, it is the key and the safety of the Great Seal and the prevention of all the errors which can arise in the Court between the King and the Baronage.[36]

The chancellor's position was of fundamental importance to the realm. He held the king's great seal, used to authenticate most royal writings. His office physically produced those acts without which the king had no public voice in the realm. The chancellor's office communicated to the governed the king's grants of land, his legislation, and his judgements and edicts. Of the six chancellors of Alexander III's reign, one was abbot of Dunfermline, four were (or became) bishops and the last (of whose professional dedication abundant evidence survives) was Thomas Charteris (or *de Carnoto*), a long-trusted royal servant who had previously been archdeacon of Lothian, and was already an experienced chancery clerk and former clerk of the rolls.[37] The chancellor was also responsible for further clerks of the household, who were chaplains and physicians to both king and chancellor. The chancery, or king's writing office, was run under the direction of the chancellor by clerks ('as many clerks as are required in reason'), themselves all educated clerics who could expect to develop significant ecclesiastical careers. They administered the issue of documents, kept the records, and one particularly dependable clerk was sometimes given power to deputise

35 Bateson, 'The Scottish King's Household'. This is an indispensable source of closely contemporary information and must reflect the situation as it prevailed in the later thirteenth century, although the extent to which it presents an ideal view, as opposed to reflecting day-to-day practice, must be open to doubt. Bateson surmised that this treatise was written for King Edward I as he compiled his ordinance for the government of Scotland in 1304/5; Barrow, *Kingdom of the Scots*, p. 93 suggests, more persuasively, that it was written for John Balliol in 1292/3. The brief description of the thirteenth-century royal administration which follows also relies largely on G.W.S. Barrow's excellent introductory material to *RRS*, i & ii, and on the briefer analysis of the acts of Alexander III by Cynthia J. Neville and Grant G. Simpson in the introduction to *RRS*, iv pt. 1. David Carpenter, 'Scottish Royal Government in the Thirteenth Century from an English Perspective' also has an important analysis of the nature of the kingdom's administration. All of the above sources should be considered, however, in the light of the most detailed, and most recent, study of the development of Scottish governmental and judicial machinery – Taylor, *Shape of the State* – which offers a different view of the underlying nature of government.

36 Bateson, 'The Scottish King's Household', pp. 31–32, 38.

37 *Handbook of British Chronology*, p. 181; Charteris: see Watt, *Graduates*, pp. 85–86.

for the chancellor when other duties monopolised his time.[38] The chancellor also played a key rôle in the chamberlain's court (see below). The clerk of the rolls, a member of the chancellor's staff (who, like Thomas Charteris, sometimes deputised for the chancellor), was responsible for the important task of maintaining the records of government, including the financial records created by the chamberlain's office.[39]

The king's *camera* (chamber) – effectively the royal counting-house (it is inaccurate to refer to a Scottish exchequer in this period; incoming revenue was deposited in the *camera*) – was presided over by the chamberlain. 'The Scottish King's Household' tells us that the position of chamberlain should be an appointment made communally by the king's council and the barons of the kingdom, and should be filled by someone able to manage the economic affairs of government, including the revenues gained from royal demesne lands, the burghs, customs and taxation, and the profits of justice, wardships and other feudal dues. The chamberlain was also responsible for purchases and should

> regulate the King's dwelling, by the assent of the King himself, and the state of his household according to the season of the year, so that the household may live by purveyance without ravaging the country.[40]

Since the mid twelfth century, the chamberlains had usually been high-ranking members of the lay aristocracy, who travelled with the king: their regular presence at court is proven by the frequency with which they witnessed royal acts. The chamberlain was thus a member of the coterie of supporters and followers of the king, a close political ally, and occupied a position that was deemed important enough in the wielding of the authority of the crown, with an impact on all levels of society, to justify appointment – in theory at least – by the whole governing community. Having gradually gained in status and importance from the early twelfth century onwards, the rôle was still developing, as the kingdom's economy and methods of accounting became more complex and sophisticated. It can be assumed that most of the day-to-day financial business was left to a staff – known as the clerks of the chapel – whose responsibility was for the physical security of the king's riches as well as for the accounting duties which inevitably followed the administration of justice, the levying of taxation and

---

38 *Chron. Fordun*, i, p. 297 (trans. ii, p. 293). Robert, dean of Dunkeld held the seal for the chancellor in 1257. Thomas Charteris, mentioned above, is another example of such promotion.
39 Bateson, 'The Scottish King's Household', pp. 32, 39; for a description of record-keeping practices, see Taylor, *Shape of the State*, ch. 7.
40 Bateson, 'The Scottish King's Household', pp. 32, 38. For discussion of the chamberlain's rôle, see Taylor, *Shape of the State*, pp. 244–62.

customs dues, and for the general administration of the royal court. The chamberlain, however, was the officer to whom the other officials, in the localities, were held accountable for their own financial duties. Those who were responsible for collecting royal revenues, the sheriffs for example (and even the chamberlain himself), had personally to render annual accounts, which were audited by the chamberlain. These were presented at a formal sitting attended by the chamberlain, the chancellor (or deputies appointed by them) and a number of other responsible, educated men, often bishops and abbots.[41] The local officials might be called to the royal court when it was in their locality, or they might have to attend a sitting of itinerant accounting sessions known as chamberlain's ayres. Though presentation of accounts might not be regular, accurate accounting records were nevertheless required. 'The Scottish King's Household' states (perhaps more in hope than expectation) that the auditors should meet annually to hear the account of all who owed one, and that the auditors should be 'people of substance and discretion enjoined by commission with the Chancellor and the Chamberlain to take such account and make reasonable deductions to the King's profit'.[42]

The domestic arrangements of the king's household were nominally the preserve of the steward and his staff. There is some evidence, however, that by this period the day-to-day running of the household – and in particular its provisioning – was in the hands of an office known as the *prebenda* or provend, and that there were similar officials (although of subordinate status) responsible for the kitchens, the wardrobe and the livery; and of course there were the bakers, brewers and cooks. The steward, by this time a hereditary holder of the office from which the later royal family name derived, was not as regularly present at court as had once been the case, and it can be assumed that the *clericus regis de prebenda*, while in status a subordinate of the steward, in fact had a considerable degree of autonomy. The king's butler (*pincerna*) was another office of some status, always held by a noble of knightly rank. The duties of the thirteenth-century constable, a secular office also held by a high-ranking nobleman, elude precise definition, but are said to have included 'general charge of the knight-service and feudal forces'; the constable does not seem to have been generally regarded as of higher military standing than the earls, however, who would lead their own territorial forces.[43]

---

41 If the chancellor and/or chamberlain (or their nominated deputies) were absent, the sitting was not deemed competent: see, e.g., *ER*, i, p. 22 (. . . *in hoc computo non decidunt, propter absenciam cancellarii et camerarii*).

42 Bateson, 'The Scottish King's Household', pp. 32, 38.

43 For the steward, provender, liverance and constable, see Bateson, 'The Scottish King's Household', pp. 32–35, 39–41; see also *RRS*, ii, pp. 34–38; quotation from p. 38.

Perhaps the most fundamental duty of the medieval monarch was the administration of justice: the ruler held a vital personal rôle in judicial proceedings. The legal administration had also grown considerably, as the law itself had developed throughout the previous two or three centuries, with an increasing definition of the distinction between canon law, which regulated ecclesiastical affairs, and the secular law, which settled disputes of a lay character.[44] The key official appointed by the king to represent his own judicial function in the locality was the justiciar. By the early decades of the thirteenth century, two such officers can be detected in the records, having responsibility for Scotia – Scotland north of the Forth – and Lothian, with a third, Galloway, following from the late 1250s.[45] These offices were usually held by high-ranking barons, sometimes earls and occasionally by bishops. It seems possible that there might sometimes have been more than one justiciar for each area. Their rôle, through the holding of regular justice ayres (itinerant courts) which dealt with cases beyond the authority of the sheriffs, was 'to provide law and justice to poor as well as rich, and to preserve and control the rights of the king in all matters which pertain to his crown'.[46] In addition, those who held land of the crown retained important judicial functions, cooperation between crown and aristocracy being essential to governance.

Sheriffs, wielding royal administrative authority in the localities, had been appearing since the 1120s, with the development of the territorially – and jurisdictionally – defined sheriffdom gradually following over the next half century.[47] By the early thirteenth century, there were 20 or more sheriffs in place (with a further 10 or so instituted during the reigns of Alexanders II and III). Most of these were, naturally, in the areas of the kings' most settled power base, the eastern and southern lowlands. The extension of royal authority was also supported by additional shrieval appointments, and by early in Alexander II's

---

44 There is an excellent summary of the state of these developments during the first half of the thirteenth century in Hector L. MacQueen, 'Canon Law, Custom and Legislation: Law in the Reign of Alexander II', in Oram, *Alexander II Essays*, pp. 221–51; see also Taylor, *Shape of the State*, ch. 5, which presents an alternative view to MacQueen's, and which stresses once again the crucial rôle played by local aristocratic courts in upholding the rule of law throughout the kingdom.

45 Taylor, *Shape of the State*, p. 212.

46 Bateson, 'The Scottish King's Household', pp. 36–37, 42 (translation quoted is by G.W.S. Barrow, *RRS*, ii, p. 46). See also Taylor, *Shape of the State*, pp. 210–43, which provides the most comprehensive study of the office of justiciar since the earlier work of G.W.S. Barrow, 'The Justiciar', in *Kingdom of the Scots*, pp. 83–138.

47 There is a brief description of the development of the shrieval system, and a list of known incumbents, in Reid and Barrow, *Sheriffs*; a much more significant analysis (which corrects some errors in the description given by Reid and Barrow) is to be found in Taylor, *Shape of the State*, pp. 192–210.

reign sheriffs were active in, for example, Moray, Inverness, Galloway and Dumfries.[48] Local nobility, of both middling and high status, were selected for this rôle throughout the thirteenth century, and by its later years there was a marked movement towards tenure by well-established baronial figures, and even a discernible tendency towards an element of heritable succession. The sheriff represented the king in tenurial affairs, in fiscal activity (the gathering, disbursement and accounting of royal income) and, over time, in the administration of royal courts as well as representing the king in local lords' courts. The revenues collected included the fruits of justice (both of his own courts and those of the justiciars) and other levies and dues owed from the locality, a considerable proportion of which was paid in kind, and had to be accounted for in just the same way as coin. The sheriffs were also responsible for much expenditure: their accounts would include the costs of hosting the royal court, for instance, and frequently the fees of royal officials were paid out of revenues collected by them.[49] By the later thirteenth century the sheriff had in addition a local military function, often as the constable of a royal castle situated at the sheriffdom's *caput*, or headquarters. It is possible that this local military function was more pronounced both in periods of English domination, when the rôle perhaps more closely resembled the English model,[50] and in times of warfare, when a greater military emphasis was inevitable. The rôle was indeed one of 'ubiquitous activity and indispensability'.[51]

The monarch, although in person the ultimate source of justice, had also to swear an oath to make and uphold good laws. Judicial and legislative functions were assumed to be fulfilled through the use of good counsel. When medieval monarchs fell foul of their people it was frequently accusations of bad counsel which were used to justify rebellious action.[52] By the mid thirteenth century,

---

48 See the maps by Hector MacQueen in McNeill and MacQueen, *Atlas*, pp. 192–94.

49 For the earliest extant sheriff's accounts (which survive only in partial seventeenth-century transcripts), see *ER*, i, pp. 1–34. For the most recent detailed work on the accounting processes, as well as governmental record-keeping, see Taylor, *Shape of the State*, chs 6 and 7.

50 G.W.S. Barrow, *Feudal Britain* (London, 1971), p. 261, describes how the thirteenth-century English sheriff 'ceased to be a farmer of his county, and became . . . a salaried custodian'.

51 *RRS*, ii, p. 41; pp. 39–42 provides a detailed discussion of the office of sheriff.

52 A prime example is the letter by which King John Balliol surrendered his kingdom to Edward I in July 1296; doubtless worded by Edward or his advisors rather than by Balliol himself, it asserted that his offence to Edward had been caused by his being led 'by evil and false counsel' (*par mauvoys consail e faus*); Stones, *Anglo-Scottish Relations*, pp. 146–47. The preamble to Bateson, 'The Scottish King's Household' (p. 31, translated pp. 37–38) makes it clear that good counsel was a prerequisite of good rule, and its final paragraph (p. 37, translated p. 43) makes it explicit that parliament was by this date (early 1290s) regarded as the most elevated form of royal council. Practical evidence for the king's actual use of counsel in this way is found in the wording of the proceedings of a legal suit heard in the parliament (or *colloquium*)

the king's council was beginning to become organised into the institution now recognised as parliament, although its representative nature, or even its structure and function, were barely regularised: the first meeting in Scotland which deserves the name of 'parliament' took place as late as 1235.[53] That meetings of this kind were convened with increasing regularity during the reigns of Alexander II and Alexander III confirms both that the expectations of kingly rule were becoming more formalised, and that there was a group of high-ranking individuals around the king who regarded themselves as having, *de jure*, a rôle in governing the kingdom. In such a position, the rôle could be both of advisor and, when necessary, of counterbalance to the monarch. The concept of aristocratic responsibility in government, though still ill-defined in the mid thirteenth century, would come sharply into focus in providing the constitutional justification for action in time of crisis at the end of the century when, in the absence of a monarch following the death of Alexander III, and again following the deposition of John Balliol, the community was to self-govern through the appointment of guardians.[54]

A primary objective of the settled rule of a kingdom is to ensure a stable and prosperous economy. Scotland's population, though far lower than at present, was then more evenly spread throughout the country, with a far smaller proportion (perhaps 10 per cent, as opposed to today's 80 per cent) living in urban centres, and with a significantly lower comparative density in the southern and eastern areas of the kingdom. Estimates tend broadly to agree on a populace numbering roughly one million – a little under one-fifth of the modern figure.[55]

at Holyrood on 13 January 1256, when a dispute involving the abbot and convent of Dunfermline was settled by the king 'by the common counsel of his magnates' (*per commune consilium magnatum suorum*); *RPS*, 1256/1. Bower, writing in the fifteenth century about the early years of Alexander III's reign, indulges in a moralising sermon regarding the necessity for a king to have good counsel: *Chron. Bower*, v, pp. 302–05.

53 See Keith M. Brown and Roland J. Tanner (eds), *Parliament and Politics in Scotland, 1235–1560* (*The History of the Scottish Parliament*, i; Edinburgh, 2004), especially the Introduction, and ch. 1: Alison A.B. McQueen, 'Parliament, the Guardians and John Balliol, 1284–1296' (pp. 29–49), where we are warned that even by 1286 'parliament was not yet a defined, structured body with any steady or permanent rôle within Scottish political society' (p. 32).

54 See Norman Reid and Michael Penman, 'Guardian – Lieutenant – Governor: Absentee Monarchy and Proxy Power in Scotland's Long Fourteenth Century', in Frédérique Lachaud and Michael Penman (eds), *Absentee Authority Across Medieval Europe* (Woodbridge, 2017), pp. 191–218; Norman Reid, 'The Kingless Kingdom: The Scottish Guardianships of 1286–1306', *Scottish Historical Review*, 61 (1982), pp. 105–29.

55 For the modern population, see the report *Rural and Urban Areas: Comparing Lives Using Rural/Urban Classifications* (Tim Pateman, Office of National Statistics, 2010/11; http://www.ons.gov.uk/ons/rel/regional-trends/regional-trends/no--43--2011-edition/index.html). For description of medieval settlement patterns and population estimates, see R.A. Dodgshon, 'Medieval Settlement and Colonisation', in M.L. Parry and T.R. Slater (eds), *The Making of the Scottish Countryside* (London 1980), pp. 45–68; the first chapter, 'Land and People', of Barrow, *Kingship*

The thirteenth-century climate was warm, encouraging cultivation of a greater amount of marginal land than was possible either previously or subsequently, and making feasible the growth of at least limited amounts of wheat, a valuable crop which was dependent on benevolent conditions. Even in the warm thirteenth century, however, most arable land produced hardier crops, such as oats and barley (or bere), primarily for local consumption.[56] Royal edicts demanding increased agricultural productivity may indicate that population growth was exceeding food supply, and also that the crown saw the opportunity to increase mercantile activity.[57]

Underlying the edicts, however, was a further issue: land was being turned away from the plough and given up to grazing for sheep, creating shortages of grain to provide the staples of everyday life. In 1209, William I decreed that 'the earls, barons and free-holders . . . should not waste their lands and the country with a multitude of sheep and beasts, thus leading God's people into penury, poverty and destruction'.[58] The growth of sheep-rearing indicates both that Scotland was in the process of moving away from a largely subsistence economy during the twelfth century, and that there was profit to be made from sheep. Another benefit of the warmer climate was the ability to produce high-quality sheep's wool, and since much of Scotland was suitable more for grazing than arable cultivation, it was therefore the production of wool which became the mainstay of the developing export market.[59] In the thirteenth century, Scottish wool was in great demand by the primary European cloth-producing centres in Flanders – second in quality only to that of England. Salmon, herring, cod, salt, coal and a variety of animal skins had been exported for centuries to enable the import of manufactured and exotic goods (an indication in itself that Scotland's was a relatively primitive economy), but it was

---

and Unity (which gives a lower population estimate of about 0.5m); Cowan, 'Norwegian Sunset – Scottish Dawn', pp. 24–25, reminds us of the perceived wealth of the Hebridean area in the Middle Ages.

56 Alastair Dawson, *So Foul and Fair a Day: A History of Scotland's Weather and Climate* (Edinburgh, 2009), pp. 96–99, urges caution in ascribing 'wonderful' climatic conditions to eleventh- and twelfth-century Scotland; written evidence suggests that it was a period with often turbulent, severe weather. See below, pp. 299–303.

57 *APS*, i, p. 397.

58 *Item statuit quod comites barones et libere tenentes regni conservent pacem et iusticiam in servis suis et quod vivant ut domini de terries et redditibus et firmis suis et non ut husbandi non ut pastores devastantes dominie sua et patriam cum multitudine ovium et bestiarum penuriam paupertatem et distructionem in populo Dei inducentes. APS*, i, p. 382. The authority of the attribution to William is uncertain, but the material within these later compilations is genuine. See Alice Taylor, '*Leges Scocie* and the Lawcodes of David I, William the Lion and Alexander II', *Scottish Historical Review*, 88 (2009), pp. 207–88.

59 For the importance of the wool trade to the Scottish economy, see Stevenson, 'Trade', ch. 1, especially at pp. 1–5, 18–21.

the expansion of the wool trade during the thirteenth century which was the engine driving Scotland's economic development. When, from the early fourteenth century, the climate started to deteriorate significantly, it seems that one effect was to reduce the quality of the wool,[60] with a concomitant diminution of demand which was severely to the detriment of the Scottish economy. Although the long war between Scotland and England which broke out at the end of the thirteenth century certainly played its part in the creation of the relative poverty which characterised late medieval and early modern Scotland, changing climate was undoubtedly another significant factor.

Thanks to some medieval chroniclers who claimed that Scotland in this period was endowed with abounding wealth, a myth has evolved of a thirteenth-century 'Golden Age'. Although modern scholarship has tempered the more fanciful historiographical excesses,[61] it cannot be denied that the Scotland which Alexander III inherited basked in an atmosphere of flourishing commercial development and economic growth.

Through use of the burgh, an increasingly monetised trading economy was promoted. Although burghs were not a new idea – they were known in Scotland from at least the early twelfth century, and most of the medieval Scottish burghs had already been founded before Alexander II acceded to the throne in 1214[62] – trade was increasingly channelled through them, and their development was fostered by the thirteenth-century kings. Despite the fact that the population was more evenly spread than in later times, it is nonetheless clear from the distribution of the emerging burghs (which were overwhelmingly situated on the eastern seaboard of the kingdom) that Scotland was becoming, in economic terms at least, an eastward-facing nation.[63] The nature of the burgh was, quite simply, 'a community organised for trade'.[64] Burghs had the right to hold a market, at which the produce of the surrounding country and imported goods were sold. Further, some

60 Stevenson, 'Trade', pp. 22–25. See also M.L. Parry, 'Secular Climatic Change and Marginal Agriculture', *Transactions of the Institute of British Geographers*, 64 (1975), pp. 1–13.

61 See, for example, Mayhew, 'A Silver Age', and Reid, 'Historiography'.

62 See E. Patricia Dennison, 'Burghs and Burgesses: A Time of Consolidation?' in Oram, *Alexander II Essays*, pp. 253–83, an excellent description of the thirteenth-century burgh, from which the following brief summary is largely drawn. See also the description of the development of the burghs in Stevenson, 'Trade', pp. 137ff., and the more recent E. Patricia Dennison, *The Evolution of Scotland's Towns: Creation, Growth and Fragmentation* (Edinburgh, 2018), pp. 11–16.

63 See the distribution maps by A.A.M. Duncan in McNeill and MacQueen, *Atlas*, pp. 196–98. Note, however, the comment by Elizabeth Ewan that 'Overseas trade was only one element in a burgh's economy, and the fact that the burghs were able to achieve recognition of their political importance in a period of declining exports suggests that it was not always the most important one.' ('An Urban Community: The Crafts in Thirteenth-Century Aberdeen', in Grant and Stringer, *Medieval Scotland*, 156–73, at p. 173. This essay also gives a vivid picture of life in the thirteenth-century burgh.)

64 Dennison, 'Burghs and Burgesses', p. 254.

burghs had the sole right to trade throughout a large area around them: the inhabitants of that area were obliged to buy and sell only through the burgh market. The burgesses exacted custom from those who bought and sold at their market; they also had freedom from payment of such customs at other burgh markets, which gave them nationwide economic advantage over those who lived outwith the burghs and over foreign merchants. The burghs thus became the focal points of the kingdom's commercial activity, and the privilege and economic power of merchants, who by the late twelfth century were beginning to form themselves into guilds within the major burghs, increased steadily throughout the thirteenth century. The importance of the burghs became such that by the early fourteenth century their representatives had taken their place within the developing parliament.[65] The crown, and others who (with permission from the crown) founded burghs, benefitted through the extraction of customs from the market, as well as the levying of burgh rents.

Burghs were generally situated in locations which had existing settlements, often of considerable antiquity, which had grown because of advantageous strategic or trading conditions, and were therefore frequently also the sites of castles. There is a striking regularity in the issuing of royal acts from burghs: well over half of the place-dated *acta* issued by Alexander III were issued at burghs, and almost half of the rest were issued from major religious houses. It would be a mistake, however, to assume that burghs were necessarily large towns, or that they were in any way physically impressive. They had populations of only a few hundred, and although rendered distinctive and separate from the surrounding landscape by their wooden palisades and their gates (sometimes with stone gatehouses, although only Perth had stone walls to match), they would have lacked splendour, other than in the architecture of conspicuous religious or fortified structures which dominated some of them. The layout was usually a single-street or occasionally (as at St Andrews and Haddington) a double-street plan, with a central marketplace. Dwellings were largely mean affairs of wood and wattle with thatched or turfed roofs; domestic building in stone would have appeared only rarely before the fourteenth century. The land was divided into evenly sized burgage plots, with strips of arable land behind the houses on the street-front. Outside the burgh boundaries was common ground for grazing and the lifting of peat and turf.[66]

---

65 The earliest parliament at which burgh commissioners are known to have been present is the 1326 parliament of Robert I held at Cambuskenneth. See A.A.M. Duncan, 'The Early Parliaments of Scotland', *Scottish Historical Review*, 45 (1966), pp. 36–58; Ranald Nicolson, *Scotland: The Later Middle Ages* (Edinburgh, 1974), pp. 115–16.

66 See the description of the built environment of the burghs in Dennison, *The Evolution of Scotland's Towns*, pp. 16–31. See also below, Map 3, p. 298.

Although the planting of burghs in the twelfth and thirteenth centuries enhanced royal administrative and political control of the kingdom,[67] their primary purpose was nonetheless economic. The levying of taxation or toll, much of which was payable ultimately to the crown, and the increasing centralisation within the burghs of trade and import/export activities encouraged the increasing trend away from a barter economy towards monetisation. Money – gold and silver coin – had been circulating in Scotland from the later eleventh century,[68] although on a relatively small scale, largely in the hands of the royal treasurer, wealthy merchants and the church (the monastic houses were major economic players, especially in the wool trade[69]), and was channelled through the burghs. The evidence of surviving coin hoards suggests that English money tended to be significantly more plentiful in Scotland than the output of Scottish mints, which largely followed the English lead both in the patterns of their coins and in the timings of re-coinages. There was also a fair amount of Continental coin in Scotland, confirming the fact that the thirteenth-century prosperity was indeed built upon overseas export. That coin would have been brought to Scotland, overwhelmingly, in exchange for wool.

The pattern of Scottish export, with relatively few shipments, often in convoys, and using ships larger than average for the period, illustrates the hazardous nature of the activity. Ships sailed, for instance, about 385 miles from Leith to Bruges (or to its port, at Sluys), which was 'by far the greatest point of exchange for waterborne traffic between northern and southern Europe', and northern Europe's primary marketplace.[70] Before the end of the thirteenth century – and perhaps earlier – the Scots had established an effective trading community within Bruges, which gained privileges there, the precursor to the formal establishment in the fourteenth century of a Scottish 'staple', effectively

67 Dennison, 'Burghs and Burgesses', p. 274, gives the example of Alexander II's establishment of Dumbarton and Dingwall, at the 'extremity of secure royal control'.

68 See D.M. Metcalfe, 'The Evidence of Scottish Coin Hoards for Monetary History, 1100–1600' (pp. 1–59), and Nicholas Mayhew, 'Money in Scotland in the Thirteenth Century' (pp. 85–102), both in *Coinage in Medieval Scotland (1100–1600): The Second Oxford Symposium on Coinage and Monetary History* (British Archaeological Reports, 45; 1977); and Mayhew, 'A Silver Age', for discussions of medieval Scottish money supply.

69 See David Ditchburn, 'Saints and Silver: Scotland and Europe in the Age of Alexander II', in Oram, *Alexander II essays*, pp. 179–209, especially at pp. 185–92, for a description of thirteenth-century Scottish Cistercian economic activity; and Elizabeth Ewan's map of Scottish monastic wool production in McNeill and MacQueen, *Atlas*, p. 237.

70 See Stevenson, 'Trade', pp. 12–16, for a description of Bruges' mercantile pre-eminence, and pp. 165–73, for the nature of the Scottish fleet and maritime habits. Although Stevenson's evidence is for a later period, his description seems likely to apply equally to the thirteenth century.

a trading colony.[71] Certainly, customs duties were levied on both exports and imports in the thirteenth century.[72]

The growing economy also demanded increased production of Scottish coin, however, and the number of active Scottish mints seems to have increased from four in the early years of the century to perhaps sixteen in 1250.[73] Although that figure dropped slightly by the later years of the century, it is suggested that overall production had nonetheless increased. It has been tentatively estimated that the amount of coin in circulation in Scotland rose from around £20,000 at the beginning of the century to perhaps £150,000 at its end,[74] reflecting as much the monetary expansion in England as that in Scotland. The size of the Scottish economy, however, seems to have remained roughly in proportion to that of the English, equivalent to their respective populations (approximately 1:6), giving the lie to the popularly held notion that Scotland was always proportionately poorer than her southern neighbour.

This picture of relative prosperity has to be tempered by the question posed by one commentator: 'for whom was the age so golden?'[75] The point has already been made that the increasing money supply, certainly for most of the thirteenth century, was in the hands of only a few – the wealthier merchants, the church and the crown. It is a commonplace of medieval history that the great majority of the population has left virtually no mark on the written record, and that historiography tends therefore largely to ignore them. In Scotland as elsewhere, it is difficult to draw more than very general conclusions based on scant archaeological evidence about the daily lives of at least 95 per cent of the population. Perhaps few of them would ever have owned many, if any, of the circulating silver coins. Their lives were still largely those of subsistence farmers, dwelling in small ferme touns of a few dozen inhabitants, scattered across the landscape. Land was divided regularly, with each family having its house or cottage, byre and allocation of cultivable land as well as a share in the common arable and grazing surrounding the toun. The nature (nucleated or dispersed) of the community, how much land was allocated, units of measurement and the methods of tillage would all vary in different parts of the country, largely according to the nature and quality of the land available. Householders would have raised livestock – pigs, cows, goats and hens – and would have grown oats, barley and

71 Stevenson, 'Trade', pp. 16–18.

72 Customs were levied on exported wool, woolfells and hides. See Stevenson, 'Trade', pp. 150–51 and p. 231 n. 63; although amounts collected are unknown before the reign of Robert I, there is reference to these tolls being levied at Berwick in a listing of the Scottish archives held in Edinburgh castle in 1292 (*APS*, i, pp. 113–17, at 114).

73 Mayhew, 'Money in Scotland', pp. 85, 87 (fig. 1).

74 Mayhew, 'Money in Scotland', p. 85.

75 Mayhew, 'A Silver Age', p. 53.

perhaps occasionally (when conditions were favourable) wheat, although such a fine crop would normally have been produced for sale to the finer-living lords or monastic communities, rather than for self-consumption. There is some evidence that, as more land was brought under cultivation, new methods (including ox-, or perhaps occasionally horse-drawn ploughs) were introduced – so it may not be the case that the lives of ordinary folk remained unchanged across centuries, without innovation or alleviation.[76] Nonetheless, it seems that agricultural method continued to be somewhat primitive, leading to low yields and a populace vulnerable to shortage, even famine. Any surplus beyond family needs and the payment of rents and duties had to be traded at a local burgh market, with payment of a share of the toll for buying, selling (or, most often presumably bartering) there. The developing wool trade did not necessarily lead to improved living conditions either: as Scotland discovered again dramatically in the later eighteenth and nineteenth centuries, the turning over of land to sheep entailed relocation and distress for those who had lived on the land. Royal edicts discouraging livestock production at the expense of arable activity must have been at least partially motivated by a perceived need to protect the populace from hardship. Diet would have been monotonous and daily routines harshly energetic and entirely devoid of modern comforts. Life was tough, and, compared to modern times, short. Yet the image often portrayed of medieval peasants as pawns in a colourless, brutal, joyless society cannot be entirely accurate; activities such as hunting, sports, drinking, gaming, storytelling and enjoyment of the entertainment provided by travelling players would have alleviated the drudgery of even the humblest of lives.[77]

It is not sufficient to depict a society divided between a small number who held privilege and wealth, and the overwhelming majority who held neither. The chronicler Walter Bower obviously gave vent to social snobbery when he stated that 'a peasant is inferior to a dog';[78] but his fulmination against peasants has to be seen in the context of his description of the English fourteenth-century peasants' revolt, which threatened social order as Bower understood it, and

---

76 See Duncan, *Making of the Kingdom*, pp. 310–11, and, for a more detailed description of the land and its people in this period, the chapters generally on 'The Land' (pp. 309–25), 'The Sorts of Men' (pp. 326–48), and 'The Conditions of Men' (pp. 349–67). There is a briefer summary in the first chapter of Barrow, *Kingship and Unity*, and excellent accounts of many aspects of Scottish medieval society in Barrow, *Kingdom of The Scots*. For region-specific discussion of land use, see Cynthia J. Neville, *Native Lordship in Medieval Scotland: The Earldoms of Strathearn and Lennox, c.1140–1365* (Dublin, 2005), ch. 3.

77 For a description of everyday life in the burghs, see Dennison, *The Evolution of Scotland's Towns*, pp. 47–76; several chapters within Edward J. Cowan and Lizanne Henderson (eds), *A History of Everyday Life in Medieval Scotland, 1000 to 1600* (Edinburgh, 2011), add rich detail on specific aspects of daily life.

78 *Chron. Bower*, vii, p. 394–95; *rusticus degenerior est cane.*

which led him to create a falsely unified peasant caste. Certainly, there was a significant gap between those who held their lands in chief of the crown – the predominant families and the major religious institutions – and the great majority of those who lived as tenants on their lands. The husbandmen who farmed the lands, and paid rents and other types of service to their lords, themselves used the labour and rents of lower-class peasants, varying in rank down to those with no landholding of their own, who depended on the fruits of their labour to survive. Social mobility was very limited, and it was not long since men, women and their families had been bought and sold along with the land on which they lived. That distinction between free and unfree was fading by the thirteenth century, but at the lowest level of society freedom must have been a dubious concept. It has been proposed that it was the breaking in of new land which was the catalyst for this change:[79] the bestowal on previously unfree tenants of land which became newly workable because of the warm climate and developing economy, giving them the opportunity to work their 'own' land in return for labour and rent owed to their lord, had changed the norms at the lower end of the social spectrum during the course of the twelfth century. At all levels of society, there seems to have been an assumption of heritable possession: as long as certain key obligations were met, landholding would normally pass from one generation to another. Heritable succession was not inevitable, however: in 1305 Edward I received a complaint from 'poor husbandmen' in Scotland that they had no security of tenure.[80] At each level, the superior had judicial powers over the inferior, to whom fines or even physical punishment could be meted out for misbehaviour. Payments (teinds) were also due to the local parish church, with the result that even the lower ranks of the clergy usually assumed a relatively elevated social status.

At the other end of the social spectrum, for the earls and barons, society had also changed significantly during the course of the twelfth century. Part of the process by which the kingdom had been gradually defined, and crucial to the recognition of royal authority, was the innovation in landholding. The influx of many Anglo-Norman families into Scotland, largely at the behest of the twelfth-century kings who offered them lands on a feudal basis – that is, that the lands were held of the crown in return for military and/or other services – had changed the social landscape of the country, and the new forms of landholding became ubiquitous, with consequent changes both in legal practice and, to some extent, in the nature of the relationship between nobility and crown. This was not, as has sometimes been portrayed, a takeover of the

79 Duncan, *Making of the Kingdom*, p. 348.
80 Quoted in Barrow, *Kingship and Unity*, p. 9, without citing source.

traditional ruling class of Scotland by incomers. Existing aristocratic families retained their lands, and the nature of their lordships gradually modified to fit within the new framework; through a natural process of assimilation by the mid thirteenth century there was probably little perceived division between the 'new' and the 'old' aristocracies.[81] It is noticeable that whereas in the earlier twelfth century it was common for royal charters to begin with a greeting which specified the various nationalities – Scottish, English, French and, sometimes, Galwegian – that constituted the *probi homines* (responsible men) of the realm, by the end of the century this had all but disappeared in favour of the more general address to 'all responsible men of his whole land' (*omnibus probis hominibus totius terre sue*), which in some circumstances might be taken as a sign of increasing homogeneity among the landed class.[82] The change towards a feudal model of landholding was not the imposition of a foreign system: Scottish landholding, and the relationship between crown and tenant, had their own characteristics, developed gradually through the melding of new and old custom.

The most elevated of the nobles, the earls, provide an example of the blend of evolution and continuity. Their positions had developed over centuries out of earlier pre-national territorial leaderships. As the holdings of the older provincial leaders, *mormaír*, became gradually more territorialised by the early thirteenth century and as the kin-based element of their authority diminished, it became accepted that their provincial power lay in authority over the *comitatus*, a concept which evolved into the earldom, and which was bestowed by gift of the king. While the link between the older *mormaership* and the earldom was strong, therefore, there was nonetheless a significant difference in the nature of the earldom, as an arm of royal authority.[83] Earls were accepted as natural rulers of the kingdom, in partnership with the crown.

---

81 See the useful summary of how the earlier kings went about introducing feudal landholding, first using their own 'demesne' estates, in Barrow, *Kingship and Unity*, ch. 3. Keith Stringer, 'Periphery and Core in Thirteenth Century Scotland: Alan son of Roland, Lord of Galloway and Constable of Scotland', in Grant and Stringer, *Medieval Scotland*, pp. 82–113, describes Alan of Galloway as 'a magnate who was typical of the greater nobility of thirteenth-century Scotland in that his power rested on aspects of both Celtic and feudal lordship, and who, like most "native" lords, moved easily in the dominant Anglo-French milieu' (pp. 98–99).

82 See the detailed description of the address clause of Scottish twelfth-century charters in *RRS*, ii, pp. 76–77. See also Barrow's comments on the expression *probi homines* in *Robert Bruce and the Community of the Realm of Scotland* (4th edn, Edinburgh, 2005), pp. 36–37.

83 Taylor, *Shape of the* State, pp. 38–53 gives a detailed explanation of the development from *mormaer* to earl. Barrow, *Kingship and Unity*, pp. 44–45 emphasised the point: 'in marked contrast with England the earldoms remained surprisingly intact and still identifiable as provincial governorships until the fourteenth century. But if the earls preserved their position in the front rank of the aristocratic class, they were nonetheless included by the twelfth-century kings among the "barons and knights" of the crown.'

A similar process of change affected the lower ranks of the aristocracy. Those leaders of localised kin-groups known as thanes saw their positions similarly territorialised during the twelfth and early thirteenth centuries, and by the mid thirteenth century 'thanes were conceptualised not only as landlords but also as having equivalent responsibilities to barons and knights': they held local courts, and raised armed forces from their lands when required by the king, and might also manage estates on behalf of the king or earls. The term 'thane' continued in use, but the meaning seems to have widened to incorporate a 'wide and increasing variety of statuses, functions and lordships that no doubt overlapped with one another in practice'.[84]

It is perhaps because of the extent to which the ancient aristocracies of Scotland maintained their positions in this new social framework that there remained a firmer concept of mutual responsibility for good governance in Scotland than in some other European nations. The Scottish king was less separate from his nobility, in both dynastic and administrative terms. The Scottish kingship – by the thirteenth century in the mainstream of European kingship in the sense that its power lay primarily in territorial lordship and judicial and political supremacy over his subjects – still bore hallmarks of a much older royal tradition, in which the king was drawn from within a group of native ruling families and governed with their (at least theoretical) consent. Both the royal and other aristocratic dynasties were by now of mixed lineage, strands in the complex web of family relationships which spanned Scotland, England, France and other parts of Europe. This broad genealogical inheritance, common to all of the realm's elite, gave further meaning to the concept of the king as *primus inter pares* (first among equals). It is indisputable that there was, if not necessarily a developed theory, then at least an intuitively accepted practice of partnership in government in Scotland in this period. Truly, the Scottish court in the thirteenth century was 'an impressive agency of authority, affiliation and "community"'.[85]

The influx of French-speaking aristocrats into Scotland in the twelfth and thirteenth centuries also prompted a cultural shift, which would affect the entire population of considerable areas of the kingdom. From the later eleventh century onwards, there was an increasing influence of Anglo-Saxon and Norman French culture in lordly and royal circles, which would eventually lead to a decline in the use of Gaelic. The retreat of Gaelic as the predominant vernacular spoken language, although already in evidence by the mid thirteenth century, was not

---

84 Taylor, *Shape of the State*, pp. 64–66.

85 Keith Stringer, 'The Scottish "Political Community" in the Reign of Alexander II (1214–1249)', pp. 53–84, at p. 67. He later commented that 'there is little doubt that Alexander [II] ruled according to the principle that subjects should participate in and influence governmental decision-making' (p. 75).

far advanced, and it is not yet fair to speak of the divide between the Gaelic and Anglo-Saxon worlds which became such a feature of the Scottish polity in later times.[86] It is still reasonable to see Scotland, at least north of the Forth, as a primarily Gaelic culture: the rôle played by the *fili* in the inauguration ceremony and his continuing place as a prominent member of the king's household not only demonstrates that the thirteenth-century kingship retained its connection with Gaelic society, but also that the aristocratic community understood that fact to be integral to their position in society.

If the nature of Scottish political culture had not mutated entirely, despite the innovations in landholding and government, it should come as no surprise that the native lordly families do not appear to have been opposed to, or to have resisted, the societal changes which characterised the period. The lords of Galloway, for instance, were deeply involved in the introduction of reformed monasticism, despite Galloway having been among the areas most resistant to the spread of royal power in the reigns of William and Alexander II.[87] Further, the late twelfth- and early thirteenth-century northern monastic foundations at Saddell, Iona, Ardchattan and Fearn – cited above as examples of implantation in the interests of centralised monarchy – were all founded by local lords of native stock. It has been demonstrated, too, that the thirteenth-century native earls of Lennox displayed adherence both to the new ideas and to older Gaelic custom and tradition in the administration of their lands.[88] The legal and ecclesiastical changes which permeated the period should be seen, at least to some extent, as a mutual project between crown and native aristocracy.

Such cooperation in government, however, was a two-sided coin. Later, for example, in 1320, in the famous Declaration of Arbroath, the barons of Scotland would threaten to oust King Robert I if he failed to protect the freedom of the kingdom:

86 See Alexander Grant, 'Scotland's "Celtic Fringe" in the Late Middle Ages: The MacDonald Lords of the Isles and the Kingdom of Scotland', in R.R. Davies (ed.), *The British Isles, 1100–1500: Comparisons, Contrasts and Connections* (Edinburgh, 1998), pp. 118–41, at p. 119, where he contrasts the Scottish situation with that of Wales and Ireland in the same period: 'Scottish Celts did not suffer from the institutionalised racialism found in Wales and Ireland . . . Instead of the divisions within Wales and Ireland – which became stronger during the thirteenth century – in Scotland there is a growing sense of Scottishness.'

87 See, Keith J. Stringer, 'Reform Monasticism and Celtic Scotland: Galloway, c.1140–c.1240', in E.J. Cowan and R. Andrew McDonald (eds), *Alba: Celtic Scotland in the Medieval Era* (East Linton, 2000), pp. 127–65.

88 Neville, *Native Lordship*, pp. 91–92, and 108–16. *RRS*, iv pt. 1, no. 19 is a royal confirmation by Alexander III of (among others) a grant made by Máel Domnaig, earl of Lennox to Patrick Graham: native aristocracies played their part in the 'feudalisation' of their own lands. See also the discussion of this issue in Fiona Watson, 'Adapting Tradition? The Earldom of Strathearn 1114–1296', in Oram and Stell, *Lordship and Architecture*, pp. 26–43.

> if he should give up what he has begun, seeking to make us or our kingdom subject to the king of England or to the English, we would strive at once to drive him out as our enemy and as a subverter of his own right and ours, and we would make some other man who was able to defend us our king.[89]

The Declaration, though requiring careful interpretation, asserts a philosophically ancient constitutional right or duty to depose a tyrannical ruler.[90] Scotland was far from unique in articulating such theories, but an underlying truth relating to the nature of Scottish society also emerges. If through a mutually beneficial contract the king of Scots depended on a level of governmental support from his aristocratic peers, he had also inevitably to expect both their insistence that they would be allowed effective participation and consequent conflict within the ruling group. Essential to successful rule was the ability to garner effective support through favour and patronage: implementing the system of feudal landholding and encouraging the development of a prosperous economy were therefore deeply in the king's interests. The monarchy nurtured support based on principles of mutual royal and aristocratic collaboration and responsibility, to achieve effective government.

While there were forces at work which made the maintenance of a strong centralised monarchy in the common interest of the king, the nobles, the church and the kingdom as a whole, there were other personal, familial, cultural, political and economic forces which could lead towards fragmentation. Any breakdown in the relationship between the crown and local magnates would threaten the effectiveness of royal control.[91] This had been demonstrated with particular ferocity in Galloway during the reign of Alexander II, and in Moray in both his and his father's reigns.[92] Alexander II had also taken the opportunity,

89 Quoted from A.A.M. Duncan's translation, in Edward J. Cowan, *'For Freedom Alone': The Declaration of Arbroath, 1320* (East Linton, 2003), p. 146. In the same volume (p. 62), Professor Cowan quotes the perceptive comment of the seventeenth-century Patrick Gordon of Ruthven: 'The Kinge of Scots is Kinge of men both because he is not intituled efter the countrie as other Kinges, but efter the natione, as lykwayes it is not his wealth or great revenues that maintains his royall dignitie and so long continewance of his throne, but the resolutione, the curradge, and the valour of his subjects.' See also Cowan's interesting essay on 'Contract, Kingship and Prophecy', *'For Freedom Alone'*, pp. 62–82.

90 Thomas Aquinas (1225–1274), whose work was heavily influenced by the writings of Aristotle, stated in his *Summa Theologica* that the overthrow of unjust, tyrannical government, did not constitute sedition. (A.P. D'Entrèves (ed.), *Selected Political Writings of Thomas Aquinas* (Oxford, 1974), pp. 160–61.)

91 See Grant, 'Celtic Fringe', p. 121.

92 For a study, for example, of the ambivalent relationship between strong local power and the ever-extending royal influence over Galloway, and the cross-cultural nature of the lords of Galloway in the thirteenth century, see Stringer, 'Periphery and Core'.

on the death of the earl of Caithness and Orkney in 1231, to ensure the succession of a more amenable heir. The earl had been at best ambivalent in his allegiance to the Scottish crown, and was succeeded, with royal intervention, by a member of the family of the earls of Angus. Loyalty in the northern mainland was also assured by a sympathetic bishop of Caithness, Gilbert Murray, and the creation of a new earldom of Sutherland.[93]

If there were inevitably tensions within the Scottish ruling community, which might lead to disjunction and dispute, there were also threats to the kingship on the international stage. The conflicting loyalties caused by cross-border landholding, an inevitable outcome of the inward migration of feudal lords, has already been mentioned. In the same context, the status of the Scottish kings themselves as feudal vassals of the English kings for lands held south of the border, and the tensions inherent in the disputed status of the national church, were issues of significant challenge. The relationship between Scotland and England, however, was not the only foreign dimension with the potential to cause political difficulties. More than just two kings ruled over the British isles, and it is thus necessary to take account of the Irish Sea dimension in the politics of both England and Scotland. By the thirteenth century the kings of Norway had managed to establish a formal overlordship over the Kingdom of Man and the Isles (which was ecclesiastically subject to Trondheim) but, remote enough from either Scottish or Norwegian royal authority, its kings and magnates were often able to plough a largely independent furrow.[94] This presented a strategic threat to the Scottish king and, with much of the land on the western seaboard in the ownership of the same lords who owed allegiance to the Norwegian crown for their island territories, there was a further element of cross-border lordship which weakened Scottish control even of parts of the mainland. Alexander II died while pursuing an ambition to extend Scottish royal control westwards. It has recently been cast into doubt that he, as the Norse saga accounts would have it, sought to acquire the islands for his own kingdom through diplomatic means in 1244, and that the expedition of 1249 was a response to the failure of his diplomatic efforts. It has been pointed out that earlier military intervention in the area had been aimed at clarifying

93 Oram, *Alexander II*, pp. 103–04; Barbara E. Crawford, *The Northern Earldoms: Orkney and Caithness from AD 870 to 1470* (Edinburgh, 2013), pp. 274–86.

94 The eleventh- and twelfth-century development of the kingdom(s) of Man and of the Hebrides, and of their strategic importance, is fully described in McDonald, *Sea Kings*, especially ch. 4. The explicit recognition of the royal status of the kings of Man is discussed in *Sea Kings*, ch. 10, and further evidence regarding the self-image of the sons of Somerled in the Hebrides is offered in R. Andrew McDonald, 'Images of Hebridean Lordship in the Late Twelfth and Early Thirteenth Centuries: The Seal of Raonall Mac Sorley', *Scottish Historical Review*, 74 (1995), pp. 129–43. Formal subservience to either Scotland or Norway (or, indeed, to England) was by no means assumed.

Scottish authority over the western mainland, rather than the isles, and that no Scottish sources support the contention that any diplomatic mission was sent by Alexander II to Norway in the 1240s: a supposed agreement between Scotland and Norway in 1098 and subsequent diplomacy can justifiably be seen as Norwegian propagandist attempts to legitimise Norwegian claims to their western colonies, and a signal of their awareness that the Scots were likely to challenge their possession, a supposition which had been proven true during Norwegian action in the isles in 1230–31.[95]

Rather than being a sudden upsurge of interest in the western seaboard and islands, the events at the end of Alexander II's reign were entirely consistent with his actions in the 1220s and 1230s with regard to Galloway, Man and the Isles, and Caithness, with his continuing infiltration of the new forms of landholding into the west throughout the 1230s and 1240s, and with his successful exertion of control over the bishopric of Argyll in the early 1240s. Following the death in May 1237 of the king of Man, however, Hákon IV of Norway took considerable pains to re-exert his control over the Kingdom of Man and the Isles, during a period of turbulent instability in the area caused by dynastic rivalries. This threatened to undermine some of the gains made in the western mainland by Alexander II. In particular, the strengthening relationship between Hákon IV and Eógan, son of Donnchad mac Dubhgaill, the representative of one of the primary families of the area, who had previously given apparently firm allegiance to Alexander II for his extensive mainland territories, must have been a matter of great concern to Alexander. When, in 1249, Hákon appointed Eógan as caretaker king of Man, it was a challenge to his own authority which Alexander II could not ignore, but by then the military action had already been decided upon, probably at a royal council meeting held in February. It is possible that a further spell of unrest in Galloway, quashed in 1247, followed by the deteriorating situation on the western seaboard, was influential in persuading the king to a course of action aimed at reaffirming stable Scottish hold on the western mainland, and particularly at bringing the recalcitrant Eógan to heel. It is significant that the fleet assembled not in Galloway (which would have been the logical starting point for an attempt to take the Kingdom of Man and the Isles), but probably near Tarbert on Loch Fyne, from where it headed to the Firth of Lorne, pausing at Kerrera, only a few miles away from Eógan's fortress at Dunstaffnage. Whether Alexander II intended

---

95 See Oram, *Alexander II*, pp. 97–103, 175–91 for his detailed analysis of the events leading up to Alexander's action in the isles in the summer of 1249; the following brief summary of events is drawn largely from Oram's account, which differs in important aspects from Noel Murray's account of the same events: Noel Murray, 'Swerving from the Path of Justice: Alexander II's Relations with Argyll and the Western Isles, 1214–1249', in Oram, *Alexander II Essays*, pp. 285–305. See also McDonald, *Kingdom of the Isles*, ch. 3, and McDonald, *Sea Kings*, ch. 4.

to do more than exert mastery over Eógan can only be speculation, given the circumstances in which the expedition came to its premature end.

Returning, then, to the boy-king as he embarked on his regnal journey on Tuesday 13 July 1249, what were the strengths and weaknesses of his position? Certainly, there seems to have been no overt threat to his succession: his dynasty appears to have been unquestioned, and the kingdom which he inherited was a more cohesive political and social unit than had been the case even 35 years earlier, when his father's reign had begun. It cannot be doubted that one of the effects of Alexander II's reign had been to strengthen the concept of the 'kingdom of Scots', through continuation of the existing royal policy of enforcing acceptance of the king's supremacy over an increasingly defined territorial domain. Even although Alexander II had failed in his attempt to consolidate his authority over the western seaboard, the territorial boundaries of the kingdom were certainly more clearly defined than they had been at the beginning of the century. He had strengthened royal control over the church and had presided over an apparently flourishing economy; both of these factors were to the young king's advantage, as was the stable relationship with Henry III of England. If the contention is accepted that three fundamental requirements of a kingdom were 'defined territorial frontiers, institutionalised governance, and the notion of the realm as a "community"',[96] then it certainly seems that Scotland was a kingdom: the sense of community in government, the notion of the king as *primus inter pares*, must surely be seen as a strength of Alexander III's nascent monarchy.

If secure in some respects, however, his position was vulnerable in others. The unfinished business in the west left Alexander III in a weak position in relation to Hákon IV, and to the powerful lords in Argyll and the isles. The very sense of community in government which tended towards stability could also lead to dispute: the king did not have absolute domination over the rule of the kingdom. There were cultural, dynastic and social issues which could tend towards fragmentation, and the uncertain status of his kingship, particularly in the eyes of the English monarchy, was an ever-present threat. But the greatest vulnerability of all arose purely from the accidents of birth and death. A young child, thrown prematurely onto the throne, he was entirely dependent on the noble community to guide both him and the realm, and to uphold his authority in a manner which would be to the benefit of the kingdom as a whole. The developments of the previous decades were at great risk; ruin could all too easily triumph. Hence Bower's cry from the heart, 'woe to the land whose king is a boy'.[97]

---

96 Stringer, 'Scottish Political Community', p. 53.

97 *Chron. Bower*, v, pp. 302–03; *Ve terre cuius rex puer est.*

CHAPTER 3

A Kingdom in Perplexity

The immediate legacy left to Scotland by Alexander II was the constitutional quandary posed by an underage king. A royal minority was not entirely unprecedented, but when Máel Coluim IV had succeeded his grandfather David I in 1153, he had been 12 years old, perhaps a little more able to exert personal authority than could be expected of his (not quite) 8-year-old great-nephew. The concept of government by the community described above may have helped to maintain a sense of order, but someone had to lead the community and take charge of the person of the king, if only for his security. In later royal minorities it would be clear that whoever gained control of the king controlled the government of the kingdom. In contrast, prior to Alexander II's death no arrangements had been made regarding either regency or guardianship, and there is no evidence of any formal deliberations on the subject thereafter. As would happen in 1286 and on several occasions during the decade following Balliol's downfall in 1296, the Scottish approach to a monarch's incapacity for personal rule in this period was to govern through a committee of the noble community.[1]

The speed with which the royal inauguration was carried out certainly indicates that there was a clear understanding of the process which had to be followed, even if 'the ritual was not something fixed and ancient, but could be adapted to reflect current concerns'.[2] It can be conjectured that the queen herself would have had some influence, particularly over the person of the young king, and that the chancellor as holder of the great seal and the chamberlain as having authority over the household would both also have had some part in the organisation of the ceremony. Other than the *fili*, the key characters that have

1 For Scottish government by committee of guardians in the thirteenth and early fourteenth centuries, see Norman Reid and Michael Penman, 'Guardian – Lieutenant – Governor', pp. 191–218.

2 Broun, *Scottish Independence*, p. 181.

been identified as having been present at the ceremony itself or in the events immediately preceding it are the bishops of St Andrews and Dunkeld and the abbot of Scone, the earls of Fife, Strathearn and Menteith, and Alan Durward, the justiciar of Scotia (along with 'many other nobles', unspecified). A brief biographical sketch of these central figures will serve to provide an idea of the nature of the governing community which surrounded the king in the early years of the minority.

Although it is not stated in any of the accounts of the inauguration ceremony, it seems inconceivable that Alexander II's queen, Marie de Coucy, would not have been present as her son became king.[3] Marie and Alexander had been married at Roxburgh in May 1239, little more than a year after the death of his first queen, Joan, the sister of Henry III of England. Marie, then aged about 20, was the daughter of Enguerrand de Coucy, a French nobleman related to the French royal house. The future Alexander III had been born a couple of years later, in September 1241.[4] The part that the queen played in the upbringing of her son is not easily established, but evidence from the following generation seems to suggest that she would have wielded considerable influence. The young Prince Alexander, son of Alexander III, was established with his own household budget in infancy, but did not have an official guardian appointed for his care until 1279, when he was 15, perhaps indicating that at that point he was deemed to have ended his tutelage. His mother, Queen Margaret, is thus likely to have had primary oversight of his upbringing until her early death in 1275. Although there is no specific evidence regarding the young Alexander III's situation, it is unlikely to have been radically different.[5] There is no doubt that Queen Marie was involved in affairs of state. In 1242, for example, during the crisis which engulfed the kingdom caused by the murder of Patrick of Atholl,[6] she is reported to have offered her personal oath regarding the innocence of Walter Bisset in the affair.[7] It is assumed that she was with the young prince when the news of the king's death was brought to them in July 1249, and she seems also to have accompanied him to the ceremonies in June 1250 when the

3 It should be noted that Queen Ermengarde had not been present at the inauguration of her son, Alexander II: she is said in *Gesta Annalia* (*Chron. Fordun*, i, p. 280; trans. ii, pp. 275–76) to have remained at Stirling with the body of King William. The situation in 1249 was different, however: unlike Ermengarde, Marie was not with her husband when he died, and the tender age of the heir would also increase the importance of her rôle.

4 Oram, *Alexander II*, pp. 155–57; for Marie's lineage, and for a different attitude to the effect of the French marriage on Alexander II's relations with the English king, see Pollock, *Scotland, England and France*, p. 145, and pp. 132, 143–44, 148.

5 See Neville, 'Preparing for Kingship'.

6 See below, pp. 86–87.

7 *Chron. Bower*, v, pp. 178–79.

relics of his recently canonised great-great-great-grandmother, Queen Margaret, were translated to a new shrine at Dunfermline.[8] Bower describes the attendees at the translation ceremony as 'the king and the queen his mother along with the bishops and abbots and other magnates of the realm': clearly her status was above the rest, on a par with the king alone. Only a few months later, however, she left Scotland to return to France, and the situation changed.[9] Her early departure has sometimes been taken to indicate that she had, or wished to have, a position of power beyond that with which the ruling party in the early days of the minority was comfortable, but an alternative interpretation can be offered. It is possible that she did not remain away from Scotland for as long as has been suggested: she may have been again resident in Scotland, departing once more to visit France in the spring and summer of 1254.[10] She did remarry, to Jean de Brienne, Butler of France and son of Jean, King of Jerusalem, but it seems likely that the marriage did not take place until 1256 or 1257,[11] and was not therefore the reason for her departure in 1250. That she certainly returned and was involved in government in 1257–58, and returned again in 1268, remaining until close to her death in 1284, suggests that she did retain a position of considerable status within Scotland. After her death, her body is said to have been returned to Scotland to be interred in a tomb which she had had prepared in Newbattle abbey: surely, she regarded Scotland as her home.[12] Marie de Coucy, representative of a leading French aristocratic family, was a prominent force in Scottish politics for much of the reign.

At the time of Alexander II's death the chancellor was probably William Bondington, the bishop of Glasgow. (He was still chancellor in February 1247, at least, and there is no indication of his successor being in post before 1250.[13]) A long-standing royal servant, he had served as clerk to two previous chancellors, and had held the post since 1231. This life in royal service had paralleled an equally eminent ecclesiastical career, in which his early years were spent as parson of Eddleston in Peeblesshire (probably the area from which he originated), before he became first the archdeacon of Lothian, and then, from 1233,

8 Duncan, *Making of the Kingdom*, p. 554; *Chron. Bower*, v, pp. 296–97.

9 See below, p. 99, n. 92.

10 See below, p. 113.

11 Two safe conducts were issued to Marie and her retinue travelling through England, in September 1256 and June 1257 (*CDS*, i, nos. 2064, 2083, 2084): the first does not mention her husband, whereas the second names him as one of the travelling party. It is likely, therefore, that the marriage was celebrated between these two dates. He was also known as Jean d'Acre, from his birthplace, Acre in Palestine.

12 See below, p. 258.

13 Oram, *Alexander II*, p. 211; he witnessed a charter of Alexander II, as chancellor, on 8 February 1247: *Melrose Liber*, i, no. 266.

the bishop of Glasgow. He brought to the government a considerable weight of administrative, political and diplomatic experience: he was, for example, a signatory to the treaty of York in 1237, was one of the envoys used by Alexander II to negotiate his marriage to Marie de Coucy, and was a very regular witness to *acta* of Alexander II, clearly spending much time in his company.[14] By late 1250 he had been replaced as chancellor by another very senior ecclesiastic, Robert Keldeleth, the abbot of Dunfermline. Keldeleth was ousted from the chancellorship in 1252, and it is not known who immediately replaced him, but in 1255 Gamelin, the bishop of St Andrews, was appointed. The succession of experienced, high-status men who held this post is indicative both of the importance of the office and of the level of administrative skill on which the king could expect to draw.

The chamberlain, Richard of Inverkeithing, had been appointed at most three or four years earlier, but first appears described as chamberlain only in April 1249, when he witnessed a document for the king. Nothing definite is known of his career before this, but it seems likely that he had been a canon of Dunkeld, since he was elected in 1250 as bishop of Dunkeld in succession to Geoffrey, son of Martin, who died in November 1249. He was a graduate by the time he appears on record in 1249, but it is not known where he studied, or when.[15]

The bishop of St Andrews, David Bernham, was already a graduate by the time he appears (as a witness to episcopal documents) in the *familia* of the previous bishop, William Malveisin, in the early 1220s. Although it is not known where Bernham had studied, it seems likely that he had trained in law, perhaps at Oxford or Paris, in both of which his nephew was later a student. Probably in 1235 he had been appointed Alexander II's chamberlain, a post which he held until his consecration as bishop in 1239. His election as bishop owed not a little to the influence of Alexander II: on the death of Bishop Malveisin in July 1238, the St Andrews cathedral chapter immediately elected Geoffrey, son of Martin, the bishop of Dunkeld, to the vacant see, but this election was not approved by the pope, who instructed a re-election. Alexander II used his influence to involve two members of the former St Andrews *Céli Dé* community of St Mary (by this time a collegiate church associated with the priory) in the new election, which saw Bernham promoted to the see in July 1239.[16] By 1249,

14 *PoMS*, and sources cited; and see Oram, *Alexander II*, pp. 156, 211–12.

15 Watt, *Graduates*, pp. 280–82.

16 One of the St Mary community involved was Richard Vairement. He has been identified as *Veremundus*, the author who supplied one of the principal sources for Fordun's fourteenth-century history, and who had only very recently, in May 1239, come to Scotland as a member of the household of Marie de Coucy. See Broun, *Scottish Independence*, p. 252–58; Watt,

therefore, Bernham was advanced in his career (and perhaps in years: he died in the spring of 1253), and had much experience of both ecclesiastical administration and royal service.[17] He was not a universally popular character, however: there was significant dispute between him and the cathedral chapter,[18] and Bower says of him that he 'behaved with harshness and inhumanity towards his [cathedral] community; he harassed them with various exactions, tolls and extortions'.[19]

Geoffrey son of Martin, the bishop of Dunkeld, had been Bernham's rival for the episcopal seat in St Andrews. He was known as Geoffrey *de Liberatione* because he had previously been clerk of the Liverance, a senior official in the royal household.[20] Indeed, he may have been in the royal service well before that: he claimed that he had been present in the king's council at the time of the grant of the church of Errol to the abbey of Coupar Angus in 1219, and a cartulary copy of a charter of January 1218 has as witness a clerk of the Liverance named Gilbert, quite possibly a misreading for Geoffrey.[21] Well known in court circles, he had been elevated to the bishopric in 1236. Although most of the evidence concerning him after 1236 relates to affairs touching on his own diocese, as an ecclesiastical magnate he did continue in royal service: he was used as a witness to various royal grants in the 1236–49 period, most often for grants to religious houses; he witnessed two secular grants of the king on 23 and 25 October 1237 (which might be inferred to represent attend ance at a council meeting), as well as the king's grant of the earldom of Lennox in July 1238 (given at Selkirk); and he was one of the three bishops and four barons who swore on behalf of the king to remain loyal to Henry III of England, at Newcastle in August 1244.[22] He appears to have had a good reputation as bishop: Walter Bower (whose island abbey of Inchcolm actually lay within the Dunkeld diocese, and who was thus perhaps not an entirely

---

Graduates, pp. 559–60. Vairement was one of the messengers sent by the king to the pope with regard to Bernham's election in 1238 (*Vet. Mon.*, no. 100): he was a trusted advisor.

17 For a more detailed biographical sketch, see Watt, *Graduates*, pp. 41–44; see also the detailed analysis of his career as bishop, in Marinell Ash, 'The Administration of the Diocese of St Andrews, 1202–1328' (unpublished PhD thesis, University of Newcastle upon Tyne, 1972), summarised in Marinell Ash, 'David Bernham, Bishop of St Andrews, 1239–1253', in David McRoberts (ed.), *The Medieval Church of St Andrews* (Glasgow, 1976), pp. 33–44.

18 See Ash, 'The Administration of the Diocese of St Andrews', pp. 43–45.

19 *Chron. Bower*, iii, pp. 394–95. However, Bower also described him (v, p. 315) as 'a man admirable in every respect'.

20 For the position, see Bateson, 'The Scottish King's Household', pp. 31–43.

21 James Wilson, 'Original Charters of the Abbey of Cupar, 1219–1448', *Scottish Historical Review*, 10 (1913), pp. 272–86, at pp. 278–80; *Charters of the Hospital of Soltre, of Trinity College, Edinburgh, and of other Collegiate Churches in Midlothian* (Bannatyne Club, 1861), Soutra, no. 20 – dating from *PoMS*, no. 2/10/153.

22 *PoMS*, nos. 1/7/268, 1/7/269, 1/7/274, 1/7/306.

impartial witness) said of him that he had 'enriched [the church] with lands and possessions, . . . shaped [it] with rules and customs, . . . adorned [it] with vestments and furnishings, [and] enhanced [it] in almost all respects'. He described him as 'the glory, shield and sword of the Dunkeld clergy'. In his description of the inauguration of Alexander III, Bower takes the opportunity to praise Geoffrey (in contrast to Bernham) again: 'There were present among the others David Bernham bishop of St Andrews and Geoffrey bishop of Dunkeld, who was then still alive, a man beloved by clergy and people, careful in his administration of matters temporal and spiritual'.[23]

In the Middle Ages, abbots of prestigious monastic houses were to be regarded as ecclesiastical magnates equal in rank to bishops. They frequently controlled not only their own houses, but many dependent churches, as well as significant landholdings, and thus wielded considerable economic power. Scone, probably the site of a religious foundation from early times, had the prestige one would expect to be associated with the royal inauguration centre.[24] The abbot of Scone in 1249 was Robert, who had been in post since the beginning of the decade,[25] but despite the high status of his office which led him to participate in the royal inauguration, he does not appear as witness to any royal acts, and there is no evidence to suggest that he was politically or governmentally active. Nonetheless, Scone hosted frequent visits of the royal court.[26] Politically active or not, there is no doubt that Robert (who remained abbot until 1270) would have been a figure who became well known to the king.

The earl of Fife participated in the inauguration ceremony as a leader, a representative of the entire body of earls. His presence was crucial: his position as the head of a family closely associated with the kingship gave him a well-attested and pre-eminent rôle to play in the ceremony – the actual seating of the king on the royal seat; in 1249 it seems that he may also have presented the new king with his royal sword.[27] As has been pointed out, it is no coincidence

23 *Chron. Bower*, v, pp. 192–93, 258–59.

24 For details of the history of the abbey at Scone, see Ian B. Cowan and David E. Easson, *Medieval Religious Houses: Scotland* (London, 1976), pp. 97–98; *Liber Ecclesie de Scon* (Bannatyne & Maitland Clubs, 1843), pp. 1–3; D.E.R. Watt and N.F. Shead (eds), *The Heads of Religious Houses in Scotland from Twelfth to Sixteenth Centuries* (Edinburgh, 2001), p. 198; Barrow, *Kingdom of the Scots*, pp. 170–71.

25 Watt and Shead, *Heads of Religious Houses*, p. 199.

26 See above, p. 53, and below, p. 215.

27 See above, pp. 11–13. As head of a family probably descended from earlier kings, the pre-eminence of Fife among the earls may have stemmed from the practical requirement of the more modern royal dynasties to acknowledge their historical status, in order to maintain their support. See Duncan, *Kingship of the Scots*, pp. 139–40; John Bannerman, 'MacDuff of Fife'. There is evidence that the family had tried to win the kingship as recently as the late twelfth century (Bannerman, 'MacDuff of Fife', p. 36n). The presentation of the sword by the earl of Fife is based

that the twelfth-century Earl Donnchad of Fife was 'the first native Scot on record to have the territory that he controlled within the existing kin-based society turned into a feudal fief'[28] – another indication that the process of feudalisation was designed to be, and was accepted as, inclusive rather than aggressive. Máel Coluim, the second earl of Fife to bear that personal name, had succeeded his uncle to the earldom in 1228, and was married (perhaps through the influence of Henry III) in the early 1230s to Susanna, the daughter of the Welsh prince Llywelyn ap Iorwerth,[29] Máel Coluim's was a family of elevated status. He was among those who swore on behalf of Alexander II to keep the terms of the treaty of York in 1237,[30] and, in company with both the bishops named above, he was also among those who swore on behalf of the king in August 1244. He witnessed relatively few acts of Alexander II (only six), but a couple of them were of considerable importance, including the foundation gift to the new Pluscarden abbey in Moray (April 1236).[31] While he was perhaps not frequently in the king's company, he was nonetheless of sufficient prestige to be inevitably involved in affairs of state.

Strathearn was another of Scotland's pre-eminent earldoms. It seems likely that the earl of Strathearn had shared with the earl of Fife the duty of placing the king on the throne, as his grandfather had probably done in 1214; the centrality of his rôle in 1249 suggests that it was customary. He has been described as 'the other, possibly the original, enthroning official'.[32] The earl in 1249 was Máel Ísu. Presumably a young man, he had been married to Margaret, daughter of the eminent Northumbrian baron, Robert Muschamp around 1243 (through whom he inherited significant border lands in 1250) and inherited his earldom on the death of his father in 1244. (The first apparent reference to him as earl is in the 1244 bond of loyalty to Henry III noted above, to which, along with the two bishops and the earl of Fife, he was party.[33]) Unlike his father,

on the later illustration in Bower's *Scotichronicon* (Bannerman, 'The King's Poet', pp. 132–33); the family's claim to a critical rôle in royal inauguration is clearly recorded in the early fourteenth century: *RRS*, v, no. 72.

28 Bannerman, 'MacDuff of Fife', pp. 22–23.

29 See Kathryn Hurlock, 'The Welsh Wife of Malcolm, Earl of Fife (d.1266): An Alternative Suggestion', *Scottish Historical Review*, 88 (2009), pp. 352–55.

30 Stones, *Anglo-Scottish Relations*, pp. 38–53; *CDS*, i, no. 1655 (and see *CDS*, v, pp. 25–26 for dating correction).

31 *PoMS*, no. 1/7/244.

32 Bannerman, 'MacDuff of Fife', p. 37, and see also p. 22 and Bannerman, 'The King's Poet', p. 258, which postulates both that the earl of Strathearn had a family relationship with the royal house, and that that the proximity of Strathearn to Scone may have given him a rôle in maintaining the inaugural site on behalf of the royal dynasty.

33 Neville, *Land, Law and People*, pp. 119–20. The date of his succession to the earldom is assumed from the 1244 bond of loyalty. Cynthia Neville, 'The Earls Of Strathearn from the Twelfth to the Mid-Fourteenth Century, with an Edition of their Written Acts' (unpublished

Robert, who had been relatively little in evidence at the royal court or in the politics of Alexander II's reign, Máel Ísu would become a central figure in Scottish politics during the difficult years of Alexander III's minority, maintaining a position of eminence throughout. Muschamp, in arranging this marriage for his daughter 'had hitched his wagon to a rising force on the Scottish political scene'.[34]

Although it is unlikely that Walter Comyn, earl of Menteith had an official part to play in the inauguration, he was certainly present. He was a representative of one of Scotland's 'new' noble families, and one which had already achieved a high status.[35] Towards the end of the thirteenth century, the Comyns reached the zenith of their territorial and political influence in Scotland, having climbed steadily since the middle of the previous century. The beneficiaries of significant royal land grants in Northumbria and southern Scotland in the twelfth century, the family was brought into the mainstream of the Scottish aristocratic milieu when Richard, the first of his kin to own significant land in Scotland, procured alliance with the royal house by marrying Hextilda, the granddaughter of King Domnall Bán (the brother of Máel Coluim III). Such a marriage was a sign of royal favour, as was Richard's very frequent presence at the court of King William, and especially his appointment by the king to the important position of justiciar of Lothian. Richard's son and heir, William, continued the trend in the early thirteenth century, further extending the landholding in the southern, western and northern parts of the kingdom. He became the first representative of any Anglo-Norman family to hold a Scottish earldom when, in 1212, he gained the earldom of Buchan through marriage to the earldom's heiress, Margery. This was his second marriage: it is not known who his first wife was, but both marriages established lines which were to continue to have great prominence within Scotland for many decades. William, like his father, was given an important rôle in the judicial administration of the kingdom, being both sheriff of Forfar and justiciar of Scotia – 'the first major sign of a deliberate royal policy to involve the family in the consolidation of royal

PhD thesis, University of Aberdeen, 1983) pp. 80, 101 and elsewhere, on advice from A.A.M. Duncan, gives the date of the death of Earl Robert as shortly before November 1245 (and misdates the Newcastle meeting to 1245, in York – an error introduced by the chronicler Matthew Paris); this cannot, however, be correct, given Malise's official presence in Newcastle in August 1244 and at a Scottish royal council in February 1245 (*APS*, i, p. 403) (C.J. Neville, email correspondence, March 2015).

34 Neville, *Land, Law and People*, p. 120.

35 The following summary of the rise of the Comyn family in twelfth- and thirteenth-century Scotland is drawn largely from chs 2 and 3 of Young, *Robert the Bruce's Rivals*, and the sources cited therein.

authority in the north'.[36] He was a constant presence in royal military campaigns and in diplomatic activities, and was very frequently at court. His acquisition of vast landholding in Buchan and elsewhere in the north was doubtless related to the strategy pursued by both King William and Alexander II of reinforcing royal power in the northern parts of the kingdom. In the mid to later thirteenth century, members of the Comyn kindred held the earldoms of Buchan, Menteith and Angus and the lordships of Badenoch, Kilbride and Kirkintilloch among others. Through marriage, they also dominated the earldoms of Atholl, Ross and Mar, and gained extensive landholdings and familial connections with many of the most influential in both Scotland and England. Walter, the second son of William Comyn's first marriage, added the earldom of Menteith to the portfolio when, in 1233, he married Isabella, the heiress of the earldom. He had been a regular attender at court during the reigns of both William and Alexander II, and already held the Lordship of Buchan, probably through gift of Alexander II. Briefly in 1235 he held the title earl of Caithness, demonstrating his rôle as a royal agent in the north, and he was further entrusted with enforcing royal authority in Galloway in the late 1230s. In 1237 his status as the king's right-hand man was emphasised by his being chosen to swear on the king's soul to uphold the terms of the treaty of York: here was a man at the forefront of Scottish politics. By 1249 he had been at the centre of Scottish royal government for close to three decades.

By a curious coincidence, the Durwards, who were to become rivals of the Comyns in the mid thirteenth century, were also descended from Hextilda, granddaughter of Domnall Bán. After Richard Comyn's death in *c.*1179 Hextilda's second marriage was to Máel Coluim, earl of Atholl, and their daughter (whose name is not known) married Thomas Lundin, the king's 'doorward' (or usher), whose son was the Alan Durward present at the inauguration ceremony of 1249. On his paternal side, he seems to have been a great-grandson of Gilla Críst, earl of Mar. Thus, although in the early thirteenth century his family was not in the first rank of Scottish nobility, he could nonetheless lay claim to close connections with two of the foremost earls. The Durwards in the thirteenth century typify both the desire of 'second-tier' nobility to rise in the social order and the opportunity offered by the kings' requirement to have supportive families in positions of power, especially in the areas of the kingdom where royal authority was

---

36 *RRS*, ii, no. 513 (p. 463), and cf. comments, *RRS*, ii, p. 40 and Young, *Robert the Bruce's Rivals*, pp. 20, 21. Young has also pointed out the extreme importance of the rôle, and the seriousness with which it was regarded by those who rivalled each other to hold it: Alan Young, 'Noble Families and Political Factions in the Reign of Alexander III', in Reid, *Alexander III Essays*, pp. 1–30, at p. 4.

weakest.[37] Thomas's office of *hostarius* or 'doorward' may by this time have been to some extent 'an ancient and honourable office which had come in practice to be performed by various deputies'.[38] He was at court very infrequently under King William, but more regularly in the early years of the reign of Alexander II, and was used by the king as sheriff of Inverness and as a military leader in the north, where he was one of those entrusted with quelling the rebellion of Godred meic Uilleim in 1211. For his efforts on behalf of the king, he was given the lordship of Urquhart on Loch Ness, and other members of his family were similarly rewarded. Thomas had at least two sons: when he died around 1230, Colin seems to have inherited the lordship of Lundie, and Alan the lordship of Mar and other lands in Angus.[39] It was Alan who was to lead the Durward family to a position of prominence in the mid thirteenth century: he was justiciar of Scotia in the 1240s and married an illegitimate daughter of the king. From this position of power, he was able to challenge for influence rivalling that held by the longer-established aristocracy. In the mid 1230s, Alan Durward also briefly gained possession of the earldom of Atholl, but his hold on the earldom seems to have been short-lived because of a counter-claim by Patrick, the son of the previous earl, supported by Walter Comyn, earl of Menteith. Alan Durward was thus close to the earldoms of both Mar and Atholl, but able to establish permanent tenure of neither. The promotion of his family's interests throughout the first half of the thirteenth century had led to rivalries with some of the most senior noble kindreds of the kingdom.

The received view of the minority of Alexander III is that it was a period of turbulence caused primarily by factional conflict among the nobles surrounding the young king.[40] There is no doubt that there were rivalries: potential competition has already been noted, for example, between the families of Durward and the earl of Menteith, and between the bishops of St Andrews and Dunkeld. However, the events of the minority can be interpreted differently.

A dispute which is reported to have taken place even before the inauguration took place has usually been cited as the first indication of the factional split

---

37 Matthew Hammond, '*Hostiarii Regis Scotie*: The Durward Family in the Thirteenth Century', in Steve Boardman and Alasdair Ross (eds), *The Exercise of Power in Medieval Scotland c.1200–1500* (Dublin, 2003), pp. 118–38. This brief account of the rise of the Durward family is drawn largely from this source.

38 Hammond, '*Hostiarii Regis Scotie*', pp. 119–20 (n.7), quoting G.W.S. Barrow.

39 On Mar, see Richard Oram, 'Continuity, Adaptation and Integration: The Earls and Earldom of Mar, c.1150–c.1300', in Steve Boardman and Alasdair Ross (eds), *The Exercise of Power in Medieval Scotland, c.1200–1500* (Dublin, 2003), pp. 46–66.

40 The fullest treatment of the minority period to date, which has become the historiographical benchmark, is Watt, 'Minority'.

which would characterise the minority years. The late thirteenth-century *Gesta Annalia* described the scene thus:

> . . . as soon as they were gathered together, there arose a dispute among the nobles. For some of them would have made not a king, but a knight, on that day, saying that it was an Egyptian day. Now this was said not because of the Egyptian day, but because the lord Alan Dorwart, then justiciary of the whole of Scotland, wished to gird Alexander with the sword of knighthood on that day. While they were arguing, the lord Walter Comyn, Earl of Menteith, a man of foresight and shrewdness in counsel, answered and said that he had seen a king consecrated who was not yet a knight, and had many a time heard of kings being consecrated who were not knights; and he went on to say that a country without a king was, beyond a doubt, like a ship amid the waves of the sea, without rower or steersman. For he had always loved King Alexander, of pious memory, now deceased – and this boy also for his father's sake. So he moved that this boy be raised to the throne as quickly as possible, – for it is always hurtful to put off what may be done at once; and, by his advice, the said bishops and abbot, as well as the nobles, and the whole clergy and people, with one voice, gave their consent and assent to his being set up as king.[41]

Bower, writing in the fifteenth century, added the detail that the king was indeed knighted on that day, not by Durward, but by the bishop of St Andrews.[42] In fact, only a knight could perform the ceremony of knighting; but Bower's account should not be completely dismissed, as it seems that he may well have been using sources, perhaps from St Andrews, which had not been available to Fordun or to the writer of *Gesta Annalia*.[43] If the king had been knighted in any sense on the day of his inauguration, however, his knighting was repeated in 1251 by Henry III of England on the occasion of Alexander's marriage to Princess Margaret.

The argument surrounding Durward's proposal that Alexander should be knighted before his inauguration is not easy to interpret, but it is crucial to an understanding of the relationships at the heart of the minority government. *Gesta Annalia* suggests that the dispute was motivated by Durward's

---

41 *Chron. Fordun*, i, p. 293 (trans. ii, p. 289). An 'Egyptian day' was said to be unlucky: see *Chron. Bower*, v, p. 436. See Broun, *Scottish Independence*, pp. 215–29 for the complex relationships between Fordun's work, his earlier sources and *Gesta Annalia*.

42 *Chron. Bower*, v, pp. 292–93.

43 *Chron. Bower*, v, pp. 435–39; Broun, *Scottish Independence*, pp. 173–74; Duncan, *Kingship of the Scots*, pp. 131–33.

desire to knight the king himself, implying that by doing so he would place the king in a position of obligation to him, thus strengthening his own personal connection to the royal house, and boosting his authority within the minority government. Because the counter-argument was led by Walter Comyn, earl of Menteith, it has been assumed that the dispute had its roots in the rivalry which it is known already existed between the two families. The rivalry was real enough: both Comyns and Durwards had been involved in the crisis surrounding the murder of the young Patrick, heir of the earl of Atholl, which took place in Haddington in 1242. Various chronicles give accounts of the event, with divergent detail,[44] but it is certain that there was a strong suspicion that the murder was the work of members of the Bisset family. The most closely contemporary source, the *Chronicle of Melrose*, concurs with the later versions of Bower and Wyntoun (both of whom used a contemporary St Andrews account) in stating so quite explicitly.[45] The head of that family, Walter Bisset, had been hosting a visit from the king and queen in his castle of Aboyne at the time, and while it was thus obvious (and, according to Bower, stated in his defence by the queen herself) that Walter Bisset had not been involved first-hand, there was nonetheless grave disquiet about the rôle his family – and perhaps therefore he himself – might have had in the affair. The murdered Patrick of Atholl was related to the Comyn family, probably through his mother, and it is therefore no coincidence that Alexander Comyn (the heir to the earldom of Buchan) and his nephew John Comyn (later lord of Badenoch), were in the forefront of the action which saw Bisset's north-eastern lands savagely plundered. Patrick, earl of Dunbar, a close associate of the Comyn family, and who had had close personal links with the murdered earl of Atholl, was also in the vanguard of the Bissets' accusers. Despite their protestations of innocence and apparent support from the king and queen, opinion against the Bissets on the part of a large section of the nobility remained unswervingly hostile, and protracted royal council proceedings eventually resulted in the outlawing and exile of Walter Bisset, his nephew John and others of the family. Walter, however, was back in Scotland, in the king's favour, by early in 1249 (and perhaps earlier).[46]

Alan Durward's part in all this is not obvious. Durward ambitions in the north, as has been seen, had previously brought them into conflict with the

---

44 The narrative of events given here is based on the version told by Walter Bower (*Chron. Bower*, v, pp. 178–87), which seems to be based on an earlier source, perhaps the late thirteenth-century St Andrews work which seems to inform much of Bower's treatment of this period. For a more detailed discussion of this episode and its aftermath, as well as the sources for it, see Oram, *Alexander II*, pp. 158–70.

45 *Chron. Melrose,* Faustina B. IX, fo.46v (trans. Anderson, *Early Sources*, ii, pp. 530–31, 533–34).

46 See Oram, *Alexander II*, p. 174.

Comyn family, especially over disputed succession to the earldoms of Mar and Atholl. The Bissets too had been establishing their north-eastern holdings as a result of royal patronage in the same period, providing both them and the Durwards with good reason for mutual hostility towards the Comyns. After Alexander II was forced to exile Walter Bisset, despite his attempts to protect him from persistent accusation, he replaced his two justiciars of Scotia, who had been ineffective (perhaps because they were pro-Comyn in their sympathies) in preventing the Comyn attacks on Bisset's land. The justiciarship was given instead to Alan Durward, whose position as a counterbalance to the powerful Comyn presence in the north was thus strengthened, and who at the same time became a crucial office-bearer in the government of the kingdom – a right-hand man of the king. At the same time, it seems that the standing of the Comyns in government was waning.[47]

So, when Alan Durward proposed that the young Alexander should be knighted before his inauguration in July 1249, he did so from a position of existing potency. In seeking to establish his position as *de facto* leader of the government, Durward could be regarded as doing no more than Alexander II would have encouraged him to do.[48] However, the significance of Durward's quest to knight the king prior to the inauguration may have been overstated or given extra lustre through the benefits of hindsight. It should be noted that the author of *Gesta Annalia* implied that Durward wished to knight the king himself, but did not relate that Durward himself stated such a wish. It has also been suggested that there was further intrigue – a counter-plot mounted against Durward by the earl of Menteith, who is said to have contacted Robert Bruce, lord of Annandale, 'the man who may have had something of a legal claim to the regency', soon after the inauguration.[49] The contact, however, was no more than Comyn's acting as witness to a land grant in favour of Bruce; it does not imply any personal contact between the two men, and was an entirely run-of-the-mill business transaction, the likes of which continued unhindered during the minority.[50] If indicative of anything at all beyond its primary purpose, it hints at business as usual. That by seeking to knight the king Durward was 'thereby conferring the first of the insignia and probably staking a claim to be

47 See Young, *Robert the Bruce's Rivals*, pp. 37–45 for a detailed description of the developing relationships between Comyns, Durwards and Bissets, and the eclipse of Comyn power towards the end of Alexander II's reign. There is also a useful summary of the rise of Durward power at the expense of Comyn, in Watt, 'Minority'.

48 Young, *Robert the Bruce's Rivals*, p. 48; Watt, 'Minority', pp. 1–7.

49 Watt, 'Minority', p. 7, citing *CDS*, i, no. 1763.

50 See below, p. 127: the continuity of this type of transaction during the minority, even between those who were supposed to be factional opponents, is striking.

regent',[51] is entirely speculative, and perhaps misleading. Knighting, even if it had taken place, was not an element of the insignia of kingship, and there can in any case have been no argument about who should assume the regency (meaning the sole responsibility for government during the absence, minority or incapacity of a monarch), since regency was not at this stage a feature of the Scottish polity. The supposition of such a motivation is an unwarranted imposition of the English monarchical tradition onto the Scottish situation.

In the event, Durward's proposal was not carried: the king remained, for the moment, unknighted. If Durward had harboured an ambition to knight the king himself in order to achieve his supposedly nefarious objective of leading the minority government, then it is perhaps surprising that he nonetheless emerged as the apparent kingpin of that government. Comyn's advice against the knighting may have swayed the gathering in favour of the immediate inauguration of the king, but it did not have the effect of placing him in any more powerful a position than he had held in the latter days of Alexander II's reign, and there is no evidence to suggest that he made any attempt at that point to challenge Durward's leading rôle. (It is important to remember, however, that Durward does not appear to have taken any formal part in the inauguration ceremony itself, which was conducted, as usual, by those with dynastic claims to precedence in such affairs.) Knighting the king before coronation was indeed 'a growing convention in thirteenth-century Europe',[52] and it may therefore be quite reasonable to see Durward's action before the ceremony as no more than an attempt, from a position of undisputed dominance in government, to conduct the ceremony in what he saw as a contemporary fashion. It has already been noted that the inauguration ceremony was not an entirely traditional, unchanging affair: was Durward simply suggesting an innovation in order to bring it up to date? Alexander II had already attempted to upgrade the apparent status of the Scottish crown by seeking from the papacy the rites of coronation and unction; Durward's government would repeat that request in 1250–51, demonstrating a desire to achieve for the crown of Scotland an evident parity in status with other European monarchies, entirely consistent with his suggestion of knighting the king before inauguration.

The leadership of Scotland seems to have remained fairly stable as the minority began. Durward, as justiciar of Scotia and husband of the young king's half-sister, continued to enjoy the favoured position he appears to have had

---

51 Duncan, *Making of the Kingdom*, p. 555; see also Watt, 'Minority', p. 7.

52 Duncan, *Making of the Kingdom*, pp. 554–55. In France, by 1250 it was an integral part of the coronation ritual; Jacques Le Goff, 'A Coronation Program for the Age of St Louis: The Ordo of 1250', in János M. Bak, *Coronations: Medieval and Early Modern Monarchic Ritual* (Berkeley, 1990), pp. 46–57, at pp. 50–51, 54.

under Alexander II. The queen may have used her own influence to ensure as great a continuity of administration as possible. No one is known to have gained any additional position of power in the care of the person of the king, so we must assume it remained primarily in the hands of his mother. It was a situation perhaps comparable to that in France in 1226, when Queen Blanche, the mother of the youthful Louis IX, ruled as regent during his minority; in 1249 Blanche was again regent, during the absence on crusade of her son, an example of which Marie de Coucy, related to the French royal line, would have been fully aware. Marie had been only six years old in 1226, but as she grew up she may have spent time at the French royal court and may have had personal knowledge of Blanche, who was 30 years her senior. She would have been well acquainted with the French political situation, experience which she would have brought to Scottish affairs in the years after her marriage to Alexander II in 1239.[53] Parallels have also been drawn between the situation in Scotland after the death of Alexander II and that of England in 1216, when the nine-year-old Henry III was knighted by William Marshal, who then became *rector* of the kingdom. It has been suggested that Durward had his eye on this example when he proposed delaying Alexander's inauguration to allow for his knighting.[54] If Scotland looked for a precedent in 1249, however, it is more likely that it would have been found through the family background and aristocratic contacts of the queen.

The administration of the kingdom weathered the establishment of the minority regime with a remarkable degree of continuity. The business of government continued as before: at least one royal council met, probably at the beginning of June 1250 in Edinburgh; although the post may have been vacant earlier, by January 1250 there appears to have been an active justiciar of Lothian; and a record of court proceedings held in Forfar in November 1250 proves both that Alan Durward continued to act as justiciar of Scotia and that sheriffs continued to act in their judicial capacity.[55] A further indication of

53 Marie was the granddaughter of a niece of Louise VII. See Pollock, *Scotland, England and France*, p. 145. Her father had been opposed to the regency of Blanche in 1226, but was later restored to her favour. Blanche was also a granddaughter of Henry II of England, giving rise to Louis IX's claim to the English throne. She was thus deeply involved in the politics not only of France, but also of England, an example of which Marie de Coucy would not be insensible.

54 Young, *Robert the Bruce's Rivals,* p. 48; Watt, 'Minority', pp. 6–7; Powicke, *The Thirteenth Century, 1216–1307*, p. 2.

55 *APS*, i, 425 refers to a council, which was probably held in early June 1250: two of the three surviving acts of the year 1250 are dated in Edinburgh on 1 and 3 June (*RRS,* iv pt. 1, nos. 1 and 2); *CDS,* i, no. 1768; C.C.H. Harvey and J. Macleod (eds), *Calendar of Writs preserved at Yester House, 1166–1503* (Scottish Record Society, 1930), no. 15. There is no reason to suppose that the system of sheriffs did not continue as before: records are sparse, but there were active sheriffs of Berwick in 1250 (J. Raine, *The History and Antiquities of North Durham* (London,

administrative normality was the recoinage carried out in 1250 by the Scottish mints (following the English example, as was usual), replacing the 'short-cross' with 'long-cross' coins, exhibiting a continuity with the later years of Alexander II's reign in monetary and economic policy (Plate 12).[56] Tension there may have been between Walter Comyn and Alan Durward, but it did not disbar Comyn from the table: he was the initial secular witness to the first known act of Alexander III, a grant to the abbey of Paisley, given on 1 June 1250.[57] That he witnessed the act presumably places him at the royal council, suggesting that the traditional picture of government through warring faction has been at best overstated, and may in fact be completely misleading. Although too young to be able to wield personal power, the first of Alexander III's *acta* makes it clear that authority in the kingdom was nonetheless deemed to emanate from the king himself:

> Alexander, by the grace of God king of Scots, to all responsible men of his whole land, greeting. Know ye that, with the counsel of our magnates, we have given . . .[58]

Very early in the reign, a seal was struck for the authentication of the acts of the minority government in Alexander's name, which serves to emphasise the duality of the governmental situation. In practice, of course, Alexander did not wield ultimate power, but it was his name and his position which bore authority. The seal, which was in use by the council of June 1250,[59] is much smaller than the usual great seal with which public acts of the king were normally authenticated. It shows the king, wearing a crown, seated on a throne, with a sword lying across his lap and bearing a staff. The legend round the seal reads *Esto prudens ut serpens et simplex sicut columba* ('be as wary as the serpent, and as innocent as the dove'), words of moralistic wisdom which had the happy benefit of both a biblical source[60] and a play on the word 'Columba'. The reverse of the

1852), Appendix, nos. 183, 187), and of Perth in 1251 (R. Milne (ed.), *The Blackfriars of Perth* (Edinburgh, 1893), no. 2).

56 Duncan, *Making of the Kingdom*, p. 518 and sources cited; *Chron. Bower*, v, pp. 298–99.

57 *RRS*, iv pt. 1, no. 1.

58 A completely standard greeting clause for a royal charter, with no implication of any unusual circumstance: *Alexander Dei gratia rex Scottorum omnibus probis hominibus tocius terre sue salute. Sciatis nos de consilio magnatum nostrorum dedisse . . .* (*RRS*, iv pt. 1, no. 1).

59 Its only surviving example is appended to the act of 3 June 1250: NRS GD 90/1/18/1; text in *RRS*, iv pt.1, no. 2. See the more detailed descriptions of the seal, and the divergent interpretations of its meaning, in *RRS*, iv pt.1, pp. 30–32; Duncan, *Making of the Kingdom*, p. 556; Duncan, *Kingship of the Scots*, pp. 151–53; and Grant G. Simpson, 'Kingship in Miniature: A Minority Seal of Alexander III, 1249–1257', in Grant and Stringer, *Medieval Scotland*, pp. 131–39.

60 It is a paraphrase of Matthew 10:16.

seal repeats the legend, and depicts a triangular shield carrying the royal arms – the lion rampant within the heraldic device known as a double tressure. It has been convincingly demonstrated that the double tressure, a recent innovation in Scottish royal heraldry, was introduced by Alexander II after the birth of his son in 1241, as a way of emphasising both the status of the Scottish crown (through the inclusion of the *fleur de lis*, a symbol of royalty) and the association with France of the Scottish royal house, through Queen Marie.[61] A second version of this seal (Plates 1, 2) was made within two years, similar in every respect, except that it added a second legend to the face of the seal, identifying it as the seal of *Alexander, Dei gratia rex Scottorum* (by the grace of God, king of Scots), rather than the more common Scottish style of *Deo rectore* (ruling under God's guidance). *Dei gratia* was a style which for centuries had been used in the mainstream of European monarchies, and the addition of this style to the seal should be seen as an update, in (futile) anticipation of the success of the renewed approach to the pope for granting of the rites of unction and coronation, and intended to represent the Scottish crown as in all respects equal to the other monarchies of Europe. The small size of both versions of this seal, the portrayal of the sword lying across the king's knees rather than held upright in typical royal fashion and the replacement of the normal image of the king on horseback on the reverse side of the seal by the royal arms are symbolic representations of the king in minority. This is a seal whose symbolism is entirely redolent of royal authority, while indicating the minority status of the king's person. Perhaps acts authenticated with this seal were intended to be confirmed later, under the great seal of the adult king.[62]

It is difficult, however, to be too dogmatic about the symbolism of the sigillography. The situation is complicated by the fact that there was also a full-sized great seal, in traditional form – the king enthroned, with regalia, on the obverse, and on horseback on the reverse, and with the legend in the *Deo rectore* form – in use during part of the minority. It first appears in use as early as 3 December 1250 and continues in use throughout 1251.[63] Whether there was a difference between the nature of the acts each seal was intended to authenticate, or in the authority they carried, cannot now be distinguished because of the very scant surviving evidence. The great seal was probably broken during the events of 1252 described below, and perhaps it was at that point that the second version of the small seal was made. Certainly, there are no surviving examples of the use of the first small seal after the first great seal appears in late 1250, and no surviving

61 John Malden, 'Alexander II and the Double Tressure', in Oram, *Alexander II Essays*, pp. 211–19.
62 This suggestion was made by A.A.M. Duncan (*Making of the Kingdom*, p. 556).
63 *RRS*, iv pt.1, pp. 31–33.

examples of the use of the first great seal after the second small seal makes its appearance in June 1252. It has been suggested that the use of a great seal, normally a sign that the king is deemed to be of an age to be wielding full power, as early as 1250 'represents a decisive shift of power . . . into the hands of Alan Durward'.[64] The evidence, however, is sparse: only one example of the first small seal survives, and five fragmentary examples of the first great seal;[65] no example of the second great seal of Alexander III has survived on any document issued before 1264, by which time it had almost certainly been in use for several years. It is not clear, either, why the use of a great seal would have benefitted Durward in particular, rather than the entire governing council.

One person who does appear to have lost his official position at court not long after the death of the king was the chancellor, William Bondington. Robert Keldeleth, abbot of Dunfermline was described as chancellor in November 1250, when he acted as a papal judge-delegate in a legal case concerning a dispute between the prior and convent of St Andrews on the one hand and the *Céli Dé* community there on the other.[66] Bondington, however, did not leave the top table altogether: like Walter Comyn, he appears to have been at the council of June 1250, heading the list of witnesses (which, as previously observed, includes Comyn) to the charter in favour of Paisley abbey. It is not impossible that the change in chancellorship took place at that council meeting or soon thereafter, perhaps in response to Bondington's involvement in a dispute between the ecclesiastical and the secular leaders of the kingdom: a letter to the king from Bondington and the bishops of St Andrews, Aberdeen, Dunblane, Brechin, Ross and Caithness protesting about the infringement of church liberties may have been a catalyst.[67] Bondington does seem to have been at odds with the ruling regime: he was received into the king's peace in April 1251, which implies a previous period of disfavour.[68] The reason for it, however, is not entirely clear,

64 Duncan, *Making of the Kingdom*, p. 559.

65 See *RRS*, iv pt.1, nos. 2, 3, 7, 11, 12, 13.

66 NLS, MS. Adv. 15.1.18, no. 30. The document is abstracted in *PoMS* no. 4/32/92. The document is discussed in Barrow, 'The Clergy at St Andrews' (*Kingdom of the Scots*, pp. 215–16). There has been some discussion of whether Bondington may have been replaced as chancellor before the death of Alexander II: see Watt, *Graduates* p. 462, followed in *RRS*, iv pt. 1, p. 28. (Watt's opinion may have been coloured by his assumption of strict factional divides emerging in the later years of Alexander II's reign, presaging the divisions of the minority; I have followed the opposing view, favoured by Stringer in 'The Scottish "Political Community" in the Reign of Alexander II', p. 58(n)).

67 See *PoMS*, no. 2/10/241 (NLS, Adv. MS 15.1.18, no. 16); printed in J. Robertson, *Concilia Scotiae* (Bannatyne Club, 1866), ii, pp. 241–42, and translated in David Patrick (ed.), *Statutes of the Scottish Church, 1225–1559* (Edinburgh, 1907), pp. 211–12; see below, pp. 95–96 & n. 78 for discussion of this document.

68 *RRS*, iv pt. 1, no. 8.

and his relatively hasty restoration indicates that he was not thoroughly *persona non grata*. It is too easy to let hindsight dictate that all the events of the minority should be seen through the prism of factionalism: there is no evidence that, as has usually been stated, it was a pro-Comyn sympathy rather than another issue which prompted Bondington's loss of the chancellorship, or a pro-Durward sympathy rather than appropriate qualifications which led to Keldeleth's appointment.[69] Instead, it might be presumed that his loss of the chancellorship was not a result of his close association with any faction, since when Keldeleth was deprived of the chancellorship at the end of 1251 when Durward's influence temporarily waned, Bondington did not resume the position. He lived until 1258, at the end of the minority, but, irrespective of which party was in power, he appears only to have witnessed one further surviving act of the king during that period, in April 1252.[70]

The chamberlainship also changed hands around the same time, but the reason is more obvious. Richard of Inverkeithing was elected bishop of Dunkeld in 1250, in succession to Geoffrey, son of Martin, who had died in the previous November.[71] It is likely that he gave up the chamberlainship in order to take up his episcopal duties. That he was elected bishop during 1250 must imply that he was not out of favour with the ruling group. His successor, Robert Menzies, is first recorded with the title of chamberlain in February 1251.[72]

The first phase of the minority, during which Alan Durward was a key figure, was to be short-lived, but was not without incident or achievement. Perhaps most striking was the ceremony in which the relics of Queen Margaret, the great-great-great-grandmother of Alexander III, who had recently been canonised, were moved or 'translated' to a new shrine at the east end of the recently enlarged abbey of Dunfermline, on 19 June 1250. This was the culmination of some years of lobbying: the abbot of Dunfermline, soon to be (if not already) royal chancellor, had been a prime mover in the negotiations regarding her canonisation, over several years, and the papal approval seems to have been given in September 1249.[73] That Robert had been entrusted with this delicate and important task by Alexander II is another signal that his appointment as chancellor to replace Bondington (who had also been appointed by Alexander II)

69 See, for example, Ash, 'The Church in the Reign of Alexander III', pp. 36–37, where Bishop Bernham is 'identified with the Comyn faction', Keldeleth's 'Durwardite' allegiance led to his appointment as chancellor, the St Andrews cathedral chapter was 'Durwardite', and the successful blocking of Henry III's attempt to gain a papal tax from Scotland was 'Durward-inspired'.

70 *RRS*, iv pt.1, no. 15 – a gift to the friars preachers of Glasgow, place-dated at Edinburgh.

71 Watt and Murray, *Fasti*, p. 124.

72 *Arbroath Liber*, no. 250.

73 See the various sources cited in Anderson, *Early Sources,* ii, pp. 7–8n.

was not the work of a discontinuous regime. The ceremony of translation was indeed 'an event of supreme national religious and political significance'.[74] As the progenitors of the current royal line, Máel Coluim III and Margaret were venerated in a self-conscious dynastic cult, now given the added lustre of religious sanctity. Here indeed was proof that their descendants, rather than any other claimants to royal descent, were the rightful monarchs. The account of the ceremony given by Bower adds to the more pedestrian narrative of *Gesta Annalia* a colourful description of all attempts to move Margaret's coffin failing until they moved Máel Coluim's along with it – implying the unity of the couple in both matrimonial and saintly terms. It stated, too, that as soon as Margaret's tomb was opened, the church was filled with the scent of flowers, a reference to the common belief that the remains of a saint were incorruptible. The occurrence of miracles at the shrine strongly invigorated the cult of St Margaret, who it was said 'illuminated the western shadows with the splendour of her light, like the radiant morning star'. Miracles of physical healing and spiritual restoration, as well as association of Margaret with events of national significance (such as the reported vision by Sir John Wemyss of St Margaret on the eve of the battle of Largs, guaranteeing a Scottish victory) also bolstered the status of the kingship which descended from her. The suggestion that the ceremony in which her relics were translated to the new shrine was 'a carefully staged event' has much to recommend it.[75]

Closely related in purpose to the canonisation of Queen Margaret was a renewed attempt to achieve papal approval for the unction and coronation of Scottish kings. This too seems to have been entrusted to the diplomatic expertise of Robert Keldeleth, abbot of Dunfermline, who emerges as a lynchpin of the administration, and who it has been suggested may have been appointed chancellor specifically because of his familiarity with the papal curia.[76] Alexander II had made application to the papacy for this symbol of independent sovereign

74 Ash, 'The Church in the Reign of Alexander III', pp. 31–32.

75 *Chron. Bower*, v, pp. 296–99; *Chron. Fordun*, i, p. 295 (trans. ii, pp. 290–91); Ash, 'The Church in the Reign of Alexander III', pp. 31–32. Ash also makes a plausible connection between the story of Margaret's reluctant relics and those of Margaret's own favourite saint, Cuthbert of Durham. The miracles ascribed to her are found in a fifteenth-century manuscript of a work written probably in the mid thirteenth century: Robert Bartlett (ed. and trans.), *The Miracles of Saint Æbbe of Coldingham and Saint Margaret of Scotland* (Oxford, 2003); quotation from p. 71.

76 Duncan, *Making of the Kingdom*, p. 559. Expert he was: he had also achieved the elevated status of mitred abbot for the head of the Dunfermline community, and, by September 1249, the office of papal chaplain for himself (*Dunfermline Reg.*, no. 290). It is thus quite possible that Bondington's loss of the chancellorship (if, indeed, he lost it rather than resigning it voluntarily) had more to do with the positive qualities that Keldeleth would bring to the position, than with the negative effects of dispute.

kingship in 1221 (and perhaps again in 1233), the request having been knocked back primarily through negative pressure exerted on behalf of the English king. As it had been in the reign of Alexander II, the request for unction and coronation was unsuccessful: our record of the event is a papal letter dated 6 April 1251 which refused to grant the request of Henry III that any such grant to the Scots should be only with the permission of the English king, but nonetheless agreed not to grant anything to the Scots that might prejudice the English crown.[77] There is no direct evidence of the nature of the Scots request, but that a counter-claim had been lodged from England in time for a response by April 1251 must indicate that the Scots were busy at the curia before the end of 1250. The abbot could hardly have been absent from the translation ceremony at Dunfermline in June, but quite soon thereafter he may have left for Lyons, where the papal curia was then sitting.

The translation ceremony indicated a 'coming of age of the national church', and thus the beginnings of a change in its relations with the crown, which became 'less personal and more bureaucratic', a trend which was similar to developments throughout Europe. As the rights of crown over church (in, for example, the appointments to bishoprics) continued to be exerted, especially during the minority, a new style of relationship between them was forged. The only significant known outcome of the royal council meeting of June 1250 was a dispute between church and state. Seven bishops protested to the king about the treatment of church lands, specifically those of St Andrews.[78] On 31 May

77 See Oram, *Alexander II*, pp. 66–68, 134–35. The papal letter of April 1251 is printed and translated in Stones, *Anglo-Scottish Relations*, pp. 58–59.

78 The quotations are from Ash, 'The Church in the Reign of Alexander III', p. 32. Robertson, *Concilia*, ii, pp. 241–42; translated in Patrick, *Statutes of the Scottish Church*, pp. 211–12. The date of the letter is uncertain, but the known royal council of June 1250 provides a plausible context. Watt suggested that it should be dated to just after the translation ceremony, in June 1250, on the grounds that it was signed by the same number of bishops that were stated to have attended the celebration. However, between November 1249 and the autumn of 1251 there were only eight bishops who could possibly have signed it. (Dunkeld was without a consecrated bishop between the death of Geoffrey, son of Martin in November 1249 and the consecration of Richard of Inverkeithing in August x October 1251. The diocese of Argyll was subject directly to the pope until the fifteenth century (and was in any case vacant at this point); Galloway (Whithorn) was subject to York; the Isles and Orkney were subject to Trondheim in Norway.) One of them, Simon, bishop of Moray was to die in 1251, and throughout his episcopate he left traces only in records relating exclusively to the ecclesiastical or tenurial affairs of his diocese (see *PoMS* database, under 'Gunby, Simon de'). It would thus have been unusual for him to be signatory to the letter, leaving a total of only seven active bishops in the period. The coincidence of seven episcopal signatories is therefore of no consequence, except that it implies a date before the consecration of Richard of Inverkeithing to Dunkeld, by October 1251. Even if later than June 1250, the bishops' letter certainly pertains to a council held during the period of Durward's ascendancy, no later than the spring of 1251. For discussion of the letter and its date, see Ash, 'The Church in the Reign of Alexander III', p. 37; Watt, *Graduates*, pp. 6, 42; Watt, *Medieval Church Councils in Scotland*, p. 71; Duncan, *Making of the Kingdom*, pp. 289–90.

1251 Pope Innocent IV responded to the complaint of the Scottish bishops by writing to the bishops of Lincoln, Worcester and Lichfield, mandating them to compel the counsellors of the king of Scots to desist from their actions against the Scottish church and to make restitution.[79] The bishops' complaint, clearly, had been made not only to the king and his council.

The specific point at issue was that, notwithstanding the Scottish royal council's dictate that the church should enjoy the same rights and privileges as it had during the reign of Alexander II, the priory of St Andrews had been despoiled of lands given in alms, and the dispute taken before lay courts rather than ecclesiastical ones. The pope's letter, however, is much lengthier than the bishops', and makes it clear that the issue ran deeper and was of longer standing than the bishops' first appeal seems to indicate – this was a matter of policy, not of a simple breach of the law. The supposition may be correct that this was a renewed pursuit of an old gripe by the bishops, who had lost ground to the secular authority earlier, in the reign of Alexander II, and who took advantage of the new situation of the minority, and of a fresh instance of their general complaint, to attempt to regain the upper hand.[80] The publication, from provincial councils, of a set of statutes for the Scottish church in the 1240s, had been 'a positive reminder to Alexander II of the liberty which the Church expected to enjoy'.[81] The bishops' protest of 1250 is therefore symptomatic of the forging of a new relationship between church and state in this period, and cannot be taken at face value as a straightforward attack on misgovernance during the early years of the minority.[82]

The national church and the state were not entirely disunited, however. One issue which seems to have drawn them together was that of papal taxation. Even as the youthful Alexander III came to the throne, events were unfolding in the far-off Holy Land which would have a significant impact on

79 *Registrum Episcopatus Moraviensis* (Bannatyne Club, 1837), no. 260; translated in Patrick, *Statutes of the Scottish Church*, pp. 212–17. It is curious that the papal letter survives in the cartulary of the bishop of Moray, rather than that of one of the signatory sees. Duncan (*Making of the Kingdom*, pp. 289–90) suggested that this resulted from connections between the sees of Moray and Lincoln: the bishop of Moray may have petitioned for the papal letter. Simon was, as usual, absent from the occasion at which the bishops' letter was composed, but his connections with Lincoln may nonetheless have been used to promote the case against the Scottish government.

80 Duncan, *Making of the Kingdom*, pp. 289–90.

81 D.E.R. Watt, 'The Provincial Council of the Scottish Church 1215–1472', in Grant and Stringer, *Medieval Scotland*, pp. 140–55, at p. 153, and for statutes, pp. 148–52.

82 See Ash, 'The Church in the Reign of Alexander III', p. 32. That papal letters regarding a similar issue affecting the diocese of Glasgow were given in 1253 indicates that it was not a problem unique to the minority government of 1249–51 (*Glasgow Reg.*, i, no. 198); the issue was still live at the end of 1259: Ferguson, *Papal Representatives*, App. IV, no. 13.

his later reign. Invasion by the armies of Sultan al-Salih Ayyub of Egypt and his mercenary allies in 1244 had wiped out the Christian hold on Jerusalem, Syria and southern Palestine, which had been established by the crusades of a few years earlier. The survival of the Christian kingdom of Jerusalem was in doubt. In response, Louis IX of France led a new crusade in 1248–50. Gathering in Cyprus, the crusading force successfully attacked the port of Damietta on Egypt's Mediterranean coast in early June 1249; but the following campaign was strategically weak and lacked understanding of the wider context of the politics of the region. It failed to build upon its early success and disintegrated in the face of robust Egyptian defence. It ended in April 1250 with the ignominious surrender and captivity of Louis IX himself. Part of the price paid for his freedom (with the survivors of his army) was the restoration of the captured city of Damietta. For all its crippling expense, the crusade had achieved nothing.[83] Yet the crusading mentality was firmly entrenched in western political and devotional life, and the failure of this campaign was the spur to more that would follow. In support of the enormous outlay of funds required for such a venture, the first Council of Lyons had in 1245 approved the imposition of ecclesiastical taxation and, through papal instruction, similar levies were again to be raised in the 1250s and 1260s, when a further crusade, with the wholehearted support also of England, was being promoted. It was not only France and England, however, that were taxed to pay for these projects: Christendom as a whole was responsible, and so the papal levy was applied also to Frisia, the Low Countries, Aragon, Sicily and, of course, Scotland. The principle of support for the great cause of Christendom was not in doubt: Scots would take the cross, fight and die in foreign parts alongside others of many nations. There was, however, an issue of national and ecclesiastical integrity at stake, tangential to the vexed issue of subservience of the Scottish church to the English, when the *ecclesia Scoticana* was taxed manifestly in support of English activity. This had been contested towards the end of the reign of Alexander II,[84] and the minority government of 1249–51 similarly made representations to Pope Innocent IV, who in September 1251 renewed an earlier concession that crusading tithes raised in Scotland should be used for the support of Scots who took the cross themselves.[85] If the dispute was thus quietened for a time, it would raise its head again before long.

---

83 For a detailed description of the crusading ventures of the second half of the thirteenth century, see Christopher Tyerman, *God's War: A New History of the Crusades* (London, 2006), pp. 770–822.

84 See Macquarrie, *Crusades*, pp. 50–51.

85 *CDS*, i, no. 1806.

Despite the tension which doubtless surrounded the issues of coronation and resistance to papal taxation, the first government of the minority achieved striking diplomatic success when negotiations for the marriage of the young king to Margaret, the daughter of Henry III of England were completed. The principal of the match had been settled earlier, in (or by) 1244, when tense relations with England in the aftermath of the Bisset affair had been pacified by an agreement at York that Alexander II would avoid making treaties with any of Henry III's enemies.[86] (It may be correct to suppose that these unspecified enemies would include the king of France, given the close associations with France brought about by Alexander's marriage to Marie de Coucy.[87]) *Gesta Annalia* tells us that the 'magnates' of the Scottish kingdom, 'by the advice of the clergy', sent an embassy to Henry III, asking for him to affirm the 1244 accord by arranging for the marriage to take place soon. The 'magnates' are presumably to be identified with the king's councillors, who were described in the same source as 'the greatest men of the whole kingdom'.[88] Nonetheless, the standard historiographical assumption has been that the approach to Henry was led by the Comyn party, in an attempt to oust the ruling Durward faction, and that they gained support from the church because of its disaffection as a result of the issue which had led to the bishops' complaint.[89] It is inconceivable, however, that the marriage was achieved without the cooperation and leadership of the government in power in Scotland at the time. The negotiations for the marriage must have been in progress from the earliest days of the minority, if not even earlier. The quite closely contemporary chronicle of Thomas Wykes (a canon from the abbey of Osney in Oxfordshire) ascribes the marriage to negotiations which took place after May 1251, on the initiative of the English king, following a military campaign caused by Scottish incursion into northern England.[90] It is not possible, however, that an event of such importance could have been negotiated and agreed in the short time suggested by Wykes. Some disenchanted

86 *CDS*, i, no. 1654.

87 Watt, 'Minority', p. 4n.

88 *Chron. Fordun*, i, pp. 295–96 (trans. ii, p. 291). The date of this supposed embassy is uncertain: it has left no trace in formal record. *Gesta Annalia* places it immediately after the account of the translation of Queen Margaret's relics, beginning the passage with the word 'meanwhile' (*interea*), perhaps implying the summer of 1250; Watt ('Minority', p. 9) assumes summer 1251, placing it after the clerical protests to the papal curia – but there is no evidence to support the assumption.

89 See, for example, Watt, 'Minority', p. 9 – 'a presumably Comyn-inspired embassy arrived from the Scottish magnates asking for him [Henry III] to intervene and to confirm his involvement in Scottish affairs by arranging for the marriage forthwith . . .'; Duncan, *Making of the Kingdom*, p. 560, however, is less certain, stating that 'the need for good relations with England was presumably appreciated by all Scots'.

90 *SAEC*, p. 362.

Scots were no doubt whispering in the ear of Henry III, but the records do not indicate that they saw an opportunity to manufacture or manipulate the marriage in order to gain power. The marriage can only have been the result of successful diplomatic negotiations carried on through normal governmental channels, probably throughout the entire period since July 1249.

The modern historiographical convention has been to describe opposing factions: the Comyns pro-English, and the Durwards anti-English. The marriage, designed to pull the two kingdoms closer together, is thus assumed to have been against the wishes of the Durwards. The initial agreement in 1244, though, had been entered into after the decline of Comyn influence, in the shadow of the Bisset crisis, when Alan Durward was already on the rise. It had been entered into when the queen, who presumably favoured French connections, had been in full command of her position; and although the marriage actually took place after Marie had left Scotland, she was nonetheless present at York to witness it.

The departure of Marie for France in the autumn of 1250 has been seen as a sign that she was at odds with the regime led by Alan Durward and had been 'denied . . . any place in the regency'.[91] In reality, however, there seems little indication that Marie's situation in Scotland changed significantly after the death of her husband. Government continued in 1249 with a marked continuity, and the likelihood is that the queen's rôle in that government, as the individual with primary responsibility for the young prince, then king, continued uninterrupted. Durward is likely to have depended on her compliance in order to undertake a programme of governance. That she left Scotland in the autumn of 1250, possibly for reasons more related to her French family than to events in Scotland, does not indicate that she was at odds with the Durward regime: had that been the case, it is unlikely either that she would have intended to return quickly, as she evidently did, or that her presence in York at Christmas 1251 would have been welcomed.[92]

The situation cannot be characterised as a straightforward oppositional division. That Walter Comyn, earl of Menteith was not ousted from his influential magnatial position, attending the June 1250 royal council, is one indication. The

91 Watt, 'Minority', p. 8.

92 She apparently travelled through England, and sailed from Dover in October 1250: *CDS*, i, nos. 1785, 1791, 1795. The initial safe conduct allows also for her return to Scotland and is valid until June 1251; that the safe conduct was later renewed (in September 1251), valid until Easter 1252, might indicate that the date of the wedding, 26 December 1251, had not yet been fixed when she left Scotland. She left with her uncle, Thomas de Coucy, whose safe conduct (issued on the same day) also permitted his return, but, curiously, was valid until Martinmas (11 November); he also travelled with her to York in 1251. *CDS*, i, nos. 1785, 1786, 1791, 1795, 1804, 1807.

career of Bishop Albin of Brechin is another.[93] Labelled Durwardite because of the part he played in attempting to prove Durward's claim to the earldom of Mar, a broader examination of his activities is warranted. His rôle in the Mar question amounted only to his referring the case to papal jurisdiction. He took little or no part in government, his only appearance in official record between 1249 and 1251 being his signature on the bishops' letter of protest against the anti-ecclesiastical activities of the Durward-led government. He appears as an assessor and witness in a court of Alexander Comyn, earl of Buchan; he is a papal mandatory to protect Bishop Bondington of Glasgow (said to be Comynite) from anti-clerical behaviour; he is not known to have supported the attempted election of the (Durwardite) priory candidate for the vacant see of St Andrews in 1253, but did support his rival; he was not involved in the ousting of the Comyn-led government of 1255, and he acted in close association on several occasions with the supposedly Comynite bishop Clement of Dunblane. Throughout, others who are said to have had strong factional allegiance were similarly involved in cross-factional activities.

When the old king died in July 1249, the government, doubtless with its personal, political and dynastic rivalries and allegiances intact, continued to function as it had done before. The only serious dispute on record, the matter of the lay interference in ecclesiastical tenurial affairs, seems to have had its roots earlier, in the reign of Alexander II, would continue in the years and decades to come irrespective of supposed factional ascendancy, and was a case brought against the government by a group composed of supporters of both of the presumed rival groupings. The general picture seems to be of a government which achieved stability, took actions to boost the status and welfare of both crown and church, supported the economy, and achieved the successful conclusion of negotiations for the king's marriage. It was, further, a government which included within the governing community those who might not be its natural supporters.

The high-point of the first period of minority came just less than two and a half years after the inauguration of the king, when, at York, he was knighted on 25 December 1251, using a specially procured sword 'with scauberg [scabbard] of silk, and silver pommel, well and ornately covered, and a fair belt attached',[94] and then, on the following day, married his eleven-year-old bride, Princess Margaret. She was the second child of Henry III and Eleanor of Provence, just over a year younger than her brother Edward, who would succeed

93 He is described (along with others) as 'Durwardite' by Watt (*Graduates*, pp. 6, 42), who also (p. 6) describes his career.

94 *CDS*, i, no. 1824.

his father to the English throne. Marie de Coucy and her retinue had travelled to England from France to attend the ceremonies. Alexander was knighted by Henry III himself. Walter Bower, who had said that the young king had been knighted by the bishop of St Andrews in July 1249, backtracked, explaining that 'a man who is not a knight cannot make a knight', and that therefore when the bishop had knighted him previously, it was in the way of 'giving him the sword for the defence of the church', and that Henry gave him the temporal sword as 'a means for the commendation of the good and the punishment of evildoers'.[95] The marriage was clearly lavishly celebrated: instructions survive from Henry to have provisions sent to York for Christmas, including 7,000 hens, 1,650 partridges, 125 swans, 115 cranes, 120 peacocks, 290 pheasants, 400 rabbits, 1,300 hares, 670 boars and swine, 250 salmon, 5 lasts (i.e. *c.*70 barrels) of herring, 1,000 mullets, 10,000 haddock, 500 eels and at least 825 deer, as well as wine, and much ceremonial clothing, furnishings and other gifts for the royal couple and others. It was indeed a feast for 'an exceedingly numerous host both of the clergy and of the knighthood of either realm'. [96] Perhaps the revelry went too far: the contemporary English chronicler Matthew Paris tells a story that the Scots, 'for precaution', had been lodged together in one street, but came to blows over the allocation of accommodation – perhaps an anticipation on Paris's part of the apparently factional disruption which was soon to arise. Paris goes on, however, to recount more detail of the banquet:

> And if I should expound more fully the abounding diversity of the banquets, the variety of changed robes, the pleasure of the applauders of jesters, the great numbers of those at table together, the extravagant narrative would arouse derision in the ears and minds of those who were not there.

He also tells us that Alexander did homage to Henry III for the lands which he held in England, and adds:

> And when in addition to this the king of Scotland was required to do homage and fealty with allegiance to his lord the king of the English, by reason of the kingdom of Scotland, as his predecessors had done to the English kings, according as it is clearly written in the chronicles of many

95 *Chron. Bower*, v, pp. 300–01.

96 *CDS*, i, nos. 1815, 1816, 1818, 1819, 1822, 1823, 1825–1835, 1838–1844, 1846. Matthew Paris, *Chronica Majora*, quoted in *SAEC*, p. 364. See also Kay Staniland, 'The Nuptials of Alexander III of Scotland and Margaret Plantagenet', *Nottingham Medieval Studies*, 30 (1986), pp. 20–45.

> places, the king of Scotland replied that he had come thither in peace and for the honour of the king of England, and by his own command, to wit to be allied to him by mediation of a matrimonial alliance, and not to reply to him about so difficult a question. For he had not held full deliberation or suitable counsel concerning this with his chief men, as so difficult a matter demanded.[97]

Henry III, we are told, backed down, rather than create conflict at the happy occasion. This story must be of very dubious veracity. It is possible that, as a pure formality, the request for homage was made in order to keep the ancient claim to overlordship of Scotland alive, but the lack of any reference to such an important constitutional issue either in any official record or in any other English or Scottish chronicle makes this extremely doubtful. Matthew Paris did not write with hindsight, after the constitutional crises of the late thirteenth century, since he was to die in 1259; rather, he fabricated the story to maintain the well-known claims of the English monarchy to superiority over Scotland. If something of the sort did happen, it is probable that both the request and the refusal were negotiated – and scripted – in advance. Otherwise, it is an exchange which reflects well on the quick thinking and the confidence of the young king of Scots. Another story told by Paris, with similar overtones, relates how the English earl marshal claimed that he had a right to the king of Scotland's horse following his knighting by the English king, to which Alexander responded that he could have been knighted by any prince or knight, but had chosen freely to be knighted by Henry as a recognition of his distinction and that the earl therefore deserved no such customary gift.[98] Doubtless these stories were included in Paris's work in order to illustrate what he believed was 'a truth', rather than 'the truth' in a strictly literal sense.

The real challenge to Scottish independent government lay ahead. Within a couple of days, the Scottish royal party, including the new queen, was on its way back north.[99] Even before their departure, immediately after the nuptial celebrations, Henry III seems to have immersed himself in Scottish affairs,

97 Matthew Paris, *Chronica Majora*, quoted in *SAEC*, p. 364 and pp. 365–66. For much useful information about Matthew Paris and the St Albans 'School of Historiography', see Antonia Gransden, *Historical Writing in England, c.550 to c.1307* (London, 1974), pp. 356–79, and Chris Given-Wilson, *Chronicles: The Writing of History in Medieval England* (London & New York, 2004), pp. 85–97.

98 *SAEC*, pp. 366.

99 The sheriff of Northumberland was instructed to give them new year's gifts when they reached Newcastle, and on 2 January letters of protection were issued for Matilda Cantilupe, 'who has gone to Scotland by the king's command with his daughter Margaret Queen of Scotland' (*CDS*, i, nos. 1851, 1858, and see also no. 1867).

apparently playing some part in the demotion of Scottish royal officials who, for reasons unspecified, were regarded as unsatisfactory.[100] The sole documentary source for this episode, a letter of Henry III declaring that their having resigned their offices outwith Scotland would not act to the prejudice of the Scottish king or kingdom, mentions no names or offices: it merely says that the 'bailiffs' (*ballivi*) of the king of Scotland had resigned their bailiaries to their lord (i.e. Alexander III) 'at his own instance'. The wording is nonspecific, and only other, narrative, sources suggest that these 'bailiffs' (a curious word to use in the context) were in fact senior members of the royal council.[101] The principal sources for this period are *Gesta Annalia* and the *Chronicle of Melrose*. Melrose tells us that Alan Durward and others were accused 'before the king of Scotland', of treason; some resigned their offices there and then, and others turned in flight back to Scotland. This episode has customarily been regarded as a coup by the disaffected Comyn-led lords in Scotland, assisted by Henry III, whose intervention they had sought; Edward's letter has been taken to suggest that 'there was a certain pretence that Alexander made the changes himself; but clearly the Scottish magnates as a whole accepted the guidance offered by Henry and preferred to have justiciars, a chamberlain and a chancellor who were all adherents of the Comyn following'.[102] If one accepts as truth the idea that the marriage itself was a Comyn-inspired attempt to achieve Henry III's intrusion (for which there is no evidence), there is obvious logic in this view. However, to consider this a coup seems to overemphasise the extent to which it was comprehensive, faction-based or urgently effected. Obviously, at the age of only ten, Alexander's personal rôle in proceedings can at best have been limited and may have been purely a fiction. Henry III was certainly not without influence in the events. It was recognised later that there had been suspicion of his motives: being aware that 'some fear he proposes to weaken the state of Scotland or its liberties', Henry declared in 1255 that 'nothing was done on the occasion of the marriage of Alexander and his daughter Margaret at York, concerning the state of his councillors and their bailiaries, calculated to injure his kingdom or its liberties'.[103] As Margaret's father, Henry would doubtless have inserted his nominees into the Scottish government whatever its hue, but his exaggerated protestation of innocence suggests that his part in the overall change in the Scottish regime was greater than that. Whatever Henry's rôle, it is significant that the re-establishment of the government was carried out later, in Scotland,

100 *Calendar of the Patent Rolls, Henry III, A.D. 1247–1258*, p. 122.

101 It is noteworthy that in August 1255, when this episode is again referred to, the terminology is a little different – *super statu consiliariorum & balliorum*. (*Foedera*, i.i, p. 367).

102 Watt, 'Minority', p. 10.

103 *Foedera*, i.i, p. 367; translation from *CDS*, i, no. 1995.

and apparently without general retribution towards those who had been accused of treason.

A personal accusation of potentially treasonable activity was levelled at Alan Durward himself: the *Chronicle of Melrose* reports that he had petitioned the pope to legitimise his daughters (who were also the daughters of the king's half-sister), thus giving them a claim to the throne should any misfortune befall the king himself. 'And if he had obtained this, none doubted that he would have turned traitor to the king and queen.'[104] *Gesta Annalia* broadly agrees with this Melrose account, but adds the detail that the accusations were made by Walter, earl of Menteith and William, earl of Mar. The king, with advice from the king and magnates of England, 'arranged and regulated everything with moderation, [and] went home again with his consort, and, disguising his intentions, awaited better times for correcting excesses of this kind'. It is the chancellor, Robert Keldeleth, abbot of Dunfermline, whom *Gesta Annalia* holds responsible for the attempt to legitimise ('by the great seal') the king's half-sister, Durward's wife (rather than their children, as Melrose would have it), so that she (and, by implication, Durward himself, through her right) would become the king's heir. *Gesta Annalia* implies that the chancellor came back to Scotland from the celebrations at York after the king, and that immediately thereafter the great seal was broken up, the chancellor was deprived of his position and the former counsellors of the king were ousted and replaced.[105] Bower, following *Gesta Annalia*, does not state that Robert was ousted from his abbacy or otherwise punished: rather, it is said that because he was in serious dispute with his abbey community (because of his 'insufferable stubbornness'), he resigned his abbacy and took the monastic habit in the Cistercian house of Newbattle.[106] Robert did not, however, retire into obscurity: in 1260 he was sufficiently trusted by both kings to be one of a high-ranking group of 'special messengers' used by Henry III to bring Alexander and Margaret safely on a visit to England[107] – hardly a rôle expected of one who had been convincingly accused of treason less than a decade earlier. If there had been animosity, it had been

104 *Chron. Melrose,* Faustina B. IX, fos. 55v–56r (trans. Anderson, *Early Sources*, ii, p. 571).

105 *Chron. Fordun*, i, pp. 296–97 (trans. ii, pp. 291–92).

106 *Chron. Bower,* v, pp. 300–03.

107 *CDS*, i, nos. 2198, 2199, 2202, 2208. I am grateful to Professor Mark Elliott and Dr Bill Hyland for advice on the use of the term 'frater' to describe him: here used loosely to indicate a man in holy orders – 'brother' (as rendered in the *Calendar of Patent Rolls* entry for *CDS* i, no. 2198), rather than the more specific 'friar', as given by Bain in *CDS*. Movement from the Benedictine order to the stricter Cistercian order would have been acceptable under canon law and was not without precedent in this period: Andrew, prior of Pluscarden (a Valliscaulian house) became prior of Newbattle and then abbot of Kinloss (Cistercian) in the later thirteenth century: Watt and Shead, *Heads of Religious Houses*, pp. 131, 178.

quelled. In 1269, whatever his offences had been, he was elevated to the prestigious position of abbot of Melrose.

The veracity of the accusation against Durward cannot now be ascertained. There is no evidence to be found in English, Scottish or papal archives, and it is noteworthy that Matthew Paris, who seems generally to have been well informed about events, included nothing of this in his account of these events. It is also perhaps surprising that Durward was not forced into exile, as one might have expected after so serious an accusation. He was still in Scotland in July 1252, when Henry III issued a safe conduct for him and some companions travelling to England.[108] His disfavour on the part of either king, or indeed the Scottish government in power, seems not to have been too severe. The *Chronicle of Melrose* and *Gesta Annalia*, on the other hand, are also well-informed sources, and although their versions differ in important detail, it seems likely that at least rumours of such machinations were circulating, if perhaps no more than malicious propaganda. On the other hand, Queen Marie appears to have maintained relations with Durward (she certainly returned to Scotland when he was once again in power, in 1257, if not previously[109]), suggesting that any plot on his part to oust (or worse) the young king was improbable.

A further detail of the rearrangement of the Scottish king's council is supplied by Matthew Paris; Henry (as was his right, as the father of a bride still in her minority) arranged for two knights, Robert Norris and Stephen Bauzan, along with 'a certain noble dame endowed with all honour', Matilda Cantilupe, to join the young queen of Scotland's household as his representatives to ensure her well-being. A marginal note also states that Robert Ros, lord of Wark in Northumberland, the son of Isabella, an illegitimate daughter of King William (and thus the young King Alexander's cousin), was assigned as a 'guardian' for her.[110] Ros's position is interesting: a Robert Ros was present at Alexander III's council meeting in Edinburgh in June 1250, and also witnessed further acts of the king in May and October 1251. If the Robert Ros commissioned by Henry III to look after his daughter's interests in December 1251 (and who was a consistent witness to the king's acts between June 1252 and February 1254, being removed from the council in the *putsch* of September 1255)[111] was the same man,

108 *CDS*, i, no. 1888.

109 See below, p. 113, for a suggestion that Marie de Coucy was not as absent from Scotland during the period 1251–57 as has usually been supposed.

110 *SAEC*, pp.368–69. Whether Ros was one of the 'other prudent and courteous men' or the 'prudent and faithful counsellor' promised by Henry is not clear from the text. Matilda's commission is clearly present in English official record (*CDS*, i, no. 1867), but the others are not. Ros's surname is spelt variously Ros, Ross and Roos. The form Ros (as in *RRS*, iv pt. 1) has here been adopted consistently.

111 *RRS*, iv pt. 1, nos. 1, 2, 10, 13, 16, 27, 28, 29, 20, 22.

then it implies at least a degree of continuity in government between the Durward-led regime of 1249–51 and the post-1251 settlement. That Ros's primary landholding was English (although he had connections with the Scottish royal house and held lands in Dumfriesshire as well as of the king of Scotland in England) might also suggest a greater degree of involvement by Henry III in the establishment of the 1249 government than has previously been considered, or than appears in any official record. Alternatively, if there are two namesakes involved, it is curious that no differentiation is made in the witness lists between the pre- and post-December 1251 witnesses, who appear so close together. It has been suggested (judging by the order of precedence in the witness lists) that the witness(es) to the early *acta* of Alexander III might indeed be two men, witnessing interchangeably – Robert (I) (d. 1270) and his son Robert (II) (d. 1274). Both, however, were firm in their allegiance to Henry III, as well as bearing their family's close association with the Scottish royal house. However one looks at it – one Robert Ros, or two – there seems to have been a greater degree of continuity in government from 1249 to 1252 than has generally been assumed.[112] A further 'counsellor' for the queen, Geoffrey Langley, is said by Paris to have been sent by Henry 'during the same time', but official record shows that he was sent to Scotland later, in November 1252; Matthew Paris, in an apparent addition to the text, has noted that Scots refused to accept him.[113]

John Balliol of Barnard Castle in Yorkshire, the father of the later king of Scots, was also sent as a representative of Henry III in the Scottish government. Although perhaps 'less familiar with Scotland' than Robert Ros,[114] Balliol had been involved enough in the Scottish court to be regarded as one of Alexander II's barons when he participated in that king's letter to the pope regarding his agreement with Henry III in 1244 and, like Ros, had witnessed a royal act of

112 I am grateful to Professor Cynthia Neville for her comments on this issue, in email correspondence, April 2016. For further information about these men, she cites Stringer, 'Periphery and Core', pp. 88–89, and Stringer, 'The Scottish "Political Community" in the Reign of Alexander II (1214–49)', pp. 69, 72 and 84, both of which place the Roberts Ros, father and son, firmly in the centre of Scottish royal politics in the reign of Alexander II. Stringer's 'Tynedale: Power, Society and Identities, c.1200–1296' in Matthew L. Holford and Keith J. Stringer, *Border Liberties and Loyalties: North-East England, c.1200 to c.1400* (Edinburgh, 2010), pp. 231–90 (at pp. 248, 250, 276), demonstrates the family's history of loyalty to both crowns. See also various references in Oram, *Alexander II*. Ros senior's Scottish credentials are also bolstered by the fact that he appears as a witness in Scotland more often in the reign of Alexander II (18 times, excluding the treaty of York; most frequently in royal documents) than he does post-1249: this was not a stranger imposed on the Scottish government by Henry III.

113 *SAEC*, p. 369 & n. He was apparently back in England by July 1253, when he was sent to Scotland again, as part of a retinue to conduct the queen of Scots on a visit to her mother, if permitted by the Scottish government (*CDS*, i, no. 1935).

114 Duncan, *Making of the Kingdom*, p. 563.

Alexander III during the first minority period.[115] He had greatly increased his Scottish landholdings throughout the southern part of the country as well as in Garioch, Perthshire and other areas, through his marriage to Devorguilla of Galloway (who was the granddaughter of Earl David, the younger brother of King William) in 1233, and was a member of a broader family which was already well established in Scotland. His uncle, Henry Balliol of Cavers, had been Alexander II's chamberlain a decade earlier, and by 1220 had been a considerable enough Scottish lord to be party to Alexander's undertaking to marry the sister of Henry III.[116] John's extensive landholding in the north of England and his position as sheriff of Cumberland brought him into close contact with Alexander II and his officers, for whose northern English lands he had to account. There is a strong case in favour of the notion that John Balliol ought to be viewed as one with primarily English identity and political commitment;[117] he was at the very pinnacle of English baronial society. Nonetheless, the fact cannot be ignored that, as with Ros, Henry III's second nominee in the Scottish government was a man with very significant political, landed and familial interests in Scotland, and with a deep knowledge of Scotland and its politics.

Henry III had indeed infiltrated the Scottish government in a way which record makes clear was designed to protect the interests and well-being of his young daughter and her husband, but which also, and without coincidence, offered distinct advantages in terms of his political ambitions regarding the Scottish crown. His intervention appears principled: his choice of counsellors, in Ros and Balliol, showed both acumen and sensitivity. They may have represented a valued continuity between the old and new councils, and neither were simply 'meddlers';[118] they were both men who possessed good knowledge of Scotland, its politics and the protagonists of its administration, and who had personal interests in achieving stable and prosperous rule.

In the early months of 1252 a new government was swinging into action in Scotland. Traditionally, this council has been viewed as representing a marked shift away from previous policy, promoting a more pro-English outlook, in contrast to Durward's opposition to English involvement in Scottish affairs.[119]

115 *CDS*, i, no. 1655; *RRS*, iv pt. 1, no. 11.

116 *PoMS*, no. 1/7/51.

117 Amanda Beam, *The Balliol Dynasty 1210–1364* (Edinburgh, 2008), pp. 2–4; it is a point which is made simply by his ubiquitous presence in English royal record: he merits no fewer than 130 index entries in *CDS*, i, named in almost 5 per cent of the documents calendared in that volume.

118 Duncan (*Kingship of the Scots*, p. 155), described Ros as 'a meddler with uncertain authority'.

119 This is the complexion that Watt ('Minority', p. 12) puts on it, although, as Watt points out, others have come to the opposite conclusion. It seems to me that neither approach is justified by the evidence.

However, the extent to which either the personnel or the policy of the king's council changed must be open to doubt. Of the 25 men who witnessed royal acts during the first period of minority, from July 1249 to December 1251, 9 also witnessed royal acts in the second period, from January 1252 to September 1255.[120] These include men who are supposed to have belonged to both predominant factions. When broader cross-factional relationships are examined, the situation becomes yet more intriguing. For example, on 17 December 1253, Walter Comyn, earl of Menteith, Alexander Comyn, earl of Buchan (and justiciar of Scotia) and William earl of Mar (the new chamberlain[121]) were among nine secular witnesses to the settlement of a dispute regarding lands belonging to Dunfermline abbey.[122] Among the other witnesses was Alexander Stewart (the steward), who had served on the 1249–51 council, was to be one of those named as 'advisors' involved in the downfall of the 1252–55 council, and was to be a member of the next new council, which was to be installed in September 1255 – a man whose colours might be assumed to be pinned resolutely to the anti-Comyn opposition. Similarly, in 1251 William, earl of Mar, who was to be one of those ousted from the council in 1255, gave a charter to his brother-in-law, Gilbert Hay, a member of the first council and of the group which replaced the supposedly Comyn council of 1252–55.[123] Hay and Mar were both also married to sisters of Alexander Comyn, earl of Buchan. If they found themselves on what we are asked to believe were opposing political sides, it seems not to have affected their familial relationship. Those who witnessed Mar's 1251 charter to Hay were Alan Durward, Alexander Comyn earl of Buchan, John Vaux, Robert Menzies, Robert Mowat (justiciar, sheriff of Forfar), Walter Bisset, Walter Comyn earl of Menteith and Robert Ros senior. Of these, Durward himself, John Vaux, Menzies and Bisset might be assumed to be Durward supporters: Durward and Menzies were active on the council in 1249–51, and again in 1255–57; Vaux and Bisset were active in 1249–51, but not in later councils, although Vaux is named as another of those who advised in the context of the 1255 replacement of the council. The two Comyns can

120 These numbers assume one, rather than two Roberts Ros; if, however, both father and son were interchangeably present throughout the period 1249–55, it strengthens rather than weakens the argument for continuity in government. Those who witnessed under both councils were: William Bondington bishop of Glasgow, Walter Comyn earl of Menteith, Alexander Stewart, Robert Ros, Richard Marshal, Thomas Randolph, Aymer Maxwell, David Lochore sheriff of Perth and Alexander Comyn earl of Buchan. For a picture of how witnessing crossed factional boundaries throughout the minority, see below, Appendix 1.

121 For Mar as chamberlain, see, e.g. *RRS*, iv pt. 1, no. 17.

122 *Dunfermline Reg.*, no. 83.

123 NLS Adv MS 15.1.18, no 68 (*PoMS*, no. 3/18/13); royal confirmation, *RRS*, iv pt 1, no. 11, on 26 July 1251.

be assumed to be in the opposing group. Ros, as noted above, seems to have represented continuity between the two sides, and the allegiance of Mowat is unclear. (It may be significant that his first appearance as sheriff is in 1250, although he does appear to have remained as sheriff throughout and beyond the minority period.[124]) What this document, among others,[125] demonstrates is that if there was factional division during the minority period, it did not apparently disrupt the normal legal and business discourse of the ruling class. Durward and his close associates did not flee in 1251, but continued to conduct their business, some of them still apparently at the centre of the royal administration. Personal, dynastic and political rivalries there may have been, but communication and mutual participation in the affairs of the kingdom continued.

Another indication that the factional divide was not as entrenched in Scotland as has been previously thought is that Alan Durward was soon back in favour at the English court. He and some companions travelled from Scotland to England in October 1252, and were allowed to hunt in Henry III's forests on their return journey in the following October.[126] Durward went with Henry to Gascony in the late summer of 1253 (where he lost his horse), and subsequently to Spain with the king's son, Prince Edward, for Edward's marriage to Eleanor of Castile in October 1254.[127] (There is no evidence that there was much enthusiasm among other Scottish nobles to heed Henry's summons to join the Gascon expedition. Henry did summon the king of Scots and his nobles to a meeting at Edinburgh in February 1254 for urgent discussions, presumably about the ongoing campaign, but there is no record of the requested meeting having taken place.[128]) Durward's position of trust at the English court is further

124 *Yester Writs*, no. 15; see Reid and Barrow, *Sheriffs*, p. 21.

125 A couple of examples: *Arbroath Liber*, no. 366 (22 June 1254), in which Gilbert Hay, William Brechin (another member of the 1249–51 and 1255–57 'Durwardite' administrations) and Robert Mowat act along with the earl of Buchan in mediating an agreement between one Peter Maule and Arbroath abbey; W. Fraser, *The Red Book of Menteith* (Edinburgh, 1880), no. 6, in which, in 1259 or 1260, Máel Coluim earl of Fife, who figures in the 1255–57 council, witnessed a grant to Hugh Abernethy alongside (among others) Alexander Comyn earl of Buchan, John Comyn lord of Badenoch, William Wishart archdeacon of St Andrews, and William earl of Mar, all of whom were removed from the council in 1255.

126 *CDS*, i, nos. 1888, 1895.

127 *CDS*, i, nos. 1984, 1985; see also *Chron. Melrose*, which blames Durward's return to favour for the forthcoming dissension among the Scottish magnates (Anderson, *Early Sources*, ii, pp. 575–76).

128 *Cal. Close Rolls, Henry III*, viii, 1253–1254, p. 108. (Note that *CDS*, i, no. 1974 dates this summons December 1254, implying that the meeting was to be held in February 1255. If Bain's assumption is correct, then it seems more likely that the subject of the meeting was the issue of the treatment of Alexander III and Margaret (see below), rather than the Gascon campaign, which was over by the end of 1254. It seems unlikely, however, that Bain is correct: the letter refers to

emphasised by his standing surety for the military service due to Henry III by the earl of Strathearn.[129]

Other than an apparently limited change of personnel in the king's council, there was no substantial alteration in either policy or activity. Two major differences from the situation which had prevailed a year earlier are apparent: Marie de Coucy was now absent, and the young king had a consort whose presence entailed for Scotland a close scrutiny of its affairs by her father, Henry III. The queen mother's absence left a void in the close control of the person of the king. Margaret's presence might be seen as partially filling that void, since she was accompanied by the counsellors and guardians appointed by Henry III, but the king's mother had held an undisputed status in Scotland which could not be matched by appointed officials of lesser rank, however sensitively or astutely chosen.

There is remarkably little record evidence for the conduct of government in Scotland between 1252 and 1255. Alexander III's *Regesta* contains only eight surviving dated royal acts of this period, compared to the (admittedly meagre) thirteen from the period between the death of Alexander II and December 1251. A glance at the records of those who witnessed royal documents during these two periods shows that they also witnessed or were party to fewer non-royal transactions during the period 1252–55 than had been the case in 1249–51.[130] Such negative evidence is difficult to interpret, however: the numbers in either period are low, and it is possible that there is no deeper cause for the apparent slow-down in activity than just the vagary of document survival: a much more comprehensive analysis of the transactional activities of a wider spectrum of people would be required before any definite conclusions could be drawn. It might be thought that a hint could be found by a crude count of the entries in some of the major repositories of such documents, the monastic cartularies. However, even there, although there is a preponderance of documents relating to the earlier period, the evidence is so sparse as to make any statistical analysis of very dubious value.[131] If the apparent reduction in activity is significant at all, it might be taken as an indication of insecurity, perhaps implying that the new regime was, by its very nature, weaker than that which had preceded it: it held

---

the king's envoys 'from Gascony', but is dated 27 December, the day (if it is 1254) of Henry's return to England.) For a brief description of the Gascon campaign, see Powicke, *The Thirteenth Century*, pp. 116–19.

129 *CDS*, i, no. 1956.

130 The analysis has been carried out through use of the *PoMS* database.

131 Examination of the *Syllabus of Scottish Cartularies* (see https://scottishmedievalcharters.wordpress.com/scottish-cartularies/) offers a total of 25 documents of Scottish origin which can be dated with reasonable certainty to the first or second minority periods; of those, 17 belong to the first minority.

power without the authority of continuity with Alexander II's council and lacked the invaluable presence of the queen mother, depending instead on self-asserted credentials and on the uncertain support of the English king. However, the general scarcity of material could equally imply that the entire minority period should, perhaps predictably, be tarred with the same brush of insecurity.[132] Nonetheless, while there is no reason to doubt that the normal, everyday activities of government and administration continued,[133] in terms of the great affairs of state the period 1252–55 sees nothing equivalent to the translation of the relics of St Margaret, the marriage and knighting of the king, or renewed pressure on the papacy to grant the rites of coronation and unction.[134]

One issue which the regime did have to contend with was the election of a new bishop of St Andrews, on the death of David Bernham on 26 April 1253.[135] The bishopric of St Andrews was crucial: a position of ecclesiastical eminence, and thus also of immense governmental importance. Typically (and as had been the case at the time of Bernham's own election in 1239), the election of his successor was challenged. The cathedral chapter elected Robert Stuteville, dean of Dunkeld. This election was disputed by the royal administration (which Bower claimed had supported the election of Gamelin, the chancellor of the see of Moray and a man trusted by the current regime, who was by then 'carrying

132 A similar examination of the *Syllabus of Scottish Cartularies* to compare the 1240s, 1250s and 1260s against each other (excluding the contents of Raine's *North Durham* (Coldingham charters), which contains a high proportion of documents of English origin) does indeed imply a downturn in activity during the 1250s: the number of documents dateable to the 1250s was only about two-thirds of the 1240s total, and approximately three-quarters of the 1260s total. Of course, many of the documents are of uncertain date, and the numbers are therefore undoubtedly incomplete; no account has been taken of local, institutional or personal issues which might also have affected business activity; and the serendipity of survival should not be discounted. Nonetheless, there is perhaps evidence enough to indicate a general trend.

133 There was, for example, a new justiciar of Lothian, Thomas Normanville, who seems to have replaced his predecessor, David Lindsay (who had been justiciar in the closing years of Alexander II's reign, and presumably continued in post until the end of 1251). (*Melrose Liber*, i, no. 322, which should be dated between early 1252 (since Gamelin is described as a royal clerk and 'carrying the king's seal', thus placing it after the abbot of Dunfermline's loss of the office of chancellor) and 13 February 1254, when (*Vet. Mon.*, no. 161) Gamelin is first seen described as chancellor.) A rare surviving record of a judicial case from 1254 also appears in the English chancery: *CDS*, i, no. 2673.

134 It is possible, but unlikely, that a further request regarding unction was made in 1252 or 1253: *RRS*, iv pt. 1, no. 181 records a comment in the *Summa Aurea* by Henry of Segusio (later Cardinal Bishop of Ostia), that the king of Scotland 'daily pursues the pope for the privilege'. The work was complete by *c.*1253, and the comment might therefore reasonably refer either to the known petition of 1251, and/or to a later attempt. If there was a repeated petition, it has left no trace in the papal archives, and surprisingly seems to have prompted no comment from the English court.

135 *Chron. Bower*, v, pp. 314–15; Watt and Murray, *Fasti*, p. 380.

the king's seal', if not yet formally royal chancellor).[136] In the event, it was neither Stuteville nor Gamelin who obtained the see, but Abel of Gullane, the archdeacon of St Andrews, one of the royal emissaries sent to the papal court to protest against Stuteville's election, who seems to have managed to gain the ear of the pope to obtain the see for himself. The dispute between Abel and Stuteville seems to have been another episode in the long-standing conflict between the cathedral chapter and the canons of the church of St Mary on the Rock, which had been a persistent problem throughout David Bernham's reign as bishop. Abel and the canons of St Mary had been deprived of a voice in the election of Stuteville, and Abel's protestation before the papal court that the election had been improperly conducted because of their exclusion was successful to the extent that their right to participate was officially confirmed.[137] Abel's sharp practice, however, in achieving for himself what neither the chapter nor the king's council had intended, cannot have endeared him in either diocesan or court circles.

There was close contact between the royal courts of Scotland and England in the years from 1252 to 1255, evidence indeed of the familial bonds between Henry, his queen and their daughter. There seems to have been a steady flow of communication between Margaret and her mother, Queen Eleanor: throughout 1252 and 1253 there are a string of accounts for payments for gifts and other expenses, and safe conducts for a variety of household members (including Margaret's valets, tailor and other messengers, and Eleanor's butler) carrying messages between them; Margaret was sent a seal for her personal use at the end of the 1252, and a gift of veils and hoods in June 1253.[138] There was also regular contact between the two courts regarding judicial and administrative matters.[139] Of particular importance must be the visit to Scotland of Simon de Montfort, earl of Leicester and Gilbert Segrave, who were dispatched to Scotland by Henry in August 1254, charged with revealing to Alexander 'some secrets causing him [Henry] anxiety'.[140] What these secrets were can only be surmised: if they were the issues of maladministration and apparent maltreatment of the young king and queen which are described in some of the chronicle accounts,[141] it is curious that it was a year later before Henry III took action to remedy the

136 *Melrose Liber*, i, no. 322: *clerico domini regis sigillum eius tunc portante.*

137 For a description of the disputed election, and biography of Abel of Gullane, see Watt, *Graduates*, pp. 225–27.

138 E.g. *CDS*, i, nos. 1872, 1897, 1903, 1928, 1929, 1930, 1932.

139 E.g. *CDS*, i, nos. 1865, 1866, 1894, 1906.

140 *CDS*, i, no. 1966.

141 E.g. Matthew Paris, *Chronica Majora*, from *SAEC*, pp. 370–71, which complains of the ill-treatment of Alexander and Margaret; *Chron. Bower*, v, pp. 302–03, 315–17, which details issues of maladministration.

situation. The Scottish royal court in this period has been portrayed as 'a kind of outlying section of the English royal household'.[142] It is an exaggeration, however: that Henry III failed to exert as much control over the Scottish household as he would have wished would be made abundantly clear by later events.

In July 1253 Henry (who was about to leave England for Gascony) requested that Margaret should be allowed to visit her mother, who was pregnant, to stay with her until after the birth of her child.[143] (Eleanor had been only 16 years old when she gave birth to Margaret in 1240.) There is no record, however, which suggests that Margaret was allowed to attend. A safe conduct had been issued in April 1253 by Henry for 'Margaret, queen of Scotland' to pass through England and return, valid until Michaelmas (29 September). It is curious, however, both that the safe conduct was issued before any request had been made to the Scottish government to allow the visit, and that its expiry date was before the due date (November) of the English queen's child. The wording, too, offering safe conduct *through* the king's territory, by land and sea, 'to her own country',[144] perhaps suggests that this safe conduct was in fact meant for Marie, queen of Scotland, the queen mother. (She was still styled queen well after Margaret became queen of Scotland.) It has been suggested that 'Margaret' is an erroneous extension of the original document's abbreviation 'M', but unfortunately this is not borne out by examination of the original, in which the name Margaret is quite clear.[145] Nonetheless, the safe conduct at this date is anomalous, and raises the intriguing suspicion that scribal error may have obscured the possibility that Marie de Coucy had not in fact left Scotland permanently in 1251, and was therefore not consistently resident in France from 1251 to 1257. If indeed she was visiting 'her own country' in 1253, then she must have been in Scotland for at least part of the period 1251–53, which would offer a different complexion to Henry III's later intervention in 1255, and to chronicle accounts of ill-treatment of the young royal couple. Whether this lends additional significance to the timing of Leicester and Segrave's visit in the summer of 1254 can only be conjecture; it is equally possible that it was foreign affairs, and the need for reassurance that Scotland would cause no obstruction to his diplomatic efforts in France and Sicily, which were the cause of Henry's anxiety at that point.[146]

142 Watt, 'Minority', p. 10.

143 *CDS*, i, no. 1935.

144 *CDS*, i, no. 1916.

145 The suggestion was made by Marion Campbell, *Alexander III, King of Scots* (Colonsay, 1999), p. 60 and n.9. Original: TNA C66/64 m. 13 (Patent Roll, 37 Henry III). Usually, Margaret is described in the English records as 'the king's daughter, the queen of Scotland' (see, e.g., *CDS*, i, nos. 1935, 1936); in this 1253 safe conduct she is described simply as 'Margaret, queen of Scotland'.

146 See below, p. 131.

It was becoming become clear that Henry had little confidence in his appointees to the Scottish government. The somewhat sparse account offered by record sources is amplified by details from some chronicles, which are fairly consistent in their versions of events. Matthew Paris relates how a physician, Reginald of Bath, was sent by the English queen to Edinburgh castle to check on the health of her daughter and Alexander. Margaret confided in him the cause of her apparent 'distress and pallor', as a result of which he accused the Scottish ruling council (including Robert Ros and John Balliol, Henry III's appointees), of treason, on account of their maltreatment of the royal couple. Reginald died soon after, it was claimed as a result of poisoning. Paris claims that further complaints from Queen Margaret, that she was effectively imprisoned in the castle, deprived of her choice of household, and that she and Alexander were unreasonably prevented from consummating their marriage, eventually led to the English king's direct intervention in Scottish affairs.[147] Other chronicles, although omitting the part played by the unfortunate Reginald of Bath, largely confirm Paris's version of the events that led Henry to approach the border with an armed force in 1255.[148] The *Chronicle of Melrose* gives a different version, in which an initiative to seize the king and queen comes from Alan Durward and his supporters. They effect a coup with the support of the English king, who is then invited to intervene to assist in settling affairs.[149] In both accounts, the earl of Gloucester (in the English accounts accompanied by John Maunsel) is also involved in rescuing Margaret and Alexander from their straightened circumstances, detail which is confirmed by official record.[150] Bower's *Scotichronicon* has no praise for this council:

> ... there were as many kings as there were counsellors. For in those days you could see examples of oppression of the poor, disinheriting of nobles, exactions laid upon the inhabitants, pillage of the common people, sacrilegious thefts of teinds and the violations of churches ...[151]

Curiously, Bower admits that he does not know the truth which lies behind these various versions of events leading to the downfall of the council. His own interpretation is brief, following (almost word for word) the account given in

147 Matthew Paris, *Chronica Majora*, from *SAEC*, pp. 370–73.
148 E.g. the *Annals of Dunstable* and the *Annals of Burton*, both quoted by Anderson in *SAEC*, p. 371n.
149 *Chron. Melrose*, Faustina B. IX, fos. 57r–58r (trans. Anderson, *Early Sources*, ii, pp. 580–83).
150 *CDS*, i, no. 1990.
151 *Chron. Bower*, v, pp. 302–03.

the earlier *Gesta Annalia*, simply stating that Henry came near the border 'since good judgement and justice slept in the realm of Scotland', and that, after discussion (held at Wark), the Scottish council was replaced. The capture of the king and queen, the initiative of Durward and his supporters, and the rôle of Gloucester and Maunsel are all offered by Bower as elements which he had read in other sources – 'not to omit the truthful statements of anyone'. Again copying from *Gesta Annalia*, he offers a further comment regarding corrupt practices by the old council, in relation to accounting for royal property.[152]

When Henry directly intervened in Scottish affairs in the late summer of 1255, he seems to have done so at least partially out of concern regarding the treatment of his daughter and the young king. Formal record is silent on the specifics of the complaint: on 10 August, he wrote to the 'bishops, earls, barons, knights and all others faithful to the illustrious king of Scots', requiring them to give due credence to what his envoys (the earl of Gloucester, the earl of Albemarle, John Maunsel provost of Beverley and Robert Walerand his steward, or any two of them) would say to them on his behalf, for the special benefit of King Alexander.[153] On the same day, he specifically commended to those envoys his 'friends' Patrick earl of Dunbar, Máel Ísu earl of Strathearn, Níall earl of Carrick, Robert Bruce, Alexander Stewart, Alan Durward, David Lindsay, William Brechin, Walter Murray, Robert Menzies, Hugh Gifford, Walter Stewart, John Crawford, Hugh Crawford, William Galbraith and others who would stand with him against those Scots 'who have caused or shall presume to cause damage to Alexander K[ing] of Scotland . . . or who shall be gainsayers of his dearest daughter Margaret Queen of Scotland, whose condition the K[ing] intends to redress in good faith', and gave his formal protection to the same 'friends', asserting that he had 'no design against the person or dignity of the K[ing] of Scotland', that he would not seek to dissolve the marriage, and would not make peace with the supposed malefactors over and above the others (*super predictis*).[154] Less than a week later he declared that, on the advice of his envoys, he would proceed to Scotland himself for the 'reformation and melioration' of the condition of the king and queen of Scots.[155]

It might be expected that these 'friends' of Henry III would represent a group of disaffected lords who had been disbarred from the second minority government and that, like Durward, many of their names would appear with increasing regularity in the English royal records as they curried favour, attempting to assure their position in readiness to regain power in Scotland. That assumption

152 *Chron. Bower*, v, pp. 316–17; *Chron. Fordun*, i, p. 297 (trans. ii, p. 292).
153 *CDS*, i, no. 1986; full text in *Foedera*, i.i, p. 325.
154 *CDS*, i, nos. 1987, 1988; full texts in *Foedera*, i.i, p. 326.
155 *CDS*, i, no. 1990.

underlies the assertion that Durward was responsible for Henry's intervention in the Scottish government, in the interests of his band of malcontents.[156] However, the pattern is not so conveniently clear. Of the fifteen names, only seven (the earls of Dunbar and Strathearn, Robert Bruce, Alan Durward, David Lindsay, Robert Menzies and William Galbraith) appear at all in the pages of the *Calendar of Documents Relating to Scotland* in the period from January 1252 until the document of 10 August 1255. Only the earl of Dunbar, Robert Bruce and Alan Durward appear more than twice. (Some of the entries, it has to be noted, relate to legitimate personal affairs in England: the Bruce English estates; Strathearn's daughters' status as heiresses to an English estate; and Dunbar's distraint for debts – hardly symptomatic of currying favour.) Similarly, their activity in Scotland represents no clear pattern: four of them (the earl of Dunbar, Alan Durward, William Brechin and Robert Menzies) had witnessed royal documents between the death of Alexander II and January 1252; Walter Murray, conversely, had witnessed documents subsequent to January 1252, but not in the earlier phase of the minority; Alexander Stewart had witnessed in both periods; and the remaining nine individuals had witnessed documents under neither regime. Only six of the fifteen would witness royal documents in the following council, from September 1255 to 1257 – Dunbar, Menzies and Brechin from the supposed Durward faction, Murray from the supposed Comyn faction, and Strathearn and Gifford who had apparently sat on the fence. Rather than representing the faction which had been ousted from power in 1252, it seems more realistic to characterise this group as embodying opposition – both from within and without – to current policy.

It is certain that the chronicle accounts of subterfuge and clandestine removal of Alexander and Margaret from Edinburgh castle are romantic exaggerations of the events of August and September 1255. Henry's intention to rectify the situation in Scotland was well signalled in his letters of 10 August; the attendance of Alexander and Margaret at Wark was carefully arranged, and it is clear that the meeting itself was conducted in a formal and considered manner, rather than being a knee-jerk reaction to sudden revelations. Bower's complaints of misgovernance are entirely formulaic, and there is little to support the accusations of personal ill-treatment of the royal couple. Walter Comyn and his companions were included in the discussions, and the affairs of state under consideration included more than simply the changes to the Scottish ruling council: several other judicial pleas, allowed by Henry III at the request of Alexander, Margaret and Alan Durward, were included within the business.[157]

---

156 Watt, 'Minority', p. 13.

157 *CDS*, i, nos. 2009, 2011, 2020–2022.

Nonetheless, Henry's annoyance at the situation in Scotland and his determination to have things his own way are unmistakeable. Something had prompted him to dispatch Gloucester and Maunsel to Scotland in early August, and to take up arms following receipt of their report. He had expected better of his nominees in the Scottish council, Ros and Balliol: Balliol's wardenship of the castle of Carlisle and sheriffdom of Cumberland were revoked, and it can be no coincidence that Henry made his base near the Scottish border in Ros's castle of Wark. These two characters were to feel the force of Henry's wrath, before they were able to atone for their misdemeanours.[158] Henry's intentions were serious: he instructed the gathering of the northern English feudal host and ordered his own armour to be brought to him from London. He was prepared to invade Scotland, should it prove necessary.[159]

158 On Balliol and the underlying tensions which coloured his position within the guardianship, see Beam, *The Balliol Dynasty*, pp. 58–67, where the point is also made that Henry had actually instructed the withdrawal from the Scottish government of both Ros and Balliol in August 1254. On their severe treatment by Henry III thereafter, see *SAEC*, pp. 371–74. They were both back in favour, however, within two years. Balliol regained royal favour in August 1257 (*CDS*, i, nos. 2091–92); Ros's castle of Wark was restored to him in May 1256 (*CDS*, i, no. 2049), perhaps casting into doubt the depth of Henry's rage against him and his family, as described by Matthew Paris (*SAEC*, p. 374). Ros was still not entirely in favour by November 1258, however, as in that month Henry, on the advice of other nobles, gave him respite of the charges against him as a result of Scottish affairs, and allowed him 'meanwhile' to cultivate his lands (*CDS*, i, no. 2138). He and his brother William were finally exonerated of all charges against them in November 1259 (*CDS*, i, no. 2168). Balliol had apparently lost his castle and sheriffdom of Carlisle because of his perceived disloyalty to Henry III, both in Scotland and because of a serious dispute with the bishop of Durham; however Robert Bruce, to whom it was given (and who, as a member of the new council was definitely not out of favour in 1255/56), was also deprived of it very shortly thereafter, in October 1255 (*CDS*, i, no. 2029). Perhaps it was no great loss to him: the castle was apparently in a shocking state of disrepair, not having been effectively repaired since the damage inflicted on it during the reign of King John (*CDS*, i, nos. 1167, 2034). As late as 1283, it was still said to be 'greatly dilapidated' (*CDS*, v, no. 48).

159 *CDS*, i, nos.1990–1994, 1998.

CHAPTER 4

The King Emergent

Henry's invasion was averted. Following his discussions with Henry at Wark, on 20 September Alexander issued letters from Roxburgh which detailed the removal from his council, 'because their faults so demand, as it is reported', of 25 men and 1 woman. A new council, 15 strong, was named as Richard of Inverkeithing bishop of Dunkeld, Peter Ramsay bishop of Aberdeen, Máel Coluim earl of Fife, Patrick earl of Dunbar, Níall earl of Carrick, Máel Ísu earl of Strathearn, Alexander Stewart, Robert Bruce, Alan Durward, Walter Murray, David Lindsay, William Brechin, Hugh Gifford, Gilbert Hay and Robert Menzies. The new council was to remain in place (unless otherwise agreed by Alexander and Henry or his heirs) for the period of seven years from 4 September 1255.[1] With total lack of coincidence, that date was Alexander's fourteenth birthday: the new settlement was intended to pertain until he reached the age of exactly 21. Both the seven-year term and the agreement between Henry and Alexander were qualified by a good behaviour clause: Alexander, with the advice of the rest of his council, had the power to remove any of them if 'they shall clearly have so acted as to be unworthy to take part in our councils and the business of our realm'.

Alexander's letter continued by declaring that those removed from office, and their associates, were not to be readmitted

1 *RRS*, iv pt. 1, no. 22. Translations from *RPS*, A1255/1. Those removed were: William bishop of Glasgow and Clement bishop of Dunblane, Gamelin bishop-elect of St Andrews, Walter Comyn earl of Menteith, Alexander Comyn earl of Buchan, William earl of Mar, John Balliol, Robert Ros, Aymer Maxwell and Marion his wife, John Comyn, Nicholas Soules, Thomas Normanville, Alexander Uviet, John Denmuir, David Graham, John Blund, Thomas Randolph, Hugh Gourlay and his brother William, William Wishart, archdeacon of St Andrews, Brother Richard, almoner of the order of the Templars, David Lochore, John Wishart, William Cadzow and William formerly the king's chaplain.

> to our counsels, and to the conduct of the business of our realm, or to our grace, or to any sort of intimacy, until they have fully atoned, by concord or by judgment, to King Henry and ourselves, for the offences imputed, and to be imputed to them. We shall compel them, if necessary, to do this, by every sort of just means. This also was settled and granted on both sides, that if it should happen that the realm of Scotland is invaded or attacked by an alien prince, we shall be allowed to admit and invoke the magnates now removed from our council, and any others whatsoever, to come to our help.

The governmental changes did not stop with the council: 'if sheriffs, foresters, and other lesser officials so offend that they ought to be moved from their posts, we shall cause others to be put in their place by our aforesaid council.' Castles assigned to individuals as part of this rearrangement would not be removed 'except by the common counsel of our advisers, assigned for the wardship and government of our realm, and of our person, and of that of our queen'. Other administrative affairs would similarly be handled by the Scots king with the advice and consent of his council. In a further statement which tends to strengthen the notion that Henry was at least in part motivated by the welfare of his daughter and son-in-law, there is a promise to Henry that

> we will treat and guard his daughter, our queen, in matrimonial affection, with every sort of consideration which befits our queen and the daughter of so great a prince, and we shall cause due and proper honour to be shown to her, in our realm, in every possible way.

Unspecified 'reasonable undertakings' made to Henry by the members of the new council were ratified by Alexander 'as representing our own command and desire': obviously, Henry had dictated his terms. The king of Scots swore, through the proxy of Patrick earl of Dunbar,[2] to uphold the provisions of the letter, and Henry confirmed through a personally witnessed letter patent that no prejudice would fall to the Scottish king, his heirs or his realm following the expiry of the seven-year term, after which Alexander's letter would be returned to the king of Scots.[3]

---

2 Swearing through a proxy was a reserved privilege: it was an explicit recognition of Alexander's kingly status.

3 *CDS*, i, no. 2013: Henry's letter, which recites Alexander's. The *CDS* abridgement does not include Henry's undertaking to return Alexander's letter at the end of the term; the full text is in *Foedera*, i.i, p. 329.

The document which records the settlement is distinctive, bearing a formality and precision which differs markedly from the vaguer accounts of the events of December 1251 to January 1252. There is no pretence regarding the part played by the English king: satisfaction of Henry's demands appears to have played a primary rôle in the negotiations, leading to the formal undertaking by the Scottish king to uphold the agreement. Henry had assumed a position of *de facto* overlordship, to which there seems to have been no recorded objection by the Scottish king or governing community. The personal rôle accorded to Alexander himself, though, was in marked contrast to the situation in 1251/52: the agreement was given in Alexander's own name; its provisions were to be implemented by Alexander himself, through 'common counsel'; and Alexander swore through a proxy, a right reserved for sovereign kings. The fact that Henry did not explicitly reserve to himself any 'vestigial right over the Scottish kingdom' through the use of the phrase *salvo iure nostro* can be viewed in two ways. It could have been an unnecessary assertion, since Henry was in the strong position of having negotiated the right to intervene for a period of seven years.[4] Alternatively, and more likely, Henry was dissociating himself from the day-to-day government of Scotland and acknowledging Alexander's own right to personal rule: hence the explicit recognition that internal affairs and replacements of serving councillors were to be the remit of Alexander himself and his council, and the fact that (unlike 1251/52) Henry did not appoint his own nominees to the Scottish government. Later, in the reign of Edward I, the formal language of overlordship would become a consistent feature of transactions between the two kingdoms; in this agreement it was entirely absent. This interpretation of events is supported by the fact that Alexander and Henry shared the Wark meeting both with those who were to form the new council and with members of the outgoing council, which was represented by, at least, Walter Comyn earl of Menteith, William earl of Mar and Robert Ros.[5] This was a summit in which all of the interested parties participated, and in which the king of England's concerns were addressed, but at which he was required to acknowledge the right of the Scots to settle their own affairs.

The king of Scots' letter was place-dated from Roxburgh several days after the Wark meeting. He had retired there with his council, presumably to complete the business (leaving his queen at Wark to remain for a time with her mother, who was ill). The *Chronicle of Melrose* suggests that Henry also participated in the Roxburgh conference, having been invited to do so by Alexander.[6] Place-date

4 Duncan, *Kingship of the Scots*, p. 156.

5 *CDS*, i, no. 2003.

6 *Chron. Melrose*, Faustina B. IX, fo. 57v (trans. Anderson, *Early Sources*, pp. 582–83). See also *CDS*, i, no. 2012.

evidence, however, has Henry at Wark as late as 15 September, in Carham (barely two miles to the west, and about seven miles from Roxburgh castle) on 16th, and back in Wark by 20th, the day on which Alexander's letter was dated.[7] Both Wark and Carham are on the English side of the border, and there is no evidence which places Henry on the Scottish side. Then, as now, Wark castle was sometimes known as Carham, and it is therefore possible that these place-dates do not represent any travel at all on the part of Henry III. It is most likely that the Scots, following the initial conference at Wark, withdrew over the border to settle their affairs on home turf, and that Henry waited within his own kingdom for their response.

It is not possible to identify all those who had attended the meetings at Wark, but the letter which Alexander issued from Roxburgh asserted that the settlement he had made was as a result of consultation with 25 named bishops, abbots, earls and barons of his kingdom 'and many others'. Among the named individuals are members of both the outgoing and the incoming councils, as well as some who cannot be shown to have taken any significant part in either. The 25 were: the bishops of Glasgow, Dunkeld and Aberdeen, the bishop-elect of St Andrews, the abbots of Dunfermline, Kelso, Jedburgh and Newbattle, the earls of Fife, Dunbar, Carrick and Strathearn, Alexander Stewart, Robert Bruce, Alan Durward, Walter Murray, David Lindsay, William Brechin, Hugh Gifford, Roger Mowbray, Gilbert Hay, Robert Menzies, William Douglas, John Vaux and William Ramsay.

Other than the change of council, there is little indication of any serious harassment of members of the previous regime in Scotland. It is clear from the safe conducts which allowed them to travel to England that the earls of Buchan and Mar were still in Scotland at the end of the year, although by that time it seems that Alan Durward had already made moves against the earl of Mar, attempting to win possession of the earldom.[8] Evidently, there were personal and dynastic tensions within the Scottish community. However, that the outgoing magnate group still had access to the king is made quite clear by the letter which Alexander wrote to Henry III on 4 February 1257, in which he stated that some of those ousted nobles were, in the interests of the peace and tranquillity of the realm, 'incessantly petitioning him' (*nobis instanter supplicarunt*)

---

7 *CDS*, i, nos. 2009, 2010, 2011.

8 Safe conducts: *CDS*, i, no. 2035. In December 1255 Pope Alexander IV wrote to the bishop of Brechin and the dean of Dunkeld instructing them to enquire into Durward's claim to the earldom, which appeared to have been based upon forged letters; that the pope's letters were dated December, however, indicates that Durward's claim was made significantly earlier, probably before September. The case was still in progress as late as the spring of 1257 (*Vet. Mon.*, nos. 196, 197).

regarding the complaints against them.[9] Despite the insinuation of corruption noted in *Gesta Annalia*, there seem to have been none of the accusations of treason which characterised the previous change of council. The period during which the new council was in power was brief, however, and lack of evidence makes it difficult to draw firm conclusions about what happened to the ousted councillors during that period. There is fragmentary evidence for at least a few of them carrying on their personal business: at the end of January 1256, for example, Alexander Uviet witnessed (in company with several others who had been named as present at the Roxburgh discussions) a charter in favour of David Graham, who was another of the ousted men.[10]

At the lower level of government, there is little discernible change. What meagre evidence there is for the incumbents of the sheriffdoms presents no indication of a wholesale movement at the moments of governmental crisis. The sheriffdom of Perth, for instance, was held by William Lochore in May 1251. It had passed to David Lochore (not his son, but presumably a relative, and presumably also the man who was ousted from the council in 1255) by 1255, who seems to have retained it until the early 1260s. David appeared also as sheriff of Fife by March 1253 and accounted for it still in the 1264/65 fiscal year. Similarly, Aymer Maxwell, another figure excluded from the council in 1255, seems to have been sheriff of Roxburgh from *c.*1248 until an unknown date, perhaps as late as 1264; he also held the sheriffdom of Peebles in 1262, in addition to that of Dumfries by 1264. The sheriffdom of Selkirk was monopolised in father-to-son succession by the Synton family for almost the entire thirteenth century.[11] It seems that the change of council may have had little impact in the locality: the peasant in the field would have been more concerned with the effect of bad weather on his crops.[12]

An exception from the 1252–55 council, who remained a controversial figure, was Gamelin, the bishop-elect of St Andrews. Abel of Gullane, who had obtained the see after the disputed election of 1253/54, had enjoyed the fruits of his victory only briefly, dying just a few months thereafter, probably in August 1254. Gamelin had been elected in February 1255, although the ongoing tensions between the cathedral chapter and the canons of St Mary meant that the election was disputed at the curia. He was consecrated by the bishop of Glasgow, in St Andrews, in December 1255. By this time the royal

9 *RRS*, iv pt. 1, no. 24 (*CDS*, i, no. 2077).

10 Fraser, *Menteith*, ii, nos. 3 & 4.

11 For the incumbents of sheriffdoms, see Reid and Barrow, *Sheriffs*, and the sources cited therein.

12 *Chron. Lanercost*, pp. 64–65: s.a. 1256, 1257: severe weather in 1256 caused crop failure in 1257.

council of which he had been part had been removed, and so although his election and subsequent papal confirmation had received royal approval under the previous regime, by the time of his consecration he was a less than welcome choice. (It also has to be remembered, though, that he was one of those present at the Wark/Roxburgh meetings who were named as having advised on the rearrangement of the council.) His office of chancellor had been given to the bishop of Dunkeld, and royal envoys were sent to the curia in an attempt to have his election annulled (although they are said by Bower to have died there before achieving their goal). There were persistent attacks on Gamelin by agents of the crown, and it seems that both his episcopal and personal property were confiscated amid accusations of corruption. The case dragged on, and Gamelin spent most of the next 18 months in contention at the curia. It was not until July 1257 that the pope issued his decision. The goods which had been seized from Gamelin in Scotland, and the temporalities of his see, were to be restored to him, and he was to receive guarantees for his safety so that he could return to Scotland and answer the charges that had been brought against him. Sentences of excommunication which had been brought in relation to his treatment in Scotland were to be revoked. A papal nuncio was appointed to go to Scotland to oversee the proceedings, but the scheme was rendered obsolete by another change in the Scottish political situation in October 1257.[13] His absence from Scotland has been characterised as political exile.[14] This may indeed be the case: but there remains the question of why there is little evidence of such harassment of others who had been ousted from the council in 1255. Actual (or assumed) transgression on the part of Gamelin, or the ongoing dispute within the cathedral chapter and the canons of St Mary, would tend to explain his treatment more effectively than general factional strife. A letter of 16 December 1256 from Pope Alexander IV to Henry III commended Gamelin to the English king, and asserted that his lands and goods in Scotland

---

13 Watt and Murray, *Fasti*, p. 380; Watt, *Graduates*, p. 210, and sources cited. *Chron. Bower*, iii, pp. 396–97 seems pro-Gamelin ('This bishop ruled the church quite wisely as a beloved peacemaker'), whereas at v, pp. 316–19, he is less enthusiastic, effectively accusing Gamelin of buying his way to the bishopric and attempting to pass the debt off to the Scottish monasteries. (See note relating to this in *Chron. Bower*, v, p. 451, however.) The *Chronicle of Melrose*, however, always deeply critical of the Durward-led government, paints an unsalubrious picture: in 1256 'bishop Gamelin was outlawed by the king's counsellors; both because he refused to acquiesce in their abominable plans, and because he scorned to give a certain sum of money, as if for the purchase of his bishopric. And since Scotland cast him out, and England refused him passage, he followed neptune, and went to France; and boldly approached the Roman court, in opposition to his adversaries. After his departure, the king's councillors pillaged the goods of his bishopric, and consumed it at their pleasure.' (*Chron. Melrose*, Faustina B. IX, fo. 58r; trans. from Anderson, *Early Sources*, ii pp. 585–86.) See also Ferguson, *Papal Representatives*, pp. 102–03.

14 This is the viewpoint adopted by Watt (*Graduates*, p. 210).

had been unjustly despoiled.[15] Henry seems to have been unmoved, and when Gamelin arrived in England in January 1258 en route for Scotland, he was detained and brought before the king to offer assurances for his good behaviour in return for safe conduct to continue north.[16] By this time the Scottish government was once more in a state of uncertainty, which may have prompted Henry to delay Gamelin's return. He was still in England in March, despite the situation in Scotland apparently having turned in his favour several months earlier.[17] There is nothing to indicate that he remained out of favour with Alexander himself by the time he eventually returned to Scotland, presumably in the spring of 1258.

The contention that the settlement of September 1255 was a 'constitutional strait-jacket', and that Henry intended 'to control the government of Scotland for as long as he possibly could',[18] must be open to challenge, particularly since there is little evidence that Henry actually tried to exercise such control. In that context, it is noteworthy that it was in the period following the installation of the new council that the first *colloquium* (or parliament) of Alexander III's reign was held.[19] The change of government, in the light both of the evidence provided by its own formal documentation and of the other tangential evidence surrounding it, should instead be considered a collaboration in government on the part of the Scottish community. The supposed malefactors were not wholly discredited within Scotland; they were not excluded from the discussions which aimed at addressing Henry III's complaints; and they retained the ear of the king who, within 18 months, was taking their case to Henry III. The solution to the threat of English invasion in August/September 1255 was to effect change in the ruling counsel, but that change seems to have been at least partially on Scottish terms and reveals considerable input by the king himself. The significance of the seven-year period during which Henry would be looking over Alexander's shoulder has to be weighed against both the lack of any explicit claim to English overlordship and the English king's apparently genuine concern for the welfare of his daughter and son-in-law. The image of the

15 *Foedera*, i.i, p. 352.

16 *CDS*, i, nos. 2104, 2107, 2110, 2112. Note that Anderson (*Early Sources*, iii, p. 586 n.) misdates this. These letters are, as in *CDS*, from 1258.

17 *Chron. Melrose*, Faustina B. IX, fo. 59r, claims that he was recalled to Scotland in October 1257 (*ab exilio revocatur*).

18 Watt, 'Minority', p. 15.

19 13 January 1256; see *RPS*, 1256/1 (from NLS, Ms Adv.34.1.3a, f.52v). The editors of *RPS* have regarded the meeting at Roxburgh on 20 September 1255 as a *colloquium*, presumably because of the inclusion of such a broad cross-section of the community. This may be so, but, unlike the meeting in January 1256, it is not so named in any record. In either case, it is evidence of a new phase of the reign, in which the king's personal position is more prominent.

Scottish noble community cooperating with the crown in government is clearer than the traditional view of a divided, factionalised governing elite. As in 1251/52, it is wrong to characterise the events of September 1255 as a coup: there was a necessary reorganisation of the method of government, consequent upon the fact that Alexander had reached his fourteenth birthday. Chronicle accusations of cruelty, of the couple having been kept apart, reflect the truth only that 4 September 1255 was the first day on which they could, according to canon law, consummate their marriage.[20] The rôle being played in the settlement and then in government 'through common counsel' by Alexander himself, who until this point had been little more than a symbolic presence, is now crucial. September 1255, rather than 1257 or later, marks not the imposition of a 'strait-jacket', but the beginning of the emergence of Alexander III from minority into personal rule.

The new council was an experienced group: they had all been active in the Scottish governing community since the 1240s or earlier; many of them had held positions of authority in the later days of Alexander II's reign, or in the years immediately following it.[21] Between them they had previously held both justiciarships (Lindsay and Durward) and the chamberlainship (Menzies and the bishop of Dunkeld), and in the earls of Dunbar, Fife and Strathearn there was representation of the topmost level of Scottish lordly society. More than half of them had witnessed royal acts in the early stages of Alexander III's minority. There is nothing to indicate, as has generally been assumed, that Alan Durward was in any sense the leader of this regime; if a leader there was, other than the king himself, it would have been one of the earls. The group of 'friends' of Henry III who had been recommended to his envoys in early August formed the majority of the new council, but were not all named on it (Walter Stewart, John Crawford, Hugh Crawford and William Galbraith were absent); and five others whose loyalty had not previously been mentioned (Roger Mowbray, Gilbert Hay, William Douglas, John Vaux and William Ramsay) were included in this new administration. One individual who was certainly in the Scottish royal circle in the period 1255–57, but who appears in neither list, is Roger de Quincy, earl of Winchester and constable of Scotland.[22] Of the fifteen individuals named as being on the new council in 1255, only six actually appear as witnesses to royal acts in the period in which it was in power. That only three royal acts have survived from the period, however, prevents conclusions from being drawn about the activity or inactivity of individuals.

20 For further discussion of the significance of the fourteenth birthday, see below, pp. 246–48.

21 See the voluminous data available via *PoMS* for details.

22 He witnessed a royal act in June 1257: *RRS*, iv pt. 1, no. 25.

The composition of the third minority council did not repeat that of the first. The pattern of witnessing of royal acts continues to provide evidence against the assumption of a straightforward factional division of the community. No fewer than seven of those who were removed from the council in 1255 (the bishop of Glasgow, Walter earl of Menteith, Robert Ros, Thomas Randolph, Aymer Maxwell, David Lochore and Alexander earl of Buchan) had witnessed royal acts in both the 1249–51 and 1252–55 periods, and one more (John Balliol) had witnessed during the first period but not the second. Of the new councillors, two (Alexander Stewart and Walter Murray) had witnessed royal acts in the period 1252–55, when they are supposed to have been out of favour. Seven of the new councillors had conducted non-royal business (including witnessing documents for each other) with members (11 in all) of the outgoing council. The governing community, irrespective of who was in the king's inner circle at any given time, apparently continued to cooperate in the conduct of both their personal affairs and the business of the realm, a fact which accords with the documentary evidence of discussion and negotiation in August and September 1255.

Alexander and his new council began their work in late 1255, and a formal *colloquium* was held in the following January, at which some administrative and legal affairs outstanding from the previous year were addressed.[23] Presumably by this time new officers of state had been appointed: Richard bishop of Dunkeld became royal chancellor; Alan Durward reclaimed his former position as justiciar of Scotia; David Lindsay replaced the earl of Mar as chamberlain; and Walter Murray became justiciar of Lothian.[24] There was unrest: although the situation seems to have been stable enough by June 1256 for the king and queen to plan a social visit to the English court, the safe conduct which Henry extended to them made reference to the possibility that Alexander himself might be prevented from travelling 'by war in Scotland'. Alexander's brother-in-law, Prince Edward (later to become King Edward I), was sent to Scotland on royal business about the same time, perhaps to escort Margaret and Alexander south. The visit, to be hosted at Woodstock in mid August, was prepared for with the usual extravagance.[25] It has been suggested that Henry's reference to potential war in Scotland in June 1256 represented the 'English view' that civil war was imminent.[26] The actuality may have been different.

---

23 *RPS*, 1256/1 (from NLS, Ms Adv.34.1.3a, f. 52v); printed in *Dunfermline Reg.*, no. 85.

24 *Chron. Bower,* v, pp. 316–17; for Murray as justiciar, see *RRS*, iv pt. 1, no. 25.

25 *CDS*, i, nos. 2053, 2054, 2055, 2071, 2072. No Scottish sources seem to confirm that Alexander did travel to England: the fee 'which [Alexander] is wont to draw daily . . . for his expenses' when in England, however, was instructed to be paid to him (*CDS*, i, 2056).

26 Duncan, *Making of the Kingdom*, p. 569.

During the absence of the Scots king from his kingdom, the sheriffs of the northern counties of England were instructed to assist with all their power against Scottish rebels, under the instruction of John Maunsel, who had been sent north 'to arrange the king of Scotland's affairs, as befits his dignity and advantage'.[27] Exactly what was happening is unclear, but it seems that some of those ousted in 1255 were seeking to have themselves reinstated in the king's peace, if not back around the cabinet table. In February 1257 Alexander sent envoys to Henry; they were entrusted to discuss various matters with the English king, including apparently incessant (*instanter*) pleas by Buchan, Menteith, Mar, John Comyn (who was not among those specifically excluded from power in 1255) and others against the disfavour in which Alexander continued to hold them. Henry responded by dispatching the earl of Winchester to Scotland at the end of March, whose meetings with Alexander seem to have prompted a further high-powered embassy to Scotland in July 'in order to terminate the disputes stirred up (*subortis*) between A[lexander] K. of Scotland and certain of his magnates'. They were to attend a meeting of Alexander and his magnates at Stirling at the end of August 1257.[28] This meeting, obviously intended to comprise a wider selection of the political community than just the inner council, should probably be seen as another *colloquium*.

Alexander's mother, Marie de Coucy, reclaims her place on the stage of Scottish politics at this point. She may also have intended to be present at the *colloquium*, since in September 1256 she had been authorised to visit England, returning to France by late May 1257. There is no indication that she made that journey, which may have been delayed by her marriage to Jean de Brienne, and in June 1257 she and her husband were granted a fresh conduct to travel through England to Scotland, contingent on their swearing an oath to do no harm to Henry or his kingdom, or to Alexander and Margaret or their council. The permitted visit was short: they were to return by the end of September 1257.[29] If the purpose of the visit was for Marie to attend the council, it would demonstrate her continued influence within Scotland, which, it seems, was a matter of some unease for Henry.

His references to disputes between Alexander and his magnates, and to rebels, do imply that Henry believed there was strife within the Scottish governing community, though the tone of Alexander's February 1257 letter to him does not support the contention. Rather, it seems that the disfavoured nobles were attempting to rejoin the inner circle, a prospect more troubling to Henry

27 *CDS*, i, nos. 2058, 2062, 2063.
28 *RRS*, iv pt. 1, no. 24; *CDS*, i, nos. 2080, 2090.
29 *CDS*, i, nos. 2064, 2083, 2084.

than to Alexander. If there was tension in Scotland, it may have been exacerbated instead by external forces. The letter by which Alexander announced to Henry III the plans for his new council in September 1255 had included the provision that, although the miscreants who were expelled from the council were not to be readmitted to favour without first having made full atonement to both kings,

> if it should happen that the realm of Scotland is invaded or attacked by an alien prince, we shall be allowed to admit and invoke the magnates now removed from our council, and any others whatsoever, to come to our help.[30]

In the context, the 'foreign prince' can hardly have been Henry III, and no external threat of such magnitude could have been expected from any quarter other than Norway. The troublesome issue of the security of the western seaboard, under the shadow of which Alexander had taken the throne, was raising its head again. On 21 September 1255, the day following Alexander's rearrangement of his council, Henry III took under his protection Eógan of Argyll, whose apparently strengthening relationship with Hákon IV had led to Alexander II's fatal expedition in 1249. Henry promised, as 'principal adviser' to Alexander III, to amend any forfeiture or other penalty incurred by Eógan at the Scottish court. It was not Henry's sole involvement in the politics of the west. Just a few months later, in February 1256, he ordered that Áengus son of Domnall 'or other malefactors of the kingdom of Scotland' should not be harboured in Ireland, and in the following March Henry knighted Magnus the king of Man, and offered him protection 'so long as he is faithful', and ordered his bailies (and requested the king of Scotland) not to receive Harald son of Godred, Ivar and their accomplices, who slew Rognvald, late king of Man, Magnus's brother.[31] The tensions which had been afflicting the isles for years had flared up again, causing insecurity at the centre of Scottish government. An interesting feature of the submission of Eógan is that the guarantors for the payment of his feudal dues for his restored lands were the earls of Mar, Fife and Strathearn, three of the most prominent figures

30 *RRS*, iv pt. 1, no. 19 (trans., *RPS*, A1255/1).

31 *CDS*, i, nos. 2014, 2017, 2041, 2046. For the back-history of the situation in the isles, see Norman H. Reid, 'The Political Context of the Treaty of Perth', in Alan MacNiven (ed.), *The Treaty of Perth* (forthcoming); Oram, *Alexander II*, pp. 175–91; McDonald, *Kingdom of the Isles*, esp. ch. 3; Cowan, 'Norwegian Sunset – Scottish Dawn'; Noel Murray, 'Swerving from the Path of Justice: Alexander II's Relations with Argyll and the Western Isles, 1214–1249', in Oram, *Alexander II Essays*, pp. 285–305. See also below, pp. 166–70.

in the ruling aristocracy of Scotland, who together represented both sides of the supposed factional divide.[32] One reason for the incessant pressure on Alexander III by the ousted councillors could well have been the threat of war in the west which they, in common with Henry III and others in the Scottish community, perceived as imminent.

Henry's high-level embassy to Scotland in the summer of 1257 may have had more business to transact than settling what he viewed as discord between Alexander and elements of the Scottish nobility. It was a group which blended high-status nobility with dependable administrators and legal officials: John Maunsel the provost of Beverley, Roger de Quincy earl of Winchester, Gilbert Preston, William Latimer, as well as the archbishop of York, the bishop of Durham and the prior of Durham. John Maunsel was a trusted royal clerk and a judge (also, for a time, royal chancellor), and was a regular actor in Henry's Scottish affairs. Quincy, hereditary constable of Scotland, was a figure of consequence, with long-standing experience of Scottish politics. Although his primary interests were in England, he was a major landholder in Scotland through his first wife, Helen, the daughter of Alan of Galloway, and had played an important part in Alexander II's gaining and retaining control of Galloway. He was well connected in Scotland, his daughter Elizabeth having married Alexander Comyn, earl of Buchan, giving him close family ties to at least two (Buchan and Menteith were half-brothers) of the most prominent of the ousted magnates.[33] Gilbert Preston was a royal justice, and William Latimer was the sheriff of York, who was to be regularly involved in Henry's business in Scotland in the following years.

Previously, Henry's envoys to the Scottish court had been primarily noble. The inclusion on this occasion of high-ranking ecclesiastics gives this embassy a different complexion, prompting the supposition that part of its remit was ecclesiastical. Henry's ambassadors may have been intent on pressurising the Scottish king and clergy into raising funds to support an English crusade. For that purpose, in May 1254, Pope Innocent IV had commanded his chaplain in Scotland, Master John de Frussinon, to levy one-twentieth of Scottish church

---

32 Duncan, *Making of the Kingdom*, p. 581 n.31, citing *APS*, i, p.115. I have favoured Duncan's suggested date of 1255 for this obligation, but even if the alternative later date of 1264/65 is accepted, it remains significant that Eógan was able to call upon these three individuals, at the very centre of Scottish political life, to stand surety for him. For an alternative view of Eógan's loyalties in this period, see McDonald, *Kingdom of the Isles*, pp. 105 and 117–18.

33 For the family tree of the Comyns, see Young, *Robert the Bruce's Rivals*, pp. x, xi. The family relationships of the Comyns are not without either complexity or significance: two of Buchan's sisters, Idonea and Elizabeth, were married respectively to Gilbert Hay (on the new royal council) and William earl of Mar (another of the ousted lords): personal and family interests transcended political rivalry.

income for a period of three years.[34] Payment, typically, having been resisted, the period during which this subvention could be raised was extended by Pope Alexander IV in the following year, and in February 1256 Henry declared that it should not set a precedent which was to the prejudice of the king of Scots or his heirs.[35] The long-standing issues of Scottish revenues being used to support English causes, of the disputed nature of the relationship between the Scottish church and the archdiocese of York, as well as the fracas surrounding the elevation of Gamelin to the see of St Andrews and the continuing dispute between Alan Durward and the earl of Mar were all under discussion at the papal curia between 1255 and 1257, and the pope would have been subject to persistent pressure from Scottish envoys. As a result, in September 1256 the pope partially remitted the subvention on condition that the Scottish church would provide 'liberal aid' in support of the pope's own war against the Hohenstaufen rule of Sicily.[36] But this project too was in English interests, since Henry had been offered the kingdom of Sicily for his son Edmund in return for assistance, leading to an escapade which became one of the reasons for the deterioration of the relationship between Henry III and his barons. Well aware of the sensitivities of the situation, the pope instructed his envoy in England responsible for the collection of the taxation, Master Rostand, to 'keep silence as to any privileges or indulgences to the Scottish Church, or the question of its independence'.[37] In October 1257 the pope issued a letter confirming the rights and privileges of Alexander III in ecclesiastical affairs, as had been held by his predecessors.[38] It was important that Master Rostand should keep silent, because the question of whether Scottish crusading levies should be diverted to other causes remained a festering sore. The use of such monies was a matter of both personal concern and national pride. Crusade was not a distant possibility, but a constant reality: one of those who set out on crusade around 1250, along with five knights and three of his cousins, was Richard, the brother of the Hugh Gifford who was a member of the new royal council of 1255.[39]

---

34 *Foedera*, i.i, p. 303. Frussinon also had the similarly unhappy task of collecting in Ireland, where he seems to have been more active, and where he is described as a canon of Dublin. (See various references in *Calendar of Documents Relating to Ireland*, ii; and William E. Lunt, *Financial Relations of the Papacy with England to 1327* (Cambridge, MA, 1939), pp. 284, 61.)

35 *Foedera*, i.i, p. 322; *CDS*, i, no. 2040. *Close Rolls, 1254–1256*, pp. 8–9, might also be taken as an indication that Frussinon had not so far been particularly successful in collecting the money in either Ireland or Scotland.

36 For further details of the Sicilian issue, see Powicke, *The Thirteenth Century*, pp. 120–28.

37 *CDS*, i, nos. 2065, 2066. See also Ferguson, *Papal Representatives*, pp. 100–03.

38 *Vet. Mon.*, no. 204.There is no evidence either to support or cast doubt on Watt's assertion ('Minority', p. 16) that it was Durward's proctor at the curia who achieved this papal concession.

39 *Vet. Mon.*, no. 142. For further information on the crusading effort in Scotland, and the controversies over crusading taxes in this period, see Macquarrie, *Crusades*, ch. 3.

Things were changing in Scotland. In mid August 1257 John Balliol had been pardoned by Henry III for his offences (*molestia*) against Alexander and Margaret, and within a month he was on his way back to Scotland.[40] There is no record, either Scottish or English, of the *colloquium* which was supposed to have been held in August. It may have been delayed or overtaken by events. The *Chronicle of Melrose* and *Gesta Annalia* both emphasise the importance of the Gamelin affair, and *Gesta Annalia* offers the further detail that strife within Scotland was caused by fruitless attempts to bring the previous councillors to justice for their misdemeanours. Both are agreed that the situation was brought to a head when a group of the disaffected lords, led by Walter Comyn, earl of Menteith, seized the king at Kinross and once again took power. According to *Gesta Annalia*, which dates the event to 29 October 1257, the lords took possession of the person of the king and of the great seal, thus indicating that they sought control of government. The strongly pro-Comyn *Chronicle of Melrose* puts a different spin on the affair, claiming that the king was 'restored to his kingdom' through his rescue from the hands of unrighteous men. Matthew Paris's *Chronica Majora* is perhaps responsible for the long-standing historiographical characterisation of the minority as strife between pro- and anti-English parties, since it portrays this event as being born out of frustration at misrule by Alexander III, who promoted foreigners within the kingdom to the prejudice of native people. Paris relates that the king was restrained and separated from the queen, who was blamed for bringing Henry III upon Scotland as an oppressor. Ejecting foreigners from the country, the rebellious lords thus 'held the reins of their kingdom with greater freedom and safety'.[41] It would be a mistake, however, to rely too heavily on the frequently xenophobic Matthew Paris as the sole witness to such events.

Remarkably, despite the fact that Roger de Quincy was still in Scotland at the end of the year,[42] and had presumably informed him of the situation, Henry does not seem to have reacted until mid January, when he instructed the raising of an army for an expedition to Scotland in order to rescue Alexander, since

> certain rebels have secretly taken away the K. of Scotland from the custody of the Council set over him till his lawful age, and detain him against his will, to the manifest scandal and disgrace of both kings.[43]

---

40 *CDS*, i, nos. 2091, 2092, 2094. His safe conduct was not issued until 13 September. If the *colloquium* was delayed (see below, p. 133), it might still have been possible for Balliol to attend it.

41 *Chron. Fordun*, i, pp. 297–98 (trans. ii, p. 293); *Chron. Bower*, v, pp. 318–21; *SAEC*, p. 376

42 *CDS*, i, no. 2098.

43 *CDS*, i, no. 2013.

Only a couple of weeks earlier, the first hint that Henry was aware of anything wrong in Scotland was the instruction to give over the castle and manor of Bolsover in Derbyshire to Alan Durward (instead of the annual fee which he had earlier been granted) 'to sustain himself during the king's pleasure'.[44] It has generally been assumed that Durward had been forced into exile, although there is no evidence of a widespread expulsion from Scotland. Frustration with external interference did have the potential to boil over into rebellion. Against the background of Henry's undoubted involvement in the 1255 rearrangement of Alexander's council, the appearance of an embassy which was obviously intended to influence the results of a planned *colloquium* might (particularly given the inclusion of the archbishop of York) have seemed to threaten the independence of political action, of both the Scottish church and state. It is curious that there are no surviving reports to Henry of the embassy's progress in settling Scottish affairs, and it could be conjectured that the *colloquium* did not take place precisely because of the inhibiting presence of the English embassy. Might the appearance in Scotland of Marie de Coucy also have heightened these tensions, introducing a French element to the picture which further complicated the situation? Although her return through England had been authorised only until September, there is no indication in the English records that she and her husband had travelled back to France. He seems to have left before the end of 1257, but it is likely that Marie herself remained. There is no indication of a general exclusion of English interests from the ruling group in Scotland: most of those involved at the top level in Scotland had their own personal interests south of the border. The ousted lords, who had been attempting to regain royal favour, perhaps partly because of perceived external threats to the kingdom, may have reached breaking point as they attempted to force their way back into the ruling circle. Their move may not have been discouraged by Alexander, who saw in it an opportunity to exert his own authority over the situation, and to shake off the remaining elements of control by his father-in-law.

Henry's army remained in England. Both his response and any requests which may have been made from within Scotland for his assistance lacked urgency, suggesting that the events of October 1257 were less dramatic than either *Gesta Annalia* or the *Chronicle of Melrose* claim. The further change in the controlling group at the Scottish court posed no danger to the king or queen, or even to the authority of government. It seems quite possible that Alexander was complicit in the realignment of the council in October 1257, and that rather than being a violent attempt by the Comyn family to oust the ruling regime, the change should in fact be seen as a signal of Alexander exerting his

44 *CDS*, i, no. 2099.

own pressure on the Scottish community to achieve a more consensual style of government. Given that Durward was not granted custody of Bolsover until January, it does not seem either that he left Scotland with undue haste after 29 October or that his situation was regarded as desperate. At the beginning of April 1258 he was still seeking 'safe retreat' near the border, along with Walter Murray and perhaps David Lindsay (who was paid a fee, but not specifically noted as requiring a safe haven), potentially in anticipation of joining an English expedition to Scotland.[45] By this time, it seems that the personal crisis for the king and queen, if crisis it had been, had come to an end: by early May, Henry was able to instruct the earl of Strathearn to attend the queen of Scots. Over a month earlier, Alexander had been free to send his envoys to the English court, informing Henry of a forthcoming *colloquium* which he intended to hold at Stirling in mid April, and to which he requested that Henry should send representatives. Henry's response was that the notice was short, and that the inaccessibility of Stirling, as well as a meeting of his own parliament, restricted who could be sent; but he would direct Roger de Quincy, John Balliol and the abbot of Burgh to attend, and he requested Alexander to alter the day and the location (to a place south of the Forth) for their convenience. At the same time, Henry instructed a further muster of arms in the north of England, under Robert Neville and William Latimer, so that they could assist in the event of war breaking out in Scotland, defending the king against 'certain magnates of Scotland, [who] have long been hostile to the K., and to the K. and Queen of Scotland and the K.'s friends there, and even yet are contriving their injury'. Should the hostile magnates gain the ascendancy, a further meeting with the king's friends was to take place at Roxburgh after Easter.[46] The English records contain several other references to 'war and disturbance' in Scotland in March and early April 1258,[47] but nonetheless it is clear that by now Alexander was not in the clutches of a subversive regime, and that the situation was well enough under control to allow him to plan a *colloquium* to begin the settlement of his own affairs.

Part of Henry III's apparent lassitude in dealing with the situation in Scotland may have been caused by preoccupation with other affairs. Growing unrest in Wales, and the increasing power of the challenger to English domination there, Llywelyn ap Gruffyd, who by March 1258 was daring and successful enough to challenge the future Edward I directly by styling himself 'Prince of Wales', was sufficient to make the Scottish issue a distinct inconvenience to Henry. Also, at least in part the result of Henry's actions in support of papal policy in Sicily,

45 *CDS*, i, nos. 2120, 2121.
46 *CDS*, i, nos. 2113, 2114.
47 *CDS*, i, nos. 2116–18.

the baronial reform movement had been gaining strength in England, and the years 1258–60 were to be crisis-ridden as Henry fought his own battles over who should, or should not, be in the inner circle of English royal advisors. Demands for reform of the process of government led to his acceptance, at the end of April 1258, of the 'Provisions of Oxford', by which Henry's absolutist tendencies were limited by an imposed baronial council and regular parliaments. The seeds of civil war had been sown.[48]

As Henry's attention was diverted, a new approach to government emerged in Scotland. The envoys sent by Alexander to Henry in March 1258 signal the transformation. William Hay was the brother of Gilbert Hay, who had been a member of the council appointed in 1255, and an associate of other members of that council in the ongoing dispute with the diocese of St Andrews over dispossession of lands during the Gamelin controversy.[49] In contrast, Nicholas Prenderleith, abbot of Jedburgh, was one of the clerics who pronounced sentences of excommunication over that very council due to its persecution of Gamelin. Prenderleith seems to have feared reprisal for his actions, since in December 1255 he had sought special protection from Henry III.[50] These envoys carried news to the English court of a *colloquium* to be held for the resolution of political dispute. By assigning this task to political opponents, Alexander astutely imbued the embassy with an unmistakeable symbolism. Alexander may have been merely a 'fox cub' (a description said to have been given his father by King John, which implies not only youth but also guile[51]), but as he outgrew his minority he clearly understood that the Scots kings were 'obliged to rule by consultation'.[52] Alexander's achievement in 1257 was not release from warring Scottish factions, but release from Henry III's influence over Scottish government. Henry had participated in the installation of Alexander's council in 1255, designed to remain in place until Alexander's twenty-first birthday. When Henry turned his attention to Scotland again, it is likely that his aim was the reinstallation of that council. After April 1258, when he was severely limited in his actions by the English baronial council, English policy remained unaltered, despite reduced involvement in Scottish affairs. The group now around Alexander were automatically rebels in Henry's eyes.

---

48 There is a useful summary of the situation in England in Powicke, *The Thirteenth Century*, ch. 4; for a more detailed and fresh interpretation of the period in England, see Adrian Jobson (ed.), *Baronial Reform and Revolution in England, 1258–1267* (Woodbridge, 2016). It is not irrelevant that Roger de Quincy, so regular a participant in Anglo-Scottish affairs in this period, was a leading figure in the baronial council installed under the Provisions of Oxford.

49 *PoMS*; also Ferguson, *Papal Representatives*, App. IV, no. 13.

50 *CDS*, i, no. 2036.

51 See Oram, *Alexander II*, p. 37 & n.

52 Oram, Alexander II, p. 27 & n., quoting K.J. Stringer.

Probably just after Alexander wrote to Henry with his plans for the April 1258 *colloquium*, a group of Scots lords joined with Llywelyn ap Gruffyd, Prince of Wales and his followers in 'a bond of mutual alliance and friendship', the primary aim of which was to assist the Welsh in resisting armed action against them by Henry III.[53] The Scots signatories undertook, should Alexander compel them to make peace with Henry, to attempt to persuade him and their adversaries in Scotland to adopt their own position in support of the Welsh prince; further, they agreed that merchants of both Wales and Scotland would be welcome in each other's country. They swore to uphold the agreement 'saving their allegiance to the King of Scots' (*in fide praedicti domini Regis Scotiae*). The agreement, made in the form of a chirograph,[54] has no place-date. It is likely that the initiative had been on the Welsh side, seeking alliance against the English invasion which they expected during the following summer, and which, depending on Alexander's relationship with Henry III, might involve active participation by Scottish nobles. (Only a few days later, on 28 March, William Ros and the earl of Strathearn were indeed among those ordered by Henry III to provide forces for an expedition against Llywelyn.[55]) The agreement with the Welsh is an event for which there seems to be no easy explanation; although there were familial relationships between Wales and Scotland,[56] there was no clear precedent for such apparent unity of political purpose between Welsh and Scottish lords. It undoubtedly ran the risk of seriously antagonising Henry III, Alexander III or both, and yet it seems to have aroused no retaliatory action on the part of either.

It is particularly intriguing that among the signatories to the agreement, made as it was without the authority of king or council, were three individuals who were office-holders in the Scottish government: the earl of Buchan was justiciar of Scotia, John Comyn of Badenoch (the nephew of the earl of Buchan) was justiciar of Galloway, and Aymer Maxwell was chamberlain. The other 16

---

53 *CDS*, i, no. 2155 (full text in *Foedera*, i.i, p. 370). This is misdated to 18 March 1259 in *CDS*: but by this time the principal Scottish signatory, Walter Comyn earl of Menteith was dead, and, as Duncan points out (*Making of the Kingdom*, p. 571 n.), by March 1259 the political context would have made such a treaty nonsensical. Henry III replied to Alexander's letter on 25 March 1258 (*CDS*, i, no. 2114), which must therefore have been written a week or two previously.

54 Chirograph: a document produced in two copies from a single piece of parchment, which could be matched up with each other to ensure authenticity. The Scots sealed the copy retained by the Welsh, and *vice versa*.

55 Strathearn's instruction was later rescinded: he was instructed instead to remain at the Scottish court, in attendance on the queen. *CDS*, i, nos. 2115, 2125; See also Duncan, *Making of the Kingdom*, p. 573.

56 For example, Llywelyn ap Gruffyd himself was a nephew of the earl of Fife, who had married Llywelyn's father's sister.

were the earls of Menteith, Mar and Ross, John Comyn of Badenoch's two younger brothers William and Richard, Freskin Murray, Hugh Abernethy, William Mowat, Hugh and Walter Barclay, Bernard Mowat, Reginald Cheyne, David Lochore, John Denmuir, William of Airth and Hector of Carrick. Of these, over half were related to the extended Comyn family in some way or had been members of the Comyn-led government of 1252–55. Of the rest, the Barclays may have been within the Comyn fold, given that Hugh was named in *Gesta Annalia* as one of the Kinross conspirators;[57] it is not possible to be clear about the political allegiance of Freskin Murray (who may have been related to Walter Murray, of the 1255–57 council), Hugh Abernethy, the Mowats, Reginald Cheyne (who was related to Murray by marriage), William of Airth or Hector of Carrick (who was a knight in the service of Níall, earl of Carrick (d.1256), an opponent of the Comyns, but who had been one of the advisors in the 1255 change of council). It has generally been assumed that all of the signatories must necessarily have been pro-Comyn but, given that in the aftermath of Kinross there were already efforts afoot to achieve consensus in the community, the assumption is invalid.

It is quite clear, however, that this was not a group of disaffected lords – three being in the inner circle of royal authority, and many of the others being identifiably associated with the party which was regarded by the English king as having 'rebelliously' taken hold of Alexander at Kinross. But neither was it a group which had assumed control of the government: their acknowledgement that the king's will was paramount is revealing of a new balance of power within Scotland. Alexander's own reaction to the current circumstances, in which it was possible that Scotland would suffer further military intervention from Henry III, was as yet unknown, but was crucial. It seems inconceivable that Alexander was unaware of the bond; that no retribution was exacted upon the signatories, however, may suggest that he was sympathetic, but could not support it as a matter of policy in view of the currently delicate diplomatic relationship with his father-in-law. Ultimately without long-term political effect, the curious affair of the 'bond of mutual alliance and friendship' nonetheless highlights an important phase in the drawing to a close of the minority of Alexander III.

In early May Alexander sent Henry envoys (Thomas Normanville, who was one of those removed from the council in September 1255 and Adam Malcarston, provost of the church of St Mary in St Andrews) to relate progress to Henry. Malcarston does not seem to have been involved in government in any official or administrative capacity before, but he has been ascribed Comyn sympathies.[58]

57 *Chron. Fordun*, i, p. 298 (trans. ii, p.293).
58 Watt, *Graduates*, pp. 370–73.

If correct, Alexander's choice of envoys, even after it is clear that he was no longer personally controlled by either of the magnatial groupings, is again worthy of note. The *colloquium* was now planned for early June in Edinburgh. Henry responded by requesting that it be prorogued until September, at a venue nearer the border and, in an uncharacteristically irresolute tone, he asked Alexander what he thought should be done, apparently uncertain that Alexander would comply with his request. He also instructed William Latimer and Robert Neville, the sheriff of Northumberland, to send a trustworthy messenger to Alexander to carry Henry's letter and receive the reply. He bade them attend the Scottish *colloquium* themselves, and if necessary support Henry's friends, should Alexander decline the requested delay. Henry evidently retained a genuine concern for the welfare of his daughter: as well as the earl of Strathearn, Latimer and Neville were again exhorted to visit her regularly and to ensure that she had 'necessary solace and succour'. Their continuing rôle as Henry's agents in Scotland was not purely political.[59]

If it took place, Alexander's June *colloquium* has left no record. More active negotiation seems to have been expected later in the summer of 1258, however, since in early August the English government, in Henry's name, gave power to Simon de Montfort, earl of Leicester (leader of the baronial movement against him), Peter of Savoy and John Maunsel to participate in talks aimed at achieving 'peace between the disturbers of the kingdom of Scotland'. Henry, or his advisors, appear to have assumed that their influence would be more profound than Alexander would allow, while expecting that a settlement of the political difficulties would involve the imposition of victory by one group over the other. Henry's letter of 27 August to Alexander resonated with mixed irritation and confusion: he was amazed (*miramur*) at what he had been told by Alexander's envoys (Matthew, abbot of Dunfermline, appointed only in 1256, who had not previously appeared in royal service, and William Hay, who had been similarly used in the previous March); and would reply only when he had heard the reports from his own three agents and taken advice of his council.[60] Henry's request for further delay had clearly been denied, and he had received unwelcome news of the proceedings of a *colloquium* (presumably in early–mid August, but before Henry's embassy was in attendance) at which Alexander had begun the process of building consensus within the governing community under his own authority, finally abandoning the 1255 agreement to which Henry craved adherence.

Confused chronology in the *Chronicle of Melrose* places Alexander at Melrose in March 1258 with armed forces ready to quell opposition from the ousted

59 *CDS*, i, nos. 2126 (but see correction, *CDS*, v, p. 32), 2127, 2128.
60 *CDS*, i, no. 2133.

Durward and his friends, and a failed attempt at reconciliation. It depicts Durward reneging on a promise of a further meeting at Forfar, returning instead to England to await support.[61] Although Alexander was at Melrose later in the year, the chronology offered by the chronicler may be intended primarily to discredit Durward and his supporters. A *colloquium* of some sort was apparently held in July or August without Henry's participation, but further meetings were then held at Roxburgh in September, in the presence of Henry's envoys, the earl of Hereford, the earl of Albemarle and the recently restored John Balliol. The Melrose chronicler, ever suspicious, unconvincingly claims that the English intention was not actually to negotiate, but to capture Alexander; but, overawed by the force the Scottish king brought with him (which, incidentally, despoiled the surrounding area), the English negotiated for three weeks, accepted what Alexander proposed and left to report back to their king. By 16 October, the deal completed, Alexander was in Perth.[62]

It was not until 6 November (which, perhaps coincidentally, was the same day that Robert Ros received some respite from his post-1255 persecution) that Henry acknowledged the fact that there was a new royal council in Scotland. His influence in creating it had been minimal, and it is clear that it did not represent the type of solution which he had intended. Henry, however, was powerless: he had no option except to confirm his acceptance of it. He tried to extract promises from the new council that they would rule effectively – 'to do equal justice between rich and poor, and to promote love and unity between their K. and his Queen' – and answer to him for any delinquency. To that end he sent Robert Neville and William Horton, a St Albans monk, to Scotland to obtain these signed undertakings, but there is no trace of such documents (which Henry had instructed to be formally registered), and it thus seems certain that the provision of such undertakings was declined.[63]

The new council was a group which fascinatingly demonstrates that heads had been hit together, and political opponents forced to cooperate for the greater good. Gamelin, the earls of Menteith, Buchan and Mar, Alexander Stewart, Alan Durward, Robert Menzies and Gilbert Hay were named alongside the queen mother herself and her husband, Jean de Brienne. The latter, however, can be shown to have been absent: he seems to have left Scotland by the end of 1257 (perhaps earlier, under the terms of his safe conduct), and was in Castile by February 1258 and at the French court by February 1259. There is no evidence that he visited Scotland again, and it is possible that his name was included as

61 *Chron. Melrose*, Faustina B. IX, fo. 59r.
62 Chron. Melrose, Faustina B. IX, fo. 59r–v; *RRS*, iv pt. 1, no. 26.
63 Stones, *Anglo-Scottish Relations*, pp. 70–75; *CDS*, i, no. 2140.

a formality, given his recent marriage to Marie and his consequent status in relation to her child, the king of Scots.[64] The question of whether Marie was herself in Scotland at this time, or whether her name also was included for the sake of form, is apparently unanswerable. It is unlikely that they would have been included in the settlement had neither she nor her husband been present, and the balance of probability must lie in the direction of her having remained in Scotland. If so, then it is quite possible – but unprovable – that her own influence was significant in achieving the 1258 agreement.

Although the formality of a minority continued in, for example, the use of a minority seal, it is clear that from this point Alexander was in personal control and that the overt influence of Henry III in regulation of the Scottish government had come to an end. Immediately after the new council was installed, two giants of the political scene departed: the deaths in November, within a fortnight of each other, of Walter Comyn, earl of Menteith, and William Bondington, bishop of Glasgow, are recorded side by side in the *Chronicle of Melrose*.[65] The tectonic plates of the Scottish political landscape were shifting.

How, then, is Alexander III's minority to be summarised and characterised? It is easy to see how the legend of a straightforward factional divide between the two 'parties' of Comyn and Durward arose. Equally, it is understandable that those parties could be labelled pro- and anti-English, although a weakness in this argument is that historians have contested which is which. The suggestion is probably correct that if there were 'parties' in the period 1249–58, they were pro- and anti-Comyn, rather than pro- or anti-English.[66] The overemphasis of factional conflict is based primarily on the variously partisan views of very meagre sources: *Gesta Annalia* favours the Durward side; the *Chronicle of Melrose* favours the Comyns; the documentary evidence is almost entirely from the English royal archives. There are thus inconsistencies and difficulties with the traditional view of the minority. Interplay between the two groups in the Scottish governing community was regular, both within government and in

64 Watt, 'Minority', p. 19 & n.

65 *Chron. Melrose*, Faustina B. IX, fo. 59v. Bondington: 10 November; buried in Melrose abbey on 13th; Menteith: Melrose does not give the date of his death, but he was alive on 6 November, as we have seen, and was dead by 25th (see *SAEC* p. 376 and n.). It should be noted that the version of Henry III's undertaking to support the new council, and its accompanying schedule, printed by Stones in *Anglo-Scottish Relations* and calendared by Bain (*CDS*, i, no. 2140) omits Menteith's name from the list of councillors, and must therefore have been amended when it was engrossed in the Close Rolls subsequent to his death. The earlier version carried the same date, 6 November, but its text, from the Patent Rolls (TNA, C66/73, m.15), which is calendared in *CDS*, i, no. 2139, and printed in *Foedera*, i.i, p. 378, includes Menteith's name.

66 Young, *Robert the Bruce's Rivals*, p. 61.

personal and business affairs. It is unjustifiable to assume, for instance, that support for (or antagonism towards) the election of Gamelin to the bishopric of St Andrews ran entirely along factional lines, or that all who signed the treaty with Llywelyn were unquestionably aligned with the Comyns. If it is accepted that the foremost motivation for either group was self-interest, then Alexander himself is reduced to little more than a pawn in a game dominated by more powerful players, and it becomes inevitable that the period is characterised as a struggle between those players and the (either benevolent or malevolent) attempts of Henry III to control the situation. The truth is obscured by an unhelpful rhetoric of overmighty subjects and a kingdom which, lacking leadership, descends into anarchy. That there was division within the Scottish community is indisputable; that there was one relatively consistent group largely (but not entirely) composed of senior members of the Comyn family is similarly beyond doubt; that there was an equally consistent opposition led by Alan Durward, however, is very doubtful. There is really no evidence to suggest (particularly after 1252) that the anti-Comyn group coalesced around the figure of Alan Durward. He does appear regularly in the record, was involved in political life and, in his attempt to break into the first rank of Scottish nobility, found himself at odds with the foremost noble family of the kingdom, the Comyns. Rivalry with the Comyns also brought about conflict with the broad network of support they had achieved through marriage alliance and landed interest. Other than his holding of the important justiciarship of Scotia, though, there is little evidence of Durward's actual participation in, let alone leadership of, government. The assumption of his prominence is probably based on the reported dispute over the knighting of the young king at the outset of the reign, but it is not borne out by regular attendance at court, as evidenced by the witnessing of royal acts. It should not be taken for granted, either, that the Comyn following was consistent or coherent. In reality, personal allegiances were fluid, based upon family, business and other interests which might change or conflict. Political activity, however, rested upon a more serious and fundamental responsibility which at times transcended these other bonds or rivalries.

If the minority period is viewed without the rigid underlying assumption of dynastic factionalism, a different picture emerges. There is a powerful case to be made for the unwavering support for royal government on the part of the Comyns during and after the minority.[67] The same can be said of those who are considered to have opposed them. The first minority government represented, above all, continuity with the government of Alexander II, in both

67 Young, *Robert the Bruce's Rivals*, chs 3 and 4, *passim.*

personnel and policy terms. Its pursuit of national goals, such as the rites of coronation and unction, the translation of St Margaret's relics and the marriage of the king, displayed a dedication to task which demonstrated genuine concern for good governance. With the fall of that government in early 1252, there is little evidence of persecution of the previous incumbents of office, and they were received back into Henry III's peace remarkably quickly. There is overlap in terms of witnessing of documents, both personal and royal, between the two apparently opposing governmental groups. General policy seems not to have altered, and judicial and administrative activity continued. The key shifts were the departure of Marie de Coucy and the increasing influence of Henry III, whose rôle in the change of government may have been intended primarily to engineer the insertion into the Scottish council of his own nominees.

It is unclear what caused the downfall of the longest-lasting administration of the minority, which led without apparent disruption between early 1252 and late 1255. Vague accusations of corruption (similar to those alleged against the previous administration) in the handling of royal and ecclesiastical property and revenues were inevitable propaganda, and there is no evidence of general dissension during this period. The specific allegations of maltreatment of the king and queen may be more substantial, especially given Henry III's treatment of those whom he had entrusted personally with oversight of the situation. However, again, there is an aura of propaganda about this, and the fact that Alexander seems, as little as two years later, to have borne no obvious ill-will towards those accused of the abuse, tends to affirm the impression that the Comyn-led government of 1252–55 was no less concerned for the welfare of the king and queen, or the effective rule of the kingdom, than was its predecessor.

The renewal of the council in 1255 was assuredly more organised than had been the case in January 1252, perhaps due both to the increasing rôle of Alexander himself, and to his developing relationship with Henry III. It is generally thought that the precise record-keeping of the events of 1255 was attributable to Henry III's involvement, but that assumption is unwarranted. More convincing, in light of the narrative offered here, is that Alexander himself demanded involvement in the decisions made and required the formal agreement of the various parties. From the autumn of 1255 it is possible to detect Alexander's imposition of personal control, and the beginning of his emergence from minority. The contrasting lists of those who advised on the change of council, those who were removed from the council and those who joined it, and the fact, again, that there is little evidence of persecution of the outgoing councillors (apart from Gamelin, whose situation, in the context of the disputed election to the most crucial ecclesiastical appointment in the kingdom, is in any case out of the ordinary), points to a Scottish community, despite conflict and dynastically based rivalries, acting in cooperative action to safeguard the rule of the kingdom.

In relation to the realignment of the council in the autumn of 1257, the story of the capture of the king and queen at Kinross has to be viewed sceptically. The chronicle tales, although taking typically divergent stances regarding the merits and demerits of the parties concerned, are generally consistent in relating that the couple were removed by one group from the control of the other: this much cannot be doubted. However, the unreliable notion that they had to be taken clandestinely implies an element of captivity, an unlikely scenario, given that such accusations were apparently one of the major causes of the removal of the previous council. That Henry (who had agents in Scotland, and so cannot possibly have been unaware of events) took so long to react implies that there was no sense of immediate or inherent danger; that Alexander himself seems to have been perfectly prepared to work subsequently with members of both groups demonstrates an element of respect on his part, and at least compliance, if not in fact initiative. It is perfectly feasible that the events of October 1257 were designed, with Alexander's collusion, to reduce the impact of Henry III's influence over the Scottish government, taking advantage of the fact that he was distracted by increasing opposition in England and Wales. That *colloquia* apparently became a regular tool of the Scottish administration only from 1255 further demonstrates Alexander's personal involvement in the government of his kingdom, the changes of 1257 being at his own behest. This impression is strengthened by the fact that Alexander's envoys to Henry III during 1258 seem to have been men of both (and neither) political allegiances, and that those who assumed the offices of state in 1257 continued in them after the settlement of 1258. If the events of 1255 can be seen as an early sign of Alexander's assumption of personal control, then those of 1257 demonstrate a far greater degree of authority on his part. The formal symbolism of minority continued, but by 1258 Alexander himself was in undisputed control of his kingdom. It would certainly be unsupportable to suggest that the rivalries which had suffused the minority years suddenly came to an end when Alexander forced consensus on the Comyns and those who opposed them. If there was consensus, it must have been uneasy, as is demonstrated by the continuing legal disputes regarding, for instance, the earldom of Menteith and the accusations that Earl Walter had been murdered.[68] Although such rivalries perhaps moved centre stage during the minority, the years 1249–58 should not be regarded differently from any other period.

68 For the Menteith issue, see *Chron. Fordun*, i, pp. 298–99 (trans. ii, pp. 293–94). See also below, pp. 163–65.

With this conclusion, that there was a relatively consistent attitude to the government of Scotland on the part of the Scots noble community, and that there was no clear distinction between the opposing groupings, then the key source of conflict was how, rather than whether, to support the king in the common goal of effective government. The historiographical legend of factional division and of pro-and anti-English parties in Scotland between 1249 and 1258 has its basis in the almost exclusively English source material, which is inevitably overlaid with a sheen not of deliberate bias, but of remote detachment. Henry III's policy in relation to Scotland and its consequent influence on events are thus worthy of examination.

Traditional historiography, reflecting the attitude of some chronicle accounts in which Henry is seen by Alexander as a father-figure, portrays Henry's intervention as purely paternal concern for the well-being of his daughter and son-in-law. 'Neither document nor chronicle suggests that Henry III claimed to interfere by virtue of lordship. He interfered as a neighbour and father-in-law.'[69] The tone of correspondence between Henry and various parties, including Alexander and Margaret, conveys the paternal care which did undoubtedly play a part in his policy towards Scotland. In itself, however, it is not sufficient to explain what Henry hoped to achieve through specific interventions, or through support, at different times, of both the Comyns and the opposition to them. Henry's attitude to Scotland has to be seen against the backdrop of a largely settled relationship with Alexander II. In the immediate aftermath of the old king's death, relations between the kingdoms seem to have progressed normally: an order in January 1250 to the burgesses of Lynn, for instance, to release the goods of Scots merchants, which had been seized because of debts owed in Scotland to Peter de Camera, 'the King's citizen of Bordeaux', in return for promises by the justiciar of Lothian to make satisfaction for the debts, belongs in the context of normal inter-government administrative contact.[70] There is no indication of concern regarding Henry's attitude to Scotland in the period during which the details of Alexander's marriage to Margaret must have been negotiated. Although Matthew Paris's story of the request for Alexander's homage for the kingdom of Scotland at the moment of his knighting seems

---

69 Duncan, *Making of the Kingdom*, p. 574. Donald Watt took a more measured view of Henry III's motivation, however: speaking of the Scottish attempts to achieve coronation and unction, and to resist the payment of papal taxes in support of English crusaders, he concluded that 'Such "disloyalty" in Henry's eyes made him realize that something must be done to establish a regime in Scotland that would not only be more effective but also more responsive to English interests.' (Watt, 'Minority', p. 9) Thirty years ago, Reid ('Political Rôle of the Monarchy', p. 14) took a harder line: 'Henry III was imposing his will on Scotland in a thinly veiled attempt to make good the old claim to English overlordship.'

70 *CDS*, i, no. 1768.

scarcely believable, in 1250/51 Henry's arguments in opposition to the Scots' request to the papacy for permission to crown and anoint their king demonstrates his awareness of the long-standing claims of the English kings over Scotland. Equally, his request to the papacy for a teind of the Scottish church arose in the context of entitlement expected by an overlord (a point which the pope made to him in response).[71] A king could not claim to influence the rule of another kingdom in virtue only of the fact that he was the father-in-law of that realm's king. To explain his interventions in Scotland in terms only of fatherly concern seems to deny in Henry III the attitude to Scotland held by every other English king from William Rufus to (at least) Edward III. The ancient claim to overlordship was no legend, and it was naturally promoted or exercised whenever circumstances allowed. If the request for homage was indeed made in 1251, both question and answer may well have been scripted in advance, in order to uphold honour on both sides: the Scots were as aware of the old claims to hegemony as were the English, and it seems likely that the conduct of the ceremonies in York at Christmas 1251 displayed little more than formulaic lip-service to long-held positions.

The part played by Henry III in the installation of a Comyn-dominated government in Scotland in early 1252 is not entirely clear. That our knowledge of the resignation of Scots officials comes from English record is significant, however, of the fact that at least the initial moves towards the realignment of the Scottish government took place at the time of the festivities at York. There is little evidence that the new appointees were promoted to office before the return to Scotland, but nonetheless it is clear that Henry III did have influence. He did not claim that his right to assign nominees to that government was made under any pretext other than his concern for the welfare of his daughter and son-in-law, but his astute choice of nominees must also indicate that he understood the political sensitivity of their situation. The chronicle accounts suggest that he managed the governmental change, having been persuaded by the Comyn following of the demerits of the group in power; the further suggestion that it was they who had negotiated the royal marriage, effectively to manufacture an event at which a coup could be staged, and in order to give Henry a reason for his intervention, is not credible. The chronicles' accusations against Durward appear to be without foundation, and if they were made contemporaneously, they seem not to have been taken seriously enough to warrant any significant action against him by either Scottish or English royal circles. The most likely explanation of the events of December 1251, therefore, is that the opposition to the Scottish government did indeed come from the

71 Stones, *Anglo-Scottish Relations*, pp. 58–59.

Comyn family, who saw an opportunity to reduce the power of their rival Durward, who had been in the ascendant, perhaps at their expense, since the latter part of the reign of Alexander II. The festivities at York became the stage on which the drama was acted out, doubtless with the assistance of Henry III, whom they had been courting, and whose own sense of opportunity encouraged him to play his part. The scene was then set for the saga of Anglo-Scottish relations to unfold over the ensuing years.

The regularity of communication with his various agents in Scotland demonstrates that Henry III's aim to maintain effective oversight of Scottish affairs was beyond doubt. In the event, he was disappointed in the actions of Balliol, Ros and the others to whom he entrusted the fulfilment of his Scottish policy. It is crucial in this context to understand the familiarity of Balliol and Ros with Scottish politics, and the fact that they were apparently ineffectual in enforcing Henry's will over the Scottish government must be a factor in the events of the autumn of 1255. The Comyns had used the opportunity of support from Henry as a means to gain control of the government in 1251/52; that does not, however, make them into the 'pro-English party' of historiographical legend. In the context of Anglo-Scottish relations, it is possible to look at the downfall of the 1252–55 government in two distinct lights: either the Comyn-led council was so open to English interference that their opposition gained enough support (including that of Alexander III) to effect a coup, which Henry III found himself unable to resist; or they had led a policy which was so antipathetic to English policy (or at least ineffective in pursuing it) that Henry himself lost confidence in them and supported, perhaps even incited, the attempt of the opposition (and Alexander) to take over. The truth is probably less polarised. Given the prominence of Henry in the 1255 negotiations and settlement, and the nature of the agreement reached, in which all of the major players were involved, it seems unlikely that Scottish resistance to an overtly pro-English government was the primary cause of the change in the composition of the council. Neither is it possible to accept that the change of government was entirely at Henry's behest or that its outcome was exactly as desired by him. The narrative offered above makes it more likely that he did indeed exert pressure (including the threat of invasion) to ensure that changes were made to alleviate the situation of Alexander and Margaret; but the involvement of both sides of the supposed factional divide, and the fact that the final settlement was reached by the Scots community itself in apparent consensus, give the impression that the community was united to the extent that they acted together in order to avert the threat of military action against the kingdom. It also seems overly coincidental that this action took place at the point of Alexander's fourteenth birthday, and that it was put in place for a period of seven years. It is thus probable that the communications between the two courts over the year preceding this rearrangement were preliminary not to a coup, but to a planned long-term settlement, prompted partly by Henry's unease over the situation in Scotland. Both the process by which agreement was reached and the nature of the agreement itself reveal equal unease on the part of the Scots community regarding the extent of English involvement; the inclusion in the written agreement that, in order to avoid prejudice to the status of the kingdom, Henry's copy of the agreement would be returned at the close of the seven-year period further demonstrates the sensitivity of the issue.

The nature of the third change of Scottish government, in 1257, is somewhat different. From his rhetoric, it is quite clear that Henry was completely uninvolved in what we might term 'the Kinross affair'. As noted above, it is much less clear that Alexander was innocent of involvement, or that it was seen at the time as a significant upheaval. Again, Henry involved himself when it became apparent to him that the Scottish government lacked enthusiasm for the promotion of English interests in Scotland. The 1258 settlement, displaying the undoubted influence of Alexander himself, and incorporating elements of both the opposing groups in Scotland, effectively put an end to the king's minority. Timed as it was to take advantage of the English crown's own domestic weakness, it also eradicated the overt involvement of Henry III in the rule of Scotland. By 1255, it seems that Alexander III was independent enough to be able to pay lip-service to Henry III's demands, but actually to go his own way. Thus there was no great panic in 1257, and despite, rather than because of, Henry's attempt at intervention in 1258, Alexander was able to establish his own policy (perhaps including tacit support of the Welsh treaty), and to achieve peace at home.

The events of 1258 show the first real assertion of the Scottish crown's independence by Alexander III: an attempt to create unity within the Scottish community, to avert further civil strife and to strengthen his independent rule of the kingdom. His assertion of personal rule, however, did not imply any quelling of noble power. If the notion is rejected that 'family interests rather than any political ideals guided the actions of the nobility in Scotland in these difficult years' and is replaced with an acceptance of their 'reverence for royal authority',[72] there is no need to assume a conflict between crown and nobility.

After the death of Walter Comyn, the accusation of murder levelled against his widow Isabella (in whose right Walter had held the earldom) and her second husband, and the consequent seizure of the earldom of Menteith's lands in the interests of the Comyn family, was said to have been engineered by a group

72 Alan Young, 'Noble Families and Political Factions in the Reign of Alexander III', in Reid, *Alexander III Essays*, pp. 1–30, at p. 7.

which included Durward, Strathearn, Fife and others who would previously have been in the anti-Comyn 'party', along with the leaders of the Comyn family. This reveals that the potential for gaining territory and status, and the action of the community to protect itself from unwanted intrusion, could overcome traditional family rivalries: if there were factional divisions, they were built not upon bedrock, but upon shifting sand.[73]

The foregoing account of the minority focusses heavily on relations with England and on the formation and re-formation of the various minority councils. It is an overwhelmingly political view. The question could rightly be asked whether these political ructions took place against a background of more mundane domestic events which were as influential in creating the apparent political divisions which afflicted the community as was the international or governmental situation. Unfortunately, there is little evidence either to support or to detract from such a contention. The narrative accounts of the minority concentrate entirely on the governmental situation, and the contemporary documentary evidence provides no hints of events or activities beyond the scope of the ordinary, other than the primary themes already discussed: if any impression is to be gained of life beyond the political, it is of normality, of continuity with the settled later years of the reign of Alexander II, and of economic and social activity between the noble families proceeding without undue disruption.

In conclusion, it cannot be denied that the minority of Alexander III was a period of turmoil, in which successive governments were faced by opposition both from within Scotland and from the external influence of English ambition. However, the traditional view of two implacably opposed familial factions, with pro- and anti-English bias (each at times supported or opposed by Henry III), and with the figure of Alexander himself being manipulated by either faction in their self-interested quest for power, cannot be sustained. A more realistic view is of a Scots community certainly divided by personal and familial rivalries, but nonetheless able to act in concert to pursue the just and effective administration of the kingdom, to maintain the position of their king and kingdom, and to uphold the nature of Scottish monarchy: independent of external control and truly dependent on the 'common counsel' of the king's peers, the aristocratic community. The community was divided not about whether to pursue these fundamental aims, but about how to do so most effectively. Thus there were changes in government according to the fluctuations of fortune and influence, but there was also continuity of action and policy, and a remarkable lack of persecution of adversaries. Both the Comyns and their opposition, when first

73 *Vet. Mon.*, no. 237. For a commentary on these confusing events, see Duncan, *Making of the Kingdom*, pp. 583–84. See also below, pp. 163–65.

in power, refused to govern within the strictures of English hegemony to the satisfaction of Henry III. In so doing, they followed an instinct which asserted the freedom of Scotland from such external interference. While the concepts of *corona* and *natio* may not have been fully developed in this period, and had as yet found no explicit written expression, they certainly existed and influenced political activity. Noticeably, following the unequivocal establishment of his own authority in 1257/58, Alexander himself seems to have displayed no rancour to individuals on either side during the various phases of conflict, which must indicate a recognition that all parties had conducted themselves with a sufficient degree of respect for king, kingdom and the rule of law.

CHAPTER 5

Protecting the Realm

It would be a mistake to assume that, with Alexander himself at the helm, there was a complete transformation of the Scottish government in September 1258. To an even greater extent than has been shown to be the case in the various rearrangements of the council during the minority, it is in fact easier to point to continuity. A glance at the offices of state confirms the impression. *Gesta Annalia* tells us that when the Comyns took power in 1257 the king's seal was wrested from the dean of Dunkeld, who held it for the chancellor, the bishop of Dunkeld.[1] The next chancellor on record is William Wishart, archdeacon (and later bishop) of St Andrews, an adherent of the Comyn family, who had been removed from power with the rest of the Comyn-dominated council in 1255. He is not named as chancellor until 1259, when he is said by Matthew Paris to have been one of the Scottish king's envoys to Henry III,[2] but it seems likely that he had been appointed to the chancellorship in 1257 and retained it in the post-minority administration: indeed, he was to hold it until 1273. Similarly, Aymer Maxwell, the chamberlain, was definitely in post by March 1258,[3] but it again seems most likely that, as another member of the council ousted in 1255, he replaced David Lindsay, of the opposition council, in 1257. Also named in the Welsh treaty of March 1258, we see the justiciarships of Scotia and Galloway held by Alexander Comyn earl of Buchan and his kinsman John Comyn, respectively. The justiciarship of Lothian was, by October 1258, held by Hugh Barclay,[4] a man whose earlier allegiance is unclear, but who was sufficiently central to the controlling group of 1257/58 to have been named (along with his brother) in the Welsh treaty. A year later this justiciarship

1 *Chron. Fordun*, i, p. 297 (trans. ii, p. 293).
2 *SAEC*, pp. 377–78.
3 He was so described in the treaty with Llywelyn, prince of Wales on 18 March 1258. *Foedera*, i.i, p. 370.
4 *RRS*, iv pt. 1, no. 26.

seems to have been held jointly by Thomas Normanville (one of those ousted with the Comyns, and a close associate of the Comyn family – his son married a daughter of the earl of Buchan) and one Stephen Fleming.[5] It has been suggested that the majority of the sheriffdoms whose incumbents can be identified were held by Comyn supporters.[6] On the other hand, the witnesses to the five surviving royal *acta* from the calendar year 1260 suggest that supporters and opponents of the Comyns were in the king's presence in roughly equal numbers. Overall, it has to be accepted that the data is so sparse as to make it impossible to draw any firm conclusions.[7] It might be significant of a further important continuity in the administration of the kingdom that one more lowly member of the king's household, an unidentified clerk known to posterity merely as 'Scribe A', apparently continued in post throughout the minority: the first surviving act he wrote was in June 1250, and he was still in royal service in March 1265.[8]

There are two different continuities here: firstly, as there had been throughout the minority period, the presence within the witness lists to royal acts of members both of the governing regime and of those who are said to have opposed it; and secondly, the continuing monopoly of the major offices of state by members of the Comyn family and those who joined them in government following the council realignment of October 1257. There is no doubt that Alexander had somehow achieved a power-sharing accommodation between the Comyns and their opponents. The preponderance of Comyn men in the formal administration, however, is symptomatic also of a new direction: Alexander III was distancing himself from the policy adopted by his father in the last few years of his reign, by not continuing to promote the welfare of Alan Durward, a major rival of the Comyn family. The Durward star was fading.

The early acts of Alexander's personal rule largely deal with the day-to-day administration of justice and landholding transactions. A glance at the 14 acts surviving between October 1258 and September 1262 (when, at the age of 21, his minority formally ended) reveals that half of them are confirmations of, or inquisitions relating to, land grants; one might be termed commercial – a grant of an annual fair to the burgesses of Ayr; and six are letters to Henry III, four

5 *APS*, i, pp. 98–99; see also *PoMS* no. 4/38/4.

6 Duncan, *Making of the Kingdom*, p. 574; Alan Young, *Robert the Bruce's Rivals*, p. 69.

7 *RRS*, iv pt. 1, nos. 27–31. Only eight names occur: Henry Graham, Alan Durward, Aymer Maxwell (twice), the earl of Buchan (twice), the earl of Dunbar (twice), Alexander Stewart, Hugh Abernethy and Walter Stewart (soon to be earl of Menteith). It is noticeable that only three of these people (Durward, Buchan and Alexander Stewart) were named in the list of ten councillors appointed by the king in 1258.

8 *RRS*, iv pt. 1, pp. 22–23; he wrote acts nos. 2–3 (1250); 7, 11–13 (1251); 14, 16 (1252); 19 (1253); 25 (1257); 31 (1260); and 56 (1265).

of which concern judicial matters and the others diplomatic issues.[9] It is the administration of the kingdom, from which justice and prosperity flow, which is paramount. As had been the case throughout the minority, the maintenance of peaceful relations with England was a high priority, and communication between the two royal courts continued unabated, despite the obvious reduction in the influence wielded by Henry III. Matthew Paris tells us that Henry sent a St Albans monk, William Horton, to Scotland immediately after the settlement of 1258, who spent several months in discussion with the Scots king and council. The complete nature of his mission is not clear, but it included an unsuccessful attempt to obtain the assurances of good behaviour which Henry had hoped to receive as part of the 1258 agreement.[10] He may also have been trying to gain consent for a visit of Alexander and Margaret to England. This agent of Henry's finds no place in Scottish record, and neither does the abortive high-level embassy comprising the earl of Buchan, Alan Durward and William Wishart, which Paris claims followed him back south at the end of his visit, but which, he says, failed to make any progress in regard to their (unexplained) assignment. Horton did visit Scotland, however: the letter by which Henry acknowledged the settlement of October 1258 includes an instruction both to him and to Robert Neville to go to Scotland in order to obtain the desired undertakings from the new Scots council.[11] Although there is no record of Buchan, Durward and Wishart visiting the English court, Alexander certainly did send others – John Denmuir is named in the English records as early as May 1259, and a year later he was apparently sent south again, in the company of Hugh Abernethy. Over the next couple of years at least two clerks of Alexander, John of Lindores and William Swinburne (who is later named as the queen's treasurer) were also conducting business for him at the English court, as was Gamelin, the bishop of St Andrews, who was perhaps on his way to France.[12] On his part, Henry sent Roger de Quincy to Scotland on his behalf in September 1259, possibly in the company of Henry's valet, William Bisset.[13] The diplomatic issues being pursued by the Scots in this period seem to have concentrated on three main points: procuring payment of Margaret's dowry, the promised return of the document of 1255, which was undoubtedly seen as prejudicial to the status of the king and kingdom, and, in a move which was clearly designed to take advantage of the relative weakness of the English crown in order to bolster Scottish sovereignty, the preparation of a further attempt to

9 *RRS*, iv pt. 1, nos. 26–39.

10 *SAEC*, pp. 377–78.

11 *CDS*, i, no. 2140.

12 *CDS*, i, nos. 2157, 2191, 2181, 2197, 2260; *RRS*, iv pt.1, nos. 34, 35.

13 *CDS*, i, no. 2189.

win approval for the rites of unction and coronation of their kings.[14] That neither the Scots nor the English seem to have given any ground in these various discussions is hardly surprising, but that they took place at all, that the initiative for the discussions came from Alexander and that Henry's responses tended towards procrastination rather than either denial or belligerence are all symptomatic of a new relationship between the two kings. The tone of the meagre surviving correspondence between them lacks the previous assumption of superiority on the part of Henry. Alexander was gaining strength as Henry weakened, leading to what might be regarded as a normalisation of relations between the two kingdoms. Eventually, small part-payments of the dowry were achieved in October and November 1260, and a further payment was made in 1261–62 (in addition to a sum which Henry offered on account, having assumed responsibility for a debt to three Florentine merchants which had been incurred by the Scots procurators during their earlier protracted negotiations at the papal curia).[15] The dowry was nonetheless an issue which remained a source of tension between the two kings for some years to come.

One diplomatic goal which was achieved with apparent equanimity was a visit to the English court by Alexander and Margaret. It is quite possible that Matthew Paris was right in suggesting that this was one of the aims of William Horton in his protracted visit to Scotland in 1258–59. Personal contact between the two courts was still frequent: Margaret received regular gifts from England, and she retained English noblewomen in her retinue in Scotland, through whom there was regular communication with her English family.[16] Formal letters regarding, for instance, the payment of dowry instalments were sometimes delivered through the queen's hands, and minor judicial matters in England were frequently pursued 'at the instance' of the Scots king and queen: the path between the two courts was well-trodden. Despite any inherited governmental tensions, which doubtless continued, there is an impression of warmth in the personal contact between the two royal families: on 10 June 1262, for example, in an official letter to Henry, Alexander opened by stating that 'the writer and his Queen and their daughter, by Divine favour, were well and happy'.[17] With apparently good personal relations, an agreement regarding a formal visit of Alexander and Margaret to Windsor may not have been too hard to reach. The safe conduct which Gamelin received in February 1260 to go to England to

14 *CDS*, i, no. 2157.

15 *CDS*, i, nos. 2192, 2209, 2217, 2219, 2220, 2264, 2265; *RRS*, iv pt.1, no. 35. Even as Henry made the payment in 1261–62, he was pleading poverty regarding the outstanding balance: *CDS*, i, no. 2295.

16 *CDS*, i, nos. 2159, 2183, 2186.

17 *CDS*, i, no. 2306.

speak with the 'King and Queen' was renewed in the following August, perhaps indicating that Gamelin's trip had been delayed.[18] Given the timing, his task in England was probably to tie up the details of the impending royal visit before either he returned to Scotland or continued his journey to France. His safe conduct allowed for either, as he chose, and was valid for a year. There was clearly a possibility that royal or diocesan business might take him further afield: perhaps discussions with Marie de Coucy, or even attendance at the curia, where a further dispute was brewing over the election of the new bishop of Glasgow. We cannot be certain, since there is no surviving evidence either of his onward journey or of his presence in Scotland before January 1262. On 17 August 1260 Henry sent his envoys to Scotland to ask Alexander and Margaret to return with them, along with Roger de Quincy and John Balliol, whom Henry delegated to bring the couple safely to his court.[19] De Quincy and Balliol were well known to the Scots king and queen, and to the royal council; so were Robert Neville and William Latimer, two of Henry's envoys (a third being Hugh Bolebeck, who as sheriff of Northumberland had been a regular servant of Henry in relation to Alexander II's English lands and would be known to many of the Scottish magnates, and probably also to Alexander). Henry's embassy was completed by the return to the diplomatic stage of a man who had temporarily disappeared from view, but would also have been well known to the young king: Robert Keldeleth, former abbot of Dunfermline, chancellor of Scotland and then monk of Newbattle. That Keldeleth was entrusted with such a mission, of a personal but also diplomatically sensitive nature, must indicate that he was a man who retained the respect of both royal households. Appearing on the scene at this precise moment, when the Scottish household was dominated, at the king's own behest, by those who seemed to have brought about Robert's earlier downfall, suggests again that the rivers of dissension and conflict during Alexander's minority may not have run as deep as has previously been asserted. As well as other elaborate arrangements for the accompaniment and entertainment of Alexander and Margaret as they travelled south, the extreme importance of this visit was underlined by the instruction to Henry's son and heir Prince Edward, the archbishop of York, the earls of Gloucester, Hereford and Marshal, and Hugh Bygod (the justiciar of England) to issue letters of safe conduct for

18 Henry was in France when the first safe conduct was issued to Gamelin. He did not return to England until April 1260. The wording, however, makes it clear that the reference to Gamelin's possible visit to France was not for the purpose of meeting Henry, who presumably knew that he would be back in England before Gamelin arrived there.

19 *CDS*, i, no. 2198. At that point Alexander was in Inverness, but within a fortnight was apparently heading southwards via the east coast, and had reached Selkirk by 21 September (*RRS*, iv pt. 1, nos. 28, 29 30).

the royal couple passing through their territories; these conducts were to be delivered to Keldeleth, who presumably carried them to the Scottish royal court for additional security.[20]

Preparations for the visit were typically detailed. The king was concerned that there was a shortage of wine at Windsor and ordered more to be sent; jewels were to be bought for presentation to Alexander and his retinue; the customary allowance for Alexander's expenses while in England was to be paid to him; and he was given new year gifts while on his journey homewards.[21] The St Albans continuation of Matthew Paris's *Flores Historiarum* grudgingly describes a typically opulent celebration, the cause of 'insufferable expense' to the surrounding area.[22] It also describes the Scottish king's visit as motivated primarily by an opportunity for him to pressurise Henry regarding the overdue dowry and his rights to lands in England. Clearly, even to this contemporary English chronicler, Alexander was exerting his personal authority as king of Scots. While this may have been partly a social visit, for Alexander it was mainly business.[23] Alexander, it is stated, did not linger long at Windsor: his transactions complete, he set off to return to Scotland before Christmas. Margaret, however, remained with her parents. She was pregnant, close to giving birth to her first child, and by prior agreement with the Scots king and council, remained at Windsor, where her daughter, Margaret, destined to become the queen of Norway, was born in mid to late February.[24] The St Albans chronicle claims that the Scots were unaware of her pregnancy when she left Scotland and were unhappy that she had effectively duped them into allowing her to have her child outwith the kingdom. That, however, was not the case. The issue had been the subject of some of the negotiations leading towards the visit: in September 1260, before Alexander and Margaret had left Scotland, Henry had issued letters promising not to detain mother or child in England, and to return the child to the Scottish magnates in the event of the death of Alexander himself. It was couched in vague terms – 'should [the queen] . . . become pregnant'. The child was born in February, and by September Margaret's pregnancy would already have been

20 *CDS*, i, nos. 2198, 2199, 2202, 2204, 2207, 2208.

21 *CDS*, i, nos. 2225, 2227, 2239, 2241.

22 *SAEC*, p. 378.

23 As usual, administrative and judicial business was carried on during the visit: see, e.g., *CDS*, i, nos. 2230–2235.

24 *SAEC*, pp. 378–79. For discussion of the various works by Matthew Paris (d.1259) and his continuators, see Victoria Gransden, *Historical Writing in England, c.550–c.1307* (London, 1974), ch. 16. Margaret's purification, which would take place 40 days after the birth, was held shortly after 25 March, giving a birth date of around 20 February. *Gesta Annalia* dates the birth to 28 February, which seems a little late (*Chron. Fordun*, i, p. 295 (trans. ii, p. 299)). Her reign as queen of Norway would be short: she died, probably in childbirth, at the age of 22.

common knowledge: given the closeness of the relationship between Margaret and her parents, it is inconceivable that the English court would have been unaware. The wording may reflect merely a discrete delicacy of expression; more probably, since she was still in the early months of her pregnancy, it provided a legal framework for acknowledging that the risk of miscarriage was high. (It is also possible that, since she was by now in her twenty-first year and had been married for a decade, this was not her first pregnancy; if so, the perceived risk of miscarriage may have been amplified.) Later, when Alexander agreed to leave her in England for her confinement, more elaborate precautions regarding the return of mother and child to Scotland were made: Henry would return both Margaret and her child to Scotland after her purification (more commonly known as 'churching'), the rite by which she was blessed 40 days after the birth, or by Easter 1261 at the latest. In the event of the death of either Margaret or her child, the other would be allowed to return to Scotland, and a committee of guardians was named that would have care of the child in Scotland in the event of the death of Alexander, irrespective of the political situation in either country. The birth of an heir to the throne was of crucial importance, much too significant for the kingdom to be left without safeguards for every eventuality. Margaret's purification took place soon after 25 March 1261 and was accompanied by more feasting: on that day the king ordered as many pike and bream as possible to be taken to Windsor from the see of Winchester 'against the instant purification of his daughter the Queen of Scotland'.[25] Margaret stayed in the south a little longer than planned, and was setting off homewards in May 1261, probably in the company of Roger de Quincy.[26]

The committee of guardians which was named in Henry's undertakings regarding the return of the queen and her child to Scotland must have been chosen by Alexander, presumably with the advice of his council. The Scots had demanded a commitment from Henry, and it seems unlikely, given the new order of Anglo-Scottish relations, that Henry would have tried to impose his will in the choice of guardians. The bishops of St Andrews, Aberdeen, Dunblane and Whithorn, the earls of Fife, Buchan, Strathearn, Dunbar and Mar, and John Comyn, Alexander Stewart, Alan Durward and Hugh Abernethy were to comprise the committee, which thus included only five of those named as Alexander's counsellors in November 1258, but which still represented a broad cross-section of the Scottish political community, from both sides of the pro- and anti-Comyn divide. Twenty-five years later, after Alexander's premature

25 *CDS*, i, no. 2248. For a discussion of purification, see Becky R. Lee, 'The Purification of Women after Childbirth: A Window onto Medieval Perceptions of Women', in *Florilegium*, no. 14 (1995–96), pp. 43–55.
26 *CDS*, i, nos. 2255, 2258.

death, the first act of the Scottish community was to elect a committee of six guardians (*custodes*) to uphold, in her absence, the rule of Alexander's heir, his granddaughter, daughter of this Margaret born in February 1261. The committee – two bishops, two earls and two magnates – represented not only a balance between the three primary social divisions of the community, but also between the kingdom's main family or factional interests. The similar choice at the end of 1260 of four bishops, five earls and four magnates as potential guardians for the new heir to the throne can be no coincidence. The guardians appointed in 1286, and on several subsequent occasions during the following two decades, underpinned their constitutional legitimacy through the styles and seals they used on official documents; this earlier group was not called upon to act, since the worst-case scenario of Alexander's death in 1261 did not transpire, and so there is no evidence of similar constitutional formality. Nonetheless, it is a clear signal that the business of ruling the kingdom was not entirely reactive, and was subject, even at this early stage, to a formalised set of procedures which found their roots in a developed constitutional theory.[27]

Alexander was now 19 years old. His position in Scotland, and his regal status in his relations with England, however, had been immensely elevated in the course of 1259–61. He was now a father, the head of a dynasty. The child was not the heir the Scots would wish to inherit: the succession of a female was not impossible in Scotland, as events later in the reign would demonstrate, but it was still regarded as less favourable than male succession. Alexander and Margaret were young, however: there was time for more children. The security of his position in Scotland was thus immeasurably increased, and his personal grip on government was even firmer than it had been following the events of 1258. His prestige in Scotland would have been bolstered by his readiness to stand up to Henry III, for so long a mightily dominant force in Scottish politics. It was becoming clear to all that Alexander III was a king to be reckoned with.

English records reveal that during the period 1259–62, several other high-status Scots were on the move. John Comyn of Badenoch received a safe conduct for travel to England and overseas, issued only two days before Gamelin's, in early August 1260: they may have been travelling together on royal business. He was on his way home from abroad in October, timing which would have facilitated a visit to Windsor with the king and queen at the end of the year.[28]

---

27 For further discussion of the Scottish guardianships of the late thirteenth and early fourteenth centuries, see Norman H. Reid, 'The Kingless Kingdom: the Scottish Guardianships of 1286–1306', *Scottish Historical Review*, 61 (1982), pp. 105–29.

28 Comyn was invited to go to the king at Windsor (*CDS*, i, nos. 2196, 2210, 2211). Although other safe conducts are not extant as evidence, it seems possible that other members of Alexander's

Comyn was on the move again in January 1262, perhaps on Alexander's business, if the description of him as 'the knight of' Alexander III is of significance. John Balliol received a safe conduct to go overseas in March 1259 and return by 1 November (later extended until April 1260). He seems to have been on Henry's business: by 18 May 1260 he was back in England and was rewarded for his 'laudable service' to the king in both England and France by the gift of 200 merks expenses (which still remained to be paid in September). Máel Ísu earl of Strathearn also had a safe conduct for overseas travel, from 4 May to 1 August 1259. During the summer, Strathearn borrowed money from merchants who were citizens of Cahors in southern France, although the fact that it was to be repaid at King's Lynn indicates that they may have been in England, rather than in France at that point. His voluntary subjection, in the event of non-payment, to the 'conservators of the privileges of crusaders' may give some indication of his foreign business, although the duration of his journey is too short for him to have been intending a prolonged military expedition. In 1260/61 Walter Lindsay undertook a pilgrimage to St James (Santiago de Compostela), and it is possible that Strathearn's journey was for a similar purpose.[29] If indeed these men were going on pilgrimage, or even just pursuing business affairs outside the kingdom, it is a sign that the situation in Scotland was more settled than perhaps it had been for some time. Throughout the English records, too, there is a scattering of cross-border minor judicial and commercial transactions which suggest a normality in relations between the kings and kingdoms.

The notion of an 'English party' in Scotland both before and after Alexander III freed himself from overt control on either side of the border still causes controversy in modern historiography. It has been rightly dismissed as 'legend': all of the major players in Scotland in the period leading up to 1258 were 'native and natural' counsellors, who supported effective rule of the kingdom, and recognised that stable and friendly relations with Henry III were necessary in order to achieve it. Some of them, such as Bruce, Balliol, Ros and de Quincy also owed natural allegiance to both crowns because of their status as the holders of significant lands on both sides of the border. The inclusion of Marie de Coucy and her husband in the 1258 council has been described as 'a sop to Henry III'; the same suggestion has been made about Alan Durward and his supporters, who have been described as 'the price for English acceptance of the settlement'; there is even some agreement that the 1258 council, known only from English

council were similarly present. Gifts of produce to Alan Durward may also indicate his presence and involvement in the provisioning of the meeting (*CDS*, i, nos. 2218, 2221, 2222).

29 *CDS*, i, nos. 2284, 2154, 2172, 2190, 2156, 2160, 2212.

record, is representative primarily of English ambition for Scotland.[30] However, the problem with the modern historiography of the early post-minority period, as for that of the minority itself, is that it has remained fixated upon the misleading premise of deep factionalism; the events of the early 1260s have invariably continued to be viewed through the skewed lens of Comyn versus Durward. The more reasoned view is that the 1258 settlement represented Alexander's own ambition. To seek out continuing conflict, or to suppose that the ensuing years must necessarily have seen one group dominating at the expense of the other, is surely to make the fact fit the theory and sustains a historiographical malaise which inevitably infects the longer-term view. If the Comyns were indeed 'the very pillars of monarchy',[31] then so were the other families and individuals within the Scottish governing community.

It has been said that Alexander III would have been unhappy with the favour shown by Henry III to Durward supporters in the year or two after his personal rule began, the assumption being that it ran counter to Alexander's policy of attempting to curb Durward aspirations.[32] Henry did show some favour to a few Scots. In January 1259 Alan Durward received a gift of cash, and in November 1260 further gifts of wine, fish and venison, as well as relief from taxation on his estate of Bolsover. The timing of these latter benefits, however, probably coincided with the demand for entertainment of the Scottish royal party on its way southwards to Windsor. In addition to the payment received by John Balliol in recognition of his loyal service, in February 1262 he was given custody of Nottingham castle and an additional gift. In January 1262 John Comyn and Robert Bruce were both awarded generous allowances for as long as they remained in the English king's household, and in the following month John Comyn further received confirmation of an old grant of lands in Tynedale 'so that he and his heirs shall be faithful to the K'. En route for Scotland in the same month, Comyn was allowed to hunt in the king's northern forests. Alexander Stewart had also received venison in August 1261.[33] Henry's favours to Scottish magnates hardly represent a pattern of support for subversives which was to be regarded as antagonistic to Alexander III. Durward had not lost his position in Scotland: he was a member of the council and clearly attended court

30 Duncan, *Making of the Kingdom*, pp. 574–76; Watt, 'Minority', pp. 18–20; Young, *Robert the Bruce's Rivals*, pp. 66–67.

31 Alan Young, 'Noble Families and Political Factions in the Reign of Alexander III', in Reid, *Alexander III* Essays, pp. 1–30, at p. 14.

32 Reid, 'Political Rôle of the Monarchy', p. 16: 'the continued favour which Henry III showed to some of the ousted Durward supporters may have acted against their gaining power in Scotland'. My opinion about the government of thirteenth-century Scotland has changed considerably since 1984!

33 *CDS*, i, nos. 2143, 2218, 2221, 2222, 2190, 2288, 2292, 2285, 2287, 2291, 2266.

at least occasionally, as evidenced by his witnessing of royal acts.[34] Balliol, Comyn and Bruce represented both sides of the supposed Scottish magnatial divide, had significant landholdings in England, and were rewarded for their loyalty to the English king, loyalty which did not conflict with that owed to Alexander or his kingdom. Stewart, far from being out of favour in Scotland, was to become a key player on behalf of the Scottish king. Bestowal of favour on men who were playing their part in the government of Scotland is symptomatic of a healthy balance within the cross-border noble community.

Following the death, soon after the 1258 settlement, of Bishop Bondington of Glasgow, in January 1259 the cathedral chapter elected Nicholas Moffat as his successor. Moffat was by medieval standards an elderly man, born probably around the turn of the century, and a long-standing servant of the diocese, having been archdeacon of Teviotdale since 1245. He was a regular official in both business and ecclesiastical matters affecting the diocese and the kingdom (which makes it probable that he had been trained in canon law). He had supported Gamelin's cause, for example, in the disputed election to the see of St Andrews. Moffat's election was confirmed by the king, and in the early months of 1259 he set off to the curia for papal confirmation and consecration. His mission faltered as, perhaps to both his own and the king's surprise, the pope refused to confirm the election. The reason for this refusal is not clear, but it is possible that Robert of the Provender, who had accompanied Moffat to the curia, argued against him, seeking (as Abel had done earlier for the St Andrews see) to have the bishopric for himself. Robert, a Glasgow canon and bishop-elect of Dunblane, had been involved in Moffat's election and may have had a personal dispute with him. The *Chronicle of Melrose* also tells us that Moffat had refused to pay what he regarded as unreasonable fees associated with his confirmation.[35] In the event, neither Moffat nor Robert were appointed by the pope, who by mid June 1259 had instead elevated John Cheam, a man who had no previous connection with the Glasgow diocese. Alexander's authority was challenged: episcopal elections disputed by the papacy were a constant thorn in the flesh of medieval monarchs.

A further complication was the fact that Cheam was not a Scot and had no position in the Scottish church; he was from the south of England and, when appointed to Glasgow, he was archdeacon of Bath. The pope wrote to Henry III on 13 June telling him of Cheam's appointment and asking him to 'advise and induce' Alexander to accept it. Henry eventually acted on the pope's request,

---

34 E.g. *RRS*, iv pt. 1, nos. 28, 55.

35 It should be noted that in 1261/62, the bishop of Glasgow (Cheam) still owed a sum of 200 marks (out of an original debt of 800 marks) to the papacy: procuring papal confirmation was an expensive business (*CPL*, pp. 380, 384).

and in March 1260 asked Alexander (as well as his queen and the members of the king's council) to give the temporalities of the see to Cheam. By then Cheam had been given the 'spiritualities' of the diocese and was already in possession of his episcopal authority.[36] That the pope appointed an Englishman to the see apparently out of the blue, and then wrote to Henry in such a manner, is intriguing. Alexander had protested about the election, but does not seem to have pressed the issue following the pope's refusal to reconsider. The dust having barely settled on the protracted legal process surrounding Gamelin's election to St Andrews, Alexander may have chosen to avoid further litigation. Alexander's primary objection was to the fact that the pope had instructed the bishops of Lincoln and Bath to ensure that Cheam was given the temporalities of the see: the king's envoys had complained that such an instruction infringed the ancient rights and customs of the kingdom. The pope's response was conciliatory: the new bishop was to swear fealty to Alexander and receive the temporalities from him, and the two English bishops had their commission revoked in order to erase any damage to the king or his realm.[37]

The independence of the Scottish church, as discussed above, was a matter of significant concern, especially in the shadow of issues such as the grant of papal taxation in favour of English crusading activities. The appointment of a non-native bishop and the involvement of the English king in the matter bring into question the motives behind English activity at the papal court in the early months of 1259; they seem less than consistent with Henry's promise in November 1258 to support the new Scottish government. His interference in the election of this bishop, even after the settlement of 1258, in the context of his other actions throughout the period since the death of Alexander II, tends to support the view that Henry was just as aware of, and ambitious to pursue, his dynasty's ambitions towards sovereignty over the entire island, as his forebears and successors had been. At that particular time, however, the episcopal election was not a fight in which Alexander wished to engage. (If the *Chronicle of Lanercost*'s assessment of Cheam was correct – that he was, despite his background, vehemently anti-English – then he was potentially not too unpalatable a choice for Alexander.) Irrespective of Cheam's character or opinions, however, as Alexander emerged from the chrysalis of minority he had other pressing

---

36 The story of this episcopal election is conveniently summarised in Watt, *Graduates*, pp. 399–400 (Moffat) and 96 (Cheam). Watt cites many sources; the key information used in the account given above is as follows: *Chron. Melrose*, Faustina B. IX, fos. 59v–60r (trans. Anderson, *Early Sources*, ii, pp. 595–96); *Chron. Lanercost*, p. 75 (trans. Anderson, *Early Sources*, ii, p. 661 n.); *Chron. Bower*, v, pp. 323–26 (where it is claimed that Moffat's own canons annulled his election 'by treachery' before he reached the curia); *CDS*, i, nos. 2158, 2182, 2194 (full Latin texts printed in *Foedera*, i.i, p. 387, 394, 387); *Glasgow Reg.*, i, nos. 210, 212.

37 *Vet. Mon.*, no. 225.

concerns, and so with apparent pragmatism the papal instruction was discharged and Cheam assumed the temporalities of his see without obstruction.

When Alexander took his somewhat hasty leave of the English court in December 1260, he was heading home to face another looming problem, which flowed from the political earthquake represented by the other prominent Scottish death of 1258, that of Walter Comyn earl of Menteith. Within a year of Comyn's death, apparently as a result of a fall from his horse,[38] accusations surfaced that he had in fact been murdered. Those accused of poisoning him were his widow, Isabella, and John Russell, an English knight whom she had married not long after Comyn's death. Comyn's title to the earldom had come from her. She was countess in her own right, the daughter of the previous earl, Maurice; she thus continued, with her new husband, to hold the earldom. The accusations against them came from a significant cross-section of the Scottish political community, however, and they were forced to resign the earldom in favour of John Comyn of Badenoch, the nephew and heir of Earl Walter. They were also compelled to give up their other Scottish properties, these being granted, under duress, to some of their accusers. Isabella and Russell were forced into English exile.[39] The plot was further thickened when the earldom was also claimed by Walter Stewart, a younger brother of Alexander the steward, in the right of his wife Mary, who was probably a cousin of Isabella (the daughter of Isabella's uncle, who had earlier resigned his earldom to his younger brother, Isabella's father)[40] and who thus carried a claim of her own to the earldom's succession. An attempt to find a resolution to this stramash, which threatened the new, and doubtless shaky consensus among the community, was one of the tasks facing Alexander as he returned to Scotland at the end of 1260. There is no record of a formal process by which the judgement was made. In December 1260, however, Walter Stewart was at Alexander's court, witnessing a royal charter in company with the earls of Buchan and Dunbar, Aymer Maxwell and Hugh Abernethy. At that point he had not been awarded the earldom, since he was not styled earl in the document, and is listed last of the witnesses, a sign of lower status. By the time he next appears in a royal witness list, in December 1262, he had been styling himself earl of Menteith for at least eight months.[41] He was attending court and witnessing royal documents, a clear indication both of favour and of his claim to the earldom being upheld

38 Matthew Paris, *Chronica Majora*, quoted in *SAEC*, p. 376.
39 *Chron. Fordun*, i, pp. 298–99 (trans. ii, pp. 293–94).
40 See Duncan, *Making of the Kingdom*, p. 584n. *Gesta Annalia* gives Walter Stewart the name 'Bullock' – an anglicisation of his Gaelic nickname *Bailloch*, meaning 'freckled' (*Chron. Bower*, v, p. 455n).
41 *RRS*, iv pt. 1, nos. 31, 41; *Paisley Reg.*, pp. 120–21.

by the king and council. Alexander, it seems, had managed to find a solution to the affair without alienating the disappointed John Comyn's relatives. It is an important point, because if the continuing preponderance of Comyn family members in the offices of state and the sheriffdoms was symptomatic of their continuing to run the show in Scotland, then it is surely very unlikely that Stewart would have gained the earldom at the expense of John Comyn. Stewart, it can therefore be assumed, won his case in a formal legal process, in which the king himself was probably the judge, being the only authority in the kingdom of higher status than the earls.

In Scotland the judgement of the earldom in favour of Stewart was apparently accepted. *Gesta Annalia* suggests that the persecution of Isabella and her new husband, John Russell – described as a 'low-born' English knight – was motivated by a reluctance on the part of the Scottish community to accept his sudden elevation into the most senior ranks of the Scottish nobility. It is tempting to see the persecution following Walter Comyn's death as reminiscent of the Bisset affair of the early 1240s,[42] but there is a marked difference. In 1242, the king and queen attempted, unsuccessfully, to defend Bisset against false charges. In contrast, in 1260 Alexander III seems to have worked with his nobility to prevent what was probably regarded as a common threat. During 1259 or early 1260 Isabella and her husband did grant land in Aberfoyle to Hugh Abernethy, one of the accusers. This may be a sole survivor of several such grants made at this time. The witnesses to the grant were the earls of Fife, Strathearn, Buchan and Mar, as well as John Comyn (then justiciar of Galloway), William Munfichet (who, in the 1240s had been sheriff of Perth) and William Wishart, archdeacon of St Andrews,[43] distinguished figures from across the Scottish political community, who were engaged in the process.

Isabella was understandably unwilling to relinquish her position as countess on the basis of what were almost certainly trumped-up charges, and record survives elsewhere of her attempts both to clear her name and to regain her inheritance. The case was taken to the papal curia: in January 1264, Pope Urban IV wrote to the bishops of St Andrews and Aberdeen and the abbot of Dunfermline, ordering them to make enquiries. Isabella and her husband had complained that they had been unjustly deprived of the earldom. Those cited as having acted against her were the earls of Mar, Buchan, Strathearn and Fife, Alan Durward, John Comyn, Alexander Uviet, Alan 'son of the earl' (a half-brother of the young earl of Atholl murdered in 1242, who had been ferocious in his attack on the 'upstart' Bissets accused of the murder), Hugh Barclay, David

42 See, e.g., Duncan, *Making of the Kingdom*, p. 583.
43 Fraser, *Menteith*, ii, p. 213.

Graham, David Lochore (sheriff of Perth), Reginald Cheyne, Hugh Abernethy and Freskin Murray. Most of these are names well known from the minority, from both sides of the Comyn/anti-Comyn divide. It is stated that although the earldom was given up by Isabella into the hands of John Comyn and his heirs, he was also among the group who later, 'by the authority of the king, then a minor' adjudged it to Walter Stewart and Mary. The pope assigned a judge-delegate to look into Isabella's case, who apparently overstepped his authority by calling the king and others to attend a hearing outside the kingdom to answer the charges and, when they failed to appear, issuing sentences of excommunication against them. The king protested that the procedure was invalid since they had been summoned outwith the kingdom, and the pope thus appointed the two bishops and abbot to make enquiry, to revoke the former sentences and to settle the case, 'the civil jurisdiction of the realm being respected'. Their enquiries continued 'over a long period', but it is not known what (if any) judgement they gave. Dispute over the earldom continued until April 1285, when the king in parliament is said by the fifteenth-century chronicler Andrew Wyntoun to have partitioned the lands between Walter Stewart (who retained the title) and William Comyn, a brother of John Comyn (II) of Badenoch.[44] Isabella and John Russell disappear from Scottish record after 1264; they vanish into obscurity, her claim probably dying with her long before 1285. That a Comyn bid for the earldom was made again a quarter of a century after the king's initial judgement in favour of Stewart, however, irrespective of the fact that the claim seems to have been legally weak, demonstrates that the competition between the families ran deep. Alexander had clearly mustered significant authority in 1260 and had not been dominated by the power of the Comyns, in order to make good his judgement in favour of Stewart. There seems little doubt that Isabella was unjustly deprived of her inheritance: the king and political community seem to have acted as one, necessarily at the expense of one of the claimants, in order to protect themselves from the intrusion into the aristocratic milieu of one whom they considered unworthy. This was a hierarchical society with a strong regard for status, and sometimes 'justice' acted in the interest of the community, rather than that of the individual.

A further issue which had been discussed with Henry III on Alexander's behalf by the embassy of John Denmuir in May 1259, and which might have hastened Alexander's return to his home turf at the end of 1260, had been the situation in the Isle of Man. Alexander had requested Henry not to assist the

---

44 *Vet. Mon.*, no. 237; *Chron. Bower*, vi, p. 172–73; *Chron. Wyntoun*, v, p. 138; *Chron. Fordun*, i, pp. 298–99 (trans. ii, pp. 293–94). This last is *Gesta Annalia*: note that the statement that the case was still awaiting judgement reveals the pre-1285 composition of the work. See also the account of papal involvement in Ferguson, *Papal Representatives*, pp. 104–07.

king of Man; the precise nature of the possible assistance, and the reason for Alexander's objection to it, was not made clear, primarily because Henry's answer, following the pattern of his other responses to that embassy, was entirely evasive: Henry

> informs Alexander he will neither oppose him in doing justice, nor has he been urged by anyone; but if anything is reported to him he will do what is right and honourable between himself and Alexander.[45]

The somewhat cryptic nature of this exchange obscures a developing issue regarding which there are several other hints in the English record, and which would over the next few years present Alexander with one of the most severe challenges to his kingship. A few months later, in August 1259, Alexander Stewart was apparently in Ireland: Henry ordered his justiciar of Ireland to allow Stewart to procure provisions and take them to Scotland 'for the purpose of his expedition there'. Again, in the following April the justiciar was ordered not to allow any of Alexander III's subjects to be received in Ireland 'to the said K's damage'; any Scots found there plotting against Alexander were to be distrained.[46] Clearly, trouble was once more brewing in the west. We noted earlier the decision of Eógan of Argyll to come into the king's peace in 1255, the involvement of Henry III in Man around the same time, and the apparent fear of a threat from Norway; there is nothing about these issues in Scottish record of the period, but it is clear that while the western conflicts which had afflicted the final years of Alexander II's reign had not been of the greatest priority during the troubled years of the minority, they had certainly not disappeared.

Picking up the tale of Man and the Hebrides as Alexander II was carried south to his requiem mass in July 1249, it is apparent that the summer campaign had not been as total a failure as the death of the king might have suggested. Alexander's death was of course the headline-grabber, and because there is no further mention of the army in the sources, it has been assumed that it simply dispersed without further action. That may not be the whole story, however, since the history of the Hebrides in this period is 'as complex, intricate and elusive as a Celtic artistic motif'.[47] Eógan mac Dubhgaill is barely visible in Scottish sources for several years; apparently persuaded that Scottish control, at least of his mainland territories, was unopposable and, perhaps being dispossessed, he went

45 *CDS*, i, no. 2157.
46 *CDS*, i, nos. 2163, 2185.
47 Cowan, 'Norwegian Sunset – Scottish Dawn', p. 111.

westwards in an attempt to establish a power base in the isles. In 1250 he attacked Man and proclaimed himself king of the Isles, while Harald, king of Man was in Norway answering Hákon IV's charges that he had usurped the kingdom.[48] Eógan failed to establish himself, though, and by 1253 he had given his allegiance to Hákon IV, and was campaigning with him in Denmark.[49] His cousin Dubgall mac Ruaridh was also on that campaign, raising further questions about the situation in Eógan's former Scottish mainland territories, since there is a suspicion that it was Dubgall who had supplanted him in 1249.

It is worth delving back a little, to unravel the complexities of the situation. In the mid twelfth century, the celebrated Hebridean leader Somerled had wrested control of the northern part of the Kingdom of Man and the Isles from its then king, Godred, effectively creating two separate kingdoms, of Man, and of the Isles, over which there was recurring tension between the various branches of the families descended from the sons of Somerled.[50] The situation was further complicated in the early decades of the thirteenth century by the pressure being exerted on the western seaboard and the islands, particularly the southern islands, by agents of the Scottish crown. In particular, the Stewart family were given significant tracts of land in an effort to strengthen Scottish royal influence in the west, and in the late 1220s and early 1230s Alan of Galloway was also militarily active in Man and the Isles. Thus opposition to encroachment on land and position held by the local lords became inevitably associated with opposition to Scottish royal authority. As the islesmen sought Norwegian assistance against Scottish aggression, Hákon IV tried to use the fractured familial relationships to exert his own control over the islands, with an expedition in 1230–31, one effect of which seems to have been to extend and consolidate the influence in the Inner Hebrides and Argyll of Donnchad, the son of Somerled's older son Dubgall.[51] By the mid century it seems that three main branches of Somerled's family had established themselves as lords in distinct areas of the western seaboard and the Hebrides: Donnchad (and then his son Eógan – the Macdougalls) in Lorn and Lismore; the descendants of Domnall, son of

48 *Chron. Man*, pp. 104–09.

49 Anderson, *Early Sources*, ii, p. 577 (ignoring the erroneous note suggesting that 'John' (= Eógan) is a mistake for 'Magnus').

50 A detailed description of the dynastic rivalries which afflicted Man and the Hebrides in the twelfth century, and of the division of the kingdom, is provided in McDonald, *Sea Kings*, ch. 5.

51 If Norwegian activity in the Hebrides can thus be seen as a response to Scottish aggression, it is also possible to see the Scots' actions as having been prompted by Norwegian hostility, as the Norwegian kings attempted to wrest back a level of control over the area which they had lost during the extended Norwegian civil wars of the twelfth century. McDonald, *Sea Kings*, pp. 138, 150–51.

Rognvald (the Macdonalds) in Islay, in parts of the southern islands and in Kintyre (where they were particularly under pressure from the Stewarts); and the descendants of Rúaidrí (the Macruaridhs) in Garmoran, Knoydart, Moidart, Arisaig, Morar, Rum, Eigg and parts of the outer isles. After the death of Alan of Galloway in 1234, there seems to have been a lull in activity until the late 1240s. Saga sources tell us that in 1248, Eógan and Dubgall were in dispute at the court of King Hákon over the kingship of the northern Hebrides, which was given to Eógan.[52]

> Then came from the west beyond the sea John [i.e. Eógan], Duncan's son, and Dugald, Ruadri's son; and they both endeavoured after this, that the king should give them the title of king over the northern part of the Hebrides. They remained with the king during the summer. . . . Some time after the burning of the town [of Bergen], the king gave with magnificence a feast in the royal dwelling, and gave his daughter Cecilia in marriage to Harold, king of the Hebrides. . . . And while he lay in Salteyiarsund, he gave the title of king to John, Duncan's son. And king John sat behind in Bergen during the winter; but Dugald was with king Hakon.[53]

The young king of Man, Harald, and his new bride, Hákon's daughter Cecilia, came to an untimely end in the autumn of 1248, when their ship was wrecked off Shetland on their return from Norway.[54] Hákon granted the title of king of Man to Eógan on a temporary basis, a double success, indicating both personal dominance and Norwegian favour, which may have prompted Alexander II to launch his expedition in the summer of 1249. In the following year, however, Dubgall is said in the Icelandic Annals to have been made king in the Hebrides. This may have been an attempt on the part of Hákon to 'divide and dominate'; on the other hand it has been suggested, perhaps more persuasively, that it was a response to the ousting of Eógan following Alexander II's 1249 expedition.[55] If Eógan had indeed been displaced, Alexander's death may have prevented the Scots from completing the task and installing a lord of Lorn who would owe allegiance to the Scottish crown, thus creating a vacuum which was temporarily filled by Dubgall. Further signs of an attempt to exert Scottish lordship were the presence of a royal bailiff in Argyll in 1250, and Alexander's last surviving act, given on the day he died, which gifted the church of St Bride,

52 Anderson, *Early Sources*, ii, pp. 550–51, 553–55.

53 Hakon's Saga, as translated by A.O. Anderson, *Early Sources*, ii, pp. 548–49.

54 Anderson, *Early Sources*, ii, p. 550.

55 Anderson, *Early Sources*, ii, pp. 554–55; Cowan, 'Norwegian Sunset – Scottish Dawn', p. 115; McDonald, *Kingdom of the Isles*, p. 104.

in Eógan's territory, to the see of Argyll. This gift is perhaps to be seen as a first step in the relocation of the seat of the diocese to the mainland in an attempt to restore the see, which had been vacant for most of the previous two decades, and to bring it more closely within royal control.[56] In this context, Eógan's attack on Man in 1250 can be seen as an attempt to regain what he regarded as his own. He failed, however, and by 1253 he had returned to Norway, and was in the service of the Norwegian king. What encouraged Eógan to turn instead to Alexander III in 1255 is not known, but it must surely have been connected to the perceived threat of Norwegian invasion at that time. Possibly, if he was aware that direct conflict between the two crowns was imminent, Eógan judged that his interests were more likely to be served in both short and long term by the protection of Henry III and Alexander III rather than that of Hákon IV.

The nature of the conflict in the west and the historiographical tradition of seeing it as an expansion and consolidation of the Scottish kingdom into autonomous, or indeed foreign, territory tend to lead to a depiction of the lords of that area in a light of 'otherness' – characters who were separate from Scottish noble society, who were later, to some extent, to become assimilated. This cannot be said of Eógan, however. As noted above, the willingness of the earls of Fife, Mar and Strathearn to stand surety for him, and the marriage of his daughter Mary to the earl of Strathearn, and of his son to a daughter of John Comyn, demonstrate that he was no stranger to the Scottish aristocratic caste. As the case of John Russell would show, those who tried to insinuate themselves into the ruling elite received scant welcome. (The marriage of Christiana, the niece of Eógan's cousin Dubgall, to a son of the earl of Mar is another example of the place of the western lords in the heart of the social and political life of the Scottish aristocracy.)

Less than six months after Eógan's submission to Alexander III in September 1255, Henry III made clear the continuing unsettled situation in the west when he prohibited Áengus son of Domnall (who was a Macdonald cousin of Eógan) and 'other malefactors of the kingdom of Scotland' from being received in Ireland.[57] Henry also took sides in the succession to the kingdom of Man, which was, in similar fashion to the rivalries between the descendants of Somerled,

---

56 *Paisley Reg.*, p. 135; *RMS*, ii, no. 3136. The see of Argyll had for some time been subject to administration by Clement bishop of Dunblane, who was with the king in the summer of 1249, and who was blamed by Matthew Paris (perhaps, if Duncan and Brown are right, at the prompting of Eógan himself) for the deteriorating relationship between Eógan and the king (A.A.M. Duncan and A.L. Brown, 'Argyll and the Isles in the Earlier Middle Ages', *Proceedings of the Society of Antiquaries of Scotland*, 90 (1959), pp. 190–220, at pp. 208–10).

57 *CDS*, i, no. 2041.

disputed between two branches of the family succeeding Godred, a late twelfth-century king. In 1248, following the drowning of the young King Harald, who had been knighted by none other than Henry III in the previous year, his brother Rognvald had briefly taken the throne, only to be ousted and killed by his cousin's son, another Harald. It was this Harald who was answering a summons to the Norwegian court in 1250 when Eógan attacked Man. In that expedition Eógan was not alone: he was in the company of Magnus, the younger brother of King Reginald, who was himself to be given the kingdom by Hákon IV in 1254. It was this man whom Henry knighted in April 1256, and whom he supported against Harald and his accomplices.[58] Eógan, it seems, had failed to make his allegiance to Hákon IV translate into effective lordship in either the Hebrides or Man, and his decision to seek once again the peace of Henry III and Alexander III, taking advantage of the political ferment of September 1255, must therefore be seen as recognition that his future lay instead as a mainland lord of Alexander III's Scotland.

The crowns of both England and Scotland thus took strategic interest in the tumultuous affairs of the west, and particularly of the kingdom of Man: as it had been for many decades, the Irish Sea was 'awash with English ambition', the result of strategic interest in the area following the English conquest of Ireland from the late 1160s onwards.[59] As Alexander emerged from his minority, these issues soon occupied centre stage. In April 1260 Henry repeated his exhortation regarding the reception in Ireland of any recalcitrant subjects of Alexander, a sign that matters in the west were once again, or continued to be, unsettled. It is not clear what had prompted Alexander to request that Henry would not give assistance to the king of Man. In 1260 the king of Man was still the Magnus whom Henry had supported in 1256, and Henry's evasive answer to Alexander seems to indicate that he was not prepared to commit to reversing English policy towards Magnus. Henry's policy in the west was coloured by his primary focus on the strategic need to avoid exacerbating the opposition to his rule in Wales, and he had no wish to make unnecessary enemies in, or across, the Irish Sea. Alexander, however, clearly saw danger for Scotland in Man and, given his later annexation of it, it is probable that his request to Henry presaged an imminent attack. Scottish action in the isles in 1259 and 1260, though ignored by some recent commentators, did occur and forms an important part of the backdrop to the negotiations of 1262–63. Henry's instruction in August 1259 to allow Alexander Stewart to procure provisions in Ireland for an expedition must refer to a Scottish attempt to exert

58 Anderson, *Early Sources*, ii, pp. 567–68, 587. *CDS*, i, no. 2046.
59 McDonald, *Sea Kings*, p. 123.

pressure on the isles, quite possibly including Man. If Alexander III was conducting operations in the area, it makes sense that he would ask Henry not to support Magnus against him, and equal sense that Henry was evasive in his answer: he would rather see a compliant Magnus on that throne than have Man open to strategically dangerous Scottish control. Further, that it was Stewart who seems to have led this expedition is also significant of Alexander's intent: the Stewart family had for long been promoted as Scottish royal agents in parts of the west – as early as the twelfth century the family had been given estates on the Clyde coast 'as a bulwark against the wild Scots of the Inner Hebrides', and their crown-sponsored expansion continued, a counterbalance to the power of Somerled's descendants.[60] It is possible that Alexander's action in the isles was in response to ongoing trouble there: Irish annals report raiding by 'the son of Somerled' (perhaps Dubgall, in company with Norwegian adventurers) during 1258:

> A great fleet came from the Hebrides' which, after conflict with the English sheriff of Connaught (whom, amongst many others, they killed), returned homewards 'with joy and profit from triumphant victory.[61]

Peace – or at least Scottish control – in the isles could not be brought about solely by force of arms, and the action of the late 1250s may simply have been a calculated prelude to negotiations. Clearly, the reception of Eógan in 1255, and the consequent involvement in the affairs of Man, as well as the ongoing administrative and military action in the west throughout the minority, demonstrate that Scottish policy towards the west had not been put on hold following the death of Alexander II: it remained a live issue, which was pursued when circumstances allowed. In the summer of 1261 Alexander sent an embassy to the court of King Hákon; it is generally assumed that they offered to purchase the isles. The idea was not well received, the envoys apparently being mistrusted: 'they went more with fair words than with good faith, as it appeared to the king.' Obviously failing in their mission, the two men tried to leave surreptitiously, but were caught and brought back to the court, where they were detained for some months. Detention, however, did not mean imprisonment: during his involuntary residence in Bergen, the knight, 'Sir Missel', was able to witness the coronation of Hákon's son and heir, Magnus, a spectacle which moved him deeply, since 'it is not the custom to crown kings in Scotland'.[62]

60 Cowan, 'Norwegian Sunset – Scottish Dawn', p. 112.
61 Anderson, *Early Sources*, ii, pp. 594–95.
62 Magnus, as heir apparent, was crowned in September 1261. Anderson, *Early Sources*, ii, pp. 601–04.

The identities of Alexander's seemingly unskilled diplomats remains a mystery. One was an archdeacon, the other named as a knight, Missel. Missel has been tentatively identified as a member of either the Fraser family (his name a misrepresentation of Frissel, a common variant of the surname) or the Strathearn family, possibly Malise (Máel Ísu), laird of Rossie; either identification is purely conjectural. The archdeacon presents a choice of seven known incumbents (excluding those in the tangential sees of the Isles, Caithness and Orkney), of whom the only men known to have undertaken royal service with any regularity were the archdeacons of St Andrews and of Lothian, William Wishart and Thomas Charteris, respectively. Wishart was royal chancellor, and cannot have been the anonymous archdeacon envoy, as he was in attendance on the king in both August 1261 and late March 1262,[63] at which times he would have been detained at the Norwegian king's pleasure. There is no evidence to place Charteris, who was a graduate and a member of the familia of Bishop Gamelin, either in or outwith Scotland in that period, and so he is a possible candidate. His relative youth (he would probably have been in his twenties) might explain both his anonymity and his lack of diplomatic skill.[64] Another candidate might be John Everley, the archdeacon of Dunkeld, who had legal and administrative experience, and was on several occasions used as a papal judge-delegate. A case has also been made for Master Godfrey, the archdeacon of Galloway, who, although not otherwise active in royal service, was later used as an envoy to Norway in the negotiations regarding the marriage of Princess Margaret. Appointed to the archdeaconry in the 1250s, he was by 1261 a man of some experience, and he certainly came from a diocese where he would have gained an understanding of the issues relating to Man and the Isles. It is quite feasible, given his later use in the marriage negotiations, that he spoke Norwegian, although not enough is known about his background to support the notion.[65] In any case, the hapless envoys seem not to have understood the etiquette of their position, and their lack of freedom to return home caused Alexander sufficient anxiety to lead him to seek the intervention of Henry III. The business carried before Henry III by Alexander's envoy John of Lindores in February–March 1262 included a request that Henry should use his influence to obtain their release, and a letter from Henry to Hákon in the following October suggests that he had indeed done so, and that (with or without Henry's intercession) Hákon had let them go.[66]

63 Watt, *Graduates*, pp. 590–94; *RRS*, iv pt.1, no. 33; *Registrum de Panmure*, ed. J. Stuart (Edinburgh, 1874), ii, pp. 82–83.

64 Watt, *Graduates*, pp. 85–86.

65 Watt, *Graduates*, pp. 184–85, 224–25; *APS*, i, p. 423.

66 *CDS*, ii, nos. 2289, 2295, 2320.

Whether prompted by the failure of diplomacy or not, Alexander once more had boots on the ground in the islands in the summer of 1262. Under the leadership of the earl of Ross and Kiarnak the son of Makamal, Skye (which was part of the kingdom of Man, and thus of concern both to Hákon and to Henry III) was viciously attacked:

> . . . they went out to Skye, and burned a town and churches, and slew very many [peasant] men and women. And they said also that the Scots had taken the little children, and laid them on their spear-points, and shook [their spears] until they brought [the children] down to their hands; and so threw them away, dead. They said also that the Scottish king intended to lay under himself all the Hebrides.[67]

This was the alarmed, even hysterical report to Hákon in Bergen: clearly it was feared that Alexander was intensifying his pressure on the isles with the intention of seizing them altogether (a policy which the saga had also ascribed to Alexander II in 1249). Hákon could not ignore such concerns. The use by Alexander of William, earl of Ross in the attack on Skye echoed the rôle played by his father, Fearchar, in both Moray and Galloway on behalf of Alexander II. Theirs was a powerful native family, which for many years had been well-rewarded agents of the Scottish crown in attempts to define and secure the boundaries of its authority. Little is known about Kiarnak, son of Makamal, who accompanied the earl in 1262. He reappears in the Exchequer Rolls (named as Kermac Macmaghaon, again in association with the earl of Ross) in the context of tribute taken from the area, probably in 1263,[68] and, judging by his Gaelic-sounding name, he must be similarly representative of the fact that the conflict in the west should not be seen primarily as a struggle between native Gaelic society and incomers.

Skye was not the only casualty of the Scottish expansion of 1261–62: by 1263 Walter, earl of Menteith seems also to have acquired lands in Knapdale from the mac Suibhne (MacSween) family. Such acquisitions were not necessarily either violent or opposed: in 1261 Dubgall mac Suibhne had made a grant to Paisley abbey of the patronage of churches in Knapdale in Argyll; one of the witnesses was Walter Stewart, earl of Menteith, indicating at least a working relationship between them.[69] If the Stewart takeover within the next two years is to be seen as

---

67 Anderson, *Early Sources*, ii, p. 605. See also Cowan, 'Norwegian Sunset – Scottish Dawn', p. 118 & n.

68 *ER*, i, p. 19.

69 *Paisley Reg.*, pp. 120–21, 121–22. The first is Dubgall's charter, witnessed by Walter Stewart; the second is Walter's own confirmation of the same grant. See also McDonald, *Kingdom of the Isles*, pp. 106–07, quoting Barrow, *Kingship and Unity*, p. 116. Barrow discusses this further in

colonisation, it seems to have been achieved in a spirit of at least nominal cooperation, rather than one of coercion. Nonetheless, complaints made several decades later demonstrate that Dubgall's descendants were less than happy with what they regarded as their disinheritance. Doubtless this example was not unique and, irrespective of how it was achieved, the insertion into this area of families owing unquestioned allegiance to the Scottish crown must have been an important aspect of the gradual loosening of ties to the Norwegian crown, and of the creeping realisation that the relative autonomy of former centuries was a fading dream.

It is not the case that the violence in the isles during the late 1250s and early 1260s led inevitably to war. Henry III continued to attempt to mediate. His letter to Hákon of October 1262 makes it clear that he had sought assurances that Hákon did not intend to invade Scotland 'or to excite war' and had urged a peaceful resolution to the dispute. Additionally, he told Hákon that he had requested Alexander to recompense Hákon for injuries sustained by Norway at Scottish hands. Henry also wrote to Alexander, urging him not to lead a campaign to the islands 'next summer'. The letter is not dated, but it seems likely to relate to 1263.[70] It seems probable that the Scots actions of 1260–63 were quite specifically intended to bring things to a head and to force Hákon into action; Henry cannot have been insensible of this. Henry could see his grip on Scotland weakening, and by playing the arbitrator he may have hoped to reassert his position. His stated belief as late as October 1262 that Hákon would not pick up the gauntlet so effectively thrown down by Alexander, as well as naïve ignorance of where Hákon's fleet was headed when it appeared in the summer of 1263,[71] both suggest that he was out of touch with the true nature of the situation. On the other hand, Alexander did send envoys to Henry in the early months of 1263 (on business relating again, at least in part, to the non-payment of Margaret's dowry), and it seems unlikely that they would not have carried news.[72] In reporting on the appearance of Hákon's fleet to Henry (or at least to the royal chancellor, Walter Merton), Robert Neville declared that many of those in the isles whom

---

Kingdom of the Scots, p. 373.

70 Walter Waddington Shirley (ed.), *Royal and Other Historical Letters Illustrative of the Reign of Henry III from the Originals in the Public Record Office* (London, 1862–66), ii, pp. 246–47. The editor provisionally dates this 1263. Duncan, however (*Making of the Kingdom*, p. 577), suggests that it relates to 1264 or 1265, presumably because a reference to Alexander's young child and heir implies that it follows the birth in January 1264 of Prince Alexander. In the context of Henry's letter to Hákon, I agree with Cowan ('Norwegian Sunset – Scottish Dawn', p. 118) that late 1262 or early 1263 is more probable.

71 *CDS*, i, no. 2351.

72 John Cheam, bishop of Glasgow, seems to have been one of these envoys; he was in England in February 1263, and was used by Henry as an envoy to France later in the year (*CDS*, i, nos. 2326, 2328, 2347; E.W.M. Balfour-Melville, 'John de Cheam, Bishop of Glasgow', *Scottish Historical Review*, 47 (1948), pp. 176–86).

they had thought to be loyal had now turned out to be rebellious. One gains the impression now of Henry as a bystander on the touchline, shouting futilely at both teams. The suggestion that Henry's lack of realism might actually have been wilful, and potentially nefarious, has much to recommend it.[73]

By late 1262 Hákon could no longer ignore the Scottish threat to his dominion over the isles: it was also a threat to the status of his kingship. With the advice of his council he commanded an armed expedition to be prepared over the winter of 1262–63, and his fleet, supposedly carrying the greatest host ever to have left the shores of Norway, set sail in early July, taking only two days to cross the North Sea.[74] The style of the saga-writing has imbued this story, and most of the subsequent historiographical tradition, with an atmosphere of the ninth-century Viking raid. It is easy to picture Hákon as his ship 'divided the high-ridged blue waves of the main', eager for the fight, at the prow of his great longship, built in Bergen specially for the expedition, 'entirely of oak: it had a fine dragon's head, all gilded; and so too the neck'.[75] In fact, though, this was an organised and considered military expedition, and would have depended on the same bureaucratic preparations for war which from time to time appear, drily, in the English chancery records. Even the saga tells us that in the spring Hákon had sent messengers to Orkney to warn of the arrival of the fleet during the summer and to procure pilots with local knowledge.[76] This was the nation's army called up for the defence of the kingdom. It would have been subject to the same – or greater – difficulties of logistics, finance and morale as any other force. Hákon waited for two weeks in Shetland, while tribute was raised in Caithness, and a raid on the Moray Firth (which does not seem to have been carried out) was considered, perhaps as retribution for the earl of Ross's activities in Skye. From Shetland, they moved on to Orkney. During these weeks it seems that scouts had been sent westwards to ascertain the lie of the land, and to assess the level of loyalty and support that Hákon could expect. Among the returning reports was the disappointing news that Eógan of Lorn had thrown in his lot with the Scottish king. Given that Eógan had come into Henry's and Alexander's peace almost eight

73 Cowan, 'Norwegian Sunset – Scottish Dawn', p. 118, where it is suggested that Henry and his advisors may have been 'sufficiently devious to be wilfully blind' and that 'Henry harboured some notion that Scotland's defeat might prove England's opportunity'. Further detailed analysis of the campaign is provided in McDonald, *Sea Kings*, pp. 170–80.

74 Anderson, *Early* Sources, ii, p. 606. The following chronology of Hákon's campaign relies mainly on the account given in McDonald, *Kingdom of the Isles*, pp. 107–115 and Duncan, *Making of the Kingdom*, pp. 578–80, both of which rely heavily on the detailed information provided in the fullest source, Hákon's Saga. Much of the relevant material from the saga is printed in translation in Anderson, *Early Sources*, ii, pp. 608–42.

75 Anderson, *Early Sources*, ii, pp. 610, 614.

76 Anderson, *Early Sources*, ii, pp. 610–11.

years previously, this cannot have come as a huge surprise: Hákon might at best have hoped that Eógan would be swayed to abandon the Scottish fold by a dual loyalty, based on territories held in both kingdoms and by the imminent threat from an approaching army. The saga states that Hákon would not believe the news until he heard it from Eógan himself, but confirmation was not long in coming. Hákon's cause suffered a critical blow through loss both of local recruits and of the prestige and influence carried by a lord of Eógan's standing.

If Henry III was out of touch with the situation in the period leading up to the launch of the Norwegian expedition, the same cannot be said of the leadership in Scotland. The Norwegian intention had been well signalled: as part of the inevitable propaganda surrounding such conflicts, deliberate rumours of the impending arrival of the Norwegian fleet (40 ships strong, it was said) had been circulated in the islands, in order to discourage the Scots from raiding.[77] It is fortunate that among the earliest survivals of Scottish royal financial records are the accounts of several of the sheriffs, which depict preparations for the Norwegian attack, and for the expenses incurred during the months of conflict.[78] The Norwegian fleet was watched as it made its progress round the coast: the fees of the *nunciorum explorancium* (spies, or scouts) employed by the sheriff of Ayr on three separate occasions came to the not inconsiderable sum of £1 4s 8d. Ships were built (although Alexander did not in the event dare to take on Hákon at sea), weapons made, garrisons increased, fortifications repaired and strengthened, and the storehouses stocked with grain and meat (partly procured through levies imposed on Caithness, Ross and other areas). Inverey castle (held by the earl of Buchan) and its drawbridge were repaired, a new hall was built, and a garrison of eight men was installed for a period of six months, *tempore adventus regis Norwegie*, all at the expense of the king. The location of the castle is not certain, but it could have been either 'Ulerin' near Forres (as suggested by the editor of the Exchequer Rolls) or more probably Inverie in Knoydart, on the shores of Loch Nevis. Inverie fits as part of the strategic preparation of the west, and suggests that the Scots monarch had significant naval resources at his command.[79] References are also made, however, to similar work at other, more easterly locations (including Aberdeen), which, although they are not specifically said to be in relation to the Norwegian invasion, were

77 Anderson, *Early Sources*, ii, p. 611.

78 All the information for the following description of the preparations made by the Scots for the Norwegian attack is from *ER*, i, pp. 1–34, *passim*. See also the summary in *ER*, i, pp. lxii–lxv, and the royal acts assumed to have existed from the evidence of the financial records, in *RRS*, iv pt. 1, nos. 224–27.

79 G.W.S. Barrow, 'The Army of Alexander III's Scotland', in Reid, *Alexander III Essays*, pp. 132–147, at p. 137.

being undertaken at the same time and should therefore probably be seen in the same context. In the west, fortifications were readied all the way down the coast, as far as Wigtown, where masonry work was carried out on the castle 'on account of the approach of the Norwegians'. Vigilance was heightened too: Stirling castle, for instance, had its watch increased when it was felt to be under danger from the marauders who penetrated to Loch Lomond and beyond, and the watch on the king's ships berthed at Ayr was intensified. The preparations were not merely military: as Hákon himself had done, the Scots king sought to ensure the loyalty of the far northern mainland as well as the west by taking tribute and hostages.[80] Caithness suffered twice: after Hákon had taken tribute from it in July, Alexander demanded that it had to provide no fewer than 21 hostages to be maintained at the expense of the sheriff of Inverness for a period of six months. Occasional references in the accounts also reveal that, political rivals or otherwise, the earl of Buchan and Alan Durward were jointly responsible for much of the preparation on the king's behalf: it is stated that they had 'the power of the king, by his letters patent'.

Under the watchful eyes of the Scottish spies, Hákon's fleet left Orkney, arriving at Kyleakin, where the fast-flowing narrows between Skye and the mainland are now bridged, in the first weeks of August. For the first time in half a century, a foreign force was on territory which the king of Scots regarded as part of the Scottish realm. War was now the only option.

From Skye the fleet headed south, past Mull to Kerrera, gathering support and ensuring the allegiance of as many of the island lords as could be persuaded. Eógan's cousin, Dubgall, who still retained his client-kingship of the Isles, remained loyal to Hákon, as did King Magnus of Man, both of whom supplied useful additions to the force. Dubgall, it was said, had dissuaded the Scots from attacking the isles earlier in the summer by telling them that the Norwegian fleet was imminently expected. Others came to Hákon's flag too, among them members of the mac Suibhne family, perhaps smarting from their recent dispossession by the Stewarts. The Islay branch of the MacSorley family was less certain in its allegiance, but under pressure from Hákon's forces who landed on Kintyre and threatened their mainland and island territories, they submitted to him. His forces swollen by local adherents, 'Hakon had then between one and two hundred ships; and most of them large, and well-manned.'[81] Bute fell, and it seems that Dunaverty was also surrendered. The Norwegian crown may have been effectively absent from the region for many years, but it was still, with force behind it, able

80 It is not always entirely clear within the accounts when the various expenses were incurred within the period 1263–66. It seems probable, however, that tribute and hostages were taken both in 1263 and in 1264/65.

81 Anderson, *Early Sources*, ii, p. 617.

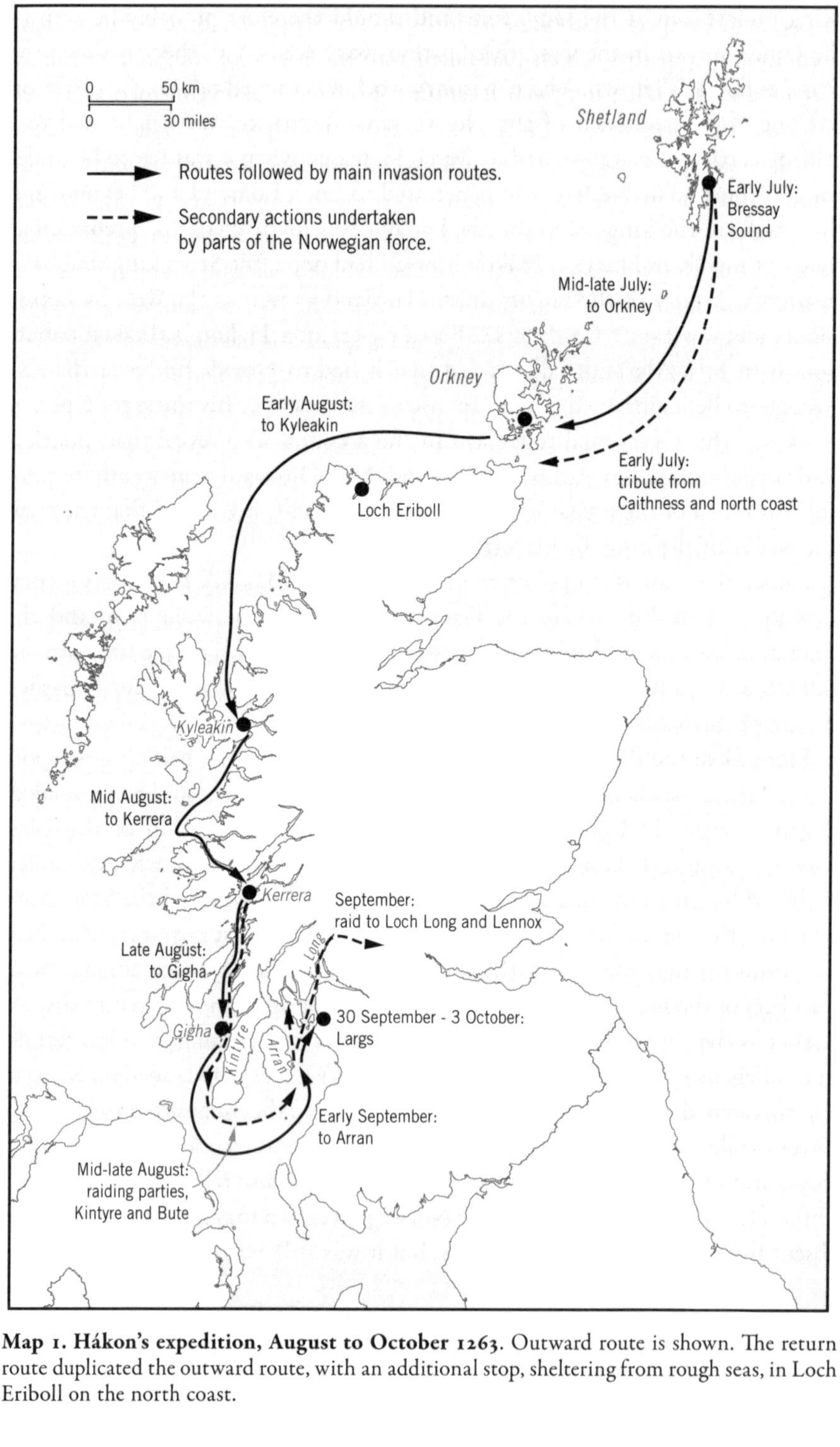

Map 1. Hákon's expedition, August to October 1263. Outward route is shown. The return route duplicated the outward route, with an additional stop, sheltering from rough seas, in Loch Eriboll on the north coast.

to command respect. Although its lordship was disputed, Bute seems to have been another territory which had fallen into the hands of the Stewart family, perhaps as early as the later twelfth century: it offered Hákon control of the Firth of Clyde, 'the gateway to the heart of the Scottish kingdom'.[82] Hákon may have been later in the season than was ideal (Dubgall mac Ruaridh is said to have urged him to hurry up), but he commanded much support and posed a serious threat to the Scottish crown. He still hoped to persuade Eógan to join him, but Eógan, citing the oath of loyalty that he had made to Alexander, and stating that he held more land of the Scottish throne than of the Norwegian, refused to give way and resigned the lands held of Hákon back into his hands. Hákon kept him prisoner for a while, but then released him without harm, and some of the saga texts claim that Eógan offered to act as a go-between for the two kings.

The expenses of Dominican friars sent by Alexander to conduct negotiations with Hákon were later recorded in the accounts of the sheriff of Inverness: Alexander's aggression over a couple of years had forced Hákon to enter the fray, but neither king wanted unnecessary loss of life or the devastation of their lands which warfare would incur. From positions of strength commanded by both kings in different ways, a negotiated settlement was preferable. The choice of Dominicans to conduct these negotiations is interesting. The Dominican order was somewhat favoured in this period in Scotland, having been introduced as recently as the 1230s. By the mid century they probably had 11 houses in Scotland, most of them foundations of Alexander II; the old king's grant of burgh ferms to the Dominicans of Perth had been confirmed by Alexander III's charter in 1251.[83] There is no evidence for the extensive selection of Dominicans for such diplomatic undertakings, although they were used in the same period as envoys to Man, and again, in late 1264, to Norway.[84] They were known for their intellectual and pedagogical activity, and it is possible that men in holy orders would have been particularly respected as impartial negotiators. It is conceivable, particularly if the chances of success were limited, that Alexander did not risk envoys of higher social or political status, fearing that they might be taken hostage. On the other hand, Clement, bishop of Dunblane, to whom Alexander II had entrusted the administration of the see of Argyll during its vacancy, and who had been with the old king on Kerrera when he died, was a Dominican. He was well educated, probably had an international scholarly reputation, and was said to be 'a man most eloquent in translating various

82 McDonald, *Kingdom of the Isles*, p. 111.

83 *RRS*, iv pt. 1, no. 10.

84 *ER*, i, p. 17. I am grateful to Drs Bill Hyland and Rory Cox for useful comments on the question of the rôle of these Dominican friars. Alexander also used Franciscans, in the negotiations leading to the treaty of Perth (*CDS*, i, no. 2373; *ER*, i, p. 26).

tongues'.[85] In royal circles at least, he may have left a legacy of respect for his order in relation to the affairs of the west.[86] Whatever their qualifications for the task, the friars seemed to have made fair progress: Hákon sent his envoys (including the two bishops of Hamar and Orkney) to the Scottish king, who declared himself ready to make peace. Several meetings seem to have taken place, but, despite apparent goodwill, an impasse was reached, the sticking point apparently being the possession of Bute, Arran and the Cumbraes, over which neither king was prepared to compromise; 'about the rest there was little [conflict] between the claims of the kings'.[87] It would appear that the Scottish king, at this stage at least, was not making a bid for possession of all of the western isles, but was prepared to reach a settlement which offered secure possession of the strategically important inner islands and western mainland. Following the stalemate Hákon issued an ultimatum: meet with their armies and either make peace or fight. The saga, hardly the most impartial of sources, relates both that the king of Scots was afraid to take on Hákon, and that Alexander's unwillingness to negotiate meaningfully was caused by duplicity: the Scots 'withdrew the terms of the peace, because the summer was nearly over, and the state of the weather began to grow worse'.[88] It was at this point that Hákon dispatched a large flotilla of ships – fast Hebridean galleys, commanded by Dubgall mac Ruaridh and his brother Alan, as well as Áengus and Murchaid, the two sons of Domnall of Islay – up Loch Long, across the narrow portage at Tarbert and into Loch Lomond. Ravaging deep into the mainland, the raiding party may have reached almost to Stirling.

> Flight-dreading ring-users of the swayer of darts'-crashing drew their boats by the broad strand-ways. The warriors of Skati, not fearful of journeying, wasted with spear-wind the islands in the widely-inhabited lake.[89]

It was a bold move, designed to emphasise that nowhere in Scotland was secure; more importantly, it has been argued that it was a deliberate attack on the Lennox and Menteith lands of the Stewarts and their kin, whose encroachments on the inner isles – particularly the disputed Bute, Arran and Cumbraes – remained an open sore, and a key element of the conflict.[90]

---

85 *Chron. Bower*, v, pp. 320–21.
86 See Oram, *Alexander II*, pp. 188, 212–13; Watt, *Graduates*, pp. 99–103.
87 *RRS*, iv pt.1, no. 223; Anderson, *Early Sources*, ii, pp. 622–23.
88 Anderson, *Early Sources*, ii, pp. 622–25.
89 Anderson, *Early Sources*, ii, p. 626.
90 Anderson, *Early Sources*, ii, pp. 625–26; see also Cowan, 'Norwegian Sunset – Scottish Dawn', pp. 121–22; McDonald, *Kingdom of the* Isles, pp. 112–13.

By this time, Hákon's main fleet was lying off Arran. If the Scots' intention in prevaricating over the negotiations had indeed been to wait for the weather to turn in their favour, it was a judgement well made. While Hákon's raiding party was laying waste the Lennox, on 30 September – 1 October a gale hit, so severe 'that men said that witchcraft was the cause of it'. Ten ships were said to have been wrecked in the storm, and, with more profound impact, some of the Norwegian ships still sheltering in the Firth of Clyde were driven ashore near Largs, the landing sailors targeted by Scots archers who retreated only when Hákon sent ashore more men. A larger Scottish force mustered on 2 October – numerous enough to persuade the Norwegians that the Scottish king himself had gathered his army to fight, as Hákon had demanded. The Scots attacked the stranded Norwegians on the shore, but were beaten back, allowing the survivors to retreat to the fleet in the bay.[91] By the fifteenth century the conflict had assumed the status of a great national victory, wrought by the intervention of none other than St Margaret herself, a tale which was to shape historiographical treatment of the period for many generations.[92] The triumphant pitched battle in reality seems to have been a disorganised series of skirmishes, which settled little and (despite the rhetoric of the sagas and of much subsequent Scottish historical writing) represented a decisive victory for neither side. Even the saga, which undoubtedly exaggerates the severity of the battle and the scale of losses, describes it rather half-heartedly: there were those on both sides who were more intent on escaping than fighting, and one repeated tactic of the Scots was to pelt the Norwegians with stones (despite the fact that they were said to have been well armed 'with bows and Irish axes').[93] It doesn't have the makings of an epic.

The aftermath of the 'battle' of Largs, though sometimes portrayed as a headlong flight on the part of the Norwegian fleet, was no such thing. Hákon took his time: he remained near Arran for some days, doubtless in full sight of the Scots forces on the mainland, before setting off northwards. His attitude seems to have been that his job was done. Despite further storms, he moved his fleet round the Mull of Kintyre and, via Gigha, back to Kerrera, where he attempted further futile negotiation with Eógan, who instead carried out 'a great shore-slaughter' on Mull. Moving on to Mull, Hákon paused to recognise the faithful service of his local supporters: Dubgall mac Ruaridh was given the island kingdom previously held of Hákon by Eógan, and others of Eógan's cousins received Bute and Arran. Although in hindsight Hákon's gifts carried

---

91 Anderson, *Early Sources*, ii, pp. 626–27.

92 *Chron. Bower*, v, pp. 336–39.

93 Anderson, *Early Sources*, ii, p. 630.

little weight, their intention was clearly to achieve continued loyalty within lands which Hákon believed would remain secure in his possession. The saga claims that Hákon had regained all of the lands taken at the end of the eleventh century by Magnus Barelegs. Still struggling against unfavourable weather, it was the end of the month before the Norwegian fleet, by way of Skye (where they took 'a tax of stores') reached the shelter of Loch Eriboll on the north coast. At that point, the saga notes another minor skirmish on land, an indication that the Scots had a force keeping an eye on the fleet as it headed northwards. They had been tracking it on its outward journey: it would make sense that they would continue to keep watch as it left. Crossing from there to Orkney on 29 October, another ship was lost to the elements, and the saga-writer hints that morale was low when he tells us that while Hákon sought refuge in Kirkwall, most of his fleet headed straight for Norway – 'some, with the king's leave; but many gave themselves leave'. Hákon had been ill throughout the summer; in the bishop's palace in Kirkwall he finally succumbed to his illness, dying in the early hours of the morning on 16 December as the sagas of his ancestors were read to him in his native tongue.[94] After his death

> the king's body was carried up into the loft-hall, and set upon a bier. The body was clothed in robes of state, and a garland was set upon his head; and in all respects things were done as they ought to be done, for a crowned king. The torch-bearers stood holding candles. The whole hall was lighted up.

After two days of lying in state, 'the peace-giving wise watcher of the northern hill-pastures' was buried in the choir of St Magnus cathedral, from where his body was moved back to Norway after the winter had passed.

94 Some accounts reported that he listened first to the Bible (or other Latin books), and then, as he weakened, to the vernacular sagas (Anderson, *Early Sources*, ii, pp. 640–41 & nn.).

CHAPTER 6

Beyond Borders

Despite his unhurried return northwards and his apparent confidence that he had reasserted his authority, Hákon IV had left his son and heir, Magnus IV, a legacy of far from peaceful dominion in the kingdom of the Isles. The nearest thing to a military disaster in Hákon's career, his campaign began late, was subject to further delays (despite the exhortations of, for instance, Dubgall mac Ruaridh), and seems to have been bedevilled by disagreement and indecision, leading to the inconclusive action at Largs. The retreat northwards was no flight, but was inevitable given the season and the mediocre level of local support. Despite his seniority and experience, Hákon had been outwitted. Magnus had little option but to negotiate: in the following spring he sent his chancellor, Askatin, an experienced diplomat,[1] along with Henry, bishop of Orkney, who had been used by Hákon as an envoy to the Scots king during the expedition in the previous year, 'to enquire about the making of peace between the lands'. They received as much of a hearing as Missel and the archdeacon had been given at the court of Hákon IV in the summer of 1261; they were threatened with death or imprisonment, and Askatin hurried home to report to Magnus that, in the wake of the devastation of so much of Scotland in the previous year, Alexander was in no mood to negotiate.[2] What Alexander was doing was playing for time until he could reinforce his position of superiority. The Icelandic Annals record that two Dominican friars went to Norway on Alexander's behalf in 1264, presumably the brother Malise and brother Simon of Berwick who appear in the accounts for 1264 as nuncios of the king

1 For Askatin, see Richard I. Lustig, 'The Treaty of Perth: A Re-examination', *Scottish Historical Review*, 58 (1979), pp. 35–57, at p. 37. Dr Lustig's article remains the best treatment of the negotiations leading to the treaty of Perth, and of the treaty itself. The account given here largely follows his argument. For source citations, unless otherwise noted, Lustig's article should be consulted.

2 Anderson, *Early Sources*, ii, p. 647.

going 'ultra mare'. In mid November of that year Malise, presumably having returned from Norway some time before, was setting out for England in the company of friar Simon de la Fontagne, presumably updating Henry (or at least his baronial 'advisors') on the situation.[3] It may not be either irrelevant or coincidental that Alexander held a formal *colloquium* in November 1264: Malise and Simon may have had more to report than just the progress of the Norwegian negotiations.[4] Bishop Henry and two Franciscan monks were also back in Scotland on behalf of the Norwegian king in the summer, and were not as harshly received; but Alexander again bought time by sending them home with the suggestion that a further, higher-powered, embassy should come a year later, in the summer of 1265. It has been suggested that the Scottish king's response was in a sense a technical one, requesting an embassy of a different type: if Bishop Henry and the monks were *nuncios*, they had the power to negotiate, but not to commit to an agreement, and the process would take more time and expense as they carried any proposals back to their masters for approval. Alexander therefore probably indicated his willingness to negotiate, but with *procurators*, who carried a fuller authority actually to make an agreement. This interpretation accords well with the surviving evidence and points to the seriousness with which the whole affair was being treated. Moreover, it was very much in the Scottish king's interests to delay the entire process for a further year.

The backdrop to the initial negotiations in 1264 was further Scottish military action in the west, Alexander aiming to press home his tactical advantage by attacking the Isle of Man and reinforcing his hold on the Hebrides. The timing was fortuitous: Alexander had sought, but not received, an assurance from Henry as far back as 1260 that he would not give assistance to the king of Man, but now had the advantage not only of having successfully weathered the storm of Norwegian invasion, but of having Henry III in no position to oppose Scottish ambitions towards Man. Following Henry's repudiation in January 1264, with the assistance of Louis IX of France, of the Provisions of Oxford (the agreement with his rebellious baronage, which he had been forced to accept in 1258), civil war had broken out in England, leading to the battle of Lewes, in May. Lewes was disastrous for Henry, who lost both the battle and his freedom. In the summer of 1264, when the beleaguered king of Man might have sought his help, Henry was effectively under house arrest, and the baronial government which held power was focused on coping with the fighting

3 *ER*, i, p. 26; *CDS*, i, no. 2373.

4 *ER*, i, pp. 30, 33; this was also several months after the battle of Lewes; the business of the Scottish envoys may also have been relevant to the Scottish king's policy towards events in England; see below, pp. 198–201.

which continued in parts of England, and on preparation for the threatened royalist invasion from France. Long before the eventual victory of the royalist cause in the battle of Evesham in August 1265, the question of the Isle of Man, for a time at least, had been settled. Alexander's army and fleet had mustered in Galloway. (Although it is difficult to differentiate, some of the entries relating to the south-west in the sheriffs' accounts for the period 1263–66 will refer to this expedition to Man, rather than to defence against the Norwegian invasion.) *Gesta Annalia* tells us that the army was gathered as soon as news broke of the death of Hákon IV, but it seems more likely that, although the project was already well in the planning before mid December, the army did not gather before the spring or early summer of 1264. In the end, Alexander had no need to take to the water: Magnus, king of Man, submitted to him at Dumfries, offered hostages to guarantee good behaviour and paid homage for his kingdom (giving an annual render of the service of ten galleys for it) in return for protection against any future Norwegian attacks. The agreement was sufficient to allow Alexander to undertake not to attack Man itself, for the time being at least. It was to be a temporary arrangement: within a year, Magnus had died, and Man was annexed to the Scottish crown and governed by Scottish-appointed officials.[5]

Immediately following the submission of Man, Alexander sent a forceful message to the Hebrides, in the form of a fleet led by the earls of Buchan and Mar and Alan Durward, where they carried fire and sword into the lands of the recalcitrant pro-Norwegian lords, bringing some of them, but not all, into the Scottish fold. Áengus of Islay was one who made his peace with Alexander as a result of this raid, and probably in this period, rather than during preparation for the 1263 campaign, he was forced to give up as a hostage his infant son Alexander (with a nurse and servant), who was held at the expense of the sheriff of Ayr. His captivity was apparently in a style befitting his status: the *per diem* cost for the infant was significantly more than for the group of 21 Caithness men held in Inverness.[6] Alexander III

5 *SAEC*, p. 380; Anderson, *Early Sources*, ii, p. 657; *RRS*, iv pt. 1, no. 232, *ER*, i, p. 17; *Chron. Fordun*, i, pp. 300–01 (trans. ii, p. 296); *APS*, i, p. 112. Also, following the Treaty of Perth, *RRS*, iv pt.1, nos. 241–46.

6 *Chron. Fordun*, i, p. 301 (trans. ii, p. 296); *ER*, i, p. 5. *Gesta Annalia*'s assertion that Buchan, Mar and Durward were personally involved in carrying out the king's policy is borne out by *ER*, i, 11 & 19–20. These correspond to *RRS*, iv pt. 1, nos. 225, 226, where they are dated 1263; following McDonald, *Kingdom of the Isles*, p. 116, I have preferred the 1264 date, which seems to make more sense in the context of the political situation. Áengus's submission, and an undertaking by other barons of Argyll to support the king should he renege on it, are no longer extant, but are noted in the lists of Scottish muniments, *APS*, i, pp. 109, 112.

then turned his attention to the far northern mainland, which saw further tribute and hostages taken from Ross and Caithness.[7] The saga sources are clear: not only is the picture painted of Caithness as a fiscal and territorial battleground, but the very believable scenario of continuing action on the part of Dubgall (and no doubt others) there and elsewhere is suggested. Further fighting followed at sea between Dubgall and a Scottish fleet in the summer of 1264 or 1265, and there is a sense of an axis of activity between the coast of Ireland and Orkney, which continued seriously to challenge the influence of the Scottish king.[8] Such activity was a tactic seen in earlier years: 'enemies' of the Scottish king (including Dubgall himself) had been active in Ireland in the late 1250s, and 'the son of Somerled' who plundered a merchant ship off the coast of Connemara in 1258 was almost certainly Dubgall himself.[9] Following the withdrawal of Hákon's fleet and the death of the Norwegian king, the disputed territories are not depicted as having waited quietly for royal diplomacy to reach a conclusion. There lingered an unresolved dissonance arising from the partly autonomous rule of local lords, who saw no reason to offer unforced allegiance to any king. Irish chronicle sources give a prominent position to Dubgall. He is mentioned frequently, and at the moment of his death in 1268 the Icelandic Annals describe him as 'king of the Hebrides'; the Irish *Annals of Loch Cé* go further and give him the more inflammatory (to the Scottish king at least) title 'king of the Hebrides and of Argyle'.[10] Despite their ambitions, neither Scotland nor Norway was widely perceived to have gained complete sovereignty over the islands and the western coastal lands. The Atlantic seaboard was also of strategic interest to England. In 1263 Hákon had considered, to the annoyance of his advisors, the offer of Irish support in return for assistance with the expulsion from Ireland of the English occupation.[11]

Throughout centuries there has been a firmly entrenched historiographical tradition which, despite successive waves of revisionism, continues to assert that the eventual victor had a right to their prize and fails to take full account of the perspectives of the vanquished. Most Scottish commentators have allowed hindsight and a centrist viewpoint to assert that the Scottish kingdom had a 'right' to rule over the western and island territories. A monarchocentric study, as this book is, could be accused of belonging inevitably to the same tradition, but fundamental assumptions have nonetheless to be challenged.

---

7 *ER*, i, p. 19–20; Anderson, *Early Sources*, ii, pp. 647–49.
8 Anderson, *Early Sources*, ii, p. 649.
9 Anderson, *Early Sources*, i, p. 594.
10 Anderson, *Early Sources*, ii, p. 660.
11 Anderson, *Early Sources*, ii, pp. 622, 634.

What right did the 'king of Scots' have to rule over these areas, and by whose dictate could they be claimed by any external authority?[12] If it is fair to characterise Argyll and the Hebrides as on the frontier of Scotland, it is equally fair to characterise the Lennox, for instance, as being on the frontier of the Hebridean kingdom: it is simply a matter of perspective. The Hebridean or Galwegian lord who ruled successfully over his lands, from the inhabitants of which he received rent and service, had no reason to accede to any external king or country's claim to higher authority, unless compelled by force of arms or circumstance. When it was in his interest to do so, there seems no reason to assume that he would necessarily choose to submit to the king of Scots, rather than one of his competitors. There were conflicting issues – regional, economic, societal, personal and familial – which affected such decisions. Equally if Alexander III aimed to incorporate this area into his kingdom, it was necessary for dominion to be achieved through military, economic and administrative pressure. The military, and, more importantly, diplomatic activity in the west has to be seen in the long-term contexts of the administrative development of Scottish government, as well as of the ecclesiastical, societal and economic developments that were described in Chapter 2.

Alexander II's last act, the gift of the church of St Bride near Oban to the see of Argyll (which may itself have been a creation, at the turn of the century, of the descendants of Somerled) can be regarded as a move towards the relocation of the seat of the diocese onto the mainland, to an area more amenable to central control. The church in question was in Eógan's territory, and the grant was therefore a challenge not only to his territorial lordship, but also to his patronage of the see (which he had allowed to remain vacant for some years) and to the effective separation of this see from the rest of the *ecclesia Scoticana*.[13] The appearance of royal bailiffs in this area as early as 1250 (and, more stridently, the attempt later to create a sheriffdom, in 1293[14]) is further evidence of an attempt to create administrative structures which would help to compel obedience. In February 1267, just as the dust was falling on both the armed conflict and its diplomatic resolution, Alexander III granted custody of the royal castle on the island of Fraoch Eilean in Loch Awe – a little to the south of Eógan's lordship of Lorne – to Gilla Críst, son of Máel Coluim MacNachtan, who, in

12 See Cowan's comments on the 'grave flaw in Alexandrian historiography' in 'Norwegian Sunset – Scottish Dawn', pp. 104–05.

13 *RMS*, ii, no. 3136; see the discussion of the history of the see, and of the significance of the king's gift, in McDonald, *Kingdom of the Isles*, pp. 211–14.

14 In 1293 King John Balliol tried to found sheriffdoms of Kintyre, Lorne and Skye. It is also noticeable that the earliest reference to the sheriffdom of Wigtown occurs in 1263. See Reid and Barrow, *Sheriffs*, pp. 28, 31, 41, 44; *APS*, i, p. 447.

the 1240s, had himself granted the church of Kilmorich (a few miles south, at the head of Loch Fyne) to the abbey of Inchaffray, which in 1257 had also received the church of St Findoc on the Loch Awe island of Inishail from Gilla Críst's brother Áed.[15] The crown was using a local family of generations-old local standing to affirm its influence in the area. Local lords were also associated with the foundation of, for example, the priories of Ardchattan (founded around 1230 by Eógan's father, Donnchad), Iona (re-founded by 1203 as a Benedictine house by Ranald, the son of Somerled) and Saddell (also founded by Ranald, at an unknown date before his death in 1207). It is also worth noting that the island lords did not restrict their donations solely to institutions within the areas ruled by them. The abbey of Paisley, for example, received gifts of the church of Kilkerran in Kintyre from Áengus Mór, of the Islay branch of the descendants of Somerled; of the church of Kilfinan in Argyll from Donnchad, son of Fearchar (whose own son, Áengus later gave a separate donation of land at Kilmory); and of the land of Skipness with its chapel of St Columba and other churches from Dubgall mac Suibhne (seen earlier in the context of loss of land to the Stewarts).[16] Equally, gifts to the religious houses in the disputed areas of the west were not given only by local donors: in the early 1250s Níall and Isabella, the earl and countess of Carrick, gave land in Ayrshire to Saddell abbey in Kintyre;[17] it was two-way traffic. The gifts of local churches have been identified as evidence of 'a strong proprietary nature to the churches in the western seaboard in the middle of the thirteenth century, as indeed there had been in Scotland generally in the twelfth'.[18]

It is evident that life on the western seaboard or in the Hebrides was not entirely distinct from that in more easterly mainland Scotland. The modern assumption of a linguistic, and therefore cultural, divide cannot be allowed either: as has been noted, virtually the whole of Scotland north of the Forth–Clyde valley was Gaelic-speaking. The apparently easy assimilation into the ruling elite of Eógan mac Dubhgaill in the years following 1255 makes it plain that he and his peers were no strangers in the kingdom ruled by the kings of

---

15 *RRS*, iv pt.1, no. 62; W.A. Lindsay, J. Dowden and J.M. Thomson (eds), *Charters, Bulls and other Documents relating to the Abbey of Inchaffray* (Edinburgh, 1908), nos. 73, 74, 85; see also Stephen Boardman, *The Campbells, 1250–1513* (Edinburgh, 2006), p. 12 & n.18. It is worth noting also that Alexander's grant to Gilla Críst was not a 'local' grant: it was made at Scone, and the witnesses were senior members of council – the earls of Buchan, Mar, Strathearn, Carrick and Alan Durward. This – which may of course have been petitioned for by Gilla Críst – was an act of policy.

16 *Paisley Reg.*, pp. 128–29, 130, 131 (Kilkerran); pp. 133–34 (Kilfinan); pp. 120–21, 121–22 (Skipness).

17 *RRS*, iv pt. 1, no. 177.

18 McDonald, *Kingdom of the Isles*, pp. 227–28.

Scots, and the long-standing use of the symbolism of knightly society by the magnates of the isles is clear evidence that they did not stand outside the norms of twelfth- and thirteenth-century European aristocracy. The notion of the west as a 'frontier society' leads to an over-simplistic view of the situation. Life in those areas was inextricably intertwined with the politics and society of Scotland, England, Ireland and – to a lesser extent by the thirteenth century – Norway. The island kingdom of Eógan and Dubgall and others may have been autonomous, but it was not separate, and the long-term competition for external control by Scotland, Norway and England, if it sometimes gave the Hebridean lords opportunities to play one off against the others, also made life politically and personally hazardous. There were those among them, therefore – most obviously (but certainly not uniquely) Eógan mac Dubhgaill – for whom a resolution of the conflict between Norway and Scotland offered as welcome an opportunity for definition of the boundaries of both territory and power as it did for the king of Scots.

If the notion of the 'otherness' of the disputed territories to the west of Scotland can be resisted, the negotiations which began in earnest in the summer of 1265 take on a different hue. The negotiators were not working on behalf of the kings alone, while 'others' to the west waited for the news with an indifference caused by generations of attempts to avoid effective rule by either party. As the provisions of the eventual treaty itself, as well as the subsequent history of the Hebrides and western seaboard, were to reveal, this was a moment of vital importance not only to the kings of Norway, Scotland and England, but to the lords, lairds and ordinary people who lived on the disputed lands, all of whom had suffered the effects of successive – and continuing – waves of violence, with its inevitable social and economic repercussions. In the spring of 1265 the Norwegian procurators, Gilbert, bishop of Hamar (whom Hákon had used as an envoy during the expedition of 1263) and the chancellor, Askatin, set off for Scotland via England.[19] They are said to have travelled via King's Lynn and York, although the continuing civil war in England would doubtless have made it difficult, if not impossible, to have meaningful discussions with either Henry III or his opponents. They may have been treated to the unusual – and undoubtedly portentous – sight of a comet which was visible in England for some weeks.[20] It was not until the battle of Evesham on 4 August (in which Simon de Montfort, earl of Leicester, the leader of the baronial opposition, died) that Henry prevailed and began to re-establish his authority over the country. By that time, however,

19 The narrative of the negotiations leading to the treaty of Perth which follows continues to rely on Lustig's 'The Treaty of Perth', and the sources cited therein, unless otherwise noted.

20 *Chron. Bower*, v, pp. 352–53, p. 469n. Bower says it was visible for 15 days; other chronicles have it for as long as three months.

it is likely that Gilbert and Askatin were already in Scotland, where they met Alexander at Perth.[21] Alexander had held a *colloquium* at Scone in the spring, at which the stance the Scots should take in the forthcoming negotiations was no doubt on the agenda, as well as their attitude to the affairs in England, about which Henry had sent envoys to the meeting. (Henry's pleas to Alexander to assist in the release of the hostages he had surrendered to the baronial council, including Alexander's brother-in-law, the future Edward I, have a ring of desperation about them.[22]) The proposal that Gilbert and Askatin made on behalf of King Magnus was that Alexander should take control of Bute and Arran (or Man, according to variant manuscripts of *Gesta Annalia*), leaving 'all the other islands which his father Hako[n] had demanded' in Norwegian hands.[23] Given both the intransigence with which the Scots had approached the brief negotiations in 1263 and the action which was still in progress in the Hebrides, it seems inconceivable that there was any expectation that such an offer would have been accepted; the hint of 'I told you so' which *Gesta Annalia* attributes to Gilbert in his report back to Magnus (he 'pointed out to his king that his trouble had been thrown away') may be fanciful, but the mental image is not hard to conjure.

Gilbert and Askatin returned to Norway, possibly accompanied by (among others) a Scottish nuncio, the monk Reginald who is so lauded in the *Chronicle of Melrose*, to persuade Magnus to think again.[24] Over the winter it seems that further discussions took place in Norway, and perhaps also in Scotland in the spring and early summer of 1266, culminating in the final agreement, the treaty which was sealed in the Blackfriars monastery in Perth on 2 July.[25] Magnus's representatives

21 Lustig ('The Treaty of Perth', p. 38n.) suggests that the hasty repairs to the castle of Wigtown because of the impending arrival of the Norwegians (*ER*, i, p. 30) was in preparation for the visit of Askatin and Gilbert. This seems unlikely, however, since travel to Perth from York seems unlikely to have been broken at Wigtown, which would add at least 100 miles to the journey for no apparent reason. It seems more likely that the record of payment for the repairs at Wigtown (which are indeed stated to fall within the 1264/65 accounting year) relate to a retrospective finalisation of accounts from the previous year, implying that the work was in preparation for the invasion of 1263.

22 *CDS*, i, nos. 2377–79.

23 This suggestion is recorded in the pages of *Gesta Annalia* (*Chron. Fordun*, i, p. 301 (trans. ii, p. 296)).

24 Lustig's argument ('Treaty of Perth', pp. 39–44) that the *Chronicle of Melrose* (Faustina B. IX, fos. 65v–66r) has greatly amplified the importance both of Reginald and of the proposal for an agreement which is contained in the chronicle, is accepted here.

25 The best printed text of the treaty is now that provided, with a good translated abridgement, in *RRS*, iv pt. 1, no. 61. Once again, the association of the Black Friars with the peace process may be noted. Given that, according to the treaty, the king with the clergy and greater magnates of the realm were there in person, it seems likely that the gathering in Perth in July 1266 should be seen as a formal *colloquium* (although the editors of the Records of the Parliaments of Scotland website have chosen not to regard it as such).

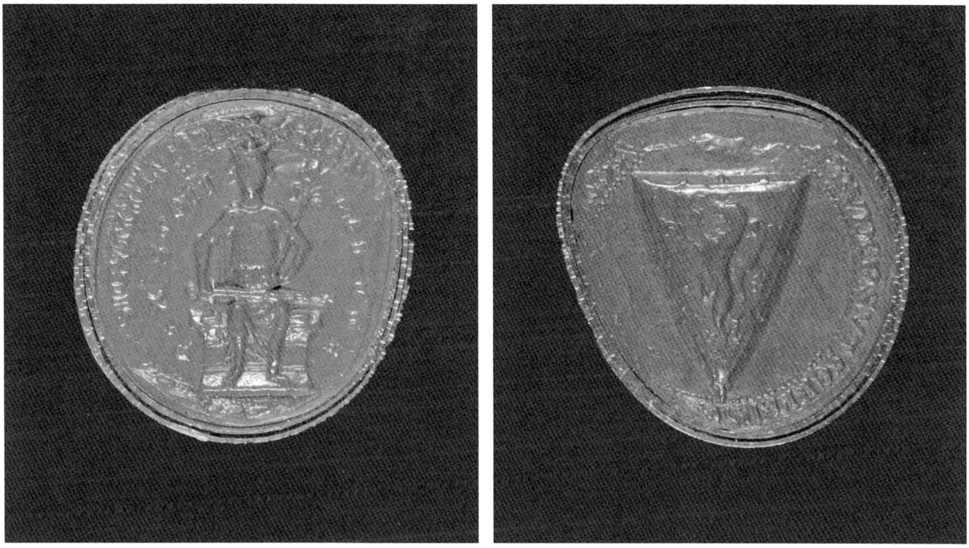

Plates 1 and 2. Casts of the obverse and reverse of the minority seal (second version) of Alexander III, from an act confirming a sale of land to the abbot and convent of Melrose, 8 June 1252.

Reproduced courtesy of the Keeper of the Records of Scotland (NRS, RH17/1/15-16, casts of seal appended to GD55/336)

Plates 3 and 4. Obverse and reverse of the Great Seal (second version) of Alexander III, from a letter regarding the marriage of Prince Alexander to Marguerite, daughter of the Count of Flanders, 4 December 1281.

Reproduced courtesy of Archives de l'État à Namur, Belgium (Chartes de Namur, no. 149)

Plate 5. (*Above*) Pluscarden abbey.

Photograph by G. Allan Little, 1971, reproduced courtesy of the University of St Andrews Library (GAL-17-412)

Plate 6. (*Right*) Sweetheart abbey, aerial view.

© HES (John Dewar Collection, SC 1555809)

Plate 7. Jedburgh abbey from the south-east.

Photograph by George Washington Wilson & Co., 1875, reproduced courtesy of the University of St Andrews Library (ALB-13-33)

Plate 8. Dryburgh abbey cloisters.

Photograph by J.M. & M. J. Playfair, 1906–1952, reproduced courtesy of the University of St Andrews Library (PLFR-12-10-53)

Plate 9. Artist's reconstruction of St Andrews cathedral as it might have appeared in the early fifteenth century, by Alan Sorrell.

Plate 10. Elgin cathedral from the west.

Photograph by J.M. & M. J. Playfair, 1906–1952, reproduced courtesy of the University of St Andrews Library (PLFR-12-11-2)

Plate 11. The face of Henry III, from the tomb effigy in Westminster abbey.

Plate 12. Image of Alexander III from a silver coin.

Plate 13. *Alexander III of Scotland Rescued from the Fury of a Stag by the Intrepidity of Colin Fitzgerald*, by Benjamin West.

Plate 14. Tantallon castle.

Photograph by J Valentine & Sons (1938), reproduced courtesy of the University of St Andrews Library (JV-A-7661)

Plate 15. Morton castle.

Photograph by the author

Plate 16. (*Left*) Castle Tioram, Eilean Tioram, Loch Moidart. aerial view.
© HES (Aerofilms Collection, SC 1269875)

Plate 17. (*Below*) Sketch of Lochindorb Castle, by W.D. Simpson.
© HES (SC 719838)

Plate 18. The inauguration of Alexander III, from a fifteenth-century manuscript of Bower's *Scotichronicon*.

Reproduced courtesy of the Parker Library, Corpus Christi College, Cambridge (ms. 171, fo. 206)

Plate 19. The funeral of Alexander III, from a fifteenth-century manuscript of Bower's *Scotichronicon*.

Reproduced courtesy of the Parker Library, Corpus Christi College, Cambridge (ms. 171, fo. 225v)

in Perth were Askatin and a baron, Andrew son of Nicholas. Made in the form of a chirograph, one copy of the treaty was sealed by King Alexander and the bishops of St Andrews and Glasgow, the earls of Buchan, Dunbar, Mar and Carrick, and Robert Menzies, and was to be held in Norway; the other part, to be held in Scotland, was sealed by King Magnus, the bishops of Bergen and Stavanger, four Norwegian barons (including Andrew son of Nicholas) and Askatin.

The provisions of the treaty are remarkable. Arguably a comprehensive victory for the Scots, aspects of it would also have been welcomed by the Norwegians. For 'the accurate preservation of memory', the treaty states, it should be known that this 'settlement and final concord' (*composicio et finalis concordia*) had been made in order to bring an end to the contentions, complaints, damages, injuries and discords regarding the isles of Man and the Sudreys (Hebrides) and the rights to them. Magnus, always a lover of peace and fosterer of justice (*amicus pacis et cultor justicie*)

> granted, resigned and quit-claimed . . . for himself and his heirs for ever, Man with the rest of the Sudreys and all other islands on the west and south of the great sea, with all right which he and his progenitors had of old therein or he and his heirs shall have in future.[26]

Alexander and his heirs were to hold and possess these lands

> with demesne-lands, homages, rents, services and all rights and pertinents of the said islands, without retention, along with the right of patronage of the bishopric of Man,

saving any rights held in the bishopric by the church of Nidaros, and specifically excluding the islands of Orkney and Shetland, 'which the said king of Norway has reserved specially to his domain'. It is further stated unequivocally that all of the inhabitants of the ceded islands, 'as well lesser as greater' (*tam minores quam maiores*), were henceforth to be subject to the laws and customs of the kingdom of Scotland. They would not be punished or disinherited on account of their activities while they were under allegiance to the king of Norway, but would 'stand peacefully therein under the lordship of the king of Scots as other free men and lieges of the said lord king who are known to enjoy the most free justice'. Moreover, the inhabitants of the isles had the option either to remain there, and become subject to the king of Scots, or to leave:

26 Quoted translations are from Gordon Donaldson, *Scottish Historical Documents* (Edinburgh, 1970), pp. 34–36.

> if they wish to retire they may do so, with their goods, lawfully, freely and in full peace; so that they be not compelled either to remain or to retire contrary to the laws and customs of the realm of Scotland and their own will.

These provisions regarding the law, and the right of people to choose under which law they should live, are exceptional, and possibly without precedent.

In return, Alexander undertook to make an annual payment, in St Magnus cathedral in Kirkwall (and thus in the lands of the king of Norway), of 100 merks sterling, 'to be counted according to the manner and use of the Roman court and the realms of France, England and Scotland' – a reminder that this treaty was being made in a European rather than a purely local context. (The merk being worth two-thirds of a pound, or 13s 4d, this amounted to £66 13s 4d sterling, a not inconsiderable sum at the time.) Additionally, a hefty lump sum of 4,000 merks (£2,666 13s 4d), was due in four annual instalments. Oaths to observe these provisions were taken by both kings, through their proxies Adam, earl of Carrick and Robert Menzies for Alexander, and Askatin and Andrew son of Nicholas for Magnus. Either side failing to adhere to the agreement would be subject to a penalty of 10,000 merks, submitting themselves to papal jurisdiction over any such issues. The kings and their queens agreed to forgive the transgressions and offences committed by them, their ancestors and their men against each other, and not to receive each other's enemies unless (in the case of criminals, but excluding traitors) they appeared to merit mercy. A final additional clause gave Norwegian sailors who might suffer shipwreck on the shores of Scotland the right to salvage their ships and goods, and to sell them or otherwise dispose of them as they wished, with criminal penalties to be imposed on anyone stealing from them. This is a clear indication that it was expected that commerce and other seaborne communication would continue between the ceded lands and Norway and its northern Atlantic territories; irrespective of which dominion was owed allegiance by the inhabitants, it would be hoped that peaceful resolution of the conflict would encourage rather than discourage such activities. The maintenance of peace and prosperity both within the kingdom and in its relationships with others was a core ambition of medieval, as modern, government.

This groundbreaking treaty had far-reaching impact. Enhancing the gradual definition of the territorial boundaries of the kingdom which had been developing for centuries, it led to further strengthening not only of royal dynasty, but also of a notion of 'togetherness' or nationhood. Additionally, it offered successive Scottish kings the opportunity to continue to consolidate their hold over the west and thus to raise increasing revenues. There were at least 20 stone castles in the disputed territories by the time of Hákon's expedition in 1263,[27] some of them impressive, imposing structures – the requirement for defence resulting from long-term instability. Such architecture is also a reminder that the Hebrides were not regarded as poor or marginal land: it was wealthy, worth fighting for, and its lords were powerful, influential individuals with money to spend.[28] For the Scots kings, too, possession of the isles offered a greater degree of control and an upper hand in the issue of strategic Atlantic coastal rivalry with England. In the long term, the treaty probably increased the destructive influence of a predominantly Anglo-Saxon society over the Gaelic culture of the west; but also, for a while at least, it might be conjectured that it increased the Gaelic influence eastwards.[29] Almost immediately, the treaty ushered in a period of much closer contact between the Scottish and the Norwegian kingdoms. A few years earlier, it would have been unthinkable that Alexander III's daughter Margaret would have married King Erik II of Norway in 1281, a union which was to provide the (sadly short-lived) successor to Alexander III himself, Margaret, the Maid of Norway. The treaty undoubtedly enabled a development of northern European relationships in social, diplomatic and commercial terms.[30] Equally, the curtailment of the kingly ambitions of the lords of the western territories, and the shift in the balance of power there towards Scotland, had profound implications for the relationship between England and Scotland. If, from a Mannian or Hebridean perspective, 'the setting of the sun on the age of the sea kings' might be lamented, the advantage gained by the Scottish kingdom was immense.[31] Without the islands' financial

27 Cowan, 'Norwegian Sunset – Scottish Dawn', p. 125, where he lists Achadun, Ardtornish, Aros, Cairnburgh, Castle Coeffin, Duart, Dunakin, Dunaverty, Dunollie, Dunoon, Dunstaffnage, Duntrune, Dunyveg, Fraoch Eilean (Loch Awe), Innis Chonnell, Kilmelford, Mingary, Castle Rarey, Skipness, Castle Sween, Tarbert and Castle Tioram. To this list might also be added Finlaggan (McDonald, *Sea Kings*, pp. 196, 259), Inverie (see above, p. 176) and Kisimul (see below, p. 322). See also Ian Fisher, 'The Heirs of Somerled', in Oram and Stell, *Lordship and Architecture*, pp. 84–95.

28 McDonald, *Sea Kings*, ch. 8, offers a detailed assessment of the environment and economy of Man and the Hebrides in the twelfth and thirteenth centuries, based on both documentary and archaeological evidence.

29 Barrow, *Kingship and Unity*, p. 121.

30 Barbara E. Crawford, *The Northern Earldoms: Orkney and Caithness from AD 870 to 1470* (Edinburgh, 2013), p. 306: 'The treaty of Perth laid the foundations for furthering the development of social and diplomatic relationships between Scotland and Norway. The period from 1266 to the early fourteenth century was one in which close contacts were established between these two kingdoms, as also with England, creating a royal and aristocratic circle of diplomatic, commercial and social networks across the North Sea.'

31 'When Scottish and Norwegian ambitions in the Isles ultimately collided in the period from the 1240s to the 1260s, it was the sea kings who were the biggest losers. The period from about 1230 until the cession of Man and the Isles to Scotland by the Treaty of Perth in 1266 therefore represents the setting of the sun on the age of the sea kings.' McDonald, *Sea Kings*, p. 155.

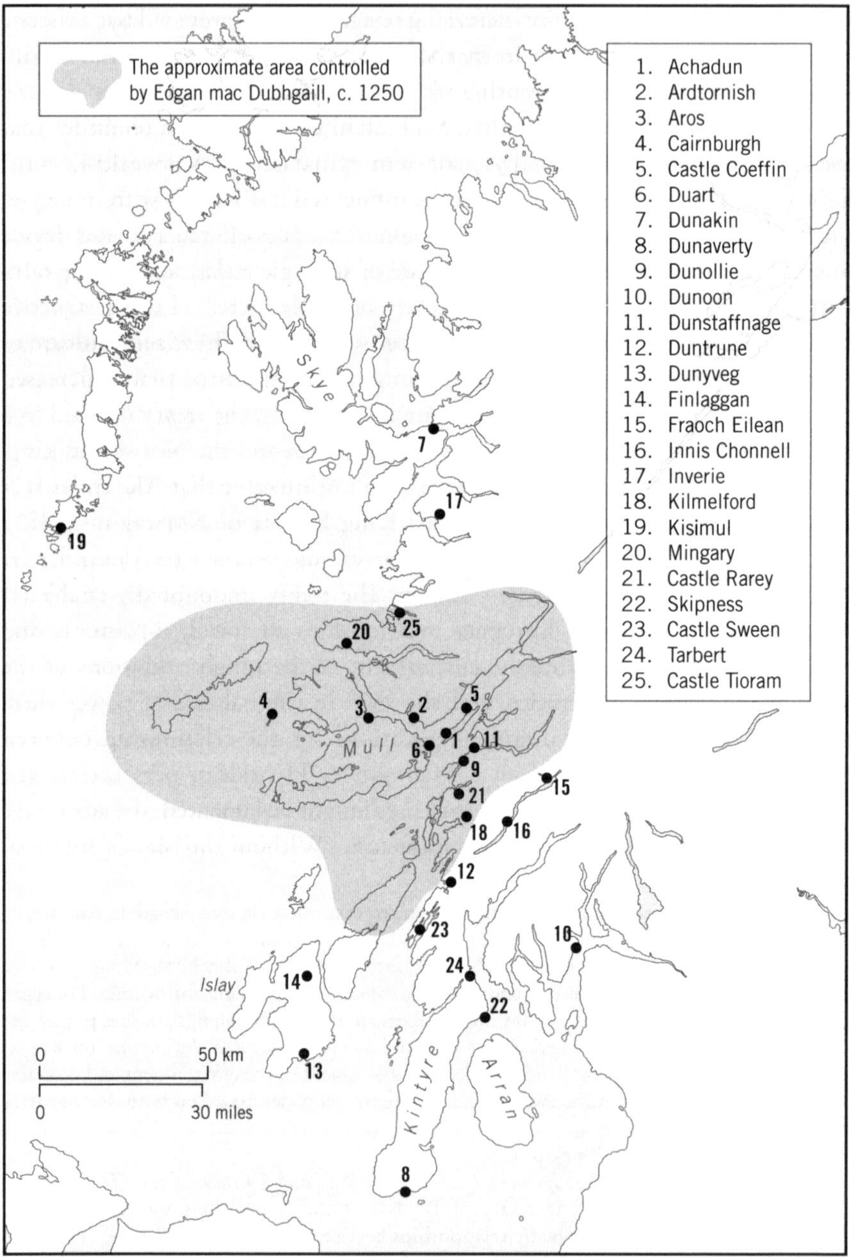

Map 2. The territory of Eógan mac Dubhgaill, c.1250, with stone castles of the west highlands and islands. The list of stone castles known to have existed in the islands and western highland mainland by the mid thirteenth century is from Cowan, 'Norwegian Sunset – Scottish Dawn', p. 125, with the addition of Finlaggan, Inverie and Kisimul (see above, p. 193, n. 27). The list is unlikely to be complete, but that over half of these are in the territory controlled by Eógan mac Dubhgaill is nonetheless testimony to the prestige and power of his family.

and military resources and without the strategic benefits provided by authority in the Hebrides, it is not certain that Scotland could have weathered the military storms of the late thirteenth and early fourteenth centuries. In 1262/63 Henry III had tried to mediate between Hákon and Alexander, doubtless very aware of his own interest in any settlement of the Scoto-Norwegian dispute. By 1264/5, however, embroiled in his own civil war, he had no space for these more remote affairs.[32] Perhaps as a consequence, a treaty was achieved which was thoroughly in the interests of both Scotland and Norway, to the long-term detriment of England.

The treaty of Perth has been portrayed by some as a halfway measure on the part of the Scots king, who, recognising that he would be unable to conquer the disputed lands, accepted the compromise of achieving *de facto* dominance through a feudal render. This archaic attitude to it has been persuasively dismissed, using the proof of the wording of the treaty itself.[33] The treaty was not a grant under which Alexander would hold the lands of Magnus, in effect as a vassal; the money was a sweetener for Magnus, not a feudal render. The suggestion that Perth represented an unhappy compromise for Alexander III must rest partially on the old attitude to his minority as a faction-ridden period characterised largely by subservience to English interventions, from which Alexander did not emerge until 1260 or 1261 (and that even then he was still dominated by a Comyn ascendancy). Such a view implies that the character of the events leading to 1263 and 1266 is of Scottish weakness in the face of Norwegian strength: the emerging youthful Scottish monarch attempting to resist the encroaching territorial ambition of a more powerful, prestigious, and more experienced Norwegian king. If, however, the alternative view of the minority is taken, in which a sense of community in government is more dominant, it follows that Alexander had left the minority period behind by 1258 or earlier, the strength of his domestic position being reflected in his trust of Buchan, Durward and Mar to lead his counter-expedition to the Hebrides in 1264. (In contrast, one of the reasons for the relative failure of Hákon's expedition seems to have been the repeated disagreement among its leaders regarding how it should be pursued.) Throughout the period leading up to Hákon's invasion, and thereafter to the treaty, the Scots' position is strong. Hákon IV was

32 Henry did write to Magnus in June 1264, but in terms limited to the settlement of Anglo-Norwegian issues, among which was a dispute regarding the seizure of English ships in Norway to add to the fleet Hákon was building against Scotland. Henry did emphasise, however, that resolution of that dispute was dependent on peace being made between Magnus and Alexander. There is no evidence that he attempted to insinuate himself into the peace negotiations themselves. *CDS*, i, no. 2355.

33 See Lustig, 'Treaty of Perth', pp. 53–55.

responding to Scottish aggression which stemmed from pursuit of established policy, which was made from a position of strength, and which should be seen as a mutual project of the governing community.

In contrast, others have characterised the treaty as a straightforward acknowledgement of military defeat by the Norwegian king – submission in the face of conquest. Magnus did indeed clearly cede sovereignty over the territories under dispute, but nonetheless had much to gain from the agreement and would not have viewed it as a defeat. Both Hákon IV and Alexander III were aggressive in their attempts to expand the territories under their control, increasingly to centralise the power they held over those territories, and to affirm the sense of dynasty which underpinned their positions. Hákon IV had without doubt been a dominant European ruler, with successful 'imperialist' ambitions over Sweden, Denmark, Greenland and Iceland.[34] The exertion of strong centralised kingship was a pan-European phenomenon in this period: these two kings were very much in the mainstream of European governmental development. While the relative wealth of the lands in dispute, and the practical benefits of controlling them, were noted above, it has nonetheless to be suspected that the issue was at least as much about power, reputation and prestige. It is true that the failure of Hákon's expedition of 1263 gave the Scots a military advantage, and that the subsequent pressing home of that advantage in 1264 and 1265 left the island lords with little pragmatic choice except to bow to domination by the Scottish king, in the short term at least, but the treaty represented neither a settlement of conqueror over vanquished, or a feudal grant with an annual render. Ultimately, the treaty of Perth was about saving face: Hákon IV might be said to have left Magnus a legacy of damage limitation. It is crucial to recognise also, however, that the face-saving agreement was equally important for Alexander III. This was a treaty which had both its roots and its character in the very nature of kingship; it was a settlement which worked for the kingly ambitions of both crowns. The Scots achieved control of the Hebrides without either conquering them or giving any homage or feudal render: it was a voluntary transfer of sovereignty, without question or limitation. Magnus received an explicit recognition of the fact that the Norwegian kings had previously held sovereign rights over the Hebrides and continued to do so over the northern isles; and he required a generous financial recompense. Most importantly of all, the treaty defined boundaries which had previously been ill-defined. As had been the case for Alexander II in the Treaty of York, that clarity of boundary in turn helped to define their respective authority as kings, a fact which was of inestimable value to both.

34 See Cowan, 'Norwegian Sunset – Scottish Dawn', p. 108.

To Alexander, recognition of his sovereign rule over the islands was vital. It was the apotheosis of a policy of settlement and colonisation which had been pursued over generations, in the context of the Scottish kings' extension of their military, ecclesiastical, economic and judicial influence across the increasing territories over which they claimed authority. Successful territorial expansion, however, was not the same as the creation of a unified kingdom or 'nation'. It was not until the first quarter of the thirteenth century that it can be stated with any confidence that 'Scotland' was synonymous with the territories ruled by the individual who called himself 'king of Scots'. The treaty of Perth is of profound importance to that view of constitutional development: it can be seen as the culmination of a period of gathering momentum, a first 'unambiguous articulation of territorial sovereignty'.[35] With its revolutionary assertion that the inhabitants of the isles would become subject to the laws of Scotland, it represents perhaps the first example of an incorporating union, further emphasising the fact that by the later thirteenth century there was a developed notion of a legal identity of the kingdom.[36]

Although these dramatic events dominated the first half of the 1260s, the normal business of administering the kingdom had to be maintained. Among other events, momentous both domestically and nationally, was the birth in Jedburgh on Monday 21 January 1264 of a second royal child, a son named Alexander, who was baptised by Gamelin.[37] Unlike the birth of

35 Broun, *Scottish Independence,* pp. 7–11: 'the idea of a "kingdom of Scotland" rather than simply the king's lands may only have become a routine feature of the mental landscape of those who drafted documents in the beginning of the thirteenth century' (p. 10). See also G.W.S. Barrow, *The Anglo-Norman Era in Scottish History* (Oxford, 1980), pp. 153–55; and MacQueen, '*Regiam Majestatem*', pp. 9–10. Although sovereignty over the isles was asserted, this does not necessarily imply cultural or governmental assimilation. See David H. Caldwell, '1266 and All That: an Archaeological Approach to Understanding the Scottish Takeover of the Kingdom of the Isles' (*Journal of the Sydney Society for Scottish History*, 20 (2022)), where it is convincingly asserted that the Scots did not take 'effective control' of the isles, and that Alexander III failed in that respect to take advantage of the Treaty of Perth.

36 The suggestion that the treaty represents quite such a legal novelty was made by Professor Dauvit Broun, in conversation. I am much obliged to Dauvit for his readiness to discuss these ideas, and for giving me sight of his (as yet) unpublished 'Regnal Sovereignty and the Creation of Political Unions in the Thirteenth Century: Some Scottish Examples', a paper given to the Conference on Comparing Political Unions in the Late Medieval and Early Modern World, 1350–1801 (Center for Renaissance Studies Programs, Chicago, 2013).

37 *Chron. Melrose,* Faustina B. IX, fo. 63r (trans. Anderson, *Early Sources*, ii, p. 643); *Gesta Annalia* miscalculates the date as December 1263 (*Chron. Fordun*, i, p. 300 (trans. ii, p. 295)). A.A.M. Duncan, 'Sources and Uses of the Chronicle of Melrose', in Taylor, *Kings, Clerics and Chronicles*, pp. 146–85, at p. 176 n., argues unconvincingly for the December 1263 date. To further confuse matters, there is a curious entry in the English Patent Rolls, apparently dated 6 May 1263, rewarding one Walter Coston, Margaret's valet, for bringing news to the English court of the birth of her son. It is possible, but very unlikely, that an earlier birth (presumably a child which did not survive) went unnoticed in the Scottish and English chronicle sources. Much more likely is that the record has been incorrectly entered in the Patent Roll.

their first child, Margaret, there was no obvious involvement of the queen's parents. It might be conjectured that the choice of Jedburgh for the birth was to ease speedy communication southwards, but Henry was in the depths of the crisis which would lead to the battle of Lewes a few months later, and he and Queen Eleanor were in fact with Louis IX of France at Amiens when their grandchild was born.[38] There is no evidence that enlightens us as to whether Alexander was himself present in Jedburgh; if so, he did not tarry for long, since he appears to have been in Scone by 10 February. (He had been in Linlithgow at Christmas, Newbattle in the following March and in Melrose in July 1264: the events in the north-west did not, at that point, require his personal intervention.)[39] The safe birth of a ruling king's child – and, in those days, especially a son – was a matter for both rejoicing and relief. The alleviation of uncertainty regarding succession, in an age when life was always precarious, offered stability within the political establishment, and thus assisted economic growth and prosperity: the birth of his son lent an added authority to Alexander III's personal rule. He was now the head of his own forward-looking dynasty. In such a patriarchal society, this must have altered attitudes to him and his rule within the governing community, and further strengthened his hand in the conduct of such vital business as the negotiations with Norway. The birth of his daughter Margaret in 1261 would have had the same effect to an extent for, as would be explicitly stated later in Alexander's reign, a Scottish female could inherit the throne; but in this period it was probably an uncomfortable truth.[40]

Less happy news came later in 1264; the festering English civil war and the calamitous (for Henry III) battle of Lewes. Lewes did present Alexander III with an opportunity: had Henry been in a position to intervene, the results of Alexander's western campaigns and negotiations might have been different. However, a threat such as that posed to Henry III by Simon de Montfort and his followers must have been unwelcome to the neighbouring king: in both personal and regal terms, Alexander would have been deeply troubled by events south of the border. For Alexander, the battle of Lewes in May represented a double blow: not only were his father-in-law and brother-in-law, the king and heir apparent of England, effectively incarcerated by a rebellious baronage, but several of the leading magnates of his own realm were captured fighting for the king. John Comyn 'who led many Scots', John Balliol and Robert Bruce had all been with Prince Edward in his successful capture of

38 Powicke, *The Thirteenth Century*, pp. 182–83.

39 *RRS*, iv pt. 1, nos. 47–49, 230.

40 See the discussion below of female inheritance, pp. 265–66.

Northampton only a month earlier; they fought again for King Henry at Lewes, and Comyn and Bruce found themselves imprisoned for their efforts. The 'many Scots' from their lands who had had no choice but to follow them into battle were less fortunate: some of the English chronicles reported also that thousands of 'unimportant men of the common people, and especially of Scots' died in the battle.[41] Bruce was still apparently in captivity in August: his wife Isabella, as well as relatives Peter and Bernard were travelling through England and Scotland during July, apparently in negotiation regarding his release, and on 9 August his son Robert was given a safe conduct to go to England 'to procure the deliverance of his father'.[42] It must be assumed that Comyn was similarly treated (the *Chronicle of Melrose* tells us that they were both imprisoned in Dover; *Gesta Annalia*, however, says London).[43] Balliol seems to have avoided imprisonment, but he suffered forfeiture of some of his lands.[44] *Gesta Annalia* suggests that these men 'had come to King Henry's rescue' at the behest of Alexander III. It is certainly unlikely that Alexander would have discouraged them, but all of them were liegemen of Henry for lands held in England, and Balliol was a key agent of the king in the north of England; it is therefore equally likely that they were there in their capacity as English barons. That they had taken men from their Scottish lands into the battle, however, might indicate a level of Scottish royal encouragement. Certainly, at the end of 1264 and in the early months of 1265 Edward and Henry were attempting to engage the Scottish king in their efforts to gain freedom for Edward, who had been given as a hostage against the king's fulfilment of the terms of the peace agreement, the 'Mise of Lewes', which had followed the battle. Alexander did send envoys to Henry in November 1264 and in May 1265 (the abbot of Jedburgh, Guy Balliol of Cavers (who, perversely, given this rôle, was to die three months later, fighting *against* Henry at the battle of Evesham[45]), Walter Lindsay and John Denmuir), and

41 *Chron. Guisborough*, pp. 188–89; *SAEC*, p. 380 & n.; *Chron. Melrose*, Faustina B. IX, fo. 64r (trans. Anderson, *Early Sources*, ii, p. 644). Henry received a letter from 'his most devoted daughter', Queen Margaret following Lewes, entreating him to do his best to procure the freedom of Richard Comyn, brother of John Comyn, who had been imprisoned (*CDS*, i, no. 2678).

42 *CDS*, i, no. 2358.

43 Anderson (*Early Sources*, ii, p. 644) translates it as Dover, but the manuscript of *Chron. Melrose*, Faustina B. IX, fo. 64r, clearly says *Castello de Dora*; *Dora* is not the Latin form for Dover (the *Chronicle of Lanercost*, for example, renders it as *Dovera, Doveria* or *Dovoria*; Bower simply uses *Dover*), but it is difficult to see where else could be meant: it may be a simple scribal error. I am grateful to Professor Richard Oram for advice on this issue.

44 *CDS*, i, nos. 2356, 2358; *Chron. Fordun*, i, p. 302 (trans. ii, p. 297); see also Amanda Beam, *The Balliol Dynasty 1210–1364* (Edinburgh, 2008), pp. 73–75.

45 *Chron. Guisborough*, p. 201; *Chron. Melrose*, Faustina B. IX, fo. 67r (trans. Anderson, *Early Sources*, ii, p. 652).

it seems that a letter had been sent by Prince Edward to the Scottish king, seeking assistance. *Gesta Annalia* claims that Alexander had prepared a force to go south to Henry's aid: he had 'levied three men from every hyde of land' for the purpose, implying that this was a calling up of the common army (although the word 'hyde' does imply that the writer has used an English source for this information). However, 'the Scots people were spared this trouble' by the battle of Evesham, which rendered the assistance unnecessary.[46] Nonetheless, there is more than a hint here of the tables having turned, and Alexander III having the upper hand in his ability to influence the course of events for Henry III. Henry had always claimed to act in the interests of Alexander and his crown (for which read, his royal status), and it cannot be doubted that, besides his strategic ambition to ensure that Scottish politics followed a path which was sympathetic to English interests, he was also motivated by personal consideration for Alexander and Margaret. In 1264–65, as a mature monarch, Alexander seems to have displayed a similar approach. From a standpoint of royal authority, he was prepared to commit Scottish power to the restoration of Henry's (and Edward's) rule, although he seems to have done so cautiously: envoys were sent, negotiations were held and a force was prepared, but held in reserve until it was seen whether or not it was needed. The nature of Henry's letters to Alexander make it clear that there was also a personal aspect to his plea for assistance; but Alexander's kingship was rooted in the Scottish community. His personal feelings for his father-in-law, or indeed his reaction to the apparent threat to royal authority in England, could not cause him to divert from the pursuit of Scottish interests in, for example, the negotiations and active campaigning regarding his Hebridean policy, or to ignore the danger to Scottish lives and livelihoods that would be brought about by large-scale intervention in English affairs. (There were bitter lessons to be learnt from his predecessors on that score.) The loyalty of Bruce, Comyn, Balliol and others to the royal cause was eventually recognised, however, as they, in common with many others, were rewarded after the battle of Evesham with lands forfeited by the defeated baronial opposition.[47] Others had to work a little harder: in November 1266,

---

46 *CDS*, i, nos. 2373, 2377–79, 2381; *APS*, i, p. 108; *Chron. Fordun*, i, p. 302 (trans. ii, pp. 297–98). For details of the 'common army', see Barrow, 'The Army of Alexander III's Scotland', in Reid, *Alexander III Essays*, pp. 132–47.

47 E.g. *CDS*, i, nos. 2393, 2399, 2490. There were also other personal rewards for loyalty: see, e.g., *CDS*, i, no. 2446, in which John Comyn was rewarded with the right to take deer from royal forests. It is to a period of near-anarchy in the aftermath of Evesham, when the many thousands of disinherited were roaming the countryside in desperate poverty, that Bower, with reluctant admiration, ascribes the adventures of Robin Hood (*Chron. Bower*, v, pp. 354–55, and p. 470n.).

Alexander Balliol (of the same family as Guy Balliol of Cavers who died at Evesham) was still negotiating his peace with Henry III.[48]

Gesta Annalia reports that, 'at length', following Prince Edward's success against some of the lingering opposition in the north of England, he visited Roxburgh where he met Margaret and Alexander and nearly all the nobility of Scotland'. The account describes it as no more than a social visit, for the purpose of 'many rejoicings and compliments made by each to the other', after which mutual back-slapping they returned home. This tale, which implies that warm personal relationships between the two royal households continued, is supported by no documentary evidence, but it does appear in variant forms in, for example, the *Lanercost Chronicle*, where the venue is Haddington rather than Roxburgh.[49] There is only one indication of Alexander having been in the right part of the country: a single act of May 1267 places him in Jedburgh, but provides no evidence of a meeting. If such a meeting did take place, its date is uncertain, but was probably in 1266 or 1267.

As regards relations with the papacy, the flow of traffic between Scotland and the curia did not slow down as the reign progressed. One of the matters raised with Henry on Alexander's behalf by John of Lindores in March 1262 was an unspecified issue which Alexander had asked Henry to write about to the pope. It is not impossible that the issue was in relation to the long-awaited papal confirmation of the election to the see of Caithness, although it might equally have been the lingering matter of ecclesiastical concern about secular influence over diocesan lands, issues relating to papal taxation or a number of other topics which are the subject of papal letters to Scotland during 1262 and 1263.[50]

Throughout the later 1250s and 1260s there was a succession of episcopal elections in addition to the disputes over the elections to St Andrews and Glasgow. In Aberdeen, bishop Peter Ramsay had died towards the end of 1256; his successor was Richard de Potton, an 'affable' Englishman who had been naturalised, according to Bower, by taking an oath of fealty.[51] There is no indication that this was another example of the pope inserting an English candidate into the bishopric against the wishes of the Scottish government, as had been done in the case of Cheam; indeed, Bower's assertion of Potton's 'naturalisation' may be specifically designed to counter any such insinuation. As far as the

48 *CDS*, i, no. 2415. See genealogical table 3(c) in Beam, *The Balliol Dynasty*, p. xx.

49 *Chron. Fordun*, i, pp. 302–03 (trans. ii, pp. 298–99); *Chron. Bower*, v, pp. 354–55 & n. p. 471; *Chron. Lanercost*, p. 81.

50 See various entries in *CPL*, e.g. pp. 379, 382, 384, 389.

51 *Chron. Bower*, v, pp. 322–33. He had been consecrated by 25 August 1258 (Watt and Murray, *Fasti*, p. 2).

meagre evidence goes, it seems that this was a peaceful election by the chapter, confirmed by both king and papacy without incident.

An interesting side-issue to the affair in the islands was the fact that the bishoprics both of Argyll and of Caithness were vacant. It seems that Caithness had been without a bishop perhaps since as early as 1255, when Bishop William last appears on record. His successor, Walter Baltroddie, a canon of Caithness, was not elected (by the chapter) until after August 1259, and his papal confirmation was not issued until 1263. Perhaps because of the long delay, his election had been annulled by then, and so the bishops of Dunkeld, Brechin and Ross were delegated to examine him and consecrate him if appropriate. Although a canon of Caithness at the time of his confirmation, it seems that he was a member of a lowland family, and it has been proposed that his election to the see was as 'an agent of the royal government'.[52] If he was indeed elected in 1259, it might indicate that an episcopal vacancy so far to the north had not been of immediate concern to the government during the troubled times of the minority. In 1259, the minority over, it is possible that Alexander's own hand can be seen drawing the area closer into the fold, already in anticipation of the impending conflict.

In Argyll, the see had been vacant for some years and had been placed under the administration of the bishop of Dunblane. Shortly before Alexander II's final expedition to the west, a papal mandate had been given to the bishops of Glasgow and Dunblane to ensure that an election was held, which did indeed happen within a year or so of the expedition (when the influence of Eógan mac Dubhgaill had waned), resulting in the choice of bishop Alan. Little is known of him, although the Melrose chronicle tells us that he died in 1262.[53] His successor, Laurence of Argyll, did not receive a papal mandate for his consecration until 31 March 1264, and so it would seem that during the crucial period of the Norwegian invasion, the see was without a bishop. Little is known of his background or career; it may be assumed from his name that he had local connections, and it is known that he was a member of the Dominican order – a fact which may be significant, given both the prominence of Dominicans in the negotiations of the early 1260s, and the fact that Clement, bishop of Dunblane from 1233 to 1258 (who, it will be remembered, had been 'caretaker' of Argyll during its vacancy) had also been a Dominican. Once more, there is no indication of dispute over either his election or confirmation, suggesting the possibility that the king had intervened, recognising that 'the evangelistic work of the mendicants was a useful adjunct to the extension of royal authority'.[54]

---

52 Watt and Murray, *Fasti*, p. 78; Watt, *Graduates*, pp. 25–26.

53 Watt and Murray, *Fasti*, p. 35.

54 Watt and Murray, *Fasti*, p. 35; Ash, 'The Church in the Reign of Alexander III', p. 41.

After the death of bishop Clement of Dunblane, Robert of the Provender was elected to the see. He had been a clerk of the provend, an official of the royal household, who seems to have come to Scotland from England sometime after the accession of Alexander III. A graduate, and probably knowledgeable in canon law, he visited the curia where he acted on behalf of Gamelin in the long-standing litigation there in the 1250s, and he may have taken advantage of his prolonged absence from Scotland to study law at Bologna. He went off to the curia again in 1259, after his own episcopal appointment, where, as well as obtaining his own confirmation and consecration, he was involved in the disputed election to the see of Glasgow. Despite his apparent duplicity regarding the Glasgow episcopate, it does not seem that his own appointment was controversial, although there is no evidence that he actually achieved consecration until 1260. The delay might suggest hesitation at the curia, but in August 1259 the pope approved petitions from him as bishop-elect regarding benefices for several Scottish clergymen and relating to means of increasing his meagre episcopal income, which must indicate that he was not held in disfavour.[55] In 1269 Albin, the bishop of Brechin died; it seems once again that his successor, William, dean of Brechin was elected without dispute, although he appears to have died before achieving consecration, and the see was still vacant in 1275.[56]

If, apart from the disputed election to Glasgow, the appointments of bishops in the early years of Alexander's personal rule were relatively non-controversial (or, at least, royal patronage was used effectively enough to minimise the threat of papal obstruction), difficult issues continued to be raised on behalf of the king and kingdom by those (bishops-elect and others) travelling to the curia. A constant flow of communication moved between Scotland and the curia regarding the ecclesiastical minutiae of benefice provision and the like, but there were other matters which touched upon more significant national issues. The involvement of the papacy in the judicial matter of the earldom of Menteith, for instance, has already been noticed. Secular seizing of diocesan lands, an issue at the beginning of the minority, was still a cause for papal concern as late as November 1259.[57] As in the 1250s, however, the major point of contention was once again papal taxation. The first overtures seem to have been low key. A Franciscan friar from Ayr named Ivo had been attempting to raise crusading funds in the early 1260s. Some money, it was claimed in papal letters, had been

55 Watt and Murray, *Fasti*, p. 100; Watt, *Graduates*, pp. 456–57; *CPL*, p. 367; see above, p. 161. For his English nationality, see *CDS*, i, no. 2440, which indicates 'special favour' towards him on the part of Henry III.

56 Ferguson, *Papal Representatives*, pp. 112–13; Watt and Murray, *Fasti*, pp. 53, 57. For an account of Albin's career, see Watt, *Graduates*, pp. 5–7.

57 *Vet. Mon.*, no. 212.

lodged with the priory of Whithorn, from where it should have been transferred to the house of the Templars in London (or, failing them, to Florentine merchants), but by early 1262 it was still unpaid, despite papal instructions to deliver it up to the nuncio, Master Leonard. (Leonard had had an unhappy time as a collector, meeting opposition in both Scotland and England, where Henry III had also been obstructive.[58]) As late as May 1266 it was still unpaid, and the latest papal collector, one Master Sinicius, was given the unpleasant task of pursuing the payment (and of compelling the prior to appear personally before the pope, should the money remain unpaid) in the knowledge that Master Leonard's messenger had not only been unsuccessful in obtaining the money, but had been beaten by the canons for his trouble![59] Ivo's mission seems to have been small-scale, but the issue of alienation of Scottish crusading levies was still of serious concern to the Scottish crown, and it is therefore probable that the refusal to hand over the cash raised by Ivo was caused by more than acquisitiveness on the part of the prior and canons of Whithorn. Master Sinicius was authorised by the pope to collect crusading monies in England, Wales, Scotland and Ireland, and the prelates of the kingdoms were instructed to supply him with horses, attendants and money for his expenses. He remained a papal collector until 1270 or later, but there is little indication that, in Scotland at least, he met with much success.[60]

Although the raising of money for operations in the Holy Land remained a high papal priority,[61] it does not seem that Master Leonard, Ivo and Master Sinicius had significant impact in Scotland. The stakes appear to have been higher, however, when a fully empowered legate was appointed. At the request of Henry III, Pope Urban IV, deeply concerned about the deteriorating political situation in England, first appointed a legate to England, Wales and Ireland in November 1263; this was Gui Foulquois, cardinal bishop of Sabina. It seems, however, that he failed even to reach England, prevented by the baronial opposition. Following the death of Urban IV in October 1264, Gui was himself elected pope, taking the name Clement IV, and in May 1265 he established a new legation, this time including Scotland, under Ottobuono de Fieshi, cardinal-deacon of St Adrian.[62] Arriving in October 1265, Ottobuono was to remain

58 *CPL*, p. 385.

59 *CPL*, pp. 384–85, 423; see also Ferguson, *Papal Representatives*, pp. 103–04.

60 *CPL*, pp. 423–24; Ferguson, *Papal Representatives*, p. 113.

61 See *CPL*, pp. 394–95 for further mandates regarding the collection of money in 1263/64; it is worth noting, too, that much can be learnt about the nature of medieval banking from the close involvement of European – particularly Florentine – merchants in the gathering and distribution of such money.

62 For further detail of the legation of Ottobuono, see Ferguson, *Papal Representatives*, pp. 108–13 and the sources cited.

in England for almost three years. It is not known for what purpose his legatine power was originally extended to cover Scotland: his initial mandate, vague in that respect, was to continue the mission begun in England by Clement himself before his elevation to the papacy 'and to be a messenger of peace in that realm, and in Scotland, Wales and Ireland'. To Henry III, Clement wrote that the primary mission of the legate was 'that the king and his house be restored to their former position and the kingdom quieted'; to Ottobuono, he gave power to further that aim by almost any means, including military. There is a hint, in a letter of 4 July, that Clement saw the English 'disquiet' as an illness which infected the entire British Isles: those who 'foster the disturbance' in England, Scotland, Wales or Ireland were to be deprived of dignities and benefices until they obeyed the orders of the legate. The campaign against those who supported the baronial opposition to Henry III was to achieve the status of a crusade, which gave a valuable (from Henry's point of view) theological dimension to the upholding of royal authority. A mandate of 4 May 1265 commanded Ottobuono to preach such a crusade 'against those who rebel against the king or the legate' in England, Scotland, Scandinavia and much of modern France and Germany – indicating that the tentacles of the disturbance in England stretched far beyond native shores. A week later, the issue of papal taxation raised its ugly head again, when Ottobuono was given the additional task of collecting a tenth of all church revenues in England, Scotland, Wales, Ireland and Norway 'to be applied to the purposes of his mission'; the bringing of peace to England was an expensive priority, which thus had far-reaching repercussions.[63]

The prospect of crusading activity in the Holy Land being elevated to another grand expedition (in contrast to the occasional forays supportive of the faltering Christian presence there over the previous decade or so) was also gaining traction. Christian ambitions in the Near East had continued to deteriorate, and the 1260s saw potentially fatal attacks on the beleaguered kingdom of Jerusalem. In 1267, Louis IX announced a further expedition, and in the following year his plans received a decided fillip by the recruitment to the cause of Prince Edward, the son of Henry III of England, which guaranteed a far stronger English contingent than had supported the catastrophe of 1248–50. Funding for such a massive undertaking, as previously, was a matter of both national and international activity.

Alexander was ready to risk papal wrath by refusing cooperation with Ottobuono. When in early June 1266 Clement granted the Scottish taxation to Henry III, 'provided that the consent of king [Alexander] be obtained', it was,

63 *CPL*, pp. 426–39 *passim*, and *Vet. Mon.*, nos. 245, 246, 249.

inevitably, an empty promise. He may have realised it: a few days later he wrote to Ottobuono, instructing him to collect the tenth in Scotland 'with that king's assent' and apply it to paying the debts of the English queen (which had been incurred in raising support in France for Henry's cause), adding that if Alexander refused to give his assent, the debts were instead to be paid from the English taxation. *Gesta Annalia* tells us that Alexander refused to allow money collected in a general taxation to be sent south, and later that a further grant, specifically for the crusade, was refused by the clergy. Further details are added in Walter Bower's *Scotichronicon* (who, incidentally, credits Ottobuono and the bishop of Rouen with the making of peace between the king and barons of England). The source for this additional information is unknown, but Alexander's refusal to cooperate with Ottobuono is interestingly associated with the raising, once more, of the issue of secular interference in episcopal lands, which Bower claims was again causing conflict between king and clergy. Bower is certainly critical of the king and his 'wicked councillors' regarding this matter, but he nonetheless fails to display much enthusiasm for the outcome of Ottobuono's mission, declaring that eventually, in 1268, the legate 'returned home with a bulging purse'.[64] Some money was in fact paid to Ottobuono, as is made clear by a receipt received by the bishop of Dunkeld on 1 May 1268,[65] but it is nonetheless obvious that Alexander, and the Scottish clergy, were vehemently opposed to any money thus raised being allocated for the use of the English crown. Bower claims that Alexander flatly refused to allow Ottobuono to enter the kingdom, which seems to be borne out by a later statement of pope Boniface VIII, who had been in Ottobuono's retinue.[66] Copies of several letters from Ottobuono to Alexander have been preserved, unfortunately undated, which give weight to the chronicle evidence that Alexander was singularly unhelpful. One of Ottobuono's messengers had been unable to carry out his duties; another had been threatened with violence; Alexander was in turn threatened with severe penalties for non-cooperation.[67] It does not seem that Alexander was excommunicated by Ottobuono, however, and the kingdom was

64 *CPL*, pp. 432–33; *Chron. Fordun*, i, pp. 303–04 (trans. ii, pp. 298–99); *Chron. Bower*, v, pp. 356–69. Ferguson (*Papal Representatives*, pp. 112–13) also points out that Bower seems to have invented at least one story, regarding the election to the bishopric of Brechin, in order to cast Ottobuono in a bad light.

65 Watt, *Graduates*, p. 281.

66 Stones, *Anglo-Scottish Relations*, pp. 170–71: 'he was certainly not admitted as a legate to the realm of Scotland until the duty of the legateship therein was committed to him by a specific papal letter'. There is, however, no evidence to support the existence of the 'specific papal letter', which Boniface suggested had later unlocked the door to Ottobuono in Scotland.

67 See Rose Graham, 'Letters of Cardinal Ottoboni', *English Historical Review*, 15 (1900), pp. 87–120; especially nos. iv (p. 90), vii (pp. 95–96), xxxiv (pp. 117–18).

not put under interdict; it is possible that the appeals which Bower claimed had been lodged to the papacy regarding the English destination of the taxation had been successful, and that the attempt to raise the money in Scotland was therefore dropped.

Ottobuono's legation was not entirely focused on the raising of cash and the settlement of the English civil war. He also dealt with a diverse range of relatively minor administrative ecclesiastical matters, as well as adjudicating on disputes relating to claimed infringements of ecclesiastical rights and privileges, and there were other more significant issues relating to doctrine and canon law which were addressed at the several church councils held in England during his three-year stay. *Gesta Annalia*, as well as some English chronicles, confirms that the Scottish church did send representatives to at least the last of these councils, which was held in London in April 1268. *Gesta Annalia* also suggests that the Scottish representation was reluctant: the legate had commanded the presence of all the bishops, and representation from the monastic houses. In the event, however, two bishops (Dunkeld and Dunblane), plus the abbot of Dunfermline and the prior of Lindores were delegated to attend, through fear that if they absented themselves altogether, the council might act in a way prejudicial to the Scottish church. There is a further claim that the legislation passed by the council was rejected in Scotland (although Duncan suggests that it is more probable that it was simply ignored), and it does seem that it had very limited effect outside England.[68] The number of papal letters referring to inhibitions which Ottobuono could impose on those who disobeyed him in any aspect of his legatine mission suggest that he encountered significant opposition – and not only from Scotland. This was hardly unusual, however: the raising of taxation was neither popular nor easy; that he seems to have played a part in the bringing of peace to England, and (if Bower is to be believed) that he returned with a bulging purse, must demonstrate that he was in fact more successful in achieving papal aims than were many other collectors.

Reluctance to part with money to the papal collectors was more a matter of national pride than of any lack of belief or piety. Certainly, at royal level, the issue was not the principle of the collection; rather, the problem was the varying papal attitude towards the status of the Scottish crown. The inconsistency with which the popes either supported or ignored the Scottish and English kings' respective pleas regarding the independence or subservience of the Scottish realm was of extreme importance in Scotland. The king and his ruling community (including, of course, the bishops and monastic prelates) could not accept

68 Ferguson, *Papal Representatives*, pp. 111–12; *Chron. Fordun*, i, p. 303 (trans. ii, pp. 298–99); Duncan, *Making of the Kingdom*, p. 291.

an action so obviously prejudicial to the kingdom. That some money was successfully collected, however, shows that there was no unreasonable antagonism to the principle of support for the unceasing fight against what was then regarded as a barbarous onslaught on southern Europe and the Holy Land. Piety and belief, however, could be demonstrated in more dramatic, and less nationally controversial, ways than the raising of cash. The pilgrimage undertaken by Walter Lindsay (and perhaps Máel Ísu, earl of Strathearn) at the end of the 1250s was noted earlier; but many more Scots answered the call for a fresh crusade to the Holy Land, joining Louis IX in what was to be 'the last of the great European crusades'.[69] In the spring of 1270 Louis' fleet left France; Edward followed in August, with a further English contingent following later in the year. In August, however, more than two months before Edward reached his French allies, by then in Tunisia, Louis had died, struck down probably by either typhus or dysentery, without seeing his crusading ambitions realised. The crusade was effectively over, and the army retreated to Sicily. Most of the army returned homeward, but Edward wintered in Sicily and led the English contingent on to Acre, in the kingdom of Jerusalem, in the spring of 1271. His army was small, however, and in practical terms achieved little, at great expense. Edward lingered in Acre until October 1272, after which he made slow progress homewards, arriving in England in August 1274. The gradual disintegration of the kingdom of Jerusalem continued until its final demise with the fall of Acre in 1291.The crusading fervour of European monarchs waned after the debacle of Louis' final attempt and, although the principle of regaining Christian control over the Holy Land continued to be promoted through papal diplomacy, and was paid lip-service by Christian kings, the increasing resistance to payment of the taxation demanded (for example by the second Council of Lyons in 1274) for such activities reveals a growing cynicism.

Gesta Annalia tells us that Adam earl of Carrick and David earl of Atholl, with many other Scots, died in North Africa. Some of them, like Louis IX, died not in battle, but rather of the diseases which were inevitably rife in such armies: this seems to have been true of both Atholl and Carrick, who died of disease at Tunis (1270) and Acre (1271) respectively. Many other Scots of significant standing are known to have been with Louis in North Africa, with Prince Edward in Sicily, and with Prince Edmund in the Holy Land between 1270 and 1274. Some saw service in more than one of those campaigns. Some, such as Robert Bruce, lord of Annandale and his son Robert, and three members of the Balliol family, returned home to tell the tale. Others did not; it seems likely that Hugh Balliol (the eldest son of the John Balliol who was

69 Macquarrie, *Crusades*, p. 63.

so prominent a figure during Alexander III's minority) died on crusade in 1271;[70] David Lindsay, a member of the 1255–57 royal council, may have been another who perished in North Africa. Clearly, a sizeable contingent of Scots nobles (and, of course, their followers who have remained largely anonymous[71]) was in action in various parts of the world following the exhortation to fight for their faith. It seems probable that the first contingent of Scots went to North Africa at the invitation of Louis IX; of those, some died at Tunis, and others then went to Sicily, where they were joined by the English force which also contained Scots, mostly those with Anglo-Scottish landholdings who therefore had cause to be in the company of one of the sons of Henry III. From there, they went in the spring of 1271 to Acre. Most of those who did come home arrived in or before 1274.[72]

In explanation of why Scotland's later thirteenth-century crusaders seem generally to have been of higher social standing than their earlier counterparts, the old argument was that the supplanting of Scotland's native aristocracy by an Anglo-Norman one during the twelfth and thirteenth centuries had given Scotland a nobility which was more amenable to such supranational causes. Although it is no longer generally believed that such social disruption actually took place, it cannot be denied that Scottish society had changed, and the nature of Scottish involvement in the crusading activity of the early 1270s does indeed point to a closer involvement with 'the corporate ventures of western Christendom'.[73] It has been suggested that the rise in social rank of crusaders may also have been influenced by the increasing cost of participation, and that the funding and equipping of a significant retinue was a symbol of both conspicuous wealth and religious zeal.[74] There is no evidence to suggest whether or not the apparent increase in Scottish interest in crusading was partly due to encouragement by the king and his royal circle, or whether, as seems to have been the case in earlier times, the decision to take the cross was an entirely individual one, made in response to the interaction of preaching and personal belief. Certainly, Alexander III and his father had no in-principle objection to the participation of Scots; individuals of the status of the earls of Atholl, Carrick or Dunbar (who

70 Hugh Balliol was dead before 10 April 1271: *CDS*, i, no. 2600.

71 Apart from the unfortunate Nicholas, a squire of Alexander Seton, who was captured, never to be seen again, when separated from the rest of his group by a 'call of nature'! (Macquarrie, *Crusades*, p. 62, quoting *Chron. Melrose*, Faustina B. IX, fo. 74r–v).

72 Macquarrie, *Crusades*, pp. 56–63. For records of some of the departures for crusading activity, see, e.g., *CDS*, i, nos. 2558, 2559, 2563, 2564, 2575.

73 Macquarrie, *Crusades*, p. 126.

74 Macquarrie, *Crusades*, p. 129; see also the comments on the funding of Louis IX's 1248–50 crusade in Christopher Tyerman, *God's War: A New History of the Crusades* (London, 2006), pp. 777–83, where both the central and personal expenses of such activity are examined.

had joined Louis IX's campaign in Egypt of 1248–50) could hardly have absented themselves from the kingdom without a degree of royal sanction. The patronage offered by crown and noble community to the Franciscan and Dominican orders (who were used by the papacy both in preaching the crusades and in taxation-gathering), and to the military orders of the Hospitallers and Templars, also suggest an openness to the concept.[75] The preaching of the cross in Scotland in the late 1260s was a responsibility which had been delegated not only to messengers of the legate Ottobuono, but also, earlier (and probably with more success) directly to the bishop of St Andrews.[76] Doubtless many of the anonymous Scots of lower social status who travelled to foreign lands did so because, in a rigidly hierarchical society, they were compelled by the nobles to whom they owed allegiance; but some of them must also have volunteered, as their predecessors had done in earlier centuries, for the good of their souls. Whether undertaken through official sanction or through personal initiative, the perceivable fact that greater numbers of wealthy Scots participated in this European venture than had previously been the case must be symptomatic of a development of society in line with the social, religious and political norms of mid thirteenth-century European kingdoms. This fact is reflected in the changing nature of the kingship: the approach to the diplomatic effort leading to the treaty of Perth; the quest for the rites of unction and coronation for their kings; the discussion of whether the king should be knighted before inauguration; the careful avoidance of statements or actions prejudicial to the crown or kingdom (including, of course, protection of the crusading levies for the purposes of Scottish crusading activity) – all point to a kingship and kingdom which was increasingly, and self-consciously, in tune with the mainstream of European politics.

Bower relates that David earl of Atholl died at Carthage on 6 August 1270.[77] Completely unrelated, three weeks later, doubtless well before Countess Isabella knew that she was a widow, the king issued a precept to Ralph Lascelles, sheriff of Fife, instructing him and his bailies to hold an inquest, presumably relating to the inheritance of land.[78] Despite the dramatic events unfolding in North Africa, the everyday business of administration and justice continued at home. Indeed, from the period between Alexander taking personal control of the

75 For the reception of the military orders into Scotland, see the introduction to Ian B. Cowan, P.H.R. Mackay and Alan Macquarrie (eds), *The Knights of St John of Jerusalem in Scotland* (Edinburgh, 1983).

76 *CPL*, p. 394: in October 1263, Urban IV had commanded the bishop of St Andrews, with other prelates and clerks chosen by him, 'to set before the faithful in [Scotland] the state of the Holy Land'. This was one of a number of such mandates sent to bishops throughout Europe.

77 *Chron. Bower*, v, pp. 374–75; cf. *Chron. Melrose,* Faustina B. IX, fo. 73v.

78 *RRS*, iv pt. 1, no. 113.

government in the autumn of 1258 and the end of 1270, around 90 royal acts have survived either in full texts, or are known to have been 'the subject of written record'.[79] This is a marked contrast to the sparser surviving record (approximately 45 acts) of the minority period, perhaps demonstrating (despite the unquantifiable vagaries of survival) that the machinery of government, having ticked over for some years, was in full swing throughout the 1260s. Some of these acts related to the diplomatic and personal communications with the English royal court, and to the major national events which have been discussed in the pages above; such acts, however, account for less than a quarter of the total. By far the majority are concerned with the commonplace of administration: inquests such as that quoted above; grants of land or other items, rights or services to both secular and ecclesiastical beneficiaries, and confirmation of grants by others; and economic and judicial minutiae.[80] The warfare in the west and the long-term effects of the resulting treaty of Perth have received many pages of description and analysis; but this is the inevitable effect of the skewed lens of hindsight. Even during the years 1261–66, the events in the west account for only a handful of the known acts: to most people who were not called on to fight, or who did not have their lands pillaged, the challenges of everyday life impacted to a far greater degree than did the events selectively discussed by historians. To that extent, perhaps the real achievement of Alexander III in the first decade of his personal reign was not to lay to rest the long-standing conflict with Norway, or to navigate the tricky diplomatic waters of papal legations and English baronial conflict; perhaps it was a much quieter achievement – the establishment and nurture of a well-functioning judiciary and administration, which in turn created an atmosphere in which goods could be produced and traded, and in which hungry mouths could be fed.

79 *RRS*, iv pt. 1, nos. 26–75, 165; plus, reasonably confidently dated to within this period, nos. 198, 202–40, 247, 250.

80 The pages of *CDS*, i for the same period offer a similar picture: minor cross-border judicial and tenurial matters far outweigh other affairs.

CHAPTER 7

Challenge and Response

The final 20 years of Alexander III's reign have sometimes been characterised as uneventful: 'even the overheated imagination of the Franciscan friar who kept the "*Lanercost*" *Chronicle* can find little that was remarkable to relate about Scotland', and 'the annals of Walter Bower pass from one pair of dead ecclesiastic's shoes to another'.[1] It is true the latter part of the reign offers none of the spectacular conflict (and conflict resolution) which had punctuated the previous few decades. However, the story is there to tell: it is a tale of a different character, but one which, as much as the dramatic scenes of the 1250s and early 1260s, moulded the Scotland that outlived Alexander into the dark days of the 1290s and beyond. As the ambassadors sailed off into the 'Norwegian sunset', treaty in hand, there was doubtless a sense of relief and satisfaction: the extension of royal authority westwards could continue legitimately and, to a degree, with the certainty of success. Diplomatic life continued with the ongoing strife in England and the business of papal legations to manage; and the matter of prominent members of the governing community leading their followers off to foreign lands for the defence of Christendom may also have posed challenges.

The affairs of government over the next few years kept Alexander on the road: from Scone in February 1267, his acts show him to have been almost constantly on the move – Jedburgh in May, Scone again in June, north to Aboyne by August and then in Berwick by the following spring. There is then a gap, before he is found as far north as Elgin in November 1268, yet back in Kelso in January, Edinburgh and on to Scone in March, after which he seems to have stayed in the south of the country (Haddington in June, Dumfries in August) for some time, presumably because of his impending journey southwards for a visit to Henry III in York in September. The pattern continues: his

1 Duncan, *Making of the Kingdom*, p. 583.

life for the next 20 years is a continual peregrination, taking in Moray, Aberdeenshire, Angus, Dundee, Perthshire, Fife, Kinross, Stirling, the Lothians, the borders, Great Cumbrae and Galloway.[2] He was required to be itinerant, visible to his people and conspicuous in his administration of justice. The judicial machinery included the ayres carried out by the royal-appointed justiciars, and the local administration by the sheriffs and other officials; but the occasional appearance of the king himself, at least in the most populated areas of the kingdom, was a necessity. So far as can be told, he does not seem ever to have visited Caithness, Ross, the north-west or the Hebrides, and the map of the place-dates of his *acta* serves to demonstrate the large proportion of his kingdom which it is not possible to prove that he graced with his presence. The reason for his apparent absence is likely to have been that these areas were less densely populated, as yet less active in the developing trading economy, and therefore produced fewer petitions requiring royal justice. The editors of Alexander's acts have suggested that royal control in the less frequently visited areas was secure enough to allow them to be administered by officials; but they have also pointed out that there was a growing tendency in this period for the chancellors and their staff to become less itinerant. As the written record of government and justice gradually became more voluminous and complex, so it became less convenient to maintain a travelling chancery. Given, too, that the attendance of the chancery clerk was more vital to the writing and authentication of a royal act on a given day than that of the king, the warning that the place-date evidence of the *acta* cannot be taken as proof of a royal itinerary is well made.[3] That the king seems to have issued few acts in the western and northern parts of the kingdom should not be taken to indicate that these areas were ignored. All of the twelfth- and thirteenth-century kings were active in trying to extend the areas which they controlled, but that activity did not always require their personal presence. Place-date data is necessarily incomplete, but the extent of the lacunae is very difficult to assess. For example, a significant proportion of royal *acta* are found in monastic cartularies, each of which naturally has a geographical bias. Non-survival of some cartularies, therefore, irreparably skews both the geographical and the chronological place-date analysis. The loss of Scottish royal records during the ensuing decades of war was very great, as is demonstrated by the inventories of archives which were held in

2 Great Cumbrae: *RRS*, iv pt. 1, no. 90, 23 September 1274, is dated at Lochcumberay, which, in the lack of more specific evidence is assumed to be Great Cumbrae. Why, unusually, he may have been in that area at that time is unknown. Unfortunately, there are no other surviving acts close to that date, so it is not possible to posit an itinerary. On 23 September he may still have been travelling homeward from his attendance at Edward I's coronation on 19 August.

3 *RRS*, iv pt. 1, pp. 4–6; see also comments above, p. 53, and below, Map 3, pp. 298–99.

Edinburgh in the 1280s and 1290s.[4] Private and ecclesiastical records must have been subject to similar loss, but no evidence exists to allow us to ascertain the scale of destruction. King William's surviving *acta*, however, comprise over 500 full texts, compared to the meagre survival of 175 from the more bureaucratically developed (and, we may therefore assume, more documentarily prolific) chancery of Alexander III.[5] It is dangerous to build a historical edifice on the quicksand of missing evidence. Neither can we be certain of the king's motivation in visiting any individual place. That a precept instructing the holding of an inquest relating to local lands was issued by the king at Montrose on 21 March 1262, for example, need not imply that it was the reason for the king's presence in the area: it is likely that the plea which gave rise to the precept was opportunistic, given the king's proximity, and the primary reason for his presence in the area at that time may just as likely have been to test-drive a new hunting steed, or the possible residence there, or in Forfar, of the queen and her household.[6] While it is therefore problematic to draw more than very general and tentative conclusions from place-date evidence, some features are nonetheless worthy of note. As the editors of Alexander III's *acta* have also pointed out, it is striking how many of Alexander's acts were dated at Scone: far more (24) than at any other place. It does indeed seem likely that this was a place which Alexander deliberately fostered as a centre of royal activity, and that he 'actively promoted the reputation of the moot hill at Scone as a cultic site and to emphasise its distinct status as both the physical and symbolic centre of the Scottish royal landscape'.[7]

In the late summer of 1268 Alexander and Margaret, at the English king's invitation, paid another social visit to Henry and Eleanor in York, 'for the sake of recreation and solace'.[8] The English royal records contain the plethora of grants and 'special favours' which usually accompanied such visits, as the protagonists carried forward petitions on behalf of others. Thus, on 24 September, 'at the instance of Margaret Queen of Scotland', William Swinburne, the queen's treasurer, received from Henry a grant of freedom for the rest of his life from juries and other services (a gift very similar to that he received five years later from Alexander III[9]); within a few days of that grant there were others to John Balliol (who died very soon thereafter), Robert Bruce, Alan Durward and others. There were settlements of mercantile disputes and judicial orders relating

4 See below, Appendix 3.
5 Numbers from *RRS*, ii & iv pt. 1.
6 *RRS*, iv pt. 1, no. 36.
7 *RRS*, iv pt. 1, p. 35 & n.
8 *CDS*, i, nos. 2482, 2486.
9 *RRS*, iv pt. 1, nos. 83, 84.

to, for example, instances of piracy: clearly, as on previous occasions, the visit included time for Alexander to conduct business as well as 'to speak with and go about with the king'.[10]

Alexander and Margaret were in England again only a year later, when (again, 'for recreation and solace') they went south to attend the translation of the relics of Edward the Confessor to the magnificent new shrine which Henry had commissioned in Westminster abbey, a ceremony which has been described as 'Henry's greatest triumph, the fulfilment of his dearest hopes'.[11] That they made the arduous journey again so soon for an event of intensely personal interest to Henry must indicate both security at home and a continuing bond of affection between the courts. This may have been the last occasion on which the two kings met. For the final few years of Henry's reign, the frequent cross-border communication which had characterised earlier times continued. In November 1268, for instance, the king's clerk, Thomas of Kinross, was sent to Scotland by Henry on business relating to the long-standing settlement of the division between the heiresses (one of whom was Elizabeth, the countess of Buchan) of the late Roger de Quincy's immense inheritance; in April 1269 Robert Bruce and three 'retainers' were about to set out for Scotland at Henry's command, 'to forward his affairs there'; the abbot of Melrose was also used as a messenger, and the routine judicial and administrative cross-border exchange continued as normal.[12] While there were issues such as injustices done to Alexander in some of his English lands and the still-awaited payment of much of Margaret's dowry, they seem to have been dealt with in a spirit of cooperation, rather than of conflict.[13]

On 20 March 1273, a little over nine years after the birth of the younger Alexander, another child, David, was born to Margaret and Alexander III.[14] Three surviving children in the course of 18 years of consummated marriage was hardly, by medieval standards, prolific, and there may have lingered some underlying tension in Scotland regarding the succession. With the birth of this new male child, however, the king's dynastic position must have seemed more secure. A few days earlier he had apparently been in Scone, but by the middle of April he was on his way to Durham, from where, on 22 April, he wrote to

10 *CDS*, i, nos. 2486, 2488–2501, *passim*. It seems likely that Margaret sought Henry's intervention in a dispute involving the Flemish merchant family of Bonebroke; later records make it clear that they conducted business on her behalf (*CDS*, i, nos. 2615–17). Swinburne also received a grant of land 'for good and laudable service' in 1269 (*CDS*, i, no. 2535).

11 Powicke, *The Thirteenth Century*, p. 224; *CDS*, i, no. 2542.

12 *CDS*, i, nos. 2544–45, 2585.

13 *CDS*, i, nos. 2578, 2579, 2580, 2588, 2627; *RRS*, iv pt. 1, nos. 78, 86 (to Eleanor, after Henry's death).

14 *Chron. Melrose*, Faustina B. IX, fo. 60v.

his mother-in-law Queen Eleanor, primarily about issues relating to his northern English estates.[15] The Eleanor to whom he wrote, however, was a widow, since Henry III had died on 16 November 1272, at the 'very old' age of 65, after 56 years on the throne. The writer of *Gesta Annalia* gave vent to artistic licence when he described Henry as 'that most peaceable king of England', who had ruled 'in the greatest peace and righteousness'; it can hardly be claimed that the England of Henry III had been entirely peaceful. If, however, his intention was to contrast the effect of the reign of Henry III on Scotland with that of Edward I, he can hardly be blamed.[16]

The relationship between Alexander III and Henry III has been the subject of considerable debate, arguments tending to revolve around whether the Anglo-Scottish events of Alexander's minority and the early years of his adult reign should be seen in the light of the personal relationship between them or through the lens of a policy of English monarchical aggrandisement.[17] In fact, any analysis of the nature of Henry's involvement in Scottish affairs must allow for both. Henry, Eleanor and their children were close, and it seems that the familial bond between the two royal houses continued into the early reign of Henry's son, Edward I. However, if there was a friendship or family relationship between Henry and Alexander, it cannot be denied that there was also a professional one. They both took seriously the responsibilities and duties bestowed upon them by their respective kingships. There was an ancient claim to English dominion over the entire island, which, when circumstances allowed, was pursued: the English monarchical attitude to Scotland was justifiably opportunistic, and there are plenty of documented actions of Henry III which make it clear that he, in common with his predecessors, harboured the long-held ambition. His request, in 1251, that the pope should not accede to the Scottish request for unction and coronation of their kings was made on the grounds that the king of Scots was his liegeman.[18] His quest for the right to use the papal taxations raised from the Scottish church and his demand for 'faithful and inviolable' observance of the agreement made regarding the Scottish governing council of 1255 are explicit in their assumption of regal authority. Another indication of his attitude to Scotland lies in his reluctance to deliver up to the Scots the document relating to the reorganisation of the royal council in 1255,

15 *RRS*, iv pt. 1, no. 86. I accept the editors' dating of 1273, rather than 1272, as given in *CDS*, ii, no. 1.

16 *Chron. Fordun*, i, p. 305 (trans. ii, p. 300); see also the note in *Chron. Bower*, v, p. 490 (l. 44), and E.B. Fryde, D.E. Greenway, S. Porter and I. Roy (eds), *Handbook of British Chronology* (London, 1986), pp.37–38; *Gesta Annalia* gives the wrong date for Henry's death.

17 See above, pp. 144–47.

18 Stones, *Anglo-Scottish Relations*, pp. 58–59.

return of which had been agreed because of the jeopardy in which it placed Scottish sovereignty.

On the other hand, notwithstanding the expectations of his own kingship, the interpretation of the minority offered above places Henry in a somewhat different light from that offered by some other commentators. His apparently light touch on affairs in 1251/52, and his giving of space to the Scots in 1255 (and in 1257/58) to arrange their own affairs, suggests that he was understanding of the character of the Scottish kingship, and his choice of representatives to uphold his royal and familial interests in Scotland throughout the minority demonstrated considerable sensitivity. Despite his crown's imperialist ambitions, his acceptance of the standing of the Scottish kingship was implicit in his agreement to Alexander swearing oaths by proxy, a fact which does not suggest that he regarded the uncrowned, unanointed, king of Scotland as of inferior status. Henry perhaps appreciated the nature of Scottish government, in a way which his son and successor demonstrably did not with disastrous result for both kingdoms.

Alexander's approach to the relationship seems to have been similarly opportunistic. As a child, he had little option but to accept the counsel both of his noble community in Scotland and of his more powerful father-in-law. When offered the opportunity to express resistance to the attempted subjugation of his kingdom, he equally had no option except to take it. If the reported refusal of homage in 1251 actually took place, it was no more than a scripted and formulaic statement of sovereign ambitions on the parts of both kings: claim and counter-claim regarding English overlordship was a traditional game played by both parties. Later, the control which Alexander exercised over the appointment of Scottish councils in 1257 and 1258 was a deliberate wresting back of lost ground, and the timing of his pursuit of aggression in the west, and of diplomacy relating to the Norwegian affair, may have been deliberately manufactured for a period when Henry was in no position to interfere. By then Alexander had been able to establish himself as an undisputed king of a sovereign kingdom. Alexander and Henry were neighbouring kings for over 20 years, during which both went through periods of strength and weakness in relation to the other. There was scope throughout much of that period for serious conflict in their relationship, and the fact that it does not seem to have occurred may be testimony to a strong personal relationship between them. As Alexander grew stronger, and Henry grew weaker, the balance of power certainly shifted; but there is no indication that the personal bond diminished.

Alexander and Henry are unlikely to have met each other on more than perhaps eight occasions (including some when Alexander was a mere child), and much of that time would have been spent in formality and ceremony: they can hardly have known each other well in personal terms. Nonetheless, it seems likely that Alexander joined Margaret in mourning the passing of her father: Henry, if at times he had provided a severe challenge to Alexander's kingship, had also offered at least remote friendship and, within the limits imposed by the very different traditions of their respective kingships, he may have been an effective mentor.

It is tempting to assume that the accession of Edward I marked a complete change in the relationship between the two kingdoms, but there is no evidence to suggest that it did so. Edward's epithet of 'hammer of the Scots' was earned in later days, after Alexander III's death, and it seems likely that the nature of the relationship between the brothers-in-law was, initially at least, quite similar to that between Alexander and Edward's father. Bower's tale of Edward's social visit to Margaret and Alexander at Roxburgh early in 1267 has already been noted; the *Lanercost Chronicle* placed it in Haddington in the absence of Alexander, where Edward met with Margaret in order to make the acquaintance of his nephew and niece. In both accounts, they parted after mutual congratulations and without further business.[19] The date may be uncertain, or there may have been more than one visit (which seems less likely): there is record of Edward having been in Scotland in the fifty-second year of Henry III's reign, which would place it during the year beginning 28 October 1267. The intention of the chroniclers in recounting these events, however, is certainly to create the impression of a familial bond and a spirit of peace and friendship between the two royal courts. Edward I should not be regarded as senior to Alexander III: he was only a couple of years older, and although Edward's deep involvement in the disturbances which characterised Henry's later years on the throne had given him plenty of experience upon which to call, Alexander had been on the throne for over 20 years by the time Edward succeeded in his early thirties. Alexander's apparent willingness to help in the crisis of the 1260s, and the loyalty to Henry and Edward which had been shown by many prominent cross-border lords must also have assisted the maintenance of warm relations. As later events were to show, the traumas of the 1260s may have given Edward a ruthless streak in the face of opposition, but for the first few years, at least, relations between Alexander and Edward displayed nothing other than cordiality.

Edward had been overseas when his father died, and almost two years were to pass before he set foot again in England. His return was carefully choreographed: in the style typical of the English court, preparations were made for ostentatious ceremonial and celebration and, although he arrived in Dover at

---

19 *Chron. Bower*, v, pp. 354–55 & n. p. 471; *Chron. Lanercost*, p. 81 (trans. & n., Anderson, *Early Sources*, ii, pp. 458–59).

the beginning of August 1274, the citizens of London had to wait in anticipation for over two weeks before he arrived there, making a theatrically staged entrance to the city only a single day before the splendour of his coronation on 19 August. It was not only the citizens of London who waited. The king and queen of Scotland were there too, with, according to *Gesta Annalia*, their children. They went, it is said, with much pomp and in the company of many of the nobles.[20] Alexander seems not to have left Scotland until after the end of July; he was presumably on his way south when he acceded to a petition from the abbot of Arbroath, at Haddington on 1 August. The safe conduct which must have been issued for the Scottish royal party travelling through England does not seem to have survived, but there is a record that the customary daily allowance of 100s., which Alexander received when he was in England on official business, was to be paid for the period of five weeks, which would have him re-crossing the border in early September. The ceremony itself, at which Edward took the oaths to observe the laws, protect the church and people, and preserve the rights of the crown, was followed by the coronations of both Edward and his queen, Eleanor of Castile. It has been suggested that the sword of state may have been carried (after some controversy) by Alexander, but this seems unlikely; there is no evidence that Alexander played any rôle in the ceremony other than as a spectator.[21] As had been the case at Alexander and Margaret's wedding in 1251, the feasting tables groaned, and there was an opulent scale of accommodation and entertainment for so vast a company. There is a tale that Alexander and five English earls came before Edward with retinues of a hundred knights each, all of whose horses were set free to be claimed by anyone who could catch them; there was, too, a pipeline of wine for the general populace: conspicuous consumption was the order of the day. Alexander, the Lanercost chronicler claimed, 'exceeded the generosity of all the others, in hospitality and gifts'.[22]

The days and weeks following the coronation during which Alexander remained at the English court show evidence of the same routine of business which characterised the other Scottish royal visits. There are the records of petitions granted, and of the settlement of a range of judicial, economic and administrative issues. On 27 August, for example, an inquest into the rights of the king of Scots and his men in the northern forests was commanded;

---

20 *Chron. Fordun*, i, p. 305 (trans. ii, p. 300).

21 H.G. Richardson, 'The Coronation of Edward I', *Bulletin of the Institute of Historical Research*, 15 (1937–38), pp. 94–99. Michael Prestwich, *Edward I* (London, 1988), p. 90 offers a persuasive rebuttal of the suggestion.

22 For a description of the event, see Prestwich, *Edward I*, pp. 89–91 and sources cited. *Chron. Lanercost*, p. 96 (trans. Anderson, *Early Sources*, ii, p. 670).

around the same time Alan Durward was again given the custody of Bolsover castle; and the outstanding issue of merchandise that had been plundered at sea from Aberdeen merchants was ordered to be settled by the king, as 'instigated by the K. of Scotland'.[23] The conduct of business between the two kingdoms seems to have continued in exactly the same way both after the death of Henry III and following the return and coronation of Edward I. The same cooperative approach prevailed in the conduct of judicial and mercantile affairs, and in the complexities of cross-border landholding. The letter issued by Alexander at the mysterious 'Lochcumberay' on 23 September, for example, informed Edward, since 'it is a duty to attest the truth', of the marriage in Scotland of Cristiana, widow of Walter Lindsay to Henry's vassal, Walter Percy (it being inadmissible for an English baron to marry without the king's permission). In a further example of royal cooperation, presumably having gnawed at the old bone of contention, Alexander was rewarded by Edward's instigating a renewed investigation into the extent of arrears remaining from Margaret's dowry. Also, 'at the prayer of his brother and liege Alexander K. of Scotland, and his sister M[argaret] Queen of Scotland, his consort' Edward granted special leave to Elizabeth, countess of Buchan (on account of her advanced pregnancy) not to have to go to him personally to receive her inheritance from her father, Roger de Quincy. In 1275 there was more correspondence, regarding Alexander's northern English lands and several other issues, and Edward sent six horses to Scotland for Alexander's use, presumably as a gift, in June 1276.[24]

The landscape of cordiality between the kings, however, may have begun to shift a little in 1275, with the death, on 26 February, of Alexander's queen and Edward's sister. According to *Gesta Annalia*, Margaret died at Cupar and was buried 'beside King David' in Dunfermline abbey.[25] More detail of her death is given by the Lanercost chronicler:

> In this year, Margaret, the queen of Scotland, and sister of the king of England, died, on the fourth day before the Kalends of March; a woman of great beauty, chastity, and humility: three qualities that are seldom combined in one person. To visit her in her illness came in great numbers both bishops and abbots; but she refused to all of them entrance to her chamber. And, after receiving from her confessor (a Minorite friar) all the

---

23 *CDS*, ii, nos. 17, 18, 20.

24 *RRS*, iv pt. 1, nos. 90, 273, 274, 275, 278; *CDS*, ii, nos. 25, 40, 55, 59, 60, 63, 78; in the pages of *CDS*, ii covering 1274 and 1275 there are many further instances of the settlement of cross-border administrative issues.

25 *Chron. Fordun*, i, p. 305 (trans. ii, p. 300).

> sacraments, she granted no audience to any others, down to the time of her death; unless it happened that her husband was present.[26]

The nature of Margaret's fatal disease is unknown, and other than a formal restoration to Alexander in May 1275 of English lands held through her right, which had been taken back into the English king's hands on her death, the official record is silent on the subject of her demise. There is little to enlighten us regarding the closeness of the relationship between Alexander and Margaret. She had been his companion since childhood, however, and it is difficult to believe that he would not have mourned her passing. In a double blow to her family, Margaret and Edward's younger sister Beatrice, who was married to John de Dreux, later duke of Brittany (and thus a relative both of Alexander's mother and of Yolande de Dreux, to whom Alexander would later remarry), died only a month later. There is little doubt that this death too would have affected Edward, and perhaps also Alexander.[27]

In the autumn of 1275 Godred, the illegitimate son of Magnus, the king of Man whose death in 1265 had led to direct rule on behalf of the king of Scotland, invaded Man. The official records of both England and Scotland are silent on the matter, and our knowledge of the event comes primarily from a remarkably detailed account in the *Annals of Furness*,[28] where it is stated that Godred was not universally accepted by the people in the first instance, 'but in a short time he subdued all to himself in fear and affection, and finally they universally and unanimously appointed him their prince'. Alexander responded by raising a fleet of over 90 ships with a sizeable force. According to Lanercost, this force came ashore on 7 October. Offered peace, Godred and his 'perverse counsellors' opted instead for battle and were routed by the more powerful and better equipped Scottish army. In a relatively rare description of the Scottish forces, which it seems were drawn mainly from Galloway, it is said that the Manxmen, 'unarmed

---

26 *Chron. Lanercost*, p. 97 (trans. Anderson, *Early Sources*, ii, pp. 671–72). Anderson (p. 672 n.) suggests that the chronicler gained the information directly from Margaret's confessor, providing evidence (p. 658 n.) that other information had been passed to the chronicler by the same source. This would explain why Lanercost provides more information than *Gesta Annalia* or Bower.

27 *Handbook of British Chronology*, p. 38; Powicke, *The Thirteenth Century*, pp. 97, 159 & n., 235. It has sometimes been commented that the choice of a French bride was a sign of a deteriorating relationship between England and Scotland; the familial relationship between Yolande and John of Brittany (who was a close friend of Edward I) may counter that suspicion.

28 The relevant passage from the *Annals of Furness* is in *SAEC*, pp. 382–83 & n. Although their accounts are briefer, some further details are added by the *Chronicle of Man* and the *Chronicle of Lanercost*: both are quoted in Anderson, *Early Sources*, ii, pp. 672–73 & nn. See also the discussion of this episode in McDonald, *Kingdom of the Isles*, pp. 137–38 and McDonald, *Sea Kings*, pp. 296–301.

and naked, could not resist the slingers, ballisteries [crossbowmen], archers and armed men'. That the fleeing Manxmen were pursued implies that at least some of these 'armed men' were on horseback. The Lanercost chronicler tells us that 'the wretched Manxmen turned their backs, and perished miserably'. Many died, but Godred himself, with his wife and some companions, escaped to find sanctuary in Wales.

The leadership of the Scottish force provides an enlightening comment on the nature of politics and government in the west. The Furness account tells us that the army was led by John de Vesci, John Comyn justiciar of Galloway, Alan son of the earl, Alexander of Argyle and Alan son of Rother. Vesci was a prominent cross-border lord, holding the lands of Alnwick and Sprouston in the eastern marches; Comyn was, of course, the lord of Badenoch, a magnate absolutely central to the conduct of Scottish crown policy throughout the reign; Alan son of the earl, an illegitimate son of Thomas of Galloway (the earl of Atholl), was 'a respected man of power, wealth and authority in Galloway and Man';[29] Alexander of Argyll was none other than the lord of Lorn, the son of Eógan mac Dubhgaill, and by now also the son-in-law of John Comyn;[30] 'Rother' is to be identified as Rúaidrí, and Alan is thus Alan mac Ruaridh, lord of Garmoran.[31] That these two families, protagonists of the western conflicts of a decade earlier, were now agents of royal power is certainly significant of a shift in the political landscape of the west. Their knowledge of the area as well as their valued ability to provide men and probably ships made them excellent choices for such a task; but their association with the mainland lords (as well as, in Alexander of Lorn's case, the marriage bond with Comyn) in such a task, is highly significant:

> Instead of opposing royal authority in the West, the MacSorleys had become agents of its enforcement, and it would be difficult to find a better example of their integration into the mainstream of Scottish society.[32]

The *Annals of Furness* level harsh criticism at the Scottish action: the suppression of the rebellion against Scottish rule was, it is claimed, brutal; many died, the abbey of Rushen was looted, the monks ejected and the land despoiled. The *Chronicle of Man* relates that the number of Manxmen who fell in the battle was 537, a figure which probably puts into perspective the actual scale of the

29 Oram, *Alexander II*, p. 169.
30 Young, *Robert the Bruce's Rivals*, p. 72.
31 For Alexander and Alan, see the genealogical trees in McDonald, *Kingdom of the Isles*, pp. 257–58; for Alan and his kindred, see also pp. 130–31.
32 McDonald, *Kingdom of the Isles*, p. 135.

engagement, but it is believable that the actions of the Scottish army thereafter were less than conciliatory. The account of the rebellion in the *Annals of Furness*, however, may not be without bias. It follows closely a description of the disputed election to the bishopric of Man, which, although ecclesiastically still subject to the diocese of Nidaros, lay in the patronage of the king of Scots. The bishop, Richard, an Englishman, but a canon of St Andrews when elected in 1253 (emphasising the already strong Scottish influence over the area by this stage), had died in England on his way home from the 1274 Council of Lyons, in March 1275. Locally, Gilbert, the abbot of Rushen, was elected in his place, but this election was rejected by Alexander III, who appointed instead Mark, a Galwegian. The Furness chronicler was deeply opposed to the Scottish king's action: he claimed that when Gilbert went to the Scottish court to seek royal confirmation, he was courteously received, but was treated with guile and treachery, his election annulled, and Mark (who it is claimed was the brother of the bailiff of Man) was intruded into the see and duly consecrated in Norway. The *Chronicle of Man*, interestingly, does not mention the disputed election, and is supportive of Mark's episcopacy.[33] It seems likely that the *Annals of Furness* (of which the Cistercian abbey of Rushen, founded in 1134, was a daughter house) was, following the rejection of Gilbert's election as bishop, vehemently anti-Scots, and this would colour the description of the election and the suppression of the revolt. Doubtless, though, the Scottish force, as had been the case in Galloway under Alexander II, would have shown little mercy in ensuring that Man would think twice about any future rebellion against the king of Scots' authority.

Although relations do seem to have remained generally good, as early as December 1275 there was a hint of frostiness in the communication between Alexander and Edward, when Alexander responded to Edward's request regarding the payment of *auxilium* from Alexander's lands in Tynedale by saying that he could not answer until he had had the opportunity to discuss the matter with his magnates.[34] Exactly what Edward had asked is not clear, but it may have been an issue that had potential to jeopardise the status of king or kingdom, since the advice of his council was required – an echo of the response which the immature Alexander was said to have given Henry III in 1251 when asked for homage for his kingdom. By the following summer there was further tension, with a serious dispute regarding the location of the border between the kingdoms, which was to fester for at least the remainder of the 1270s. Alexander

33 *SAEC*, pp. 381–82; Anderson, *Early Sources*, ii, pp. 673–74 & nn. (Note that Anderson erroneously gives the year of his death as 1274); Watt and Murray, *Fasti*, p. 261.

34 *RRS*, iv pt. 1, no. 96.

wrote to Edward on 18 August 1276 commending his envoys, the bishop of Brechin, the chamberlain Thomas Randolph and the king's clerk Master Thomas Charteris (who was soon to become the chancellor), and exhorting him to give attention to the business they would explain to him. This was the disputed border in the Berwick area; the bishop of Durham complained to Edward that agents of the Scottish crown were infringing episcopal and royal rights there by holding courts 'on land once covered by the sea and waves, as if the same belonged to Scotland', and by imprisoning an episcopal servant. The English king's response was to order that, if the situation had not been rectified by Alexander, all Scots passing through the sheriffdom of Northumberland should be arrested. There were further exchanges of correspondence, and another high-powered embassy (comprising the bishops of St Andrews and Dunblane, the earl of Carrick and Richard Straiton) was sent to Edward in July 1277; more envoys followed in September and again in the ensuing April, May and September to continue discussion of the 'excesses and outrages committed by Scottishmen on this side of Twede'. Thereafter, there seems to have been a lull for a time in the diplomatic spat,[35] but other issues arose, perhaps related, such as the injury inflicted by Edward's justices on Alexander's men in Cumberland, Westmorland and York in July 1279, which merited a visit by yet more envoys.[36] Although the tone of the correspondence is unfailingly respectful and superficially cordial, there is an unmistakeable underlying atmosphere of tension which was missing in earlier years.

Before the tetchy dispute over the border was settled, another source of tension infected relations between the two kingdoms, which has received much more historiographical attention. In February 1278 arrangements began to be made for a visit of the king of Scots to the English court, to take place in the autumn. The bishop of St Andrews and William Soulis were sent to Edward, and on 20 March Edward sent them back with his *viva voce* responses to the issues they had raised on Alexander's behalf. Over the following months, although there is little detail in the record, it is clear that negotiations were being conducted regarding the conditions under which Alexander would undertake to travel south. By late May Wishart and Soulis were back in Scotland, having delivered Edward's reply to their first embassy, and Alexander again wrote to Edward, with the response of his council. At this point, it seems that the issue was the nature of the safe conducts by which Alexander would travel south. He was willing to accede to Edward's wishes to attend upon him

35 *RRS*, iv pt. 1, nos. 99 and note, with sources cited therein, 106, 109, 110, 114, 117, 119, 121, 125; *CDS*, ii, nos. 82, 95.
36 *RRS*, iv pt. 1, no. 123.

and 'do his pleasure in reason', but 'it would greatly satisfy the people of his realm if he had the usual safe conduct of the English magnates, or at least the K.'s letter, that the coming of the Scottish K. to England should not hereafter injure him or his heirs'. There was a further request that Alexander should be escorted within England by the archbishops of Canterbury and York, and the earls of Gloucester, Warenne and Lincoln (all of whom Edward had already assigned to the task, in a draft safe conduct prepared on 20 March). Within two weeks Edward responded to this request by drafting, but apparently not issuing,[37] a letter patent declaring that Alexander's visit 'should not tend to the future prejudice of that K. or his heirs'. A week later, on 12 June, a further safe conduct was issued, with detailed arrangements for Alexander's escort for a visit to take place in September. At the beginning of September, Alexander was in the south of Scotland, sending further envoys (perhaps relating to the border issue again, rather than the subject of the visit itself) from Traquair. A curious memorandum has also survived, demonstrating that the custom of mercantile profiteering at times of high demand is not a modern phenomenon: in preparation for the progress southwards of Alexander and his considerable retinue, on 15 September Edward found it necessary to command that 'the prices of provisions, etc., be not unduly raised during the visit of the K. of Scotland to England'. But Alexander did not in fact leave Scotland until after a council meeting (or more probably a full *colloquium*) which was held at Roxburgh on and around 2 October.[38]

The reason why this visit to England seems to have been more studiously negotiated than previous ones was because of the severely contentious nature of the business to be transacted. On 17 October Edward declared that Alexander had met him at Tewkesbury on the previous day and had offered him homage. Because on that day Edward did not have his council with him, however, the issue was delayed until an unspecified day, in London. When that day came, on 28 October, during the meeting of the English parliament, it was one of pomp and circumstance: Master Elyas, the king of Scotland's harper, as well as Alexander's trumpeters and minstrels were all to receive gifts from Edward.[39] This was indeed an important occasion, since it had significant implications for the status of both kingdoms. Intriguingly, though, it seems to be the result

---

37 See Duncan, *Kingship of the Scots*, p. 160.

38 *RRS*, iv pt. 1, nos. 112, 113, 114, 115; *CDS*, ii, nos. 104, 107–09, 111–16 (some of which are erroneously dated as *c.*20 March: they must refer to September when Alexander was en route to England), 119–26. *RRS*, iv pt. 1, no. 115 is a grant to the monks of Dunfermline dated at Roxburgh on 2 October; the number and status of the witnesses (some at least of whom were to accompany him to London) make it probable that this act was made on the occasion of a *colloquium*.

39 *CDS*, ii, no. 131.

neither of subsequent events, nor of contemporary subterfuge, that there are two different accounts – one from England, one from Scotland – of the wording of the homage ceremony.[40] There are significant differences between the two accounts, although they are not mutually incompatible. In the English version, Alexander is said to have 'presented himself' to Edward in the king's chamber at Westminster, in front of a considerable gathering of the magnates and prelates of England, and to have sworn homage and 'become his liegeman'. The wording of the oath as reported is unspecific regarding the issue of the status of the Scottish kingdom:

> I, Alexander, king of Scotland, become the liegeman of Lord Edward, king of England, against all men.

The act of homage was then related without quoting the actual words used:

> And the king of England received the homage of the king of Scotland, reserving the right and the claim of the king of England, and of his heirs, to the homage of the king of Scotland, and of his heirs, for the realm of Scotland, when they wish to discuss the matter.

The oath of fealty which followed was sworn on Alexander's behalf by the earl of Carrick, such proxy being an unmistakeable recognition of Alexander's royal status, but a recognition given by Edward, it is said, 'as an act of special grace, for that occasion'. The fealty was sworn by Carrick 'on the soul' of Alexander:

> I, Alexander, king of Scotland, will keep true faith with Edward, king of England, and with his heirs, the kings of England, in matters of life and limb and of earthly honour, and will faithfully perform the services due for the lands and tenements that I hold of the king of England.

Clearly, if this was a formula which had been negotiated in the months leading up to the occasion, it was one which was designed to lay on the table, but to

---

40 Both versions are printed and translated, with notes, in Stones, *Anglo-Scottish Relations*, pp. 76–83, from which all quotations are drawn. The English account originates from the Close Rolls (printed, *Foedera*, i.i, p. 563); the Scottish version is in *Dunfermline Reg.*, no. 321. For alternative discussions of this episode, see Duncan, *Making of the Kingdom*, pp. 590–91; Duncan, *Kingship of the Scots*, pp. 160–64; Powicke, *The Thirteenth Century*, pp. 595 & n., 596 (which treats the homage very briefly, but also considers Edward's attitude to his claims over Scotland); Broun, *Scottish Independence*, p. 162; Barrow, *Scotland and Its Neighbours*, pp. 4–6. In the discussion which follows, references to Duncan's work are to his later thinking, in *Kingship of the Scots*.

avoid dealing with, on that occasion at least, the contentious question of homage for the kingdom of Scotland. On the basis of a detailed examination of the evidence, Professor Duncan was persuasive in suggesting that this English account was not in fact exactly contemporary, but was produced retrospectively, in the early months of 1279, when Edward became uneasy about the lack of an official record of the homage and fealty, as further transactions regarding the ongoing border dispute caused him to fear that the previously collegiate Alexandrian approach to Anglo-Scottish relations might be changing.[41]

The Scottish account of the occasion was copied into the Dunfermline cartulary probably in the 1320s; however, Duncan argued that it represents a contemporary version kept by the Scots and created from a text of the words decided upon, and rehearsed, at the Roxburgh *colloquium* before Alexander went south to face Edward: it was 'defensive by anticipation'. It seems quite probable, since the only surviving evidence of that *colloquium* is a grant to the abbey of Dunfermline, that the abbot of Dunfermline, one of the most senior monastic prelates of the kingdom, was present at Roxburgh; given that it is in the cartulary of Dunfermline that the Scottish record of events has survived, it is therefore also tenable to suggest that the abbot, Ralph Greenlaw, was one of those present in the king's chamber in Westminster and may have had a hand in writing up the Scottish account of the proceedings. This account does not directly contradict the English one, but it does provide additional detail, with a decidedly pro-Scottish spin. The wording of the initial homage is more specific:

> I become your man for the lands which I hold of you in the realm of England for which I owe you homage, reserving [the right of] my kingdom.

Following this, the bishop of Norwich is said to have interrupted with the words:

> and let it be reserved to the king of England, if he should have right to homage for the kingdom,

to which Alexander gives the famous retort,

> nobody but God himself has the right to the homage for my realm of Scotland, and I hold it of nobody but God himself.

41 'The English record, then, was a later ad hoc production by one who was there (though the text does not say so), for a king troubled by the independence of the Scottish realm, in a dispute over the Border.' (Duncan, *Kingship of the Scots*, p. 162).

Finally, the homage sworn on Alexander's behalf by the earl of Carrick again differs from the English version:

> my lord the king of Scotland here will be faithful to you in matters of life and limb, and of earthly honour, and will keep your counsels secret,

after which Alexander himself adds

> for the lands that I hold of you in the realm of England.

It is obvious that the Scottish version of events places considerably more emphasis on the stating and rejection of the English claim to overlordship of Scotland than does the English account. It is also more anecdotal in style. Both versions record in Latin an event in which the language used would certainly have been Anglo-Norman French, and they are thus interpreted through the filter of translation. If Duncan's analysis is accepted, it is reasonable to assume that the Scottish version records accurately the initial oath of homage spoken by Alexander: although apparently copied later, it is based on a text produced even before the event. The suggestion that the earl of Carrick used the wrong words, and that Alexander's own personal interjection following the fealty was made in order to rescue the situation, seems fanciful.[42] More likely – although still pure conjecture – is that the later ascription of those words to Alexander himself was either a further piece of theatre rehearsed by the Scots in order to make the point firmly, or a device of the writer, intended to strengthen the effect of the words in a document which was undoubtedly being written for the purposes of the upholding of national status. The latter explanation seems more plausible: for Alexander to interject personally, specifically in order to uphold his regal authority, in an oath sworn by proxy would seem counter-productive. It does seem quite possible that the bishop of Norwich's apparent blunder in admitting doubt as to whether the king of England had right over Scotland ('*if* he should have right') is an addition after the event, either deliberately or accidentally, which conveniently ascribes uncertainty within English ranks.

Overall, it is not difficult to reconstruct a plausible sequence of events out of these two accounts. The variations in quoted wording can be ascribed to the vagaries of memory and translation; otherwise, the two versions are not incompatible, but represent differences in the amount of detail and in emphasis which suit the perspectives of each side. Alexander undoubtedly swore homage; it is inconceivable that he would have sworn it for his kingdom, and it is therefore

42 Duncan, *Kingship of the Scots*, pp. 162–63.

quite probable that someone (and there is no reason to doubt that it was the bishop of Norwich) would have registered what was, from an English viewpoint, an omission. Alexander would certainly have retorted firmly. That the English account, but not the Scottish, makes the point that the fealty was sworn by proxy as a one-off act of grace on the part of Edward is again consistent with the strategies and standpoints adopted by the two sides.

Duncan's conclusion was that both sides had rehearsed their parts, and that both were temporarily thrown off balance by the other: Norwich made his hasty intervention when the Scots king unexpectedly reserved the right of his kingdom in the homage. Alexander, similarly troubled by Norwich's unexpected intrusion, reacted spontaneously, and the reiteration of the point during the swearing of fealty re-emphasised Alexander's self-assurance regarding the independence of his kingdom.

It has to be doubted, however, that an event of this formality and importance could have been conducted in such an *ad hoc* way. The similar episode in 1251, when Alexander refused to answer Henry III's request for homage for the kingdom, was a carefully rehearsed event, and the stating of right on the part of the English king, and its refusal by the Scottish king, was ritualistic.[43] There is no reason to doubt that the 1278 event was any different. It seems highly unlikely either that the Scottish king would be surprised by the request for homage for the kingdom or that the English king would expect Alexander to accede to it. It is perfectly clear that this event had been carefully negotiated over a period of some months, and therefore it is more likely that the entire event – claim, counter-claim, interruption and response – was as carefully choreographed as had been the event in 1251, when the child Alexander had said his equally pre-prepared words before Edward's father: this was just another figure in the now familiar dance. It is worth noting that *Gesta Annalia*, a closely contemporary work, stresses the Scottish version of events. Claiming that Alexander happened in any case to be in England, on a pilgrimage to the shrine of Thomas Becket, the writer tells us that Alexander, 'without prejudice to all his dignities, did homage to Edward, king of England, as he had formerly done to Edward's father also, for his lands in England'. The lands are specified, including the dowry-lands of Queen Margaret and 'the other lands and ancient honours formerly possessed by his predecessors the kings of Scotland' (except Huntingdon, which Henry, it is stated, had refused to allow him).[44] The reflection here of the careful expression of Scottish rights within the Scottish version of the 1278 ceremony, along with its association with the homage offered to Henry III, tends to

43 See above, pp. 101–02.
44 *Chron. Fordun*, i, pp. 305–06 (trans. ii, pp. 300–01).

confirm an impression that homage, being recognised as a potentially dangerous issue, was one for which there was a customary procedure, intricately designed not to rock the boat.

As would be fully demonstrated in the early 1290s, Edward I was a man obsessed by record; he would not have failed to instruct that a formal record be made of the ceremony unless the whole event had been carefully negotiated and rehearsed in advance. Duncan's suggestion regarding the causes of the subsequent creation of the two records is consistent with this approach: the lack of record was acceptable while the two kingdoms were at peace and the issue of the relationship of the two crowns was understood by both kings. However, if relations between them were to break down, then a formal stating of the disputed issue of homage became more significant to both. Rather than reducing the plausibility of a Scottish rehearsal at Roxburgh, the suggestion that the whole event was prearranged tends to increase it. It was important that everyone involved should know their rôles and their lines and, highly significant of the nature of the Scottish kingship, it was the governing community as a whole that advised on and approved the script. In the months leading up to October 1278, therefore, the envoys who travelled repeatedly between Edward and Alexander were not discussing merely the nature of Alexander's summons, nor the means, style and significance of his journey, but, much more importantly, the precise detail of the ceremony itself; if not the actual words and the actors who spoke them, then certainly the shape and import of the transaction. It was known that Alexander would swear homage, saving for his kingdom; it was known that the English claim to homage for the kingdom would be made; and it was known that Alexander would reject it. This was a ritual and formulaic stating and denial of the English crown's ambitions regarding Scotland which, as in 1251, allowed both kings to maintain their status and honour.

Traditionally, this episode has been seen as a portent of the much more turbulent relationship that characterised the years following the death of Alexander III; with the benefit of hindsight, the claim of Edward I to homage owed for the kingdom of Scotland does indeed seem to be replete with significance. However, seen in the light of the generally settled relationship between the adult Alexander III and both Henry III and Edward I, and viewed as a piece of carefully rehearsed theatre, the event can instead be seen to be significant of precisely the opposite. If the supposition concerning the reason for Edward's retrospective record-making is correct, it is further evidence that in the lead-up to the homage event it was assumed that there was no requirement for the record: there was no dispute. The positions of both crowns were clear, were understood and were accepted: it was, in effect, an agreement to disagree. Had there been a serious debate about the significance of the homage, it is perhaps unlikely that Alexander would have conceded the visit to England at all. The possibility was noted above that Edward's desire to rectify the absence of record of the homage ceremony was caused by insecurity stemming from increasing tension over the border dispute in the late 1270s. However, such disputes had arisen and been settled over decades and centuries, and should not be seen as a sign of inherent distrust between the kingdoms. There was no endemic conflict, and the nature of the relationship between the two kingdoms over most of the previous century, with the exception of a few specific episodes, was of peaceful cooperation. The steady conduct of cross-border judicial and administrative affairs, and the apparent ease with which the increasing number of Anglo-Scottish nobles conducted their business on both sides of the Tweed–Solway line must indicate that at the opening of the fourth quarter of the thirteenth century the expected norm was of collaboration between the two crowns. It has been rightly pointed out that, because of the 'deep-seated and fairly comfortable relationship based on shared kin, language and values' among the leading members of both communities, war between England and Scotland must have seemed a very distant threat.[45] One of the lessons to be learnt from Alexander III's reign – including the much-discussed question of the homage of 1278 – is that warfare between Scotland and England was not, as it has so often been portrayed, an inevitable result of deep-rooted and inextinguishable hostility between the two nations and their rulers. Following the 1278 episode, Alexander 'went home and resumed amiable correspondence with Edward I over Border disputes and family news'.[46]

It is not, therefore, surprising to note that the conduct of affairs across the border was maintained for the next few years exactly as previously. The matters afflicting the marches and the Scottish king's English lands, from Berwick right across through Cumberland, Westmorland and as far south as York in 1278 and 1279, have already been noted above as a sign of increasing tension, but these were the type of affairs which cropped up periodically, as were the various pleas which are recorded in the English rolls of assizes from this period.[47] Their records exist side by side with normal requests from one king to another, and settlement of issues: Alexander sought favour for Ingram d'Umphraville, who was trying to secure possession of his late father's English lands (whose case was also supported by Prince Alexander, the King's son, writing separately to his uncle Edward); Edward ordered of some of the lands seized from Alexander to be restored to him and other injustices righted; Alexander wrote also to his

45 Fiona Watson, *Under the Hammer: Edward I and Scotland, 1286–1307* (East Linton, 1998), p. 6.
46 Duncan, *Kingship of the Scots*, p. 164.
47 See, e.g., *CDS*, ii, nos. 146–49.

'dearest friend' Edmund, Edward's brother, seeking credence for his envoys to the English court.[48] The settlement of pleas, by both great and small, the business of administering cross-border lands by nobles and monastic houses, and the traverse of the border by merchants and traders continued as before. There was an apparently affectionate and entirely informal letter (in French) from Margaret, Alexander's daughter, to her uncle, simply giving him news that she was well and hoping the same of him; and, at Prince Alexander's request, one James Multon was pardoned of outlawry.[49] The absence of Queen Margaret seems to have been responsible, understandably, for a decrease in the number of messengers carrying news and gifts from one court to the other: there is not the same impression of the familial bond which had prevailed in the days of Henry III. It is easy to suspect that there was no particularly close friendship between Edward and Alexander, a notion strengthened by the fact that, after 1278, Alexander never again visited England; but neither is there an atmosphere of overt hostility. The two kingdoms continued to cooperate and exist, for the most part, in harmony, and the hysterical headlines created by some historians about the homage ceremony should not be taken as evidence of any impending slide into enmity.

The year 1274 (which, incidentally was also the year in which, on 11 July, Scotland's celebrated future King Robert I was born) had been momentous. The coronation of Edward I had certainly been an event of both colour and import, but of equal political note was the holding of another major church council at Lyons, which met in several sessions from May to July, presided over by the Pope, Gregory X. The business transacted at the Council of Lyons was dominated by the ecclesiastical politics and theological issues involved in an ultimately futile attempt to reunite the long-divergent Eastern and Western churches, and, of course, the ongoing issue of both achieving and financing the reconquest of the Holy Land. Bower tells us that all the Scottish bishops attended except for Dunkeld (Robert Stuteville) and Moray (Archibald),[50] and it seems likely that some other ecclesiastical dignitaries accompanied them, including abbots of some of the more significant religious houses. An innovation of this council was the inclusion of personal representatives of many monarchs (and including, remarkably, James I of Aragon in person), a recognition of the increasingly important and defined rôle of national governments in implementing papal policies. It is not known who represented Alexander III at the Council – presumably one or more of the prelates who were attending anyway – but a copy of Alexander's invitation to attend remains in the papal archives.[51] That such

48 *RRS*, iv pt.1, nos. 118; *CDS*, ii, nos. 157, 160.
49 *CDS*, ii, nos. 185, 193.
50 *Chron. Bower*, v, pp. 398–99.
51 *CPL*, i, p. 446.

events were of international importance is demonstrated by the fact that the pope wrote to Edward I expressing his disappointment that Edward would not be present at the Council because his coronation was arranged for the same time, and asking him accordingly either to hasten or to postpone the ceremony.[52] Given that he was not actually crowned until mid August, it seems that Edward acceded to the pope's wishes; the coronation was an important event too, and would require the presence not only of the king, but of many of the bishops who might otherwise have been absent at the Council.

If Bower is correct in stating that all the Scottish bishops went to Lyons except Dunkeld and Moray, that would have provided a powerful Scottish contingent. Hugh Bennum of Aberdeen (consecrated at the curia under Gregory X himself, in 1272); Laurence of Argyll; William Crachin of Brechin (who may have died in Lyons: Bower claims that he died 'at the papal court, having been there for a long time'[53]); Robert of Dunblane; Henry of Galloway; Robert Wishart of Glasgow and his uncle, William Wishart of St Andrews; Richard of the Isles (who died in March 1275, before reaching home); and Matthew of Ross (another delegate who died during the Council), along with selected abbots and perhaps others, were more than capable of representing the views of the Scottish church. The diocese of Caithness may not have been represented: following the death of Walter Baltroddie in 1270, Nicholas, abbot of Scone was elected to succeed him; in June 1273, however, the pope wrote to the dean and chapter instructing a new election, Nicholas having been rejected by the pope because of his 'intolerable lack of learning', a sad reflection on the electoral system. The new elect, Archibald Herok, received a mandate for his consecration in November 1274, but whether, as an unconfirmed bishop-elect, he attended the Council is unknown. Nicholas abbot of Scone was said by Bower to have been detained 'in Rome', presumably meaning the papal court in Lyons, on account of his debts; whether this means that he attended the council as an abbot or as a bishop-elect is not clear. He was not Bower's favourite person: he is accused of having been elected abbot of Scone when merely a novice, 'more out of fear of the lord king than out of love', and the election to the bishopric was 'a result of royal favour rather than for the merits of his life'; why (or, indeed, if) he was so favoured by the king is not known.[54]

The surviving members of the Scottish delegation returned home with deeply unwelcome news. Bower again:

---

52 *CPL*, i, p. 446.

53 *Chron. Bower*, v, pp. 398–99.

54 *CPL*, i, p. 446, Watt and Murray, *Fasti*, 78–79; for the other bishops, see Watt and Murray, *Fasti*, pp. 2, 35, 53, 100, 169–70, 190, 380–81, 261, 347 respectively, and sources cited. For Nicholas abbot of Scone, see also *Chron. Bower*, v, pp. 378–79, 400–01 and, p. 496n.

> At the said council the lord pope decreed that a tenth of all church property was to be contributed as aid to the Holy Land for six years, and that there were to be no privileged exceptions.[55]

The issue of papal taxation in support of crusading activity had raised its ugly head again. No time was wasted: as early as 20 September 1274, Master Baiamundus de Vitia (known generally in Scotland as Bagimond) was appointed papal collector in Scotland, although it remains a mystery whether his appointment was because of, or in spite of, his experience as one of the retinue of Ottobuono, who experienced considerable difficulty the last time such a task was attempted.[56] He is known to have reached Scotland by the summer of 1275, but, claiming to have set out ten months earlier, his apparent delay may have been caused by Scottish reluctance to admit him.[57] *Gesta Annalia* tells us that Bagimond summoned a council of the Scottish church at Perth on 6 August 1275, at which he made the demand of the Scottish church for the tenth. On this occasion, the principle of the payment appears not to have been disputed; instead, the contentious issue was the valuation of church property on which it was based. Bagimond insisted that, according to his commission, it was to be a tenth of the *verus valor* or 'true value', as opposed to the Scots clergy's objective of having it based on an 'old taxation', which would considerably undervalue the estate. (They were not unique in protesting about this new, more lucrative, method: at least some of the English clergy, and doubtless others, raised similar objections.[58]) Bagimond is said by the writer of *Gesta Annalia* to have acceded to the request of the Scots that he should return to Rome to present their case to the pope, but the records of his activities, which include both correspondence and more than fragmentary accounts, do not suggest that he made any trip to the curia in person before 1287. Papal approval, however, was not forthcoming for the presumed envoy who presented the Scottish case.

After this shaky start, Bagimond did achieve greater success in collecting the funds than his beleaguered predecessor of the previous decade. Within two years, some cash had been deposited for safekeeping in the cathedral of

55 *Chron. Bower*, v, pp. 398–401. Bower has taken the wording regarding 'privileged exceptions' from *Gesta Annalia*'s description of the council held by Bagimond in August 1275.

56 *CPL*, p. 448. The account of Bagimond's visit given below is based largely on that given in Ferguson, *Papal Representatives*, pp. 114–17, and on the sources cited therein. See also Ash, 'The Church in the Reign of Alexander III', pp. 44–46.

57 Ferguson, *Papal Representatives*, p. 114.

58 Annie I. Dunlop, ed., 'Bagimond's Roll: Statement of the Tenths of the Kingdom of Scotland', SHS *Miscellany*, vi (1939), pp. 1–77, at p. 6 & n.

Dunkeld. But, as in the 1250s and 1260s, it seems that opposition to the collection came not only from those who had to pay, but from the state itself. Within a few years, Bagimond asked to be recalled to the curia since he had achieved as much as he thought possible, because of the recalcitrance or even downright obstruction of some of the Scottish clergy. The pope, by now Martin IV, was stern in his refusal, however, instructing Bagimond to increase his efforts and to proceed with the threatened excommunication against those who would not pay, as had been dictated by the Council of Lyons. Revealingly, the pope also wrote to Alexander III in April 1282 asking him to allow the release from Scotland of some of the funds that had been successfully collected, a request which was still falling on deaf ears as late as July 1285, when Alexander's officials were said to have prevented the Florentine merchants who were effectively acting as papal bankers from taking money out of the kingdom, and had even arrested them.[59] It seems, then, that the very common medieval reluctance to allow the export of currency was a significant factor in the controversies which surrounded such taxations. Not only did the collection deprive the church of revenue, but it also had potentially damaging effects on money supply within the kingdom as a whole, and thus a deleterious effect on the national economy. The assertion that the approximately £18,000 collected by Bagimond in Scotland totalled roughly one-seventh of the amount collected in England (despite apparent irregularities, amounting to extortion, in the methods of English collectors) suggests that the papal officials had more trouble with the Scots than with the English, considering that the relative wealth of the churches in the two countries was approximately 1:5.[60] By July 1283, an order had already been issued instructing Bagimond's return to the curia to account for himself, since his mission had been unsuccessful.[61]

It seems that no lessons had been learnt from previous taxations: quite apart from the fundamental economic difficulties represented by taxation on such a scale, there was a serious political problem which the papacy might have anticipated. Perhaps in the hope that the king might be diverted from his concern about the destination of the very significant sums of money which were being extracted from the kingdom's coffers, in April 1282 Martin IV exhorted Alexander III either to join the crusade personally or to hand over the money to the Florentine merchants. In October of the following year, Martin IV wrote to Bagimond, ordering him to pay the money over to further named merchants, despite his pleas that he had been unable to do so 'on account of the king's

59 *CPL*, pp. 465, 481.
60 Ash, 'The Church in the Reign of Alexander III', p. 45; *CPL*, pp. 452–53; Mayhew, 'A Silver Age', pp. 59–60.
61 *CPL*, p. 469.

prohibition'. Bagimond had still failed to carry out this command by August 1284.[62] Worse, the pope answered in the affirmative a request by Edward I to have allocated to him the taxations raised in England, Scotland, Wales, Ireland, Gascony and Ponthieu, if the king should take the cross himself. The burning issue of English use of Scottish taxation was raised again in the early months of 1286, when it was compounded by Edward's request that he should be allowed to select men from Scotland for the crusade, because of his 'practical experience of the country'.[63] True, the grant of the Scottish money was contingent both upon the consent of the king of Scots and on Edward's willingness to support any Scots who joined the intended crusade, but nonetheless, the allocation of Scottish papal taxation to the English crown was, as it always had been, a red rag to a bull. The situation was further complicated by the residence in England of Bagimond for much of the period following the end of the initial six-year term of the levy, and the suspicion that he was an instrument of Anglo-papal policy,[64] which strengthened Scottish resistance to meeting the papal demand. Why successive popes continued to inflame Scottish sensibilities in this way is difficult to ascertain. It is quite possible that sensitivity to this issue and the vagaries of Anglo-Scottish relations were simply regarded as less important than the grand scheme of Christian resurgence in the Holy Land, of which the English crown was a key agent. Alternatively (or simultaneously), perhaps English agents at the *curia* were simply more effective than the Scots and were able to promote the English political message more compellingly. Resistance to taxation, however, was not unique to the Scots: over many years there were protracted and awkward negotiations between the English crown and the papacy about the collection, disbursement and export of money, and it was to be 1287 before Edward finally did take the crusading oath. However, he was never to repeat his crusading venture of 1270–74.[65] The difficulties in collecting the Scottish money continued until, and past, Alexander III's death: Bagimond submitted detailed accounts at the curia in 1287 and returned to Scotland thereafter. If his task did indeed ease following the death of the king, it may be an indication that Alexander himself was a principal actor in the Scottish

62 *CPL*, pp. 465, 469, 478. Ferguson (*Papal Representatives,* p. 115, n. 347) notes that a similar offer had been made to Alexander by Pope Innocent V in 1276.

63 *CPL*, pp. 473–74, 479–80. These were not the first indications that Scottish taxation might be made available to support English activity: see Ferguson, *Papal Representatives*, p. 115 & nn.

64 See Dunlop, 'Bagimond's Roll: Statement of the Tenths', pp. 8–9.

65 See the useful description of Edward's relations with the papacy in this period, and the ill-fated plans for a crusade, in Prestwich, *Edward I*, pp. 326–33. See also, for instance, *CPL*, p. 476 (July 1282), where Edward is reproved 'for having laid hands on the tenth in aid of the Holy Land, for doing which his letters offer frivolous excuses'.

recalcitrance.[66] Shifting political sands in the Middle East, however, had rendered the whole crusading concept of doubtful value, and the protracted nature of the attempted collection across Europe for over 15 years following the Council of Lyons, spanning no fewer than eight pontificates,[67] demonstrates widespread international obstruction of papal policy.

Because of the process of taxation there is more information than usual in this period about the condition and workings of the Scottish church: Bagimond's accounts provide some detailed evidence which would otherwise be almost entirely lacking. It is interesting to note the inconsistency with which the ecclesiastical (in contrast with territorial) boundaries of the kingdom were treated: the diocese of Man and the Isles (or Sodor), territorially now subject to Scotland, but ecclesiastically still Norwegian, was not counted part of the Scotland for this purpose; Galloway, however, territorially Scottish but ecclesiastically within the archdiocese of York, was deemed Scottish. Bagimond's detailed accounts for the archdeaconry of Teviotdale (in the diocese of Glasgow) and for the entire diocese of Moray have survived in contemporary copies, revealing the specific amounts raised from individual parishes, thus offering an appraisal of relative affluence at quite a localised level.[68] Had this information survived for a greater proportion of the country, it would have provided an unparalleled portrait of the Scottish medieval church and the prosperity of its lands across the kingdom. One point is worth noting here, however: despite the difficulties with the manuscripts (including inaccurate totals in the accounting) pointed out by the editors, it is clear that, for the most part, Bagimond does not in fact seem to have been unable to raise the money: despite his protestations to the curia, the churchmen themselves do not seem to have been fundamentally reluctant about payment. For the six years of the assessment, the Moray roll offers no example of default; Teviotdale is more complex, but in general the accounts appear to show remarkably little in the way of non-payment. The editors both concluded that during the six years of the teind, it was paid with relatively little demur. It has to be remembered, however, that these documents are not dated, and may indeed emanate from a later period, perhaps as late as the accounts which we know Bagimond submitted in 1287. Therefore, while the accounts show that the taxation based on the controversial *verus valor* was indeed paid *for* any, or all, of the

66 Ferguson, *Papal Representatives,* p. 116.

67 Gregory X, Innocent V, Adrian V (who died before consecration), John XXI, Nicholas III, Martin IV, Honorius IV, Nicolas IV (C.R. Cheney (ed.), *Handbook of Dates for Students of English History* (London, 1978), pp. 37–38).

68 Annie I. Cameron (ed.), 'Bagimond's Roll for the Archdeaconry of Teviotdale, from a Thirteenth-Century Transcript in the Vatican Archives', SHS *Miscellany*, v (1933), pp. 79–106; Revd Charles Burns (ed.), 'Bagimond's Roll for the Diocese of Moray', SHS *Miscellany*, x (1965), pp. 1–9.

years of the assessment, we cannot be sure that it was paid *in* those years. The apparently comprehensive nature of the eventual collection is thus not certain evidence of alacrity or timeousness in payment; nonetheless, it does tend to add weight to the impression that Bagimond's primary problem was not with the clergy, but with the king and his council, and therefore that the real issue with such impositions – elsewhere as well as in Scotland – was not the principle of supporting the grand crusading schemes, but rather the political and economic effects, at national level, of the payment to external sources of such large sums. The third accounting record which has survived from Bagimond's activity is an incomplete summary of his accounts, produced within the papal curia, together with an appended list of specific collections.[69] Offering a complex topographical picture of the Scottish church broken down into deaneries and parishes from which the money was raised, it is a very useful organisational benchmark against which later developments can be gauged. An impression of the apparent relative wealth of the parishes can be gained, and sometimes also even the names of some of the sub-collectors to whom the undoubtedly unpopular day-to-day business was delegated. As well as the amount of money raised, the summary also describes the way in which it was dispersed, confirming that much of it (although clearly not all), through the hands of foreign merchant bankers, did indeed find its way out of Scotland, some of it into the coffers of, for example, Charles of Anjou, king of Sicily, to whom it was lent by the merchants on behalf of the pope. The fear of loss of currency from the kingdom, and its appropriation to the uses of others, was well founded.

Throughout all the controversy, the usual business of Scottish–papal relations continued, with the administrative tasks of confirmation of prelatical appointments, granting of benefices and the like. While the pope might in one week denounce the king or some of his ecclesiastics for their refusal to meet his fiscal demands, in the next he might be entirely amenable to their requests in other areas of church affairs. Over the years of Bagimond's Scottish mission, episcopal elections were frequent. The bishop of Aberdeen, Hugh Bennum, died in 1282; as noted earlier, the bishop-elect of Brechin died in 1274/75, perhaps at the council of Lyons; there was a dispute over the uneducated bishop-elect of Caithness in 1272/73, but his successor's episcopate was short-lived and was followed again by a controversial election; Robert of the Provender, who had been bishop of Dunblane since the closing days of the minority, died in the early months of 1284; Robert Stuteville, bishop of Dunkeld since 1273, died in late 1282, and his elected successor, Hugh of Stirling, suffered the unfortunate fate of dying at the curia before consecration, in 1283. The disputed election to

69 Dunlop, 'Bagimond's Roll: Statement of the Tenths'.

the diocese of Man and the Isles has already been noted; the vacancy in the bishopric of Ross had to be filled following the death of bishop Matthew at the council of Lyons in 1274; and finally, the bishop of St Andrews appointed in 1271, William Wishart, died in May 1279. There were thus no fewer than eight episcopal as well as several abbatial appointments to be made in Scotland between 1274 and the death of Alexander III in 1286. Bower had good reason to focus on ecclesiastical succession!

Some of the episcopal appointments went smoothly. For example, there seems to have been no dispute about the election of William Comyn to the see of Brechin following the death of the bishop-elect at the Council of Lyons. The pope left it in the hands of the bishops of St Andrews and Dunkeld to enquire regarding the process of his election by the chapter as well as his fitness, and to consecrate him if they thought it appropriate. Of the family of Kilconquhar in Fife, he was the brother of Adam of Kilconquhar who married the countess of Carrick in the 1260s, and who consequently bore the title of earl of Carrick. His Comyn ancestry is not known, although his use of the name must indicate a close allegiance. A graduate by February 1267, having by then been, perhaps for some years, in the *familia* of Bishop Gamelin of St Andrews, he was a Dominican friar in the Perth house at the time of his election. Again, it is possible that royal favour assisted his election: association with the Comyn family, and his use in 1276 as an envoy to Edward I regarding the border dispute, might indicate an association with the royal household.[70] The election of Robert Fyvie, the archdeacon of Ross to replace Matthew, bishop of Ross, who had been in possession of his see for less than two years when he died at the council of Lyons, seems to have been similarly uncontroversial: he was confirmed and consecrated locally probably soon after June 1275.[71]

Not all appointments went quite so smoothly, however. The election of Henry Cheyne to Aberdeen was not entirely without incident. Henry, the precentor of Aberdeen, was elected unanimously by the chapter, but the pope at first refused to sanction the election because Henry was not an ordained priest (which does add a marginally bizarre twist to the election). 'Considering the circumstances', however, the pope (presumably after an appeal on Henry's behalf) agreed to his appointment and instructed the bishops of Glasgow, Dunblane and Caithness to ordain and consecrate him. It is not known what special circumstances persuaded the pope but, given that the new bishop was of a noble family which held extensive lands in the north-east of the country,

70 Watt and Murray, *Fasti*, p. 54; Watt, *Graduates*, pp. 107–09; *CPL*, p. 450.
71 Watt and Murray, *Fasti*, p. 347; *CPL*, p. 449.

and was closely associated with the Comyn family, it seems quite possible that the king himself had encouraged the election.[72]

Caithness seems to have been a problem diocese. Archibald Herok, whose appointment had followed the controversy over the election of the uneducated Nicholas, himself died in 1278. The chapter elected Richard, dean of Caithness, and sent their procurator to the curia to seek his confirmation, but the pope was once again dissatisfied, with concerns both about procedure and about the personal fitness of the bishop-elect, who apparently had at least one illegitimate child, and who was aged and infirm. He was persuaded to resign his election, and Harvey of Dundee, a canon of St Andrews, was elected in his place. Election to the bishopric of Caithness seems to have been a somewhat poisoned chalice, however, as by April 1282 Harvey too had died at the curia while seeking confirmation. The pope then appointed and consecrated one Alan of St Edmund, an Englishman who was at the curia at the time.[73] This may well have been a contentious appointment, as Alan was later to become a valued agent of Edward I in Scotland, but there is no record of any protest against it by Alexander III.

On the death of Robert of the Provender in 1284, the chapter of Dunblane elected William, the abbot of the Tironensian abbey of Arbroath, who was also a canon of Dunblane, as his successor. Again, there may have been some disagreement surrounding the election; intriguingly, the papal letter confirming his appointment states that, having been examined by three cardinals at the curia, he resigned the right he had to the bishopric through his election, following which the pope personally appointed him (presumably on the basis of the examining cardinals' conclusions) and ordered his consecration. It is possible, therefore, that an objection to the validity of the election had been raised at the curia, although it is not clear by whom or on what grounds. On this occasion the papal letters of confirmation were sent not to the king of Scots, but to Máel Ísu, earl of Strathearn, as the patron of the diocese.[74] The papal curia appears to have been a dangerous place: yet another bishop-elect, Hugh of Stirling, the elect of Dunkeld following the death late in 1282 of Robert Stuteville, died there while awaiting papal confirmation. The chapter then elected their dean, William, who received papal confirmation at the end of 1283. There is no record of dispute regarding

72 *CPL*, pp. 465. 467; Watt and Murray, *Fasti*, pp. 3, 12; Norman H. Reid, 'Cheyne, Henry (d. 1328)', *Oxford Dictionary of National Biography*, available online at https://doi.org/10.1093/ref:odnb/5259. The pope did write to Alexander III about the election, but that was standard practice, and does not itself indicate royal intervention.

73 *CPL*, pp. 457–58, 464–65; Watt and Murray, *Fasti*, pp. 79, 83; J. Dowden, *The Bishops of Scotland* (Glasgow, 1912), pp. 236–39.

74 Watt and Murray, *Fasti*, p. 100; *CPL*, pp. 472–73.

the appointment, but William may have been largely absent from his diocese, or even from the kingdom, since he is almost entirely missing from Scottish record throughout his episcopate, which lasted until his death in 1288.[75]

Finally, the all-important see of St Andrews became vacant following the death on 29 May 1279 of William Wishart. It is unlikely to be coincidence that the man elected to the vacancy was William Fraser, the dean of Glasgow and the royal chancellor. From a family of royal officials (his father (Gilbert) and one of his brothers (Simon) both serving as sheriffs of Traquair, and another brother (Andrew) as sheriff of Stirling), William was probably in royal service from the 1260s; he was a graduate, probably of Oxford, by 1271, and was appointed to the Glasgow deanery by early in 1273, and to the chancellorship in October 1273, on the consecration to the see of St Andrews of the previous chancellor, William Wishart. The direct influence of the king is not difficult to detect; the prior and subprior of St Andrews, the archdeacon and four canons who were delegated by the chapter to choose the new bishop are likely to have been firmly told who to elect. Nonetheless, there is, refreshingly, no recorded problem with this most important election: the pope ratified it without demur.[76] All of these processes, while not necessarily contentious, do serve to illustrate the difficulties of maintaining episcopal succession, and the potential political issues which might arise.

Aside from episcopal appointments and the difficult business of tax collection, there seems to have been relatively little business in Scotland requiring papal attention. The pages of the calendar of papal letters for the period are a more fruitful source for English history than for Scottish, but there is enough to indicate a normality in relations despite the king's fiscal intransigence: in 1277 William Fraser received papal approval to hold a third benefice besides his deanery of Glasgow and the church of Ayr; and in 1281 Pope Martin IV instructed the bishops of Dunblane and Argyll to give a dispensation, if they found it appropriate, to Hugh Abernethy, who had petitioned for it on account of his having married within the forbidden degrees of kinship. It seems to have been a rather late repentance for his sin. Admitting that he had already had 'several sons' with his wife, Mary, Hugh must by this time have been in late middle age: he had already been politically active in the 1230s. By 1288, however, it seems that his case was still outstanding, since in that year he asked Edward I to intercede with the pope on his behalf. Perhaps he sought to rectify his anomalous marriage before it was too late: he died in 1291 or 1292.

---

75 Watt and Murray, *Fasti*, pp. 124–25; *CPL*, i, pp. 469–70; Dowden, *The Bishops of Scotland*, pp. 58–59.

76 Watt and Murray, *Fasti*, pp. 380–81; Watt, *Graduates*, pp. 203–06; *CPL*, i, p. 462; Reid and Barrow, *Sheriffs*, pp. 32, 43.

Mary herself is an intriguing character: she was the daughter of Eógan of Argyll, her marriage to Máel Ísu, earl of Strathearn noted above as a symbol of her family's acceptance into the mainstream of the Scottish nobility. That, however, was her second marriage: earlier in life she had been queen of Man, married, in an apparent attempt at détente between the rival ruling kindreds of Man and the Hebrides, to Magnus, the king of Man who died in 1265.[77] Her subsequent alliance to Strathearn is thus all the more striking; one wonders what her feelings were about her brother, Alexander of Argyll, leading a Scots army against her step-son, Godred, and her former kingdom in 1275. Her time as countess of Strathearn must have been brief, since Máel Ísu died in 1271; she then married Hugh Abernethy, and after his death she was married for a fourth time, to a member of an important Welsh marcher family, Warin Fitzwarin. She outlived them all, dying probably in August 1302. She seems to have had quite an entourage in attendance at the time of her death in London, reinforcing the impression of a formidable matriarch. No fewer than 15 people were given safe conducts to return to Scotland thereafter.[78] At least half of them were 'of Argyle' or had recognisably Gaelic names (if somewhat butchered by an English clerk). The decade from the mid 1260s has been portrayed through the international dramas of the crusades and the attempts to fund them, the birth and deaths of prince, king and queen, tensions over border disputes and national status, and the politics of the west. Mary's life, touched by many of these issues, spanned the divisions through which many historians have defined the period. Though her marital career has been regarded as symbolic of cultural and political assimilation, she defies that notion by retaining her Gaelic identity to the end.

77 McDonald, *Sea Kings*, p. 301.

78 *CPL*, pp. 454, 463; J. Stevenson (ed.), *Documents Illustrative of the History of Scotland, 1286–1306* (Edinburgh, 1870) i, no. 49; *PoMS* ('Mary, queen of Man/countess of Strathearn/wife of Hugh Abernethy'); *CDS*, v, p. 173, no. 290.

CHAPTER 8

Securing Inheritance

Friction on the border, dealing with his brother-in-law, the ongoing nightmare of papal taxation – Alexander and the Scots government had such issues and more to tackle in the 1270s and 1280s. There were domestic matters of immense consequence, not least of which was the need to further fortify his dynastic position through advantageous marriage alliances for his children. The searches for spouses for his two older children seem to have been undertaken at the same time, and each came to fruition in 1281. In July, agreement was reached that his eldest, Margaret, would marry King Erik II of Norway. A few months later, by early December, Prince Alexander was betrothed to Marguerite, the daughter of Count Guy of Flanders and his wife Isabelle of Luxembourg.[1] Both of these marriages were of the utmost importance, asserting the relative status of the Scottish royal house within the pan-European aristocracy. The marriages are not indicative of a cooling of relations with England. Alexander II's marriage to Marie de Coucy does not appear to have been considered hostile in these terms, and there is no evidence which prompts different conclusions a generation later.[2] While it may appear that in negotiation of the marriage alliances of 1281 the Scots pointedly looked over the shoulder of Edward I to the European possibilities beyond, the fact that both Flanders and Norway enjoyed good relations with England suggests that neither of these matches would have been seen as antagonistic to England. There is no evidence to support the speculation that Alexander might have consulted Edward I about a possible Flemish match for the prince.[3] As Edward had daughters of his own (and there were other English aristocratic possibilities), it is unlikely that he would have encouraged Alexander to look abroad. It is also improbable that

1 Margaret: *RRS*, iv pt. 1, no. 132; Alexander: *RRS*, iv pt. 1, nos. 133–35.
2 Oram, *Alexander II*, pp. 156–58.
3 Duncan, *Making of the Kingdom*, pp. 591–92.

Alexander III would have invited English interference in an affair of such importance to the Scottish crown. That there is nothing to suggest English complicity, however, does not indicate that Edward would have interpreted the marriages as inferring either political or personal antipathy.

The closer alliance which was sought with Norway must indicate both that the peace which had been forged in the treaty of Perth was holding firm and that there was a continuing desire on both sides of the North Sea to strengthen the relationship. Although Scoto-Norwegian trade does not seem to have been a major economic factor in this period,[4] it is nonetheless quite probable that the marriage treaty carried a subtext of mutual economic advantage. Maritime trading activity had been specifically acknowledged in the clause in the treaty of Perth regarding shipwreck and salvage. Under the baronial council which advised King Erik after the death of Magnus IV in 1280, Norway was pursuing an aggressive stance in relation to Denmark and adopting instead a west-ward-facing approach. Negotiations towards the marriage alliance may not have been a break with previous policy: they may have been initiated as part of the process through which the Norwegian monarchy attempted to fortify commercial links with both England and Scotland, perhaps in the hope of ensuring payment both of an extensive dowry and of the annual sums due from Scotland as a result of the treaty of Perth, the non-payment of which may have been a source of tension between the two countries.[5]

The marriage treaty, which was signed at Roxburgh on 25 July, was detailed in its treatment of financial arrangements. Margaret's dowry, the not inconsiderable sum of 14,000 merks sterling (almost £9,250) was to be paid in four annual instalments, beginning in 1281. The first, in cash, was to be sent with Margaret to Bergen, and half of the total might, at Alexander's discretion, be paid as annual land rents from lands assigned to Erik in Scotland, an option which was taken up by Alexander, with the assignation of significant lands in the north-east and Lothians.[6] Erik was to give Margaret a gift of land in Norway worth 1,400 merks annually, to be retained by her until her death, even in the event of Erik's prior demise.

The treaty also detailed the punitive compensations which would be incurred should the marriage fail to take place by reason of default on either side. This should not be understood as a sign of lack of trust: Erik was still a minor, either 12 or 13 years old, and the provisions of the treaty included the possibility that

4 See below, p. 304.

5 Knut Helle, 'Norwegian Foreign Policy and the Maid of Norway', *Scottish Historical Review*, 69 (1990), pp. 142–56, at pp. 146–47.

6 See G.W.S. Barrow, 'A Kingdom in Crisis: Scotland and the Maid of Norway', *Scottish Historical Review*, 69 (1990), pp. 120–41, at p. 121. See also *RRS*, iv pt. 1, no. 293.

Erik might refuse the marriage when he reached his age of majority, his fourteenth birthday.[7] Margaret was to be sent to Norway immediately, and Erik was to marry her by 8 September (or 'if legitimate business prevents this', no later than 30 August in the following year), with Margaret being offered 'a castle or secure place' in which to reside until the wedding.[8] This last was not merely a practical issue or a matter of her security: the taking of a bride to the bridegroom's home was in many traditions tantamount to marriage itself. Erik's age at the proposed date of the marriage presents a problem, since he was below the age permitted by canon law. There is no evidence of a papal dispensation having been sought or granted, but there is explicit recognition of his minority, both in the clauses regarding default mentioned above and in the statement that the first instalment of the dowry would be paid after the marriage had been celebrated, irrespective of circumstances, 'as if King Erik had reached the age of maturity'.[9] There is a further statement that Erik should not have 'carnal access' prior to the celebration of the wedding, which seems to imply that consummation of the marriage would be expected at any point thereafter. Marriage in this period has usually been regarded as an act which was signalled by betrothal and completed by a ceremony which was, by this stage, a sacrament. However, lack of consummation could be a pretext for annulment of a marriage, implying that the agreement was not entirely fulfilled until consummation had taken place.[10] This suggests that marriage should instead be seen as a process which was begun with betrothal, continued with a sacramental celebration and completed in due course with consummation when both partners were of legal age.[11] Although

7 The text is *quousque dictus rex Norwagie fuerit quatuordecim annorum completorum* – 'when the said king of Norway has completed fourteen years' (not, as in *RRS*, iv pt. 1, pp. 158–59, his *fifteenth* birthday). For the importance of the achievement of the age of 14 in medieval Europe, see Janay Nugent and Elizabeth Ewan (eds), *Children and Youth in Premodern Scotland* (Woodbridge, 2015), pp. 6, 18, 174. There was some Norwegian opposition to the marriage (from a party which included the king's mother – see below, p. 249); the opportunity for Erik later to refuse it may have offered some consolation to its detractors.

8 Anderson (*Early Sources*, ii, p. 680 n. 4) transposes the two dates, suggesting that the marriage had to take place between 30 August and 8 September 1281, but the text is clear: by the festival of the nativity of the blessed Virgin (8 September) or, failing that, no later than the day following the *decollatio* of John the Baptist (29 August, therefore 1282).

9 *cum fuerit legittime etatis*: *RRS*, iv pt. 1, p. 161.

10 See David d'Avray, *Medieval Marriage: Symbolism and Society* (Oxford, 2005), ch. 4.

11 For a discussion of marriage in the period, particularly in Scandinavia, see Mia Korpiola, 'An Act or a Process? Competing Views on Marriage Formation and Legitimacy in Medieval Europe', in *Family, Marriage and Property Devolution in the Middle Ages*, ed. Lars Ivar Hansen (Tromso, 2000), pp. 31–54. It has also been stated that, in an earlier period, French canonists tended to view marriage as a process completed by consummation (Marie-Bernadette Bruguière, 'Canon Law and Royal Weddings, Theory and Practice: The French Example, 987–1215', *Proceedings of the Eighth International Congress of Canon Law (Monumenta Iuris Canonici*, ser. C, Subsidia, ix) (Vatican, 1992), pp. 473–96, at p. 476.

the 1281 marriage agreement did not specify such a process (and indeed appears to imply otherwise), it may be that there was an implicit understanding that the marriage would not be consummated before Erik's fourteenth birthday.[12] The marriage would not therefore be expected to be complete before the date on which consummation would be canonically legal, maintaining a literal upholding of the strictures of canon law.

A parallel example is the marriage of Alexander III to Margaret Plantagenet, celebrated at Christmas 1251 when he was just ten, and she only a year older. The agreement has not survived, but a similar approach to the marriage must have been adopted. When Henry III pressed for change in the Scottish council in August 1255, Alexander was not yet 14, but when on 20 September the king of Scots announced his new council, it was stated to have taken over the reins of government on the crucial date of 4 September – his fourteenth birthday. That day ushered in a new era for the king and queen, both in governmental authority and in marital status.

In contractual terms, all went to plan for Alexander's daughter and her underage fiancé. She left Scotland, according to the Lanercost chronicler, on 11 August and, despite a stormy crossing, arrived in Bergen four days later. Erik did not exercise his agreed right to refuse her, and soon afterwards the marriage was celebrated, closely followed by Margaret's crowning as queen of Norway.[13] The romantic wedding hymn written for the occasion eulogises the princess:

> From you arises, sweet Scotland, a light
> whose brightness is seen shining in Norway;
> how you will sigh when she is borne across the sea,
> when the daughter of your king is taken away.
> . . .
> To Eirik the king the royal maid is sent,
> and with highest honour there received;
> everyone breaks out in wild applause,
> the people dancing while they sing her praise.
> . . .
> How to praise this partner of the king,
> so gentle, kindly, full of prudence?

12 The precise date of Erik's birth is not known. It is possible that the later date, 30 August 1282, may have been his fourteenth birthday, although the fact that he was to be given the opportunity to refuse the marriage when he reached 14 would suggest that he was born before 30 August 1268.

13 *Chron. Lanercost*, pp. 104–05.

> Humble, she gives to all, strong in her speech,
> made lovelier yet by noble continence.
> . . .
> From you, sweet Scotland, there comes forth
> a cause to sing your praise across the earth.[14]

The return voyage for those who had accompanied her to Norway did not go according to plan: one of the ships was wrecked close to home, with the loss of Bernard Mowat and the abbot of Balmerino, among others. The earls of Buchan, with his countess, and Strathearn, who had been specifically assigned by Alexander to accompany Margaret, were among those who survived the ordeal. Salvaged items, including Scottish copies of the marriage treaty which to this day show evidence of water damage, indicate a coastal wreck.[15]

The complex arrangements which were made to safeguard against non-compliance suggest a degree of contention. The Lanercost chronicler states that the 20-year-old Margaret (in common with her friends and relatives) was underwhelmed by the prospect of her much younger consort, but was unequivocally overruled by her father, who had personally promoted the match. She was unusually old for a first marriage in this period, perhaps indicating that this union had been on the cards for some years, awaiting Erik's coming of age. Bower stated that Erik's mother, Ingibjorg, was also opposed to the marriage, an opinion which might have carried more weight than Margaret's.[16] Daughter of the Danish King Erik (d.1250), Ingibjorg was understandably hostile towards the foreign policy direction being pursued by her son's advisors. As in Scotland during the minority of Alexander III, her position in relation at least to the welfare of her young son was influential: the oaths sworn in the marriage treaty by the Norwegian ambassadors were on behalf of the young king himself, of the queen his mother, and of all the magnates of the realm. Ingibjorg's objection, however, was also overruled.

The marriage treaty relates directly to the treaty of Perth, through the provision that in the event of Erik defaulting on the agreement, Norway would not only pay the enormous sum of £100,000 in compensation, but would also cancel the annual sum due from the Scottish king for the western isles, along with the cession of all Norwegian rights to the Orkney islands. Conversely, the Scots king in case of default would incur a similar fine of £100,000 plus cession back to Norway of the Isle of Man. Neither of these scenarios would seriously have

14 For full Latin text and translation, see below, Appendix 2.
15 See *RRS*, iv pt. 1, p. 165 n.; *Chron. Bower*, v, pp. 410–11 & nn. p. 502; *Chron. Fordun*, i, p. 307 (trans. ii, p. 302).
16 *Chron. Bower*, v, pp. 410–11, and p. 502 n.

been contemplated by the respective kingdoms, and there must therefore have been a strong presumption that the marriage alliance would proceed as planned. As added surety on the Norwegian side, hostages were left in Scotland until the completion of the marriage ceremony and, as an insurance against the dangers of piracy and war, the contract stated that it might become necessary to adopt alternative methods of payment of the various cash sums.

A feature of great interest in the marriage agreement is the detail with which it stated the position of Margaret and any children of the marriage as regards their inheritance from Alexander III, both of heritable goods and of the kingdom of Scotland. Should Alexander and his sons die without legitimate children, Margaret and her offspring were to succeed 'according to Scottish law and custom'. This 'law and custom' was under active consideration in Scotland at the time because of the stark reminder of mortality provided at the end of June 1281 by the death of Alexander's younger son, David, at the age of only a little over eight. Having died in Stirling castle, of unknown causes, he was buried in Dunfermline 'amid the deep wailing of all the Scots, and the still deeper wailing of the king'.[17] Less than a month, therefore, before the conclusion of the marriage negotiations at Roxburgh, one of the king's children had been buried, without doubt both a domestic tragedy and a dynastic tremor. Margaret's threateningly difficult crossing to Bergen and the loss of life on the return of her entourage must have caused further disquiet.

For Norway, the treaty provided that should Margaret and Erik have daughters, 'they shall succeed to everything to which they have the right by Norwegian law and custom, including the kingdom itself, if this is the custom.' It is striking that the Norwegians express uncertainty regarding their succession customs: the issue of female succession had, according to the wording of the document, apparently not been previously considered. In fact, the Norwegians had gone to some lengths to codify a law of succession in 1273 (confirmed in 1280) in which it was made almost inconceivable that a woman could succeed.[18] The chaotic, troubled and frequently violent succession to the Norwegian monarchy

17 *Chron. Fordun*, i, p. 307 (trans. ii, p. 302). *Chron. Bower* (v, p. 409) gives the date as June 1280. If the marriage alliances with Norway and Flanders are to be seen as a response to David's death, then Bower's date is preferable: David's death may have given the Scots an incentive to respond positively to Magnus's overtures. On the other hand, the December 1281 outcome of the negotiations with Flanders would correspond well to being in reaction to David's death in June. Duncan (*Kingship of the Scots*, pp. 165–66) also points out that the reference in the Norwegian treaty to the 'sons' (plural) of Alexander III suggests that David was alive when it was drafted, strengthening the case for his death having occurred in 1281. The possibility should not be discounted that this was a formulaic plural, admitting the possibility that more sons might yet be born. As the more closely contemporary account, I have preferred the date given in *Gesta Annalia*.

18 See Duncan, *Kingship of the Scots*, p. 169 & sources cited.

over the previous 150 years or more had compelled them to create a law which tightly defined the rules. This law excluded women. It seems likely that the wording in the marriage agreement was left deliberately vague in order to smooth the way to a treaty which in almost every other way seemed in the long-term interests of both kingdoms. Scotland's monarchy over the same period, although hardly trouble-free, had seen no chaos comparable with that in Norway's past; no law had been required to regulate it, and thus when the situation demanded, there was a vague appeal to 'ancient custom'. Scotland's chaos was yet to come.[19] In 1281, given the youth of the Norwegian king, the succession to that kingdom must also have been a matter of concern, but the possibility of female succession had not specifically arisen because there were as yet no females in the line who might succeed. At Erik's death in 1299 he did indeed have a surviving daughter, the offspring of his second marriage to another Scot, Isabella Bruce, the sister of the future King Robert I. He had no sons, but at that point Norwegian law dictated that Erik was succeeded by his younger brother, Hákon.

As the agreement with Norway was being signed at Roxburgh, discussions must already have been taking place in Flanders regarding the marriage of Margaret's younger brother, Alexander to Marguerite, then in her early teens. The marriage contract, assuming that it ever existed in a single document, has not survived, but three documents dated December 1281 describe the monetary arrangements and the Scottish law relating to inheritance by offspring of the marriage.[20] Their wording makes it clear that the marriage had already been agreed, and at Roxburgh on 4 December the procurators of the count of Flanders swore oaths on behalf of their lord committing him to acceptance of the terms.[21] The documents, which ran in King Alexander's name, had clearly been written, in Picard French, by a Flemish clerk. The first document, which deals with the succession, had been drawn up in presence of at least most of the Scottish royal council – the bishops of St Andrews, Brechin, Aberdeen, Glasgow and Dunkeld, the earls of Buchan, Strathearn, Dunbar, Mar, Fife and Carrick, as well as John Comyn, Alexander Balliol, William Murray, William Soulis and William

---

19 There are, of course, other European examples of royal succession planning involving (or rejecting) female inheritance: see the very brief summary in Norman Reid, 'Margaret, "Maid of Norway" and Scottish Queenship', *Reading Medieval Studies*, 8 (1982), pp. 75–96, at pp. 89–91.

20 *RRS*, iv pt. 1, nos. 133–35 & nn. The language and curious diplomatic of the documents is briefly discussed in E.L.G. Stones and Grant G. Simpson (eds), *Edward I and the Throne of Scotland, 1290–1296: An Edition of the Records Sources for the Great Cause* (Oxford, 1978), ii, pp. 188–90 & nn., where the first document, relating to the succession, is also printed in full. There is a more detailed discussion of the diplomatic in *RRS*, iv pt. 1, pp. 25–26.

21 *RRS*, iv pt. 1, no. 133 n.

Sinclair. All of the seals, except for those of the bishops of St Andrews and Brechin and the earl of Strathearn, remain appended to the original document, which survives in the archives in Namur. The second document, by which King Alexander undertook to make the agreed compensatory payments to the count or his heirs in the event of Marguerite's early death, is unwitnessed, but carries the king's great seal (Plates 3, 4). By the third letter, Alexander agreed to the settlement of money and land on Marguerite in the event that, after the marriage, she survived Prince Alexander; in the same letter, Prince Alexander swore to complete the marriage by 6 October 1282. It was witnessed by the bishop of St Andrews, the earl of Mar, Alexander Balliol, William Soulis, Bernard, dean of Messines and William Mortaigne (the last two being the count's procurators), and still carries both the great seal of King Alexander and the privy seal of the prince. The latter appears to be a new seal, this being the first recorded instance of Prince Alexander's use of a seal of his own. It is a clear indication that his marriage was regarded as a turning point in his transition to adult life, which offered him a newly elevated status in the political and administrative business of the kingdom. His seal was similar in design to the small seal of minority used in the early years of his father's reign (although, unlike that seal, this proclaimed itself as a 'privy seal'). By the time the marriage agreement was renewed in 1282, following an unavoidable delay, the prince had a new seal, freshly designed, perhaps on his own authority.[22]

Why the marriage documents were written by Flemish clerks, apparently in Flanders, why their counterparts from the count of Flanders (also written by the same clerks and sharing witnesses) claim to have been sealed at Roxburgh, and why there seems to be no surviving actual marriage contract are questions which are unlikely ever to be answered with certainty. The editors of Alexander III's acts have argued persuasively that the documents were penned in the chancery of Guy de Dampierre, the count of Flanders. Given the extraordinarily high-powered list of witnesses to the succession document, however, it seems likely that it emanates from a Scottish council meeting or *colloquium* and must have been drawn up in Scotland rather than in Flanders. It is highly improbable, and quite unprecedented, that an embassy of such size and status – far weightier than the embassy which would be sent to France in 1284 to negotiate the king's own marriage – would have been sent to Flanders. (The 12 Scots who negotiated the Norwegian marriage treaty did so in Scotland, discussing the issues with a smaller group of Norwegian emissaries.) If the document is Scottish in origin,

22 Neville, 'Preparing for Kingship', pp. 167–69; *RRS*, iv pt.1, p.26, & nos. 133, 140. Note also that in her mid–late teens, Princess Margaret did not have her own seal (*CDS*, ii, no. 185 [1272 x 81], which, judging by the relatively mature tone of the letter, was probably written towards the end of the date-range).

the use of Flemish clerks to write it needs to be explained. Were it not authenticated with the seals of almost all of those named in the document (and with space left for the others), it might be assumed that it was a copy of an original Latin text emanating from the council, made by his own clerks for the reassurance of the count of Flanders. The best explanation would seem to be that it is a parallel version, drawn up by Guy's clerks who were in attendance at the council meeting as observers, of a document of which the Scottish (Latin) version has not survived. If Guy had insisted on Flemish-French copies of all of the formal documents relating to the agreement, it would also explain the apparently anomalous presence of the king's and prince's seals on the other two documents. The suggestion, however, is entirely conjectural.

Irrespective of the truth behind the unusual documentation of the event, the facts that Prince Alexander's marriage was arranged at precisely this time and that the agreement for the marriage so intricately involves the succession to the Scottish crown make it abundantly clear that a major motivation for the alliance was the urgent need to bolster Scottish dynastic security. Even more acutely than was the case with the Norwegian agreement, good relations with Flanders were vital to Scottish economic well-being: there were sound economic reasons for this particular marriage alliance. Dynastic insecurity may explain the timing of the marriages of both of Alexander's surviving children and the nature of the documentation recording them, but the choice of partners was influenced more by other factors. That Alexander III did not look to England is significant primarily of the political and economic advantages of closer alliance with Norway and Flanders, although it is also possible that a perceived strategic insecurity inherent in closer dynastic links with England was a persuasive factor. A generation earlier, Alexander III's own marriage had been planned several years in advance: agreement with Henry III had been reached in 1244, if not sooner, for a ceremony which did not take place (after months of preparation) until the end of 1251. It is very unlikely that Alexander III had not previously considered the marriage prospects of his children, which adds weight to the proposition that the diplomatic engagement leading to the Norwegian marriage contract had been initiated much earlier, perhaps by Magnus before his death in May 1280. It is not impossible that the principle of such a match was considered at, or soon after, the negotiation of the treaty of Perth, and that Erik was effectively spoken for from the time of his birth in 1268. The context of early negotiations with Flanders is less easy to identify, but Alexander must certainly have been considering the marriage of his son for some years prior to 1281. The arrangement with Flanders offered 'a prestigious match with a continental house that broadened Scotland's foreign connections, fostered expanding trade links and provided Alexander III with an opportunity to host a royal marriage in his own realm'.[23] The conclusion of both marriage agreements may well have been hastened by the untimely death of Prince David,[24] but it is likely that they were far from hastily planned.

Prince Alexander's upbringing from the moment of his birth until his sadly premature demise has been well explored.[25] His name was chosen with care, to position him 'at the nexus of both the past and the future of the dynasty'; he was from a very early age allocated funds for an appropriately regal household and personal income; he was given lands and further income which gave him 'the status of the richest magnate in the realm', and his appointment, at the age of 11, as lord of Man (following the rebellion of 1275) added further political prestige, implying his formal recognition as *rex designatus*. In Norway, as in the case of Erik II, such heirs to the throne were crowned as joint monarchs during the lives of their predecessor; the Scottish model was less formalised, but through the grant of royal appanages such as the lordship of Man, the rôle of the designated heir in the rule of the kingdom was nonetheless made clear, and the prince gained practical experience of politics and the wielding of authority. Early in 1279, the king appointed Sir William Sinclair of Roslin to be guardian for the prince. Sinclair had family connections with both Marie de Coucy and Yolande de Dreux (who would become Alexander III's second queen), and has been described as 'closer to Alexander III than any other Scot'.[26] The claim may be presumptuous at a distance of over seven centuries, but there can be no doubt that Sinclair, who was also custodian of Edinburgh castle, which contained the king's treasury, was ever-present at critical moments in the later reign. His frequent appearance in the king's acts as official, beneficiary and witness places him at the heart of royal government, and his presence in the list of councillors who sealed the document relating to the succession of the kingdom in December 1281 can be no surprise. William Sinclair's 'sure hand in implementing the Scottish royal council's designs in the matter of the prince's schooling as heir to the throne' is revealed in the astute and self-assured tone of the young prince's 1279–81 correspondence with his uncle, Edward I.[27] Such schooling would have involved not only his formal education in the arts and literature, and in diplomatic and military arts, but also his tutelage in matters such as effective building of personal and dynastic support networks through astute patronage. His gradual increase in personal authority has also been identified through his involvement

23 Dean, 'Crowns, Wedding Rings and Processions', p. 227.

24 This suggestion is made by Cynthia Neville in 'Preparing for Kingship', pp. 166–67.

25 The following passage relies heavily on Neville, 'Preparing for Kingship', and the sources cited therein.

26 Duncan, *Making of the Kingdom*, p. 588.

27 Neville, 'Preparing for Kingship', pp. 163–64.

in the settlement in the early 1280s of the recurring dispute over the earldom of Menteith. When William Comyn sought Edward I's assistance in pursuing his claim to the earldom, he wrote (in French) to ask that Edward would intercede on his behalf with King Alexander 'and his son', which Edward agreed to do, instructing 'amicable' letters to be written to both Alexanders.[28] It is clear that the prince's influence was being felt in political and judicial affairs, and it seems possible that the judgement given in 1285 (according to Andrew Wyntoun's chronicle, in parliament by Alexander III himself), when the lands of the earldom were partitioned, reflected a decision reached jointly by father and son.

The wedding of Prince Alexander and Marguerite was celebrated at Roxburgh, a little later than intended, on 15 November 1282. Roxburgh was likely regarded as an ideal wedding venue due to 'the wealth of the area, its proximity to merchant communities, and for the ease of attendance for foreign guests from both northern England and Europe'.[29]

> On the Sunday next after Martinmas, in the winter of the year 1282, the lord Alexander, son of Alexander, king of Scotland, took to wife, at Roxburgh, the daughter of the lord count of Flanders, in the presence of many Flemish knights and ladies, amid unbounded joy and compliments. A great many Scottish bishops, abbots, earls, barons and knights, and the other nobles, also, were there met together, and after remaining there for the space of fifteen days, when the wedding had been solemnized in great state, they at length hied them home again.[30]

The 'unbounded joy', however, was short-lived: the explicit recognition in both Norwegian and Flemish marriage agreements that they might be dissolved by the early death of one or other of the parties, proved sadly prophetic.

Margaret's marriage to Erik appears to have been successful, if the Lanercost chronicler is to be believed (while ignoring his patronising attitude towards northern nations):

> she bore herself so graciously towards the king and his people that she changed [his] manners for the better; taught him the idiom of France,

28 *CDS*, iv, no.1763 & text printed in App., no.5. A further example of Prince Alexander's involvement in affairs of state is the plea by Queen Eleanor of England, in which she writes to Edward I, asking him to write to the king of Scots 'and his son' in support of the bishop of Caithness. The date must be towards the end of the 1274–80 range suggested by Bain (*CDS*, ii, no. 178).

29 Dean, 'Crowns, Wedding Rings and Processions', p. 221, discussing the choice of Roxburgh for the marriage ceremony of Prince Alexander's paternal grandparents, in 1239.

30 *Chron. Fordun*, i, pp. 306–07 (trans. ii, p. 301).

> and of England; and raised him to a more honourable level in regard to clothes and food.[31]

They soon had a child, predictably named Margaret, born probably in 1283. Erik's queen, however, like so many women of her time, died apparently either in childbirth or soon thereafter, on 9 April 1283.[32]

For some time, her brother Alexander had been suffering from an illness which seems likely to have been the cause of the delay to his wedding. He was certainly seriously ill through the summer of 1282: in July he wrote an unusually personal letter to Edward I in which he described the failures of other physicians and sought approval for the continued services of Master Adam of Kirkcudbright, a physician who for some years had been in the *familia* of the Bruce family and who, he said, had already saved him 'from the gates of death'.[33] To continue in Alexander's service would require Adam to be absent from his English estates for some time, to which Edward agreed, releasing him for a period of two years. Despite Alexander's confidence in the ability of Master Adam to succeed where others had failed, his condition seems to have been beyond remedy. He had recovered sufficiently by the late summer to allow the marriage to proceed (the English safe conduct for the passage of Marguerite to Scotland was sought and approved in August), but his remission was to be relatively short-lived and, despite the ministrations of Master Adam, he died on 28 January 1284, at Lindores, leaving no heirs.[34] It is possible that by the late summer his illness was known to be terminal, and that the wedding was celebrated, rather than cancelled, in the vain hope that the couple would be able to produce an heir before the prince's inevitable demise. As with his mother, the most detailed account of Prince Alexander's death is given by the Lanercost chronicler:

> On the second festival of St Agnes, Alexander, the son of the king of Scotland, was withdrawn from the world; dying on the same day on which he had been born, aged only twenty years; changing gladness at his birth-[-day] into grief over his death: because, if he had lived, he would have been the light of his country, and the joy of his family. He was taken at

31 *Chron. Lanercost*, p. 105 (trans. Anderson, *Early Sources*, ii, p. 680).

32 *Chron. Fordun*, i, pp. 307–08 (trans. ii, pp. 302–03). The cause of Margaret's death is not known, but death in, or closely following, childbirth would not have been unusual, and the timing is otherwise coincidental. *Chron. Lanercost* dates her death to February 1284, but I agree with Duncan (*Kingdom of the Scots*, p. 166) that the date given in *Gesta Annalia* is to be preferred.

33 For Master Adam, see Watt, *Graduates*, pp. 306–08.

34 *Foedera*, i.i, p. 611; *CDS*, ii, nos. 220, 221, 222; *Chron. Fordun*, i, p. 307 (trans. ii, p. 302).

> Cupar, in Fife, by a slow ague [*per lentam acutam*]. When he had suffered for some time from wandering of the mind, he came to himself, late on Thursday evening; and he foretold (of his own death) that on the following day, at sunrise, the sun of Scotland would set . . .
>
> I heard these things from the relation of those who were present with him when he died. One of them was a knight, and his tutor; the other was rector of the church [of Cupar], and his priest.[35]

Echoing his description of the death of Queen Margaret in 1275, the Lanercost chronicler was able to introduce detail which can only have come – as he stated unequivocally on this occasion – from eyewitnesses. It seems probable that this part of the chronicle, compiled later at Lanercost, was in fact originally penned in the late 1280s and 1290s by a Franciscan friar known as Richard of Durham (perhaps to be identified with a Richard of Sleckburn, in Northumberland, within the Palatinate of Durham). He is likely to have been resident in the friary of Haddington in East Lothian.[36] His access to the Franciscan network in Scotland and the north of England, as well as local knowledge and personal familiarity with some of the kingdom's noble families clearly provided him with information which other chroniclers of Scottish affairs lacked. It is therefore reasonable to conclude that much of the detail he provides for events such as the deaths of Prince Alexander and his mother, and the 1267 visit of Prince Edward to Margaret and her children in Haddington, should be accepted. The knight, his tutor, who was with Prince Alexander when he died was presumably the much favoured Sir William Sinclair; his priest may have been Adam of Kirkcudbright, although there is no evidence to suggest that he had been given the rectorship of Cupar. The 'slow ague' from which Alexander suffered could have been malaria, a disease certainly present in medieval Britain. His death may well have been anticipated, giving added urgency to the discussions

35 *Chron. Lanercost*, p. 111 (trans. Anderson, *Early Sources*, ii, pp. 683–85). There are issues with details (and with Anderson's notes): Alexander's birthday was 21 January; the second festival of St Agnes was on 28 January. Anderson is correct to point out that *Gesta Annalia* stated that he died 'in his twentieth year', but either his birthday or a week later would fall in his twenty-first year. The 'second St Agnes' date seems clear and is to be preferred: both *Gesta Annalia* and Lanercost erroneously state that it was his birthday. Lanercost also claims that he died in Cupar, whereas *Gesta Annalia*'s suggestion of Lindores abbey (which is not far distant) is a more likely location for an infirmary in which such a high-status patient would be cared for. (See also Neville, 'Preparing for Kingship', p. 170.) Duncan (*Making of the Kingdom*, p. 592), says the date of Alexander's death was 17 January, but does not provide a source.

36 See A.G. Little, 'The Authorship of the Lanercost Chronicle', in A.G. Little, *Franciscan Papers, Lists and Documents* (Manchester, 1943), pp. 42–54; Victoria Gransden, *Historical Writing in England c.500–1307* (London, 1974), pp. 494–501. Anderson (*Early Sources*, ii, p. 672 n.) suggests that Lanercost's description of Queen Margaret's death was informed by her confessor.

regarding the rules governing succession to the kingdom which figured so largely in both marriage alliances. Marguerite returned home to Flanders in the early months of 1285, a very young widow.[37]

A further blow to Alexander III's family occurred later in 1284, with the death of Marie de Coucy. This event is recorded in a single sentence in Bower's *Scotichronicon*, which reads 'In the following year [1284] Mary the mother of Alexander III king of Scotland died abroad.'[38] Marie's presence in Scotland is almost invisible between her return to reside in Scotland following her separation from her second husband in 1268, until her death.[39] She visited the shrine of Thomas Becket at Canterbury in 1276. In December of that year, before returning to Scotland, she received both a gift of a gold cup from Edward I and further permission to go overseas, presumably to her familial estates in France.[40] If, as has been suggested, her body was returned to Scotland for burial at Newbattle, this certainly demonstrates an affinity with the kingdom in which she had made her home, and indicates both that her absence abroad was intended to be purely temporary and that her death had not been thought imminent when she left the country. Immediately prior to the birth of the future Alexander III, in 1241 (aware, of course, of the dangers of childbirth), she had bequeathed her body for burial at Newbattle, and a later description of the medieval abbey buildings described Marie's ornate marble tomb within the church. There is no record source to prove that the tomb she appears to have commissioned was actually used, but later tradition asserts that it had been. In July 1284, Alexander III made a grant of land in Midlothian to the monks of Newbattle, in return for the celebration of mass for his ancestors, children and heirs annually on 25 July; there is no way of knowing whether that grant was related to the death of Marie or to her burial there but, being the only known grant by the king to the abbey, its timing makes it feasible. The place-dates of Alexander's other *acta* in the period place him south of the Forth at Haddington and Edinburgh on 26 and 27 June, in Stirling on 1 July (where the grant to Newbattle was given) and in Dundee on 11 July; nothing places him at Newbattle in that period for a funeral, which he would surely have attended, but it is a relatively short distance from either Edinburgh or Haddington, and the evidence of the *acta* is in any case very incomplete.[41]

37 *CDS*, ii, no. 247.

38 *Chron. Bower*, v, pp. 416–17 & n. p. 505.

39 *Chron. Bower*, v, pp. 368–71, where it is stated that Alexander, using the bishop of Glasgow as his intermediary, achieved a financial settlement which gave Jean de Brienne a pension out of her dower-lands in Scotland.

40 *CDS*, ii, nos. 67, 80, 84, 85.

41 Sir J. Balfour Paul (ed.), *The Scots Peerage* (Edinburgh, 1904–14), i, p. 6; *Registrum. S. Marie de Neubotle* (Bannatyne Club, 1849), pp. xxxix–xl, 89–90; *RRS*, iv pt. 1, nos. 150–53.

It would be wrong to consider that at this stage there was already a dynastic crisis. Alexander III was in his forties, apparently healthy and had a granddaughter, the possibility of whose inheritance of the throne had already been contemplated without obvious in-principle opposition. On 20 April 1284, almost three months after the death of the prince, Alexander wrote a personal letter to Edward I. In it, he thanked Edward for the solace he had offered following 'the grievous and unbearable trials and tribulations which we have suffered, and do suffer, from the death of our dear son, your beloved nephew'. Alexander reminded Edward that 'in the providence of God much good may come to pass yet through your kinswoman, the daughter of your niece, the daughter, too, of our beloved, the late queen of Norway, of happy memory, who is now our heir-apparent'. Alexander's letter was carried to Edward by Andrew, the abbot of Coupar Angus, whom he commended as his envoy. Andrew was carrying further messages by word of mouth, and Alexander asked that he should be sent back, with news of Edward himself.[42]

It is unfortunate that small portions of this document are so damaged as to make the text unreadable, with some of the detail necessarily left to conjecture, thus tempting the historian towards overambitious interpretation. One proposal in particular seems to overreach the evidence: it has been suggested that Alexander's reference to the 'good' that might yet come through the infant Maid of Norway was an early statement of intent towards a marriage alliance between Margaret and an English husband. In hindsight, this would be Edward's son and heir, Prince Edward, to whom she would indeed become betrothed, in 1290.[43] No other source points towards such a policy as early as 1284. Indeed, it was not Alexander's place to harbour such plans: Margaret's marriage was the business of her father, the king of Norway, a point which was explicitly recognised by the Scots in the later treaty of Salisbury (1289), which arranged for Margaret to be sent to Scotland. Although the relations between England and Scotland remained apparently cordial, the tensions on the border and possible suspicions of English royal ambition regarding Scotland would seem to have made it unlikely that such a proposal would have come from Alexander. Immediately following the mention in the letter of the Maid of Norway, there are a few unreadable words – but too few to allow for a more explicit statement of intent by Alexander. It has also been suggested that the business carried to Edward by Abbot Andrew was the marriage proposal, implying that the reply

42 *RRS*, iv pt. 1, no. 146 (trans. Stones, *Anglo-Scottish Relations*, pp. 84–87).

43 Duncan, *Making of the Kingdom*, p. 593: 'with necessary, if unfeeling, practicality, King Alexander went on to indicate that "much good may yet come to pass" through his granddaughter – that is, that she would be married into Edward's family'.

which Edward was to send back with him was a reaction to it.[44] The letter, however (although again it suffers from a couple of illegible words at the crucial point), appears to do no more than to seek personal news of Edward himself. There seems no reason to read more into this letter than a personal response to condolences offered following bereavement. Alexander's mention of his granddaughter is not unfeeling; it does, however, indicate that through her, as a potential heir, the silver lining might yet appear in the storm-clouds. There is no surviving evidence either that Edward I answered Alexander's letter or that any other business was taken before him by Abbot Andrew.[45] (It seems to have been quickly known that Marguerite was not pregnant when her husband died: the possibility of a posthumous child who might inherit in precedence over Margaret does not feature in record.)

At this point, there was no cause to doubt that Alexander III could live for a further decade or two, and the focus of attention swiftly moved (if it had not already done so) towards a second marriage for him. Four knights, it is reported by *Gesta Annalia*, were sent to France early in 1285 to seek a bride for the king. In Thomas Charteris (the chancellor), William Sinclair, John Soulis and Patrick Graham, the king had an embassy of significant stature and loyalty.[46] It is tempting to assume that Marie de Coucy might also have been involved in the early stages of the search, in the months preceding her death: her knowledge and family connections could have been valuable to this venture, but the evidence is very slight, and the lack of any reference to her presence in Scotland, other than the (English) safe conducts for travel, between 1268 and her death makes it likely that she was no longer active on the political stage.[47] Bower, in reporting her death 'abroad', does not state that she was in France (although it seems likely) and makes no reference to her involvement in any formal business.

---

44 Duncan, *Kingship of the Scots*, p. 171.

45 There is a curious line in the wedding hymn of 1281, which states that 'above all England shares your joy' (see below, Appendix 2). This might be taken as a tantalising hint of a subtext in the marriage treaty that offspring of Margaret and Erik were already promised to English royal children. The assumption, however, again relies on hindsight, and the poetic line, in its context, is much more likely to refer to England as a party most interested in peace between its two neighbours.

46 *Chron. Fordun*, i, p. 309 (trans. ii, p. 304). Graham was of a family which had climbed the social ladder during the thirteenth century, and especially during Alexander's reign. Patrick seems to have been loyal to, and in the favour of, the king: he was a regular witness to royal acts in the last few years of the reign (*RRS*, iv pt.1, pp. 21, 24). Soulis was to become a strikingly prominent member of the Scottish governing community in the years following the death of Alexander III.

47 Pollock, *Scotland, England and France*, p. 189, where Marie's involvement is assumed, but not evidenced; it is also stated there that her death was in 1285; although it would add weight to the idea that she may have been involved in the marriage negotiations, I have preferred the rationale given by the editors of Bower for 1284.

It cannot be said that she had a close family relationship with the chosen bride, Yolande, the daughter of the compte de Dreux. Several generations separated the two women from a common ancestor: Marie's grandmother was a sister of Yolande's great-great-grandfather. There was, additionally, a step-relationship: Yolande's mother was a step-daughter of Jean de Brienne, Marie's estranged second husband, through his first marriage. Whether this would have helped or hindered the match cannot be said. If it remains doubtful that Marie was personally involved in the search for her son's second queen, it is nonetheless probable that the existing family connections between Scotland and the Dreux family would have helped to open doors. Such connections were not limited to the queen mother: familial ties held by others, such as Sir William Sinclair, may also have been of value. Notwithstanding the influence of the various family relationships, Yolande was a representative of the high echelons of French nobility, with kings in her ancestry: she was of suitable lineage to make an appropriate queen for a Scottish king at the height of his personal power.

Gesta Annalia comments that the search for a new bride was 'in the tenth year after the queen's death', surely a suggestion that Alexander had not forgotten Margaret and also, by implication, that he might not have sought another queen at all had it not been for the deaths of his children. The embassy's work bore fruit, and by mid August 1285 a safe conduct had been issued for the passage through England of Yolande.[48] Bower relates that this 'most beautiful of ladies' arrived in Scotland 'with great pomp and with an impressive escort of Frenchmen', in time for the wedding, which took place at Jedburgh on 14 October:

> Very many nobles of France and Scotland along with an innumerable multitude of both sexes met for the ceremonial celebration of their wedding in royal fashion. After the wedding was over the French, gladdened by all sorts of gifts, returned home in good spirits, although a few remained behind with the queen.
>
> I cannot recall having read of such a famous feast ever before in Scotland.[49]

There can be little doubt that Alexander's late second marriage was contracted with the primary aim of providing a direct heir to the throne: at 21 or 22, his second queen was neither too young nor too old to have children. It has already been noted that the marriage contracts of both of Alexander's children

48 *CDS*, ii, no. 273.
49 *Chron. Bower*, v, pp. 416–19.

included statements concerning the succession to the Scottish kingdom. The contract for Alexander's marriage to Yolande has not survived, and so it is not known if there was a similar statement therein – although it would seem likely. Even before that marriage took place, however, on 5 February 1284, very soon after the death of Prince Alexander, further discussion of the succession system and of the practicalities of putting it into effect was held in a *colloquium* at Scone. The meeting had presumably been called for that very purpose, and resulted in a statement issued by a formidable array of the governing community.[50] It is a veritable roll-call of the politically active community throughout the king's reign: the earls of Buchan, Dunbar, Strathearn, Lennox, Carrick, Mar, Angus, Menteith, Ross, Sutherland, Orkney, Fife and Atholl; Robert Bruce, James Stewart, John Balliol, John Comyn, William Soulis, Ingram de Guines,[51] William Murray, Alexander Balliol, Reginald Cheyne senior, William Sinclair, Richard Siward, William Brechin, Nicholas Hay, Henry Graham, Ingram Balliol, Alan 'son of the earl', Reginald Cheyne junior, J[ohn] Lindsay, Patrick Graham, [Herb]ert Maxwell, Simon Fraser, Alexander of Argyll, Áengus son of Domnall, Alan son of Rúaidrí, 'the barons of Scotland'. The ecclesiastical community are involved too, since the barons swear to uphold the promise they make, submitting themselves to the jurisdiction, coercion and censure in the event of their default, of the bishops of St Andrews, Glasgow, Dunkeld, Aberdeen, Moray, Brechin, Galloway, Dunblane, Caithness, Argyll and [Ross]. The nub of the document is that the signatories bind themselves to uphold the customary law of succession to the kingdom:

> Know ye, that since it has pleased the Most High that our lord Alexander, eldest son of [king] Alexander, has gone the way of all flesh with no lawful offspring surviving directly from the body of the said king, we bind ourselves and our heirs straitly by the presents to our said lord king and the heirs descended from his body directly or indirectly who by right

50 *APS*, i, p. 424. Although this undoubtedly emanates from a *colloquium*, it does not actually say so in the document, which is presumably why it has not been included in the *RPS* database. The square brackets in the following list of participants indicate *lacunae* in the manuscript and printed edition. I have conjecturally completed the missing names by reference to the witness lists of Alexander III's *acta*; the missing bishop is obvious.

51 Guines was a relative newcomer to Scotland. Perhaps arriving in Scotland as late as 1275, he was a nephew of Marie de Coucy and may therefore have sought favour. He married the daughter of William Lindsay, through whom he inherited lands in southern Scotland and northern England and, as a 'dear cousin' of the king, appears to have found considerable favour at Alexander's court in the latter years of the reign. He later became lord of Coucy. Duncan, *Making of the Kingdom*, pp. 586–87; *CDS*, ii, nos. 209, 239, 267 (= *RRS*, iv pt. 1, no. 155).

> ought to be admitted to succeed to him and in the faith and fealty by which we are bound to them we firmly and faithfully promise that if our said lord king happens to end his last day in this life leaving no lawful son or sons, daughter or daughters of his body or of the body of the said Alexander his son, we each and all of us will accept the illustrious girl Margaret, daughter of our said lord king's daughter Margaret, of good memory, late queen of Norway, begotten of the lord Eric, illustrious king of Norway, and lawful offspring descended from her, as our lady and right heir of our said lord king of Scotland, of the whole realm of Scotland, of the Isle of Man and of all other islands belonging to the said kingdom of Scotland, and also of Tynedale and Penrith with all other rights and liberties which belong or ought to belong to the said lord king of Scotland . . . and against all men . . . we shall maintain, sustain and defend [her] with all our strength and power.[52]

There are therefore no fewer than three surviving statements from the 1280s of the Scottish law of succession. The most straightforward and most practical is the last, the entail of 1284 quoted above, in which the barons of the realm state quite simply that, in accordance with custom, they will support succession by, firstly, sons or daughters of the king or of his son, failing whom, the king's existing granddaughter, Margaret. It is noteworthy, therefore that the living daughter of the king's daughter takes second place to a (hypothetical) son or daughter of the king's son, emphasising the essentially conservative nature of the succession: although the Scots do not appear, as was the custom in some kingdoms, to exclude the principle of female succession, they nonetheless give the conventional precedence to male succession.

The statements concerning the succession in the two marriage treaties are more complex, because they prepared for a more hypothetical eventuality, while two of the king's children yet lived. In the 1281 treaty with Norway, the succession issue is summarised thus:

> If it should happen that the king of Scotland die without a legitimate son, and none of his sons leaves lawful issue and Margaret has children by the king of Norway, she and her children shall succeed the king of Scotland and his children, both in the kingdom and in other goods, or she alone shall, even if she is without children, according to Scottish law and custom; and the king of Scotland agrees generally that his daughter and all her descendants shall be freely admitted to all successions and all other rights

52 Translation from Gordon Donaldson, *Scottish Historical Documents* (Edinburgh, 1970), p. 38.

> which can belong to them according to Scottish law or the custom of the said realm.[53]

The approach taken in the documents surrounding the Flemish treaty is broadly consistent, although more concerned with the financial arrangements consequent on the eventuality of Marguerite surviving her husband (for which Alexander, as added security, sought and received papal confirmation), a further indication that there was significant doubt regarding the prince's prognosis. One document, however, specifically deals with the issue of succession; in it Alexander announces that, in relation to the forthcoming marriage, he and his council have reviewed 'the ancient customs and practices of the kingdom of Scotland in use since time immemorial and now still in use for the succession to the throne'. It too is worth quoting in full:

> . . . if the son and heir male of a king of Scots has an heir and the former predeceases the king, the heir of this son remains and must remain heir to the kingdom of Scotland. Thus, if it should happen that Prince Alexander and his wife Marguerite should marry and have male issue, the latter shall be the lawful heir to the kingdom of Scotland. If Prince Alexander should predecease his father and he has brothers they shall not have any claim to the kingdom by reason of heritage. If Marguerite should predecease her husband before producing heirs male and the prince takes another wife from whom he has male issue, the latter shall become heir to the kingdom without prejudice. If the heirs male of the prince's second marriage should die without male heirs, the kingdom of Scotland shall revert and return in its entirety to the eldest female child of Prince Alexander and his wife Marguerite; the same shall happen if King Alexander should marry a second time and any heir male of that marriage fail to produce issue. Members of the royal council, and the king himself in the person of Simon Fraser, take an oath to abide by the ancient custom and practices set out here and renounce any custom or practice that might overturn them or might be prejudicial to Marguerite and her above-mentioned heirs.[54]

The king's counsellors are commanded to swear to uphold these provisions, and the pope, again, is asked to approve them. The five bishops, six earls and five

53 *RRS*, iv pt. 1, no. 132. Translation from the editors' summary, which at this point provides a full English text.

54 *RRS*, iv pt. 1, no. 133. Translation from the editors' summary.

barons whose names (and almost all of whose seals) appear on the document are also all among the signatories (or the ecclesiastical scrutineers) to the 1284 entail and must be counted, from the evidence of this document naming them as counsellors, as the inner circle of the king, rather than as an embassy sent to Flanders for the negotiation.

In its comment on female succession, this document is consistent with both the Norwegian treaty and the 1284 entail: the principle of female succession is accepted, but only after the failure of succession through the male line. Thus Margaret, queen of Norway would only have right to succeed herself or to pass on to her male or female children, should Alexander III or his sons all fail to leave heirs; and any female children of Alexander and Marguerite could only inherit should any (as yet unborn) brothers of Prince Alexander, or male children by his hypothetical second wife, die without male issue. However, because this document deals with potential succession of heirs of the king's son (rather than, as in either of the other documents, his daughter), it goes a step further and introduces a further complication which appears to go beyond any 'ancient custom' or law of the Scottish kingdom. The provision that a male heir of Prince Alexander would have precedence over a direct male heir of the king himself cannot be said to have reflected existing Scottish custom, since such a situation was previously unknown and, so far as surviving evidence suggests, had not been discussed. Nonetheless, there had indeed been previous consideration of the principles of succession, as demonstrated by the late twelfth-century king-list inserted into the Melrose chronicle, and its relevance to the situation which prevailed in 1281–84.[55] It shows that the Scots had for a century or more adopted the principle of 'anticipatory designation' in order to reduce instability and conflict, a principle which ran counter neither to primogenitive custom nor to the strong element of election which continued within the Scottish kingship. The statements regarding the succession made at the end of the thirteenth century, therefore, are not entirely novel: rather, they extended that designatory process to hypothetical (but, sadly, probable) circumstances. Due to the fact that the king had no earthly superior, it was necessary to treat the kingdom differently from an inferior fief such as an earldom, because in the latter case the king, as superior, could ensure that justice was done in the case of dispute, for example between co-heiresses. Female succession to a lesser fief was possible, but it seems that in general the rules of seniority, which dictated, for example, that an older son would inherit before a younger, did not apply to women

55 There is an extensive discussion of this, and of the ramifications of the various succession scenarios outlined in the documents of 1281–84, in Duncan, *Kingship of the Scots*, pp. 164–71. The technicalities of the issues relating to the rules of primogeniture are not recited again here.

(between whom, as in the celebrated case of the earldom of Winchester, the lands of the earldom might be partitioned). The key point was that there was in fact no custom relevant to the succession of a female to the kingdom, because the question simply had not previously arisen: the creation of political theory, as ever, was a pragmatic response to an unprecedented situation, and the necessary action – that the king, with the advice of his council, should define the custom – was no less effective or authoritative than if the custom had in reality been in use for time immemorial.

Perhaps in an attempt to satisfy the desires of all parties, the account of Scottish succession given in the Flemish treaty is overcomplicated, ambiguous and self-contradictory. In past times, when the principles of primogeniture were tempered by electoral factors related to broader kinship, suitability and seniority, the genealogical complications inherent in any attempt to codify the system were less relevant. In 1284, when a primogenitive succession system was unquestioned, it became impossible to provide a succinct statement of Scottish practice, simply because custom developed hand in hand with circumstance; there was no adequate body of precedence on which to rely, and to provide a comprehensive set of hypothetical situations was a hopeless aspiration.[56] The attempt to explain the succession system has been aptly dubbed 'a challenge to sanity', displaying a fundamental lack of logic: in attempting to create a workable 'ancient custom' which would provide them with the desired result, the Scots had done little more than re-emphasise the lack of custom governing the situation which might (and eventually did) face them.[57] The situation in the early 1280s, however, had certainly forced the Scots into facing the possibility of female succession to the crown. The explicit Scottish acceptance of female rule in the Norwegian marriage treaty as well as in the 1284 entail, and its more limited acceptance in the Flemish treaty, contrasts with obfuscation on the issue on the Norwegian side.

As the likelihood of minority, and female, succession increased with the deaths of Alexander III's remaining children, so the documentation became clearer and more specific. The entail of 1284 made specific reference to the king's granddaughter because at that point, when the provision of more heirs of the king himself must have felt at best uncertain, her succession was the most likely outcome. Saving the right of a yet unborn son or daughter (once

56 Such arguments would soon come to the fore in the immensely complicated pleadings of the 'Great Cause', the competition for the Scottish throne in 1291/92. The events, and arguments, of the Great Cause are discussed in detail in Stones and Simpson, *Edward I and the Throne of Scotland, 1290–1296*, i, *passim*; different views are offered in Reid, 'Political Rôle of the Monarchy', pp. 75–100, and in Duncan, *Kingship of the Scots*, pp. 255–315.

57 Duncan, *Kingship of the Scots*, p. 167.

again suggesting that for women the nearness of degree was more important than the seniority of line) of the king himself, or any posthumous offspring of the now deceased Prince Alexander, the lay leaders of the community bound themselves to uphold the right of the Maid of Norway. There is one significant difference, however, between this and the Norwegian marriage treaty: in that agreement, Princess Margaret and her children had been stated to succeed to the throne in the event that 'the king of Scotland die without a legitimate son, and none of his sons leaves lawful issue', implying that Margaret *and her heirs* would take precedence over the king's daughter from a second marriage; now, Princess Margaret's daughter would take second place to a daughter of the king himself. The change is not insignificant, but whether it is deliberate, or is merely a further indication of the confusion which surrounded the entire issue, cannot be said with certainty.

The apparent acceptance of female rule at the end of the thirteenth century in Scotland, as evidenced by the marriage treaties and especially by the entail of 1284, is certainly important. An equally significant issue in relation to the Flemish treaty and the entail, however, is the quite distinctly stated requirement for the wholehearted backing of the political community. The statement of succession in the Flemish agreement was made by King Alexander's entire council, and the king ensured that the entail was approved by an even wider representation of the governing community. This not only indicates that the issue was both critical and potentially controversial, but it also casts light on the nature of Scottish royal government. Had the law of succession been readily known, there would have been no need for such elaborate arrangements; because 'law and custom' were effectively being created, or at least codified, for purposes which could potentially have major impact on the future of the kingdom, it was necessary that the community gave its wholehearted, and public, backing to the policy being espoused. It is, again, irrefutable evidence of the king as *primus inter pares*, and of the noble community playing its essential rôle in the governance of the realm. By achieving the approval of the community for his succession planning, Alexander III was not merely attempting to ensure compliance: he was validating the policy itself, giving it legislative weight. Through the power of the whole governing community, it thus gained the authority of custom. In that respect, it is also important that the entail asked more of the community than just their declaration of support for the infant Margaret (or whoever else would eventually succeed the king); it also involved their obligation to effect payment of all amounts due under the executry of the king's will.[58] This

58 This important passage has often been overlooked: it is, for example, entirely omitted from Donaldson's translation in *Scottish Historical Documents*, without editorial indication of the

requirement, over and above the general obligation to support the heir to the throne, demonstrates the crucial rôle of the community in ensuring that crown revenue is effectively administered and that the conduct of good government thus remains possible. This document therefore anticipates the election of guardians which was to take place after Alexander's death: it is the rôle of the community to maintain stable government, with or without the king. The course of Alexander's reign may have seen that rôle become more explicit and more clearly expressed, but it was not new: as noted above, a council of guardians consisting of the usual mixture of bishops, earls and barons had been appointed expressly to cover the eventuality that Alexander might die before his first child, Margaret, could be brought to Scotland after her birth at Windsor in 1261.[59] The fundamental nature of Scottish royal government had not changed, but circumstances in the 1280s had demanded that it be clearly and openly expressed.

If Princess Margaret's and Prince Alexander's marriages had been short-lived, their father's marriage to Yolande was destined to be even shorter, since after only a single winter she was left a widow. On 18 March 1286, just five months into their marriage, Alexander was attending a meeting of his council in Edinburgh. One piece of business, we are told by the Lanercost chronicler, was to make a decision regarding a request from John Balliol to release from confinement the now very aged Thomas, son of Alan of Galloway, who had been under house arrest in Barnard castle in Yorkshire (in the hands of Balliol kindred – he was Devorguilla Balliol's half-brother) for half a century – ever since his surrender in 1236 following an abortive rebellion in Galloway in the previous year. The council appears not to have been favourable to him; the memory of the Galloway uprisings seems to have run deep, and Thomas may still have been felt to represent a threat to royal authority. (It was to be 1296, and on the orders of Edward I, perhaps as a deliberate challenge to King John Balliol's authority, that he was eventually released, by then a very old man indeed.[60]) After the council meeting, Alexander set out to return to Yolande, who was at Kinghorn in Fife, where there was a royal demesne and residence. There are various later versions of events, but all that can be known with certainty is that, inexplicably separated from his escort, he was found the next day, not far from Kinghorn, dead. A spot traditionally associated with the discovery of his body is marked today by an obelisk, erected to celebrate the 600th anniversary of his death. It has been confidently stated with false authority that his horse went over the

omission. It implies that Alexander had written a last testament by, or around, the death of his daughter in April 1283 (*RRS*, iv pt. 1, no. 298).

59 *CDS*, i, no. 2229.

60 Oram, *Alexander II*, pp. 149–50; G.W.S. Barrow, *Robert Bruce and the Community of the Realm of Scotland*, 4th edn (Edinburgh, 2005), p. 145.

cliff, that it stumbled and threw him, that he went off the path to find shelter on what was a stormy night, even that he was murdered. In reality, all that is known is that he died on the night of 18–19 March 1286, apparently while riding to Kinghorn.[61] There are no closely contemporary Scottish sources which offer any detail. The 'Scottish Poem' in the *Liber Extravagans*, written probably *c.*1304, gives a very brief account of the reign:

> This third Alexander reigned for almost thirty-seven years.
> Pity those Scots who have not experienced
> a prince so gracious, generous, mild and successful,
> who was fifty-first in the order of kings.
> In 1285
> this prince in an untimely manner
> paid his debt to life at Kinghorn
> on 19 March,
> on which day it is appropriate to commemorate the funeral rites which
> had to be completed,
> so that the monks who dwell at Dunfermline may not observe his obit
> as a day of slothfulness; but he lies buried there.[62]

Gesta Annalia I, having been completed during 1285, was written shortly before his death; *Gesta Annalia II,* the best part of a century later, says very little: after noting the king's wedding, the writer simply says that on 19 March, 'this Alexander of goodly memory, the illustrious king of Scotland, died at Kinghorn, and was buried in state at Dunfermline'.[63] A note inserted in the fourteenth century into the *Chronicle of Holyrood* (the chronicle's only reference to events in Scotland between 1249 and 1286) adds the detail that Alexander died in an 'accidental fall' (*casu fortuito*) while journeying towards Kinghorn.[64] As time

61 There are a couple of Alexander's acts dated at Kinghorn, a grant of a weekly market to the burgh in 1285 and grants from the lands of the burgh to Dunfermline and Arbroath abbeys (*RRS*, iv pt.1, nos. 9, 102, 103, 159, 185 & p. 234). *RRS*, iv pt. 1, no. 103 specifically notes a grant to Dunfermline made by Alexander II from the demesne of Kinghorn and Crail. An undated act, ascribed to Robert I in *RMS*, i (Appendix i, no. 84), but which does not appear in *RRS*, v, refers to *manerio nostro de Kingorne*. It is tempting to assume that the establishment of the weekly market 'for the improvement of the burgh' in June 1285 was more than coincidentally related to the intention imminently to establish a household there for Yolande, who would become queen only four months later.

62 Edited and translated by Dauvit Broun with A.B. Scott in *Chron. Bower,* ix, pp. 54–127; the passage on the death of Alexander III is at pp. 74–77.

63 *Chron. Fordun*, i, p. 309 (trans. ii, p. 304).

64 M.O. Anderson (ed.), *A Scottish Chronicle known as the Chronicle of Holyrood* (Edinburgh, 1938), pp. 172–73 & n. (trans. p. 194).

went on, the story was elaborated, perhaps – or perhaps not – with the use of authoritative sources. Bower, writing in the 1440s, felt it necessary to introduce an omen of the king's death, in the shape of a ghostly apparition which appeared at the wedding feast:

> While everything was going on at the royal wedding according to due custom, a kind of show was put on in the form of a procession amongst the company who were reclining at table. At the head of this procession were skilled musicians with many sorts of pipe music including the wailing music of bagpipes, and behind them others splendidly performing a war-dance with intricate weaving in and out. Bringing up the rear was a figure whom it was difficult to decide whether it was a man or an apparition. It seemed to glide like a ghost rather than walk on feet. When it looked as if he was disappearing from everyone's sight, the whole frenzied procession halted, the song died away, the music faded, and the dancing contingent froze suddenly and unexpectedly. Laughter is [always] mixed with grief, and mourning takes over from extremes of joy: after such splendour the kingdom lamented ingloriously, when a short time afterwards it lost itself and as a consequence its king.[65]

Further, Bower offers us the earliest rendition of the well-known prophecy of Thomas of Earlston ('Thomas the Rhymer'), who is said to have told the earl of Dunbar, when asked what the next day would bring, that it would be 'a day of calamity and misery'.

> . . . before the stroke of twelve a strong wind will be heard in Scotland the like of which has not been known since times long ago. Indeed its blast will dumbfound the nations and render senseless those who hear it; it will humble what is lofty and raze what is unbending to the ground.

The following day his meaning became clear, when the news of the king's death was brought to the earl.[66]

Bower does not expand on the kingdom 'losing itself', or on his implication that the loss of the king was a consequence of some national failure or sin. He was never hesitant to moralise, as it was one of his primary purposes in writing, and it is unsurprising that other medieval sources also note portentous happenings in the period immediately preceding the king's death. The Lanercost

65 *Chron. Bower*, v, pp. 418–19.
66 *Chron. Bower*, v, pp. 427–28.

chronicler, writing perhaps only a decade after the event, ascribes the king's death to divine vengeance; he had been punished for his immoral behaviour in his lifetime through the deaths of his children, but had not reformed, and so paid the ultimate price himself. The event, Lanercost claims, had been widely heralded: for a year it had been rumoured in Scotland that the Day of Judgement would fall on that day; there had been violent storms, thunder-claps and lightning 'which, in the judgement of the wise, prognosticate the fall of princes'. On 18 March there was a dreadful storm, a further warning, 'although he did not understand it'.[67]

Portent or prophecy were commonly deployed in medieval writing, as indication of God's purpose was sought through association of distinct events: 'not just eyewitness testimony, but Godwitness testimony'.[68] Thus, when Bower recalled the prophecy of Thomas the Rhymer, he was offering evidence of God's will in an event which seemed, in his pro Alexandrian stance, so cataclysmic and illogical as to be almost ungodly: to quote the portent and prophecy, and thus to reveal the divine intention, was not equivalent to judging any demerits which brought it about. Lanercost used prophetic language differently: his moralistic criticism of Alexander III was given added weight by his assertion that Alexander and those close to him were unable to decode the God-sent messages warning them of the dire consequences of their behaviour. For both writers, however, their use of portent on this occasion had the effect of amplifying the significance of the particular event they were describing: in signalling the event itself in this way, they signalled also the extraordinary consequences which it would have for future generations. Implicitly, through their own ability to decode the portentous messages, these writers also bolstered their authority as trustworthy historians. Trope was no doubt an element too, as found in Bower's insertion of the ghostly vision into his account of the wedding feast, and in the common motifs of famine and extreme weather heralding Judgement Day.[69]

Bower goes on to describe the king's death, explaining that he was crossing from north to south (which, given the consensus of other sources, and the plausible story of the Edinburgh council meeting, is almost certainly incorrect) but was prevented from doing so by the weather, and turned instead to

67 *Chron. Lanercost*, pp. 115–16 (trans. Anderson, *Early Sources*, ii, pp. 698–99).

68 Chris Given-Wilson, *Chronicles: The Writing of History in Medieval England* (London & New York, 2004), p. 38. See, generally, Chapter 2, 'Godwitness Testimony'. See also the interesting discussion in Marjorie E. Reeves, 'History and Prophecy in Medieval Thought', *Medievalia et Humanistica*, n.s., 5 (1974), pp. 51–75.

69 'The author of the *Annales Londoniensis*, for example, stated that the dreadful storms and famine which struck England in the summer of 1260 led some people to suspect that "the day of Judgement was now imminent"' (Given-Wilson, *Chronicles*, p. 40).

'Kinghorn Regis' with an escort of knights. His horse stumbled on the sand, and he fell, 'too negligently attended by his followers', breaking his neck.[70] The *Book of Pluscarden*, written probably just a couple of decades after the *Scotichronicon*, on which it relies heavily, does not repeat Bower's prophetic passages but, in generally following Bower's description of the events leading to the king's death, adds further (probably invented) detail: near the shore, his horse's legs sank into soft sand, the horse stumbled and fell, crushing the king, who died of a broken neck.[71] Lanercost, having described the dismissive attitude of the king and his counsellors to the threat of judgement, relates that the king set out to visit Yolande, 'whom he had brought a little while before from foreign parts, to his own sorrow, and the perpetual injury of the whole province'. Whether the chronicler's scornful attitude to Yolande was through an aversion to her French birth, to an innate misogyny, or was intended to sustain his moralistic message, is unknowable. It might not be irrelevant, however, that his accusation of immorality against Alexander was based on an alleged frailty in the face of sexual temptation. Certainly, the chronicler had no love for Yolande: he claimed also that she was brought to Scotland and married to the king 'by considerations of charity only'.[72] Despite repeated warnings against travel in such weather by those he met on the way – the ferry-master at Queensferry and the master of the salt-works in Inverkeithing – Lanercost tells us that the king persisted and, becoming separated from his companions (who, somewhat unbelievably, were just a couple of farmers from Inverkeithing whom he asked to guide him), took a wrong road, fell from his horse and died of a fractured skull.

The tale is told in various other English sources, with minor variants. The *Historia Anglicana* of Thomas Walsingham (which for the thirteenth century is largely copied from earlier St Albans works), for example, merely states that, visiting his wife in darkness, his horse stumbled and he fell, injuring himself gravely, and died. There is no reference to omens or portents, or indeed any judgemental comment on the king or his reign; the chronicle simply goes on to relate the dynastic crisis which resulted. Similarly, the mid fourteenth-century *Scalachronica* by Sir Thomas Gray, recites the basic facts that, riding one night to visit his wife, Alexander 'fell from his palfrey near Kinghorn, and broke his neck, to the great confusion of the two realms'.[73] Many other English sources, which might have been expected to use the opportunity to moralise against the

70 *Chron. Bower*, v, pp. 418–21.

71 F.J.H. Skene (ed.), *Liber Pluscardinensis* (Edinburgh, 1877–80), i, pp. 111–12 (trans. ii, p. 80).

72 *Chron. Lanercost*, p. 116 (trans. Anderson, *Early Sources*, ii, pp. 690, 693–94).

73 Thomas Walsingham, *Historia Anglicana*, ed. T. Riley (Rolls Series, 28, London, 1863), i, p. 31; Thomas Gray, *Scalachronica*, ed. and trans. H. Maxwell (Glasgow, 1907), p. 5.

Scots and/or their king, are completely silent on the issue: the king's death is not even mentioned in the chronicles of Guisborough or Meaux, both rich sources for some periods of Scottish history, or in the vehemently anti-Scottish Anglo-Norman verse chronicle of Peter Langtoft. It is later, in the sixteenth century, that variations on the tale reoccur, perhaps picking up and embellishing Bower's tale: Hector Boece, for instance, whose *History of the Scottish People* was first published in 1527, has him riding fast on a 'fierce horse', which threw him on steep ground, breaking his neck. By the time Raphael Holinshed's *Chronicles of England, Scotland and Ireland* were printed 50 years later (a work which for Scottish material leaned heavily on Boece, and particularly on his translator into Scots, John Bellenden), Alexander was

> gallopping on a fierce horsse at Kingorne, forcing him in his race somewhat rashlie, he was throwne over the west cliffe towards the sea by a woonderfull misfortune so rudelie, that he brake his necke, and so therewith immediatelie died.[74]

Holinshed did not find the cliff in either Boece or Bellenden (who, did, however, repeat Bower's prophecy by Thomas the Rhymer), but Holinshed's topographical detail must indicate a relatively local source: the tradition already existed. Picked up by later historians in the eighteenth century, this new tradition that Alexander III died by falling over the cliff at Kinghorn has remained an almost unshakeable feature of popular memory. Sadly, for most Scots this image, almost certainly fictitious, is all that this important king means to them. Later interpolations and wild conspiracy theories are entirely without substance and are unworthy of attention.

Following Alexander's death, there was a suspicion that Yolande was pregnant. Perhaps predictably, the Lanercost chronicler accuses her of 'employing a womanish trick' which was eventually futile, since, he claimed, 'woman's cunning always has a miserable result'.[75] There is nothing to support his assertion that she attempted to pass off another woman's child as her own, and, her subterfuge exposed, left the country in disgrace. Bower, on the other hand, claims that the guardians who had been appointed following the king's death gathered at Clackmannan in November, when her child was due, but that 'this

74 Hector Boece, *Scotorum Historiae a prima gentis origine* . . . (Paris, 1527), fol. ccci v. – cccii r.; John Bellenden, *The History and Chronicles of Scotland: written in Latin by Hector Boece, canon of Aberdeen; and translated by John Bellenden, archdeacon of Moray, and canon of Ross* (Edinburgh, 1821), 2 vols; R. Holinshed, *Chronicles of England, Scotland and Ireland* (London, 1808), v, p. 321. Holinshed also repeats the weather-related portents.

75 *Chron. Lanercost*, pp. 117–18 (trans. Anderson, *Early Sources*, p. 693).

event failed to take place or there was a still-birth'.[76] No more closely contemporary source mentions this, however, and there is thus a lack of authoritative evidence to support any assertion of pregnancy, miscarriage or still-birth. Whatever the truth of Yolande's pregnancy, no living posthumous child of the king was born. Yolande, as dowager queen, certainly retained status in Scotland: entries in accounts rendered by the sheriffs of Stirling and Lanark for 1288–90 indicate both that the guardians ensured that lands and revenues were assigned to her as part of her dower, and that she probably remained in the country for at least part of that period.[77] When she eventually left Scotland is unknown, but it was certainly prior to 1294, when she remarried, taking as her second husband Arthur, count of Brittany. It is reasonable to speculate that after the death of Alexander's granddaughter Margaret, when it became clear that the direct royal line from Alexander was extinct, thus leaving her no dynastic rôle, she returned to France.

Little detail of the king's funeral obsequies is provided in any of the sources. The sole illustration of the funeral, from the fifteenth century (Plate 19), only shows a coffin, with a hint of carved elaboration, draped in tasselled cloth and adorned simply with a cross, being borne by four apparently richly dressed pall-bearers, followed by a choir.[78] Bower's description is brief: he was buried 'in the monastery of Dunfermline, as befits a king'. Further, he relates:

> He lies buried beneath the church at Dunfermline
> Amidst his kingly forbears; he reigned three times ten plus seven years,
> And was not quite eight years older.
> His noble heart rests in peace at Perth.
> And thus after those events may God ordain regarding this kingdom.[79]

This is the only reference to separate heart burial for Alexander. If true, it might be conjectured that his heart was taken for burial in the Blackfriars, which had

76 *Chron. Bower*, vi, pp. 10–11, where he states that the guardians were at Clackmannan on St Catherine's day (25 November). Bower's contention is perhaps supported by the fact that two of the guardians witnessed a document at Stirling only two days later (*Liber S. Thome de Aberbrothoc*, i (Bannatyne Club, 1848), no. 293). A.A.M. Duncan, 'The Community of the Realm of Scotland and Robert Bruce: A Review' (*Scottish Historical Review*, 45 (1966), pp. 184–201, at pp. 187–89) discusses the question of Yolande's pregnancy, concluding (in my view, unjustifiably) that by November, if not earlier, the pregnancy was feigned.

77 *ER*, i, pp. 39, 40, 46. An additional entry (p. 43) regarding a stud which she had near Jedburgh is not evidence of her presence in the country, since it refers to the stud which she 'used' (*solebat*) to have.

78 The illustration is from the Corpus Christi College, Cambridge, manuscript of Bower (ms. 171, fo. 225v); see Plate 19.

79 *Chron. Bower*, v, pp. 420–21.

been the site of perhaps his greatest triumph, the treaty of Perth, and the recipient of largesse from both Alexander III and his father.[80]

Alexander was laid to rest near his childhood companion and queen, two of his children, and many of his predecessors, including the saintly Margaret and her husband, Máel Coluim III, historical figures of almost legendary status, whom he had fêted as the royal progenitors of his dynasty. None of these tombs are nowadays identifiable, doubtless due partly to the 'cleansing' of the building by religiously zealous vandals in 1559 and 1560.[81] The 'Scottish Poem' in the *Liber Extravagans* berated the monks of Dunfermline for their 'slothfulness' and suggests that, even within two decades of his death, his tomb was uncared for:

> The tomb of such a great man should have been polished with better care
> on the part of the craftsmen, but he should have had a sympathetic funeral.
> After Death's savage bite, affection turns its back:
> love ends with the end of life.[82]

It is a sombre note on which to close the life-story of one who in later times was to become so celebrated.

80 Doubt has been cast on Bower's assertion: see Grant G. Simpson, 'The Heart of King Robert I: Pious Crusade or Marketing Gambit?', in Barbara E. Crawford (ed.), *Church, Chronicle and Learning in Medieval and Early Renaissance Scotland* (Edinburgh, 1999), pp. 173–86, n. 23. There seems little reason to be quite so negative about the suggestion, however. Simpson himself states (p. 174) that 'by the thirteenth century the practice had certainly become a cult at the higher levels of society, and was fairly frequent among the royalty and aristocracy of western Europe', and there is nothing inherently improbable about Bower's statement.

81 Richard Fawcett, 'Dunfermline Abbey Church', in Fawcett, *Royal Dunfermline*, p. 56. See also, however, Martin Macgregor and Caroline Wilkinson, 'In Search of Robert Bruce, Part 1: Medieval Royal Burial at Dunfermline, and the Investigations of 1818–19', *Scottish Historical Review*, forthcoming, for a fascinating discussion of the evidence for the location of the royal tombs in Dunfermline and the plausible identification of one of them, which was revealed in the early nineteenth century. Their conclusion largely supports that of the earlier analysis of Iain Fraser, 'The Tomb of the Hero King: The Death and Burial of Robert I, and the Discoveries of 1818–19', in Fawcett, *Royal Dunfermline*, pp. 155–76.

82 *Chron. Bower*, ix, pp. 76–77. See also nn., pp. 114–15, speculating on the reason for the anti-Dunfermline tone.

CHAPTER 9

'That Scotland Led in Lauch and Le'

Regiam Majestatem, the earliest surviving example of a systematic digest of medieval Scots law, was compiled during the early fourteenth century to 'rebuild the vanished structure' of Scottish common law which had been developing throughout the twelfth and thirteenth centuries and which had been largely destroyed during the struggle for independence.[1] Along with other legal compilations of similar date, it was an element of the conscious rebuilding of Scottish identity in the later years of Robert I's reign: an effort to re-establish a legal framework for effective rule and consciously to promote 'displays of legitimate kingship'.[2] In common with other early tracts, *Regiam Majestatem* contains material originating from various periods, perhaps widely divergent. Nonetheless, it forms the clearest guide to the nature of Scots law as it existed during the reign of Alexander III. It focuses on the status and responsibility of the monarch in upholding law and order: the king is the fount of justice, the upholder of good and the crusher of evil. Through his maintenance of justice, the people of his realm are protected from oppression and wrong. The opening of the prologue reads:

> The King's majesty should not only be made glorious by military power to be applied against rebels and those who rise against the King and his

1 The date and the reason for its compilation follow the arguments in A.A.M. Duncan, '*Regiam Majestatem*: A Reconsideration', *Juridical Review*, n.s., 6 (1961), pp. 199–217 (quotation from p. 217). Duncan's argument for the fourteenth-century date (probably during the later reign of Robert I) is still generally accepted.

2 Alice Taylor, 'The Assizes of David I, King of Scots, 1124–53', *Scottish Historical Review*, 91 (2012), pp. 197–238, at p. 234. For further discussion of *Regiam Majestatem*, see MacQueen, '*Regiam Majestatem*'; Alan Harding, '*Regiam Majestatem* Amongst Medieval Law-Books', *Juridical Review*, n.s., 29 (1984), pp. 97–111; Taylor, *Shape of the State*, esp. at pp. 124–27 and sources cited; Hector L. MacQueen, *Common Law and Feudal Society in Medieval Scotland* (Edinburgh, 2016), especially at pp. 89–98.

> realm, but should also be strengthened by laws for the government of those whom he has overcome and his peaceful subjects; so that, alike in peace and war, our illustrious King, who rules over this realm and who has no superior but God himself, the Creator of heaven and earth and ruler of all, and the holy Roman Church, may with such felicity conduct himself and govern the realm committed to his charge by God that by the might of his strong right hand he may crush the insolence of the violent and unruly and with the sceptre of equity may moderate justice to all humble and obedient folk, and may thus all the days of his life be victorious in subduing his foes and be recognised as a just and impartial judge in governing his subjects.
>
> No one will question the art, the vigour and the skill with which the King has employed the force of arms in time of war in withstanding the malicious conspiracy of his enemies. No one can doubt the justice, the discretion and the mercy which he, who is a lover and author of peace, has displayed in time of peace to his subjects. Such is the spirit of uprightness and equity which pervades his courts of justice that no judge has ever been so shameless and so insolently presumptuous as to dare to deviate by one hair's breadth from the path of justice, or to trespass one step beyond the bounds of truth. In these courts the powerful adversary cannot oppress the poor, nor can love, favour or grace of friends drive any man from the seat of judgement.[3]

The concept that justice must emanate from the monarch is consistent across the ages. The prologue is based on material found within the sixth-century *Institutes* of Justinian and was used in varying forms by several medieval jurists (including in the English tract known as Glanvill, which was a source for considerable portions of *Regiam Majestatem*). The king must be the ultimate secular judge; the Scottish account of Alexander III's response to the bishop of Norwich's suggestion that he should pay homage to Edward I for his kingdom in 1278 used words very similar to those in the prologue: 'nobody but God himself has the right to the homage for my realm of Scotland, and I hold it of nobody but God himself'. Independently of other political reasons, the judicial status of the king alone demands his independence from other rulers.

Law and judicial administration had been central to the development of the kingdom.[4] The extent to which a single rule of law holds sway over the

---

3 Lord Cooper (ed. and trans.), *Regiam majestatem and Quoniam attachiamenta: Based on the Text of Sir John Skene* (Edinburgh, 1947), pp. 57 (trans. p. 58, & n.).

4 MacQueen, '*Regiam Majestatem*', p. 1: 'in a very literal, even physical, sense law and jurisdiction do indeed define what is Scotland'. See also the sources MacQueen cites for further

territory claimed by a ruler is integral to the identity of those who live there; it follows that the ability of the ruler to make good that rule of law through effective institutions and administration is vital to the royal authority which he claims. Thus the treaty of Perth, which asserted that the people of the lands ceded by Norway to Scotland would henceforth be subject to the laws and customs of Scotland, can be seen as vital to the establishment of a Scottish identity, assuming that actual subjection to those laws and customs could be achieved. Law, the upholding of good governance, is central both to the 'sense of solidarity' that gives people a common identity,[5] and to the very existence of royal authority. Similarly, the long-running dispute between Scotland and England over the line of the border centred on the incursion of Scottish officials into English territory; if the lands were subjected to the imposition of Scottish law and administration, they effectively became part of Scotland.

This distinctiveness in its law and administration of a single jurisdiction (which thus quite explicitly excluded other, external, laws and traditions) applied also in ecclesiastical affairs: the business of Scotland's church was to be dealt with in Scotland and nowhere else, 'save through the process of appeal to Rome'.[6] The independence of the Scottish church from the sees of Canterbury or York, insistence on the separation of papal taxation raised in Scotland from that of England, and the refusal (expressed clearly and regularly in treaties following the death of Alexander III) to allow Scots to be called to justice, secular or ecclesiastical, outside their kingdom were all elements of that most fundamental duty of the king to uphold the freedom and welfare of his people – freedom from injustice, but freedom also from foreign interference or oppression. The summoning of King John Balliol to answer for what were, in Edward I's eyes, shortcomings of the judicial process in Scotland, is one of the most oft-cited causes both of Balliol's downfall and of the Scottish rebellion against English authority in the 1290s. Edward I did not disrespect Scottish law; rather, he stated that he wished to uphold it. His usurpation of the right to administer it, however, and especially to do so from beyond the boundaries of the kingdom, was unsustainable from a Scottish point of view. The upholding of justice had a conceptual as well as a practical aspect. The definition of law and custom was an important element in the creation of a coherent identity and effective royal authority, but the effectiveness and practicalities of application and enforcement were just as crucial. Further, the idea that law was central to good governance

consideration of law as an important element in Scottish national identity.

5 MacQueen, '*Regiam Majestatem*', p. 2, quoting Susan Reynolds, *Kingdoms and Communities in Western Europe, 900–1300* (Oxford, 1984), p. 253.

6 MacQueen, '*Regiam Majestatem*', p. 2; see also p. 9.

was not restricted to 'officials, clerics and academics but . . . [was] widely held in society at large'.[7]

There is no specific documentary evidence of Alexander III as a law-maker, although he was credited by his enthusiastic eulogists with being a sage legislator. (The development of law as it was practised, as opposed to specific royal legislation, is discoverable through documentary evidence and has been extensively studied. It is not the subject of further discussion here.[8]) *Gesta Annalia* and Bower attributed to Alexander III laws which had impact, in one way or another, on aspects of economic life. These laws may be fictitious, designed to promote the writers' ideal of Alexander as a just king who, through his wise law-making, fostered the conditions for prosperity and equity. It is highly probable that Alexander did legislate, since he governed through counsel and held fairly frequent *colloquia*; it is impossible, however, to know the extent, nature or value of any legislation passed, because most of his *colloquia* are not the subject of surviving record. Some of the legislation which, after his reign, compilers attributed to kings from the periods before Alexander III, perhaps in an attempt to give it a spurious air of ancient authority, might in fact have been the product of Alexander III's reign. It is simply not possible either to state or refute such a case with any confidence.

The same cannot be said, however, of Alexander as upholder of the law. When *Gesta Annalia* was scathing about the governments of the minority, the criticism centred on the lawlessness of their leaders:

> But these councillors were so many kings. For he who saw the poor crushed down in those days, the nobles ousted from their inheritance, the drudgery forced upon citizens, the violence done to churches, might with good reason say, 'Woe unto the kingdom where the king is a boy!'
>
> When, therefore, judgement and righteousness in the kingdom of Scotland were slumbering . . .[9]

---

7 MacQueen, '*Regiam Majestatem*', p. 7, discussing A. Grant, 'Aspects of National Consciousness in Medieval Scotland', in C. Bjorn, A. Grant and K.J. Stringer (eds), *Nations, Nationalism and Patriotism in the European Past* (Copenhagen, 1994), pp. 69–95.

8 For the development of law in this period, see particularly: MacQueen, *Common Law and Feudal Society*; MacQueen, 'Scots Law under Alexander III', in Reid, *Alexander III Essays*, pp. 74–102; Taylor, *Shape of the State* (esp. ch. 5); Neville, *Land, Law and People*; and a briefer summary in Andrew R.C. Simpson and Adelyn L.M. Wilson, *Scottish Legal History*, i, 1000–1707 (Edinburgh, 2017), Parts 1 and 2.

9 *Chron. Fordun*, i, p. 297 (trans. ii, p. 292). 'But these councillors were so many kings' (*sed quot fuerunt consules, tot fuerunt reges*): the expression is not intended to mock kingship, but rather the plurality, and thus inconsistency, of approach. Rather than one king, upholding the nation's interest, there were many, each upholding their own.

This statement is designed specifically to contrast with the prosperity later enjoyed under Alexander's personal rule, which, the annalist tells us, was notable for fairness and discipline. The 'most free justice' which the men of Scotland were 'known to enjoy'[10] came about through good choice of justiciars and other royal officials, and strict attention both to their conduct and to judicial practice. Only by ensuring that the law was fair, and that it was enforced in a manner designed to benefit the litigants rather than the judiciary, could men enjoy 'free justice'. Alexander III certainly made use of the judicial system established by his predecessors, which it had been claimed had been so abused during his minority. Whether or not it was accurate, *Gesta Annalia*'s accusation of misgovernance in the course of the minority did at least serve its function of providing a contrast with the picture the annalist wished to paint of the mature king's reign.

Although the record is not seamless, it is nonetheless possible to demonstrate fairly conclusively that throughout the reign (including the minority) justiciars were in post in all three of the traditional judicial territories of Scotia, Lothian and Galloway.[11] Probably from the time of the king's assumption of power in 1258, Alexander Comyn, earl of Buchan, was justiciar of Scotia, and held itinerant courts at which, if he himself was not available, a substitute of similar rank and standing took his place.[12] He held the position until his death in 1289. Hugh Barclay was justiciar of Lothian, also from 1258; after a period in 1259–(?)62 when Thomas Normanville and Stephen Fleming are found in that office, Barclay returned to hold it until *c.*1279, when William Soulis was appointed, remaining probably until his death in 1292/93. In Galloway, John Comyn of Badenoch was justiciar from 1258 at least until 1264, and possibly until the latter part of the reign. There is a reference to Aymer Maxwell as justiciar of Galloway in 1264, but Comyn was again in the rôle later; he died probably in 1277, and seems to have been replaced by William Sinclair, although there is no record of him in post before 1287. There is thus no doubt that justiciars were in post, and while record of their judicial activity is not plentiful, it

10 Treaty of Perth, *RRS*, iv pt. 1, p. 102: *qui liberiori iusticia gaudere dinoscuntur.* It is noticeable that in the treaty of Perth Alexander is also described as being 'a zealot for truth and a lover of peace and concord' (*veritatis zelator et pacis et concordie amator*) (p. 102).

11 It has been suggested that Durward was for a time 'sole justiciar' of the whole of Scotland, but this is a misreading of *Gesta Annalia*'s phrase *totius . . . Scociae justiciarius*, meaning justiciar of the whole of Scotia, i.e. Scotland north of the Forth. A table of known justiciars is given in Barrow, *Kingdom of the Scots*, pp. 237–38, from which the following list of justiciar appointments is taken.

12 See, e.g., J. Anderson (ed.), *Calendar of the Laing Charters, 854–1837* (Edinburgh, 1899), no. 8, a record of a justiciar court in 1266, in which Adam earl of Carrick took the place of Buchan as justiciar of Scotia 'before the full court of Fife and Fortherif'.

is present.[13] References to such bodies as 'the full court of Fife', to figures such as 'dempsters' or *iudices* and to the money raised from judicial process are further evidence of the activity of the local judiciary, even if its actual effectiveness cannot easily be gauged.[14] The *iudex* has been described as 'a survival from pre-twelfth-century Scotland', and he thus represented a firm continuity between older and more modern society and judicial practice. Not a government official in the normal sense, but rather a public official of almost hereditary status with legal training, his presence in the record is a further indication of awareness of the importance of the judicial process at local level, and of the continuing use of local hierarchies in the pursuit of royal control.[15]

There is abundant evidence that, in both the minority and the personal rule, Alexander's reign saw full use of the system of sheriffs. Indeed, it was primarily through a network of loyal sheriffs that government kept control of the kingdom: given the decentralised model of Scottish administration, judicial and fiscal organisation would have been effectively non-existent without the sheriffs. As noted above, the extension of Scottish royal dominance over the western seaboard and the isles included the appointment of royal bailiffs as early as 1250 and, although there is no positive indication of the establishment of sheriffs in the area until the reign of John Balliol, the award of the custody of royal castles to local lords, as in the case of Gilla Críst MacNachtan, was indicative of a policy which aimed to establish a local administration of similar character.[16] Justiciars were necessarily non-local, and their courts were itinerant and thus occasional; the sheriff was the permanent representative of royal authority in the locality. The names of many sheriffs have survived from this reign, showing that practically all (if not all) of the 30 or so sheriffdoms which existed in the mid thirteenth century were in the hands of active incumbents.[17]

Sheriff courts were held to inquire into both civil and criminal cases, and to pass on to the justiciars, or to the royal court, those matters which could not be resolved at the local level. For example, in a court held at Peebles in July 1259

---

13 Barrow, *Kingdom of the Scots*, pp. 83–138, *passim*.

14 *St Andrews Liber*, p. 246: a memorandum from a justiciar's court held at Perth in 1260, before Freskin Murray, David Lochore and John Cameron, acting in place of the earl of Buchan, justiciar of Scotia. Two of the witnesses are described as *judices*. There is also a *judex* among the witnesses to *Inchaffray Charters*, no. 103 (dateable 1268 x 84).

15 Barrow, *Kingdom of the Scots*, pp. 69–82, at p. 69; for dempsters/*iudices*/*breitheamhnan* in this period, see also: MacQueen, 'Scots Law under Alexander III', pp. 81–82; Taylor, *Shape of the State* (Part 2, *passim*, see index); Neville, *Land, Law and People* (*passim*, see index).

16 See above, pp. 187–88.

17 See *ER*, i, pp. 1–34, *passim*, where no fewer than 27 sheriffdoms are mentioned, with named sheriffs; many other references exist in charters and other record evidence: see Reid and Barrow, *Sheriffs*, for a list of incumbents, with sources for their first and last appearances; around four dozen names are provided for this reign.

before the joint justiciars of Lothian, Thomas Normanville and Stephen Fleming, ten of the twelve named jurors (opposed by the other two) found that a previous inquisition into the ownership of certain lands had been properly carried out by Sir Gilbert Fraser (who had been sheriff in the 1230s). The case still being in dispute almost 30 years later, it had been remitted upwards to the justiciar's court.[18] At the other end of the country, in August 1261 the king issued a precept (or instruction) to Alexander Montfort, sheriff of Elgin, instructing him to hold an inquest (using 'good men of the shire, and burgesses of Elgin') into the rights claimed by Robert Spinc, a crossbowman, and his wife Margaret, to hold the king's garden and its adjoining land in Elgin. A fortnight later the inquisition was duly held 'at the sheriff's full pleas', finding in favour of Robert Spinc; Margaret's ancestors had indeed held the garden, and they should therefore inherit it (saving the rights of the king to produce from it when he was resident in Elgin).[19] This case demonstrates the effective downward communication of justice between king and locality; the lack of delay in holding the inquest upon receipt of the precept shows that the system worked; and the testimony of the 12 named jurors brought local knowledge to bear on the case. It is also noteworthy that Robert Spinc himself was 'the bearer' of the precept: he had personally sought recognition of his family's claims at the hands of the king himself. This was his route to local justice, opening the gates of the judicial process to him. The personal rôle of the king was integral to the administration of justice. Matters could move downwards to the local courts from the king, as well as upwards; the king was the ultimate court of appeal.

A little more than a year later, at the end of 1262, a further inquisition was held at Inverness before Alexander Comyn, justiciar of Scotia, accompanied by both the bishop of Ross and, once again, Alexander Montfort sheriff of Elgin. On this occasion no fewer than 17 men – including several who had taken part in the inquisition at Elgin in the previous year (among them Thomas Wiseman, the provost of Elgin) – testified that Ewan, thane of Rathenech (who had also been part of the previous year's jury) was the rightful heir to land, a house 'within the castle of Elgin' and a net on the River Spey, held in chief of the crown by grant of King William in return for the provision of one sergeant and service in the 'Scottish army'.[20] Ewan's title was another survival from earlier society, but it serves again to remind that the process of administrative reorganisation was a gradual process, and that it built on, rather than replaced, the

18 *CDS*, i, no. 2162.

19 *CDS*, i, nos. 2271–72; printed in full in *APS*, i, p. 89.

20 *CDS*, i, no. 2323. For a discussion of 'the Scottish army' and other forms of military service, see G.W.S. Barrow, 'The Army of Alexander III's Scotland', in Reid, *Alexander III Essays*, pp. 132–47.

existing administrative and social organisation. Ewan, as thane, was doubtless responsible for raising the required military levies in his thanage of Rathenech, and his house in the castle is a reminder of his traditional duty of supervising the king's residence. In the later thirteenth century, Ewan's position still retained its associated hereditary rights, as well as a duty to act alongside the official who by that time had become his superior in the local administration, the sheriff. Ewan's thanage (then in the hands of his successor, William) was still the subject of record a few decades later, when Edward I marched as far as Elgin in 1296.[21]

Other cases cast at least a faint light on the operation of these courts: the interplay between the justiciar and sheriff courts is again demonstrated by a suit of 1255/56 regarding lands claimed by Dunfermline abbey.[22] In April 1268, the king commanded Simon Fraser, the sheriff of Traquair, to hold an inquest into the diversion of the water course on land near the Gala Water owned by Melrose abbey. Whether the monks had diverted the course to the prejudice of others, or had suffered through the action of their neighbours, is not known; nonetheless, the cause had come directly to the attention of the king, who instructed the local judiciary to enquire and report back to him.[23] Similarly, Thomas Randolph, sheriff of Roxburgh was ordered to hold an inquest to discover who had been responsible for the plundering of the lands of Horndean in Berwickshire, and whether the stolen goods had been reset in his bailiary; again, he was to report back to the king's chapel.[24]

Such detailed evidence regarding the rôle of king, justiciar or sheriff in criminal cases in this period in Scotland is rare, but the accounts of the sheriffs make it clear that the monetary fruits of justice – *lucra justiciarii* – were significant. As in civil matters, criminal activities were subject to judicial process at all levels. Two prosecutions serve as examples: one malefactor named John Girve was executed by beheading for an unspecified crime, and Richard, son of Robert, son of Elias was exonerated (through a plea of self-defence) for having killed Adam the Miller, a known thief.[25] That the king was personally involved in the dealing of justice to his people is also made clear by the inventory of records held in Edinburgh in 1292, which reveal that many records of a judicial nature, involving the participation of the king himself, have been lost.[26] The English

21 On the thane, see G.W.S. Barrow, *Kingdom of the Scots*, pp. 7–68, especially at pp. 46–49, where the thanage of Rathenech is discussed; and Taylor, *Shape of the State* (*passim*, see index; for Ewan himself, see especially p. 60 n.).

22 *RRS*, iv pt. 1, nos. 186, 187.

23 *RRS*, iv pt. 1, no. 67.

24 *RRS*, iv pt. 1, no. 70.

25 *ER*, i, pp. 1–34, *passim*; MacQueen, 'Scots Law under Alexander III', p. 92; *APS*, i, pp. 97–98.

26 MacQueen, 'Scots Law under Alexander III', pp. 84–85; *APS*, i, pp. 114–15.

records also enlighten: as previously mentioned, they note occasions on which individuals were pardoned of offences, or given liberties, by the English king 'at the instance of' the king or queen of Scots, demonstrating that access to the royal person to plead a cause for oneself or on behalf of others was commonplace.

A few examples survive in Scottish record. In one, Emma, the daughter and heiress of Gilbert Smeaton, took her plea regarding lands disputed with Dunfermline abbey before the king's council in December 1253; she lost, and was required to acknowledge the abbey's ownership, but was in return awarded a pension for her life from the abbey.[27] Even during the minority, it was a feature of the judicial system to have access to the person of the king (who, it was stated, had seen the abbey's charter from David I, and had it read to him) in council. Clearly, the minority councils were not as unheeding of the rule of law as some chroniclers would have us believe. Celebrated actions, such as Bordeaux merchant John Mason's pursuit of payment for Alexander's unpaid wine bill, were in later days to come before the English judiciary. These have been rightly regarded as symbolic of the submission of Scotland to England after the competition for the crown, which was the consequence of the deaths of Alexander III and his granddaughter; but they are also telling of a Scottish judicial system which, if it did not always provide the remedy which the appellants wanted, was undeniably active. Mason, whose debt was disputed by the Scottish crown, had presented a plea before the Scottish king's officials and even suffered temporary imprisonment for his perseverance.[28] Individuals such as Mason, Emma Smeaton or even Robert Spinc of Elgin had the ability to present their cause to a council meeting, or even to a full *colloquium*; a forum of this sort was not restricted to high-status cases such as the disputed earldom of Menteith (which, as noted earlier, the king settled in parliament in 1285).

From an early age, Alexander appears to have succeeded in bringing together a fractious community to provide the good counsel recognised to be essential for the effective government of the kingdom. Generally, it must be assumed, the king acted in council, a gathering of at least a quorum of the 'inner circle' which was in almost constant attendance. Lists of members of most of the councils of the minority have survived in written record, indicating a likelihood that there was a formal process for appointment, although no details have survived.[29]

27 *RRS*, iv pt. 1, nos. 18, 182, and *APS*, i, p. 426.

28 For the Mason case, which was under active consideration by 1284, see *CDS*, ii, nos. 252, 255, 264 and other entries following the death of Alexander III.

29 Duncan (*Making of the Kingdom*, p. 608) notes that there is no record of any oath being required of the councillors appointed in 1255; it is possible, however, that Henry III's attempt to extract undertakings of good government from the councillors appointed by Alexander in

While *colloquia*, meetings of the nascent parliament, were convened on at least ten occasions between 1258 and the end of the reign, it has to be recognised that these were not equivalent to the more ubiquitous gatherings of the council.[30]

The *colloquium* was 'a genuine meeting place where the needs of king and government could be expounded and at the same time confronted by the needs, objections, and petitions of the king's subjects'; it was also 'the guarantee of the integrity of the Scottish realm, the sole body capable of giving political expression to the community of that realm'.[31] The personal involvement of the king in justice and administration, though vital to his regal function, was circumscribed by the essential use of good counsel through the wise choice of royal officials, the constant dependence on the inner circle or royal council, and the approval and acclamation by the entire community, as representative (although not in the modern democratic sense) of the kingdom. The king was neither outside nor above that community: he was, essentially, part of it. Thus the *colloquium* dealt not only with matters of great national import, such as marriage treaties, the succession, and the making of peace and war; it also involved itself in matters such as the settlement of the dispute over the earldom of Menteith, and many lesser affairs. In January 1256, therefore, i*n pleno colloquio* ('in full colloquium'), and *cum commune consilium* ('with common counsel') of the magnates gathered there, Alexander is said to have given judgement over the disputed lands of Dunfermline abbey.[32]

During the adult reign of Alexander III, the key offices of the royal household were effectively held by trusted servants. In the appointment as chancellors of William Wishart, archdeacon of St Andrews (1258), William Fraser, dean of Glasgow (1273) and Thomas Charteris (1279 x 1285 – perhaps 1279, when Fraser became bishop of Andrews), Alexander ensured in this key position men of learning (all graduates), with considerable administrative experience.[33] Charteris, with a lesser ecclesiastical career than the others, seems to have been primarily an administrator: although not without experience of royal diplomacy, it is his name which heads the list of clerks who prepared the inventory of records held in Edinburgh castle in 1282 (perhaps, although not necessarily, before he became chancellor). His appointment may be indicative of a desire to increase the

---

1258, should be taken as circumstantial evidence of the existence of such an oath of office (see above, p. 139).

30 See the list of Alexander III's 'parliaments' in *APS*, i, pp. 68–70; Duncan, *Making of the Kingdom*, pp. 609–11 also discusses some of these meetings, the evidence of their nature, and the language used to describe them.

31 Barrow, *Kingship and Unity*, p. 128.

32 *RRS*, iv pt. 1, nos. 186, 187 (*RPS*, 1256/1).

33 See Watt, *Graduates*, pp. 85–86 (Charteris), 203–06 (Fraser), 590–94 (Wishart).

efficiency of the chancellor's rôle and the office of which he was the head.[34] That only three men held the office over a period of almost three decades certainly indicates a valuable continuity in this most vital element of the royal administration; the quality of the incumbents is testimony to the importance of the office. The chancellor was a right-hand man of the king in government; his faithfulness, efficiency and integrity were invaluable assets to the king. Alexander III's reputation as a good ruler must have rested largely upon his choice of officials, particularly his chancellors.

The financial duties of the chamberlain were central to good rule, for should he fail to find the necessary income for the household, the king would be forced to impose unduly upon his subjects, perhaps to an extent constituting oppression. The tract known as 'The King's Household' makes it clear that the chamberlain's duty was to provide for the king and his court without placing such burden on the land. *Gesta Annalia*'s comments regarding the 'poor crushed down' and 'the drudgery forced upon citizens' in 1252–55, and the 'grinding of the poor' in 1255–57,[35] may have been little more than formulaic criticisms which were designed to contrast the minority with strong personal rule, but they do draw attention to the financial oppression which would be the inevitable result of bad government.

The accounts presented by the chamberlain in 1264 for an 18-month period depict a Scottish monarchy which was neither opulently cash wealthy, nor in penury. The recorded income from the fruits of royal estates, feudal renders of various types and the profits of justice amounted to a little over £5,400,[36] which represents less than half the equivalent payments to the English treasury in the same year, during which the English state was riven by the civil war which undoubtedly depressed its income. Accepting an estimated average annual English royal income of about £30,000, the Scottish figure (pro-rated for a 12-month period) represents roughly one-eighth of the English king's revenue. Additionally, in that period Alexander III had expended unusual sums on the war with Norway, and the actual income was probably greater, boosted by some receipts not revealed in the fragmentary surviving accounts and, from time to time, by one-off levies.[37]

34 See the comments in *RRS*, iv pt. 1, p. 37. Although the editors have opted for Charteris as being still, at that point, a senior clerk under Fraser as chancellor, it is not certain that he was not yet chancellor himself. Charteris is not found with the title until 1285, but neither is Fraser found with it after 1279, when he became bishop of St Andrews; given that Wishart gave up the chancellorship on his promotion to that see, it is not unreasonable to suggest that Fraser did likewise.

35 *Chron. Fordun*, i, pp. 297–98 (trans. ii, pp. 292–93).

36 *ER*, i, p. xlvii (calculated from the account transcribed on pp. 10–11); quoted by Mayhew, 'A Silver Age', p. 53, and by Taylor, *Shape of the State*, p. 387.

37 Taylor, *Shape of the State*, p. 387.

The Scottish royal income, therefore, although predictably much smaller than the English, may have been proportionately comparable.[38] It is significant to the understanding of the nature of Scottish monarchy, however, to recognise that this level of income far exceeded that of even the most senior aristocratic families of the kingdom. Coherent data does not exist for the extent of the revenue which nobles might expect to raise from their own estates, feudal income and judicial activities, but there is some evidence to suggest that the sizeable estates of, for instance, the earls of Fife or Roger de Quincy might generate at best one-seventh of the royal income.[39] Even the aggregated wealth of various branches of the mighty Comyn family, therefore, is unlikely to have provided serious competition with royal resources. Though the Scottish king was *primus inter pares* in a governmental sense, he could hardly have been regarded by his nobility as a financial equal.

The apparent lack in Scotland of economic antagonism between crown and nobility has been persuasively attributed not to financial parity in the echelons of power, but rather to the mediation of regal power through the aristocracy. As the arms of royal government, the nobility could ensure that, in normal circumstances at least, exploitative income generation through unreasonable taxation, a cause of recurring strife south of the border, did not occur in Scotland.[40] In 1326, however, Robert I was to impose a tax on the community because the war had so drained the royal coffers that the estate of the crown could not be upheld 'without intolerable charges and inconveniences to his people'.[41] The Scottish style of government certainly helped prevent the recurring financial conflict which scarred English medieval politics, but it did not render it impossible.

The chamberlain's office was usually (although not exclusively) a magnatial appointment, a normality fully reflected under Alexander III, at least until the closing years of the reign.[42] By March 1259 (perhaps in the autumn of 1258) David

38 See above, p. 64, where a Scottish economy worth roughly one-sixth of the English (more or less proportionate with the respective populations) is postulated.

39 Cynthia J. Neville, *Native Lordship in Medieval Scotland: The Earldoms of Strathearn and Lennox, c.1140–1365* (Dublin, 2005), pp. 126–27; pp. 126–30 offer a useful discussion of magnatial income. The one-seventh figure roughly equates the £500 estimated by Neville to the very conservative estimate of £3,600 *per annum* royal income.

40 See the extensive discussion of royal income in Taylor, *Shape of the State*, ch. 6, especially at pp. 387–89.

41 *RPS*, 1328/1.

42 An exception to this rule was the chamberlain appointed in the closing stages of Alexander II's reign, Richard of Inverkeithing. He was no longer chamberlain by early 1251: he may have resigned when elected to his bishopric of Dunkeld in 1250 (Watt, *Graduates*, pp. 280–82). David Bernham, later bishop of St Andrews, had also served as chamberlain for several years during the reign of Alexander II.

Lindsay, who had held the office from 1255, had been replaced by Aymer Maxwell; between the end of 1260 and the early months of 1262 William, earl of Mar resumed the office, which he had held during the second period of minority from 1252 to 1255; from 1267, for a couple of years, Reginald Cheyne held the title, followed by Thomas Randolph (1269–1277/78), John Lindsay (1277/78–1281 x 1286) and (perhaps) Weland Stikelaw (1281 x 1286). These names are all familiar from the political events of the reign, except Stikelaw, about whose appointment there is some uncertainty. The close involvement of these nobles in the administration of the royal household is an indication that the noble community had not only a right, but also a responsibility and duty, to be part of the governmental process. Stikelaw, however, was out of the usual mould: he was a graduate, perhaps the son of a former steward of Bishop Gamelin of St Andrews, and himself a canon of Dunkeld. In royal service as a clerk by the early 1280s, he was among the clerks who supported John Lindsay in the rôle. By late in 1287, Alexander Balliol was in the office, and a few years later Stikelaw was in Norway, in the retinue of Isabella Bruce (who was to become Erik II's second queen), with whom he had family connections.[43] Although it was later said that he had been chamberlain, there is no contemporary record which styles him so, and it is possible that Lindsay did in fact continue in office until after the death of the king (although perhaps largely as an absentee). Whether as stand-in or senior official for the absent Lindsay, or as chamberlain in his own right, Stikelaw must represent the efficient, clerical aspect of the rôle.[44]

Before considering the attitude of Scottish medieval writers to Alexander's kingship, it is worth pausing first to consider to what extent, in terms of the provision of effective justice and administration, this reign matches up to the theoretical, philosophical approaches to medieval European kingship. Political theory in the thirteenth century was a field of study which reflected the transition and crisis affecting Christendom at that time. The development of self-aware political units – kingdoms – with monarchical systems of government, was still a relatively new phenomenon, and created an environment in which it became necessary to articulate the parameters within which such authority should be wielded. There remained in medieval Europe, therefore, a duality of thought:

> On one side was the old idea of the fundamental unity of mankind, expressed in a universal Empire and in a universal Church. On the other,

43 For a fuller biography of Stikelaw, see Watt, *Graduates*, pp. 516–17.

44 It is tempting to speculate that Stikelaw may have been appointed chamberlain around the same time as Charteris became chancellor, as part of a drive towards administrative efficiency; there is, however, no evidence to support the notion.

> the new and modern experience of a number of independent communities, gradually becoming aware of their independence.[45]

Thomas Aquinas (1225–74), a close contemporary of Alexander III, and one of the period's most influential theorists, concluded that any political unit, of whatever nature, required regimentation, and that the most effective method was rule by one man who carried the authority of the *communitas*. This laid immutable responsibilities on the chosen ruler: 'it is of the nature of kingship that there should be one to rule and that he should do so with a view to the common good without seeking private gain'. In a state of tyranny (defined as that state where the ruler wields power in his own interest, rather than in that of his people) 'there is no security, and all is uncertain: for there is no law'.[46] Dante Alighieri (*c.*1265–1321), less than a generation later, agreed: 'the people [do not exist] for the sake of the king; on the contrary, the king is for the sake of the people'.[47] The connection between good rule and material prosperity is also explicit: 'a just king makes rich the earth, but the miser destroys it'.[48] The material and spiritual welfare of the ruled are thus placed at risk by the bad ruler; to avert this danger, the choice of king has to be carefully made: he must be of the true kingly character and ability. In this, Aquinas's and Dante's work rested on the bedrock of Aristotelian philosophy, ubiquitous throughout the medieval period, which they developed in the context of Christendom. They were in tune with, for example, the almost contemporary writings of Marsilius of Padua (*c.*1275–*c.*1342), who, in defending the prerogatives of the Holy Roman Empire against encroachment from the papacy in his treatise *Defensor pacis* (1324), developed further the idea that political authority stemmed from the people; only they had the intrinsic power to create, discipline or remove their rulers.[49]

To the medieval theorists, the logical conclusion of the king's duty to support the interests of his people, who were also the bestowers of royal power, is that the power had necessarily to be restricted. A ruler could not be bound by laws which he himself had made, as this would place the law above its creator, a concept with deeply unsettling theological implications. He should nonetheless submit himself to the laws voluntarily, being aware of his moral responsibilities

45 A.P. d'Entrèves (ed.), *Selected Political Writings of Thomas Aquinas* (Oxford, 1974), pp. xxiv–xxv.

46 Thomas Aquinas, *De regimine,* in d'Entrèves, *Selected Political Writings*, pp. 9, 17.

47 Dante Alighieri, *Monarchy: and Three Political Letters*, ed. and trans. D. Nicholl and C. Hardie (London, 1954), p. 20.

48 Aquinas, *De regimine*, in d'Entrèves, *Selected Political Writings*, p. 17.

49 See Marsilius of Padua, *The Defender of Peace*, trans. Alan Gewirth (New York, 1967).

and of the judgement of God upon him. Stepping beyond the bounds of his authority created a state of tyranny, to which there was a right, even a duty, of resistance. This most fundamental responsibility, to promote and uphold the common weal, finds expression in two basic ways: the king must establish 'peaceful unity' and uphold equitable justice. Through these two kingly functions, liberty and stability would be found, in which the people would be able to live at peace, increase their material prosperity, and through love for their fellowmen, grow spiritually and be led closer to God. One leader was required for a kingdom to achieve that unity and peace, whose very purpose was 'to provide freedom and peace for men as they pass through the testing-time of this world'.[50] It was not merely physical safety and material welfare which the well-ruled kingdom provided; it was, more importantly for the medieval writers, a state of spiritual well-being. The centrality of law, justice, unity and peace did not inhibit or absolve the ruler from the duty to utilise might and warfare when necessary. These were tools of kingship, however, to be used only in the interests of justice. When the integrity of the kingdom or the rule of law demanded the resort to arms, God would come down on the side of righteousness. In this way, God controlled the temporal conflicts of mankind and, by his judgement, gave authority to those who ruled men. The apparently contradictory authorities of God, people and kings was thus logically worked out within the parameters of a worldview in which God, as creator and ruler of all, delegated authority to rulers who held their power through the choice, consent and support, and in the interests, of their subjects.

In this context, the comments in *Regiam Majestatem* on the rights and responsibilities of the royal office can be recognised as a practical expression of current political theory, amply reflecting the philosophy of good rule as expounded in the thirteenth century. The reciprocal duties of the king and his subjects are propounded, as are the legal and moral obligation on the king to uphold law and justice, the limitation of his power (specifically in relation to alienation or diminution of the realm and infringements of the rights of his subjects), and the position of the king as deriving his authority directly from God, with no other human superior. Most emphasis, however, is laid on his absolute duty to provide equitable justice and fair laws, through which the realm could find peace and stability. The king is, above all, 'the lover and author of peace'; his majesty might indeed be made glorious in warfare, but only in pursuit

50 Aquinas, *De regimine*, in d'Entrèves, *Selected Political Writings*, p. 9: 'the most important task for the ruler of any community is the establishment of peaceful unity'; Dante (*Monarchy*, pp. 11, 14, 8, 93): 'every kingdom divided against itself shall be laid waste', 'the world is best ordered when justice is at its strongest'. Humanity could only fulfil its true potential 'in the quietude or tranquillity of peace'.

of peace, to curb rebels or other challengers of his authority who threaten the well-being of the community at large.

These concepts were richly promoted by Bower in the fifteenth century when formulating his moralistic tale of Alexander III's reign. In expounding the failings of the minority (and particularly of the government of 1249–51), he used Cicero, the eleventh-century Persian philosopher Avicenna and Plutarch to emphasise the essential requirement for good counsel:

> In exercising government nothing is more advantageous for a king than to have good counsellors. For if his councellors should be false, then his own chief men are a king's enemies, for they give him advice which is not expedient for one in his position. These [evil counsellors] are particularly dangerous in any community because, just as the honour, well-being and success of a king and of the state of which the king is a head depend most of all on good counsellors, so confusion and the overthrow of the state arise especially from the presence of evil counsellors.

Quoting from Cicero's *De Senectute*, he likens the counsellor (the equivalent in the medieval kingdom of the Roman senator, as described by Plutarch) to the helmsman of a ship, who keeps it on course irrespective of the work of the rest of the crew. He ascribes to Avicenna (although without specific reference) the similar idea that 'the counsellor's function is to lay down the blueprint according to which everyone else has to work and be guided'. Examples from both Old and New Testaments serve to confirm his assertions.[51] Bower's insistence on the absolute requirement for good counsel fits well with his ambition in telling the story of Alexander III. Nonetheless, it also effectively describes the essential aspect of community which infuses the Scottish medieval kingship.

In theoretical terms, therefore, Scotland was on a par with other European countries in her political development. The conduct of his reign seems to demonstrate that the adult Alexander III managed to match the demands of the theory in most respects. He successfully defended the physical realm against Norwegian threat, and thereby extended its boundaries, using warfare where peaceful negotiation had failed. The very wording of the treaty of Perth reflects aspects of the theory: it was made 'with the counsel of his magnates'; it was an agreement 'between the foresaid kings, their kingdoms, and the kingdoms' inhabitants'; and in allowing those in the isles to leave if they so wished, in threatening punishment of disturbers of the peace, and in offering amnesty towards those who had trespassed under the previous regime, the treaty claimed to be on behalf of, and in the interests of, all

51 *Chron. Bower*, v, pp. 302–05.

the people of both kingdoms. The tenet that government must be exercised in the pursuit of truth, peace, law and unity is also expressed within the treaty. King Magnus was said to have participated in the agreement because he was 'a friend of peace and a fosterer of justice', and out of 'reverence for God and for love and diligent observance and cherishing of peace, the expulsion of danger to friends, and the avoidance of slaughter of men'. In turn, Alexander was described as 'a devotee of truth, and lover of peace and concord', who took part 'for good peace, and so that harassments and troubles may be averted'; and of course, the 'most free justice' enjoyed by the Scots would henceforth apply to all the inhabitants of the ceded lands, 'as well lesser as greater'. Recognising the ultimate superiority of God (alone), for the greater security of the treaty's terms, both kings subjected themselves to papal sanction (specifically including excommunication) if they failed to uphold it. Their authority was derived from God, a fact which they explicitly accepted in the acknowledgement of the power of his delegate on earth to sanction them should they fail in their duties to uphold peace and justice.

Explicit reference to the king governing with, and for, his subjects is not unusual: for example, the preamble to the 1277 confirmation of the lands and privileges of Dunfermline abbey states that the confirmation is given by royal authority, with the consent of the bishops, earls and barons, and with the agreement of the clergy and people of the kingdom.[52] The marriage treaty of 1281 stated that Alexander acted with the consent not only of his daughter and son, but also of his whole council. Other such references to government by counsel of the community, and in the interests of the realm as a whole, are commonplace: in theory at least, government was exercised in the interests of all.

The defence of the common weal was demonstrated also in the care exercised in ensuring stable succession. The deficiency of government under a weak king and divided community had been evident in Alexander's minority: his duty to the kingdom, in the interests of unity, stability, peace and justice, was to provide for firm rule after his death. That Margaret and all three of their children predeceased him was thus a national as well as a personal tragedy. There is no way of knowing anything of the personal relationship which may have developed between Alexander and Yolande de Dreux, but, irrespective, the marriage itself was a fulfilment of his royal duty.

In general, the adult reign of Alexander III saw the maintenance of generally amicable relations with England and with Scotland's other trading partners. Naturally, there were from time to time issues which caused conflict between

---

52 *RRS*, iv pt. 1, no. 102: . . . *ego Alexander Dei gratia rex Scottorum filius Alexander illustris regis Scottorum auctoritate regia. ac potestate episcoporum comitum. baronumque regni mei consensu atque testimonio. clero ettiam adquiescente et populo . . .*

the inhabitants of the kingdoms, but through those episodes it is possible to see the effective use of 'law and custom' to defuse tension and to maintain the peaceful relationship in the interests of all.[53] The holding of parliaments, the administration of justice and the effective conduct of government further promote the idea that Alexander did attempt to live up to the expectations of the governed. The conduct and documentation of Alexander III's reign do assert that his government was founded upon awareness of his duties and responsibilities, and largely achieved the prosperous and peaceful results which were consistent with contemporary theories of good kingly rule.

From a twenty-first century viewpoint, the well-known inequalities of medieval society, in which the gap between rich and poor was almost immeasurable, inevitably create a degree of cynicism about the extent to which government in this period was conducted in the interests of all. The judgement, however, has to be made from within the context of the social framework of the period, and of the limitations imposed by technological, communicative and administrative systems. The concept of government was necessarily more limited than in modern times and was far less pervasive in the daily lives of individuals. That is not to say that there were no attempts to address specific issues – the legislation cited in Chapter 2, attempting to control the extent to which land was turned over to sheep rather than being used for arable production, provides an example – but the solutions were seen as being in the general interests of the realm, and consequently for the common weal. What might be termed good government, therefore, was use of a broad brush, aimed at safeguarding and benefitting all of the kingdom's communities within their own social situations. To that extent, it is justifiable to claim that Alexander III's administration did live up to the theoretical demands of medieval government.

'A just king makes rich the earth, but the miser destroys it.' If there was an element of sacral kingship[54] in Aquinas's philosophy and in the attitude of medieval writers towards the Scottish crown, there was also an entirely pragmatic

53 See, e.g., *CDS*, ii, no. 183, where a dispute over possession of a stolen horse was to be settled 'according to the law of the march of Scotland'; *Calendar of the Close Rolls of the Reign of Henry III, 1264–1268*, pp. 88–89, where justice was to be done to Scottish merchants whose ships and goods had been impounded at Great Yarmouth; *CDS*, i, no. 2337, where the two crowns appear to be cooperating in the attempt to restore the ship and cargo of a burgess of Berwick, which had been stolen by his servants, who were then 'wandering about as vagabonds and fugitives on the sea'; *CDS*, ii, no. 59, which shows Alexander using the 'laws and customs of his own realm' to bring to justice 'sea-robbers' said to have taken refuge in Scotland.

54 Sacral kingship: the concept that through the position of the king as the representative of God, the good king brought about divinely instigated benefits, while the bad king brought divine retribution in the form of ruin; prosperity or lack of it was thus a theological, rather than a purely economic, phenomenon. The bad king might, for example, be the cause of adverse weather, the failure of crops, etc.

implication: good rule, the pursuit of peace and justice, created the right environment for successful trade and thus for both national and individual prosperity. Much of Alexander III's subsequent reputation has been built upon the grandiose claims of Bower and others that he was successful in building an economic prosperity which was unparalleled, before or since. The 'Golden Age of Alexander III' (expanded by some historians to become a feature of the entire thirteenth century) is a historiographical concept which has survived across centuries. To what extent is it possible to support the general impression of Alexander as a successful king in terms of judicial and administrative activity and of contemporary political theory with an assessment of his economic performance?

The national economy was undoubtedly much simpler than its modern equivalent: the provision of services such as health and education were unheard of as state responsibilities. The very incomplete surviving accounts of the sheriffs suggest that the royal coffers profited quite effectively from the fruits of rents paid for crown lands, trade, customs, services and justice.[55] That income was balanced by the expenditures on household and other expenses of the king and his officials in the localities, as well as outlays on repair and maintenance of royal properties, the payments of (for example) gifts and allowances to the religious houses, salaries and other allowances to royal servants. The maintenance of the king's household and status, however, although a significant element of the crown's costs, was not the only expense for which the king, as the embodiment of the state, needed money. As in the case of the conflict with Norway, defence of the realm entailed considerable expense, including fortifications and the expense of maintaining and equipping large bodies of fighting men. The machinery of justice and administration was also expensive; each royal official, from the chancellor to the gardener, required his fee. (The chancellor's annual fee in 1288 was £100, a sizeable sum; the gardener at Forfar was paid £5 in 1264. The chancellor must have seemed unimaginably wealthy to the gardener: the income relationship (without considering the chancellor's additional revenue gained from his estates and other income) of 1:20 compares, in 2017, to an equivalent relationship of roughly 1:7 between an average gardener wage and the UK Chancellor of the Exchequer's salary.[56]) A sizeable element of royal income came also from wardships; when estates were inherited by minors, for example, or were escheated to the crown through misdemeanour, their wardships, worth significant amounts of money, fell to the crown; fees were also payable to the crown for marriages, inheritance fees and the like. When the

---

55 *ER*, i, pp. 1–34.

56 *ER*, i, pp. 46, 8; http://www.bbc.co.uk/newsbeat/article/31970289/the-uks-highest-paid-politicians-who-gets-what; https://www.totaljobs.com/salary-checker/average-gardener-salary.

countess of Carrick (the widow of earl Adam, who died on crusade in 1270), married Robert Bruce (son of the lord of Annandale) without royal consent a year or two later, her lands and castle of Turnberry were taken into royal custody until she was pardoned the offence.[57] Similarly, the secular fruits of vacant bishoprics were the property of the crown, and, with a rare trace of criticism, Bower suggested that Alexander deliberately prolonged such vacancies:

> In the following year [1271] five bishoprics were vacant at the one time. These were the bishoprics of Glasgow, Brechin, Aberdeen, Caithness and St Andrews. The king held them all in his own hand, and deliberately [in practice] took an annual levy from the bishops-elect of those bishoprics, because [also at that time] the apostolic see was vacant on account of dissension amongst the cardinals.[58]

The nature of the surviving accounts (known only through later, abbreviated copies) is not sufficient to offer a complete picture of the financial affairs of the localities, but, although it is clear that the use of cash was gaining ground, Scotland's rural economy was still essentially subsistence in nature; that a high proportion of the income was paid in kind emphasises the fact. Oats was the most commonly produced crop, with barley and 'fodder' (hay) also appearing; livestock included pigs, sheep, cattle and poultry. Malt was commonly produced from both wheat and barley; the cattle were kept for their hides, which were of ubiquitous use (and were an export item), for dairy produce and (for those who could afford it) for the dinner table. Sheep, kept primarily on the great lowland estates of the religious houses for wool production and export, were less common than pigs, which provided by far the most common meat for human consumption. All of this produce had cash value for accounting purposes, and doubtless much of it found its way to the burgh marketplace. In an unusually full account for 1263–64, the sheriff of Forfar accounted for income from cows, pigs, poultry, cheese, eels, malt, barley-flour and fodder; but much of this produce appeared also on the other side of the equation, *expense in servicio regis* – expended in the service of the king. Accounted in this way, the produce was paid for, but nonetheless, where the king held court in a royal residence, the demands on the local community could be considerable.[59]

---

57 *Chron. Fordun*, i, pp. 304 (trans. ii, pp. 299–300). *Gesta Annalia* misidentifies her as Adam's daughter; she was his widow, through whose right he gained the title of earl, which was later held by Bruce. The case was a *cause célèbre*, since she was said to have detained him against his will, and effectively forced the marriage. One of their sons was the future King Robert I.

58 *Chron. Bower*, v, pp. 380–81 & n., p. 486.

59 *ER*, i, pp. 6–9.

Although there is no doubt that the burghs were increasingly being used as conduits through which goods – for both local consumption and export – could be channelled in order to raise income for the crown, there is little direct evidence of Alexander III's own activity in this area: he seems not to have initiated any new burghs, and record evidence of his direct support or encouragement of the burghs' economic activity is very sparse. He did grant an annual fair to the burghs of Ayr and Aberdeen; he confirmed the gift by kings William and Alexander II to the burgesses of Inverkeithing of toll and custom on all goods, moving by land or on water, between the rivers Leven and Devon, and he increased their rights and liberties to match those of the burgesses of Perth and Aberdeen; 'for the improvement of the burgh' (*ad melioracionem burgi*) he granted the burgesses of Elgin the right to have a merchant guild, as in other burghs; and Kinghorn was granted a weekly market.[60] The most detailed royal act relating to a burgh is the confirmation, given very close to the end of the reign, of the rights and privileges of the burgh of Lanark. Lanark had been founded as a burgh in the twelfth century, but in November 1285 Alexander III confirmed it in all of the customary burghal rights and privileges: no one except the burgesses were to pursue trade in wool, hides or other goods, or to carry on commerce (and specifically the making of cloth); anyone (including foreign merchants) purchasing goods within the sheriffdom from anyone other than the burgesses was to be seized and their goods held; the burgesses were to hold their accustomed common land, and those bringing wood or timber for the maintenance of the burgh were to be able to pass in and out without hindrance.[61] Whether this confirmation (which probably added little to the existing rights and privileges of the burgh) was connected to a campaign of expansion of its activities cannot be said with certainty; nonetheless, it serves to illustrate the advantage that the burghs held in commercial activity, and thus the level of central control which was exerted through the burghs over the economic activity of the kingdom as a whole. If these examples tend to suggest that Alexander did indeed make significant effort to encourage the prosperity of the burghs, that impression has to be tempered by the reminder that these acts constitute only half a dozen out of over 300 surviving royal acts of the reign and by the comparison with the number of grants, totalling over 60, which were given to religious houses. Around half of the latter were confirmations of grants given by other lay donors (including the king's predecessors), but the remainder, representing new grants to over 20 religious establishments, seem to demonstrate a commitment to the church which was considerably greater than that to

60 *RRS*, iv pt. 1, nos. 31, 44, 69, 87, 159.
61 *RRS*, iv pt. 1, no. 163.

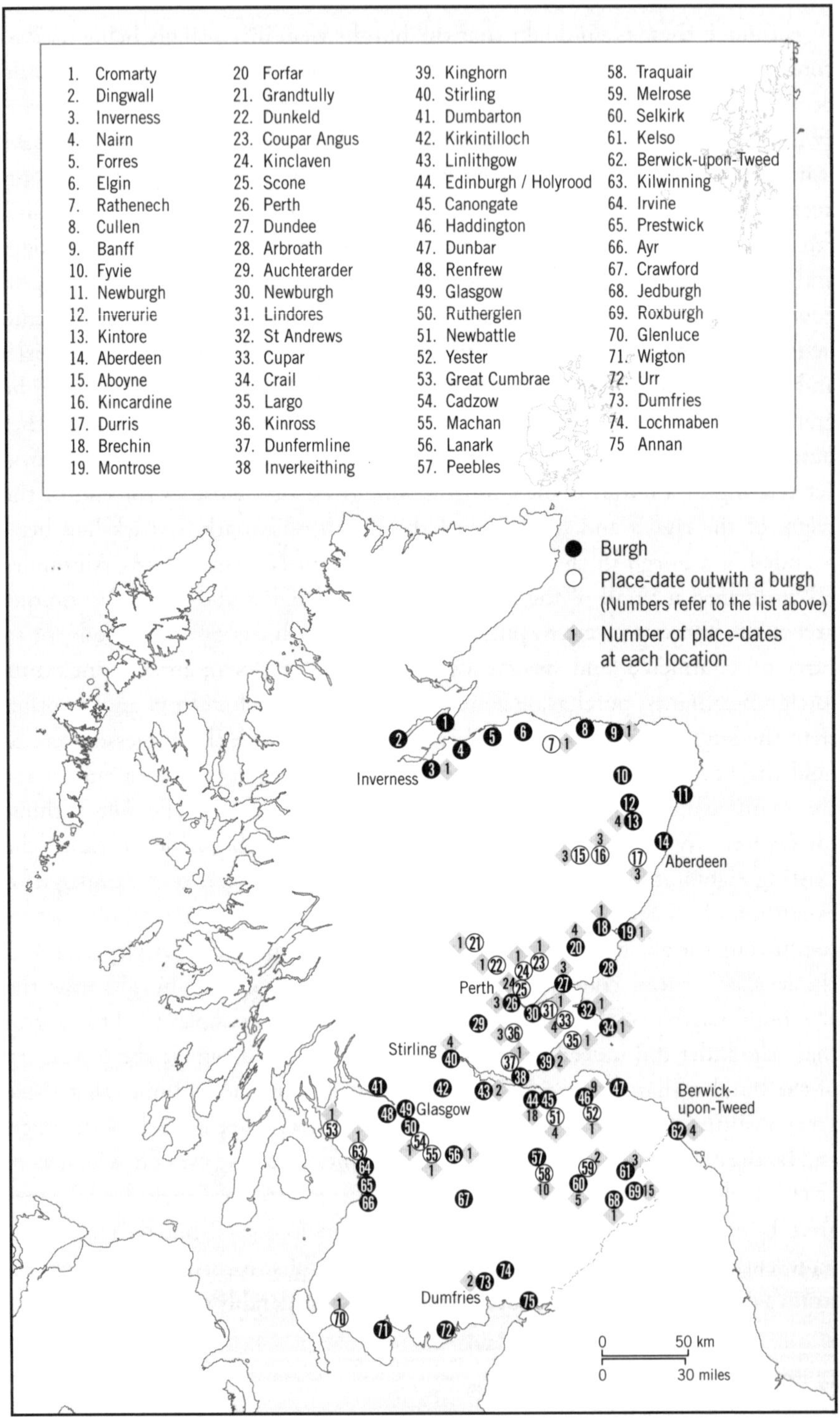
1. Cromarty
2. Dingwall
3. Inverness
4. Nairn
5. Forres
6. Elgin
7. Rathenech
8. Cullen
9. Banff
10. Fyvie
11. Newburgh
12. Inverurie
13. Kintore
14. Aberdeen
15. Aboyne
16. Kincardine
17. Durris
18. Brechin
19. Montrose
20 Forfar
21. Grandtully
22. Dunkeld
23. Coupar Angus
24. Kinclaven
25. Scone
26. Perth
27. Dundee
28. Arbroath
29. Auchterarder
30. Newburgh
31. Lindores
32. St Andrews
33. Cupar
34. Crail
35. Largo
36. Kinross
37. Dunfermline
38 Inverkeithing
39. Kinghorn
40. Stirling
41. Dumbarton
42. Kirkintilloch
43. Linlithgow
44. Edinburgh / Holyrood
45. Canongate
46. Haddington
47. Dunbar
48. Renfrew
49. Glasgow
50. Rutherglen
51. Newbattle
52. Yester
53. Great Cumbrae
54. Cadzow
55. Machan
56. Lanark
57. Peebles
58. Traquair
59. Melrose
60. Selkirk
61. Kelso
62. Berwick-upon-Tweed
63. Kilwinning
64. Irvine
65. Prestwick
66. Ayr
67. Crawford
68. Jedburgh
69. Roxburgh
70. Glenluce
71. Wigton
72. Urr
73. Dumfries
74. Lochmaben
75 Annan
Burgh
Place-date outwith a burgh
(Numbers refer to the list above)
Number of place-dates at each location
Inverness
Aberdeen
Perth
Stirling
Glasgow
Berwick-upon-Tweed
Dumfries
0 50 km
0 30 miles

the burghs. Further, some of these religious grants included payments out of burgh revenues: for example, a gift of the large sum of 100s. per annum to a priest in the cathedral of Glasgow for masses to be said for the souls of Alexander and his ancestors and heirs, was to be paid out of the income of the burgh of Rutherglen;[62] the abbey of Lindores was given the town of Newburgh with burghal rights; the abbey of Melrose held gifts which were to be paid out of burgh fermes; the Dominicans in Elgin, Perth, Inverness, Ayr and Aberdeen all received income from their burghs; and the hospital at Soutra, Kelso abbey and the Knights Hospitaller received grants out of the revenues of Traquair, Perth, Rutherglen and other burghs.[63] The list is not comprehensive. If Alexander's support for burghal prosperity might therefore be regarded as somewhat minimal, it may have been due less to lack of interest than to the fact that the burghs were doing well enough not to need additional royal investment: if the economy was buoyant, trade would come to and through the burghs without additional royal encouragement.

The climate, generally recognised to have been relatively warm throughout most of the thirteenth century, may have been a significant factor in the development of the Scottish economy. A recent study of evidence for summer temperatures in the Cairngorms, extracted from tree-ring data of 'subfossil' wood preserved in lochs, suggests (although with caveats regarding the uncertainty of the earliest data) that the 1280s were a significantly warm decade, 'suggesting the possibility of previous warmer conditions during the late Medieval'. Very tentatively, it is suggested that three out of the five warmest

62 *RRS*, iv pt. 1, no. 148.

63 See, e.g., *RRS*, iv pt. 1, nos. 48, 58, 57, 64, 71, 91, 149, 154, 234, 323, 329; see also *ER*, i, p. lviii–lix for further comment on the income granted to the church.

Map 3. Burghs in the mid thirteenth century, with place-dates for the *acta* of Alexander III. The list of burghs, including those whose privileges were granted by the king as well as by other lords, follows that given by A.A.M. Duncan, 'Burghs in Existence by 1300', *Atlas of Scottish History to 1707*, ed. Peter G.B. McNeill and Hector L. MacQueen (Edinburgh, 1996), p. 198. The place-dates of royal *acta* follow the identifications made by N.H. Reid in *Atlas of Scottish History*, p. 163, with additional and corrective information gained from *RRS*, iv pt. 1. (Non-extant *acta* whose places of issue are known are included here, but were excluded from the map in both the *Atlas* and *RRS*, iv pt. 1. Acts dated outwith Scotland are excluded.) Of the 169 acts noted here, 93 were issued in burghs; but the number of burghs involved (22) is almost identical to the number of non-burgh sites (21). The area frequented by the king is generally equivalent to the area populated by burghs, revealing the inter-relationship of economic and administrative activity, but clearly the burghs did not always provide accommodation fit for a king. Many (although not all) of the extra-burghal sites are religious houses. The relative paucity of place-dates in western and northern areas of the kingdom is also illustrative of the largely settled nature of Alexander III's reign, in which there were few occasions on which military activity required the king's presence outwith his usual ambit.

summers between 1200 and 2010 were 1282, 1284 and 1285.[64] Evidence of climatic clemency, however, can be overstated. Scotland's position makes it prone to wide fluctuations in both weather and climate. The effect of the Gulf Stream makes it warmer than many places at such a northerly latitude, but it also lies in a zone where warm and cold air masses collide, with consequent instability and high rainfall. Scotland exists 'on the edge of warm and cold, of rainfall and drought, of storminess and calm conditions'.[65] Even if Scotland was warmer in the thirteenth century than it had been a couple of centuries earlier, the weather was undeniably turbulent. There seems to have been a large volcanic eruption (evidenced by spikes in volcanic sulphates occurring in ice cores from both Greenland and Antarctica) towards the end of the 1250s, and it is likely that the climate cooled and became more unpredictable in its aftermath.[66] In 1260, for instance, Bower tells us that

> there was a great food shortage in parts of Scotland, so much so that a boll of flour was being sold for four shillings. Dreadful claps of thunder were heard, and there were terrifying flashes of lightning which burned up men in the fields and animals far and wide, and destroyed crops and trees in several places by burning them up. A wet autumn choked the harvest [with weeds]. After the autumn, gales of wind wrecked houses and caused a vast amount of destruction.[67]

This was not an isolated instance. He tells us of another 'great famine caused by the harvest being ruined' in 1261 or 1262; in 1267 'worms and caterpillars destroyed the vegetable crop like locusts throughout almost the whole of England and Scotland', and a sudden violent storm in October (such as 'had not been seen since the time of Noah') resulted in massive coastal flooding 'and caused a great deal of damage in many places, but especially between the rivers Tay and Tweed'. The following winter was 'very harsh, with continual whirlwinds of hail, snows and rain'; in 1268 'the spring was windy and rainy; and the summer was likewise windy, cold and rainy', causing high mortality among deer, ponies, 'but most of all sheep'. The next winter was no better, so harsh that 'nobody could plough or work the land', and the whole of 1270

64 M. Rydval, N.J. Loader, B.E. Gunnarson *et al.*, 'Reconstructing 800 Years of Summer Temperatures in Scotland from Tree Rings', *Climate Dynamics*, 49 (2017), pp. 2951–74 (https://doi.org/10.1007/s00382-016-3478-8). I am grateful to Dr Rob Wilson, one of the co-authors of this paper, for advice on this issue.

65 Alastair Dawson, *So Foul and Fair a Day: A History of Scotland's Weather and Climate* (Edinburgh, 2009), p. 6.

66 Dawson, *So Foul and Fair a Day*, pp. 74, 99–101.

67 *Chron. Bower*, v, pp. 324–25.

was characterised by 'a great dearth and much rain'. 1272 seems to have been particularly bad:

> In the year 1272 there was a great lack of productivity on the land and unfruitfulness at sea, as well as turbulence of the air, as a result of which many people fell ill and many animals died. On the Saturday of Epiphany week [8th January] about midnight a strong north wind, suddenly rushing down and bringing hail, overturned houses, smothered those sleeping within and flattened high buildings. And fire arising from the vehemence of the storm burnt the church of Arbroath and many others. A great famine hit France, England, Scotland and many areas, for the cattle mostly died, the crops failed, and the poor died of their poverty. Treasure was being transported to the Holy Land and to Rome by pilgrims and clerics, and the common people were in great danger.[68]

The *Lanercost Chronicle* reports similar events: appalling weather in 1256 caused famine in 1257, and in 1275 'there was a universal sickness throughout the whole stock of sheep in England'.[69] The love of medieval writers for portents has already been cited, and comets and other omens – including unusual weather – appeared with marked regularity. However, the detail which some of these accounts provide of the effects of these weather events suggests that many of them were faithfully reported as incidents of importance, even if the writers were unable to identify what they meant in terms of their spiritual worldview.[70] If Bower, for instance, had deliberately inserted such events in order to presage the calamitous end of the king's reign, he would not have entered them so frequently between 1260 and 1272, and then ceased. Climatic instability is supported by other sources: the *Chronicle of Guisborough*, for example, also reports famine throughout England in 1257–58, and an appalling rainstorm at Canterbury in 1271.[71] There is evidence that sea-ice around Iceland and Greenland, often an indicator of conditions further south, was very extensive in the 1270s.[72] Such periods of

68 *Chron. Bower*, v, pp. 334–35, 358–61, 368–73, 384–87. The storm of 1272 was probably also responsible for the partial collapse of the as yet incomplete nave of St Andrews Cathedral (*Chron. Bower*, iii, pp. 398–99).
69 *Chron. Lanercost*, pp. 64–65, 97.
70 Bower himself comments on the weather as portentous when, in relation to the events he described in 1260, he stated 'Thus many portents appeared in that year' (v, pp. 324–25). The comment should not be taken, however, as an indication that the disastrous weather was a portentous invention, inserted to offer retrospective warning of subsequent events.
71 *Chron. Guisborough*, pp. 184, 212.
72 Dawson, *So Foul and Fair a Day*, p. 100.

extreme, which continued into the 1280s, were unfavourable for agriculture, and famine was not uncommon. So if in general terms the climate had been mild for some decades, it does seem that the later thirteenth century was witnessing the end of the warm period, with, as in the present, changing weather patterns and unusually severe one-off events being symptomatic of developing longer-term change. It has been suggested that the conditions which had fostered the expansion of Scotland's upland cultivation were in fact deteriorating between 1250 and 1300, during which period the effective climatic limit of cultivation in the Lammermuirs had fallen by some 50m.[73] Even if individual events caused short-term hardship, it would take time for such gradual deterioration to have a fundamental effect on the amount or quality of, for instance, exportable wool. Such evidence has nonetheless generally been assumed to indicate that the failure of the Scottish economy in the fourteenth century cannot be blamed entirely on the wars of independence and governmental instability.

Caution is required, however, in interpreting such evidence. Recent studies in the Glen Affric area, using pollen analysis, demonstrate that cultivation (or lack of it) in upland areas did not necessarily correlate with periods of what we would nowadays regard as appropriate climatic conditions. It may therefore be an oversimplification to suggest that climate change is the only, or even the primary, cause for changes in land use.[74] The outstanding population and economic growth of the thirteenth century had created an environment in which agricultural output had necessarily increased and was inevitably turning towards a model less predominantly subsistence, and more heavily commercial. Population growth increased pressure on land, and the resulting social, economic and probably technological pressures, as new techniques, such as the transhumance evidenced in the Lammermuirs and other upland areas, were developed, may have been as much a factor in the increased cultivation of marginal land as the relatively warm (but, it seems, unstable) climate.[75] If climate may, therefore, be assumed to be less of an influence than has sometimes been claimed in

---

73 M.L. Parry, 'Secular Climatic Change and Marginal Agriculture', *Transactions of the Institute of British Geographers*, 64 (1975), pp. 1–13.

74 Althea L. Davies, 'Upland Agriculture and Environmental Risk: A New Model of Upland Land-Use Based on High Spatial-Resolution Palynological Data from West Affric, NW Scotland', *Journal of Archaeological Science*, 34 (2007) pp. 2053–63. I am grateful to Dr Davies for her advice, and for directing me to this paper.

75 See R.A. Dodgshon, 'Medieval Settlement and Colonisation', in M.L. Parry and T.R. Slater (eds), *The Making of the Scottish Countryside* (London 1980), pp. 45–68, at pp. 48–49, where it is suggested that the earlier twelfth-century royal exhortations to cultivate are the consequence of a food supply issue (because of rising population and other social factors), rather than of land shortage.

the expansion of Scottish agriculture and trade in the thirteenth century, it follows that it may also have been less influential in its later decline, and that those who place the lion's share of the blame for the 'utter debasement' of the kingdom's economy on the English aggression of 1296 onwards,[76] may have a strong case.

Even despite the paucity of Scottish economic data for this period, it is very easy to see that the peaceful pursuit of foreign trade was a major concern of government. Bower claimed that Alexander III discouraged Scottish merchants from exporting goods on the grounds that merchandise was in too short supply to risk its loss at sea; as a result, foreign merchants came to Scotland bringing goods with them, and the economy boomed.[77] The presence of a Scottish merchant community in Bruges disproves Bower's tale: and that Alexander III levied customs on some exports as well as imports demonstrates that he was able to see the benefit of the movement of goods in both directions.[78] There are many references in the records to Scottish merchants in England or elsewhere, and to foreign merchants coming to Scotland. Naturally enough, it was often when something went wrong that the merchants became the subject of record. Not infrequently it is the judicial or diplomatic settlement of acts of piracy, wrongful impounding of goods, unjust imposition of taxes and duties, or disputed and unpaid accounts which reveals the activities of merchant traders to the historian. Had John Mason not been plying the trade in Bordeaux wine, he would not have had the disputed account which brought him to our attention. Similarly, David Taylor and Adam Wales of Berwick, whose cargo, freighted on two Flemish ships, had been impounded at Great Yarmouth during the English civil war of 1264–65, were obviously engaged in trade with Flanders, and there is little doubt that among their 'diverse merchandise' was Scottish wool on its way to the lucrative Flemish markets. Great Yarmouth was at the centre of controversy again in 1273, when Thomas Ker, John of Aberdeen and Walter de la Bothe, Aberdeen merchants, complained that their ship had been attacked at sea near that port by John Adrian of Winchelsea. Fortunately, the complainants listed the cargo which had been stolen from them: wool, salmon, oak and lamb-skins, as well as ox- and deer-hides.[79] In 1276 another Scottish pair of Berwick merchants, Philip Ridale and Patrick Scot somewhat naively accepted the offer of help from one Adam of Arderne when their ship, loaded with wool and other merchandise, was driven ashore on its way to Dieppe. The unscrupulous Adam seems to have helped himself to what he

76 Donnelly, 'Berwick Shipping Trade', p. 3.
77 *Chron. Bower*, v, pp. 424–25.
78 See above, pp. 63–64, nn. 71, 72.
79 *CDS*, ii, no. 9.

wanted and left the rest unguarded on the ship, which was then plundered by locals.[80] Seagoing trade was not limited to the prosperous east-coast burghs: there is record of Alexander soliciting Edward I's help to have a ship freed which belonged to Alexander mac Dubhgaill of Argyll, and which had been detained on suspicion of piracy when it called in to Bristol.[81]

Trade routes across the North Sea to Scandinavia, although apparently geographically obvious, were perhaps less busy in this period than might be assumed: Scotland and Norway (the closest overseas neighbour) were too similar in their agricultural production, and in their need to import manufactured goods, for the principle of 'complementary markets' to encourage regular trade.[82] Direct Scottish–Norwegian trade probably did not become economically significant until the growth of the Norwegian timber industry in the fifteenth century. Nonetheless, when Henry III wrote to King Magnus Hákonsson in June 1264 to offer condolences for the death of his father,[83] his letter was careful to speak of peace between the realms as much in terms of mercantile affairs as military. Indeed, the trading benefits of peace were made very clear: Henry wished that merchants of the two nations could come and go freely, on condition that peace was achieved between Magnus and Alexander III. Unsettled relations between two nations not only disrupted normal trading activities between them, but made the already perilous sea crossings yet more hazardous for merchants of other nations as well. The increasing dominance of German merchants in the Baltic and Scandinavian trade probably meant that their ships called into Scottish ports on their journeys to and from England: that there is little evidence for direct trade between Scotland and Scandinavia does not negate the possibility that merchants of other countries acted as intermediaries.[84] Henry's letter and the clause in the treaty of Perth relating to the salvage of ships and cargoes in Scottish waters is certainly evidence that trade across the North Sea, whoever owned the ships and wherever their destination, was valued, and should not be inhibited in the long term either by the recent conflict or by the means of its resolution.

80 *CDS*, ii, no. 74.

81 *RRS*, iv pt. 1, nos. 92, 278.

82 David Ditchburn, 'A Note on Scandinavian Trade with Scotland in the Later Middle Ages', in Grant G. Simpson (ed.), *Scotland and Scandinavia, 800–1800* (Edinburgh, 1990), pp. 73–89, where it is pointed out that Norwegian wrecks off Scotland could indicate voyages past Scotland en route to Dublin, as well as direct trade with Scotland.

83 *CDS*, i, no. 2355.

84 David Ditchburn, 'Scandinavian Trade with Scotland', pp. 75–76; a small amount of thirteenth-century Scottish pottery has been found in excavations in Bergen, but not enough to indicate regular direct commerce (p. 74).

If Scandinavia was not yet a major trading partner, the same cannot be said of other traditional haunts of the Scottish merchant in France, the Netherlands and the Baltic, which were being actively worked in this period. The famous invitation by William Wallace to the merchants of Lübeck and Hamburg (and no doubt to other trading partners) to resume their trade with Scotland, newly freed (if only temporarily) from English domination in 1297, is certainly evidence not only of the habitual presence of German merchants in Scotland, but also of the fact that the trade had been disrupted, if not completely obliterated, by the outbreak of war.[85] A recent study of the fourteenth-century Berwick shipping trade suggests that the background was a context of 'considerable economic growth' throughout the thirteenth century.[86] Scotland's thirteenth-century economic records are paltry, but using English and papal taxation records, the same study has demonstrated that the period following 1296 (rather than 1286) saw a catastrophic downturn in Scottish economic fortunes. Papal records show that at its best (particularly in the diocese of St Andrews, which had its economic heartland in the fertile Lothians) the thirteenth-century Scottish church was as wealthy, or wealthier, than most of the English church.[87] The traditional view of Scotland, formed from many generations of fundamentally English-focused historiography, is of a country on the margins of European trade, which was inevitably poorer than its southern neighbour. While its economy (as one would expect with a population perhaps one-quarter or one-fifth that of England's[88]) was undoubtedly more limited in scale, it nonetheless seems, before the outbreak of war, to have been buoyant. For example, the suggestion that in the mid fourteenth-century Berwick (by then in English hands) was the fifth-busiest customs port in the British Isles, makes it likely that it may have been comparatively wealthier in the thirteenth century, before Scotland's share of trade and custom declined.[89]

It is impossible to separate the local agrarian economy from the development of overseas trade, and thus of its bedfellow, an increasingly monetised economy; the agricultural output, particularly of wool and hides, was the mainstay of the

---

85 J. Stevenson (ed.), *Documents Illustrative of Sir William Wallace, his Life and Times* (Maitland Club, 1841), p. 159; Barrow, *Robert Bruce*, pp. 14–15, points out that earlier in 1297 Lübeck merchants were said to owe money for customs on exports of wool and hides from Dundee; this may be evidence that the trade had not stopped completely in the interim period.
86 Donnelly, 'Berwick Shipping Trade', p. 2.
87 See also Bruce M.S. Campbell, 'Benchmarking Medieval Economic Development: England, Wales, Scotland and Ireland, c.1290', *Economic History Review*, 61 (2008), pp. 896–945: 'England may have had by far the greater number of parishes, but Scottish parishes were on average wealthier' (p. 902). Some of Campbell's assumptions are questionable, but his overall conclusions on the relative prosperity of the four countries are revealing and persuasive.
88 Campbell, 'Benchmarking Medieval Economic Development', pp. 928–30.
89 Donnelly, 'Berwick Shipping Trade', p. 8.

trading economy. As commercial trade increased, centred on the growing burghs, the demand for commercially available grain (much of which came from the Baltic kingdoms) and for other food products to supply the urban populations and to alleviate shortages in bad-harvest years, also grew.[90] The scale of Scottish export of wool, woolfells and hides was considerable; the imports from, particularly, England, Flanders and the Baltic of manufactured goods and grain to supply the Scottish deficiency in, for example, wheat, were thus made possible by the commercial undertaking of large-scale animal husbandry.[91] Even papal taxation, while resisted, could have the effect of stimulating trade, since the Italian merchants who represented the papacy sent agents to Scotland whose activities encouraged increasing local participation in 'a web of international trade and finance'. 'Where external taxation threatened to withdraw silver, primary exports could balance the payments with trade', and of course as trade increased it offered the opportunity to bolster royal coffers through the imposition of customs duties.[92] There is some evidence that Alexander III did indeed make use of this opportunity, although the very scant nature of it – the merest references in the Scottish archival inventories of 1292 and 1296 – has led to dispute regarding its interpretation.[93]

The question of money supply is a vital element of the economy in the context of thirteenth-century Europe. Scotland's gradual shift from a subsistence and barter economy to a cash economy was an inevitable feature of the kingdom's increasing involvement in external trade, and was a development being experienced by almost all the states of Europe. As previously noted, although Scotland successfully participated in overseas trade, much of the crown's income was still paid in kind, symbolic of the fact that for much of the century the penetration of the money economy into some areas of the kingdom was at best superficial. However, it is misleading to caricature Scotland as a cash-starved economy, 'a poor land with a scanty coinage circulating almost entirely in burgh markets'.[94] It has been argued that merchant prosperity was encouraged by low levels of customs in the thirteenth century, a state of affairs doubtless made possible by

90 See Nils Hybel, 'The Grain Trade in Northern Europe Before 1350', *Economic History Review* 55 (2002), pp. 219–47. There is relatively little evidence of direct export of Baltic grain to Scotland, but it was certainly carried there via other supply points, especially in England.

91 Donnelly, 'Berwick Shipping Trade', p. 3.

92 Donnelly, 'Berwick Shipping Trade', p. 4; see also, J. Donnelly, 'Thomas of Coldingham, Merchant and Burgess of Berwick upon Tweed (died 1316)', *Scottish Historical Review* 59 (1980), pp. 105–25, where (p. 105) the actions of the foreign papal collectors as wool merchants are discussed.

93 Donnelly, 'Berwick Shipping Trade', p. 6 and discussion in n.; the references from the inventories are in *APS*, i, pp. 114, 118 (and see facsimile, facing p. 113).

94 William W. Scott, 'The Use of Money in Scotland, 1124–1230', *Scottish Historical Review*, 58 (1979), pp. 105–31, at p. 105.

the relative peace and stability of the kingdom in that period. The rise of a merchant class – based exclusively in, and trading from, the burghs – both encouraged and depended on the use and availability of cash. Credit was known, and some of the wealthier merchant houses of Florence and Venice (among others) acted as bankers for the papacy and for kings; but, especially when pursued by smaller players, and in the context of a society in which the banking system was at best in its infancy, trade necessarily remained a predominantly cash-led activity. Even in the reign of Alexander II cash was not uncommon in areas beyond the burghs, as evidenced by cash grants to religious houses, and the use of cash for payment of secular rents and judicial fees, for instance.[95] When Alexander III negotiated the dowry payments for his daughter and his son, the documentation makes it clear that most, if not all, of the sums were expected to be paid in cash. It seems very probable that one of the reasons why Alexander was so reluctant to allow the sums gathered by the various papal collectors to leave the country, quite apart from the issues of sovereignty raised by their allocation to English activities, was because the export of such large amounts of cash, with no trading benefit in return, would have a significantly adverse effect on the nation's balance of payments. Bower's stricture, quoted above, regarding the export of 'treasure' during a period of famine, to the great detriment of the common people, reminds us of the logic behind the fact that a key economic objective of Alexander's government was to encourage the import of money into the kingdom, and to attempt to limit its export. In this, there seems to have been considerable success: 'It is perfectly clear that money supply in Scotland grew impressively in the thirteenth century, especially during the reign of Alexander III.'[96] It has been estimated that Scottish monetary growth over Alexander III's reign may have reached 300 per cent, in contrast with a probable figure of about 55 per cent in England: 'Scotland was earning silver at a very much faster rate than England', doubtless as a result largely of the burgeoning wool trade, which seems to have peaked at the end of the thirteenth century.[97] The figure of 300 per cent is astonishing, however, and cannot be accounted for entirely by successful external trading activity. Although much higher than in previous reigns, and apparently continuing to increase during Alexander III's reign, the output from Scottish mints seems still to have been relatively low, and it is incontrovertible that a great deal of English and other

95 Scott, 'The Use of Money in Scotland', *passim*.
96 Mayhew, 'A Silver Age', p. 61.
97 Mayhew ('A Silver Age', pp. 62–63) discusses possible causes for inaccuracy in the growth rates, based on mint output figures and the evidence of coin hoards: nonetheless, even if the 300 per cent figure is a considerable overestimate, the growth remains, according to Mayhew, 'outstanding'.

foreign coin was in circulation in Scotland. The increase in coin was therefore the result both of a buoyant economy and of a deliberate policy of monetisation, actively promoted by government, even during the minority.

As the money economy accelerated, the increase in cultivable land which the economic upturn demanded (and which, according to one model at least, may have been facilitated by the climate) was inevitably exploited in order to achieve greater production, both for local trade and for export. The earlier kings' strictures regarding the need to maintain land in arable production has already been noted, a reminder that Scotland's economy was indeed still largely agrarian and subsistence. If the great religious houses, the magnatial class and the royal coffers saw increasing wealth through the production of wool and other exportable goods, much of the population would have benefitted little from it: 'the arithmetic of prices and wages' was barely favourable to the mid thirteenth-century peasant, when compared to later, post-plague days. Increasing population meant more mouths to feed; an increase in cultivated land (even with rising population) may have entailed longer hours in the fields; the effect of a buoyant market is to increase prices, and, with an increasing working population, to reduce wages. The 'sub-historical prôletariat' – 'those with only their labour tò sell' – may indeed have 'cast something of a pall over the golden landscape of Alexandrine Scotland'.[98] Most people still depended on goods which were locally produced and locally consumed; for the ordinary person in the field the short-term view was therefore more relevant than long-term trends. However one interprets the conflicting evidence of climate and land use, one year's failure of crops could mean starvation.[99] It is not necessarily the case, however, that the 'trickle-down' effect was entirely negligible in this period, since the increasingly monetised economy also meant that jobs were available through the use of capital in, for example, large- and small-scale building projects (both secular and ecclesiastical), and through the inevitable requirement for skilled labour in a variety of occupations required to support trading activities.[100] These waged workers brought cash into local communities, and therefore, while early in the thirteenth century it probably was the case that outside the burghs the money economy was largely restricted to the upper echelons of society, as the trading economy developed in the course of the century it seems likely that the infiltration of cash into all areas of society accelerated. Cash may not have been

98 Mayhew, 'A Silver Age', pp. 59, 66.

99 See Parry, 'Secular climatic change'. Although dealing primarily with a later period, the scientific evidence for the effect of, for example, summer wetness on the production of oats, is compelling.

100 Donnelly, 'Berwick Shipping Trade', pp. 17–22; see also further comments on the 'trickle-down' effect on pp. 29–30.

entirely ubiquitous by the late thirteenth century, but there can be no doubt that it was more commonplace at the end of Alexander III's reign than it had been at the beginning.

It is certainly true that in order to come to a realistic view about the economy of Alexander III's reign, one must have 'laid aside the golden spectacles'.[101] There really is insufficient evidence to justify the suggestion that Alexander III was an economic miracle worker: the economy of his reign does seem to have been sound and prosperous, but that was an achievement of (at least) the whole century rather than just its second half, and if Alexander can be congratulated on creating a good economic environment through the pursuit of peace and stable government, he can hardly be credited with other contributing factors, such as (perhaps) a generally amenable climate and a beneficial European-wide trading environment which together seem to have encouraged the increased production of crops and saleable-quality wool. It is true, however, that Scotland's ability to participate in the 'mainstream of European trade'[102] had the effect of increasing money supply, which in turn stimulated economic growth; it also seems to be true that generally competent and consistent government in this period enabled Scottish merchants to make the most of the favourable prevailing conditions. It has been stated that in terms of its economy, Scotland on the eve of the union of 1707 'remained a relatively retarded member of Western European society'.[103] Though perhaps an uncomfortably harsh assessment, it reflects the fact that Scotland's economy had not developed as effectively as most other European states' had over the fourteenth to sixteenth centuries. In the thirteenth century, though, it seems to have been largely comparable in both nature and method to the economies of its major trading partners. The failure in the later development of the Scottish economy can be blamed partly on the lack of stable government: the Scottish kings of the fourteenth to sixteenth centuries did not 'ensure uniform administration of law and order – the fundamental requirement for economic progress'.[104] In contrast, the twelfth and thirteenth centuries had seen stable, largely peaceful rule, by long-lived kings (the shortest reign being that of Alexander I, for 17 years; the longest, William, for almost half a century). The warfare which followed the death of Margaret, Maid of Norway in 1290 severely disrupted effective judicial, administrative and economic structures, but in the reign of Alexander III it can be confidently asserted that the Scottish economy was functioning as effectively as that of most

---

101 Mayhew, 'A Silver Age', p. 66.

102 Mayhew, 'A Silver Age', p. 66.

103 S.G.E. Lythe and J. Butt, *An Economic History of Scotland, 1100–1939* (Glasgow & London, 1975), p. 70.

104 Lythe and Butt, *An Economic History of Scotland*, p. 72.

other states. That there was indeed so catastrophic a downturn right at the end of the thirteenth century, substantially caused by the collapse both of stable government and of peaceful relations with England, is not simply an impression gained from chroniclers who wrote through a haze of nostalgia. In England too, the rapid growth of the economy until the end of the thirteenth century was matched by an equally rapid decline in the following decades (although neither as far nor as severe as in Scotland), as the two kingdoms 'locked themselves into patterns of (not quite mutual) assured destruction'. Scotland's economic growth has to be seen in this broader context: an export-led economic boom, exploiting conditions which encouraged the development, particularly, of the wool trade, turned Scotland into one of the 'economic tigers of the North-Sea rim', until disastrously disrupted by the war with England.[105]

In the very early years of the fifteenth century Andrew Wyntoun, the Prior of Loch Leven, started to write his metrical history of Scotland. Beginning with the story of creation, he intended to write seven books (echoing the seven ages of universal history), and to complete his story with the catastrophic death of Alexander III.[106] Thus, although the original plan was soon extended, continuing the work into Wyntoun's own time, the oft-quoted 'sang' with which Wyntoun lamented the death of the king was originally intended to form the closing lines of the work, the final words of which were an invocation to Christ as the saviour both of Scotland and of humankind.

Sen alexander our king wes deid
That scotland left in luf & le
Away wes sons of aill & breid
Off wyne & walx of gamyn & gle
The gold wes changeit all in leid
The frute falȝeit on everilk tre
Ihesu succour and send Remeid
That stad Is in perplexite[107]

105 Donnelly, 'Berwick Shipping Trade', pp. 25–26.

106 The comments on the structure of Wyntoun's work, and on the text of the 'sang', are based on Chris Jones, 'Inclinit to Diuersiteis: Wyntoun's Song on the Death of Alexander III and the "Origins" of Scots Vernacular Poetry', *The Review of English Studies*, 64 (2013), pp. 21–38. I am grateful to Professor Jones for several stimulating discussions regarding this text.

107 The version of the text quoted here is that from the privately owned Wemyss castle manuscript of Wyntoun, as transcribed by Jones. He identifies this manuscript as representing a text from the earliest stage in the composition of the work. My only change to his transcription of the version given in that manuscript is to transpose the second and third lines; the original order, which disrupts the rhyming scheme and makes less grammatical sense, is here assumed

Wyntoun claimed that these lines were quoted – implying that they were a contemporary lament for the dead king. On that basis, they have frequently been cited as the earliest surviving instance of Scots vernacular literature. Whether that is so, or whether Wyntoun borrowed and elaborated lines from the earlier vernacular work of John Barbour, is a conundrum best left to linguists.[108] It is unquestionable, however, that these few lines represent an early stage in the formation of the historiographical tradition which depicts Alexander III as the archetypal *Good King*.

The foregoing analysis of Alexander's pursuit of the monarchical ideal has concentrated on his activities as upholder of law and justice, on firm and effective governmental administration, on rule through good counsel in the interests of all the people of the kingdom, on his safeguarding of the kingdom from foreign aggression, and on his pursuit of a successful economy. The poem is a mirror to many of these ideas. In some versions, the second line reads 'That Scotland led in lauch and le', stating that the king 'led' (rather than 'left') the realm through law and loyalty. Either version indicates the supposed view of society at large: until his death the king ruled the kingdom in righteousness, deserving the loyalty shown to him by his people. The dearth of the staples of everyday life (ale, bread, wine, wax), and the consequent loss of 'gamyn and gle' (sport or playfulness, and merriment), and the failure of crops, effectively echo the Aristotelian principle of material well-being as the consequence of good rule. The economy ceased to flourish, with the almost alchemical, counter-miraculous transformation of gold into lead. Finally, the corollary of the invocation to Christ to succour the stricken nation is that it was the loss of divinely inspired leadership that had reduced the kingdom to its desperate situation.

Irrespective of the historiographical context of Wyntoun's attitude to Alexander III, the lines with which he chose to end the first version of his chronicle were a reminder both of the ideals and of the value of strong and just medieval monarchy. After critical scrutiny, Alexander III's reign can be seen largely to have matched these ideals, suggesting that he should indeed be regarded as a successful monarch.

---

to be a scribal error. (But see Jones's comments, 'Inclinit to Diuersiteis', p. 33, for an alternative approach to the issue.)

108 See the discussion of this issue in Jones, 'Inclinit to Diuersiteis', pp. 23–25.

CHAPTER 10

Man and Myth

The inherent difficulty of identifying personality in a medieval king is exacerbated when source material is scarce, limited in its nature and highly partisan. Unfortunately, Alexander III provides a prime example of the problem: only a fraction of the official records which we know existed at the end of his reign survived either the war which ravaged the kingdom within a decade of his death or the centuries of wilful neglect which followed their removal from Edinburgh by the conquering Edward I. Scotland has a very limited store of narrative writing which survives from as early as the thirteenth century, and our native historiographical traditions therefore tend to be filtered both through the external view of English contemporary writings and through the interpretation of events by later Scottish and English writers; in both cases, the motivation which inspired the writers' approach to events has to be carefully considered.[1] The search for Alexander III suffers an additional impediment, in that his adult reign, apart from the events of 1263, was not punctuated by severe threat, disaster, rebellion or misrule; in medieval times, as now, dramatic events earned more column-inches. It is challenging to find the character of a man in sources which, with little else to report, merely 'pass from one pair of dead ecclesiastic's shoes to another'.[2] The problem is compounded further in a monarchical system which relies on rule through consensus and council, since the modern commentator cannot be certain of the extent to which the king himself influenced any decision or course of action.

If the source material does not permit a straightforward analysis of the man, at least it is possible to garner an impression of the world he inhabited; exploration of the courtly environment surrounding him reveals aspects of his lifestyle. Distinguished Scottish royal consorts such as Ermengarde Beaumont,

1 See below, Appendix 3.

2 Duncan, *Making of the Kingdom*, p. 583.

Marie de Coucy and Alexander's own two queens, Margaret Plantagenet and Yolande de Dreux, would have assumed accoutrements of fine living to match other courts of Europe, particularly in a period in which the Scottish economy was buoyant and the royal court consequently affluent. The descriptions of the inauguration ceremony include royal robes, crown and an inaugural stone dressed in silk and golden cloth; English records reveal that Alexander and Margaret received gifts of wine and produce, rich clothing, jewels, books, chalices and even horses from their English family;[3] and when the couple attended the coronation of Edward I in 1274 their display of pomp was particularly noted by the Lanercost chronicler, Alexander himself being exceptionally unstinting in his generosity.[4] Later dispute over the unpaid wine bill about which John Mason from Bordeaux litigated, the accounts of the sheriffs who claimed their expenses in connection with provisioning the itinerant royal court, and the extravagant preparations made for the Scottish royal party on their visits to England leave no doubt that the attendees at the Scottish royal court were as conspicuous in their consumption as other European aristocracies. Lavish eating and drinking apart, instrumental and vocal music, poetry, storytelling and theatre would all have featured in the entertainment at court. Thomas of Earlston, a documented contemporary soothsayer and poet who was credited, among other prophecies, with foretelling the death of Alexander III, has perhaps left traces of his storytelling and poetry within the later (fourteenth- or fifteenth-century) romance and oral tradition ballad known as 'Thomas the Rhymer'.[5] Bower describes pipers playing at the wedding feast of Alexander and Yolande, and we know without doubt that Elyas, the king's harpist, as well as trumpeters and minstrels accompanied Alexander to the English court in 1278.[6] The court would also have resounded to the sounds of drum and horn, fiddle, cittern, psaltery and rebec.[7]

Elyas may have been the harpist present at Alexander's inauguration as an essential assistant to the king's *fili*.[8] Or, as he appears again as late as 1296, when Edward I ordered the sheriffs of Perth and Fife to restore his lands to him

3 *CDS*, i, nos. 1851, 1872, 1903, 1930 2227, 2242 (in which the amount to be spent on the gift of jewels was an impressive £100); *CDS*, ii, no. 78.

4 *Chron. Lanercost*, p. 96.

5 Purser, *Scotland's Music*, pp. 59, 62; *PoMS*, no. 3/0/0; Tim Clarkson, *Scotland's Merlin: A Medieval Legend and its Dark Age Origins* (Edinburgh, 2016), pp. 119–20.

6 *Chron. Bower*, v, pp. 418–19; *CDS*, ii, no. 131. Although the translator of this passage of Bower has used the word 'bagpipe', it is unlikely that the bag-blown pipe would have been in use in thirteenth-century Scotland: see Purser, *Scotland's Music*, pp. 75–76, where the pre-fifteenth-century evidence for bagpipes is disputed.

7 Purser, *Scotland's Music*, p. 62.

8 Bannerman, 'The King's Poet', pp. 266–70.

(at which point he is described as a tenant of the heir to the earl of Fife), he may have been the successor to the harpist at the inauguration. He held land of the earl of Fife which administratively involved the sheriffs of both Fife and Perth, perhaps indicating that his home was close to that of the *fili,* whose estates lay near to the boundary of Fife and Perthshire. He was thus of landholding status, presumably a university graduate, and probably the representative of a family who held a hereditary position at court.[9] Clearly, the occupation of king's harpist was not that of a low-class entertainer.

The instrument itself, as well as the distinctive way in which it developed in Scotland, influenced the nature of more than the harp repertoire, since its versatility, greater than that of the lyre, which was more common in some countries, encouraged part-singing: the Scots were renowned, it was stated by the twelfth-century Gerald Cambrensis, for the beauty of their music.[10] In the greater churches, the increasingly popular organ would also have been present.[11] Some Scottish music of the period, written specifically for St Andrews, has survived within a mid thirteenth-century manuscript, now held in the Herzog August Bibliothek in Wolfenbüttel, one of several which were removed from St Andrews priory just a few years before the Reformation.[12] Named the *St Andrews Music Book* by a recent commentator, the manuscript contains French music of the period, along with Scottish material which exhibits elaborate creativity and skill.[13] The musical and Latin textual traditions of the Celtic church have also survived within a manuscript written in the late thirteenth century on Inchcolm Island (whose abbey, as indicated by its name, was dedicated to Columba). Certainly reflecting earlier styles, this music displays beauty in its inventiveness and cultural distinctiveness, and would have been in use for many generations before the date of the manuscript. It has been conjectured that Walter Bower himself,

9 See John Bannerman, 'The Clàrsach and the Clàrsair', in Bannerman, *Kinship, Church and Culture*, pp. 398–417, at p. 408, where it is commented that King James I in the early fifteenth century had a reputation as a fine harpist. It is tempting to indulge in the aimless speculation that, educated at court, Alexander III might have been similarly accomplished. Watt, *Graduates*, p. 256, doubts that Elyas was a graduate, suggesting instead that the 'master' may refer to his training as a harpist: 'Elyas the master harper', then, rather than 'Master Elyas the harper'. The generally precise way in which the term *magister* is used, however, must cast doubt on the suggestion, and Watt himself was unsure enough to justify including him in the list of graduates.

10 Purser, *Scotland's Music*, p. 50.

11 Purser, *Scotland's Music*, p. 50. We know with certainty that there were organs in the cathedral of St Andrews in the early fifteenth century, when Bower describes their use in the services which celebrated the opening of the University (*Chron. Bower*, viii, pp. 78–79).

12 See James Houston Baxter, *Copiale Prioratus Sanctiandree* (Oxford, 1930), pp. xx–xxxi, for a description of how the manuscripts reached Wolfenbüttel. The manuscript has been published in facsimile: James Houston Baxter (ed.), *An Old St Andrews Music Book* (London, 1931).

13 For a brief description of the manuscript and its significance, and an eloquent and enthusiastic analysis of the music it contains, see Purser, *Scotland's Music*, pp. 50–56.

as abbot of Inchcolm, may have sung these chants.[14] Outwith the liturgical context, the wedding hymn written for the marriage of Princess Margaret to King Erik in 1281, *Ex te lux oritur, o dulcis Scotia* has been described as having the dual nature of both hymn and romance, and the tune as 'one of the loveliest of the mediaeval repertoire'.[15] On 12 January 2017, the eve of the feast of St Kentigern (also known as Mungo, to whom Glasgow cathedral is dedicated), the First Vespers for St Kentigern, reconstructed from another thirteenth-century manuscript, were sung in the cathedral for the first time since the Reformation.[16] The hypnotic flow of the music, within the magnificent building for which it was written, left the enthralled listener in no doubt that thirteenth-century Scotland was far from being an uncultured or uncivilised land.

Although specific evidence is less abundant, it is demonstrable that in cultural and intellectual terms the Scottish court would not have seemed out of step with its European counterparts. There is good reason to believe that, both through his education and out of simple necessity, Alexander would have been conversant at least in Scots/English, French (both Anglo-Norman and Continental), Gaelic and Latin; it would be unsurprising if he was also competent in Flemish and/or Norwegian. At the age of 12 he had a Latin charter of David I to the abbey of Dunfermline read to him, so that he might make judgement in a dispute concerning its lands.[17] The presence in Scotland (in the possession of the Macdougall family of Lorne, through family connections with the original owner), within a few years of the end of this reign, of the high-status illuminated devotional book known as the Murthly Hours is another signal of the type of aesthetic environment in which the Scottish elite existed.[18] Probably written in Oxford, it has been persuasively argued that the illuminations were commissioned from a Paris workshop, likely in the 1280s. The Murthly Hours presents 'a statement of aristocratic values' reinforcing the notion that Scotland

14 Purser, *Scotland's Music*, pp. 39–46.

15 Purser, *Scotland's Music*, pp. 59, 60–61. The song is known from a manuscript in Uppsala University Library, Codex Upsalensis C233. There is a facsimile and free translation in Revd John Beveridge, 'Two Scottish Thirteenth-Century Songs, with the Original Melodies, Recently Discovered in Sweden', *Proceedings of the Society of Antiquaries of Scotland*, 73 (1939), pp. 276–88, where the Scottish (rather than Norwegian) authorship of the piece is proposed. The other piece discussed in the article is a hymn in honour of St Magnus, a two-voice setting, written probably in Orkney in the 1270s. A better translation of *Ex te lux oritur*, by Gilbert Márkus, is given in Thomas Owen Clancy (ed.), *The Triumph Tree: Scotland's Earliest Poetry AD 550–1350* (Edinburgh, 1998), pp. 295–96. For full text and translation, see below, Appendix 2.

16 From the Sprouston Breviary (NLS Adv. MS 18.2.13B). See Greta-Mary Hair and Betty I. Knott (eds), *Vespers, Matins and Lauds for St Kentigern, Patron Saint of Glasgow* (Glasgow, 2011).

17 *RRS*, iv pt. 1, no. 18.

18 For a detailed study of the Murthly Hours, see John Higgitt, *The Murthly Hours: Devotion, Literacy and Luxury in Paris, England and the Gaelic West* (London, 2000).

participated in the mainstream of European literary and artistic development.[19] Importantly, one of the book's historiated initials depicts its female owner herself, reading the book.[20] If such items were in circulation among the Scottish aristocracy, they were also owned and used in the royal court. The books that are known to have existed in the libraries of Scotland's religious houses even before this reign attest the scholarly activity common among the ecclesiastical hierarchy, many of whom had received a philosophical and theological education in the universities of Europe (and, less frequently, England). They frequented the royal court and were often the officers of state. Similar intellectual effort would have been evident in many of the clerks of the household, among whose number would be individuals charged with elements of the education of the young king and his bride. Within religious houses, too, there were scriptoria, producing distinctive and high-quality texts such as the copy of Bede's commentary on the Song of Songs written, probably in the early thirteenth century, in the abbey of Lindores.[21]

Contemporary artistic fashions in decor, furnishings and clothing would have been current at the Scottish court. Even the Lanercost chronicler – not generally an admirer of the Scots – acknowledged this when he praised young Princess Margaret for having 'changed [King Erik's] manners for the better'.[22] Comparison with the courtly cultures of England and Continental Europe might imply that Scotland's creative activity was purely receptive, or lacked originality. Not so: styles, as elsewhere, were transformed to suit local tastes, conditions, materials and traditions. The celebrated Lewis chessmen probably date from the later twelfth century, and rare survivals of jewellery and other objects illustrate that Scotland was home to those who produced, and who used and loved, beautiful objects. The monumental carving tradition in the West Highlands and islands, drawing on Romanesque, Pictish, Anglo-Saxon and Scandinavian influences, seems to have emerged in the later thirteenth century, or possibly earlier. Stone funeral effigies of both secular and ecclesiastical figures from throughout the thirteenth century are extant in various parts of Scotland,[23] and the quality of architectural stone carving in the religious buildings of the thirteenth century is testimony to the skill of Scottish masons.

19 Higgitt, *The Murthly Hours*, pp. 151–53.

20 Higgitt, *The Murthly* Hours, pp. 145–46; for discussion of literacy, and especially female literacy, in this period, see pp. 173–76 and sources cited.

21 For some illustrated examples of Scottish artefacts from the period, see National Museums of Scotland, *Angels, Nobles and Unicorns: Art and Patronage in Medieval Scotland* (Edinburgh, 1982).

22 See above, pp. 255–56.

23 See John Bannerman, *Late Medieval Monumental Sculpture in the West Highlands* (Edinburgh, 1977). The earliest dateable example is the effigy of King William (d.1214) at Arbroath (Bannerman, *Late Medieval Monumental Sculpture*, p. 23).

Architectural undertakings – notably in the great monastic and diocesan buildings which were often the subject of royal patronage – displayed an awareness and understanding of contemporary European styles, without slavish copying. Church buildings of the middle part of the thirteenth century were being designed 'by masons who now had the confidence to take only those elements that they wanted from such English buildings as they were consulting, while creating a blending of ideas that was specifically attuned to the tastes – and pockets – of their patrons'.[24] In the soaring Gothic lines of Glasgow cathedral, much of the work on the rebuilding of which was undertaken during the reign of Alexander III and which he must surely have seen in progress, we have 'one of the greatest masterpieces of Scottish medieval architecture'.[25] Although the thirteenth-century additions to Dunfermline abbey seem to have been limited primarily to the chapel (and associated alterations to the existing church) built to house the relics of the newly canonised Queen Margaret, 'great expense' was involved in their pursuit, doubtless due to the quality demanded for such an exceptional shrine.[26] At Melrose, the construction of a new abbot's residence by Abbot Matthew in the central decades of the thirteenth century was an ostentatious expression of wealth, demonstrating that the Cistercian order's quest for asceticism and austerity was waning by the reign of Alexander III. Although only foundations remain, they provide evidence of a sizeable structure containing a public hall and private chambers, the primary elements of aristocratic homes; additionally, it was located so as to provide 'a most attractive residence, in an almost idyllic setting'.[27] Matthew had a reputation as a conventual leader who increased the material welfare of his community, but his own residence must have contrasted sharply with the abbey's older, simpler church building, which remained unaltered until its reconstruction in the fourteenth century.[28] At Arbroath and later Dunfermline, impressively militaristic gatehouses likewise suggest the lordly nature of major religious institutions.[29] In St Andrews, the cathedral building was, right from its twelfth-century

---

24 Fawcett, *Scottish Medieval Church*, p. 106. Chapters 3 and 4 provide a detailed guide to the development of Scotland's ecclesiastical architecture in the mid and later thirteenth century.

25 Fawcett, *Scottish Medieval Church*, p. 114. Although none of Alexander's surviving acts bear a place-date to prove that he visited Glasgow, it is highly unlikely that he would not have visited the seat of such an important diocese.

26 Richard Fawcett, 'Dunfermline Abbey Church', in Fawcett, *Royal Dunfermline*, pp. 49–50.

27 Richard Fawcett and Richard Oram, *Melrose Abbey* (Stroud, 2004), pp. 198–99.

28 Richard Oram, 'Prelatical Builders: A Preliminary Study, c.1124–c.1500', in Oram and Stell, *Lordship and Architecture*, pp. 1–25, at pp. 12–13.

29 Oram, 'Prelatical Builders', p. 16.

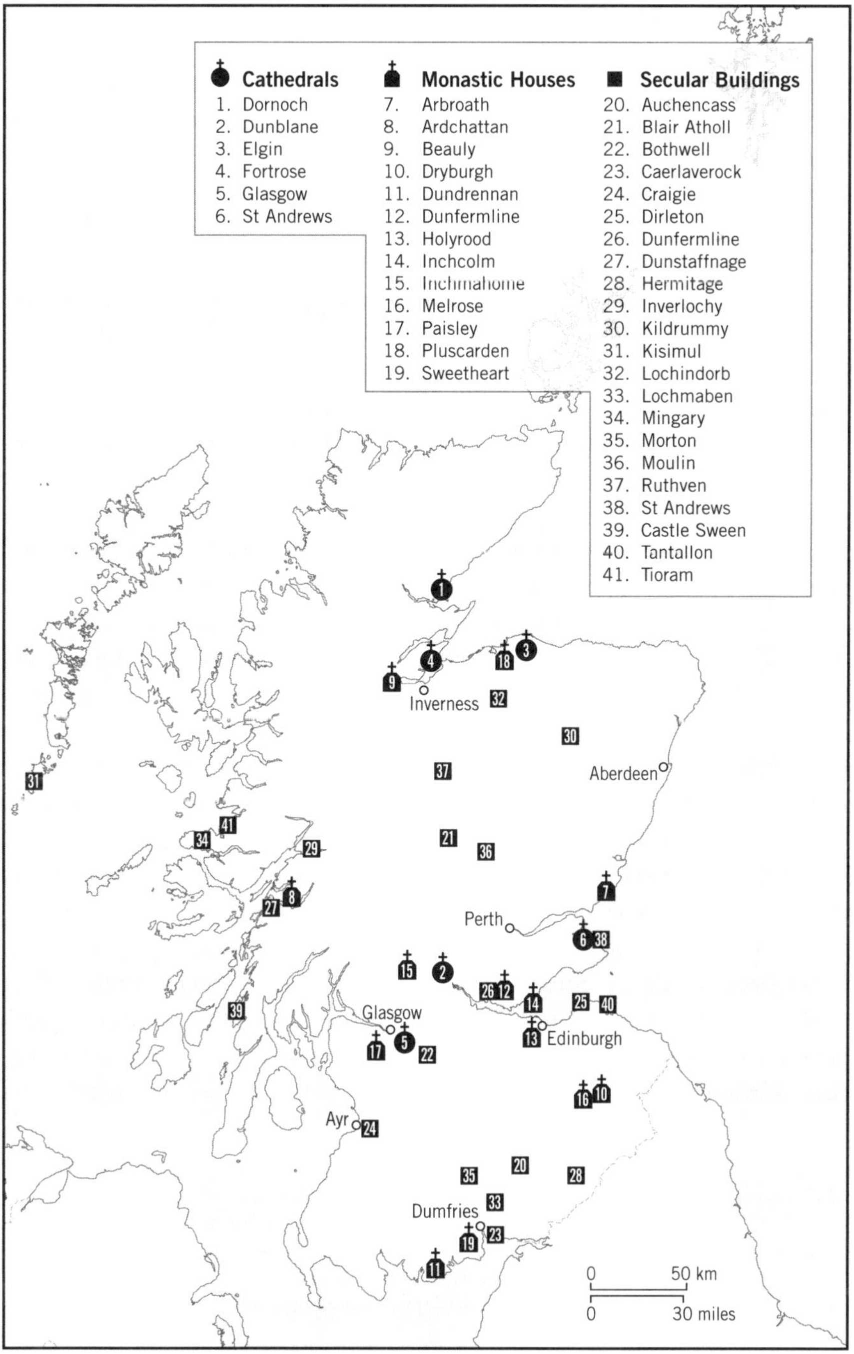

Map 4. Building work in progress, c.1250. Ecclesiastical and secular building operations noted in the text as probably underway during the reign of Alexander III. The list is undoubtedly incomplete, but the spread of building activity across so much of the country is indicative of the fact that cash flow was relatively abundant well beyond the areas economically dominated by the burghs.

beginnings, 'a building in the very latest fashion of northern English Gothic', precociously intended to reveal both skill and grandeur.[30] Itself providing inspiration for further new work elsewhere, when the decision was taken around 1250 to extend the (already impressively long) nave of the church westwards, the architecture was changed to a fashionably contemporary pointed Gothic style, involving some redesign of work already completed.[31] Holyrood abbey in Edinburgh also displays ambition in its engineering, with its unusual rib-vaulted roof probably constructed during the 1260s.[32] Projects of such scale and complexity took time to complete – for both St Andrews and Holyrood, over 150 years. These buildings were designed to astound, both in size and in artistic style, and to illustrate 'the cosmopolitan outlook and wide terms of reference of patrons who understood where to recruit the master masons best able to express their ambitions'.[33]

But long-term and aspirational building work could incur grievous expense, even from within relatively burgeoning institutional coffers, and in a period of comparative plenty. When the still incomplete nave of St Andrews was partially destroyed in a storm in 1272, Bower claims that it was rebuilt at the personal expense of Bishop Wishart. If the church itself had not the means to repair the damage, it seems that this ecclesiastical magnate did.[34] The abbey of Dryburgh suffered similar strain on its resources: even with powerful and wealthy cross-border patrons (the Moreville family), the building campaigns of the early thirteenth century came at exorbitant cost, and by the time the young Alexander III took his throne, the abbey was deeply in debt, enmired in litigation and dependent on papal generosity to help it out of potentially terminal crisis.[35] Nonetheless, with a confidence presumably inspired by an atmosphere of general prosperity, building continued at Dryburgh and, in common with the operations of the 1270s in Elgin cathedral, there are stylistic parallels with work of only a few decades earlier at no less prestigious a building than Westminster abbey.[36]

30 Ronald G. Cant, 'The Building of St Andrews Cathedral', in David McRoberts (ed.), *The Medieval Church of St Andrews* (Glasgow, 1976), pp. 11–32, at p. 14.

31 Cant, 'The Building of St Andrews Cathedral', pp. 22–23. For St Andrews, see also the digital reconstruction of the building as it is thought to have existed at consecration in 1318, at https://www.openvirtualworlds.org/st-andrews-cathedral-c1318/.

32 Stewart Cruden, *Scottish Medieval Churches* (Edinburgh, 1986), pp. 147–48; Fawcett, *Scottish Medieval Church*, pp. 107–10.

33 Richard Fawcett, 'The Medieval Ecclesiastical Architecture of St Andrews as a Channel for the Introduction of New Ideas', in Brown and Stevenson, *Medieval St Andrews*, pp. 51–83, at pp. 58, 79–80.

34 *Chron. Bower*, iii, pp. 398–99.

35 Richard Fawcett and Richard Oram, *Dryburgh Abbey* (Stroud, 2005), pp. 16–17.

36 Fawcett and Oram, *Dryburgh Abbey*, pp. 75–76.

Founded by Devorguilla Balliol in 1273, Sweetheart abbey in Kirkcudbrightshire (Plate 6) was the last Cistercian house to be established in Scotland. Its building (although lacking neither creative features nor stylistic parallels elsewhere in both Scotland and England) is thought to be architecturally less ambitious than some earlier foundations, harking back to traditional Cistercian austerity. A happy consequence of the plainer approach may have been a less fraught building campaign: the church at least was in a state of completion sufficient to allow Devorguilla herself to be laid to rest there in 1289.[37] In contrast, Pluscarden in Moray, one of three Valliscaulian foundations in Scotland (all founded in northern Scotland in 1230, and the only houses of the order outside France), is 'among the finest achievements of a notable period', the work of a skilled and imaginative architect who was well versed in developments elsewhere.[38] It is striking that design elements of the great monastic and cathedral buildings across the length and breadth of the country show similarities which clearly indicate that they influenced each other: obviously there was close communication between patrons, builders and their ecclesiastical clients across Scotland and well beyond. If it cannot be claimed that there was a cohesive school of religious architecture in thirteenth-century Scotland, a strong case can certainly be made for a self-consciously active, and well-funded, architectural community. Although the evidence is more elusive, there can be no doubt that the same assertion is true for the smaller-scale developments represented by parish churches and lordly chapels.

The contention that Alexander III's Scotland was not an impoverished land is further reinforced by the kingdom's secular architecture. The financial burden on the church of large-scale building endeavours must have paled into insignificance against the comparative expense of secular initiatives funded out of private (including royal) purses. At Dunfermline, it seems that earlier royal residential apartments were extended or rebuilt in stone in the later thirteenth century, probably on Alexander III's instruction, to a standard which even Edward I saw as acceptable for his own temporary residence there in the early years of the fourteenth century.[39]

The earls of Strathearn, in common with their counterparts in what might be termed the Scotian heartlands of the older kingdom, appear to have eschewed the increasing vogue for mighty fortification as expressions of aristocratic

37 Cruden, *Scottish Medieval Churches*, pp. 137–44; Fawcett, *Scottish Medieval Church*, pp. 175–80.

38 Stewart Cruden, *Scottish Medieval Churches*, pp. 146–47; Fawcett, *Scottish Medieval Church*, pp. 139–45.

39 Aonghus Mackechnie, 'The Royal Palace of Dunfermline', in Fawcett, *Royal Dunfermline*, pp. 101–38, at pp. 105, 112–13, 117.

status.[40] Nonetheless, there is ample evidence elsewhere in Scotland of such lordly secular construction in the second half of the thirteenth century. It is unsurprising that the Comyns, the mightiest, and presumably also the wealthiest of Scottish noble families, were avid patrons of new building throughout their widespread estates in both England and Scotland. Most spectacularly visible today, at Lochindorb near Grantown-on-Spey (Plate 17) are the remains of a massive four-walled castle with round corner towers built on an artificial island in a loch; and at Inverlochy near Fort William, the castle built *c.*1270–80 survives as a large (about 840m²) quadrangular enclosure with walls which still stand to a height of nine metres, protected by projecting corner towers, not unlike the majestic late thirteenth-century castle at Harlech in Wales. Such influence is not unique to Inverlochy: elsewhere too there are architectural features echoing that 'perfect synthesis of stone and wall' which typifies military architecture in the England and Wales of Edward I.[41] Defensively masterful, both Lochindorb and Inverlochy also exhibit excessive expenditure on the symbolic display of lordly status and power. They were not unique examples, however, even of Comyn activity: the Badenoch branch of the family alone seems to have been responsible for both Inverlochy and Lochindorb, as well as castles at Blair Atholl, and at Ruthven near Kingussie (both now overlaid with more modern work), and several other sites in the south of Scotland and northern England.[42]

The remarkable concentration of stone castles on the western seaboard and islands, the work of many of the families who locally controlled those areas, has already been mentioned.[43] Castle Sween in Argyll is an excellent example of the impressive stone keeps of the thirteenth century. Tioram on the shores of Loch Moidart (Plate 16), Mingary near Kilchoan in Ardnamurchan and Dunstaffnage, which commands the mouth of Loch Etive near Connel, are curtain wall castles, and persuasive architectural evidence has been adduced to include Kisimul castle on Barra within this group of thirteenth-century structures, 'the work of the same school of military architects'.[44] Although without corroborating evidence secular architecture is notoriously difficult to date with any certainty, some at least of this extensive work, along with secular patronage of ecclesiastical

40 Fiona Watson, 'Adapting Tradition? The Earldom of Strathearn, 1114–1296', in Oram and Stell, *Lordship and Architecture*, pp. 26–43; Cynthia J. Neville, *Native Lordship in Medieval Scotland: The Earldoms of Strathearn and Lennox, c.1140–1365* (Dublin, 2005), pp. 116–124.

41 Stewart Cruden, *The Scottish Castle* (Edinburgh, 1963), p. 11.

42 Alan Young, 'The Comyns to 1300', in Oram and Stell, *Lordship and Architecture*, pp. 60–83. See also Cruden, *The Scottish Castle*, pp. 61–62 (Lochindorb), 58–63 (Inverlochy); and for all named monuments, Historic Environment Scotland's invaluable database, *Canmore*, at https://canmore.org.uk.

43 See above, p. 193.

44 Cruden, *The Scottish Castle*, pp. 38–49.

buildings, undoubtedly belongs to the period between the death of Alexander II and the Norwegian invasion in 1263, and/or to the process of consolidation of Scottish control which followed the events of 1263.[45] The obvious requirement for defence in the west was not the only impetus for such activity, however, since similar projects were being pursued across the kingdom. Building work at Dirleton and Tantallon (Plate 14) in East Lothian, St Andrews in Fife (built by the bishop as his palace), Lochmaben, Caerlaverock and Auchencass in Dumfriesshire, Moulin in Perthshire, Bothwell in Lanarkshire and Kildrummy in Aberdeenshire can all have cases made, on stylistic grounds, for construction during the later part of the thirteenth century, and can be identified as military architecture in a grand European tradition.[46] Defensive residential buildings on a smaller scale will have been constructed also by less affluent nobles, such as the hall-houses evident at Morton in Dumfriesshire (Plate 15), Craigie in Ayrshire and elsewhere.[47]

For religious, defensive and residential purposes alike, the financial implication of stone building of such ubiquity (and those named can be no more than a few examples out of many) speaks eloquently of the ample means at the disposal of much of the Scottish aristocracy – both lay and ecclesiastical – in this period, and of a thriving economy. The architectural similarities with projects in England and elsewhere similarly testify to a constant experiential interplay between the aristocracies of Scotland and their peers to the south and across Continental Europe. As leader of that lordly community, Scotland's king was required to be at the forefront in a culturally aware and powerfully ambitious environment, rivalling that of his European contemporaries.

The pastimes of the court were not confined to the indoors. Alexander's fondness for the hunt is evidenced both by investment in royal parks and by the high number of his acts which were dated at places known to have been royal hunting reserves, especially in the borders and the north-east. He also kept kennels and birds of prey at several locations.[48] The sheriff of Forfar accounted for expenses incurred in keeping the king's horses and falcons for a considerable part of 1263: while the place-date evidence does not suggest that the king spent the 29 weeks there which the account suggests, it is quite possible that he visited from time to time, and that the domestic household – the queen (who was pregnant) and the young Princess Margaret – remained relatively

---

45 Cruden, *The Scottish* Castle, pp. 22–26; Ian Fisher, 'The Heirs of Somerled', in Oram and Stell, *Lordship and Architecture*, pp. 84–95, at p. 89.

46 Cruden, *The Scottish Castle*, pp. 64–72.

47 For a discussion of the thirteenth-century hall-house, see Cruden, *The Scottish Castle*, pp. 91–99.

48 See the editors' comments in *RRS*, iv pt. 1, p. 36 & n., and the cited references to John M. Gilbert, *Hunting and Hunting Reserves in Medieval Scotland* (Edinburgh, 1979).

static. Provisions (including a considerable amount of wine) being sent to Forfar, and repairs being made to the fabric of the building, would certainly suggest that it was occupied for at least part of the period. It is not known where the queen spent those months of her pregnancy during which travel would have been arduous, but the preparations of Forfar during 1263 seem to make it a likely venue.[49] Forres figured also in the same period: in 1264, two falconers spent 14 weeks there; the king also spent considerable sums on constructing new parks in Stirling and Kincardine (and on repairing the old one at Stirling), and on maintaining four falconers for a period of two years at Dunipace, near Falkirk.[50] Hunting was not a pastime restricted to the king: he seems to have participated enthusiastically in a leisure activity which was popular with the aristocracy in Scotland as elsewhere.[51]

Although it seems probable, it is not certain that Alexander heard the service for St Kentigern; but he undoubtedly heard many other such works. In an age dominated by Christian observance, attendance at devotional acts was routine; religious belief was unquestioned, but the extent of Alexander's personal piety cannot be ascertained. In an attempt to identify feast-days on which he did not conduct business, and to ascertain where he chose to spend significant festivals, a study of the place-dates of his acts concludes that Alexander was perhaps less strictly 'conventional' in his religious activity than his father had been.[52] Alexander's religious itinerary was discernibly political in its nature, designed to enhance royal and dynastic authority, and to reinforce Scotland's religious reputation. In that political context, which included an agenda of fostering national identity, it is unsurprising that there emerges a greater emphasis on the celebration of native Scottish saints such as Columba and Kentigern, along with adopted Scots such as Andrew and Ninian.[53] The encouragement of historical interpretation of Scotland's past within the cloister, especially in St Andrews, should be seen in the same light. Similarly, late in his reign Alexander increased his devotion to the dynastic mausoleum at Dunfermline, and sponsored new building there, as this was the site at which Queen Margaret, both of their sons and Alexander himself would be buried. It is possible also to read political intent into his probable

---

49 *ER*, i, pp. 7–8. The Preface to *ER*, i (at pp. li–lii), commenting on the sheriff's account, suggests that the king spent over six months at Forfar. Place-date evidence demonstrates that Alexander travelled extensively throughout the southern part of the kingdom in 1263 and 1264. He was probably never resident in one place for as long as six months. Prince Alexander was born in January 1264.

50 *ER*, i, pp. 15, 21, 24.

51 See Gilbert, *Hunting and Hunting Reserves*, Chapter 2, especially at pp. 24–29.

52 The following paragraph is largely based on Penman, 'Royal Piety', and the sources cited therein.

53 Penman, 'Royal Piety', pp. 22–23.

accompanying of Prince Edward on a pilgrimage to Whithorn in 1256, in his own pilgrimage to St Cuthbert's shrine at Durham in 1273, and perhaps in a gift of alms (out of the income of Arbroath abbey) to the shrine of St Thomas (to whom Arbroath was dedicated) at Canterbury in 1279.

If aspects of Alexander's religious observance were either formulaic or politically motivated, there are nonetheless hints of personal devotion to be found. *Gesta Annalia* reports that an ancient cross was found in Peebles on 9 May 1261, followed a few days later by the discovery of an urn containing apparent relics of a holy martyr. Miracles having been observed, the king had a church built on the site, displaying a pious intent, which the author links (through juxtaposition) with the safe delivery of the first child of Alexander and Margaret a few weeks later.[54] Some doubt has been cast on Alexander's rôle as the founder of this church (which later became a community of Trinitarian friars, and the ruins of which remain to be seen near the centre of the modern town), but the architectural remains and the early date of *Gesta Annalia* provide a reasonable level of evidence. None of Alexander's acts is place-dated at Peebles, although Traquair, only a few miles away, was one of his more frequent destinations.[55] Other than the likelihood of his patronage of the Cross Kirk at Peebles, there appear to be no new religious foundations by Alexander III: it was a vogue which was waning by this period, and the number of noble foundations was also decreasing rapidly. Rather than creating new foundations, Alexander supported existing houses: his generosity towards religious houses was discussed in Chapter 9. There is no reason to suggest that Alexander III was less supportive of the church, both secular and monastic, than would have been expected.

Unlike some other medieval kings, Alexander is rarely the subject of fulminations against degenerate moral standards. Only the author of the *Chronicle of Lanercost* is stridently critical of him in anything like personal terms. In portraying the deaths of Alexander's children as divine punishment for his sins, the chronicler offers a generic accusation of sexual profligacy, which is countered by the lack of any corroborating testimony and the king's apparent lack of illegitimate offspring.[56] Although the nature of the man as a husband and father is undiscoverable, it is possible to detect in dry official records a sense of warmth in some of the king's personal relationships. During the minority, the dynamic of the relationship between England and Scotland meant that any personal

54 *Chron. Fordun*, i, p. 299 (trans. ii, pp. 294–95). See also *RRS*, iv pt. 1, no. 217, which (following Ian B. Cowan and David E. Easson, *Medieval Religious Houses: Scotland* (London, 1976), pp. 109–10) suggests a date of 1262, on the basis of *Gesta Annalia*'s statement that it took place during Alexander's thirteenth regnal year.

55 *RRS*, iv pt. 1, map at p. 275 and index entries.

56 *Chron. Lanercost*, pp. 111, 116 (trans. Anderson, *Early Sources*, ii, pp. 685 & n., 690).

communication was very limited. Later, however, the close contact between the English and Scottish royal courts, as Alexander and Margaret established and conducted their own relationship with her parents, occasionally allowed a degree of sentiment to be expressed. The gifts and the good familial wishes which were exchanged, as well as the apparently easy business relationship which seems to have surrounded the visits of Alexander and Margaret to the court of Henry III indicate a lack of tension, at least.[57] It does seem that there were some visits between them which may have been purely social: the reported visit of Prince Edward in 1267, to Margaret and Alexander at Roxburgh (or Haddington), may be an example.[58] That this meeting took place just as Edward was mopping up in the north of England after the rebellion against Henry III may indicate that there was a considerable element of political news-giving involved in the visit: that no evidence of it has survived in formal record, however, also suggests that it was more personal than official in nature. This episode is typical of the difficulty of differentiating between the official and the personal. The nature of most of the extant correspondence is too formal to draw any firm conclusions about personal relationships: only five of Alexander's acts surviving in full texts were written in French, the informal, day-to-day language of the English court, none of which contains communications with, or relates to anyone in, the English court. The surviving communication is entirely in Latin, and almost unstintingly official; it is only by reading between the lines that it is possible to draw any conclusion about personal matters.

When Alexander readied himself to intervene in the English civil disturbance, it is very difficult to tell whether he was motivated to do so by personal family concern, political partisanship, a desire to uphold the principle of royal authority or a mixture of these considerations, all of which must have guided the relationship with Henry III and his family at different times. It is also possible that the appearance of familial warmth on the part of Alexander III is coloured by the close ties which do seem to have existed between Henry III, Eleanor and their children, and it seems probable that the nature of those family relationships were at times influential in the conduct of affairs. To distinguish between personal and political relationships becomes even more problematic after the deaths of both Henry III and Margaret when, in the last decade of Alexander's reign, political tensions intensified between England and Scotland. That Alexander did not return to England after 1278 may be significant. Nonetheless, Edward did write to Alexander to offer condolences on the death

57 See above, pp. 216–22.

58 *Chron. Fordun*, i, pp. 302–03 (trans. ii, pp. 298–99); *Chron. Bower*, v, pp. 354–55 & n. p. 471; *Chron. Lanercost*, p. 81.

of Prince Alexander in 1284, and Alexander's reply, referring to his 'grievous and unbearable trials and tribulations' (*tristissimas et intollerabiles angustias et eventus*), seems heartfelt.[59] Two months later, in June 1284, Alexander sent Edward a gift of four falcons, apparently an amicable gesture.

There is a complete lack of intimate comment regarding the deaths of Queen Margaret, Prince David or Princess Margaret in both English and Scottish record. Alexander's care to ensure that they were buried together in Dunfermline may be a sign of familial affection, especially when it is remembered that neither King William nor Alexander II shared a mausoleum with their spouse.[60] It is possible that the timing of Alexander's pilgrimage to the shrine of St Cuthbert at Durham might also be reflective of a concern for family: only a month after his third child was born after a wait of almost a decade, it may have been a pious act of thanksgiving to a saint with whom he had a personal connection, having been born on 4 September, the feast of the translation of St Cuthbert.[61] It is not known if Margaret accompanied Alexander on his constant journeys throughout Scotland or (more probably) maintained a relatively static household of her own. There is no more than a vague impression of fondness to be gleaned, and perhaps a suggestion from the meagre place-date evidence that he may have been resident with her for the birth of at least two of their children. He created in her honour a chapel dedicated to St Laurence, in Forres,[62] perhaps an intimate memorial, reflecting a more individual, personal, local preference than would have been represented by a more grandiose or ostentatious offering. The king's grant to Newbattle around the time of his mother's death (the only surviving act of Alexander which specifies that masses should be said for him, his ancestors and his heirs) echoes an earlier grant to Scone, specifically in the name of Margaret and their children.[63] This does not represent a large body of material celebrating the lives of those close to him, but it does contrast with the fact that Alexander II seems to have left commemoration of his first wife, Joan, entirely to her brother, Henry III.[64] If indications of affection for Alexander's family are scarce, they are entirely lacking in relation to anyone else. While it is probable that he held high regard for characters such as Sir William Sinclair of Roslin and others of the inner circle such as Thomas Charteris, who was promoted to royal chancellor perhaps beyond his expectations, it is not possible

---

59 *RRS*, iv pt. 1, no. 146.
60 William, Ermengarde, Alexander II and Marie were buried in Arbroath, Balmerino, Melrose and Newbattle, respectively.
61 *RRS*, iv pt. 1, no. 86.
62 *RRS*, iv pt. 1, no. 279. The choice of Forres, one of the residences used for the hunt, for this chapel may indicate that it was a place of shared memory.
63 *RRS*, iv pt. 1, nos. 146, 169.
64 Penman, 'Royal Piety', p. 19.

to discern whether they were simply trusted servants or might have been regarded as friends.[65] Certainly, some of those in very regular attendance at court would have been almost constant companions.

A few elements of Alexander's character can be postulated through the conduct of his rule. The death of his father and thereafter the frequent, and sometimes long-term, absence of his mother meant that he was initiated into the ways of the royal court from an early age. He thus gained an understanding of the patterns of behaviour of those around him to a degree probably greater than most others so young. One can imagine that in the first few years of his reign his rôle was primarily restricted to that of an observer, but he was clearly able to play his part, if the reports of the request for his homage in December 1251 are to be believed. Within half a dozen years, he was apparently able to begin to stamp his own authority on the situation. Although the factionalism of the minority was neither as deep nor as overt as has usually been suggested, it cannot be denied that the Scottish aristocratic community was fractious, which makes it probable that the selection of councillors in 1257 and 1258, and the choice of envoys to communicate with the English court, reveal more than a trace of Alexander's own initiative. His lessons had been well learnt and, even in these early days of his personal rule, he demonstrated astuteness and an understanding of the political system within which he had to operate, qualities which would serve him well. His continued use within government of individuals who rivalled each other, as in the selection of Alan Durward and Walter Comyn for the task of making preparations against the impending Norwegian invasion in 1263, confirmed his insight.

Alexander III's personal reign was largely peaceful, undisturbed by civil unrest other than the rebellion in the Isle of Man in 1275.[66] The untroubled reign may itself reveal a king whose behaviour did not court controversy. The root of the insurrection in Man lay not in actions taken specifically by Alexander III, but in the events of several decades past. The way with which it was dealt, however, is instructive. Those selected to lead the counter-offensive on behalf of the king were both trusted political adherents of the king and members of the lordly families of the mainland and isles, which establishes both that there was by this stage a considerable degree of mutual trust and that the centrality of the western seaboard to the Scottish polity was beyond question. The sources from which details of the incident are gleaned are not generally sympathetic to Scottish action or ambition. Nonetheless, we are told that the insurgents were offered terms for peace; it was the aspiring king of Man,

65 Sinclair was the recipient of some largesse: see *RRS*, iv pt.1, nos. 126, 130, 268. See also the comments in *RRS*, iv pt. 1, p. 19 – citing Duncan, *Making of the* Kingdom, p. 588.

66 See above, pp. 222–24.

Godred, led by 'perverse counsellors', who opted instead for battle. After the resulting rout by the much superior Scottish force, the account given by the *Annals of Furness* claims, the fleeing rebels were slaughtered and the Scots were harshly repressive. It is uncertain whether this represents the truth or is an account embellished by a hostile commentator, or to what extent the actions of the Scottish commanders in 1275 were in response to instructions from the king. An attempt to quell support for any future rebellion is a possibility, but there seems to be no indication that Alexander III shared the reputation of his father as fiercely vindictive in such situations. However, Alexander III had to face nothing approaching the seriousness of the challenges to his authority faced by his father in Galloway: he was not tested in that way. In relation to the Norwegian invasion of 1263, Alexander's action in levying tribute and taking hostages was certainly firm, but no accusations of injustice or wanton violence have survived in that connection, other than the somewhat formulaic accusations of atrocity levelled against his forces in the isles in 1262.

In the field of judicial activity, Alexander appears equally balanced: the relatively meagre extant record suggests that his judgement, both in politically explosive cases (such as the settlement of the earldom of Menteith) and in more mundane affairs (such as disputes regarding boundaries), seems to have been largely accepted without complaint. One suit which was the subject of future controversy was the litigation by the merchant John Mason of Bordeaux regarding his claim for non-payment.[67] The Scottish authorities challenged the extent of the underpayment, claiming that an account to prove the debt had not been provided. That the proceedings were so protracted (the account was said to be already 'long overdue' when the case initially appears in records in May 1284 and was still a live issue a decade later), and were the cause of several communications between Edward I and Alexander III, indicates that the judicial process was open to appeal and that the king became personally involved. In May 1284 Alexander asked Edward to encourage Mason to come to Scotland to render his account and receive payment. Edward seems to have complied with the request, but the result was not as Mason expected, since by the time he wrote to Edward I again (an undated letter), he was in a Scottish prison. The suit was not straightforward, however, as debts owed by Mason to other merchants were also involved. Whether Mason had in fact been unjustly deprived of his money is not clear, and the long drawn-out nature of the dispute may suggest at least that the system lacked efficiency; but that the case continued and was subject

67 See *CDS*, ii, nos. 252, 255, 264, and the later explanation of the Scottish position in no. 688 (1293; misdated in *CDS* to 1294); see H.G. Richardson and George Sayles, 'The Scottish Parliaments of Edward I', *Scottish Historical Review*, 25 (1928), pp. 300–17, at p. 303n.

to repeated hearings, and that Mason was obviously released from prison before pursuing his cause again later, demonstrate a respect for process, rather than coercive vindictiveness, on the part of the king.

Alexander was undoubtedly a character to be reckoned with. As early as December 1251, at the age of ten, he asserted his refusal to acknowledge the superiority of the English crown over Scotland; as a teenager he effectively grasped the reins of power in 1257/58, to the amazement of his father-in-law;[68] in 1263, still only in his early twenties, he and his council masterminded the protection of the kingdom against foreign invasion; in the later 1270s, he again defended the status of his kingship against Edward I; and he commanded the respect of his noble community in judgements such as that in favour of Walter Stewart as earl of Menteith in 1261/62 (presumably against a degree of opposition from the powerful Comyn family).[69] As well as an understanding of the nature of his kingship, Alexander displayed determination and an ability to govern.

Though evidence is too scarce to discern how likeable a person Alexander was, some general qualities can be detected: he was an individual who was educated and cultured, who appears to have established effective personal relationships with those around him; he had a firm understanding of the political dynamics of the society in which he lived; he had the intelligence and strength of character to fulfil his rôle as monarch, and was astute enough to navigate the political maze and gain sufficient respect to be a commanding presence in the kingdom. If Alexander the man must remain a shadowy character, in personal as well as political terms he can nonetheless be shown to have been an effective king.

It has long been recognised that 'Fordun' was a mirror to the later fourteenth-century kings in whose era it was written.[70] It aimed to strengthen the image of strong kingship, independent of English hegemony, which had been challenged in the period between Alexander's death and the reign of Robert I in the early fourteenth century. The kingship was challenged again in the minority and rule of Robert's son, David II, whose adult reign saw defeat in battle against the English, the consequent temporary imprisonment of the king himself and, later, rebellion against him. Before it was understood that the work which used

---

68 *CDS*, i, no. 2133.

69 See above, pp. 163–65.

70 The discussion of the historiography of the reign which follows develops that given in Reid, 'Historiography', to take account of the more recent clarity which has been provided regarding Fordun's *Chronica Gentis Scotorum*, especially in the cited works by Dauvit Broun. Reid, 'Historiography', however, contains more detail on some of the writers, and a fuller chronological survey, than is provided here and should be referred to for additional information.

to be known as John Fordun's *Chronica Gentis Scotorum* is in fact composed of several independent texts, written and revised over a wide timeframe, it was suggested that the whole treatment of Alexander's reign was intended to provide a moral framework for kingship in the later days of David II.[71] Current understanding of the nature of this part of the work, which is not the work of Fordun himself, and part of which was written much earlier, obviously necessitates a partial revision of that view. The treatment of Alexander III's minority in *Gesta Annalia I* (written by 1285), which was formerly interpreted as a deliberate contrast with the settled days of the adult reign in order to heighten the contrast between weak and strong rule, cannot now be taken as a coded message for Scotland in the 1360s or 1370s. The message of *Gesta Annalia I* – a 'sophisticated attempt to project [the] image of kingdom and country as one into the primordial past and furnish it with a continuous regnal narrative up to the present' – has been clearly explained, though, and is not inconsistent with the approach of the fourteenth-century writers.[72]

The encomium which follows the death of Alexander III is part of the later continuation, termed *Gesta Annalia II*, which was designed to contrast Alexander's reign with the catastrophic difficulties which later beset the kingdom: 'How worthy of tears, and how hurtful, his death was to the kingdom of Scotland, is plainly shown forth by the evils of after times.'[73] It seems likely to have been written, by a contemporary of John Fordun, between the early 1360s and the late 1380s.[74]

> All the days of the life of this king, the Church of Christ flourished, her priests were honoured with due worship, vice was withered, craft there was none, wrong came to an end, truth was strong, and righteousness reigned. Moreover, rightly, and by reason of the merits of his uprightness, was he called king: seeing that he ruled himself and his people aright, allowing unto each his rights; and if, at any time, any of his people rebelled, he curbed their madness with discipline so unbending, that they would put a rope round their necks, ready for hanging, were that his will and pleasure, and bow themselves under his rule. By reason whereof he was

71 See Reid, 'Historiography', pp. 190–91.

72 Broun, *Scottish Independence*, p. 275.

73 *Chron. Fordun*, i, p. 309 (trans. ii, p. 304).

74 See the conclusion to Broun, *Scottish Independence* for a summary of his argument regarding the construction of the work previously regarded as Fordun's *Chronica Gentis Scotorum* and its predecessors. For the important distinction between *Gesta Annalia I* and *II*, see Broun, *Scottish Independence*, pp 175, 216–17, 261 and Dauvit Broun, 'A New Look at *Gesta Annalia* Attributed to John of Fordun', in Barbara E. Crawford (ed.), *Church, Chronicle and Learning in Medieval and Early Renaissance Scotland* (Edinburgh, 1999), pp. 9–30.

> looked upon with equal fear and love, both far and near, not only by his friends, but also by his adversaries, – and especially by the English. And all the time he lived upon earth security reigned in steadfastness of peace and quiet, and gleeful freedom. O Scotland, truly unhappy when bereft of so great a leader and pilot; while – greater unhappiness still! – he left no lawful offspring to succeed him. Thou hast an everlasting spring of mourning and sorrow in the death of one whose praiseworthy life bestowed, on thee especially, such increase of welfare.[75]

Having been written perhaps a century after the death of the king, this eulogy cannot be taken as evidence either of Alexander's exemplary nature, or of the apparently utopian nature of Scotland during his reign. *Gesta Annalia (I* and *II)* do not present the reign of Alexander III as outstanding: the narrative treatment of the reign itself is relatively muted. The same is true of contemporary sources such as the *Chronicle of Melrose* and the earlier English chronicles (the *Chronicle of Lanercost*, and the *Chronica Majora* of Matthew Paris, for example), which are for the most part relatively uneffusive in either praise or criticism. In death, however, he is here given the qualities which exemplify the ideal king: by the later fourteenth century, the view of his reign had been transformed, creating out of Alexander 'a true paragon of kingship'.[76] As in the Wyntoun song discussed in Chapter 9, a sketch is drawn of a kingdom led in piety and justice by a king who earned respect and loyalty, thus bringing peace, freedom and 'increase of welfare' to the people. The settled, strong and prosperous rule of the mature Alexander III became the antithesis not only of the weakness of a troubled minority, but also of the tyranny of a usurping foreign power. The still-current historiographical tradition of factionalism and self-serving, which has bedevilled the interpretation of the minority (and which has been extended to cast doubt on the integrity of the nobility in subsequent periods), probably had its roots in the ambitions of these fourteenth-century writers who strove to emphasise, by comparison, the good kingly qualities of the adult Alexander.

Only a few decades later, in the first decades of the fifteenth century, Andrew Wyntoun carried the process a step further with an even more elaborate eulogy, which particularly emphasised the kingly qualities of piety, virtue, generosity and equity in justice. Further, he credited Alexander with regulations that promoted agricultural development, leading to abundance and affordability of food. Notably, Wyntoun stated that this period of plenty came to an abrupt

75 *Chron. Fordun*, i, pp. 309–10 (trans. ii, pp. 304–05).
76 Reid, 'Historiography', p. 191.

end with Alexander's death.[77] Wyntoun's claim (further elaborated through the 'sang' discussed above) that destitution immediately followed the demise of the king was echoed only a few years later by the abbot of Inchcolm, Walter Bower. Written in the early 1440s, Bower's *Scotichronicon* was a continuation and development of Fordun and its associated content, and his extravagant praise of the king *post mortem* both quoted extensively and inflated the account given in *Gesta Annalia II*. He lamented that 'the losses of the times which followed clearly show how sad and harmful his death was for the kingdom of Scotland' and hinted at unspecified 'calamities that were to come'.[78] No contemporary description of Alexander's physical appearance exists: no examination of his remains, as has taken place for some English medieval kings, has been possible, and there are no sufficiently detailed accounts of his funeral obsequies to enlighten us regarding his stature or other personal details.[79] The images on seals and coins are mostly too worn to allow analysis or comparison; for the first time, therefore, in Bower we find a personal description of the king: he was

> exceptional in appearance, physically well-built, thick-set and tall in stature, though he could not be called fat. He had a jovial face, a steadfast heart, a devout spirit. He was affable in his speech, likeable in appearance, gifted with wisdom, famed for his moderation, unshakeable in his inner strength and well-tried in his outward strength, unwavering in the severity of his justice, unremitting in his forbearance, strong in patience, gentle in humility, unstinting in his charity and fair in all things.[80]

The description is, of course, entirely fanciful and, especially in the depiction of an impressive physique, predictably formulaic; it nonetheless served its purpose in giving human as well as kingly qualities to a figure who was to Bower less of a historical character than a moral exemplar. Much of the information which Bower provided in addition to his chief sources (Fordun and *Gesta Annalia*) was designed to enhance the status and independence of the Scottish kingship in the period before the wars of independence. For example, Bower made the extravagant claim that Alexander was both crowned and anointed in 1249, before discussing at length the concept of Christian

77 *Chron. Wyntoun*, v, p. 142. Wyntoun claims that Alexander 'insisted' that everyone who had an ox should have land under the plough; he did not say that it was a law, and I have not therefore categorised it as legislation. It is nonetheless consistent with the evidence for increased arable production.

78 *Chron. Bower*, v, pp. 420–21, 426–27.

79 For such evidence concerning English kings, see D.A. Carpenter, *The Reign of Henry III* (London, 1996), ch. 20.

80 *Chron. Bower*, v, pp. 420–23.

kingship; he also related the vision of St Margaret and her sons on the eve of the battle of Largs, implying a divine intervention in the battle as well as emphasising the dynastic eminence of the king.[81] Bower's eulogy continued the embellishment of earlier sources: the good firm rule conducted by Alexander III brought wealth, peace and prosperity; he was not afraid to mingle with his people and conducted regular ayres to bring royal justice to their doors; he legislated to benefit all (including the extraordinary law that every poor person was to dig at least seven square feet daily to avoid the idleness which he saw as the root of many other ills leading to impoverishment of the kingdom); his wise legislation created an environment in which trade thrived to the great benefit of the merchant community and thus the whole populace. So great was his reputation that

> many came from east and west and the ends of the earth to hear the justice, to view the orderly government, to size up the potential of the kingdom and [to admire] the wisdom of the king.[82]

One particular group who were deeply impressed were traders from Lombardy, who offered to build a city on an island in the Forth, so that they could benefit from the riches of the burgeoning Scottish economy.[83]

Curiously, in the midst of his enthusiasm for the peace and plenty which Alexander's rule bestowed on Scotland, Bower was not afraid to describe also the unstable weather which caused harvest failures and famine; he it was who claimed that the storm of 1267 was the worst since Noah's flood.[84] Bower may have had an overriding purpose in his writing, but he had enough of the historian's instinct to be unable to omit interesting detail when his sources presented it to him, even when it appeared to contradict his didactic ambition. This is not the only inconsistency in Bower's approach. In 1267, for instance, although Alexander was 'well advised in all his business . . . at the instigation of his courtiers he began to rebel against the church and the clergy', taking sides against Bishop Gamelin in the ongoing dispute about the temporalities of the diocese. The king and the church came to terms, the errant knight (John Denmuir) sought absolution for his wrongdoing and harmony was restored.[85] Again, an episode is related which falls short of enhancing the flawless reputation which, for the most part, Bower wished to give the reign.

---

81 *Chron. Bower*, v, pp. 336–39.
82 *Chron. Bower*, v, pp. 422–25.
83 *Chron. Bower*, v, pp. 424–27.
84 *Chron. Bower*, v, pp. 322–25, 368–69, 384–87.
85 *Chron. Bower*, v, pp. 360–61.

It is to Walter Bower that the concept of the Alexandrine 'golden age' must be ascribed. Moving beyond the portrayal of a ruler who exemplified the qualities of good kingship, Bower did more than simply amplify and embellish the contents of his earlier sources. He wrote within two decades of the release of James I from English captivity, and only about five years after the same king's violent assassination. As he put pen to paper, the kingdom was again undergoing the trials of royal minority, and had in the recent past suffered from both famine and plague.[86] His work bore an unmistakeable message for his own day: personal or factional considerations must be outweighed by strong personal rule, following the precepts of Christian kingship and in the national interest (that is, independent of foreign influence or oppression). Only through such a course could the nation be rescued from impending catastrophe. The reign of Alexander III thus became an elaborate allegory of just and righteous rule, a moral lesson for the leaders of a Scotland fractured by political difficulty in the mid fifteenth century.[87]

Although it is to Bower that we should ascribe the 'decisive flourish' in the creation of what has been termed 'the Alexander myth',[88] his work's enormous popularity and influence throughout several centuries ensured that later writers also played their part in securing this king's image in popular culture and folk memory. Successive historiographical generations developed and embellished the notion that Alexander III represented the high point of Scottish kingship. Only two or three decades after Bower wrote, and heavily reliant on his work, the *Liber Pluscardinensis* added to Bower's version of the inauguration details of the myth which related the legend of Scottish origins in Egypt and Greece, and added an extensive passage eulogising the achievements of those civilisations. The writer thus figuratively extended the lineage of the kingship into the great civilisations of the past. Significantly, Pluscarden laid less stress on the turmoil of the minority by ascribing the removal of the first council not to Henry III, but to good counsel provided by the Scottish parliament, thus offering a model of communal leadership which was effective against evil counsel, even despite the limitations imposed by the age of the king.[89] If the Pluscarden writer's assertion that Bagimond had sought a reduction in the level of papal taxation on account of the kingdom's poverty in the 1270s seems at odds with the notion of a Scotland flourishing economically, it is consistent with an approach which, even more than Bower's, pushes a strongly

86 For the dating of Bower's writing, see *Chron. Bower*, ix, pp. 210–14.
87 The *Scotichronicon* has been described as 'a key advisory text'. For its didactic purpose, see Sally Mapstone, 'Bower on Kingship', *Chron. Bower*, ix, pp. 321–38.
88 Reid, 'Historiography', pp. 192, 194.
89 *Liber Pluscardinensis*, i, pp. 80–81, 85 (trans. ii, pp. 55–56, 59).

independent Scottish agenda, and provides an even more exaggerated portrait of Alexander as the perfect king.

The historiographical trend continued across several centuries, although, as historical technique developed, as primary sources became more available, and as evidence was both sought and cited, a more critical approach to the reign became evident. In *Annals of Scotland* by Sir David Dalrymple of Hailes (first published in 1776) reference was frequently made to primary sources, and the multifarious versions of events supplied by earlier writers were subject to analytical synthesis; but still the conflict at Largs in 1263 was portrayed as a major national victory for the Scots (in which 24,000 Norwegians lost their lives), and the reign was characterised by good justice, peaceful relations with England, effective safeguarding of the church and a king who demonstrated 'temperance and purity of manners'.[90] If Bower's more obvious excesses in terms of legislation and material prosperity had by this time been sacrificed on the altar of critical analysis, his continuing influence over the general analysis of this reign as a high-point of the medieval period is clear. This process of historiographical development continued in the nineteenth and early twentieth centuries, with large-scale publication of primary source material fuelling the production of new, multivolume, histories. If critical analysis became more stringent, mythology still abounded. Tales of the king's death as a result of being thrown from his horse over the cliffs at Kinghorn, and of unprecedented material wealth, survived unscathed in some, if not in all, works of the period. In the late 1860s, John Hill Burton's seven-volume *History of Scotland from Agricola's Invasion to the Revolution of 1688* used the evidence of surviving architecture to suggest that Scotland was not a poor country in the later thirteenth century; Burton overdeveloped the theme, however, to claim (while acknowledging that the evidence was slender) that Scotland under Alexander III was richer than it had ever been, or would be again. Burton did characterise this reign as a watershed, a period which was crucial to the understanding of later events, and thus devoted more space to it than many previous historians had done. He was sceptical of the extravagant treatment given by others to the battle of Largs; on the other hand, he did not even attempt to reach a deep understanding of the minority period, stating that it was too confusing, laden with intrigue: 'neither can the actors nor the policy they pursued be brought out so distinctly as to enable us to take an interest in them'.[91] The turmoil of the minority was symptomatic of weak rule which gave rise to the scourge of

90 Sir David Dalrymple, Lord Hailes, *Annals of Scotland from the Accession of Malcolm III to the Accession of the House of Stewart* (Edinburgh, 1819), i, pp. 213, 223–24.

91 John Hill Burton, *History of Scotland from Agricola's Invasion to the Revolution* (Edinburgh and London, 1867–70), ii, pp. 21–24.

domination by overmighty subjects. Burton and other late nineteenth- and early twentieth-century writers (among them Peter Hume Brown, the author of a much-loved popular three-volume history of Scotland), largely rejected the historiography of the sixteenth to eighteenth centuries, purporting instead to offer more critical analysis based on primary sources. In so doing, they in fact reverted to the supposed truth as promoted by Bower and others, while giving it a veneer of evidential authority. The myth of the golden age thus lingered in the historiography which was to influence generations of schoolchildren and a public which throughout the twentieth century became voracious consumers of popular history.

These late Victorian writers still formed the bedrock of Scottish historical scholarship in the early and mid twentieth century. In that period, the rise of nationalism fostered a societal atmosphere which was warmly receptive to the narratives provided by Fordun, Bower and others, which were focused on successful, prosperous rule, independent of England.[92] The renaissance of Scottish culture, which had its roots in the Celtic revivalism of the late nineteenth century and which was fervently promoted by such literary luminaries as Christopher Murray Grieve (Hugh McDiarmid) from as early as the 1920s, was fertile soil for the propagation of a national history which had been tentatively challenging the pervasive Britishness of post-Union Scotland ever since the novels of Sir Walter Scott in the early nineteenth century.[93] Irrespective of political leanings, the romantic myths of Scottish history, so effectively promulgated by these writers, became the staple diet of Scots themselves, encouraged by the appetite of developing tourism (and particularly, in more recent times, ancestral tourism). The notion that some rulers gained 'popular' support in a period when no such concept could have existed, is a useful example. Hume Brown, followed three decades later by Sir James Fergusson in the first monograph devoted entirely to Alexander III's reign, claimed that the 'anti-English' Comyn party of the minority were supported by the common people of the kingdom against the 'pro-English' (and, by implication, more distantly aristocratic) Durwards.[94] From such an approach develops the apparently inextinguishable myth, for example, that William Wallace and King Robert Bruce were the heroes of the ordinary folk of the land.

---

92 The Scottish National Party was formed in 1934, through the amalgamation of two slightly earlier nationalist organisations.

93 This bald statement belies a complicated and controversial subject, with a copious literature. For different interpretations, see (for example) Christopher Harvie, *Scotland and Nationalism: Scottish Society and Politics, 1707–1977* (London, 1977); H.J. Hanham, *Scottish Nationalism* (London, 1969); Andrew Marr, *The Battle for Scotland* (London, 1992).

94 P. Hume Brown, *History of Scotland* (Cambridge, 1902), i, pp. 118–19, 121.

James Fergusson's *Alexander III, King of Scotland* (1937) has been described as a 'depressing disappointment' – in the main 'a simplistic recitation of a careful selection of contemporary and near-contemporary narrative sources'.[95] With a miniscule list of sources and completely unreferenced, it did not claim to be a scholarly work. Although critical of the traditional treatment of the battle of Largs on the basis of topographical research, which he used to back up his reading of both Scottish and Norwegian narrative sources, Fergusson nonetheless recited again, without any attempt at critical analysis, the Bowerian mantra of unprecedented wealth and unrealistic legislation, and padded it with unevidenced supposition. (In contrast to other periods, the peasantry were, apparently, 'contented' under Alexander III.[96]) Fergusson later, in 1949, became Keeper of the Records of Scotland: his work on Alexander III betrays little use of the records for which he would have curatorial responsibility for two decades.

William Croft Dickinson's *Scotland from the Earliest Times to 1603* (1961) was the first of a new generation of modern, revisionist histories. Dickinson's introduction (written in 1959) stated unequivocally that it was published in order to replace Hume Brown's work as the 'standard account': 'a real need has arisen for a new "History of Scotland", written from a somewhat different approach and taking full account of our advancing knowledge'.[97] This presaged a new outpouring of scholarship on medieval Scotland throughout the later twentieth and early twenty-first centuries, characterised by entirely fresh approaches. Understanding of the society, institutions and economy of the kingdom, and of discrete sections of society (in particular, the nobility) was immeasurably deepened by forensic analysis of a wide range of primary evidence, presented in a cornucopia of groundbreaking works. Long-accepted narratives were revisited, and long-held beliefs abandoned. At last, Bower's account of Alexander's mercantile legislation was revealed for what it really was – 'garbled nonsense'![98] The eight contributors to the volume of essays on aspects of *Scotland in the Reign of Alexander III, 1249–1286* were active participants in this resurgence of Scottish medieval studies and made an important contribution to the historiography of Alexander III.[99] Specific mention must also be made of D.E.R. Watt's monumental achievement in producing, along with a nationwide team of experts, a new critical edition of Bower's *Scotichronicon*, replacing at last the eighteenth-century edition by Goodall, and providing the

95 Reid, 'Historiography', p. 203.

96 James Fergusson, *Alexander III, King of Scotland* (London, 1937), p. 156.

97 W. Croft Dickinson, *Scotland from the Earliest Times to 1603*, 3rd edn, revised by A.A.M. Duncan (Oxford, 1977), p. vii.

98 Duncan, *Making of the Kingdom*, p. 603.

99 Reid, *Alexander III Essays.*

first ever complete English translation.[100] Over the last two decades, the work primarily of Dauvit Broun in unpicking the complexities of the constituent parts and predecessor texts of Fordun's *Chronica Gentis Scotorum*, and his analysis (with Julian Harrison) of the *Chronicle of Melrose* have revolutionised the historian's ability to interpret the most important narrative sources.[101] Similarly, detailed analysis, by a number of scholars, of documentary sources (for example, the groundbreaking *Regesta Regum Scotorum* series) has changed the understanding of, and approach to, legal, administrative and governmental issues. D.E.R. Watt also made his own highly influential contribution to the historiography of the reign of Alexander III with his study of the minority, published in 1971.[102] If more recent research has led to different conclusions, Watt's was nevertheless an original approach, attempting to analyse the motivations and behaviour of the protagonists in their historical and socio-dynastic context, to cast a fresh light on events.

The populist end of the modern market has largely failed to follow the lead: where, all too rarely, this important reign receives any significant attention, still there are pro- and anti-English 'parties' in the minority; still the golden age weaves its magic spell; still Alexander dies, 'bruised and broken', at the foot of a cliff (the result of his 'devotion' to Yolande, from whom 'he could not bear to be parted').[103] It is common to find that the manner (rather than the significance) of Alexander III's death occupies a completely disproportionate amount of space within an otherwise meagre account of the reign.[104] In Alistair Moffat's, *Scotland: A History from Earliest Times*, Alexander and his council were carousing in Edinburgh in celebration of his marriage to the 'beautiful French countess'; 'fuelled by Gascon wine', Alexander stated that he was in the mood to visit her and so took off in the deadly storm, dying when his horse 'plunged with its rider over the cliffs'.[105] The requirement to recite and embroider the

100 *Chron. Bower;* Goodall edition: W. Goodall (ed.), *Joannis de Fordum Scotichronicon cum Supplementis et Continuatone Walteri Boweri* (2 vols, Edinburgh 1759).

101 *Chron. Melrose*; Dauvit Broun, 'Becoming Scottish in the Thirteenth Century: The Evidence of the Chronicle of Melrose', in Beverley Ballin Smith, Simon Taylor and Gareth Williams (eds), *West Over Sea: Studies in Scandinavian Sea-Borne Expansion and Settlement Before 1300* (Leiden, 2007), pp. 19–32. For Broun's work on Fordun, see the Bibliography.

102 Watt, 'Minority'.

103 A few examples: R.L. Mackie, *A Short History of Scotland* (London, 1930), quote from p. 96; John Prebble, *The Lion in the North* (Harmondsworth, 1973), quote from p. 68; James Sharp, *The Flower of Scotland: A History of Scottish Monarchy* (Perth, 1981); Alistair Moffat, *Scotland: A History from Earliest Times* (Edinburgh, 2017), pp. 200–01.

104 This is true, for example, of Neil Oliver, *A History of Scotland* (London, 2009), where 20 per cent of the total treatment of the reign is given over to Alexander's demise at the foot of the cliffs. There is no analysis of the significance of the reign, and the account is an undifferentiated mixture of fact and fiction.

105 Alistair Moffat, *Scotland: A History from Earliest Times*, pp. 200–01.

romantic myth of the king's death has again overwhelmed both fact and significance. The council meeting was during Lent – not a time for carousing; the marriage was already some five months old; and, as has been noted, there is no evidence of a fall from the cliffs. To render good history popularly accessible is laudable; wilfully to mislead is not.

In 1999 Marion Campbell published the only monograph-length treatment of the reign other than Fergusson's, *Alexander III, King of Scots*.[106] Its bibliography almost completely ignored the entire corpus of Scottish historical writing of the previous 20 years. The author freely admitted that she had 'applied a novelist's reasoning to disentangle some puzzles',[107] and although printed documentary sources were cited frequently, the narrative largely followed the chronicle accounts. Despite a novelistic style which tends to obscure the boundary between fiction and fact, the work did have serious intent, included useful broadly European contextual information and concluded that one of the legacies of Alexander was that he had 'fused the ancient consultative processes of Celtic kingdoms into those of a feudal state, to produce a mature and balanced system of government'. He thus left a country which was strong and self-confident enough to cope with the difficulties of the ensuing decades: 'the Community of the Realm . . . was Alexander's lasting bequest to his people'.[108] Despite this promising final analysis, which is not dissimilar to that of Duncan's *Making of the Kingdom* of a quarter of a century earlier (which does not appear in Campbell's bibliography), in this, as in much of the populist genre, Bower still wears his crown as the supreme interpreter of the reign.

The closing paragraph of Archie Duncan's *Scotland, The Making of the Kingdom* almost anticipated the notion of mutual responsibility of aristocracy and monarch which underpins the premise of this book:

> During the thirteenth century the kings of Scotland had created a political atmosphere whose essential quality was harmony, by distributing office in the state widely among the magnates so that they acquired insight into the methods and problems of government and became fit – that is, constructive – advisers of the king. The sources do not speak of the 'community of the realm' before 1286 but this 'abstract expression' acquired its meaning in Alexander III's Scotland when the king sought common counsel of his barons. If unity of opinion was a fictitious 'consensus', it became real when opinion was accepted by the king and so

106 Marion Campbell, *Alexander III, King of Scots* (Colonsay, 1999).
107 Campbell, *Alexander III*, p. xii.
108 Campbell, *Alexander III*, pp. 236–37.

> transformed into the policy of government. Essential to the community as a source of political responsibility was the king whose authority provided the men of thirteenth century Scotland with their political ideas and vocabulary. Together they made a kingdom.[109]

It is a view more overtly monarchocentric than would generally be expressed today. Although Duncan pointed to an important truth about the nature of Scottish medieval political discourse, he characterised the consensual nature of Scottish government as an achievement of – a change wrought by – the thirteenth-century kings, rather than as a foundational precept of Scottish kingship itself. The difference between the view expressed by Duncan and the one which underlies the present volume lies in the approach to the societal and legal changes of the twelfth and thirteenth centuries. If the 'feudalisation', or territorialisation of aristocratic power which occurred under David I and his successors is truly regarded as a mutual project rather than as an imposition of a foreign system (even one into which older structures were assimilated), then the resulting judicial and administrative structures reveal a deep-seated tradition of shared aristocratic responsibility lying at the heart of Scottish royal government. It is this fact which makes Alice Taylor's *The Shape of the State in Medieval Scotland, 1124–1290* so fundamental to a new interpretation of the reign of Alexander III. The end point of this brief historiographical survey, Taylor's vision of the crucial importance to Scottish kingly rule of aristocratic power enables a synthesis of much of the important work of the last few decades, itself based on detailed study of documentary and narrative sources, to reveal both the nature and the importance of Alexander's reign.

109 Duncan, *Making of the Kingdom*, pp. 614–15.

Conclusion

In the National Gallery of Scotland hangs a painting by Benjamin West, an American-born artist who achieved very considerable success in late eighteenth-century Britain. It bears the grandiose title *Alexander III of Scotland Rescued from the Fury of a Stag by the Intrepidity of Colin Fitzgerald* (Plate 13). West's massive painting, 'a tour de force of pictorial theatre', was commissioned by Francis Humberston Mackenzie, the chief of the Seaforth line of the Clan Mackenzie, and was first exhibited at the Royal Academy in London in 1786.[1] The canvas depicts a family legend, apparently first written down in *The Genealogie of the Mackenzies Preceeding Ye Year MDCLXI* by Sir George Mackenzie (1669), which relates that Colin Fitzgerald, a political exile from Ireland who had been given protection in Scotland by Alexander III (and who had given loyal service during the Norwegian invasion of 1263), rescued the king from a stag during a hunt. Mackenzie's text reads, '. . . A Hart pursued him, and with probability to have hurt him, If Colin Fitz-Gerald had not killed him in his approach with ane arrow . . .',[2] and the tale in its context seems to relate more to the design of the subsequent Mackenzie coat of arms than to an act of singular heroism. The king is said to have given Fitzgerald the lands of Kintail (by implication, as a reward), and he thus became the progenitor of the Mackenzies of Kintail (later, in the seventeenth century, earls of Seaforth). Mackenzie quotes an obviously spurious charter of Kintail by Alexander III in support of his contention.[3] A century later the painting dramatically, and romantically,

1 Timothy Clifford, Michael Gallacher and Helen Smailes (ed. Duncan Thomson), *Benjamin West and the Death of the Stag: The Story Behind the Painting and its Conservation* (Edinburgh, 2009), p. 5. The painting is indeed on a grand scale: it measures 12 × 17 feet (p. 11).

2 [George Mackenzie], *The Genealogie of the Mackenzies Preceeding Ye Year MDCLXI* (Edinburgh, 1829), p. 3.

3 The charter, quoted in *The Genealogie of the Mackenzies*, p. 3, purports to be dated at Kincardine (which was, certainly, a favoured hunting ground) on 9 January a.r. 16. This would be January 1265 (rather than 1266, as stated by Mackenzie), but, quite apart from the highly

exaggerates the scene. The king, apparently thrown from his horse, seems in peril of his life, but for Fitzgerald's single-handed wrestling and spearing of the stag. In its seventeenth-century published form, the legend may have had a previous life in oral tradition, and was used as a means of conferring an Anglo-Irish pedigree on the family, rather than the less fashionable Gaelic genealogy which more closely resembled the truth. A more ambitious purpose may be identified over a century later in the commissioning of the painting. The family had been subject to forfeiture after the 1715 rebellion for its Jacobite sympathies, and by the 1780s, although partially reinstated, it still required to rehabilitate itself in the eyes of the British establishment. The grand and extravagant work may have served its purpose; Mackenzie received a peerage, with the title of Lord Seaforth, in 1797.[4]

In most respects the story of the painting is associated more with the politics and society of the eighteenth century than it is with the reign of Alexander III. It is intriguing, however, to contemplate why these two Mackenzies, more than a century apart, chose a tale of fervent allegiance to this thirteenth-century Scottish king on which to rebuild their family honour. Alexander's own reputation, after all, was founded on fourteenth- and fifteenth-century writers' adulation of him as a defender of Scotland's independence from southern oppression. The painting did carry a simple message of unswerving loyalty to a monarch, intended for George III, who was already an admirer and patron of West, and who certainly saw the work. The selection of Alexander III as the subject of the legendary progenitor's potentially self-sacrificial act of heroism as opposed to that of a more ancient, and a more British, object of allegiance, however, is striking. For George Mackenzie, writing in the 1660s, before the Union of Parliaments, who had no need of the profound familial rehabilitation required by his later descendant, the choice of an overtly Scottish royal patron may not have been an obstacle to advancement; but a more saintly or valiantly patriotic king (David I – whose own legendary tussle with a stag is said to have led to the foundation of Holyrood abbey – or Robert I?) might have been a more obvious candidate. In any case, it would not have been surprising if by the time the painting was commissioned the legend had been modified, both to reflect the greater need for strengthening the family's reputation and to

---

improbable diplomatic of the charter, the witnesses include Archibald bishop of Moray (1253–98), Thomas Durward (*Hostiarius*), sheriff of Inverness (1220s), and Henry 'de Balcock', chamberlain. If Balcock is a misreading for Balliol (the only Scottish thirteenth-century chamberlain named Henry, 1231–35 and 1241–49), there is no date in the reign of either Alexander II or Alexander III which would accommodate any two, let alone three, of these individuals.

4 Clifford *et al.*, *Death of the Stag*, pp. 11–12.

harmonise with the infinitely more pervasive expectation of British identity which dominated the post-Union period. Instead, Alexander III remained the preferred model of ideal kingship. In demonstrating the legendary progenitor's loyalty to the perfect king, Francis Humberston Mackenzie implied an analogous contemporary loyalty to his own ideal king, George III.

The painting exemplified civilised and generous patronage of the arts at the heart of the British establishment; it asserted an ancient British lineage underlying title to the lands in question as well as a long-standing respect for and loyalty to monarchy. Importantly, in achieving these ends it flattered the king whose approval was sought. Allusion to a 'golden age' for both monarchy and kingdom would serve to bathe the present in a golden light. It was a message which could only be effective in a society in which Alexander III was understood to be a King Arthur figure: a paragon of kingship, in a mythologically perfect kingdom.

The problem with this approach to the reign is that biography becomes hagiography; the ill-defined notion of a golden age is 'an irrelevance and a hindrance to deeper study'.[5] The politically motivated exaggerations of Bower and others have profoundly influenced the understanding of this reign through half a millennium into present times, as demonstrated by the persistent weakness of its treatment in populist histories. Removal of the Bower-filter, now made possible by deeper understanding of both documentary and narrative sources, enables a more realistic assessment of the achievements and significance of the reign. Though in certain respects unspectacular, the adult reign was largely peaceful and lacked any severe threat to royal authority; the economy was good, but not as fabulously prosperous as later accounts would have us believe; external relations were generally settled, but there were fractures which required healing; the church seems generally to have flourished, but dispute was not uncommon as its relationship with the newer style of secular authority developed. Apart from the royal succession (and the apparently rough coastal path to Kinghorn), there were no disasters, but neither were there dramatic triumphs. Though life in Alexander III's Scotland seems to have been better for many than it was in other periods, it is important to retain a realistic image of a society in which life was grossly unequal, insecure, harsh, heavily male-dominated, disease-ridden and, all too frequently, short.

Aspects of this reign, though, in contrast with the grim decades which followed, offer glimpses of Scottish medieval society at its best. In that respect, there is value in viewing this reign as a watershed: 'a grasp of the true nature of this settled period is of vital importance to our understanding of what followed';

5 Reid, 'Historiography', p. 207.

but it is not necessary to conclude that the 'watershed' nature of the reign comprises its 'primary importance'.[6] If such an approach is taken, there is a danger of simply assuming that everything appears rosy in hindsight, and thus of denigrating, or ignoring, real achievement. There are thus fine balancing acts to be performed in the final analysis: to strip out unhelpful historiographical embellishment while holding on to true achievement; to make use of the available image of the kingdom poised before its plunge from the metaphorical cliff-edge, while accepting that the view is in some ways inevitably distorted; to discern the merits of good government while acknowledging that it is to a great extent the product of earlier developments; and to recognise the achievements of an able ruler and governing community while remaining largely ignorant of their individual personalities and accomplishments and of the nature and practicalities of their working relationships.

The development of a law common to the entire kingdom provided a profound element of the peace and prosperity which forms the most basic characteristic of the reign. It was that peace, the protection from strife in both national and local contexts, which allowed people throughout society to get on with their daily lives. For much of the reign, all that was stormy was the weather: crops may sometimes have been ruined by flood or pestilence, but they were allowed to regrow without being trampled by armies. The huge increase in the amount of circulating silver coin reveals a governmental drive towards a money and trading economy, the benefits of which would to some extent filter down through society. It is unarguable that as the meteorological, political and economic climates deteriorated in the subsequent decades, the quality of life worsened for all.

This reign marks the fruition of two centuries of administrative, legal and societal change and development. Alexander III's ability to rule was founded on a bedrock of process and structure which had been built and extended by his twelfth and thirteenth predecessors, and which he adapted and further developed. Much older, older even than the dynastic kingship which he represented, was the tradition of consensual rule, which was a core principle of the Scottish monarchy. By the later thirteenth century these two strands, of modern territorial-based administration and ancient consensus, had blended to form a model of kingship which served Scotland well, both then and in the troubled years to come. The 'community of the realm' did not find written expression until after Alexander's death, but there can be no realistic doubt that it was a vital concept which was well understood in Alexander III's day (and earlier). More than a concept, it was an actuality within the kingdom. It did not owe its existence to the skill and acumen of Alexander III, but was a fundamental

6 Reid, 'Historiography', p. 207.

component of the kingship he embodied. The community of the realm had been essential to the kingship for centuries, evolving with other social and governmental structures. It was political necessity in time of crisis which led to its being articulated in writing because that was when it became essential to elucidate the conceptual underpinning of the Scottish state.[7] This model of government, eased by benign conditions, rendered Alexander's reign exceptional. It is not unreasonable to postulate that it was the very success, territorially, economically and politically, of Alexander III's Scotland which was a primary motivator of Edward I as he lined the kingdom up in his sights from 1291 onwards: a strong, successful Scotland was too much of a threat. The contrast between Scotland and the more bureaucratic, centralist and monarch-dominated governmental system to the south is striking: England's method of rule offered some advantages, but in this period had led to conflict rather than consensus between crown and aristocracy. An understanding of these two distinct models is essential to any study of either internal affairs or the relationship between the two kingdoms.

Alexander III was undoubtedly an able ruler who gained the respect of his peers both in Scotland and beyond. He was also fortunate in the timing of his reign: following an extended period of administrative and legal development, at the culmination of a lengthy, and conscious, drive towards achieving the self-identity of a nation, in a benevolent economic climate which bathed the whole of Europe, and, most importantly, in a period of relative political stability. It is not therefore realistic to ascribe to this single individual the achievements which his reign appears to exhibit. Describing the English state of the fifteenth century (although it is as relevant to the thirteenth or fourteenth) as 'a vehicle for powerful, potentially predatory, kingship', Chris Given-Wilson has commented that

> its dependence on active and cooperative kingship and the power which it invested in the person of the monarch was also its Achilles heel, for it relied disproportionately on the aptitude of each king to make it function in a way that was acceptable to the polity, and aptitude was not something that the lottery of heredity could guarantee.[8]

7 Barrow, *Kingship and Unity*, pp. 128–29; also, p. 125: 'As we should expect, the idea came in advance of the actual phrase required to express it.' Barrow's discussion of the lack of a vernacular English phrase for this concept (pp. 124–25) reminds us again of the intrinsic difference between the English and Scottish systems of rule: he makes the useful point that this was a concept which was foreign to the English monarchy until forced on it by the upheavals of the 1250s and 1260s.

8 Chris Given-Wilson, *Henry IV* (Newhaven and London, 2017), p. 7.

Scotland was perhaps lucky: heredity dealt a good hand in Alexander III. But, stretching *Gesta Annalia II*'s metaphor, although after Alexander III's minority the ship *Scotland* did indeed have an able steersman, she also had the multiple benefits of having been well designed, of being crewed by an effective and cooperative team, and of sailing a calm sea. Hindsight, from the viewpoint of the ensuing political and economic catastrophe, does not provide a sufficient analysis of the reign of Alexander III: 'golden age' is an unhelpful term. Rather, the happy circumstance of able and consensual rule grounded on a governmental and societal order which had evolved over centuries, and in a period of economic prosperity and political security, allows us a view of what might justifiably be termed the zenith of Scottish medieval kingship.

APPENDIX 1

Witnesses to Royal Acta and Members of Royal Council, 1249–1262

The table below lists all those who appear as witnesses to royal *acta*, as well as those named in relation to the change of royal council in September 1255, and demonstrates the witnessing activity of each, from the beginning of the reign in July 1249 until Alexander III's twenty-first birthday, in September 1262.

The names of the 68 men and 1 woman are presented in the order in which they first appear in the *acta*; the divisions within the table represent the dates at which minority governments changed (with the document of September 1255 represented as a segment on its own, lying between the second and third minority councils). Grey shading indicates that an individual witnessed during this period; no shading indicates they did not. The eight central columns refer, in order, to:

- witnesses to *acta* issued during the first minority council of July 1249 to December 1251; *RRS*, iv pt. 1, nos. 1–13;
- witnesses to *acta* issued during the second minority council of January 1252 to September 1255; *RRS*, iv pt. 1, nos. 14–21;
- those named as having advised the king on the reorganisation of the council in September 1255; *RRS*, iv pt. 1, no. 22;
- those named as having been removed from the council in September 1255; *RRS*, iv pt. 1, no. 22, who are, for clarity, further marked with **X**;
- those named as having been appointed to the new council in September 1255; *RRS*, iv pt. 1, no. 22;
- witnesses to *acta* issued during the third minority council of September 1255 to October 1257; *RRS*, iv pt. 1, nos. 23–25;
- a blank column, indicating the total lack of surviving *acta* for what might be termed the fourth minority council, between the Kinross

affair in October 1257 and Alexander's independent appointment of a council in September 1258;
- witnesses to *acta* issued during the period October 1258 to September 1262; *RRS*, iv pt. 1, nos. 26–39.

The final column identifies the relevant documents for each individual, as numbered in *RRS*, iv pt. 1. By referring to the numbers it can therefore be ascertained how many times each individual witnessed during any given period.

Several editorial considerations should be noted:

1. Not all documents of the period are represented, since one (no. 21) bears no witnesses, and six (nos. 29, 34–39) are witnessed solely by the king – '*teste me ipso*'.
2. Personal names are given in the form in which they appear in the text of the book.
3. Since it is impossible to distinguish one from the other in the *acta*, the table treats Robert Ros, father and son, as one individual.
4. Known dates of death are noted in those cases where they died between July 1249 and September 1262. Dates are not presumed purely because the individuals disappear from record.
5. The approximate dates, where known, of office-holding is provided for chancellors and chamberlains. Other offices are noted only if they are specified in the *acta*.

Both the low number of documents and the unevenness with which they are spread across the period make it unwise to draw firm conclusions about the make-up of the minority governments. However, if the table supported the contention of strict factional division within the minority, the expectation would be, for example, that names appearing in column 1 (1249–51) would not also appear in column 2 (1252–55), but might reappear in columns 5 and/or 6. Certainly, the table would have a less random aspect. When the witnessing activities of these individuals is further examined, through the evidence provided in non-royal documents (discoverable through the *PoMS* database), the picture becomes even clearer: business between those who might be assumed to be political rivals continued as usual despite governmental changes. A table using the resultant quantity of data would be impractical: the more limited picture provided solely by the royal *acta* is thus offered here.

	Witness 1249–1251	Witness 1252–1255	Named as advisor in 1255	Removed from council in 1255	Member of new council in 1255	Witness 1255–Oct. 1257	Oct. 1257–Sept. 1258 – no *acta*	Witness Oct. 1258–Sept. 1262	*RRS*, iv pt.1 refs (no.)
William (Bondington), bishop of Glasgow (d. November 1258)				X					1, 15, 22
Walter Comyn, earl of Menteith (d. Nov. 1258)				X					1, 11, 14, 15, 16, 18, 19, 20, 22, 26
William of Menteith									1
Alexander Stewart									1, 7, 8, 14, 18, 22, 30
Robert Ros				X					1, 2, 10, 13, 16, 17, 18, 19, 20, 22
Robert Menzies, chamberlain (1251)									1, 2, 5, 6, 8, 10, 11, 12, 13, 22, 23
Gilbert Hay									2, 3, 5, 9, 12, 22
John Vaux (d. 1256–57?)									2, 5, 6, 7, 9, 12, 13, 22
Richard Marshall									2, 17
Thomas Randolph (d. 1262)				X					2, 19, 22
Richard, bishop (-elect) of Dunkeld (chancellor, 1255–57)									3, 13, 22
Roger, abbot of Newbattle (d. 1256)									3, 22
Alan Durward, justiciar of Scotia									3, 11, 22, 28
Walter Bisset									4, 7,
David of Haddington									4,
John of Hermiston									4, 6, 9, 13
William Hay									4,

	Witness 1249–1251	Witness 1252–1255	Named as advisor in 1255	Removed from council in 1255	Member of new council in 1255	Witness 1255–Oct. 1257	Oct. 1257–Sept. 1258 – no *acta*	Witness Oct. 1258–Sept. 1262	*RRS*, iv pt.1 refs (no.)
David Menzies									5,
Aymer Maxwell (chamberlain, 1259–60)				X					7, 16, 17, 22, 28, 31
William Hadden									7
Patrick, earl of Dunbar									8, 22, 23, 24, 25, 30, 31
David Lochore, sheriff of Perth				X					10, 19, 22
John Balliol				X					11, 22
Alexander Comyn, earl of Buchan, justiciar of Scotia				X					12, 16, 18, 19, 20, 22, 30, 31
William Brechin									12, 22, 25
William, earl of Mar (chamberlain 1252–55, 1262–66)				X					14, 15, 16, 17, 18, 19, 22, 26
David (Bernham), bishop of St Andrews (d. 1253)									15
Matthew, abbot of Melrose (deposed/resigned, 1261)									17
Walter Murray, justiciar of Lothian									17, 22, 25
Clement, bishop of Dunblane (d. 1258)				X					18, 19, 22
Richard, abbot of Cambuskenneth									18
Nicholas Soulis				X					18, 19, 22
David Graham				X					18, 22
Gamelin (bishop (-elect) of St Andrews) (chancellor, 1254–55)				X					18, 22

	Witness 1249–1251	Witness 1252–1255	Named as advisor in 1255	Removed from council in 1255	Member of new council in 1255	Witness 1255–Oct. 1257	Oct. 1257–Sept. 1258 – no *acta*	Witness Oct. 1258–Sept. 1262	*RRS*, iv pt.1 refs (no.)
William the Chaplain				X					18, 22
Alexander of Corbridge									18
John Blund				X					18, 19, 22
John Salvain									18
Peter, bishop of Aberdeen (d. 1256)									22
(John) abbot of Dunfermline (d. 1256)									22
(Robert) abbot of Kelso (d. 1258)									22
(Nicholas) abbot of Jedburgh									22
Máel Coluim, earl of Fife									22
Níall, earl of Carrick									22
Máel Ísu, earl of Strathearn									22, 25
Robert Bruce									22
David Lindsay (chamberlain, 1255–57)									22
Hugh Gifford									22, 23
Roger Mowbray									22
William Douglas									22
William Ramsay									22
Marion Maxwell				X					22
John Comyn				X					22

	Witness 1249–1251	Witness 1252–1255	Named as advisor in 1255	Removed from council in 1255	Member of new council in 1255	Witness 1255–Oct. 1257	Oct. 1257–Sept. 1258 – no *acta*	Witness Oct. 1258–Sept. 1262	*RRS*, iv pt.1 refs (no.)
Thomas Normanville				X					22
Alexander Uviet				X					22
John Denmuir				X					22, 33
Hugh Gourlay				X					22
William Gourlay				X					22
William Wishart, archdeacon of St Andrews (chancellor, 1257?x59–73)				X					22, 33
Richard, almoner of the Knights Templar				X					22
John Wishart				X					22
William Cadzow				X					22
Roger de Quincy, earl of Winchester, constable of Scotland									25
Hugh Barclay, justiciar of Lothian									26
Henry Graham									27
Hugh Abernethy									31, 32
Walter Stewart									31
John Park									33
William Sinclair									33

APPENDIX 2

Et te lux oritur, o dulcis Scotia

The Wedding Hymn for Princess Margaret of Scotland and King Erik II of Norway, 1281

Latin text taken from the manuscript facsimile in *Proceedings of the Society of Antiquaries of Scotland, lxxiii* (1939), pp. 276–88 (plate lxxxiii). Translation by Gilbert Márkus, from Thomas Owen Clancy (ed.), *The Triumph Tree: Scotland's Earliest Poetry AD 550–1350* (Edinburgh, 1998), pp. 295–96. Translation reproduced by courtesy of Gilbert Márkus and Thomas Owen Clancy.

Ex te lux oritur o dulcis scocia *qua vere noscitur fulgens norwagia.* *Que cum transvehitur trahis suspiria* *tui subtrahitur quod regis filia.*	From you arises, sweet Scotland, a light whose brightness is seen shining in Norway; how you will sigh when she is borne across the sea, when the daughter of your king is taken away.
Cum pax accenditur que sui gracia *regnis indicitur redit leticia.* *Applaudunt undique terrarum spacia* *tecum sed utique congaudet anglia.*	When the flame of peace is kindled, its grace proclaimed to the nations, gladness makes reply. Every nation's length and breadth now celebrates, but above all England shares your joy.
Ad regem mittitur Eyricum regia *virgo suscipitur summa cum gloria.* *Gens tota solvitur In plausus eya* *cantus extollitur fiunt tripudia.*	To Eirik the king the royal maid is sent, and with highest honour there received; everyone breaks out in wild applause, the people dancing while they sing her praise.
Cleri celebriter occurat concio *orat salubriter sacra religio.* *Prodit celeriter omnis condicio* *et sexus pariter resultans gaudio.*	A crowd of clergy solemnly comes forth, and wholesomely the holy priesthood prays. Swiftly now come every class of folk, men and likewise women, joy resounding.

Rex ducit virginem dulce coniugium *per mundi cardinem producit gaudium.* *Salvet compaginem deus hanc omnium* *horum propaginem det et in medium.*	The king leads forth the maid – a cause of joy throughout the world is their sweet union. May the God of all pour blessings on this bond and of their marriage grant them children.
Regina residet in regni solio *iniuncta possidet coronam regio.* *In cultu presidet digna fastigio* *sit qui sic providet laus dei filio.*	One flesh with the king, the queen now sits upon the kingdom's throne and wears the crown, worthy to preside and guide the nation's life. Praise be to him who makes it so, God's son.
O quam laudabilis hec regis socia *mitis affabilis plena prudencia.* *Cunctis dat humilis pollet facundia* *venustat nobilis quam continencia*	How to praise this partner of the king, so gentle, kindly, full of prudence? Humble, she gives to all, strong in her speech, made lovelier yet by noble continence.*
Viro sit ut fuit rachel amabilis *ut regi placuit ester placabilis.* *Ut lya genuit sit prole fertilis* *degat ut deguit susanna stabilis.*	May she be loving to her man as was Rachel; may she be pleasing to the king, as Esther was. as Leah begot, may she be fertile in offspring, and like Susannah may she live in steadfastness.
Manentes iugiter dei servicio *Senescant taliter felici senio.* *Ut vite labilis de curso stadio* *semper durabilis sint digni bravio.*	Living conjoined in the service of God, may they in happiness grow old that when the race is run of this, their passing life, they may be worthy of a lasting reward.
Ex te progreditur o dulcis scocia *qua late spargitur laudis materia.*	From you, sweet Scotland, there comes forth a cause to sing your praise across the earth.

* The Latin *continencia* means continence in the sense of self-restraint or purity.

APPENDIX 3

A Note on Sources

For those readers not familiar with the rigours of researching medieval Scotland, a very general note regarding sources might be helpful. This is not intended to present a list of the sources available, but rather to give an impression of their nature. There is an almost innate assumption by many Scots that inevitably their country is severely lacking in source material; the age-old Scottish inferiority complex, encouraged by centuries of Anglocentric education, leads us to assume that the evidence of Scotland's past is naturally far inferior to that of our southerly neighbour. For reasons which will be touched on below, there is sadly an element of truth in this regarding the amount of material available within Scotland, but it has to be emphasised that the situation is not as bleak as is sometimes imagined.

Medieval Scotland, as explained in Chapter 1, had a largely decentralised government. One effect of this was that the astounding series of government records created by the English and some other centralised administrations are largely lacking here, particularly for the thirteenth and earlier centuries. The magnificent English Patent Rolls, Close Rolls, Fine Rolls and other series, which provide so detailed a picture of royal and aristocratic activity throughout the southerly kingdom, have no equivalent in Scotland in this period. For the reign of Alexander III, the official record of government is largely contained firstly within the slender volume, very recently published, in which has been gathered excellent modern editions of the few hundred surviving acts of the king himself, and, secondly, in part of the first volume of financial records known as the Exchequer Rolls, which was made available in printed form in the late nineteenth century. The royal *acta* comprise a variety of record types: charters recording transactions of the king, by which he granted lands or other benefits to individuals, religious establishments and burghs; records of state events, such as treaties and agreements; documents emanating from judicial cases; and, just occasionally, personal correspondence of the king. The original financial records of Alexander's reign, comprising just a tiny percentage of the mainly later printed series, now exist only in a selective seventeenth-century transcript, providing partial copies of sheriffs' and chamberlains' accounts for the crucial period of the early–mid 1260s. They are a tantalising glimpse of those documentary riches which have not survived. Fragmentary as they are, they reveal much about how the kingdom was administered, how its economy, landholding and judicial systems worked, and how it was organised to withstand the exigencies of war. Similar types of document are found in greater quantity in non-royal sources. The great monastic houses and cathedrals kept their own records of land transactions and legal proceedings which affected them, and they may sometimes have acted as repositories of proof for transactions which did not directly involve them. The records they held, selectively transcribed into the books known as cartularies, or into bishops' registers, contain thousands of documents which add immeasurably to our understanding of how the kingdom worked: the relationships – legal and financial, but only rarely personal – between people and institutions. Other bodies, such as burghs, kept records of their activities and property, which add further to our stock of knowledge. Some private individuals and families at the aristocratic end of the social scale retained copies, in charter chests and copied into registers, of documents providing evidence of their landholdings and rights in relation to their neighbours, superiors (including the king) and tenants. Finally, there is in various collections (often of later transcriptions) a broad range of legal, legislative and other material, some of which is difficult to date accurately, but which provides further evidence to assist in the interpretation of what can be an elusive past. Much of this documentary material has been, in the course of the last two centuries, edited and published to make it more readily accessible. As with the sources for the medieval history of any country, even in published form it presents linguistic challenges: an overwhelming percentage of it is written in Latin, with small amounts in Anglo-Norman French, Gaelic and, just occasionally, other languages.

The documentary evidence outlined above tells us much about how the social, legal and economic framework of the kingdom operated. It also helps in the construction of a narrative of the reign: the lists of witnesses to dated documents, for example, tell us more or less reliably who was where, and when; treaties and agreements place events in time; and the rare snippets of correspondence can further place a few pieces in the challenging jigsaw of constructing a narrative of events. To a great extent, however, the story of the reign depends on the accounts given in narrative sources – the accounts of events which were written down, as history, at the time and soon thereafter. Again, Scotland cannot compete with the extraordinary outpouring of historical narrative which flowed from English monasteries in the medieval period. We do not have dozens of medieval chronicles which can be compared, analysed and sometimes mediated against each other to help construct a chronological framework of events. We know that Scotland did have such work being carried out in its monastic houses, especially at St Andrews. Much of the early work, however, has survived only in shadowy form, sometimes barely distinguishable, as sources, now lost, used by later historians. Of such works contemporary to the thirteenth century only the majestic chronicle written at Melrose and a few other shorter pieces and fragments survive in their original form. (There is a small amount of material relating to thirteenth-century events in the chronicle of Holyrood, but it takes the form of later additions to a chronicle which otherwise stopped in the later twelfth century.) It is now clear, however, that much of the fourteenth-century work which was published in the nineteenth century as John of Fordun's *Chronica Gentis Scotorum* ('Chronicle of the Scottish People') is in fact a separate work, *Gesta Annalia*, the earlier part of which was written probably during the reign of Alexander III himself. Our new understanding of 'Fordun', and of the sources which he used to compile his own elements of the narrative, offers us the opportunity to use his slightly later work, as well as the earlier *Gesta Annalia*, with a fresh insight into how it can help to build a trustworthy narrative. *Gesta Annalia* and Fordun's *Chronica* were also among the many sources used in the fifteenth century by Walter Bower, the abbot of Inchcolm, in writing his *Scotichronicon*, which (along with some other more or less contemporary works heavily reliant on both Bower and other writings) is another invaluable well of information regarding the events of the period under discussion. Similarly, the rhyming vernacular chronicle by Andrew Wyntoun, a fifteenth-century abbot of St Serf's near Kinross, provides crucial information based on earlier sources, now lost. While Scotland's narrative historical tradition prior to the fifteenth century, therefore, was never as abundant as England's, it did exist, and despite grievous loss of much of that early work in its original form, can nonetheless be mined.

In the comments above, the notions of loss and survival have been mentioned several times. One of the difficulties of researching medieval history is the knowledge that sources which once existed no longer do. Inevitably, whether through accident, negligence or deliberate destruction, in the course of over seven centuries many items have ceased to exist which, had they survived, would have provided further enlightenment. This is true of all countries, but Scotland has suffered particularly badly in this respect. Among other documents printed in the first volume of the nineteenth-century edition of the Acts of the Parliaments of Scotland, which draws together many disparate items relevant to Scotland's pre-fifteenth-century history, are inventories of the content of the Scottish royal archives as they existed in Edinburgh castle in 1282, 1291/92 and

1296. They reveal a treasure-trove of material, including records of judicial processes, land grants, financial records and documents relevant to the great affairs of state and relations with other realms and the papacy. The earliest of these was the result of a survey ordered by Alexander III and undertaken, with assistance, by the indefatigable Thomas Charteris, who was perhaps already royal chancellor at that date. Tragically for the historian, only a small fraction of the material listed still exists. The reason for the immense loss is ironically revealed by the very existence of the later inventories: they were compiled on the instruction of Edward I of England, as he initially made his bid for the superiority of Scotland during the competition for the crown which followed the death of Alexander III's granddaughter Margaret in 1290, and again later, when his conquering army removed King John Balliol from the throne, and Edward thus assumed, for a time, direct rule over Scotland. He firstly ordered that the Scottish archives should be searched for evidence relating to the claims of the various competitors for the Scottish throne, and that the documents should be brought to Berwick-upon-Tweed; further documents were removed from Edinburgh to Roxburgh for the purposes of a financial audit being conducted on Edward's orders; and finally, a triumphant Edward removed the remnant in 1296. Most of the material removed from Edinburgh on these three occasions was sent eventually to Westminster; a few items, however, were left in Berwick, and some financial records were returned to Edinburgh for current administrative purposes. The record material removed from the royal archives of Scotland at this time, along with symbols of the kingdom's sovereignty such as the Stone of Scone and the royal insignia, were not merely the spoils of war: the wholesale removal of the evidence of Scotland's former status as a sovereign kingdom must be seen as part of a conquering regime's deliberate policy of obliteration from the historical record of Scotland's independent existence. When the first phase of the war of independence came to an end with the treaty of Edinburgh–Northampton in 1328, one of the treaty's clauses dictated that the Scottish muniments and other material should be returned to Scotland. This agreement, soon superseded by further warfare, was not honoured. Further loss was suffered in the seventeenth century when more records were removed (perhaps including the early financial material) to the Tower of London by the invading armies of Oliver Cromwell, while others were dispersed in panic into private hands. Some of the material sent to London was returned a few years later, but more was lost at sea in 1660 in the course of its return. Some further records were returned from London during the course of the twentieth century. Not all of the material removed at the end of the thirteenth century had survived its captivity; and the history of Scottish record-keeping, particularly during the eighteenth century, was also one of sad neglect. The result is that only meagre fragments survive today of the undoubted wealth of record material which once formed what was, as early as the 1280s, an organised royal archive. The scale of loss is immense and immeasurable.

This state of near perdition of medieval governmental record is compounded by the situation relating to private and institutional records. Virtually nothing, for example, from the great cathedral and priory of St Andrews – which it is known had impressive medieval libraries, as well as the records of the administration of the diocese and its extensive landed estates – survived the iconoclastic 'cleansing' ravages of the Reformation in the mid sixteenth century. It is not the only major medieval religious house which is now represented by virtually no literary or record survivals. Private archives too would suffer similar fates: reverence of antiquity for its own sake is a relatively recent phenomenon, and so neglect, deliberate destruction, war and civil disturbance, fire, flood and other threats have all taken their toll. The surprise is perhaps not that so much has been lost, but rather that so much has survived.

The Scottish situation is not as irredeemably dismal, however, as the above paragraphs might suggest. Fortunately, then as now, national isolationism was not only undesirable, but impossible. As with any country, some of the source material, generated by relationships with those beyond our own shores, lies elsewhere. Mention was made above of the impressive surviving governmental records of medieval England: as much of this book has demonstrated, the relationship between England and Scotland dominates many aspects of the reign, and so English royal, ecclesiastical and private archives provide a wealth of material which support, fill lacunae and assist with the interpretation of the surviving Scottish material. This is true in times both of conflict and of peace: the English Patent Rolls, for instance, include details of movement of high-status individuals to, from and through England, and many other matters of interest for the conduct of ordinary and extraordinary affairs between the two kingdoms. Similarly, the papal archives, which over the last half century or so have been thoroughly researched in pursuit of Scottish material, provide enlightenment not only regarding Scottish–papal relations, but also on Scottish ecclesiastical history, some judicial cases, and the relationship between the church and the state. There are similarly valuable sources for the affairs of medieval Scotland in overseas archives, including those of Norway and France. Narrative output from beyond the kingdom is equally helpful: as well as the English monastic chronicles mentioned above (which, it has to be said, vary considerably in their treatment of Alexandrian Scotland, from near-obsession to total lack of interest), the Scandinavian sagas and Irish annals are examples of further sources which can be called upon to support Scottish historical endeavour. That so much of the evidence is to be found in English and other sources should not be taken to imply an intrinsic bias. All sources, whatever their origin, have to be interpreted carefully, with consideration of the underlying purpose, context and background of their production. There is an advantage to reliance on external sources: Scotland's dependence, for the medieval period, on the documentary and literary riches of other countries has inevitably created a relatively outward-looking, rather than introspective, historiography; it simply is not possible to achieve a view entirely from within.

The archival evidence, whatever its source, provides a view of history which, reflecting both the society which produced it and the nature of events which it records, is heavily male- and upper-class dominated. Quite rarely does the record, or the contemporary historical narrative, penetrate beyond the lives of the privileged few. We can learn something about the lives of sections of the population by reading between the lines, especially of the financial record (which reveals the types of crops which were grown, and to an extent fluctuations in prices, for example); the chronicling of serious weather events is another example of information which can offer a momentary glimpse into the life of the woman-in-the-field. More can be gleaned, of course, from archaeological evidence: the surviving material culture of medieval Scotland can demonstrate, better than any document, how people lived. Standing architecture and art similarly offer information about those who could afford either to build homes substantial enough to stand for many centuries, or to decorate them. It is the archaeologist, and increasingly the scientist, who can sometimes elucidate the lives of ordinary people in the towns and countryside.

Select Bibliography

PRIMARY SOURCES (UNPUBLISHED)

The National Archives

TNA C66/64 m. 13 (Patent Roll, 37 Henry III).
TNA, C66/73, m.15 (Patent Roll, 43 Henry III).

National Records of Scotland

NRS GD 90/1/18/1 (Charter of Alexander III, 1250, bearing fragment of minority seal; text in *RRS*, iv Pt. 1, no. 2).

PRIMARY SOURCES: CALENDARED, PUBLISHED, CRITICAL, FACSIMILE AND ONLINE EDITIONS

Documentary

The Acts of the Parliaments of Scotland, ed. T. Thomson and C. Innes, i (Edinburgh, 1884).
Bateson, Mary (ed.) 'The Scottish King's Household and other Fragments from a Fourteenth Century Manuscript in the Library of Corpus Christi College, Cambridge', Scottish History Society *Miscellany*, 2 (1904), pp. 3–43.
Baxter, James Houston (ed.), *An Old St Andrews Music Book* (London, 1931).
Beveridge, Revd John (ed.), 'Two Scottish Thirteenth-Century Songs, with the Original Melodies, Recently Discovered in Sweden', *Proceedings of the Society of Antiquaries of Scotland*, 73 (1939), pp. 276–88.
The Blackfriars of Perth, ed. R. Milne (Edinburgh, 1893).
Burns, Revd Charles (ed.), 'Bagimond's Roll for the Diocese of Moray', Scottish History Society *Miscellany*, 10 (1965), pp. 1–9.

Calendar of the Close Rolls of the Reign of Henry III, 1227–1272, 14 vols (London, 1902–38).

Calendar of the Close Rolls of Edward I, i, 1272–79 (London, 1900).

Calendar of Documents Relating to Ireland, ii, 1252–1284, ed. H.S. Sweetman (London, 1877).

Calendar of Documents Relating to Scotland, ed. Joseph Bain, 4 vols (Edinburgh, 1881–88); vol. 5, ed. Grant G. Simpson and James D. Galbraith (Edinburgh, n.d.).

Calendar of Entries in the Papal Registers Relating to Great Britain and Ireland; Papal Letters, i, *A.D. 1198–1304*, ed. W.H. Bliss (London, 1893).

Calendar of the Laing Charters, 854–1837, ed. J. Anderson (Edinburgh, 1899).

Calendar of the Patent Rolls, Henry III, 1247–72, 4 vols (London, 1908–13).

Calendar of Writs preserved at Yester House, 1166–1503, ed. C.C.H. Harvey and J. Macleod (Edinburgh, 1930).

Cameron, Annie I. (ed.), 'Bagimond's Roll for the Archdeaconry of Teviotdale, from a Thirteenth-Century Transcript in the Vatican Archives', Scottish History Society *Miscellany*, 5 (1933), pp. 79–106.

Charters, Bulls and other Documents relating to the Abbey of Inchaffray, ed. W.A. Lindsay, J. Dowden and J.M. Thomson (Edinburgh, 1908).

Charters of the Hospital of Soltre, of Trinity College, Edinburgh, and of other Collegiate Churches in Midlothian (Bannatyne Club, 1861).

Close Rolls of the Reign of Henry III, 1251–53, 1254–56, 1261–64, 3 vols (London, 1927, 1931, 1936).

Concilia Scotiae: Ecclesiae Scoticanae Statuta Provincialia quam Synodalia quae Supersunt, 1225–1559, ed. J. Robertson (Bannatyne Club, 1866).

Cooper, Lord (ed. and trans.), *Regiam majestatem and Quoniam attachiamenta: based on the text of Sir John Skene* (Edinburgh, 1947).

Dunlop, Annie I. (ed.), 'Bagimond's Roll: Statement of the Tenths of the Kingdom of Scotland', Scottish History Society *Miscellany*, 6 (1939), pp. 1–77.

Exchequer Rolls of Scotland, ed. John Stuart and George Burnett, i, 1264–1359 (Edinburgh, 1878).

Foedera, Conventiones, Litterae et Cuiuscunque Generis Acta Publica, ed. T. Rymer, 17 vols (London, 1816–69).

Fraser, W., *The Red Book of Menteith* (Edinburgh, 1880).

Hair, Greta-Mary and Knott, Betty I. (eds), *Vespers, Matins and Lauds for St Kentigern, Patron Saint of Glasgow* (Glasgow, 2011).

Liber Cartarum Prioratus Sancti Andree in Scotia (Bannatyne Club, 1841).

Liber Ecclesie de Scon (Bannatyne & Maitland Clubs, 1843).

Liber S. Marie de Calchou, 2 vols (Bannatyne Club, 1846).

Liber Sancte Marie de Melrose (Bannatyne Club, 1837).

Liber S. Thome de Aberbrothoc, 2 vols (Bannatyne Club, 1848, 1856).

Records of the Parliaments of Scotland to 1707, ed. K.M. Brown *et al.*, available online at www.rps.ac.uk.

Regesta Regum Scottorum, i, *The Acts of Malcolm IV*, ed. G.W.S. Barrow (Edinburgh, 1960).

Regesta Regum Scottorum, ii, *The Acts of William I*, ed. G.W.S. Barrow (Edinburgh, 1971).

Regesta Regum Scottorum, iv pt 1, *The Acts of Alexander III*, ed. Cynthia J. Neville and Grant G. Simpson (Edinburgh, 2013).

Regesta Regum Scottorum, Handlist of the Acts of Alexander II, 1214–1249, ed. James M. Scoular (Edinburgh, 1959).

Registrum Anglie de libris doctorum et auctorum veterum, ed. R.A.B. Mynors, R.H. Rouse and M.A. Rouse, in *Corpus of British Medieval Library Catalogues*, 2 (London, 1991), pp. 303–08.

Registrum de Dunfermelyn (Bannatyne Club, 1842).

Registrum Episcopatus Glasguensis (Bannatyne and Maitland Clubs, 1843).

Registrum Episcopatus Moraviensis (Bannatyne Club, 1837).

Registrum Monasterii de Passelet (Maitland Club, 1832).

Registrum de Panmure, ed. J. Stuart (Edinburgh, 1874).

Registrum S. Marie de Neubotle (Bannatyne Club, 1849).

Shirley, Walter Waddington (ed.), *Royal and Other Historical Letters Illustrative of the Reign of Henry III from the Originals in the Public Record Office*, 2 vols (London, 1862–66).

Somerville, Robert (ed.), *Scotia Pontificia: Papal Letters to Scotland before the Pontificate of Innocent III* (Oxford, 1982).

Statutes of the Scottish Church, 1225–1559, ed. David Patrick (Edinburgh, 1907).

Stones, E.L.G. (ed. and trans.), *Anglo-Scottish Relations, 1174–1328: Some Selected Documents* (Oxford, 1965).

Stones, E.L.G. and Simpson, Grant G. (eds), *Edward I and the Throne of Scotland, 1290–1296: An Edition of the Record Sources for the Great Cause*, 2 vols (Oxford, 1978).

Vetera Monumenta Hibernorum et Scotorum Historiam Illustrantia, ed. A. Theiner (Rome, 1864).

Narrative

Anderson, Alan Orr, *Early Sources of Scottish History A.D. 500 to 1286*, 2 vols (Edinburgh, 1922; Stamford, 1990).

Anderson, Alan Orr, *Scottish Annals from English Chroniclers, A.D. 500 to 1286* (London, 1908).

The Anglo-Saxon Chronicle, According to several Original Authorities, ed. Benjamin Thorpe (London, 1861).

Bartlett, Robert (ed. and trans.), *The Miracles of Saint Æbbe of Coldingham and Saint Margaret of Scotland* (Oxford, 2003).

Bower, Walter, *Scotichronicon*, ed. and trans. D.E.R. Watt *et al.*, 9 vols (Aberdeen and Edinburgh, 1987–98).

Broun, Dauvit and Harrison, Julian, *The Chronicle of Melrose Abbey, A Stratigraphic Edition*, i, *Introduction and Facsimile* (Edinburgh, 2007).

The Original Chronicle of Andrew of Wyntoun, ed. F.J. Amours, 6 vols (Edinburgh, 1903–14).

The Chronicle of Man and the Sudreys, ed. P.A. Munch (Douglas, 1874).

The Chronicle of Walter of Guisborough, ed. Harry Rothwell (London, 1957).

Chronicon de Lanercost, MCCI–MCCCXLVI, ed. Joseph Stevenson (Bannatyne Club, 1839).

Dante Alighieri, *Monarchy: and Three Political Letters,* ed. and trans. D. Nicholl and C. Hardie (London, 1954).

Fordun, Joannis de, *Chronica Gentis Scotorum*, ed. W.F. Skene, 2 vols (Edinburgh, 1871–72).

Gray, Thomas, *Scalachronica*, ed. and trans. H. Maxwell (Glasgow, 1907).

Liber Pluscardinensis, ed. F.J.H. Skene, 2 vols (Edinburgh, 1877–80).

Marsilius of Padua, *The Defender of Peace*, trans. Alan Gewirth (New York, 1967).

The Orkneyinga Saga, ed. Joseph Anderson, trans. Jon A. Hjaltalin and Gilbert Goudie (Edinburgh, 1975).

Paris, Matthew, *Chronica Majora*, ed. Henry Richards Luard, Rolls Series, 57, 7 vols (London, 1872–84).

The Saga of Hacon and a Fragment of the Saga of Magnus with appendices, ed. and trans. G.W. Dasent, Rolls Series, Icelandic Sagas, iv (London, 1894).

'The Scottish Chronicle', Benjamin T. Hudson, *Scottish Historical Review*, 77 (1998), pp. 129–61.

A Scottish Chronicle known as the Chronicle of Holyrood, ed. M.O. Anderson (Edinburgh, 1938).

Thomas Aquinas, *Selected Political Writings*, ed. and trans. A.P. d'Entrèves (Oxford, 1974).

Walsingham, Thomas, *Historia Anglicana*, ed. T. Riley, Rolls Series, 28, 2 vols (London, 1863).

SECONDARY SOURCES

NB Where all or most essays within a collection have been used, only the collection itself is cited; where only a small number of the essays in a collection have been used, they are cited individually and the collection is not listed separately.

Adams, Jonathan and Holman, Katherine (eds), *Scandinavia and Europe, 800–1350: Contact, Conflict and Coexistence* (Turnhout, 2004).

Anderson, M.O., *Kings and Kingship in Early Scotland* (Edinburgh, 1974).

Ash, Marinell, 'David Bernham, Bishop of St Andrews, 1239–1253', in David McRoberts (ed.), The *Medieval Church of St Andrews* (Glasgow, 1976), pp. 33–44.

Avray, David d', *Medieval Marriage: Symbolism and Society* (Oxford, 2005).

Bagge, Sverre, *From Gang Leader to the Lord's Anointed: Kingship in Sverris saga and Hákonar saga Hákonarsonar* (Odense, 1996).

Bagge, Sverre, *From Viking Stronghold to Christian Kingdom: State Formation in Norway, c.900–1350* (Copenhagen, 2010).

Bagge, Sverre, *Cross & Scepter: The Rise of the Scandinavian Kingdoms from the Vikings to the Reformation* (Oxford, 2014).

Bannerman, John, *Late Medieval Monumental Sculpture in the West Highlands* (Edinburgh, 1977).

Bannerman, John W.M., 'The Clàrsach and the Clàrsair', in John W.M. Bannerman, *Kinship, Church and Culture: Collected Essays and Studies* (Edinburgh, 2016), pp. 398–417.

Bannerman, John W.M., 'The King's Poet and the Inauguration of Alexander III', in John W.M. Bannerman, *Kinship, Church and Culture: Collected Essays and Studies* (Edinburgh, 2016), pp. 252–82.

Bannerman, John W.M., 'MacDuff of Fife', in John W.M. Bannerman, *Kinship, Church and Culture: Collected Essays and Studies* (Edinburgh, 2016), pp. 230–51.

Bannerman, John W.M., 'The Residence of the King's Poet', in John W.M. Bannerman, *Kinship, Church and Culture: Collected Essays and Studies* (Edinburgh, 2016), pp. 283–94.

Bannerman, John W.M., 'The Scottish Takeover of Pictland and the Relics of Columba', in John W.M. Bannerman, *Kinship, Church and Culture: Collected Essays and Studies* (Edinburgh, 2016), pp. 209–29.

Barrell, A.D.M., 'The Background to *Cum universi*: Scoto-Papal Relations, 1159–1192', *Innes Review*, 46 (1995), pp. 116–38.

Barrow, G.W.S., *Feudal Britain* (London, 1971).

Barrow, G.W.S., *The Kingdom of the Scots: Government, Church and Society from the Eleventh to the Fourteenth Century* (London, 1973).

Barrow, G.W.S., 'The Idea of Freedom in Late Medieval Scotland', *Innes Review*, 30 (1979), pp. 6–34.

Barrow, G.W.S., *The Anglo-Norman Era in Scottish History* (Oxford, 1980).

Barrow, G.W.S., *Kingship and Unity: Scotland 1000–1306* (London, 1981).

Barrow, G.W.S., 'The Scots Charter', in *Studies in Medieval History Presented to R.H.C. Davis*, ed. H. Mayr-Harting and R.I. Moore (London, 1985), pp. 148–64.

Barrow, G.W.S, 'Frontier and Settlement: Which Influenced Which? England and Scotland, 1100–1300', in Robert Bartlett and Angus Mackay (eds), *Medieval Frontier Societies* (Oxford, 1989), pp. 3–21.

Barrow, G.W.S., 'A Kingdom in Crisis: Scotland and the Maid of Norway', *Scottish Historical Review*, 69 (1990), pp. 120–41.

Barrow, G.W.S., *Scotland and Its Neighbours in the Middle Ages* (London, 1992).

Barrow, G.W.S., 'Observations on the Coronation Stone of Scotland', *Scottish Historical Review*, 76 (1997), pp. 115–21.

Barrow, G.W.S., *Robert Bruce and the Community of the Realm of Scotland*, 4th edn (Edinburgh, 2005).

Beam, Amanda, *The Balliol Dynasty 1210–1364* (Edinburgh, 2008).

Birch, Walter de Gray, *History of Scottish Seals from the Eleventh to the Seventeenth Century* . . . (Stirling, 1905).

Blakely, Ruth M., *The Brus Family in England and Scotland, 1100–1295* (Woodbridge, 2005).

Boardman, Steve 'Dunfermline as a Royal Mausoleum', in Richard Fawcett (ed.), *Royal Dunfermline* (Edinburgh, 2005), pp. 139–53.

Boardman, Stephen, *The Campbells, 1250–1513* (Edinburgh, 2006).

Broun, Dauvit, 'Dunkeld and the Origin of Scottish Identity', *Innes Review*, 48 (1997), pp. 112–24.

Broun, Dauvit, 'Defining Scotland and the Scots Before the Wars of Independence', in Dauvit Broun, R.J. Finlay and Michael Lynch (eds), *Image and Identity: The Making and Re-making of Scotland Through the Ages* (Edinburgh, 1998), pp. 4–17.

Broun, Dauvit, *The Irish Identity of the Kingdom of the Scots* (Woodbridge, 1999).

Broun, Dauvit, 'A New Look at *Gesta Annalia* Attributed to John of Fordun', in Barbara E. Crawford (ed.), *Church, Chronicle and Learning in Medieval and Early Renaissance Scotland* (Edinburgh, 1999), pp. 9–30.

Broun, Dauvit, *Scottish Independence and the Idea of Britain* (Edinburgh, 2007).

Broun, Dauvit, 'Becoming Scottish in the Thirteenth Century: The Evidence of the Chronicle of Melrose', in Beverley Ballin Smith, Simon Taylor and Gareth Williams (eds), *West Over Sea: Studies in Scandinavian Sea-Borne Expansion and Settlement Before 1300* (Leiden, 2007), pp. 19–32.

Broun, Dauvit, 'The Presence of Witnesses and the Writing of Charters', in Dauvit Broun (ed.), *The Reality Behind Charter Diplomatic in Anglo-Norman Britain* (Glasgow, 2011), pp. 235–90.

Broun, Dauvit, 'Regnal sovereignty and the creation of political unions in the thirteenth century: some Scottish examples', an unpublished paper given to the Conference on Comparing Political Unions in the Late Medieval and Early Modern World, 1350–1801 (Center for Renaissance Studies Programs, Chicago, 2013).

Broun, Dauvit, 'Britain and the Beginning of Scotland', *Journal of the British Academy*, 3 (2015), pp. 107–37.

Broun, Dauvit, 'The Origins of the Mormaer', in Huw Docherty and David Crouch (eds), *The Earl in Medieval Britain* (forthcoming).

Brown, Michael, *The Wars of Scotland, 1214–1371* (Edinburgh, 2004).

Brown, P. Hume, *History of Scotland*, 2 vols (Cambridge, 1902).

Burton, John Hill, *The History of Scotland from Agricola's Invasion to the Revolution*, 7 vols (Edinburgh and London, 1867–70).

Campbell, Bruce M.S., 'Benchmarking Medieval Economic Development: England, Wales, Scotland and Ireland, c.1290', *Economic History Review*, 61 (2008), pp. 896–945.

Campbell, Ewan, 'Trade in the Dark-Age West: A Peripheral Activity?', in Barbara E. Crawford (ed.), *Scotland in Dark Age Britain* (Aberdeen, 1996), pp. 72–91.

Campbell, Ewan, 'Were the Scots Irish?', *Antiquity*, 75 (2001), pp. 285–92.

Campbell, Ian, 'The Idea of St Andrews As the Second Rome Made Manifest', in Michael Brown and Katie Stevenson (eds), *Medieval St Andrews: Church, Cult, City* (Woodbridge, 2017), pp. 35–50.

Campbell, Marion, *Alexander III, King of Scots* (Colonsay, 1999).

Cant, Ronald G., 'The Building of St Andrews Cathedral', in David McRoberts (ed.), *The Medieval Church of St Andrews* (Glasgow, 1976), pp. 11–32.

Carpenter, David A., *The Reign of Henry III* (London, 1996).

Carpenter, David A., 'Scottish Royal Government in the Thirteenth Century from an English Perspective', in Matthew Hammond (ed.), *New Perspectives on Medieval Scotland, 1093–1286* (Woodbridge, 2013), pp. 117–59.

Clancy, Thomas Owen (ed.), *The Triumph Tree: Scotland's Earliest Poetry, AD 550–1350* (Edinburgh, 1998).

Clifford, Timothy, Gallacher, Michael and Smailes, Helen, *Benjamin West and the Death of the Stag: The Story Behind the Painting and its Conservation*, ed. Duncan Thomson (Edinburgh, 2009).

Corser, Peter, 'The Brus Lordship of Annandale, 1124–1296', in Richard Oram and Geoffrey Stell (eds), *Lordship and Architecture in Medieval and Renaissance Scotland* (Edinburgh, 2005), pp. 45–59.

Cowan, Edward J. and Henderson, Lizanne (eds), *A History of Everyday Life in Medieval Scotland, 1000 to 1600* (Edinburgh, 2011).

Cowan, Ian B. and Easson, David E., *Medieval Religious Houses: Scotland* (London, 1976).

Cowan, Ian B., Mackay, P.H.R. and Macquarrie, Alan (eds), *The Knights of St John of Jerusalem in Scotland* (Edinburgh, 1983).

Crawford, Barbara E., *Scandinavian Scotland* (Leicester, 1987).

Crawford, Barbara E., *The Northern Earldoms: Orkney and Caithness from AD 870 to 1470* (Edinburgh, 2013).

Cruden, Stewart, *The Scottish Castle* (Edinburgh, 1963).

Cruden, Stewart, *Scottish Medieval Churches* (Edinburgh, 1986).

Dalrymple, Sir David, Lord Hailes, *Annals of Scotland from the Accession of Malcolm III to the Accession of the House of Stewart* (Edinburgh, 1819).

Davies, Althea L., 'Upland Agriculture and Environmental Risk: A New Model of Upland Land-Use Based on High Spatial-Resolution Palynological Data from West Affric, NW Scotland', *Journal of Archaeological Science*, 34 (2007) pp. 2053–63.

Davies, R.R., *Domination and Conquest: The Experience of Ireland, Scotland and Wales, 1100–1300* (Cambridge, 1990).

Dawson, Alastair, *So Foul and Fair a Day: A History of Scotland's Weather and Climate* (Edinburgh, 2009).

Dennison, E. Patricia, *The Evolution of Scotland's Towns: Creation, Growth and Fragmentation* (Edinburgh, 2018).

Dickinson, W. Croft, *Scotland from the Earliest Times to 1603*, 3rd edn, revised by A.A.M. Duncan (Oxford, 1977).

Ditchburn, David, 'A Note on Scandinavian Trade with Scotland in the Later Middle Ages', in Grant G. Simpson (ed.), *Scotland and Scandinavia, 800–1800* (Edinburgh, 1990), pp. 73–89.

Dodgshon, R.A., 'Medieval Settlement and Colonisation', in M.L. Parry and T.R. Slater (eds), *The Making of the Scottish Countryside* (London 1980), pp. 45–68.

Donnelly, Joe, 'Thomas of Coldingham, Merchant and Burgess of Berwick upon Tweed (died 1316)', *Scottish Historical Review*, 59 (1980), pp. 105–25.

Donnelly, Joe, 'An Open Economy: The Berwick Shipping Trade, 1311–1373', *Scottish Historical Review*, 96 (2017), pp. 1–31.

Dowden, J., *The Bishops of Scotland* (Glasgow, 1912).

Driscoll, Stephen T., 'The Archaeological Context of Assembly in Early Medieval Scotland – Scone and Its Comparanda', in Aliki Pantos and Sarah Semple (eds), *Assembly Places and Practices in Medieval Europe* (Dublin, 2004), pp. 73–94.

Dumville, David N., 'Kingship, Genealogies and Regnal Lists', in P.H. Sawyer and I.N. Woods (eds) *Early Medieval Kingship* (Leeds, 1977), pp. 72–104.

Duncan, A.A.M., 'Regiam Majestatem: A Reconsideration', *Juridical Review* (1961), pp. 199–217.

Duncan, A.A.M., 'The Early Parliaments of Scotland', *Scottish Historical Review*, 45 (1966), pp. 36–58.

Duncan, A.A.M., *Scotland: The Making of the Kingdom* (Edinburgh, 1975).

Duncan, A.A.M., 'Sources and Uses of the Chronicle of Melrose', in Simon Taylor (ed.), *Kings, Clerics and Chronicles in Scotland, 500–1297* (Dublin, 2000), pp. 146–85.

Duncan, A.A.M., *The Kingship of the Scots, 842–1292: Succession and Independence* (Edinburgh, 2002).

Duncan, A.A.M., 'The Foundation of St Andrews Cathedral Priory, 1140', *Scottish Historical Review*, 84 (2005), pp. 1–37.

Duncan, A.A.M. and Brown, A.L., 'Argyll and the Isles in the Earlier Middle Ages', *Proceedings of the Society of Antiquaries of Scotland*, 90 (1959), pp. 190–220.

Entrèves, A.P. d', *Dante as a Political Thinker* (Oxford,1952).

Ewan, Elizabeth, 'An Urban Community: The Crafts in Thirteenth-Century Aberdeen', in Alexander Grant and Keith J. Stringer, *Medieval Scotland: Crown, Lordship and Community* (Edinburgh, 1993), pp. 156–73.

Fawcett, Richard, 'Dunfermline Abbey Church', in Richard Fawcett (ed.), *Royal Dunfermline* (Edinburgh, 2005), pp. 27–63.

Fawcett, Richard, *The Architecture of the Scottish Medieval Church, 1100–1560* (New Haven and London, 2011).

Fawcett, Richard, 'The Medieval Ecclesiastical Architecture of St Andrews as a Channel for the Introduction of New Ideas', in Michael Brown and Katie Stevenson (eds), *Medieval St Andrews: Church, Cult, City* (Woodbridge, 2017), pp. 51–83.

Fawcett, Richard and Oram, Richard, *Melrose Abbey* (Stroud, 2004).

Fawcett, Richard and Oram, Richard, *Dryburgh Abbey* (Stroud, 2005).

Ferguson, Paul C., *Medieval Papal Representatives in Scotland: Legates, Nuncios, and Judges-Delegate, 1125–1286* (Edinburgh, 1997).

Fergusson, James, *Alexander III, King of Scotland* (London, 1937).

Fisher, Ian, 'The Heirs of Somerled', in Richard Oram and Geoffrey Stell (eds), *Lordship and Architecture in Medieval and Renaissance Scotland* (Edinburgh, 2005), pp. 85–95.

Foster, Sally M., *Picts, Gaels and Scots: Early Historic Scotland* (London, 1996).

Foster, Sally M. (ed.), *The St Andrews Sarcophagus: A Pictish Masterpiece and its International Connections* (Dublin, 1998).

Fraser, Iain, 'The Tomb of the Hero King: The Death and Burial of Robert I, and the Discoveries of 1818–19', in Richard Fawcett (ed.), *Royal Dunfermline* (Edinburgh, 2005), pp. 155–76.

Fraser, James E., *From Caledonia to Pictland: Scotland to 795* (Edinburgh, 2009).

Fraser, James E., 'From Ancient Scythia to *The Problem of the Picts*: Thoughts on the Quest for Pictish origins', in Stephen T. Driscoll, Jane Geddes and Mark A. Hall (eds), *Pictish Progress: New Studies on Northern Britain in the Early Middle Ages* (Leiden, 2011), pp. 15–43.

Gemmill, Elizabeth and Mayhew, Nicholas, *Changing Values in Medieval Scotland: A study of prices, money and weights and measures* (Cambridge, 1995).

Gierke, Otto, *Political Theories of the Middle Ages*, trans. F.W. Maitland (Cambridge, 1922).

Gilbert, John M., *Hunting and Hunting Reserves in Medieval Scotland* (Edinburgh, 1979).

Given-Wilson, Chris, *Chronicles: The Writing of History in Medieval England* (London & New York, 2004).

Goff, Jacques Le, 'A Coronation Program for the Age of St Louis: The Ordo of 1250', in János M. Bak (ed.), *Coronations: Medieval and Early Modern Monarchic Ritual* (Berkeley, 1990), pp. 46–57.

Graham, Rose, 'Letters of Cardinal Ottoboni', *English Historical Review*, 15 (1900), pp. 87–120.

Gransden, Antonia, *Historical Writing in England, c.550 to c.1307* (London, 1974).

Grant, Alexander, 'Aspects of National Consciousness in Medieval Scotland', in C. Bjorn, A. Grant and K.J. Stringer (eds), *Nations, Nationalism and Patriotism in the European Past* (Copenhagen, 1994), pp. 68–95.

Grant, Alexander, 'Scotland's "Celtic Fringe" in the Late Middle Ages: The MacDonald Lords of the Isles and the Kingdom of Scotland', in R.R. Davies (ed.), *The British Isles, 1100–1500: Comparisons, Contrasts and Connections* (Edinburgh, 1998), pp. 118–41.

Hammond, Matthew, '*Hostiarii Regis Scotie*: the Durward family in the thirteenth century', in Steve Boardman and Alasdair Ross (eds), *The Exercise of Power in Medieval Scotland c.1200–1500* (Dublin, 2003), pp. 118–38.

Harding, Alan, '*Regiam Majestatem* Amongst Medieval Law-Books', *Juridical Review*, n.s. 29 (1984), pp. 97–111.

Helle, Knut, 'Norwegian Foreign Policy and the Maid of Norway', *Scottish Historical Review*, 69 (1990), pp. 142–56.

Herbert, Máire, '*Rí Éirenn, Rí Alban*: Kingship and Identity in the Ninth and Tenth Centuries', in Simon Taylor (ed.), *Kings, Clerics and Chronicles in Scotland 500–1297* (Dublin, 2000), pp. 62–72.

Higgitt, John, *The Murthly Hours: Devotion, Literacy and Luxury in Paris, England and the Gaelic West* (London, 2000).

Higgitt, John (ed.), *Scottish Libraries*, Corpus of British Medieval Library Catalogues 12 (London, 2006).

Historic Environment Scotland, *Canmore*, available online at https://canmore.org.uk.

Hurlock, Kathryn, 'The Welsh Wife of Malcolm, Earl of Fife (d.1266): An Alternative Suggestion', *Scottish Historical Review*, 88 (2009), pp. 352–55.

Hybel, Nils, 'The Grain Trade in Northern Europe Before 1350', *Economic History Review*, 55 (2002), pp. 219–47.

Hybel, Nils, *The Nature of Kingship c.800–1300: The Danish Incident* (Leiden, 2018).

Jobson, Adrian (ed.), *Baronial Reform and Revolution in England, 1258–1267* (Woodbridge, 2016).

Jochens, Jenny M., 'The Politics of Reproduction: Medieval Norwegian Kingship', *The American Historical Review*, 92 (1987), pp. 327–49.

Jones, Chris, 'Inclinit to Diuersiteis: Wyntoun's Song on the Death of Alexander III and the "Origins" of Scots Vernacular Poetry', *The Review of English Studies*, 64 (2013), pp. 21–38.

Kantorowicz, Ernst H., *Laudes Regiae: A Study in Liturgical Acclamations and Mediaeval Ruler Worship* (Berkeley/Los Angeles, 1946).

Kantorowicz, Ernst H., *The King's Two Bodies: A Study in Mediaeval Political Theology* (Princeton, 1997).

Korpiola, Mia, 'An Act or a Process? Competing Views on Marriage Formation and Legitimacy in Medieval Europe', in Lars Ivar Hansen (ed.), *Family, Marriage and Property Devolution in the Middle Ages* (Tromso, 2000), pp. 31–54.

Lee, Becky R., 'The Purification of Women after Childbirth: A Window onto Medieval Perceptions of Women', *Florilegium*, 14 (1995–96), pp. 43–55.

Legge, M.D., 'The Inauguration of Alexander III', *Proceedings of the Society of Antiquaries of Scotland*, 80 (1945–46), pp. 73–82.

Little, A.G., 'The Authorship of the Lanercost Chronicle', in A.G. Little, *Franciscan Papers, Lists and Documents* (Manchester, 1943), pp. 42–54.

Lunt, William E., *Financial Relations of the Papacy with England to 1327* (Cambridge, MA, 1939).

Lustig, Richard I., 'The Treaty of Perth: A Re-Examination', *Scottish Historical Review*, 58 (1979), pp. 35–57.

Lythe, S.G.E. and Butt, J., *An Economic History of Scotland, 1100–1939* (Glasgow and London, 1975).

McDonald, R. Andrew, 'Matrimonial Politics and Core-periphery interactions . . .', *Journal of Medieval History*, 21 (1995), pp. 227–47.

McDonald, R. Andrew, 'Images of Hebridean Lordship in the Late Twelfth and Early Thirteenth Centuries: The Seal of Raonall Mac Sorley', *Scottish Historical Review*, 74 (1995), pp. 129–43.

McDonald, R. Andrew, *The Kingdom of the Isles: Scotland's Western Seaboard, c.1100–c.1336* (East Linton, 1997).

McDonald, R. Andrew, *The Sea Kings: The Late Norse Kingdoms of Man and the Isles, c.1066–1275* (Edinburgh, 2019).

Mackechnie, Aonghus, 'The Royal Palace of Dunfermline', in Richard Fawcett (ed.), *Royal Dunfermline* (Edinburgh, 2005), pp. 101–38.

[Mackenzie, George], *The Genealogie of the Mackenzies Preceeding Ye Year MDCLXI* (Edinburgh, 1829).

McNeill, Peter G.B. and MacQueen, Hector L., *Atlas of Scottish History to 1707* (Edinburgh, 1996).

Macniven, Alan, *The Vikings in Islay: The Place of Names in Hebridean Settlement History* (Edinburgh, 2015).

Macquarrie, Alan, *Scotland and the Crusades, 1095–1560* (Edinburgh, 1985).

McQueen, Alison A.B., 'Parliament, the Guardians and John Balliol, 1284–1296', in Keith M. Brown and Roland J. Tanner (eds), *Parliament and Politics in Scotland, 1235–1560* (Edinburgh, 2004), pp. 29–49.

MacQueen, Hector L. '*Regiam Majestatem*, Scots Law, and National Identity', *Scottish Historical Review*, 74 (1995), pp. 1–25.

MacQueen, Hector L., *Common Law and Feudal Society in Medieval Scotland* (Edinburgh, 2016).

Márkus, Gilbert, *Conceiving a Nation: Scotland to AD 900* (Edinburgh, 2017).

Mayhew, Nicholas, 'Money in Scotland in the Thirteenth Century', in D.M. Metcalfe (ed.), *Coinage in Medieval Scotland (1100–1600): The Second Oxford Symposium on Coinage and Monetary History*, British Archaeological Reports, 45 (Oxford, 1977), pp. 85–102.

Metcalfe, D.M., 'The Evidence of Scottish Coin Hoards for Monetary History, 1100–1600' in D.M. Metcalfe (ed.), *Coinage in Medieval Scotland (1100–1600): The Second Oxford Symposium on Coinage and Monetary History*, British Archaeological Reports, 45 (Oxford, 1977), pp. 1–59.

[National Museums of Scotland], *Angels, Nobles and Unicorns: Art and Patronage in Medieval Scotland* (Edinburgh, 1982).

Neville, Cynthia J., *Violence, Custom and Law: The Anglo-Scottish Border Lands in the Later Middle Ages* (Edinburgh 1998).

Neville, Cynthia J., 'Scottish Influences on the Medieval Laws of the Anglo-Scottish Marches', *Scottish Historical Review*, 81 (2002), pp. 161–85.

Neville, Cynthia J., *Native Lordship in Medieval Scotland: The Earldoms of Strathearn and Lennox, c.1140–1365* (Dublin, 2005).

Neville, Cynthia J., *Land, Law and People in Medieval Scotland* (Edinburgh, 2010).

Neville, Cynthia J., 'Neighbours, the Neighbourhood, and the Visnet in Scotland, 1125–1300', in Matthew Hammond (ed.), *New Perspectives on Medieval Scotland, 1093–1286* (Woodbridge, 2013), pp. 161–73.

Neville, Cynthia J., 'Preparing for Kingship: Prince Alexander of Scotland, 1264–1284', in Janay Nugent and Elizabeth Ewan (eds), *Children and Youth in Premodern Scotland* (Woodbridge, 2015), pp. 155–72.

Oram, Richard D., 'A Family Business? Colonisation and Settlement in Twelfth and Thirteenth-Century Galloway', *Scottish Historical Review*, 72 (1993), pp. 111–45.

Oram, Richard D., 'Continuity, Adaptation and Integration: The Earls and Earldom of Mar, c.1150–c.1300', in Steve Boardman and Alasdair Ross (eds), *The Exercise of Power in Medieval Scotland, c.1200–1500* (Dublin, 2003), pp. 46–66.

Oram, Richard D., 'Prelatical Builders: A Preliminary Study, c.1124–c.1500', in Richard Oram and Geoffrey Stell (eds), *Lordship and Architecture in Medieval and Renaissance Scotland* (Edinburgh, 2005), pp. 1–25.

Oram, Richard D. (ed.), *The Reign of Alexander II, 1214–49* (Leiden and Boston, 2005).

Oram, Richard D., 'Royal and Lordly Residence in Scotland, c 1050 to c 1250: An Historiographical Review and Critical Revision', *Antiquaries Journal*, 88 (2008), pp. 165–89.

Oram, Richard, *Alexander II, King of Scots 1214–1249* (Edinburgh, 2012).

Parry, M.L., 'Secular Climatic Change and Marginal Agriculture', *Transactions of the Institute of British Geographers*, 64 (1975), pp. 1–13.

Penman, Michael, 'Royal Piety in Thirteenth-Century Scotland: The Religion and Religiosity of Alexander II (1214–49) and Alexander III (1249–86)', in Janet Burton, Phillipp Schofield and Björn Weiler (eds), *Thirteenth Century England XII: Proceeding of the Gregynog Conference 2007* (Woodbridge, 2009), pp. 13–29.

People of Medieval Scotland, 1093–1314, available online at http://www.poms.ac.uk/.

Pollock, M.A., *Scotland, England and France after the Loss of Normandy, 1204–1296* (Woodbridge, 2015).

Powicke, Maurice, *The Thirteenth Century, 1216–1307* (Oxford, 1962).

Prestwich, Michael, *The Three Edwards: War and State in England, 1272–1377* (London, 1980).

Prestwich, Michael, *Edward I* (London, 1988).

Purser, John, *Scotland's Music: A History of the Traditional and Classical Music of Scotland from Early Times to the Present Day* (Edinburgh, 1992).

Raine, J., *The History and Antiquities of North Durham* (London, 1852).

Reeves, Marjorie E., 'History and Prophecy in Medieval Thought', *Medievalia et Humanistica*, n.s. 5 (1974), pp. 51–75.

Reid, Norman H., 'The Kingless Kingdom: the Scottish Guardianships of 1286–1306', *Scottish Historical Review*, 61 (1982), pp. 105–29.

Reid, Norman H., 'Margaret, "Maid of Norway" and Scottish Queenship', *Reading Medieval Studies*, 8 (1982), pp. 75–96.

Reid, Norman H. (ed.), *Scotland in the Reign of Alexander III, 1249–1286* (Edinburgh, 1990).

Reid, Norman H., 'The Prehistory of the University of St Andrews', in Michael Brown and Katie Stevenson (eds), *Medieval St Andrews: Church, Cult, City* (Woodbridge, 2017), pp. 237–67.

Reid, Norman H., 'The Political Context of the Treaty of Perth', in Alan Macniven (ed.), *The Treaty of Perth* (forthcoming).

Reid, Norman H. and Barrow, G.W.S. (eds), *The Sheriffs of Scotland: An Interim List to c.1306* (St Andrews, 2002).

Reid, Norman and Penman, Michael, 'Guardian – Lieutenant – Governor: Absentee Monarchy and Proxy Power in Scotland's Long Fourteenth Century', in Frédérique Lachaud and Michael Penman (eds), *Absentee Authority Across Medieval Europe* (Woodbridge, 2017), pp. 191–218.

Reynolds, Susan, *Kingdoms and Communities in Western Europe, 900–1300* (Oxford, 1984).

Richardson, H.G., 'The Coronation of Edward I', *Bulletin of the Institute of Historical Research*, 15 (1937–38), pp. 94–99.

Richardson, H.G. and Sayles, George, 'The Scottish Parliaments of Edward I', *Scottish Historical Review*, 25 (1928), pp. 300–17.

Ruiz, Teofilo F., 'Unsacred Monarchy: The Kings of Castile in the Late Middle Ages', in Sean Wilentz (ed.), *Rites of Power: Symbolism, Ritual, and Politics Since the Middle Ages* (Philadelphia, 1999), pp. 109–44.

Rydval, M., Loader, N.J., Gunnarson, B.E. *et al.*, 'Reconstructing 800 Years of Summer Temperatures in Scotland from Tree Rings', *Climate Dynamics*, 49 (2017), pp. 2951–74; available online at https://doi.org/10.1007/s00382-016-3478-8.

Sanmark, Alexandra, *Viking Law and Order: Places and Rituals of Assembly in the Medieval North* (Edinburgh, 2017).

Scott, William W., 'The Use of Money in Scotland, 1124–1230', *Scottish Historical Review*, 58 (1979), pp. 105–31.

Scott, W.W., 'Abbots Adam (1207–1213) and William (1215–1216) of Melrose and the Melrose Chronicle', in Barbara E. Crawford (ed.), *Church, Chronicle and Learning in Medieval and early Renaissance Scotland* (Edinburgh, 1999), pp. 161–72.

Sellar, W. David H., 'The Common Law of Scotland and the Common law of England' in R.R. Davies (ed.), *The British Isles, 1100–1500: Comparisons, Contrasts and Connections* (Edinburgh, 1988).

Simpson, Andrew R.C. and Wilson, Adelyn L.M., *Scottish Legal History, Vol. 1: 1000–1707* (Edinburgh, 2017).

Simpson, Grant G., 'The Heart of King Robert I: Pious Crusade or Marketing Gambit?', in Barbara E. Crawford (ed.), *Church, Chronicle and Learning in Medieval and Early Renaissance Scotland* (Edinburgh, 1999), pp. 173–86.

Simpson, Grant G., 'Kingship in Miniature: A Minority Seal of Alexander III, 1249–1257', in Alexander Grant and Keith J. Stringer, *Medieval Scotland: Crown, Lordship and Community* (Edinburgh 1993), pp. 131–39.

Skene, William F., *Celtic Scotland: A History of Ancient Alban*, 2 vols (Edinburgh, 1886, 1887).

Staniland, Kay, 'The Nuptials of Alexander III of Scotland and Margaret Plantagenet', *Nottingham Medieval Studies*, 30 (1986), pp. 20–45.

Steinsland, Gro, Sigurðsson, Jón Viðar, Rekdal, Jan Erik and Beuermann, Ian (eds), *Ideology and Power in the Viking and Middle Ages: Scandinavia, Iceland, Ireland, Orkney and the Faeroes* (Leiden, 2011).

Stevenson, John Horne and Wood, Marguerite, *Scottish Heraldic Seals: Royal, Official, Ecclesiastical, Collegiate, Burghal, Personal*, 3 vols (Glasgow, 1940).

Stringer, Keith J., 'Reform Monasticism and Celtic Scotland: Galloway, c.1140 – c.1240', in E.J. Cowan and R. Andrew McDonald (eds), *Alba: Celtic Scotland in the Medieval Era* (East Linton, 2000), pp. 127–65.

Stringer, Keith J., 'Tynedale: Power, Society and Identities, c.1200–1296', in Matthew L. Holford and Keith J. Stringer, *Border Liberties and Loyalties: North-East England, c.1200 to c.1400* (Edinburgh, 2010), pp. 231–90.

Stringer, Keith J., 'The Scottish "Political Community" in the Reign of Alexander II (1214–1249)', in Matthew Hammond (ed.), *New Perspectives on Medieval Scotland, 1093–1286* (Woodbridge, 2013) pp. 53–84.

Syllabus of Scottish Cartularies; available online at https://scottishmedievalcharters.wordpress.com/scottish-cartularies/.

Taylor, Alice, '*Leges Scocie* and the Lawcodes of David I, William the Lion and Alexander II', *Scottish Historical Review*, 88 (2009), pp. 207–88.

Taylor, Alice, 'Historical Writing in Twelfth- and Thirteenth-Century Scotland: The Dunfermline Compilation', *Historical Research*, 83 (2010), pp. 228–52.

Taylor, Alice, 'Common Burdens in the *regnum Scottorum*: The Evidence of Charter Diplomatic', in Dauvit Broun (ed.) *The Reality Behind Charter Diplomatic in Anglo-Norman Britain* (Glasgow, 2011), pp. 166–234.

Taylor, Alice, 'The Assizes of David I, King of Scots, 1124–53', *Scottish Historical Review*, 91 (2012), pp. 197–238.

Taylor, Alice, *The Shape of the State in Medieval Scotland, 1124–1290* (Oxford, 2016).

Taylor, Simon, 'Babbet and Bridin Pudding or Polyglot Fife in the Middle Ages', *Nomina*, 17 (1994), pp. 99–118.

Taylor, Simon, 'Pictish Place-names Revisited', in Stephen T. Driscoll, Jane Geddes and Mark A. Hall (eds), *Pictish Progress: New Studies on Northern Britain in the Early Middle Ages* (Leiden, 2011), pp. 67–118.

Taylor, Simon, 'From *Cinrigh Monai* to *Civitas Sancti Andree*: A Star is Born', in Michael Brown and Katie Stevenson (eds), *Medieval St Andrews: Church, Cult, City* (Woodbridge, 2017), pp. 20–34.

Thurlby, Malcolm, 'St Andrews Cathedral-Priory and the Beginnings of Gothic Architecture in Northern Britain', in John Higgitt (ed.), *Medieval Art and Architecture in the Diocese of St Andrews* (Leeds, 1994), pp. 47–60.

Tyerman, Christopher, *God's War: A New History of the Crusades* (London, 2006).

Ullman, Walter, *Law and Politics in the Middle Ages* (London 1975).

Watson, Fiona, 'Adapting Tradition? The Earldom of Strathearn 1114–1296', in Richard Oram and Geoffrey Stell (eds), *Lordship and Architecture in Medieval and Renaissance Scotland* (Edinburgh, 2005), pp. 26–43.

Watt, D.E.R., 'The Minority of Alexander III of Scotland', *Transactions of the Royal Historical Society*, 5:21 (1971), pp. 1–23.

Watt, D.E.R., *A Biographical Dictionary of Scottish Graduates to A.D. 1410* (Oxford, 1977).

Watt, D.E.R., 'Scottish University Men of the Thirteenth and Fourteenth Centuries', in T.C. Smout (ed.), *Scotland and Europe, 1200–1850* (Edinburgh, 1986) pp. 1–19.

Watt, D.E.R., *Scottish Church Councils in the Middle Ages* (Edinburgh, 2000).

Watt, D.E.R. and Murray, A.L. (eds), *Fasti Ecclesiae Scoticanae Medii Aevi Ad Annum 1638* (Edinburgh, 2003).

Watt, D.E.R. and Shead, N.F. (eds), *The Heads of Religious Houses in Scotland from Twelfth to Sixteenth Centuries* (Edinburgh, 2001).

Welander, Richard, Breeze, David J. and Clancy, Thomas Owen (eds), *The Stone of Destiny: Artefact and Icon* (Edinburgh, 2003).

Woolf, Alex, *From Pictland to Alba: 789–1070* (Edinburgh, 2007).

Patrick Wormald, 'The Emergence of the *Regnum Scottorum*: A Carolingian Hegemony?', in Barbara E. Crawford (ed.), *Scotland in Dark Age Britain* (Aberdeen, 1996), pp. 131–60.

Yeoman, Peter, *Medieval Scotland: An Archaeological Perspective* (London, 1995).

Young, Alan, 'The Political Role of Walter Comyn, Earl of Menteith, During the Minority of Alexander III of Scotland', in K.J. Stringer (ed.) *Essays on the Nobility of Medieval Scotland* (Edinburgh, 1985), pp. 139–41.

Young, Alan, *Robert the Bruce's Rivals: The Comyns, 1212–1314* (East Linton, 1997).

Young, Alan, 'The Comyns to 1300', in Richard Oram and Geoffrey Stell (eds), *Lordship and Architecture in Medieval and Renaissance Scotland* (Edinburgh, 2005), pp. 61–83.

THESES

Ash, Marinell, 'The Administration of the Diocese of St Andrews, 1202–1328', University of Newcastle upon Tyne, 1972.

Dean, Lucinda H.S., 'Crowns, Wedding Rings and Processions: Continuity and Change in the Representations of Scottish Royal Authority in State Ceremony, c.1214–c.1603', University of Stirling, 2013.

Hawes, Claire, 'Community and Public Authority in Later Fifteenth-century Scotland', University of St Andrews, 2015.

Neville, Cynthia J., 'The Earls of Strathearn from the Twelfth to the Mid-Fourteenth Century, with an Edition of their Written Acts', University of Aberdeen, 1983.

Reid, Norman H., 'The Political Rôle of the Monarchy in Scotland, 1249–1329', University of Edinburgh, 1984.

Stevenson, Alexander W.K., 'Trade Between Scotland and the Low Countries in the Later Middle Ages', University of Aberdeen, 1982.

Index

Personal names: individuals known by patronymics or descriptors (e.g. Eógan mac Dubhgaill, John the Scot) are indexed under their Christian names; individuals with an obvious surname (e.g. David Bernham) are indexed under their surname.